www.wadsworth.com

Criminal Law

Eighth Edition

Thomas J. Gardner

Attorney at Law

Terry M. Anderson

Creighton University School of Law

THOMSON
WADSWORTH

Australia • Canada • Mexico • Singapore • Spain
United Kingdom • United States

Executive Editor, Criminal Justice: *Sabra Horne*
Criminal Justice Editor: *Shelley Murphy*
Assistant Editor: *Dawn Mesa*
Editorial Assistant: *Lee McCracken*
Technology Project Manager: *Susan DeVanna*
Marketing Manager: *Dory Schaeffer*
Marketing Assistant: *Neena Chandra*
Advertising Project Manager: *Bryan Vann*
Project Manager, Editorial Production: *Jennie Redwitz*
Print/Media Buyer: *Judy Inouye*

Permissions Editor: *Stephanie Keough-Hedges*
Production Service: *Linda Jupiter, Jupiter Productions*
Text Designer: *Lisa Devenish/Adriane Bosworth*
Photo Researcher: *Linda Rill*
Copy Editor: *Barbara Coster*
Proofreader: *Henrietta Bensussen*
Cover Designer: *Ross Carron*
Compositor: *Thompson Type*
Text and Cover Printer: *Edwards Brothers, Ann Arbor*

Printed in the United States of America
1 2 3 4 5 6 7 06 05 04 03 02

For more information about our products, contact us at:
Thomson Learning Academic Resource Center
1-800-423-0563
For permission to use material from this text,
contact us by:
Phone: 1-800-730-2214
Fax: 1-800-730-2215
Web: http://www.thomsonrights.com

ExamView® and *ExamView Pro*® are registered trademarks of FSCreations, Inc. Windows is a registered trademark of the Microsoft Corporation used herein under license. Macintosh and Power Macintosh are registered trademarks of Apple Computer, Inc. Used herein under license.

Library of Congress Control Number: 2002105119

Student Edition ISBN 0-534-59481-6
Instructor Edition   ISBN 0-534-59484-0

Wadsworth/Thomson Learning
10 Davis Drive
Belmont, CA 94002-3098
USA

Asia
Thomson Learning
5 Shenton Way #01-01
UIC Building
Singapore 068808

Australia
Nelson Thomson Learning
102 Dodds Street
South Melbourne, Victoria 3205
Australia

Canada
Nelson Thomson Learning
1120 Birchmount Road
Toronto, Ontario M1K 5G4
Canada

Europe/Middle East/Africa
Thomson Learning
High Holborn House
50/51 Bedford Row
London WC1R 4LR
United Kingdom

Latin America
Thomson Learning
Seneca, 53
Colonia Polanco
11560 Mexico D.F.
Mexico

Spain
Paraninfo Thomson Learning
Calle/Magallanes, 25
28015 Madrid, Spain

Dedicated to Lauren Demet on the occasion of her 18th birthday

About the Authors

Thomas J. Gardner, after earning a Bachelor of Science degree in economics, served three years as a naval officer in the South Pacific during and immediately after World War II. He then attended and graduated from Marquette Law School with a Juris Doctor degree in 1949. During the Korean War he worked in procurement for the Air Material Command. He also earned a Master of Arts degree in political science. His long association with the criminal justice system began as a criminal defense lawyer. He then worked as a prosecutor, a police legal adviser, and in police in-service legal training. He was a member and president of a police and fire commission.

For twenty-eight years, he taught courses in Criminal Law, Criminal Evidence, and Arrest, Search and Seizure at the Milwaukee Area Technical College complex of campuses. He lives in Milwaukee, Wisconsin, with his wife, Eileen.

Terry M. Anderson, Professor of Law, is a Visiting Professor at the Denver University College of Law. He will return to Creighton University School of Law in Omaha, Nebraska, for the 2002–2003 school year. He received his Bachelor of Arts degree in 1968 and Juris Doctor degree in 1971 from the University of North Dakota, where he was a member of the Order of the Coif and the Case Editor of the *North Dakota Law Review.* After earning a Master of Laws degree from Harvard Law School in 1972, he joined the Creighton Law School faculty. He has also been a Visiting Professor of Law at the University of New Mexico. He teaches Contracts, Insurance, and Secured Transactions in Personal Property. His next project is co-authoring a new edition of *Criminal Evidence.*

Contents in Brief

Contents

PART 4
Crimes Against Property

Preface

Thomas J. Gardner co-authored the first edition of this text more than twenty-five years ago. The authors' goal then was to introduce law enforcement personnel and others interested in criminal justice to the main principles of American criminal law. To accomplish this goal, they integrated excerpts from case law with a sound and practical textual discussion of the criminal law.

In subsequent editions, Terry M. Anderson joined as a co-author. In those editions, we increased the coverage of the text to reflect its use in more broadly based criminal justice programs. We also increased the number of case excerpts and case references in the text, believing that understanding criminal law demanded an understanding of the importance of court decisions to the growth and development of the criminal law. However, our goal of providing a practical, commonsense discussion of criminal law remained an important part of the text's mission. Throughout the history of this text, readers and reviewers have pointed to the straightforward, readily understandable manner in which it is written as one of its primary strengths. We have endeavored to retain that strength with each new edition.

New to This Edition

Our goals in this eighth edition of *Criminal Law* mirror those of previous editions: to incorporate the most recent developments in criminal law into the text while at the same time retaining the basic organization and pedagogical approach that we believe best suits this subject. We have accordingly integrated criminal law decisions of the U.S. Supreme Court and the highest state courts from as late as January of 2002 into the text. We have also included discussions of significant legislative acts enacted since the seventh edition, such as the Federal USA Patriot Act of October 2001.

We have made several changes in the subject matter covered in this edition, both in the nature and the extent of that coverage. In Part 1, Chapters 1 and 2 have been reorganized and expanded to include more discussion of the common law in federal and state courts. In Chapter 4, the discussions of conspiracy and criminal attempt have been reorganized and rewritten, and an expanded discussion of the application of factual and legal impossibility has been added to reflect the modern treatment of those issues. In Chapter 6, our discussion of the use of force and physical restraints by law enforcement officers and the use of force in disciplining children has been updated. We updated the many affirmative defenses discussed in Chapter 7, and, in some cases, such as mistake of fact and double jeopardy, we rewrote them. In Chapter 8, in the discussion of criminal punishment, we expanded and reorganized the discussion of corporal punishment, focusing on the different tests for the use of such punishment when administered in prisons or by state school officials. We also added a new box on the death penalty as applied to juveniles and the mentally retarded; there is some likelihood that the U.S. Supreme Court soon may be prepared to give more definitive answers to those questions. Finally, in Chapter 9, we extensively expanded the discussion of tribal jurisdiction over criminal acts and added a new section on the jurisdiction of military tribunals to try suspected terrorists following President George W. Bush's 2001 order to hold such trials.

In Part 2, we attempted to edit the coverage of the balancing of constitutional rights with need for public order, in the belief that this area is increasingly the subject of a separate course in the criminal justice curriculum. We hope we have retained the essential material for those who wish to cover it in the criminal law class.

The organization of Part 3 remains unchanged. New materials regarding child "safe haven" laws and so-called end-of-life decisions have been added to Chapter 13. In Chapter 14, we added a new section discussing hate crime laws and court interpretations of some of those laws.

In Part 4, we rewrote Chapter 15 to more fully discuss basic property concepts and their relationship to theft of property. Treatment of the theft crimes was also rewritten to better illustrate the elements of those offenses. We have also included an expanded discussion of carjacking. In Chapter 16, the coverage of shoplifting has been updated and includes new materials, such as recent cases explaining more fully when the crime has occurred and recent legislative responses to the liability of store owners who cause customers to be stopped and searched or questioned. A new section on computer crimes has been added that includes computer crime statutes. We substantially edited Chapter 17 to eliminate discussion of some less important crimes, and added coverage of more contemporary issues such as Internet securities fraud. Because of its enormous popular interest, we added a discussion of the events leading up to the Enron scandal in 2001–2002. Though criminal charges against Enron or its officers have not been filed as of the publication of this edition, such charges may come about in the near future.

In Part 5, we rewrote Chapters 18 and 19 to reflect ongoing developments in sex-related crimes and criminal activity. Chapter 19 has an expanded discussion of child pornography, with emphasis on the use of the Internet in that activity. That chapter also includes an exercise devoted to examination of the Child Pornography Prevention Act of 1996 and the *Free Speech Coalition v. Reno* case construing that act. The U.S. Supreme Court has taken certiori of that case, and its decision obviously will have an enormous effect on Internet activities.

Part 6 includes a new chapter on terrorism, in which we discuss the various terrorist actions of past and recent periods and the statutory responses to those acts. It includes a review of a major part of the U.S. Congress's legislation concerning terrorism enacted in the past one hundred years.

Supplements Available with This Edition

Supplemental materials available to accompany this new edition consist of the following:

Instructor's Manual

This revised and updated *Instructor's Manual* includes the following for every text chapter: detailed chapter outlines, learning objectives, key terms, critical thinking questions, and a test bank. The completely new test bank features the following for each text chapter: thirty multiple-choice, twenty-five true/false, twenty fill-in-the-blank, and five essay questions.

ExamView®

FREE to adopters, this unparalleled program helps you create and deliver customized tests and study guides (both print and online) in minutes. ExamView guides you step by step through the process of creating tests, and its unique "what you see is what you get" capability allows you to see the test you are creating on the screen exactly as it will print or display online. It includes:

- **Complete word-processing capabilities.** Allows you to add an unlimited number of new questions or edit existing questions. Undo, cut, copy, paste, find and replace, create tables, and much more!
- **So much variety.** Create tests of up to 250 questions in length and choose from twelve question types and five methods of question selection.
- **Internet tests and study guides.** Simply choose "Save as an Internet Test" after you have built your test. You can then deliver the test via the Internet, and student results will be automatically e-mailed back to you.
- **Online Test Wizard.** Offers the opportunity to deliver your test over a local area network and then control who takes the test and when it may be completed.

A New Book-Specific Web Site

So many great tools to enhance learning for every chapter of the text:

- Tutorial quizzing activities
- Relevant Web links
- InfoTrac College Edition exercises
- Internet activities
- Chapter updates (includes chapter-related case and news updates)

It's easily accessible from Wadsworth's full-service Criminal Justice Resource Center: **http://www.cj.wadsworth.com.** This Web site provides instructors and students alike with a wealth of free information and resources, such as:

- The Criminal Justice Timeline
- What Americans Think

- BookFinder
- Terrorism: An Interdisciplinary Perspective
- National Criminal Justice Reference Service Calendar of Events

The Wadsworth Criminal Justice Video Library

So many exciting, new videos, so many great ways to enrich your lectures and spark discussion of the material in this text! Your Thomson/Wadsworth representative will be happy to provide details on our video policy by adoption size. The library includes the *A&E American Justice Series, Films for the Humanities*, and the *National Institute of Justice Crime File Videos*.

Court TV Video Selections: Seminal and high-profile court cases

Choose from sixteen absorbing and instructive videos, each featuring a different high-profile court case. Available free to qualified adopters based on adoption size. Cases include *California v. Powell et al.; Florida v. Smith; Vermont v. Grace; Cabey v. Goetz; New York v. Nelson; Massachusetts v. Woodward; The Greatest Trials of All Time: The Scottsboro Boys; Michigan v. Kevorkian; Florida v. Campbell; Florida v. Wuornos; New Mexico v. Gilbert; The Greatest Trials of All Time: Sam Sheppard; Karla Faye Tucker: A Question of Mercy; Maximum Security: New Jersey v. Landano;* and *Florida v. Miller.*

Crime Scenes: An Interactive Criminal Justice CD-ROM

Recipient of several *New Media* magazine Invision Awards, this interactive CD-ROM allows your students to take on the roles of investigating officer, lawyer, parole officer, and judge in excitingly realistic scenarios!

Mind of a Killer CD-ROM

Voted one of the top one hundred CD-ROMs by an annual *PC* magazine survey, *Mind of a Killer* gives students a chilling glimpse into the realm of serial killers with over eighty minutes of video, 3-D simulations, an extensive mapping system, a library, and much more.

Internet Guide for Criminal Justice, Second Edition

Intended for the novice Internet user, this completely updated eighty-page booklet explains the background and vocabulary for navigating the World Wide Web and offers criminal justice-related Web sites and Internet project ideas.

The Criminal Justice Internet Investigator, Third Edition

This colorful trifold pamphlet lists the most popular Internet addresses for criminal justice-related Web sites. Categories include policing, investigations, courts, corrections, research, juvenile delinquency, victimization, and more.

Key Cases, Comments, and Questions on Substantive Criminal Law

This book by Henry F. Fradella examines numerous cases with comments, analysis, and fully integrated pedagogy to help students grasp challenging material and test their knowledge through discussion questions.

Careers in Criminal Justice Interactive CD-ROM, Release 2.0

The *Careers in Criminal Justice Interactive CD-ROM,* Release 2.0, provides extensive career profiling information and self-assessment testing. It is designed to help students investigate and focus on the criminal justice career choices that are right for them. It also offers links and tools to assist students in finding a professional position. The 2.0 version includes seventeen new career profiles and eight new video interviews.

Seeking Employment in Criminal Justice and Related Fields, Fourth Edition

This book by J. Scott Harr and Kären M. Hess includes a free copy of the new *Careers in Criminal Justice CD-ROM,* Release 2.0. This supplemental book is designed to help students develop a job search strategy through resumes, cover letters, and interview techniques. It also provides extensive information on various criminal justice professions, including job descriptions, job salary suggestions, and contact information.

Guide to Careers in Criminal Justice, Second Edition

This updated sixty-page booklet helps students review the wide variety of careers in the criminal justice field. Included are job descriptions, salary suggestions, and contact information.

State Guides to Criminal Law (for California, Florida, Maryland, New York, Tennessee, and Texas)

These concise booklets include topics, laws, and other information related to criminal law specific to each state. State crime enforcement, court procedures, correctional systems, and juvenile justice programs are just a few of the issues covered.

Finally, *Criminal Law,* Eighth Edition, has several new features. Every chapter now has questions and problems and a brief summary at the end of the chapter, a keyword list at the beginning of the chapter, and at least two exercises designed to introduce the InfoTrac College Edition Internet resource to students (available free with the Eighth Edition). We trust these additions will add to the Eighth Edition's pedagogical value.

We hope you find that this new edition of *Criminal Law* retains the best features of past editions while adding material that will enhance the student's understanding of the course. As always, we welcome your comments and suggestions.

Explanatory Note

The authors have presented the general principles of criminal law in this textbook. However, a few states will vary somewhat in their laws because of statutes or court decisions within that state.

For this reason, it is recommended that students and law enforcement officers consult with their legal advisers before assuming that the law applicable in other states is used in their state.

Acknowledgments

The authors wish to thank the following persons who reviewed the seventh edition of *Criminal Law* in preparation for the eighth edition. Their thoughtful and incisive comments were extremely helpful to its completion:

Frank L. Fischer, Kankakee Community College

Sandra J. Gourley, Lake Land College

Milo Miller, Southeast Missouri State University

Steven D. Murray, Community College of Rhode Island

Richard E. Priehs, Saginaw Valley State University

Darrell L. Ross, East Carolina University

Steve Russell, University of Texas—San Antonio

The authors also wish to thank Sabra Horne, Jennie Redwitz, Shelley Murphy, Linda Jupiter, and Barbara Coster for their help and contributions to the text. Terry Anderson wishes to thank Creighton Law School and Denver University College of Law for providing him with the time and assistance to work on the text.

Thomas J. Gardner
Milwaukee, Wisconsin

Terry M. Anderson
Denver, Colorado

I

Criminal Law Generally

CONTENTS

KEY TERMS

public law

tort

nulla poena sine lege

felony

misdemeanor

void for vagueness

overbreadth

ex post facto

bill of attainder

due process

Criminal Law in a Democracy

Crime has been part of the human condition since people began to live in groups. Ancient documents indicate that conduct such as murder, theft, and robbery was defined as criminal by civilizations that existed before biblical times. The Bible recounts stories of crimes such as Cain killing Abel and the parable of the Good Samaritan, who came to the assistance of a man who had been assaulted and robbed (Luke 10:25–37).

Criminal laws regulate human conduct and tell people what they cannot do and, in some instances, what they must do under certain circumstances. Throughout history, all societies have had criminal codes regulating conduct.

The Law as the Will of the People Within a Democracy

Democracies have always sought to translate their basic principles and ideals into achievable goals through a system of laws that balance the rights of individuals with the compelling needs of society as a whole. These goals include public order, domestic tranquility, and protection of the basic rights of individuals.

Because governments in democracies are the servants and not the masters of the people, laws should be the product of the will of the people. Criminal justice systems in democracies operate most successfully when the majority of the people believe that laws are fair and that the system can operate efficiently and effectively.[1]

The issue of what laws should be enacted often causes intense public debate. Laws are enacted by elected representatives of the people. They are enforced, administered, and interpreted by civil servants and elected officials in other branches of government. In the United States, those branches are as follows:

1. *The legislative branch.* Laws (including criminal laws) are enacted by the legislative branch. The chief executive officer participates in the legislative process by signing or vetoing proposed laws. State governors and the U.S. president provide leadership on many proposed laws by either supporting or opposing them and by providing information about proposed laws.

2. *The executive branch.* Agencies within the executive branch of government administer and enforce laws. Law enforcement agencies are found within the executive branch of government and are charged with the enforcement of criminal laws, in addition to the performance of other duties.

3. *The judicial branch.* People who are charged with crimes have a right to be tried before a judge or a jury in a court in the judicial branch of government. Fact finders (jury or judge) determine the issues in cases presented to them, including the issue of guilt or innocence. Judges in the United States have the power of judicial review in determining the constitutionality of laws or ordinances.

The debate over public policies and which laws should be enacted commences in many instances when candidates seek election to public office. Candidates for public office state their positions on what laws they will seek to enact. Debates then continue in the state legislative body and in the Congress of the United States.

Government Regulation of Conduct

Government may regulate conduct of persons by means of

- fines or forfeiture for civil offenses (for example, speeding is ordinarily a civil offense punishable by a fine and forfeiture of points)
- imprisonment for some criminal offenses

Law enforcement officers do not make laws. Their traditional tasks are to enforce laws and maintain public order. They are also called upon to provide a wide range of other public services, such as minimizing traffic problems, mediating violent family disputes, rendering aid to injured persons, coping with community tensions, guiding community crime prevention efforts, and responding to emergencies and disasters.

Criminal Law and Related Fields of Law

Public and Private Law

In early England, crimes such as robbery, murder, and theft were classified as private matters, which made victims responsible for remedying their own problems. Victims and their families usually responded with violence if they knew or suspected the identity of the offender. They also had the option of bringing the matter before a civil court, but such courts were few and the chances of success minimal.

During the reign of Henry II (1154–89), English law began to recognize that crime was more than a personal affair between the victim and the perpetrator and that punishment should not be left to individuals.

Today, criminal law in England and the United States is *public law.* Apprehension and prosecution of criminals are public matters. Public law enforcement agencies, public prosecutors, courts, jails, and correctional institutions make up the criminal justice systems in both countries. Crime victims can bring lawsuits in civil courts if the offender is known and has resources to pay money judgments.

Private law deals with relationships between individuals in matters such as divorce, contractual issues, real estate law, and private inheritance.

Criminal Procedure

Criminal procedure is a subfield of criminal law and consists of the steps that are followed from the criminal incident through punishment and release of the offender.

Criminology and criminalistics are fields that are separate from but related to substantive criminal law. **Criminology** is the sociological and psychological study of the causes of crime, the control of crime, and the conditions under which criminal law developed. Criminalistics is the professional and scientific discipline directed to the

Why Some Conduct May or May Not Be Designated as Criminal

Reasons a Legislative Body Might Designate Specific Conduct as Criminal

- To protect the public from violent or dangerous conduct
- To protect public health
- To maintain public order
- To protect the right of privacy of individuals
- To protect public morality
- Because no other apparent way to promote a desired public policy is available

Reasons a Legislative Body Might Not Designate Specific Conduct as Criminal

- The government does not have constitutional power to prohibit such conduct.
- The conduct in question is constitutionally protected.
- No influential public or private groups or individuals have demanded the regulation of such conduct.
- Enforcing a law criminalizing such conduct would not be economically feasible.
- Passing a law criminalizing such conduct would not be politically popular.

recognition, identification, individualization, and evaluation of physical evidence by application of the natural sciences. Criminology is a branch of sociology; criminalistics is the application of science to criminal investigation and encompasses forensic science.

Substantive Criminal Law

Substantive criminal law is an important branch of public law. It defines the standards of conduct that the society and the community require for the protection of the community as a whole. It establishes the standards necessary to preserve public order and to protect property rights. It seeks to protect the right of individual privacy and the right to move about freely without fear of molestation. It does this primarily by defining conduct that is unacceptable and punishable.

In ancient times and on the frontiers in America, people had to protect themselves and thus moved about armed with weapons. If the law could not (or would not) punish an offender, the victim or the victim's family and friends would punish the offender themselves. Such retaliations could trigger blood feuds that went on for years between families and clans.

With the establishment of a system of laws and the growth of public confidence in the ability of the criminal justice system to preserve ordered liberty, people have generally ceased taking the law into their own hands. Public confidence that the government, as an agent of the people, has the ability and the desire to maintain public order is an indispensable ingredient of a successful criminal justice system.[2]

Legal Wrongs

Legal wrongs are either civil or criminal. A *civil wrong* is a private wrong, such as a tort or a contract violation, done to a person or property. A *criminal wrong* is one in which the state and the public have declared an interest. Ordinarily, when a private wrong occurs, only the injured party or the party's representative may seek civil redress in a civil court of law. Nearly every large American community has three or four times as many civil courts, which hear civil cases of alleged private wrongs, as criminal courts, which hear criminal cases involving public wrongs. In cases of public wrong, the state may either begin a criminal action in a criminal court or take the alleged public wrong to a civil court, as is done occasionally in obscenity, antitrust, or consumer fraud cases.

Distinction Between a Crime and a Tort

A **tort** is a civil wrong done to a person or to his or her property. Of the civil private laws, the law of torts is the closest to criminal law. Often the same wrong may constitute both a tort and a crime. For example, battery, rape, theft, criminal libel, and criminal damage to property are all torts and also crimes. Both civil actions by the injured parties and criminal actions by the state may be brought against the offenders. The offenders may be convicted of the crime in a criminal court and then found to be civilly liable in a civil court and ordered to pay compensatory and punitive damages to the victims for the torts that were committed.

A person who has thrown rocks at the windows of a private building, breaking ten windows and injuring one of the occupants, has committed both crimes and torts. Not only may a criminal action be brought against this person for the actual conduct, but civil tort actions may also be brought by the person who was injured and by the person whose property was damaged. However, someone who has seriously injured another person in an automobile accident, in which the police and a prosecutor determine that neither a criminal violation nor criminal negligence has occurred, cannot properly be charged with a crime. In this case, only a civil action may be brought by the injured person or his or her representative. If the defendant were found to be civilly liable, the case would then be an example of a tort that was not also a crime.

Criminal Law and Moral Law

Criminal laws are strongest when they reflect the moral and ethical beliefs of the society. Murder, for example, is considered morally wrong, and most people would not murder

---

Distinguishing Crime, Tort, and Moral Wrong

Type of Wrong		Court Determining Wrong
Crime	A public wrong against society	Criminal court
Tort	A private wrong against an individual or individuals	Civil court
Moral wrong	Violation of a moral or religious code	No punishment unless the moral wrong is also a crime or tort

A crime may also be a tort and a moral wrong. For example, murder is a crime, a tort, and also a moral wrong.

Factors Influencing Whether to Commit a Crime

Why a Person Would Not Commit a Crime	*Why a Person Would Commit a Crime*
Moral or ethical commitment to obey the law ("law behind the law")	Insufficient moral or ethical restraints
Fear of arrest and punishment	Belief in ability to get away without detection, arrest, and punishment
Social and peer pressures of friends, associates, family, and community	Peer pressure
Fear of embarrassment to self, family, and friends	Belief that detection and associated embarrassment can be avoided
Lack of motive or compelling drive to commit crime (no compelling desire to steal, murder, assault, rape, and so on)	Compelling desire or motive to achieve illegal objective (narcotic addiction, for example, provides motive for person who would probably not otherwise commit crime)
Lack of opportunity, or lack of capacity or skill, to commit crime	Opportunity combined with capacity and skill
Fear of economic sanction, such as loss of job or promotion, lawsuit and damages, or loss of license (driver's license, liquor, lawyer, doctor, nurse, and so on)	Sees crime as a quick, easy way of obtaining money, drugs, power, or other objectives (Even if caught, the odds are good that the person will not go to prison. Few persons convicted of nonviolent felonies go to prison.)

another person even if it were not forbidden by all jurisdictions in the United States. Murder, then, is forbidden not only by the criminal law but also by the moral law. This moral or ethical commitment to the law is known as the *law behind the law*. The importance of the law behind the law is the fact that it compels most people to conform to standards necessary for public order regardless of whether a police officer is watching them. Public order is not possible without the law behind the law, because not enough police are available to enforce criminal law without this moral and ethical backing.

The standards set by moral laws are generally higher than those set by criminal laws. Moral law attempts to perfect personal character, whereas criminal law, in general, is aimed at misbehavior that falls substantially below the norms of the community. Criminal conduct is ordinarily unjustifiable and inexcusable.

Criminal law alone cannot bring all conduct into conformity with the standards expected by the community. Society uses many sanctions besides criminal law to encourage people to behave properly. A person with a good job and savings is not likely to assault, rape, or libel other people, knowing that a substantial money judgment could be obtained by any victim. A spouse beater could end up in a divorce court instead of a criminal court. A person who is rude, abusive, and vulgar will lose friends and social standing. An employee who cannot get along with other people or who punches another employee in the face could be fired by the employer. Suspension of a driver's license and the revocation of a liquor license are other examples of sanctions used to regulate behavior.

The Principle of "No Punishment Without a Law for It"

A basic principle of both English and American law is that no one can be lawfully punished for his or her conduct or omission unless that conduct or omission has been clearly made a crime by statutory or common law of that jurisdiction. The Latin maxim **nulla poena sine lege** ("no punishment without law") long ago established this principle.

This principle was made part of American law in 1791 by the enactment of the Fifth Amendment of the U.S. Constitution, which provides that "No person shall be . . . deprived of life, liberty, or property without due process of law."[3]

Although the "prior notice" doctrine requires that fair warning be given in language that the ordinary person will understand, it does not require that the statute list in detail the many ways in which a forbidden wrong may be committed. The following example illustrates this:

EXAMPLE: Criminal homicide can be committed by many different unlawful acts such as using a gun, knife, poison, a crowbar, a truck, or other vehicle; pushing off a cliff or a bridge or down stairs; or strangulation. Murder statutes do not have to list the hundred or more ways of committing murder. Such statutes forbid the defined evil and clearly provide notice as to the act or acts forbidden.[4]

Therefore, in view of the principle of no punishment without a law for it, the following questions must be asked before any person is arrested, charged with a crime, or convicted: What has the person done that violates the statutes of the state? Was the person legally (not just morally) obligated to act and then failed to perform this legal (not moral) duty?

Classifications of Crimes

Many acts have been designated as criminal offenses in the United States. The President's Commission on Crime reported in 1966 in *The Challenge of Crime in a Free Society* (p. 18) that the federal government alone has designated more than 2,800 offenses as crimes and noted that "a much larger number of State and local" offenses exist.

The large number of crimes in the United States may be classified as follows:

- According to their sources, as statutory, common law, administrative, or constitutional crimes (see Chapter 2)

- As felonies or misdemeanors, which determines the method in which they are tried and, in many states, affects the law of arrest for such offenses. Many states classify felonies and misdemeanors as class A, class B, and so forth. In this way, punishment can be standardized: a class B felony is generally a twenty-year felony; a class C felony is a ten-year felony, and so on (see the next section on Felony and Misdemeanor)

- According to the harm or wrong that occurs (see individual state criminal codes for classifications of crime, such as "crimes against the person" or "crimes against property")

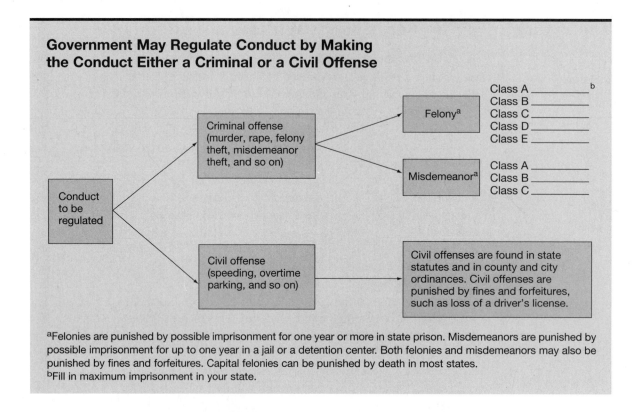

Government May Regulate Conduct by Making the Conduct Either a Criminal or a Civil Offense

[a]Felonies are punished by possible imprisonment for one year or more in state prison. Misdemeanors are punished by possible imprisonment for up to one year in a jail or a detention center. Both felonies and misdemeanors may also be punished by fines and forfeitures. Capital felonies can be punished by death in most states.
[b]Fill in maximum imprisonment in your state.

Felony and Misdemeanor

The felony/misdemeanor classification is the most common and most important classification of crime. A **felony** is the most serious crime and generally is punished by one year or more in prison or a penitentiary. Most states and the federal government have laws providing for the death penalty for a few very serious felonies.

A **misdemeanor** is a less serious offense and may be punished by imprisonment in the local jail or house of correction for a period of time less than a year (for example, thirty days, sixty days, or longer lengths of time).

An offense that does not provide for possible jailing or imprisonment is generally not classified as a crime but rather as a civil offense. For example, ordinary speeding is punished by a fine and loss of points but is not a "crime."

Whether a crime is a felony or a misdemeanor is important for the following reasons:

1. Conviction of a felony would, in most states, stand in the way of some types of employment, affect credit rating or the ability to adopt a child, and prevent a person from entering the armed forces, becoming a law enforcement officer, or obtaining a license as a nurse, doctor, lawyer, and so on unless a pardon is obtained.[5] A misdemeanor conviction would not ordinarily have these effects.

2. People charged with felonies have the right to a preliminary hearing or a "presentation or indictment of a grand jury."[6]

3. The law governing making an arrest for a felony differs from the law governing making an arrest for a misdemeanor in the following ways:

When Failure to Act Is a Crime

State and federal criminal codes, as do the Ten Commandments, forbid specific conduct, for example, do not murder and do not steal. Such offenses are called *crimes of commission.*

    A small percentage of crimes in criminal codes are crimes of omission—failure to act when a duty or obligation is imposed upon persons under certain circumstances. The following are examples of crimes of omission that can be found in state criminal codes.

Statute number of the offense in your state. (If not a crime, indicate status of this conduct in your state.)

1. Failure to remain at the scene of a vehicular accident in which a person was involved (also list other responsibilities of the person required in your state)   *Commission*

2. Failure to aid an officer when requested to do so   *Omission*

3. Failure to report the death of a child   *Commission*

4. Failure to report the location of a human corpse   *Commission*

5. Failure by parent, guardian, or others to provide adequate food, clothing, shelter, medical care, supervision, and so on, for a child in his or her care when harm results or might result   *Omission*

6. Failure by parent, guardian, or others to come to the aid of a child in his or her care when such aid would not place the adult in any serious danger

7. Failure to aid, come to the assistance of, or summon police for a crime victim when having knowledge that a crime of bodily harm has occurred and when such aid would not place the informer in any serious danger   *Omission*

8. Failure to leave or withdraw when ordered by a public official who has declared that an unlawful assembly exists

9. Failure to move on or to leave a place when properly and lawfully ordered to do so by a law enforcement officer

10. Failure to properly identify oneself and explain one's conduct when properly and lawfully ordered to do so by a law enforcement officer (see Section 250.6, Loitering or Prowling, of the Model Penal Code)

11. Failure to submit to a Breathalyzer test (or other similar test) when properly and lawfully requested to do so by a law enforcement officer   *Omission*

12. Failure to obey a proper and legal order of a court (see Chapter 22, on contempt)   *Commission*

13. Homicide by omission

Victimless Crimes

The term *victimless crimes* is used to designate crimes that do not directly inflict personal or property harm on another person in the sense that murder, robbery, rape, and theft do. The term is controversial when applied to crimes such as drug violations because the deadly drug trade in the United States results in many victims.

Examples of Victimless Crimes[a]

Possession or use of a small amount of a drug such as marijuana

Public drunkenness (decriminalized by many states)

Prostitution

Gambling (many forms of gambling are now legal)

Obscenity offenses involving consenting adults

Fortune-telling

Dueling (both parties consent but can result in victim)

Loan-sharking (when both parties voluntarily enter agreement)

Examples of Victimless Crimes That Have Been Abolished by Many States

Fornication

Adultery

Homosexual relations

Cohabitation

Between consenting adults in a nonpublic place

Examples of Victimless Crimes That Have Been Declared Unconstitutional

Use of contraceptives (even by married couples)—*Griswold v. Connecticut,* 381 U.S. 479 (1965)

Possession of or reading obscene material in privacy of one's home—*Stanley v. Georgia,* 394 U.S. 557 (1969)

Drug addiction as a crime in and of itself— *Robinson v. California,* 370 U.S. 660 (1962)

[a]Some people take the position that society is the victim of many of these offenses.

a) There is broad authority for law enforcement officers to make a felony arrest; however, law enforcement officers in states using the "in presence" requirement cannot arrest for misdemeanors unless the misdemeanor is committed in their presence or unless other statutory or common law authority exists.

b) "Citizen's arrest" is generally limited to felonies committed in the presence of the citizen unless the statutes or common law of a state provide additional authority.[7]

General Constitutional Limitations on Criminal Laws

States' Power to Enact Criminal Laws

The U.S. Supreme Court stated that "[b]roadly speaking, crimes in the United States are what the law of the individual States make them, subject to (constitutional) limitations."[8]

States, therefore, have broad authority to create criminal laws. But criminal laws cannot violate rights of persons protected or granted by the U.S. Constitution or the constitution of that state. States cannot criminalize conduct protected by the First Amendment freedom of speech, freedom of religion, or freedom to move about freely (see Chapters 10, 11, and 12). Nor can a state impose a punishment that violates the Eighth Amendment prohibition against "cruel and unusual punishment" (see Chapter 8). Chapters 6 and 7 on defenses also present other constitutional limitations. Other general limitations on criminal laws follow.

Ex Post Facto Laws

Article I, Sections 9 and 10, of the U.S. Constitution forbid the U.S. Congress and all states from enacting "**ex post facto** (after the fact) laws." Therefore, no state or the U.S. Congress can create a new crime in November and make the law retroactive so as to punish conduct that was lawful in September or October of that year. Most state constitutions also forbid ex post facto laws. Ex post facto restrictions apply only to criminal laws and not to civil laws such as tax laws. The ex post facto clause also is only a limitation on the power of state and federal legislation bodies and does not apply to the judicial branch of government. (See the May 2001 U.S. Supreme Court case of *Rogers v. Tennessee,* 149 L.Ed.2d 697.)

The ex post facto clause forbids the following: (1) creating a criminal law and making it retroactive so as to make conduct before the enactment of the law a criminal violation; (2) laws that aggravate a crime retroactively (for example, making a misdemeanor a felony as of a date six months before the enactment of the legislation); (3) laws that increase the punishment for a crime retroactively; and (4) laws that alter the legal rules of evidence and permit conviction on less or different evidence than the law required at the time of the commission of the offense.[9]

The ex post facto clause protects conduct that is innocent when performed and requires that "persons have a right to fair warning of conduct which will give rise to criminal penalties." (U.S. Supreme Court in *Marks v. United States,* 430 U.S. 188, 97 S.Ct. 990, 992 [1977]).

Bill of Attainder

Article I, Sections 9 and 10, of the U.S. Constitution also forbid Congress and the states from enacting any **bill of attainder.** A bill of attainder is a legislative act that inflicts punishment without the person (defendant) already having had a trial in a court before a judge. In 1965, the U.S. Supreme Court stated the history of the bill of attainder in *United States v. Brown,* 381 U.S. 437:

> The bill of attainder, a parliamentary act sentencing to death one or more specific persons, was a device often resorted to in sixteenth, seventeenth and eighteenth century England for dealing with persons who had attempted, or threatened to attempt, to overthrow the government. In addition to the death sentence, attainder generally carried with it a "corruption of blood" which meant that the attained party's heirs could not inherit his property. The "bill of pains and penalties" was identical to the bill of attainder, except that it prescribed a penalty short of death, e.g., banishment, deprivation of the right to vote, or exclusion of the designated

party's sons from Parliament. Most bills of attainder and bills of pains and penalties named the parties to whom they were to apply; a few, however, simply described them.

In forbidding bills of attainder, the U.S. Constitution and state constitutions limit legislatures to the task of writing laws (rule making). Persons charged with a crime can go before a court to determine guilt or innocence.

Void-for-Vagueness Doctrine

In writing a criminal statute or ordinance, a legislative body must use clear and precise language that gives fair and adequate notice of the conduct that is forbidden or required. If the language of a statute or ordinance is vague, it may be held unconstitutional under the **void-for-vagueness** doctrine.

The void-for-vagueness test asks whether a statute or ordinance on its face "is so vague that men of common intelligence must guess at its meaning and differ as to its application."[10] A vague criminal statute or ordinance creates uncertainty as to what the law requires and may have some or all of the following results:

1. It may trap those who desire to be law-abiding by not providing fair notice of what is prohibited.[11]
2. It may cause arbitrary and discriminatory enforcement because those who enforce and apply the law have no clear and explicit standards to guide them.[12]
3. When a vague statute "abut(s) upon sensitive areas of First Amendment freedoms, it operates to inhibit the exercise of (those) freedoms. Uncertain meaning inevitably leads citizens to steer far wider of the unlawful zone . . . than if the boundaries of the forbidden areas were clearly marked.[13]

The void-for-vagueness doctrine recently was applied by the U.S. Supreme Court to declare a Chicago, Illinois, "gang congregation" ordinance unconstitutional. *City of Chicago v. Morales*[14] involved a Chicago ordinance that sought to control gang violence by giving the police permission to arrest gang members who are loitering in a public place. The ordinance permitted a police officer who believed a gang member was one of a group of people loitering in a public place to order the entire group to disperse. Refusal to do so was a criminal offense. The U.S. Supreme Court declared the ordinance unconstitutionally vague, because it did not require the police to determine the purpose of the group before ordering it to disperse. The police therefore had virtually unlimited discretion to determine what conduct was criminal, which violates the second factor listed above. The ordinance also violated the Due Process Clause because it did not give fair warning of prohibited conduct and did not adequately inform the public what prompt dispersal meant.

Overbreadth

Criminal statutes and ordinances may also be held to be unconstitutional if the manner in which they are written violates the **overbreadth** doctrine. In 1967, the U.S. Supreme Court stated that overbreadth "offends (when the words of a statute or ordinance) . . .

sweep unnecessarily broadly and thereby invade the area of protected freedoms."[15] A vague statute or ordinance may be overbroad if its uncertain boundaries leave open the possibility of punishment for protected conduct and thus lead people to avoid such protected activity in order to steer clear of violating the uncertain law.[16] However, a clear and precise statute may also be overbroad if it prohibits constitutionally protected conduct.

The void-for-vagueness test and the overbreadth test are separate and distinct. However, when First Amendment rights are at issue, the U.S. Supreme Court uses the two tests in a manner that makes them virtually one doctrine. From the cases, it can be stated that statutes and ordinances that regulate conduct must comply with the following requirements:[17]

- Fair and adequate notice must be given of the conduct that is forbidden or required.

- A precise standard of conduct must be specified in terms of results that can reasonably be expected.

- The statute or ordinance cannot permit or encourage arbitrary and discriminatory law enforcement that may result in erratic and arbitrary arrests and convictions.

- The statute or ordinance cannot violate or infringe on rights that are secured or granted by the U.S. Constitution.

"Status" Crimes

A state may regulate and control the use of such drugs as heroin, cocaine, and crack in a number of ways. The government may and does forbid the importing or manufacturing of the drugs; the law forbids possession and transportation of the forbidden drugs; the sale, use, or possession of such drugs is also forbidden. All of these specific acts (conduct) have been determined to be harmful to others or to the society as a whole. But can a state make addiction to heroin, cocaine, or crack, by itself, a crime?

To do something about its increasing heroin problem in the late 1950s, California passed a law making heroin addiction, by itself, a crime. The issue before the U.S. Supreme Court in the 1962 case of *Robinson v. California* was whether a person could be arrested and convicted for what he or she is or was.[18] The U.S. Supreme Court considered the question of whether a state could make a "status" or a "chronic condition" a crime in itself.

In pointing out the many ways in which government may legitimately attack the evils of narcotics trafficking, the U.S. Supreme Court reversed the defendant's conviction. In holding that a state law that made the "status" of narcotic addiction a criminal offense for which an offender might be prosecuted and imprisoned at any time, the Court held that such a criminal statute inflicted a "cruel and unusual punishment" in violation of the Eighth and Fourteenth Amendments of the U.S. Constitution. The Court stated that "even one day in prison would be a cruel and unusual punishment for the 'crime' of having a common cold."

In the 1968 case of *Powell v. Texas,* the defendant was an alcoholic with approximately one hundred arrests for acts of public intoxication.[19] In this case, the defendant argued that because he was compelled to drink and because he could not control his "status," the state did not have the power to punish him for his acts of public intoxica-

Due Process, Void for Vagueness, and Overbreadth

The **Due Process** Clause of the U.S. Constitution, made binding on states by the Fourteenth Amendment, requires that criminal legislation clearly identify prohibited conduct so as to give a reasonable person fair notice of that conduct. A criminal statute written so broadly as to invade the area of constitutionally protected rights, like free speech, is unconstitutional under the overbreadth doctrine. The following are representative cases on the void-for-vagueness and overbreadth doctrines.

Vagueness

Coates v. City of Cincinnati
Supreme Court of the United States
402 U.S. 611 (1971)

Ordinance made it illegal for three or more people gathered on a sidewalk to "annoy" passersby. Because what annoys one person may not annoy another, the Court held that "[t]hus the ordinance is vague . . . in the sense that no conduct is specified at all."

Papachristou v. City of Jacksonville
Supreme Court of the United States
405 U.S. 156 (1972)

Ordinance making being a "vagrant" a crime and defining vagrants as "rogues and vagabonds," "dissolute persons," or "common night walkers" held unconstitutional. The ordinance did not give fair notice of prohibited conduct.

Warren v. State
Florida Supreme Court
572 So.2d 1376 (1991)

Statute making it a crime to keep a "house of ill fame" unconstitutionally vague.

State v. Reba
Minnesota Court of Appeals
474 N.W. 2d 360 (1991)

Ordinance making it a crime for failure to keep a dwelling "in a clean and sanitary condition" vague, because it did not adequately give notice of prohibited conduct.

State v. Lara
Kansas Court of Appeals
853 P.2d 1168 (1993)

Statute making criminal "excessive and unusual" motor vehicle noises held not void for vagueness.

State v. Bohannon
Washington Court of Appeals
814 P.2d 694 (1991)

Statute making it a crime for causing a minor to engage in "sexually explicit conduct" held not void for vagueness.

Overbreadth

City of Houston v. Hill
Supreme Court of the United States
482 U.S. 451 (1987)

Ordinance making it unlawful to "interrupt policeman in execution of his duty" held overbroad, because it made otherwise protected speech a violation of the ordinance. (A citizen who interrupted a police officer to tell the officer of a bank robbery could lawfully be arrested under this ordinance.)

tion. The U.S. Supreme Court, however, affirmed Powell's conviction, holding that he was arrested and convicted for what he did (being drunk in a public place) and that Powell was not convicted for what he was (status). In refusing to extend the rule of law that had been established in the case of *Robinson v. California*, the Supreme Court held:

Traditional common-law concepts of personal accountability and essential considerations of federalism lead us to disagree with appellant. We are unable to conclude, on the state of this record or on the current state of medical knowledge, that chronic alcoholics in general, and Leroy Powell in particular, suffer from such an irresistible compulsion to drink and to get drunk in public that they are utterly unable to control their performance of either or both of these acts and thus cannot be deterred at all from public intoxication.

Equal Protection of the Laws

If a state made the crime of burglary in that state applicable only to males, the first man charged with burglary in that state would challenge the statute, arguing that it violated the Fourteenth Amendment requirement of "equal protection of the laws." Women could commit burglary in that state, but for the same conduct, a man could be convicted and sent to jail.

The Equal Protection Clause of the Fourteenth Amendment requires that states must treat all people alike, not only in enacting criminal and civil laws but also in enforcing rules. For example, probably all states have consanguinity laws forbidding marriages between brothers and sisters and other close relatives. Consanguinity laws apply to all persons, regardless of status, race, or religion.[20] They represent a valid exercise of the police power of a state because children born to closely related parents are more apt to be deformed.

But can a state make it a crime for blacks to marry whites, or for people of different races to live together? In the early 1960s, some states had such laws, which forbade marriage between persons of different races (miscegenation laws).[21] The following is one of the cases challenging miscegenation laws before the U.S. Supreme Court:

Loving v. Virginia

Supreme Court of the United States (1967) 388 U.S. 1, 87 S.Ct. 1817

Richard Loving, a white man, and Mildred Jeter, a black woman, were lawfully married in Washington, D.C. They then moved to the state of Virginia, which forbade interracial marriages. The Lovings were criminally indicted and pleaded guilty to the charges. They were sentenced to one year in jail. However, the trial judge suspended the sentence on the condition that the Lovings leave Virginia and not return for twenty-five years. The convictions and sentences were appealed to the U.S. Supreme Court. The Court noted that "Virginia is one of 16 States which prohibit and punish marriages on the basis of racial classifications." In declaring such laws unconstitutional, the U.S. Supreme Court held:

These statutes . . . deprive the Lovings of liberty without due process of law in violation of the Due Process Clause of the Fourteenth Amendment. The freedom to marry has long been recognized as one of the vital personal rights essential to the orderly pursuit of happiness by free men.

Marriage is one of the "basic civil rights of man," fundamental to our very existence and survival. . . . To deny this fundamental freedom on so unsupportable a basis as the racial classifications embodied in these statutes, classifications so directly subversive of the principle of equality at the heart of the Fourteenth Amendment, is surely to deprive all the State's citizens of liberty without due process of law. The Fourteenth Amendment requires that the freedom of choice to marry not be restricted by invidious racial discriminations. Under our Constitution, the freedom to marry or not marry a person of another race resides with the individual and cannot be infringed by the State.

SUMMARY

Criminal law is public law. That is, even though individual citizens may be the direct victims of criminal behavior, society as a whole is also wronged by that conduct. As a result, determination of what conduct should be made criminal is generally left to the public, usually through its elected representatives in state legislatures and the U.S. Congress. These bodies are charged with the responsibility of making the substantive criminal law, classifying each law as a felony or misdemeanor according to its perceived importance, and providing punishment for violations.

Although the elected representatives in the various states have broad authority to identify what behavior shall be made criminal, important limitations on that authority exist in the U.S. Constitution. Some of these limitations are explicit, such as the constitutional prohibition against ex post facto laws and bills of attainder. Other limitations, such as the *nulla poena* principle and the void-for-vagueness rule, are part of the due process guarantee of the Fifth and Fourteenth Amendments. These limitations help to strike a balance between the public's right to control objectionable conduct and the private citizen's right to freedom of expression.

WWW   BOOK-SPECIFIC WEB SITE

For chapter-related Web links, quizzing activities, and case and news updates, go to the *Criminal Law,* Eighth Edition, book-specific Web site at **http://info.wadsworth.com/ gardner.**

QUESTIONS AND PROBLEMS

1. Pestinikas and his wife verbally agreed to provide food, medicine, and other necessities to a sick and elderly 92-year-old man. Unfortunately, Pestinikas and his wife failed to provide the food and medical care they had been paid to provide. The state can prove that the 92-year-old man's death was caused by this failure and that the man died of malnutrition and exposure.

Under the criminal code of your state, could criminal charges be brought against Pestinikas? What possible charge could be issued? *Commonwealth v. Pestinikas,* WL 364218 (Pa. Super. 1992). For a discussion of criminal liability for negative acts, see Perkins, *Criminal Law,* 2d ed. (Mineola, N.Y.: Foundation Press, 1969). *Omission, murder*

2. A 5-year-old child is in sudden peril when a big wave hits him while in shallow water at the beach. All the following people could have saved him with no risk to themselves, but all fail to come to the child's assistance. Indicate the legal liability of each and whether that person can be charged in your state with the death of the child.

a) The father of the child *Guilty*

b) The lifeguard on duty *Guilty*

c) A stranger sunning on the beach who took pictures of the child's death *not guilty*

3. Ten-year-old Johnnie is punished by his mother for eating all the cookies in the cookie jar. Which of the following instructions by the mother, given just before she left the house for an hour, would not violate the void-for-vagueness principle?

a) "Be a good boy, Johnnie."

b) "Don't do anything naughty, Johnnie."

c) "Don't go into the cookie jar, Johnnie."

d) "Don't eat anything and spoil your appetite, because we are going to have dinner in an hour."

e) (c) and (d) are correct

Explain your answer.

4. Michael was almost 18 years old. Around midnight on a summer's night, he approached a 16½-year-old girl, Sharon, and her sister as they waited at a bus stop. The girls had been drinking. Michael and Sharon moved away from the others and began to kiss. When Sharon objected to Michael's sexual advances, Michael struck her in the face. Sharon then submitted to sexual intercourse. If the California prosecutor had charged Michael with rape, the state would have had a difficult time obtaining a criminal conviction. Therefore, based on the statements of the parties and witnesses (and other evidence), Michael was charged with violating California's "statutory rape" law. This law in California forbade sexual intercourse with a female under 18 (who is not a wife of the perpetrator). Another term for this offense is SIWAC (sexual intercourse with a child). Because the statute makes men alone criminally liable, Michael attacked the statute as violating equal protection of the laws. Does California have a valid state interest in enacting a statutory rape law and making it applicable to men only? Explain. *Michael M. v. Superior Court of Sonoma County,* 450 U.S. 464, 101 S.Ct. 1200 (1981).

5. The *Morales* decision, page 12 of this chapter, seems to make it difficult for the police to break up gangs congregating in the streets. Gang violence is undoubtedly a serious problem in many cities. In Chicago, for example, gang-related homicides increased from 51 in 1987 to 132 in 1991, the year the ordinance ruled unconstitutional in *Morales* was passed. Gang homicides peaked in Chicago in 1994 at 240.[22] What can the city do about street crimes and gang activity if ordinances such as the one in *Morales* are invalid because of the discretion given police? Could a city pass a curfew law, banning *all* persons below a certain age from gathering on the streets during certain hours? See *Hutchins v. Dist. of Columbia,* 188 F.3d 531 (D.C.C. 1999). Is this the best way to deal with the *Morales* problem?

INFOTRAC COLLEGE EDITION EXERCISES

1. Recall the case of *Carnell v. Texas* discussed in the ex post facto section of this chapter. Then read *Rogers v. Tennessee,* 121 S.Ct. 1693 (2001). Do you think *Rogers* was correctly decided? Go to InfoTrac College Edition, click on *Keywords,* and, using the search term *ex post facto law,* find the article in the *New Jersey Law Journal* discussing the *Rogers* case. Do the conclusions of the author of that article agree with yours? Why or why not?

2. For a look at how one Canadian city deals with one aspect of vagrancy, go to InfoTrac College Edition, click on *Subject guide,* and, using the search term *vagrancy,* click on View 14 Periodical references, and find the article "Cracking Down on the Down-and-Out" (May 18, 1998), which describes Vancouver, British Colombia's, response to certain kinds of panhandling. Click on View <u>text and retrieval choices</u>. Would the Vancouver ordinance be unconstitutional under the void-for-vagueness rule if adopted by, say, Seattle? Why or why not?

3. Go to InfoTrac College Edition, click on *Subject guide,* and, using the search term *vagrancy,* click on <u>See also</u> 2 Related Subjects. Click on <u>See</u> begging. Click on <u>View</u> 53 Periodical references. Find the article "Brother, Can You Spare a Dime?" (Dec. 1999) describing a panhandling case in Fort Lauderdale, Florida. Click on View <u>text and full content retrieval choices</u>. What was the argument made that the ordinance was unconstitutional?

NOTES

1. See James Q. Wilson's book, *Thinking About Crime* (New York: Basic Books, 1983), in which he states, "the average citizen thinks it obvious that one major reason why crime has increased is that people have discovered they can get away with it." This reflects a belief that the criminal justice system is neither efficient nor effective.

2. Failure to protect citizens breeds crime. When the government fails to protect citizens, some persons are likely to take the law into their own hands. An example of private justice (vigilantism) may have occurred in a New York City subway in December 1984. Bernhard Goetz told New York police that he believed he was about to be robbed and that he produced a gun, shot his presumed assailants, and then left the scene. A New York grand jury would not indict Goetz for the shooting but did indict him for the illegal possession of a handgun. He was convicted and punished for that offense.

3. See Appendix A of this text for applicable sections of the U.S. Constitution.

4. See the case of *United States v. Bass,* 404 U.S. 336, 92 S.Ct. 515 (1971), in which the U.S. Supreme Court held that "a fair warning should be given . . . in language that the common world will understand."

5. When good reasons are given, state governors are likely to grant a pardon for a felony or misdemeanor conviction. The pardon will wipe the slate clean for the person. Depending on the law of the state, governors have the authority and power to grant clemency in different ways. They may grant a pardon, or commute or modify a sentence. Such clemency could be conditional if authorized by the state law.

6. Fifth Amendment to the U.S. Constitution.

7. Some states authorize store employees to arrest persons for shoplifting, which in most cases is a misdemeanor or is charged as an ordinance violation. The shoplifting statutes of other states authorize the store employees to detain the suspect until the police or sheriff arrives.

8. *Rochin v. California,* 342 U.S. 165, 168, 72 S.Ct. 205, 207 (1952).

9. See the May 2000 U.S. Supreme Court case of *Carnell v. Texas,* 146 L.Ed.2d 577, where the sexual assault conviction of the defendant was reversed because a Texas law retroactively reduced the amount of proof necessary to support the sexual assault conviction in violation of the ex post facto clause.

10. *Connally v. General Construction Co.,* 269 U.S. 385, 46 S.Ct. 126 (1926).

11. See *Papachristou v. City of Jacksonville,* 405 U.S. 156, 162, 92 S.Ct. 839, 843 (1972); and *United States v. Harriss,* 347 U.S. 612, 617, 74 S.Ct. 808, 811 (1954).

12. See *Coates v. City of Cincinnati,* 402 U.S. 611, 614, 91 S.Ct. 1686, 1688 (1971); and *Shuttlesworth v. City of Birmingham,* 382 U.S. 87, 90–91, 86 S.Ct. 211, 213–214 (1965).

13. *Grayned v. City of Rockford,* 408 U.S. 104, 109, 92 S.Ct. 2294, 2299 (1972).

14. 119 S.Ct. 1849 (1998).

15. *Zwickler v. Koota,* 389 U.S. 241, 250, 88 S.Ct. 391, 396 (1967).

16. See *Grayned v. City of Rockford,* 408 U.S. 104, 109, 92 S.Ct. 2294, 2299 (1972); and *Dombrowski v. Pfister,* 380 U.S. 479, 486, 85 S.Ct. 1116, 1120 (1965).

17. See 119 S.Ct. 1849 (1999).

18. 370 U.S. 660, 82 S.Ct. 1417 (1962).

19. 392 U.S. 514, 88 S.Ct. 2145 (1968).

20. State statutes also often provide that marriage licenses may be issued to women beyond childbearing age who wish to marry a close relative. Under such statutes, two first cousins could marry if the woman meets the requirements of the state statute.

The results of six major medical studies reported in 2002 concluded that only small medical risks are seen in children born to first cousins who marry. The report recommended that the term "incest" should not apply to sexual relations between cousins—only to sexual relations between siblings and between parents and children. (See the *New York Times* article "Few Risks Seen to the Children of First Cousins," April 4, 2002.)

21. It is reported that there are now more than one million married interracial couples living in the United States. For example, U.S. Supreme Court Justice Clarence Thomas is a black man married to a white woman.

22. See *Gang Loitering, the Court, and Some Realism About Police Patrol,* 1999 S. Ct. Rev. 141, 147-48.

2

Purposes, Scope, and Sources of Criminal Law

CONTENTS

KEY TERMS

police power

common law crimes

Magna Carta

habeas corpus

state courts

federal courts

administrative crime

Goals and Purposes of Criminal Law

Background of the U.S. Criminal Justice System

People in all societies have the inherent right to protect their society and those living in that society from vicious acts that threaten either the society or the people. Societies throughout history have exercised this inherent right and have had either written or unwritten laws forbidding and punishing acts or omissions considered detrimental to the group or the individual.

From colonial days through World War I, the criminal codes of the various American states were generally small and usually embodied only those crimes that were considered serious wrongs against the society. Because these criminal laws were used to define and enforce public morality, the traditional attitude of lawyers and judges was that a crime was essentially a moral wrong.

The United States in those days was primarily an agricultural society with a simple style of life. Because most people lived in rural areas or small towns, the criminal codes could confine themselves primarily to conduct that was considered a serious threat to society. In those days, religious institutions, the family, and social pressure from the neighborhood and the town were generally capable of regulating behavior in other respects.

The 1920s saw the beginnings of rapid change of the United States from an agricultural society to an industrial society. This transformation, plus the unbelievable array of economic, social, and political changes that accompanied it, hastened the arrival of today's mass industrial society. These changes reduced the influence of American religious institutions, the community, and the home in molding and shaping behavior (particularly of youth) to the standards expected by society. To compensate for this change, many new criminal laws were enacted. The burden of maintaining public order and safety gradually shifted to local, state, and federal governments.

Today, the U.S. criminal justice system is large and assumes a greater role than ever before. Fear of and concern for crime have caused many changes. Everyone takes precautions today that were not taken thirty years ago. Doors are locked. Businesses and corporations take sophisticated measures to protect their employees, customers, and property. Private security personnel now outnumber law enforcement personnel. Alarm systems in businesses, homes, schools, and vehicles are common. Private attempts to deal with crime have become an important complement to the criminal justice system.

Goals and Purposes

The U.S. Constitution is the supreme law of the United States. Its preamble states that the purposes of the U.S. Constitution are to

> establish Justice, insure domestic Tranquility, . . . promote the general Welfare, and secure the Blessings of Liberty to ourselves and our Posterity.

The U.S. Supreme Court stated that the "most basic function of any government is to provide for the security of the individual and his property." *Lanzetta v. New Jersey,* 59 S.Ct. 618 (1939).

The signing of the U.S. Constitution from a painting in the Smithsonian Institution in Washington, D.C.
© Bettmann/CORBIS

The generally recognized goals and purposes of the criminal justice system are to

- discourage and to deter people from committing crimes
- protect society from dangerous and harmful people
- punish people who have committed crimes
- rehabilitate and reform people who have committed crimes

The U.S. District Court for the District of Columbia expressed the objective and purpose of criminal law in these terms in the first-degree murder case of *United States v. Watson*:

> The object of the criminal law is to protect the public against depredations of a criminal. On the other hand, its purpose is also to prevent the conviction of the innocent, or the conviction of a person whose guilt is not established beyond a reasonable doubt. The Court must balance all these aims of the trial. This view was eloquently stated by Mr. Justice Cardozo in *Snyder v. Commonwealth of Massachusetts*, 291 U.S. 97, 122, 54 S.Ct. 330, 338, 78 L.Ed. 674: ". . . [J]ustice, though due to the accused, is due to the accuser also. The concept of fairness must not be strained till it is narrowed to a filament. We are to keep the balance true."[1]

In forbidding burglary, assault, rape, robbery, and other crimes, criminal laws protect the right of privacy of individuals. The U.S. Supreme Court recognized this important function in the 1967 case of *Katz v. United States*, 88 S.Ct. 507, when the Court wrote:

The protection of a person's general right of privacy—his right to be left alone by other people—is, like the protection of his property and his very life, left largely to the laws of the individual States.

The Permissible Scope of Criminal Laws in the United States

Dictators such as Hitler and Stalin used the criminal laws of their countries to rule by brute force and terror. However, in a democracy, criminal laws and the criminal justice system are essential parts of the democratic system, providing for public order and basic freedoms. Such a system is used to serve the people and cannot be used to master and suppress the people, as is done in totalitarian countries. Therefore, in order to prevent misuses of the criminal justice system, constitutional limits are placed on the power of government to regulate the conduct and lives of its citizens through the use of criminal laws. Some of these constitutional limitations are presented in Chapter 1. Other limitations are presented in Chapters 5, 6, and 7 and in Part Two of this text.

The Use of the Police Power to Maintain Public Order

Each state is responsible for the maintenance of public order and public safety within that state. To do this, states enact criminal laws and establish a criminal justice system under the police power of that state. The police power is an inherent power vested in each state. The Tenth Amendment of the U.S. Constitution provides that "[t]he powers not delegated to the United States by the Constitution, nor prohibited by it to the States, are reserved to the States respectively, or to the people."

The term **police power** refers to the broad legislative power of a state to pass laws that promote the public health, safety, and welfare. In the 1949 case of *Kovacs v. Cooper,* the U.S. Supreme Court stated:

The police power of a state extends beyond health, morals and safety, and comprehends the duty, within constitutional limitations, to protect the well-being and tranquility of a community. A state or city may prohibit acts or things reasonably thought to bring evil or harm to its people.[2]

In the 1974 case of *Village of Belle Terre v. Boraas,* the U.S. Supreme Court sustained a zoning ordinance restricting land use to single-family dwellings, stating:

The police power is not confined to elimination of filth, stench, and unhealthy places. It is ample to lay out zones where family values, youth values and the blessing of quiet seclusion, and clean air make the area a sanctuary for people.[3]

Limitations on the Police Power of a State to Regulate Conduct

In enacting criminal laws through the use of the police power, the state is regulating the conduct of citizens within the state by telling them what they may not do or what they must do. The state may not regulate conduct arbitrarily.

**Goals and Purposes of Criminal Law
and the Criminal Justice System**

- To discourage and deter people from committing crimes
- To protect society from dangerous and harmful people
- To punish people who have committed crimes
- To rehabilitate and reform people who have committed crimes

In enacting criminal law, the state must be able to show

- a compelling public need to regulate the conduct the state seeks to regulate, and that the power to regulate is within the police power of the state. The U.S. Supreme Court held in *Lawton v. Steele* that "it must appear, first, that the interests of the public generally . . . require such interference; and, that the means . . . are not unduly oppressive upon individuals;"[4]

- that the law does not contravene the U.S. Constitution or infringe on any of the rights granted or secured by the U.S. Constitution or the constitution of that state; and

- that the language of the statute or ordinance clearly tells people what they are not to do (or what they must do) and that the law prohibits only the conduct that may be forbidden.

To understand these limitations, suppose some of the states create the following offenses as misdemeanors:

State A enacts a law requiring that all people in the state go to a church of a specific religion every Sunday.

State B enacts a law forbidding skateboarding.

State C enacts a law forbidding the sale, use, or possession of any tobacco product.

State D enacts a law requiring operators and passengers of motorcycles to wear protective headgear.[5]

Not only would State A violate First Amendment rights to the freedom of religion by passage of a law of this nature, but also this statute is not within the police power of a state because it serves no valid function of government.

Regulation of skateboarding could be done by governmental units, such as cities and school districts, for public safety reasons and to minimize interference with pedestrian and motor vehicle traffic. But no compelling public need exists to completely forbid such conduct because of public health, safety, or morals; therefore, such regulations could hardly stand under attack. The right to be free from interference by government was stated as follows in 1975:

No right is more sacred, or is more carefully guarded, by the liberty assurance of the due process clause than the right of every citizen to the possession and control of his own person, free from restraint or interference by the state. The makers of our Constitution conferred, as against the government, the right to be let alone—the most comprehensive of rights and the right most valued by civilized man.

* * *

However, personal freedoms are not absolute, and the liberty guaranteed by the due process clause implies absence of arbitrary interferences but not immunity from reasonable regulations.[6]

State C could show that its regulation is within the police power of the state because medical studies show that the use of tobacco products does affect people's health. To date, states and cities have not outlawed smoking completely. Rather, they have prohibited smoking in parts of (and in some places all) public buildings. Enforcement of a complete ban has not been advocated by any group because it would be difficult if not impossible to enforce. A total ban on smoking could lead to the kind of lawlessness associated with attempts to outlaw alcohol in the 1920s.

Sources of Criminal Law

Substantive criminal law can be found in the following sources, each of which is discussed in the next sections:

- Criminal law, on rare occasions, can be found today in the common law of some states.

- Most criminal law is found in the statutes of each state and in the statutes of the federal government.

- Criminal law can also be found in commercial, sanitation, health, financial, and tax administrative regulations that have criminal sanctions. These regulations are enacted by state and federal administrative and regulatory agencies.

- A few sections of state constitutions and one section of the U.S. Constitution contain criminal law. Treason is the only crime defined by the U.S. Constitution. For material on treason, see Chapter 21 on terrorism.

Common Law Crimes

Because the common law was the first and earliest source of criminal laws, it is presented first. And because the historic source of U.S. criminal law lies in the common law of England, a review of the development of criminal law in England and in the American colonies is necessary.

When the English kings gained control of the whole of England in the Middle Ages, royal judges began deciding civil and criminal cases throughout all of England, thus supporting the Crown by preserving the peace and dispensing justice. Few people in those days could read or write, and England was not yet a democracy. The king, the judges, and the ecclesiastical authorities played important roles not only in creating (sometimes inventing) criminal laws but also in defining the elements and the scope of the criminal offenses. Judges became familiar with the general customs, usages, and moral concepts of the people and based judgments on them. In doing so, the judges determined which customs and moral concepts should prevail as law.

By the early 1600s, with only a few criminal statutes, the criminal law of England was composed primarily of the mandatory rules of conduct laid down by the English judges. In formulating the **common law crimes** of England, the royal judges believed that their decisions represented the best interests of the king and of the country as a whole. These decisions became the common law of England. As authoritative precedents, they were followed and applied in future cases wherever English common law was used and followed.

During this period of development of the criminal law in England, the English Parliament enacted a few criminal statutes, such as embezzlement, false pretense, and incest. The English ecclesiastical courts (religious courts) formulated and punished offenses that violated the moral code but were not public offenses, such as private acts of fornication, adultery, and seduction.

The English settlers who began colonizing North America in the early 1600s brought with them the English common law. This formed the basis of the law in each of the individual colonies. Modifications and adjustments were made to meet the needs of the frontier life of each of the colonies. A great deal of discretion was vested in colonial governors, councils, and judges with respect to the enforcement and scope of offenses and with respect to the creation of new laws. However, for the most part, English common law crimes continued as the common law crimes in each of the colonies.

During the American Revolution and for some time after, a great deal of hostility was directed toward the English in America; this hostility extended to the common law. Justice Hugo L. Black of the U.S. Supreme Court referred to this situation in his 1958 dissenting opinion in *Green v. United States,* in which he stated:

> Those who formed the Constitution struck out anew free of previous shackles in an effort to obtain a better order of government more congenial to human liberty and welfare. It cannot be seriously claimed that they intended to adopt the common law wholesale. They accepted those portions of it which were adapted to this country and conformed to the ideals of its citizens and rejected the remainder. In truth, there was widespread hostility to the common law in general and profound opposition to its adoption into our jurisdiction from the commencement of the Revolutionary War until long after the Constitution was ratified.[7]

Many American lawyers and judges knew the value of many of the English common law principles, which at that point had been developing for more than two hundred years. But the public wanted American law for Americans, and many changes were thus made by the new state legislative bodies, which transformed English common law into statutory law.

Common Law Crimes in the U.S. Federal Courts

In 1812, the case of *United States v. Hudson and Goodwin* came before the U.S. Supreme Court.[8] The defendants were charged with the common law crime of criminal libel because they wrote in a newspaper that the president of the United States and the Congress had secretly voted to give $2 million as a present to Napoleon Bonaparte. No federal

Important Documents of the English-Speaking World

Magna Carta, 1215 A civil war in England forced King John to sign the Magna Carta ("great document"), which provided:

- There will be no criminal "trial upon . . . simple accusation without producing credible witnesses to the truth therein."

- "No freeman shall be taken, imprisoned . . . except by lawful judgment of his peers or the law of the land."

The signing of Magna Carta in 1215 was the first step toward democracy in England, as it was the first time that a king relinquished some of his power to the people. Until Magna Carta, English kings ruled with almost absolute power under the concept of "divine right of kings," and the people had only the little freedom the kings chose to give them.

The writ of **habeas corpus** developed in English common law to protect the new rights of English people under Magna Carta. In 1679, the English Parliament enacted the first habeas corpus statute. The U.S. Constitution of 1788 guarantees and protects the writ of habeas corpus in Article I, Section 9. All of the original thirteen states guaranteed the writ in their original constitutions. Today, people who believe they are illegally being detained can use the writ of habeas corpus to challenge their imprisonment.

Mayflower Compact, 1620 As the *Mayflower* rode at anchor off Cape Cod, some of the passengers threatened to go out on their own, without any framework of government. To avoid this threat of anarchy, the Mayflower Compact agreed that "We . . . doe . . . solemnly and mutually . . . covenant and combine our selves together into a civil body politike for our better ordering and preservation . . . and by vertue hereof to enact . . . such just and equal laws . . . unto which we promise all due submission and obedience."

English Bill of Rights, 1689 Because of the numerous attacks on personal liberty, the English Parliament forced King James II to abdicate, and Parliament produced a Bill of Rights. This document served as a guide for Americans and provided:

- "Suspending laws . . . without consent of Parliament is illegal";

- "Keeping a Standing Army within the Kingdom in Time of Peace unless it be with Consent of Parliament is against the law";

- "Election of Members of Parliament ought to be free";

- "Freedom of Speech . . . ought not to be impeached or questioned."

Declaration of Independence, July 4, 1776 After King George declared the American colonies to be in a state of rebellion and the English Parliament forbade all trade with the colonies, an eloquent statement of the American democratic creed was made in the Declaration of Independence:

> We hold these truths to be self-evident, that all men are created equal, that they are endowed by their Creator with certain unalienable Rights, that among these are Life, Liberty and the pursuit of Happiness.—That to secure these rights, Governments are instituted among Men, deriving their just powers from the consent of the governed,—That whenever any Form of Government becomes destructive of these ends, it is the Right of the People to alter or to abolish it, and to institute new Government, laying its foundation on such principles and organizing its powers in such form, as to them shall seem most likely to effect their Safety and Happiness.

U.S. Constitution, ratified 1788 Because of the failure to achieve a workable government under the Articles of Confederation, delegates from the American states met in Philadelphia in 1787. George Washington presided for months over the debates and arguments that led to the adoption and ratification of the Constitution used by the United States since that time.

The Bill of Rights (first ten amendments) was made part of the U.S. Constitution in 1791. See Appendix A of this text for applicable sections of the U.S. Constitution.

statute made libel a crime, but criminal libel was a common law crime. The Supreme Court pointed out that *state courts* could punish a person for a violation of the common law crime of libel under their police power if they chose to adopt and incorporate the offense as part of the crimes of that state. But the Supreme Court held that *federal courts* had only that power and jurisdiction given to them by the U.S. Constitution and the Congress and had no power to adopt common law crimes. The rule that there are no federal common law crimes has been affirmed many times over the years. In 1949, Justice Robert H. Jackson wrote that "it is well and wisely settled that there can be no judge-made offenses against the United States and that every federal prosecution must be sustained by statutory authority."[9]

Common Law Crimes in State Courts

Many states have abolished criminal common law crimes, but all states have continued to use common law rules of criminal procedure. Some states, however, have not abolished common law crimes and continue to allow prosecution for common law crimes. In those states, prosecution is rare and not often successful.

For example, Dr. Jack Kevorkian, the medical doctor who championed assisted suicides, was charged in Michigan with the common law crime of assisting two suicides. Angry over being charged with an "unwritten" law, Dr. Kevorkian shouted a number of times in court during his trial, "This is not a trial! This is a lynching! There is no law! No law!" The jury acquitted Dr. Kevorkian of the common law charges. (Later, using the Michigan criminal code, Dr. Kevorkian was charged and convicted of murder in 1999 and sentenced to ten to twenty-five years in prison.)

Because of the difficulties and limited success of prosecuting for common law crimes, prosecutors use the modern statutory crimes that are available in the criminal codes of their state.

Statutory Crimes

After the American Revolution, the new state legislatures began converting common law crimes to statutory form. Through the police power of the state, they had the power to amend, affirm, change, extend, abolish, modify, or alter any common law crime or rule. In many instances, state legislatures kept the common law crime intact by merely restating the law in statutory form. In other instances, legislatures created new crimes by forbidding and punishing conduct that was not a crime in common law. In still other instances, they redefined the common law crime by changing elements of the crime or removing common law limitations and extending the crime to cover conduct not included in the common law crime. If the common law punishment was considered too severe, changes were made in the degree or form of punishment. Attempts were made to clarify areas of doubt or uncertainty in common law crimes.

Practically all criminal laws that are enforced today are statutory laws enacted by legislative bodies. Many of today's statutory crimes were unknown in common law. Most of these criminal laws have been enacted in the past thirty or forty years to meet the problems of our mass industrial society.

Administrative Crimes

In 1911, the case of *United States v. Grimaud* came before the U.S. Supreme Court.[10] Congress had passed a statute authorizing the Secretary of Agriculture to make regulations concerning the use of government forests in order to preserve and maintain these areas as forest reserves. Violation of regulations created by the Secretary of Agriculture was made a criminal offense by Congress. The defendant (Grimaud) had continued to graze his sheep on U.S. forest lands without obtaining permits as required under a regulation issued by the Secretary of Agriculture. Because the federal courts were divided on the question of whether a violation of such regulation constituted a crime, the government appealed the case to the U.S. Supreme Court.

The Supreme Court held that Congress may constitutionally delegate to an administrative agency the power to make regulations that are enforced by criminal penalties established by that legislative body. The Court stated that the Secretary did not exercise the legislative power of declaring the penalty or fixing the punishment for grazing sheep without a permit, but the punishment is imposed by the act itself. The offense is not against the Secretary but, as the indictment properly concludes, is "contrary to the laws of the United States and the peace and dignity thereof."

Today, established practice allows Congress and most state legislatures to delegate to an administrative agency the power to make rules, and the legislature may provide by statute that such rules may be enforced by criminal penalties. In a few states, this procedure has been held to be unconstitutional. But in the majority of states, criminal laws may be created by the legislature establishing the framework and the administrative agency providing the specific regulation or rule within that framework. The delegation of such authority is constitutional in the majority of the states if

- the legislative act sets forth sufficient standards to guide the administrative agency, and the act provides for criminal penalties for the violation of the administrative regulations created within the guidelines, and if

- the administrative agency stays within the guidelines established by the legislative body in creating rules enforced by the criminal penalties; but

- the rules of the administrative agency "must be explicit and unambiguous in order to sustain a criminal prosecution; they must adequately inform those who are subject to their terms what conduct will be considered evasive so as to bring the criminal penalties of the Act into operation,"[11] and

- the determination (adjudication) of whether a violation of the **administrative crime** has occurred is made by a court with proper jurisdiction and is not made by the administrative agency.

Publication of Administrative Rules Having Criminal Sanctions

People who are subject to the criminal law cannot be presumed to know the law if information as to the contents of the law is not available to them. This information is ordinarily available at public libraries or from governmental agencies on request. However, in 1933 and 1934, information as to the administrative rules having criminal sanctions was sometimes not readily available from any source. The National Recovery Administration (NRA) and other New Deal agencies of the federal government were issuing reg-

Common Law, Statutory, and Administrative Crimes

Common Law Crimes (used in the early days of the United States)	Custom, usage, or moral values, and concepts of a community built up over a period of many years	plus	Adoption by judges of these customs or concepts in court decisions as crimes
Statutory Crimes (make up the vast majority of crimes today)	Enactment of bills by a legislative body	plus	Signing of the bills by the chief executive officer (governor or president)
Administrative Crimes (used in the fields of health, drugs, stock market, taxation, and other areas the government must regulate)	Enactment of sufficient guidelines by a legislative body that are signed into law by the governor or president	plus	Authorized regulatory agencies that create rules within the guidelines established by law

ulations having criminal sanctions at an unprecedented rate because of the economic emergency that existed at the time. A committee of the American Bar Association (ABA) estimated that the NRA alone issued 2,998 orders in a one-year period and that these regulations were made known to the public through 5,991 press releases. Lawyers had to inform themselves of the law by reading the newspapers and hoping that the reporters had accurately reflected the facts. The ABA committee reported as follows:

> The total legislative output by, or in connection with, this one administrative agency staggers the imagination. Any calculation involves guess-work but a safe guess would be that the total exceeds 10,000 pages of 'law' in the period of one year. . . . Under these circumstances not only citizens but even lawyers are helpless in any effort to ascertain the law applicable to a given state of facts. The presumption of knowledge of the law becomes, to term it mildly, more than violent. Is it too much to expect that before these legislative enactments be given force and effect, they be subjected to simple formalities such as those suggested in the committee's conclusion?[12]

In 1935, the Federal Register Act was passed, and in 1936 the Federal Register became the agency by which federal regulations and administrative orders were made known to the public. Today, states also publish and make known their state administrative orders and regulations through a state agency from which the public and business groups can obtain copies of regulations and orders.

Federal and state administrative codes are used to regulate such activities as the stock and bond markets, the marketing of food and drugs, taxation, and public health and safety.

SUMMARY

Goals, purposes, scope, and sources of criminal law are discussed in this chapter.

Common law crimes are the first and earliest source of criminal law. Today, the federal government and all the fifty states each have more than two thousand statutory criminal laws. Common law crimes are rarely charged today in the states that have not abolished common law crimes. Many rules of criminal procedure continue to be used today. Regulatory or administrative crimes are used in many (but not all) states. These rules are created by regulatory agencies created by the state in which they function.

 BOOK-SPECIFIC WEB SITE

For chapter-related Web links, quizzing activities, and case and news updates, go to the *Criminal Law,* Eighth Edition, book-specific Web site at **http://info.wadsworth.com/ gardner.**

QUESTIONS AND PROBLEMS

1. The defendant out of spite placed a dead animal in his neighbor's well, intending to poison the water in the well. The state in which this happened had no specific statute making poisoning well water a crime. It did have a common law crime of "selling unwholesome food or drink or poisoning food or drink intended for human consumption." Can the defendant be charged with a crime under these facts? If so, will such a crime be a "new," judge-made crime? See *State v. Buckman,* 8 N.H. 203 (1836).

2. Creek was charged with the crime of kidnapping a child. During the entire kidnapping, the child, Adam, remained asleep. Under relevant state tort law, Adam could not recover damages from Creek for the tort of false imprisonment, because to do so, a victim must be conscious during the imprisonment.

   Creek contends that because he could not be held liable for the tort of false imprisonment, he cannot be guilty of kidnapping where the victim is asleep or unconscious. Is he correct? Are the goals of tort law and criminal law the same? Should different goals produce different results here? See *Creek v. State,* 588 N.E.2d 1319 (Ind. App. 1992).

 INFOTRAC COLLEGE EDITION EXERCISES

1. The common law tradition in the United States has been responsible for the creation and refinement of much of our law. Go to InfoTrac College Edition, click on *Keywords,* and, using the search term *common law,* find the article "The Common Law in the Twentieth Century: Some Unfinished Business" (James Gordley, Dec. 2000). Click on View text and full content retrieval choices. This article provides a good historical description of how the common law works to create and refine law.

2. After finding the reference to the article cited in Exercise 1, click the link that appears on the citation page. Then click on Periodicals under common law and find the article "Scalia Contra Common Law Adjudication." The article is critical of Supreme Court Justice Scalia's view of the common law. What does the author see as the faults in Justice Scalia's conclusions?

NOTES

1. *U.S. v. Watson,* 146 F.Supp. 258, 262 (D.D.C. 1956), judgment reversed, 249 F.2d 106 (C.A.D.C. 1957).

2. *Kovacs v. Cooper,* 336 U.S. 77, 69 S.Ct. 448 (1949).

3. *Village of Belle Terre v. Boraas,* 416 U.S. 1, 94 S.Ct. 1536 (1974).

4. *Lawton v. Steele,* 152 U.S. 133, 14 S.Ct. 499 (1894).

5. State laws that require motorcycle operators and passengers to wear protective headgear have generally been upheld by state and federal courts as being a valid use of the police power of the state. The Supreme Court of Nebraska reviewed these cases in *Robotham v. State,* 488 N.W.2d 533 (1992), in which the Nebraska motorcycle helmet law was upheld.

However, some motorcycle groups have mounted considerable political opposition to state helmet laws. In Wisconsin, for example, hundreds of motorcyclists converged on the state capitol building in Madison to protest the Wisconsin helmet law. The motorcyclists slowly drove around Capitol Square in downtown Madison, tying up traffic for blocks in all directions. After a number of such demonstrations in which mo-torcycle drivers and passengers did not wear helmets, the state legislature repealed the Wisconsin law requiring drivers and passengers on motorcycles to wear protective headgear.

6. *Bykofsky et al. v. Borough of Middletown,* 401 F.Supp. 1242, Affr. (3d Cir. 1976), 535 F.2d 1245, review denied, U.S. Supreme Court, 89 S.Ct. 2033, 97 S.Ct. 394 (1976).

7. *Green v. U.S.,* 356 U.S. 165, 78 S.Ct. 632 (1958).

8. *U.S. v. Hudson and Goodwin,* 11 U.S. (7 Cranch) 32, 3 L.Ed. 259 (1812).

9. *Krulewitch v. U.S.,* 336 U.S. 440, 69 S.Ct. 716 (1949).

10. *U.S. v. Grimaud,* 220 U.S. 506, 31 S.Ct. 480 (1911).

11. *M. Kraus & Bros., Inc. v. U.S.,* 327 U.S. 614, 66 S.Ct. 705 (1946).

12. American Bar Association's Special Committee on Administrative Law, 59 A.B.A. Rep., pp. 552–55 (1934).

3

Essential Elements of a Crime

KEY TERMS

strict liability

reasonable doubt

actus reus

mens rea

specific intent

scienter

motive

proximate cause

presumption

inference

Since the development of common law and until modern times, all crimes consisted of two essential elements: (1) the physical act or omission and (2) a mental requirement known as criminal intent or purpose. Some writers refer to such crimes as *true crimes*. Today, true crimes continue to make up a considerable number of crimes in any criminal code.

With the industrialization of the United States in the 1920s and 1930s, state legislatures began creating criminal laws that did not require the mental element essential to true crimes. This relatively new type of crime is called a *strict liability* crime, or regulatory offense. Strict liability crimes can be found in criminal laws pertaining to traffic violations, narcotics, liquor, sanitation, hunting, and pure food requirements. In strict liability crimes, the government does not have to prove intent or purpose, but must show only that the accused performed the act or omission charged or brought about the results that are alleged and shown.

Crimes Requiring Proof of Mental Fault

Before a person may be convicted of a crime that requires proof of mental fault, the government must prove the following elements beyond a *reasonable doubt:*

The external physical act: That the conduct or act forbidden by the law of the jurisdiction was in fact committed by the defendant

The internal mental element: That the act or omission was accompanied by a state of mind required by the criminal statute

The Latin term **actus reus** ("guilty act") is used by the courts and writers to describe the essential physical act, and the term **mens rea** ("guilty mind") is used to describe the essential mental requirement. This mental requirement of criminal intent is embodied in criminal statutes in the following degrees:

- Acted intentionally (the highest degree of mental fault)
- Acted knowingly
- Acted recklessly
- Acted negligently

The U.S. Supreme Court has never created and announced a doctrine requiring proof of *mens rea* in all crimes and in all cases before an accused can be held accountable for his or her acts.[1] Therefore, the states are generally free to create criminal laws that do not require proof of *mens rea* or to create criminal laws requiring different degrees of mental fault or mental guilt. But if a degree of mental guilt is made an element of the crime by law, the prosecutor must then prove this essential element of the crime.

Simultaneous Occurrence of the Forbidden Act and the Mental Element

Thinking of committing a crime without performing a criminal act is not a crime. If a person with criminal thoughts does nothing to carry out his or her thoughts, no crime has occurred. Government cannot punish thoughts alone. To show that a true crime has occurred, the state must show that the external physical act and the internal mental state essential to that crime occurred at the same time. Even crimes such as conspiracy, in which two or more persons share their thoughts about a crime, require that the conspirators do at least one physical act in furtherance of the conspiracy (see Chapter 4).

In some instances, an act without the required mental state (guilty mind) is no crime. For example, a person incapable of entertaining the required criminal mind because of legal insanity has not committed a crime. A student who picks up someone else's book or briefcase by mistake has performed a physical act, but without the guilty or criminal state of mind necessary for the crime of theft, no crime has been committed. However, suppose that the student keeps the book or briefcase for two days and then, realizing the mistake, decides to keep the property. The taking and keeping of the property for two days has been a continuous act in the eyes of the law. The crime of theft occurred when the intent to deprive the true owner of permanent possession concurred with the act of taking and retaining possession.

Although the forbidden act and the guilty mind must concur, the results do not necessarily have to take place at the same time.

EXAMPLE: While A is on vacation, X rigs a spring gun to A's front door (forbidden act), setting it with the intention that A be killed when he opens the door (guilty mind). Two weeks after the spring gun is set in place, A returns from vacation and is shot and killed when he opens his door.

In the example given, the *actus reus* and the *mens rea* concurred, but the results did not occur until A opened the door two weeks after the act with intent to kill was performed.

Actus Reus: **The Forbidden Act or Omission**

Most criminal laws forbid specific acts, and a few punish the failure to carry out a legal duty. The act forbidden or commanded by the law is described in the definition of each particular offense, usually in terms of the harm or the wrong that occurs. In the crime of murder, the death of the victim caused by the defendant's forbidden act or omission is the harm and the wrong. In the crime of larceny, the loss of personal or movable property caused by the defendant's wrongful taking and carrying away is the harm and the wrong.

The manner in which the harm or wrong can be caused varies considerably. A murder can be committed by use of a gun, a knife, a blow, poison, or by any one of many different acts. The harm or the wrong done usually varies from crime to crime, but sometimes two crimes embody the same harm or wrong. All criminal homicides share the same harm or wrong, which is the death of a person. These crimes differ from one another primarily because of the differing states of mind of the offenders at the time they cause the harm or wrong, which is the death of another person.

Actus Reus **for Different Elements of Parties to a Crime**

A *party to a crime* could be (1) a person who actually and physically commits the crime, (2) a person who conspires in the planning of the crime or orders that the crime be committed, or (3) a person who aids and assists in the commission of the crime. All state

Elements of a Crime

Crimes May Consist of Combinations of the Three Human Activities of Thought, Communication, *and* Actions (*or Conduct*):

1. *Thoughts* alone cannot be punished as crimes; however, thoughts can constitute the required mental element *(mens rea)* for verbal offenses or acts that have been designated as crimes.

2. *Communications* (spoken or written words, symbols, and so on) may be offenses in themselves or may be combined with either thoughts or actions to constitute crimes (see Chapter 10).

3. *Human acts* alone may constitute strict liability crimes in which the state is required to show only that the defendant committed a forbidden act or omission. When the state is required to prove a specific mental element *(mens rea),* it must then prove the required intent, purpose, or knowledge that is an essential element of the crime.

criminal codes define parties to a crime and make each of the parties to a crime equally liable for the crime (see Chapter 4 for further material).

The different *actus reus* for parties to a crime are illustrated by the following example:

EXAMPLE: A hires B and C to murder X. A tells B and C how and where she wants X to be murdered. B is the vehicle driver and lookout while C commits the murder.

C's act in killing X is the *actus reus* of the direct commission of the crime. B's acts as aider and abettor are the *actus reus* of assistance. A jury could easily find that all three parties (particularly A) conspired and agreed in the planning of the murder, which is the *actus reus* of agreement.

The state has the burden of proving beyond a reasonable doubt the *actus reus* element of every offense, and the jury must unanimously agree that the state has proved the *actus reus* elements before they may find a defendant guilty.

Because the *actus reus* element for each category is different, the jury must agree unanimously on which *actus reus* or which category the state has proved.

Mens Rea: **The Guilty Mind**

A cardinal principle of criminal law pertaining to true crimes was long ago expressed in Latin as *actus non facit reum nisi mens sit rea* ("an act does not make a person guilty unless the mind is guilty").

The term *mens rea* means evil intent, criminal purpose, and knowledge of the wrongfulness of conduct. It is also used to indicate the mental state required by the crime charged, whether that be **specific intent** to commit the crime, recklessness, guilty knowledge, malice, or criminal negligence.

Criminal liability usually requires "an evil-meaning mind [and] an evil-doing hand."[2] But the late Justice Robert H. Jackson complained of the "variety, disparity and confusion" of judicial definitions of the "requisite but elusive mental element" required in the proof of crimes. In 1970, the National Commission on Reform of Federal Criminal Laws complained of the "confused and inconsistent ad hoc approach" of federal courts to this problem and called for a new approach.

In the 1980 case of *United States v. Bailey,* the U.S. Supreme Court pointed out that in "common law, crimes generally were classified as requiring either 'general intent' or 'specific intent.' This . . . distinction, however, has been the source of a good deal of confusion."[3] As the Court pointed out, this problem has led to a movement away from the common law classifications of *mens rea.* Citing Section 2.02 of the Model Penal Code and LaFave and Scott's book *Criminal Law,* 2d ed. (Belmont, Calif.: West/Wadsworth, 1986), the Court suggested the following categories "in descending order of culpability: purpose, knowledge, recklessness, and negligence."

The following example illustrates situations in which the harm done is the same in all cases, but the mental element varies:

EXAMPLE: X, a construction worker, is working on the fourth floor of a building under construction in the downtown area of a city. His conduct caused the death of W, who was hit on the head by a crowbar as she was walking on the sidewalk past the building.

1. X deliberately dropped the heavy crowbar so as to hit W on the head.
2. X did not want to kill anybody but wanted to see the people scatter when he dropped the crowbar to the sidewalk.
3. X threw the crowbar at another worker in a fight, but missed. The crowbar fell, killing W on the sidewalk below.
4. X came to work drunk and accidentally pushed the crowbar off the edge of the building.
5. Another worker called for the crowbar and X threw it to him, but the throw was bad and the crowbar hit W on the sidewalk below.
6. X was knocked unconscious when a crane collapsed, causing him to drop the crowbar, which hit and killed W.

In your jurisdiction, what degree of criminal liability should X be charged with in each example with respect to his conduct and mental state? Because a jury could be the final judge in determining whether the "evil-meaning mind [and] evil-doing hand" existed, what arguments could a prosecutor and defense lawyer make to prove their cases?

See *United States v. U.S. Gypsum Co.,* in which the U.S. Supreme Court stated that in the case of most crimes, "the limited distinction between knowledge and purpose has not been considered important."[4]

In *United States v. Bailey,* the U.S. Supreme Court stated that in a "general sense, 'purpose' corresponds loosely with the common-law concept of specific intent, while 'knowledge' corresponds loosely with the concept of 'general intent.'"[5]

Proving Criminal Intent or Criminal State of Mind

When criminal intent or another mental element is an essential element of a crime, the state has the burden of proving the required *mens rea.* Proof of the mental element may be made by

- showing the acts of the defendant and the circumstances that existed at the time of the crime. Because most people know what they are doing and also know the natural and probable consequences of their acts, a judge or jury may reasonably infer that the defendant intended the natural and probable consequences of his or her deliberate acts.[6] Thus, a person who pointed a loaded gun at another person and pulled the trigger knew what he or she was doing and desired the natural and probable consequences of the acts;

- producing evidence to show the statements of the defendant at the time of the crime as well as statements made after the crime. Statements of a defendant before or after a crime may be incriminating and may include admissions or a confession of guilt.

Only rarely is written evidence of intent or purpose of a defendant available to the state. The following jury instruction on intent was approved by the Fifth Circuit Court of Appeals in the 1975 case of *United States v. Durham:*

> It is reasonable to infer that a person ordinarily intends the natural and probable consequences of his knowing acts. The jury may draw the inference that the accused intended all the consequences that one standing in like circumstances and possessing like knowledge should reasonably have expected to result from any intentional act or conscious omission. Any such inference drawn is entitled to be considered by the jury in determining whether or not the government has proved beyond a reasonable doubt that the defendant possessed the required criminal intent.[7]

Although one can reasonably infer that a person ordinarily intends the natural and probable consequences of his or her knowing and deliberate acts, one cannot extend that inference to conclude that a person intends results that are not the natural, reasonable, or probable consequences of a voluntary act.

The Requirement of Scienter

Scienter is sometimes made an essential element of a crime that the state must prove beyond a reasonable doubt. **Scienter** is a legal term meaning a degree of knowledge that makes an individual legally responsible for the consequences of his or her acts. Scienter is alleged in a criminal complaint through charging that the accused person had sufficient knowledge to know that his or her act was unlawful. Examples of crimes in which state statutes most often require scienter include the following:

- In battery or assault on a law enforcement officer, knowledge that the victim is a law enforcement officer

- In refusing to aid a law enforcement officer, knowledge that the person requesting assistance is a law enforcement officer

- In obstructing a law enforcement officer, knowledge that the person obstructed is a law enforcement officer

- In receiving stolen property, knowledge that the property received is stolen property

- In possession of obscene material, knowledge of the nature of the material

Innocent Acts That, If Done with Forbidden Intent, Are Crimes

Innocent Acts	*Forbidden Intent*	*Resulting Crimes*
Possessing a tool or other instrumentality	To use such a device to break into a depository or building and steal therefrom	Possession of burglarious tools
Traveling in interstate or foreign commerce	To avoid prosecution for a state felony or to avoid giving testimony in such a prosecution	Fugitive felon or witness violation; 18 U.S.C.A. §§ 1073 & 1074(a)
Traveling in interstate or foreign commerce	For the purpose of engaging in nonmarital sexual activity with a person under 18 years of age (twenty-one countries now permit police to arrest for this offense in an effort to stamp out the sex trade in children between nations)	Mann Act 18 U.S.C.A. § 2423
Traveling in interstate or foreign commerce	With intent to incite a riot (statute requires an overt act, but such act could be a lawful act)	18 U.S.C.A. § 2101(a)(1)
Using U.S. mail, telephone, or interstate wire facilities	To participate through racketeering in a criminal enterprise	RICO violation; 18 U.S.C.A. §§ 1961–68 (see Chapter 22)
Using the U.S. mails	To advance a fraudulent scheme	Mail fraud; 18 U.S.C.A. § 1341
Using a fictitious name or address	To further a fraudulent mail scheme	18 U.S.C.A. § 1342
Associating with other people who advocate, and even membership in an organization that advocates, the overthrow of government by force or violence	Knowledge of the aim to use force or violence in the overthrow of government and an intent to bring it about	18 U.S.C.A. § 2385
Entering a train	With intent "to commit any crime or offense against a person or property thereon"	18 U.S.C.A. § 1991
Going on "any military, naval, or Coast Guard reservation, post, fort, arsenal, yard, station, or installation"	"For any purpose prohibited by law or lawful regulation"	18 U.S.C.A. § 1382
Teaching or demonstrating the use, application, or making of a firearm, explosive, or incendiary device, or a technique capable of causing injury or death	"Intending that the same will be unlawfully employed for use in, or in furtherance of, a civil disorder which may in any way or degree obstruct, delay, or adversely affect commerce" or the performance of any federally protected function	18 U.S.C.A. § 231(a)(1)

- In bribery of a public official or a juror, knowledge that the person is a public official or juror

- In harboring or aiding a felon, knowledge that the person aided is a felon

EXAMPLE: As you are driving your car down a busy street, you see a hitchhiker. You pick up the hitchhiker, and a mile down the road you are stopped by police. The hitchhiker had committed an armed robbery of a store minutes before you picked him up in your car. What scienter element must be shown to justify your arrest and conviction for either the offense of party to the crime of armed robbery or harboring and aiding a felon?

The following cases have appeared before the U.S. Supreme Court in recent years.

United States v. Feola

Supreme Court of the United States (1975) 420 U.S. 671, 95 S.Ct. 1255

Feola and others assaulted two men. Feola argued that he did not know the men he assaulted were undercover federal agents and, for that reason, his convictions of assaulting federal officers should be reversed.

In their "assault on law enforcement officer" statutes, most states require proof of scienter (knowledge that the victim was a law enforcement officer). But the U.S. Congress did not put this element into the federal crime of assaulting or battering a federal officer.

The U.S. Supreme Court refused to read the scienter element into the federal crime written by the U.S. Congress. The Court pointed out that the defendants may have been surprised when their victims turned out to be federal officers, but they knew from the beginning that the planned course of conduct was unlawful. The Court held:

> A contrary conclusion would give insufficient protection to the agent enforcing an unpopular law, and none to the agent acting under cover.

United States v. Falu [8]

Federal Court of Appeals, Second Circuit (1985) 776 F.2d 46, 38 CrL 2142

The federal "schoolyard statute," 21 U.S.C.A. § 845a(a), provides for doubling the sentence of a person convicted of selling drugs within one thousand feet of an elementary or secondary school. The federal statute does not require the government to prove a defendant had knowledge of the school's proximity. Perez sold heroin to a federal undercover agent brought to him by his friend, Falu. The sale occurred within one thousand feet of a public school that could not be seen from the location where the sale occurred. Perez and Falu were convicted of "knowingly or intentionally" selling the heroin. Perez directly committed the crime and Falu was an aider and abettor to the crime. Increased penalties were given to both defendants under the schoolyard statute, as Congress's clear purpose was to deter drug distribution in and around schools. The Court of Appeals affirmed the convictions and increased penalties, stating:

> The defendant argues that without a requirement that a defendant be aware of the key element under the schoolyard statute, namely, proximity to a school, the statute fails to provide fair notice that the prohibited conduct is subject to enhanced penalties. Falu attempts to distinguish the schoolyard statute from a statute like 18 U.S.C.A. § 111, which makes assaulting a federal officer a federal offense regardless of the defendant's knowledge of the victim's identity. See *U.S. v. Feola,* 420 U.S. 671, 684 (1975). Section 111, he argues, seeks to effectuate the legislative aim—protection of federal officers—directly, while the schoolyard statute operates only indirectly to benefit school children.

The Motive for Committing a Crime

Motive and intent are sometimes thought of as being one and the same. However, the law contains a clear distinction between the two. Intent is the mental purpose or design to commit a specific act (or omission), whereas motive is the cause, inducement, or reason why an act is committed.

EXAMPLE: A man entered a crowded tavern. When the man saw the person he was looking for, he went up to him and killed him by plunging a large knife into his body.

When this case was tried, the state easily proved intent to kill through the many eyewitnesses to the crime (that is, the jury easily inferred intent to kill from the action of the defendant). But the state had no admissible evidence as to motive (why the defendant sought out and killed the victim). However, the state had inadmissible hearsay evidence that the victim had sold the defendant a bad batch of heroin. The heroin caused the defendant to become ill. As soon as the defendant could get on his feet, he went out and killed the supplier of the heroin.

Intent is an essential element of many crimes and must be proved beyond reasonable doubt when required. Motive, however, is seldom made an essential element required for a criminal conviction.[9] For example, in the 1991 case of *State v. Famiglietti,*[10] the Supreme Court of Connecticut held that the state did not have to prove the motive or reason the defendant set fire to his store after it was shown that the fire was intentionally set by the defendant.

Motive, however, is always relevant evidence that, if available to the state, can be used to show why the person committed the crime. In this sense, motive can be used to help prove intent or another degree of *mens rea* in that it provides the trier of fact with more information and may remove doubt by answering the question "why." Motive alone is not sufficient to convict; however, a person may be lawfully convicted even if there is no motive or if a motive cannot be shown.

Criminal homicides are committed for different motives, such as hatred, anger, greed, and revenge. However, homicide and other offenses may be committed for "good" motives. Robbing a bank to give the money to the poor and needy is still a crime, even if the stolen funds are used for a good purpose.

Motive can be important evidence in determining punishment or sentencing. An elderly man who kills his terminally ill wife because of her great pain and suffering would be charged and sentenced differently than a man who brutally killed an innocent person while committing a crime such as rape or robbery.

Strict Liability Crimes

In enacting statutes to enforce rules having to do with traffic, liquor, purity of food, hunting, and narcotics offenses, modern legislative bodies often choose not to create true crimes, but rather strict liability (or liability without mental fault) statutes.

Except for narcotics offenses, the penalties for strict liability offenses are usually lighter. The offenders are often not generally considered criminals in the full sense of the word, and the state is not required to carry the burden of proving criminal intent or

Degrees of Mental Fault

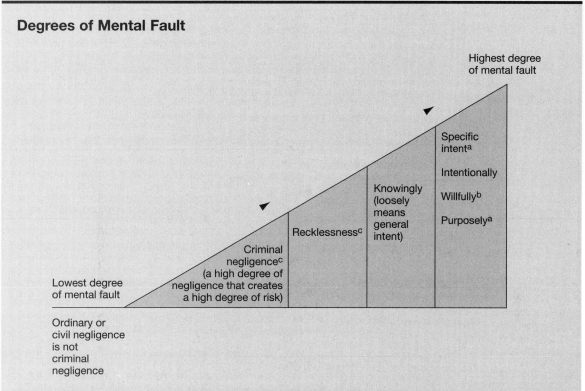

[a]See pp. 216–27 of *Criminal Law*, 2d ed., by LaFave and Scott (Belmont, Calif.: West/Wadsworth, 1986) for a discussion of general intent and specific intent.

[b]The English police officer's handbook (*Moriarty's Police Law*, 28th ed., Butterworths, 1972) states on p. 5 that "when a person of his own free will does an act he is said to do it willfully."

[c]See pp. 231–37 of *Criminal Law*, 2d ed., by LaFave and Scott for a discussion of recklessness and negligence.

other mental fault. The defendant is liable, regardless of his or her state of mind at the time of the act.

The motor vehicle codes, hunting regulations, and the food and liquor laws of most states contain strict liability statutes. A bartender cannot ordinarily use as a defense the fact that the person to whom he sold liquor looked 22 when in fact the person was only 17. The driver of an overweight truck cannot argue that the company scales were faulty; nor can an adult male, in most states, argue that he did not know the age of the 15-year-old girl with whom he had sexual intercourse.

In referring to strict liability crimes, the U.S. Supreme Court pointed out that "Congress has rendered criminal a type of conduct that a reasonable person should know is subject to stringent public regulation and may seriously threaten the community's health or safety."[11]

Courts sustained strict liability laws in the following cases:

Firearms	Unregistered hand grenades, *United States v. Freed*, 91 S.Ct. 1112 (1971); unregistered machine guns, *United States v. Evans*, 978 F.2d 1112 (9th Cir. 1992); the

	offense of carrying a concealed weapon, *People v. Combs,* 408 N.W.2d 420 (Mich. 1987).
Motor vehicle safety laws	Defective headlight, *Queen v. State,* 189 Ga.App. 161, 375 S.E.2d 287 (1988); running a red light, *Hoffer v. State,* 192 Ga.App. 378, 384 S.E.2d 902 (1989).
Intoxicating liquor or beer	Sale to underage person, *State v. Jones,* 57 Ohio App.3d 155, 567 N.E.2d 313 (1989).
Drug-related deaths	A number of states have enacted Len Bias laws making persons who illegally manufacture, distribute, or dispense illegal drugs strictly liable for drug-related death. See *State v. Ervin,* 242 N.J.Super. 584, 577 A.2d 1273 (1990), in which the defendant's girlfriend died of cocaine she obtained from the defendant. His conviction for the New Jersey crime of causing a drug-induced death was affirmed.
Public health laws	Corporation officers can be convicted of Federal Food and Drugs Act violations even when "consciousness of wrongdoing [is] totally wanting." See *United States v. Dotterweich,* 64 S.Ct. 134 (1943), in which adulterated and misbranded drugs were shipped.
Other laws	Littering, *State v. Waugh,* 72 Ohio App.3d 253, 594 N.E.2d 632 (1991). Prior to discharge from service, Air Force colonel negotiated for a civilian job and was involved in contract negotiations that violated the laws against taking government action while having conflicting financial interest. *United States v. Hedges,* 912 F.2d 1397 (11th Cir. 1990).

Strict Liability Laws That Seek to Protect Children

The age of a minor is an essential element of such crimes as SIWAC (sexual intercourse with a child), contributing to the delinquency of a child, violating liquor laws or child pornography laws, or giving or selling a minor a pistol, drugs, cigarettes, and so on.

Such laws seek to protect children. To provide further protection to children, many states take away the defense of mistake of age from some or all of the offenses that seek to protect children. When this defense is taken away, defendants cannot argue that they made an honest mistake as to the age of a child (see Chapter 7 for a discussion of the defenses of honest mistake of law or fact).

By taking away the defense of honest mistake as to the age of a child, the state then makes the offense a strict liability offense, and defendants can be proved guilty by showing only that they committed the forbidden act.

EXAMPLE: An adult has sex with a minor. The state has to show only that the sex occurred and the age of the parties. Consent cannot be used as a defense by the adult,

Examples of Strict Liability Laws	Conduct Justifying Criminal Convictions	Case
Minnesota prohibited "promoting, employing, using, or permitting a minor (to engage in) a sexual performance" (Minn. Stat. 617, 246).	After checking the identity of a young woman, Eve White hired her to dance nude on her bookstore dance floor. The young woman was only 17. White could not argue that she honestly believed the girl was 26.	*Minnesota v. White,* 464 N.W.2d 585, review denied U.S. Supreme Court, 112 S.Ct. 77 (1991)
To protect minors from the illegal drug trade, Congress enacted 21 U.S.C.A. § 861,[12] which forbids an adult to "employ, hire, [or] use" a minor to avoid detection or apprehension in committing a drug crime or to "receive a controlled substance" from a minor other than an immediate family member.	Convictions were affirmed in the *Chin* and *Cook* cases, in which the defendants argued that they did not know their drug suppliers were minors. Proof of knowledge of age is not required for conviction.	*United States v. Chin,* 981 F.2d 1275, review denied U.S. Supreme Court, 113 S.Ct. 2377 (1993). *United States v. Cook,* 76 F.3d 596 (4th Cir. 1996)
The White Slave Traffic Act increases the punishment for transporting a minor for immoral purposes in interstate or international commerce. Proof is required to show knowledge that the person is being transported for immoral purposes, but proof is not required to show knowledge that the person transported is a minor.	Hamilton could not argue that he did not know the person he was transporting was a minor, or that he made an honest mistake of fact.	*United States v. Hamilton,* 456 U.S. 171, review denied U.S. Supreme Court, 92 S.Ct. 2051 (1972)

as the minor is incapable of giving consent. Mistake as to the age of the minor cannot be used if this defense is prohibited by state law.

Proximate Cause or Causation

Crimes are defined in terms of conduct that is forbidden or required and the mental state existing at the time of the forbidden act or omission. Crimes can also be defined in terms of the harm done or the wrong that occurs.

In crimes in which a harm has occurred, the state must prove that the wrongful act or omission of the defendant was the ordinary and probable cause of the harm that resulted. The harm to the victim could occur immediately, such as a bloody nose resulting from a blow to the face or death from being shot at point-blank range. In other instances, a victim could be dangerously injured in a chain of events in which the victim's death does not occur until days or weeks after the crime. In all such cases, the state must prove beyond reasonable doubt that the unlawful and wrongful act of the defendant was the ordinary and probable cause of the harm that resulted. The following cases illustrate court rulings in which the victim's death did not occur immediately:

In the 1992 case of *People v. Roberts,* 826 P.2d 274, death did not occur immediately following eleven stab wounds. The Supreme Court of California pointed out that **proximate cause** of a death is "a cause which, in natural and continuous sequence, produces the death, and without which the death would not have occurred" (CALJIC #8.55). The Court pointed out that California follows the old rule, holding:

> If a person inflicts a dangerous wound on another, it is ordinarily no defense that inadequate medical treatment contributed to the victim's death.
>
> * * *
>
> To be sure, when medical treatment is grossly improper, it may discharge liability for homicide if the maltreatment is the sole cause of death and hence an unforeseeable intervening cause.

- The highest court in New York State held in 1993 that a gunshot to the victim's head was a sufficient, direct cause of the victim's death two months later to establish causation beyond a reasonable doubt. In the case of *People v. Velez,* 159 Misc.2d 38, 602 N.Y.S.2d 758 (1993), the victim pulled out his feeding tube, refused food, and ingested only ice water and other liquids. The defense lawyer argued that the victim committed suicide, but the court held that the victim's acts did not operate as an intervening act excusing criminal liability.[13]

- In the case of *McKinnon v. United States,* 1988 WL 125652, the defendant was convicted of first-degree murder after he slashed his girlfriend's throat. The woman died six weeks later from the injury and from hepatitis, which experts testified probably was caused by blood transfusions or the drug therapy necessary to treat the wound. Neither this case nor the California *Roberts* case presented any claims that medical treatment was grossly improper.

Unintended Harm Resulting From a Misdemeanor or Other Minor Offense

A defendant who accidentally or unintentionally causes death while committing a felony of violence (robbery, rape, arson, and so on) can be charged with felony murder. Examples of causation in felony murder cases are presented in Chapter 13 of this text.

The following cases illustrate situations in which unintended harm occurs while a defendant is committing a misdemeanor or other offense. For a prosecutor to charge and a jury or fact finder to convict, the state must be able to prove that the harm was the natural and probable consequence of the wrong done by the defendant. Many of the following convictions are for involuntary manslaughter, which is a lesser offense than felony murder.

Conduct of Defendant	Resulting Harm/Criminal Conviction	Case
Repeatedly allowing vicious animals to run loose	Vicious dogs killed a jogger/ Involuntary manslaughter	*State v. Powell,* 109 N.C.App. 1, 426 S.E.2d 91 (1993)
Permitting an inexperienced youth or intoxicated person to drive his or her vehicle	Death of child or other person/ Involuntary manslaughter	*State v. Travis,* 497 N.W.2d 905 (Iowa App. 1993) and other cases
Leaving cocaine in a place where a child could easily obtain it	Infant daughter died after eating cocaine/Manslaughter and drug abuse	*State v. Grunden,* 65 Ohio App. 3d 777, 585 N.E.2d 487 (1989)
In Howard Beach, New York, six white teenagers (several of whom had weapons) taunted and threatened three black men. Several of the youths chased Michael Griffith, who ran from the threatening teenagers.	Car killed Griffith as he attempted to cross a busy six-lane highway. Defendants could not use as a defense that "Griffith chose the wrong escape route."	Convictions for manslaughter, assault, and conspiracy affirmed, *People v. Kern,* 554 N.E.2d 1235 (1990)
A girlfriend who was being beaten fled defendant to avoid the beating.	Car crushed the fleeing victim/ Third-degree murder conviction affirmed.	*Commonwealth v. Rementer,* 410 Pa.Super. 9, 598 A.2d 1300 (1991) and other cases
Urging a distressed person talking of suicide to go ahead and do it and providing a gun	Victim committed suicide/Second-degree manslaughter	*People v. Duffy,* 79 N.Y.2d 611, 584 N.Y.S.2d 739, 595 N.E.2d 814 (1992)
Leaving infants or children alone for long period of time	Babies left at home while mother went out for evening were killed in fire/Involuntary manslaughter	*Commonwealth v. Skufca,* 321 A.2d 889, review denied 419 U.S. 1028, 95 S.Ct. 510 (1974)
During a fight, the defendant hit his brother in the side with a baseball bat, causing the victim to collapse in a hallway. The defendant then kicked his brother several times. The victim died as the result of the injuries.	Defendant charged with second-degree murder but convicted of voluntary manslaughter after seeking a reduction to assault with intent to do great bodily harm	*People v. Bailey,* 549 N.W.2d 325 (Sup.Ct. Mich. 1996)
After starting a fight by striking the first blow and causing the victim to fall to a concrete floor, the defendant then kicked the victim one or more times.	Victim died as a result of bleeding inside his head caused by the injury/Manslaughter	*State v. Jones,* 598 So.2d 511 (La. Ct. of App. 1992)
Defendant, who was angry over a highway incident, followed a man home and continued to threaten and make menacing gestures to the victim even after being warned that the older man (victim) had a bad heart.	Victim died of a heart attack while his wife was calling the sheriff; the threats and gestures were held to be an assault/Involuntary manslaughter	*State v. Nosis,* 22 Ohio App.2d 16, 257 N.E.2d 414 (1969)
Providing liquor to a minor or an intoxicated adult	See "dramshop laws" in Chapter 20, which discusses civil and criminal liability for taverns and social hosts for resulting harm.	*Anderson v. Moulder,* 183 W.Va. 77, 394 S.E.2d 61 (1990)

When the Illegal Act Would Not Support a Manslaughter Conviction

When the death or injury of a victim is not a foreseeable risk of a defendant's illegal act, courts will not permit a manslaughter or other felony conviction to stand. The following cases illustrate:

- The defendant stole money from a church collection plate—a misdemeanor. One of the members of the church had a heart attack and died from the heart attack as he chased the defendant in his car. In reversing the defendant's conviction of manslaughter for the victim's death, a Florida Court of Appeals held in 1992 that

    the petty theft did trigger a series of events that concluded in the death [of the victim] . . . and was, in that sense, a "cause" of death. . . . [But] the petty theft did not encompass the kind of direct, foreseeable risk of physical harm that would support a conviction of manslaughter. *Todd v. State,* 594 So.2d 802.

- The defendant was a capable driver and had been driving for some years but did not have a driver's license. The victim's death occurred when an intoxicated passenger grabbed the wheel from the defendant, causing the car to go out of control. In holding that not having a driver's license was not the proximate cause of the death, the court reversed defendant's manslaughter conviction. *Frazier v. State,* 289 So.2d 690 (Miss. 1974).

The Ancient "Year-and-a-Day" Murder Rule

The year-and-a-day rule goes back hundreds of years in the law to 1278, when medical science was primitive.[14] Sir William Blackstone described the rule before the American Revolutionary War as follows: "In order . . . to make the killing murder, it is requisite that the party die within a year and a day after the stroke (blow) received, or cause of death administered; in the computation of which the whole day upon which the hurt was done shall be reckoned the first."[15]

Under the year-and-a-day rule, a defendant could not be convicted of murder if the victim did not die within a year and a day. The rule made sense years ago when medical knowledge was limited. But with medical science today, the rule serves little purpose. Many states have abolished the rule or increased the time of the rule. In California, the rule is three years and a day. However, a surprising number of states continue to use the old rule.

Most states have no statute of limitations for murder, so that a murder trial could commence any time an offender is taken into custody (see Chapter 7). However, the year-and-a-day rule would apply in states using the rule if the victim does not die within that time. In the following case, the defense lawyer sought to use the year-and-a-day defense:

State v. Hefler

Supreme Court of North Carolina (1984) 310 N.C. 135, 310 S.E.2d 310

The defendant drove a car after he drank a lot of beer, swallowed quaaludes, and smoked marijuana. While intoxicated in this way, the defendant hit a jogger with his car, seriously injuring the man. The man never regained consciousness and died more than fourteen months after

---

Essential Elements of a True Crime

To obtain a conviction, the state must prove the following essential elements when charging a *true crime:*

- The *act* element: the forbidden act (or failure to act)
- The *mental* element: the state of mind required for the crime (the guilty mind); usually proved by use of inferences drawn from the acts of the defendant
- The *harm* element: the wrong done (killing, physical injury, property damage, loss, and so on)
- The *cause* element: the harm done was the natural and probable result of the wrongful act

Some crimes require proof of additional essential elements, such as scienter, possession (actual or constructive), and others.

---

being run down by the defendant. The defendant was not charged until after the victim's death. The North Carolina courts held that the year-and-a-day rule applied only to murder cases and would not extend the rule to the involuntary manslaughter charge of which the defendant was convicted.

The *Hefler* case is unusual in that Hefler was not criminally charged until more than fourteen months after the criminal act. Most suspects who seriously injure other persons in criminal acts are immediately taken into custody. If a suspect is in custody, a prosecutor must issue a criminal charge or release the person. When a criminal charge is issued, the speedy trial requirements commence running. In most states, *speedy trial* means that a defendant must be tried within 90, 100, or 120 days. Failure to try a defendant within this time limit is a complete defense to the criminal charges (see Chapter 7).

Therefore, in such cases, prosecutors bring such charges as attempted murder, aggravated assault (or battery), and injury by intoxicated use of a motor vehicle, and go to trial on lesser charges. Defense lawyers are not likely to waive a speedy trial and wait until a victim dies.[16]

Possession Alone as a Crime

All states make the possession of certain objects a criminal offense. Examples of such crimes are the possession of illegal drugs, carrying a concealed weapon, possession of an instrument of a crime, possession of stolen property (vehicles, credit cards, and so on), and possession of graffiti instruments (in some cities and states). The following jury instruction defining *possession* is used in federal courts:

[T]he law recognizes different kinds of possession. A person may have actual possession or constructive possession. . . . A person who has direct physical control of something on or around his person is then in actual possession of it. A person who is not in actual possession but who has both the power and the intention to later take control over something . . . is in constructive possession of it. . . . Whenever the word "possession" has been used in these instructions it includes actual as well as constructive possession. [17]

Because of public safety, all states forbid carrying an unauthorized concealed weapon (see Chapter 12). *Carrying* requires a showing of actual possession. If a pistol is in the trunk of the car and not within the immediate reach and control of a person, it is not within actual possession.

Illegal drugs could be in actual possession of a defendant, or a defendant could have constructive possession of the drugs. The term *constructive possession* is used to indicate control over property and objects that the defendant does not have in actual possession. The object may be in his or her car parked two blocks away, in a desk drawer in the home or office, or in a suitcase stored somewhere for which he or she has a baggage claim check or key. Constructive possession would not be sufficient to sustain a conviction for carrying a concealed weapon, as a showing of actual possession is necessary. However, constructive possession would sustain a conviction for the possession of contraband, such as narcotics.

The mental element that must be proved in possession offenses is generally that of intention or "knowledge." These mental elements are usually easy to prove, because a person with a loaded revolver or two pounds of marijuana in his or her pocket cannot argue convincingly that he or she did not know that the contraband was in actual possession. The intent to possess, then, is a state of mind existing at the time the person commits the offense. In seeking to determine the state of mind of the alleged offender in order to decide whether an intent existed, the jury or the court may base its decision on the defendant's acts, conduct, and other inferences that can be reasonably deduced from all the circumstances.

Possession is one of the rights of ownership of property. Criminal statutes do not require that ownership be proved. A person who possesses heroin may or may not be the owner of the heroin. Possession of personal property is presumptive evidence of ownership, and possession accompanied by the exercise of complete acts of ownership for a considerable time is strong evidence of ownership. In the absence of evidence showing otherwise, objects and articles in a vehicle, dwelling, or a business place lead to a strong inference that they are in the constructive possession of the person controlling the vehicle, dwelling, or business place. Therefore, heroin found in an apartment searched under the authority of a search warrant is in the constructive possession of the person controlling and occupying the apartment, unless the person can show otherwise (also see Chapter 20 on drug abuse).

The Possession of Illegal Contraband Inference

A strong inference of possession of illegal contraband can be made when the contraband (such as cocaine or an illegal gun) is found (1) under the front seat of a car driven by the owner of the vehicle, (2) in the home of a person who is the sole occupant of the house or apartment, or (3) in other situations in which a reasonable inference of possession can be drawn.

When Possession Alone Is a Crime

Possession May Be	*Possession May Be*	*Possession of a Controlled Substance May Be*
Actual or	In one person (sole), or	Of a *usable amount,* or
Constructive (not in actual possession)	Joint (in possession of more than one person)[19]	Of a *trace amount,* or
		Within the body of the suspect, or
		A combination of any of the above

Most states will not permit a criminal conviction for drug possession based only on a showing of illegal drugs within the body of a defendant. Some states will not sustain a conviction of drug possession on only a showing of a trace amount alone. The strongest cases are those in which a usable amount or a large amount (possession with intent to deliver) is proved (see Chapter 20 on drug abuse).

Examples were used by the U.S. Supreme Court in 1994 to illustrate when conclusions of illegal possession could not be inferred. The following innocent persons should not be arrested or charged, as pointed out in the case of *United States v. X-Citement Video, Inc.*:[18]

- "[A] Federal Express courier who delivers a box" containing the illegal contraband
- "[A] new resident of an apartment receives mail (containing contraband) for the prior resident and stores the mail unopened"
- "[A] retail druggist who returns an uninspected roll of developed film to a customer," unaware that the film is illegal sexually explicit child material

Because these innocent persons could be improperly charged with the possession of illegal contraband, the Supreme Court forbade making such possessions strict liability crimes.

The Use of Presumptions and Inferences in Criminal Law

Presumptions are used in criminal law. The first and earliest presumptions were common law presumptions created by courts. In modern times, most presumptions are created by legislative bodies. The best-known **presumption,** and probably the oldest, is the presumption of innocence until proven guilty. The presumption of innocence until proven guilty is a rebuttable presumption, which means it may be overcome by evidence proving otherwise. The presumption of innocence may be overcome by evidence showing that a defendant is guilty beyond a reasonable doubt.

Some writers identify another form of presumption, called *conclusive presumption.* A *conclusive presumption* is a statement of substantive law that cannot be overcome with evidence showing otherwise. Of the few conclusive presumptions, probably the best known is the rule of law that a person under age 7 has not reached the age of reason and therefore is not capable of committing a crime.

Elements That May Be Essential to the Proof of a Crime

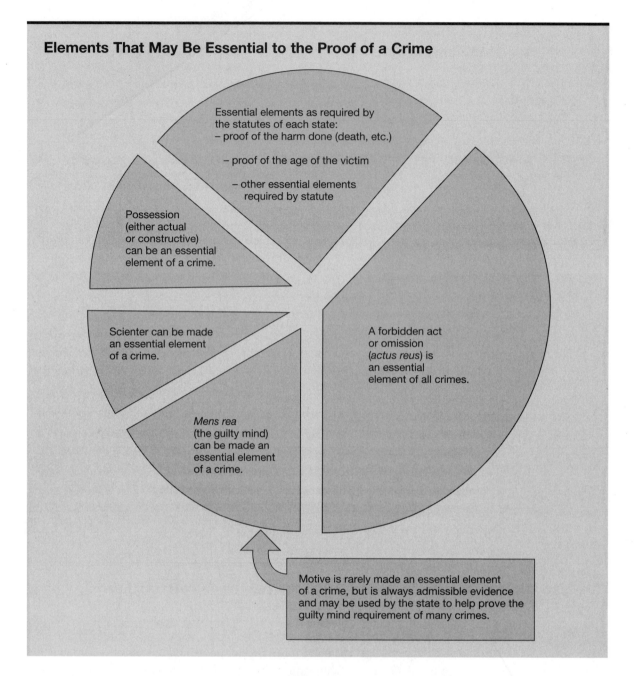

Essential elements as required by the statutes of each state:
– proof of the harm done (death, etc.)
– proof of the age of the victim
– other essential elements required by statute

Possession (either actual or constructive) can be an essential element of a crime.

Scienter can be made an essential element of a crime.

A forbidden act or omission (*actus reus*) is an essential element of all crimes.

Mens rea (the guilty mind) can be made an essential element of a crime.

Motive is rarely made an essential element of a crime, but is always admissible evidence and may be used by the state to help prove the guilty mind requirement of many crimes.

Functions of Presumptions

Presumptions are created to permit orderly civil and criminal trials.[20] The Supreme Court of Pennsylvania and the Supreme Court of Indiana defined the function and legal significance of presumptions as follows:

> A presumption of law is not evidence nor should it be weighed by the fact finder as though it had evidentiary value. Rather, a presumption is a rule of law enabling the party in whose favor it operates to take his case to the jury without presenting evidence of the fact presumed. It serves as a challenge for proof and indicates the

party from whom such proof must be forthcoming. When the opponent of the presumption has met the burden of production thus imposed, however, the office of the presumption has been performed; the presumption is of no further effect and drops from the case.[21]

Inferences Distinguished From Presumptions

A presumption is an assumption the law expressly directs that the trier of fact (jury or judge) *must* make. Because most presumptions may be disputed, they may be outweighed or overcome with evidence showing otherwise. Unless presumptions are overcome with other evidence, judges and jurors *must* accept the presumption as true.

The purpose of civil and criminal trials is to determine the truth of the issues presented to the fact finder. Criminal trials commence with the presumption that the defendant is innocent. To overcome this presumption, the state must present evidence proving beyond a reasonable doubt in the minds of the jury the guilt of the defendant. Each essential element of the crime charged must be proved beyond a reasonable doubt.

Fact finders must use good common sense and their knowledge of everyday life. In their reasoning process, juries and judges must use inferences. An *inference* is a conclusion or deduction that a jury or judge *may* draw from a fact or a group of facts presented to them. A common inference used in criminal trials is that persons intend (desire) the natural and probable consequences of their deliberate acts. The following example illustrates this:

EXAMPLE: X is charged with either attempted assault with a deadly weapon or attempted murder. X is a strong, 30-year-old man who did the following:

Conduct of X	Inferences That Can Logically Be Drawn From X's Conduct:
Reliable witnesses testify that X repeatedly attempted to hit Y on or about Y's head with a baseball bat. Bystanders stopped X.	Fact finders can easily conclude that a baseball bat is a deadly weapon in the hands of a strong man who exhibited an intent to kill or seriously injure.
Same facts as stated above, except that X used a rolled-up newspaper to strike at Y.	Fact finders cannot logically conclude that a rolled-up newspaper is a deadly weapon or that the defendant exhibited intent to kill; therefore, neither charge could stand.

The Presumption That All Persons Are Sane, Normal, and Competent

An important presumption assumes that all adults are sane, normal, and competent. Adult witnesses in civil and criminal cases are assumed to be sane, normal, and competent. However, attorneys in civil or criminal proceedings may challenge this presumption, if necessary, and show otherwise. Before young children can testify, the trial judge would have to question (voir dire) them and then rule as to whether they meet these requirements of a witness.

California statutes, like most states, provide that defendants in criminal cases are presumed to be competent to stand trial. A defense lawyer challenging this presumption has

Permissible and Impermissible Inferences

In criminal trials, fact finders may draw reasonable inferences from facts presented in a case. Stacking of inferences, or basing an inference solely upon another inference, is not permitted. For example, a jury could properly infer that a tire jack used with such force as to cause the victim to fall after being hit in the head/neck area was a deadly weapon and that an intent to kill existed. This particular example was held not to be inference stacking in *State v. Jacks,* 63 Ohio App.3d 200, 578 N.E.2d 512 (1989).

The leading U.S. Supreme Court case on inferences is presented as Questions and Problems 1 in this chapter. The murder charges against O. J. Simpson were based upon circumstantial evidence from which inferences needed to be drawn. Following are other examples of permissible and impermissible inferences:

Defendant forced a young girl into a secluded area and forced her to take off her clothes and lie on the ground. He threatened her with a gun as he loosened his pants. Nothing was said of his intent and he fled at this point.	Can an inference be made as to the intention of the defendant?	Yes, conviction for attempted sexual assault affirmed. See *Green v. Connecticut,* 194 Conn. 258, 480 A.2d 526 (1984), review denied 469 U.S. 1191, 105 S.Ct. 964, 36 CrL 4178 (1985).
In the middle of the day, police saw defendant walking out of an empty warehouse. Defendant was cooperative, did not run, and had nothing in his possession. He told police that he had to go to the toilet and entered the building looking for a lavatory.	Can an inference of intent to steal be drawn to justify a conviction of burglary (illegal entry with intent to steal)?	No, see *Commonwealth v. Muniem,* 225 Pa.Super. 311, 303 A.2d 528 (1973).
Police with a search warrant stop a United Parcel Service (UPS) truck carrying more than two hundred parcels on city delivery. The warrant authorizes the opening of one of the parcels, which was found to contain two pounds of heroin.	Can an inference be drawn based on this information to conclude probable cause to justify an arrest of the UPS driver by the police?	No.
X is present in a store while the store was robbed.	Would mere presence at the scene of a crime justify an arrest?	No, further information would be needed.
A murder is committed, and only two people were at the scene of the crime. They could have committed the crime together, or one could be guilty and the other innocent.	Would these facts justify a conclusion that probable cause exists to arrest either or both?	Yes, see Restatement of Torts (2d) Sec. 119 (1965).

(continued)

Permissible and Impermissible Inferences (continued)

Defendant was one of the crew aboard a small boat carrying 22,000 pounds of marijuana on a long trip to the United States. Defendant claims he had no knowledge of the illegal enterprise.	From the facts, can inferences be drawn that defendant was a party to the illegal enterprise?	Yes, see *United States v. Guerrero-Guerrero,* 38 CrL 2235, 776 F.2d 1071 (1st Cir. 1985).
Police sought to catch a thief who had been stealing property at a Veterans Administration hospital. Money in a wallet was left in a room with invisible dye on the wallet. The dye became visible when it came in contact with moisture. Defendant was seen leaving the room with blue dye on her hands. The money in the wallet was gone.	Are these facts and the inferences drawn from them sufficient to sustain a conviction for petty theft?	Yes, see *United States v. Baker,* 769 F.Supp. 137 (S.D.N.Y. 1991).
Defendant was arrested with cocaine in his possession. He also had a scale for weighing the cocaine, baking soda for cutting it, more than $1,000 in $20 bills, and other drug items. At his jury trial, a woman testified that she bought cocaine from the defendant on the day of his arrest.	Would this evidence justify the jury's finding of possession of cocaine with intent to deliver?	Yes, see *Sams v. State,* 197 Ga.App. 201, 397 S.E.2d 751 (1990).

Inferences of guilt cannot *be drawn from the following:*

- The fact that a defendant in a criminal case does not get on the witness stand and testify in his or her own behalf. *Griffin v. California,* 85 S.Ct. 1229 (1965); *Carter v. Kentucky,* 101 S.Ct. 1112 (1981).

- A Detroit Police Department policy providing for the automatic arrest of all occupants in a vehicle wanted in connection with a felony. The car in question was stopped forty-eight hours after a burglary and all occupants arrested. The policy based on impermissible inferences was condemned by Michigan courts. *People v. Harrison,* 163 Mich.App. 409, 413 N.W.2d 813, 42 CrL 2153 (1987).

- Prosecutors, judges, and police officers cannot comment on the fact that a defendant asserted his or her Fifth Amendment right to remain silent after being given Miranda warnings. *State v. Marple,* 98 Or.App. 662, 780 P.2d 772 (1989).

- In a period of six months, four elderly women were sexually assaulted in their homes. The unique pattern of the crimes indicated that one single perpetrator was committing the crimes. After defendant was arrested, the series of very similar crimes stopped. Most state and federal courts hold that evidence of the inference of guilt drawn from the fact that a series of similar crimes stopped when the defendant was arrested and held in jail was inherently unreliable to prove guilt. See *Commonwealth v. Foy,* 612 A.2d 1349 (Sup.Ct.Pa. 1992).

the burden of coming forward with evidence to prove that a defendant is incompetent and cannot be tried. In 1992, the U.S. Supreme Court heard the case of *Medina v. California,* 505 U.S. 437, 112 S.Ct. 2572, in which defense lawyers sought to have this presumption held unconstitutional. Medina was convicted of three murders committed during robberies and shooting sprees. The U.S. Supreme Court followed the ruling of the California Supreme Court in holding that California Penal Code Sec. 1369(f) does not violate any right granted or protected by the U.S. Constitution. The *Medina* decision followed the 1952 case of *Leland v. Oregon,* 72 S.Ct. 1002, in which the U.S. Supreme Court held that states may require defendants seeking to use the insanity defense to carry the burden of proving the defendant's insanity beyond a reasonable doubt. Most states and the federal government place the burden of proof upon the party alleging insanity.

SUMMARY

When conduct is made criminal, the statute doing so describes the actions or state of mind that constitute the crime. These are called the elements of the crime. The elements may include acts *(actus reus),* for example, breaking into a dwelling place, as well as a mental state *(mens rea),* for example, knowingly possessing stolen property. Most crimes require proof of some kind of mental intent, although so-called strict liability crimes require only proof of acts.

The prosecution must prove every element of a crime by introduction of proof beyond a reasonable doubt. It is not enough to prove it was more likely than not that an element of the crime was true. The proof must be such that a reasonable person could not conclude the element was not true. The beyond reasonable doubt requirement applies to both proof of acts and mental states identified in the statute creating the crime.

Presumptions and inferences are used in criminal law and in both criminal and civil trials. All criminal trials start with the mandatory presumption that the defendant is innocent until proven guilty. This is a rebuttable presumption that the state may overcome with evidence that carries the burden of proof beyond reasonable doubt.

BOOK-SPECIFIC WEB SITE

For chapter-related Web links, quizzing activities, and case and news updates, go to the *Criminal Law,* Eighth Edition, book-specific Web site at **http://info.wadsworth.com/gardner.**

QUESTIONS AND PROBLEMS

1. The defendant, James Jackson, admitted that he had shot and killed his friend, Mrs. Cole. Jackson also testified that he was not drunk at the time of the shooting but that he had been "pretty high." He testified that Mrs. Cole had taken off some of her clothes and then attacked him with a knife when he had resisted her sexual advances. Jackson testified that he had fired warning shots and then reloaded the gun. When the victim attempted to take the gun from him, it "went off," killing her. Without seeking help for the victim, he drove her car to another state. No other person was at the scene of the shooting,

and defendant argues not only self-defense but also that he was too intoxicated to form the specific intent necessary for conviction of first-degree murder.

A deputy sheriff also testified at the trial. He knew the defendant and Mrs. Cole and had seen them in a restaurant just before the shooting. Because Jackson appeared intoxicated, the sheriff offered to hold Jackson's revolver until Jackson sobered up. Jackson said that this was unnecessary because he and Mrs. Cole were about to engage in sexual activity.

Jackson waived his right to a jury trial and was tried before a judge. The fact finder (the judge) found him guilty of first-degree murder. Should the U.S. Supreme Court hold that the evidence and the inferences drawn from the evidence were sufficient to support the conviction? Explain. *Jackson v. Virginia,* 443 U.S. 307, 99 S.Ct. 2781 (1979).

2. A New York police officer made a lawful stop of a speeding vehicle. Four men were in the car (two in the front seat and two in the rear). The officer smelled burnt marijuana coming from the vehicle and, as he was standing next to the vehicle, saw an envelope marked "Supergold" on the floor of the car between the two men in the front seat. The officer had probable cause to believe that the envelope contained marijuana. Would these facts justify a conclusion (inference) as to which of the men were in possession of marijuana (all four? only two? only one?)? Which of the men would the officer have authority to arrest (or cite)? Explain your answer. *New York v. Belton,* 453 U.S. 454, 101 S.Ct. 2860 (1981).

INFOTRAC COLLEGE EDITION EXERCISES

1. Go to InfoTrac College Edition, click on *Keywords,* and, using the the keyword term *strict liability crimes,* find the <u>Ignorance of Law</u> article. Click on <u>Links</u>. Click <u>View</u> under strict liability. Find the article that raises the question, When should corporations be held criminally liable? What standard of fault, that is, intentional, negligent, or strict liability, does the author think is best in defining corporate crime?

NOTES

1. *Powell v. Texas,* 392 U.S. 514, 535, 88 S.Ct. 2145 (1968).

2. *Morissette v. United States,* 342 U.S. at 252 (see Chapter 7).

3. 444 U.S. 394, 100 S.Ct. 624, 26 CrL 3065 (1980).

4. 438 U.S. at 445, 98 S.Ct at 2877 (1978).

5. 444 U.S. 394, 100 S.Ct. 624, 26 CrL 3065 (1980).

6. See 22 Corpus Juris Secundum Criminal Law, Secs. 30–36.

7. 512 F.2d 1281 (5th Cir. 1975).

8. In the 1995 case of United States v. Lopez, 115 S.Ct. 1624, 57 CrL 2031, the U.S. Supreme Court held that the federal law forbidding the possession of a firearm in a school zone was invalid. The Court held that as the possession of guns near schools did not affect interstate commerce, the federal government did not have the authority to enact the law under the commerce clause of the U.S. Constitution. In her concurring opinion, Justice Sandra Day O'Connor pointed out that states have authority to enact gun-free school laws and that forty states have enacted such statutes.

9. Because motive is the reason and belief that could cause a person to act or refrain from acting, motive could be the basis for enhancing or increasing a

criminal penalty. Increasing or enhancing a penalty because of motive therefore punishes the person's thought. Antidiscrimination laws prohibit acts committed with a discriminatory motive. Treating a person less favorably than others because of race, color, religion, sex, or national origin is forbidden because of discriminatory motive, which is often proved from the inference drawn from difference in treatment.

10. 595 A.2d 306 (Sup.Ct.Conn. 1991).

11. See pages 242–50 of LaFave and Scott, Criminal Law, 2d ed. (Belmont, Calif.: West/Wadsworth, 1986).

12. The Comprehensive Drug Abuse Prevention and Control Act of 1970, as amended.

13. In the 1991 case of *Dill v. State,* 600 So.2d 343, the victim was shot in the head during a robbery but did not die until nine months later when he pulled out his feeding tube and suffered dehydration. The conviction for capital murder was affirmed with the Court holding that the victim's death was caused by the gunshot wound. For further cases and material on causation, see pages 277–99 of LaFave and Scott, Criminal Law, 2d ed. (Belmont, Calif.: West/Wadsworth, 1986).

14. See *People v. Stevenson,* 416 Mich. 383, 331 N.W.2d 143 (1982).

15. Blackstone, Commentaries 197.

16. The victim in the Hefler case was brain-dead a short time after he was hit by the defendant's car. If a victim is brain-dead, could the state go into court and have the person declared legally dead, clearing the way to issuing criminal homicide charges? In such situations, the family of a victim is tempted to "pull the plug," which would also clear the way for criminal homicide charges. See Chapter 13 for more material in this area.

17. See *United States v. Winchester,* 916 F.2d 601 (11th Cir. 1990), having to do with persons who cannot possess a firearm under the Federal Gun Control Act of 1968.

18. 115 S.Ct. 467 (U.S. Sup.Ct. 1994).

19. Charges of joint possession are commonly brought in cases in which a large amount of illegal drugs is seized by law enforcement officers. See the U.S. Supreme Court case of *Ker v. California,* 374 U.S. 23, 83 S.Ct. 1623 (1963) for an example of a conviction based upon joint possession of illegal drugs by a husband and wife.

20. Because taxpayers have possession of their tax records, the burden of proof is on the taxpayers to prove the accuracy of their tax returns. Federal courts have held for many years that rulings of the Commissioner of the Internal Revenue Service are presumed to be correct. (See *Welch v. Helvering,* 290 U.S. 111 at 115, 1933.) During the debate on the new federal tax code in 1998, changes were urged by members of Congress, and many writers predicted that this presumption and burden of proof would be changed in the new tax law. However, the 1998 Tax Reform Act modifies the old rules only slightly, and the presumption and burden of proof remain practically the same as they have been for many years.

21. *Commonwealth v. Vogel,* 440 Pa. 1, 17, 268 A.2d 89, 102 (1970); Sumpter v. State, 261 Ind. 471, 306 N.E.2d 95 (1974).

4

Criminal Liability

CONTENTS

KEY TERMS

preliminary, anticipatory, or inchoate crimes

crime of solicitation or incitement

crime of conspiracy

crime of attempt

Wharton Rule

parties to the principal crime

aider and abettor or conspirator

common design or plan

accomplice

"what one did, they all did"

unindicted co-conspirator

post-crime offenses

material witnesses

Preliminary, Anticipatory, or Inchoate Crimes

When Is a Crime Committed?

Not all crimes are planned in advance. Some crimes are committed impulsively, the decision to commit the crime being made on the spur of the moment or almost spontaneously with the commission of the offense.

Nor are all crimes completed. In some instances, the person (or people) who has carefully planned to commit a crime decides, for one reason or another, not to. Crimes are also not completed because of events that prevent their completion.

A person who has plans in mind to commit a crime has not yet violated any law. He or she may even in some instances express vocally the intention to commit a crime without committing an offense. However, in some instances, such a person may be subject to arrest or to detention for expressing such intentions. The following examples illustrate this point:

EXAMPLE 1: A 14-year-old high school boy warned several classmates that "something big was going to happen" and that they should get out of the way.

EXAMPLE 2: X, who has previously attempted to commit suicide, states that he is going home to kill his wife, his children, and himself.

EXAMPLE 3: Y states that he is going to embezzle money from his employer, who is not paying him enough.

Example 1 is the warning that the 14-year-old boy in West Paducah, Kentucky, gave about a week before he fired on a prayer circle outside his high school, killing three students and wounding seven. Law enforcement officers state that three of the other boys in the eight school shooting incidents of 1997–98 gave similar warnings.

Before the shocking school shootings of 1997–98, such statements by teenagers were often ignored. Adults hearing of such a statement should make inquiries and an investigation as to what was meant by the statement. Example 2 is a very specific threat of violence, and preventive action should be taken. Example 3 is a threat of theft in which lives and safety are not involved.

Officers in different jurisdictions might handle these situations in different ways. Possible courses of action are as follows:

1. Take the person into custody under the emergency detention laws of that state, as the person appears irresponsible and dangerous to himself or others (in Example 2).

2. If the person is carrying a concealed weapon, or there is probable cause for an arrest for another offense, take the person into custody.

3. Warn potential victims and take protective steps to prevent harm (such as securing firearms and other weapons).

In some instances, a threat to commit a crime is a crime itself:

EXAMPLE: 8 U.S.C.A. § 871 makes it a federal offense to do the following: "(a) Whoever knowingly and willfully . . . makes any such threat (to take the life or to inflict bodily harm) against the President, President-elect, Vice President or other officer next in the order of succession to the office of President, or Vice-President-elect, shall be fined not more than $1,000 or imprisoned not more than five years, or both."

Because of the need to prevent serious social harm before it occurs, courts long ago created the three separate and distinct common law *crimes of solicitation, conspiracy, and attempt.* Although these offenses were crimes in themselves, each of these acts is *preliminary* or *anticipatory* to another more serious crime that the offender has in mind.

In considering the preliminary offenses, the following questions always arise: Where and when does noncriminal conduct become criminal conduct by a further act of the suspect? Which of the preliminary offenses, if any, has been committed by the suspect? When does the commission of the principal offense begin so as to allow the state to charge either the preliminary offense or the principal offense? Some states do not permit convictions for both the **inchoate** crime (solicitation, attempt, or conspiracy) *and* the completed crime.

Solicitation or Incitement to Commit a Crime[1]

By the early 1800s, English and American courts had recognized solicitation as a misdemeanor under the common law.[2] Solicitation may be defined as an attempt to get another person to commit a crime. It may also be described as an attempt to conspire to commit a crime. The solicitation does not have to be successful. The crime of solicitation is committed even if the person solicited refuses to cooperate and repudiates the proposal. It is also immaterial, in most instances, whether payment or reward is offered and whether it is accepted or refused. Evidence of the offer of payment or reward, however, can be important in proving solicitation.

From a practical point of view, two things are necessary for the successful prosecution of a charge of solicitation:

1. The cooperation of the person who was solicited
2. Evidence that supports and sustains (corroborates) the testimony of the cooperating state witness

The following example illustrates this point. A man (A) whose name was in the newspaper because he went into bankruptcy called the police and stated that a stranger (B) had telephoned him and asked him if he would like to make some money. When A said yes, B told him that he wanted his wife killed and would pay A to do the job. A realized that he was talking to someone with severe mental or emotional problems and pretended to be interested but said that the job would have to be done by a professional killer. A said that he knew such a man, and after B gave A his name and telephone number, A called the police.

At this point, the police had a weak case to take to court, as a denial by B could raise a degree of doubt. Law enforcement officers also realized that the story A told them could be a fabrication or a hoax. For these reasons, they had to investigate further. This is ordinarily done by using an undercover officer. (Students occasionally ask if this would be entrapment; the answer is no. See the section on entrapment in Chapter 7.)

An undercover police officer telephoned B, pretending to be a hired killer from another city. A meeting was arranged and B again repeated his offer to pay to have his wife killed. When B paid money to the officer for the killing, the officer arrested B, who was charged with solicitation to commit murder under the statutes of that jurisdiction. The undercover officer was the complaining witness. His statements were corroborated by the money bearing B's fingerprints. Statements from A were also available as evidence.

In this example, B was charged under the general solicitation statute of Wisconsin with *solicitation to commit murder*. Wisconsin, like all states, has a general solicitation statute.[3] It also has the solicitation section built into the crimes of prostitution and bribery, which are part of the Wisconsin Criminal Code. Most prostitution cases and many bribery cases are solicitations to commit those offenses. The following cases further illustrate the crime of solicitation:

- A witness for the state testified that the defendant asked him if he wanted to make $5,000 by killing "these" people. The jury believed the witness and convicted the defendant of solicitation to murder. On appeal, it was held that the conviction was supported by sufficient evidence. *State v. Clapp,* 67 Wash.App. 263, 834 P.2d 1101 (1992).

- In 1994, the Oklahoma Court of Criminal Appeals held that when one person solicits another person to commit murder, it does not matter whether the defendant solicited the person to commit the murder himself or herself or to find another to commit the murder. The Court pointed out that either act is a crime. *Moss v. State,* 888 P.2d 509 (1994).

- After the murder of a husband, the defendant and the victim's wife planned to live together and to share the insurance, land, and mobile home of the victim. The solicitation to murder became a conspiracy to murder, which resulted in the murder of the victim. Good police work solved the case and resulted in a confession and an agreement to cooperate by the defendant. *State v. Manning,* 327 N.C. 608, 398 S.E.2d 319 (1990).

- The fact that the victim saved herself from death and was not killed could not be used as a defense because the crime of solicitation to murder had occurred and was proved by the state of Michigan. *People v. Vandelinder,* 192 Mich.App. 447, 481 N.W.2d 787 (1992).

- A lawyer was convicted of "solicitation of obstruction of justice" because of his request of a store employee to obtain dismissal of shoplifting charges against the lawyer's client. *State v. Clemmons,* 100 N.C.App. 286, 396 S.E.2d 616 (1990).

- An employee of a McDonald's drive-through restaurant told a customer that he would like to have oral sex with her. The employee was convicted of solicitation of oral sodomy. However, the Virginia Court of Appeals reversed the conviction, holding that the statement did not constitute solicitation of the Virginia felony offense of oral sodomy. *Ford v. Commonwealth,* 10 Va.App. 224, 391 S.E.2d 603 (1990).[4]

Conspiracy to Commit a Crime[5]

The crime of conspiracy is the oldest of the preliminary crimes. It received some legislative recognition as early as 1292, but it was not until the early 1600s that the crime of conspiracy was developed into an offense of wide scope, capable of extensive application by the English Court of the Star Chamber. This court was created in the late 1500s to try certain high crimes without a jury. Because of the ruthless methods used, the court is sometimes referred to as the "Infamous Star Chamber."

Modern critics of the crime of conspiracy sometimes recall the ancient unsavory use of the crime of conspiracy, as did former Justice Robert H. Jackson in his concurring opinion in *Krulewitch v. United States:*

> The crime comes down to us wrapped in vague but unpleasant connotations. It sounds historical undertones of treachery, secret plotting and violence on a scale that menaces social stability and the security of the state itself. "Privy conspiracy" ranks with sedition and rebellion in the Litany's prayer for deliverance. Conspiratorial movements do indeed lie back of the political assassination, the coup d'etat, the putsch, the revolution and seizure of power in modern times, as they have in all history.[6]

The federal government (18 U.S.C.A. § 371) and probably all states have enacted statutes making conspiracy a crime in their jurisdictions. The reasoning behind such legislation generally is that when two or more persons plan a crime together, (1) the extent of potential harm to the society is often increased considerably; (2) the possibility of the abandonment of the criminal plan is greatly reduced; (3) the chances of success in the criminal venture are greater than if only one individual were involved; and (4) their actions can be more difficult to detect than individual preparation to commit a crime.

The purpose, then, of criminal conspiracy statutes is to prevent and to punish criminal partnerships in crime and to stop, if possible, such criminal combinations of people before attempts to commit substantive crimes are made.

Although the statutes of each state define conspiracy within that state, the generally accepted common law definition of conspiracy is "a combination of two or more persons, by some concerted action, to accomplish some criminal or unlawful purpose, or to accomplish some purpose, not in itself criminal or unlawful, by criminal or unlawful means."[7]

The Requirement of Two or More Guilty Persons[8]

As conspiracy was looked on as a partnership in crime, the traditional view was that the state must prove the involvement of *two or more* guilty persons. If A and B were charged with conspiracy to murder and the jury found A guilty and B not guilty, the traditional view is that the conviction against A could not stand. The reasoning for the dismissal of the charge and conviction against A is that A could not conspire alone and that two or more guilty persons are necessary in order for the conviction to stand.

Most states and the federal government follow the rule in drug cases that require proof of a sincere agreement between two or more persons in order to convict of conspiracy to violate those drug laws.

However, both the National Advisory Committee on Organized Crime and the American Law Institute Model Penal Code recommended that the old rule be changed to allow a suspect to be charged with conspiracy if the suspect agrees with an undercover officer or an informant to commit a crime. The following example illustrates a conspiracy conviction where an informant only pretended to be a party to a conspiracy to murder:

EXAMPLE: After a New York judge placed a high cash bail on a stockbroker charged with security fraud, the man offered his jail cellmate $35,000 to kill the judge. A New York jury convicted the stockbroker of conspiracy to murder after hearing the testimony of the defendant, the cellmate, and two audiotapes of the conversations between the two men regarding the proposed killing. (See "Stockbroker is Found Guilty of Conspiring to Have a Judge Killed," *New York Times,* December 23, 2000.)

The Requirement of an Overt Act

Under common law, proof of the criminal partnership was all that was required to prove the crime of conspiracy. Today, most states have written into their criminal conspiracy statutes the requirement of proof of an overt act by a defendant.

Virtually any act in furtherance of the conspiracy will satisfy this requirement. For example, making a telephone call, as in the case *United States v. Fellabaum,* 408 F.2d 220 (7th Cir. 1969), was held to satisfy the overt act requirement. In a 1993 case, the defendants agreed to rob a man. Their overt acts were the obtaining of guns and ski masks. *Burk v. State,* 848 P.2d 225.

When the U.S. Congress wrote the federal statute (21 U.S.C.A. § 846) forbidding drug conspiracies, the law required only proof of the criminal conspiracy without requiring proof of an overt act. In 1994, the U.S. Supreme Court affirmed the defendant's conviction in the case of *United States v. Shabani,* 115 S.Ct. 382, and held that the federal drug conspiracy statute was constitutional, stating:

> "[T]he language (of the federal statutes does not) require that a overt act be committed to further the conspiracy, and we have not inferred such a requirement from congressional silence in other conspiracy statutes." (The Supreme Court then quoted criminal conspiracy cases under the Sherman Act [1913] and the Selective Service Act [1945].)

Overt acts are often very convincing evidence of the sincerity of a conspiracy agreement and almost all strong conspiracy cases have evidence of overt acts. The general federal conspiracy law (18 U.S.C. § 371) expressly requires proof of an overt act done in furtherance of the criminal conspiracy that is charged.

The Wharton Rule

Some crimes cannot be committed alone but require two or more persons. Examples of such crimes are dueling, bigamy, gambling, adultery, incest, pandering for prostitution, receiving a bribe, and distributing illegal drugs. As the crime of conspiracy punishes partnerships in crime because of increased danger to society, the **Wharton Rule** states that the crime of conspiracy cannot be charged if the number of persons involved are only those necessary to commit the crime.

EXAMPLE: In order to distribute illegal drugs, there must be both a deliverer and a person receiving the drugs. Under the *Wharton* Rule, if two persons engaged in a one-time sale of a small quantity of an illegal drug, the seller and buyer cannot be charged with conspiracy.[9]

Most states and the federal government use the *Wharton* Rule and will not permit a conspiracy charge when only the persons necessary to commit the crime are named as defendants.

Mere Knowledge of a Crime Alone Is Not Sufficient to Support a Conspiracy Conviction

Mere association with criminals without agreeing to assist in the commission of a crime is not enough to prove conspiracy. For example, a live-in housekeeper who admitted she knew that drugs were in the house and that the homeowner was involved in large-scale drug trafficking was improperly convicted of drug conspiracy. On appeal, it was held that there was insufficient evidence to prove she agreed to assist in the crime. *United States v. Vasquez-Chan,* 978 F. 2d 546 (9th Cir., 1992).

In the following U.S. Supreme Court cases, both suppliers knew that their product was being used for illegal purposes. One supplied a product difficult to obtain and often used for illegal purposes, whereas the other defendant supplied a product easy to obtain and not often used for illegal purposes.

United States v. Falcone 311 U.S. 205 (1940). The defendants sold yeast and sugar (lawful products) to a man who was making illegal alcohol (bootlegger). The evidence showed that defendants knew that their products were being used for illegal purposes, but the Supreme Court held that such mere knowledge alone is insufficient to establish guilt of conspiracy. The Court held that to convict of conspiracy, there must be evidence of an agreement between the parties. In this case, there was no evidence of such an agreement.

United States v. Direct Sales, 319 U.S. 703 (1943). The defendant wholesaler continued to supply a small-town doctor with morphine after federal narcotic officials warned the defendant that the doctor was illegally supplying the morphine to addicts. Sales to the doctor continued for a long time and increased to a quantity sufficient for 400 average doses a day. The U.S. Supreme Court held that the defendant had more than mere knowledge of the illegal activity and that the continuous sales established a tacit (unspoken) agreement between the doctor and the defendant wholesaler to illegally distribute a controlled substance (morphine).

To avoid the defense of the *Wharton* Rule, criminal charges other than conspiracy could be used unless three or more persons can be charged (the federal gambling statute—18 U.S.C. Section 1955 requires "five or more persons").

In the example given, the *Wharton* Rule could be defeated if sufficient evidence was used showing that the buyer and seller have a long-standing criminal relationship involving repeated sales of large quantities of illegal drugs. The evidence would have to show an agreement beyond a simple one-time transaction. Most states would then permit substantive drug charges in addition to the conspiracy charge.

The Crime of Attempt

Attempt is the most frequently charged of the three preliminary crimes because "near" victims and witnesses will generally report attempted rapes, robberies, murders, and other crimes to the police. Moreover, such victims and witnesses are generally more cooperative about appearing in court to testify to the attempted crimes.

In defining the crime of attempt, the New York Criminal Code provides that "a person is guilty of an attempt to commit a crime when, with intent to commit a crime, he engages in conduct which tends to effect the commission of such crime."[10]

Bad thoughts alone cannot be charged as attempt or any other crime. The prosecution must show that the defendant attempted to commit the crime charged, and this requires the showing of an overt act or acts. The federal courts and many states use the Model Penal Code *substantial step test* in defining the required overt act. The "substantial

Attempt Under the Federal Criminal Code

Although there is no comprehensive statutory definition of attempt in federal law, federal courts have rather uniformly adopted the standard set forth in Section 5.01 of the . . . Model Penal Code . . . that the requisite elements of attempt are:

1. an intent to engage in criminal conduct, and

2. conduct constituting a "substantial step" towards the commission of the substantive offense which strongly corroborates the actor's criminal intent.

—*United States v. Joyce,*
693 F.2d 838 (8th Cir. 1982)

step must be conduct [showing] the firmness of the defendant's criminal intent." New York and other states hold that the state must show that the defendant performed acts that carried the "project forward within dangerous proximity of the criminal end to be attained." The following cases illustrate conduct that courts ruled to be attempts to commit the crime charged:[11]

- Defendant pointed a loaded gun at victim's face and pulled the trigger. The gun clicked but did not fire. Conviction for attempted first-degree assault. *State v. Turner,* 24 Conn.App. 264, 587 A.2d 1050 (1991).

- Mother abandoned her 15-month-old infant. When found, the baby was near death and infested with maggots. Conviction of attempted murder. Affirmed. State v. Klafta, 831 P.2d 512 (1992).

- An undercover officer was hired as a hit man and participated with defendant in detailed planning of the intended murder. The undercover officer was paid half the fee before and the balance after the defendant was falsely told the killing had occurred. Conviction for attempted premeditated murder. *United States v. Church,* 29 M.J. 679 Air Force (CMR 1989), review granted in part 30 M.J. 220 (CMA 1990).

- Defendant paid a man to murder her boyfriend's wife and son. The defendant made a sketch of the crime scene, described the victims, wrote a fake suicide note to make the killings look like murder-suicide, and pointed out the intended victims' home to the hired killer. Conviction for attempted murder and conspiracy to murder. *State v. Burd,* 189 W.Va. 415, 419 S.E.2d 676 (1991).

- Defendant shoved a woman onto a bed and told her to lie down and take off her clothes as he attempted to remove her clothes and removed his pants, exposing himself. When she escaped from the room and tried to leave the house, he caught her and struggled with her, touching her breast. Conviction for attempted rape. *Fortune v. Commonwealth,* 14 Va.App. 225, 416 S.E.2d 25 (1992).

- Defendant was alone with a 14-year-old girl and came within two feet of her, telling her to lift up her shirt or he would kill her. The girl said no and continued to back up, screaming. Defendant said he was "just joking" and left. Evidence was held sufficient for a jury to find that the defendant took a substantial step toward raping the girl. *State v. Jackson,* 62 Wash.App. 53, 813 P.2d 156 (1991).

- As two young girls were preparing to cross a street at an intersection, the defendant stopped his van, leaned out of the window, and said to the girls, "I'll pay you a dollar if you'll come . . . with me." The defendant was later found in the area and attempted to avoid being seen by police officers. Conviction for attempted kidnapping because if the girls had entered the van, their movements would have been restrained, and also because the young girls could not consent, and once in the van could have been taken to a place where they were not likely to be found. *State v. Billups,* 62 Wash.App. 102, 813 P.2d 149 (1991).[12]

Impossibility in Attempt Cases

In 1994, Francisco Duran paced back and forth on the sidewalk in front of the White House in Washington, D.C., until he saw a man he believed to be President Clinton. Duran then pulled an automatic weapon from under his coat and began firing at the man through the White House wrought iron picket fence until security forces seized him.

Duran was charged with the federal crime of attempted assassination of the president. Duran contended he could not be charged with the attempt because it was impossible to complete the crime. The man he saw and shot at was not the president, who was in fact not in Washington at the time of the attempt. The federal court rejected this defense and convicted Duran of the attempt charge.[13]

In another somewhat similar case, defendant Benny Curtis was charged with attempting to kill wild deer out of season when he shot at a deer decoy set up by game wardens in response to complaints by residents of illegal deer shootings. Curtis argued that it was impossible to complete the crime because he was shooting at a decoy, and therefore he could not be guilty of the attempt. The Supreme Court of Vermont rejected that contention, and Curtis was convicted of the charge.[14]

Courts formerly classified impossibility defenses in attempt cases into two classes: factual impossibility and legal impossibility. Attempting to pick an empty pocket is an example of factual impossibility. The only thing that prevents the crime from being completed is the fact that the pocket is empty. Attempting to receive stolen goods that were not stolen has been characterized as an example of legal impossibility. Even if the defendants completed the intended act, they would not be guilty of a crime.

Most state courts and the federal courts have abandoned the distinction between factual and legal impossibility, and have rejected the defense in both situations.[15] The Model Penal Code, Section 5.1, also rejects the impossibility defense, whether factual or legal, concluding that the culpability of the defendant should be judged by the circumstances as the defendant viewed them.

The defense of impossibility was rejected in the following cases, and the defendants were convicted of criminal attempt:

- Attempted armed robbery, even though the victim had no money in his wallet. *Brown v. Commonwealth,* 482 S.E. 2d 75 (Va. App. 1997)

- Attempted sex with a child, even though there was not a young girl in the motel room the defendant entered with the intent to have such sexual contact. *People v. Keister,* 424 P.2d 97 (Cal.App. 1996)

- Attempted statutory rape, even though the policewoman used as a decoy was 24 years old and not 16 as she pretended to be. *People v. Coleman,* 547 N.Y.S. 814 (N.Y. Ct. of App.)

- Attempted possession of illegal drugs, even though the substance sold was not PCP as defendant was told. *United States v. Fletcher,* 945 F.2d 725 (4th Cir. 1991)

- Attempt to receive stolen property, even though the property the defendant purchased was not stolen. *Commonwealth v. Henley,* 474 A.2d 1115 (Pa. 1984).[16]

Abandonment of the Criminal Purpose

In attempt, conspiracy, and solicitation, a person usually has time to change his or her mind and decide not to go ahead with the intended crime. Many states now have statutes in their criminal code on abandonment of a criminal effort. Important questions concerning abandonment of a criminal intent include: Has a preliminary crime already been committed (how far along is the criminal effort)? Was the abandonment voluntary or involuntary? What was the reason for the abandonment (did the victim scream or police arrive at the scene or a burglar alarm go off)? The following cases illustrate:

- A neighbor rang the doorbell of an elderly widow's home and, after being invited in and offered a beer, told the woman, "I am going to have you." After dragging the woman into a bedroom and throwing her on a bed, defendant forcefully took most of her clothes off. As the defendant began taking his pants off, the woman kneed him in his groin and hit him in the face. Defendant then stopped his efforts, apologized, and pleaded with the woman not to call the police. The Supreme Court of Wyoming affirmed defendant's conviction of attempted sexual assault, pointing out that the defendant did not voluntarily stop his attack and that the crime of attempt had already been completed. *Apodaca v. State,* 796 P.2d 806 (1990).

- A stranger forced a woman back into her home, told her to undress, pointed a handgun at her, shoved her onto a couch, and once threatened to kill her. The woman cried and talked about her little girl, telling the defendant that her little girl's daddy was dead. The defendant then said that if she had a little girl, he would not do anything, and left in his pickup truck. The Supreme Court of Mississippi reversed defendant's conviction of attempted rape, holding that under the attempt statute of Mississippi that when "a defendant, with no other impetus but the victim's urging, voluntarily ceases his assault, he has not committed attempted rape." *Ross v. State,* 601 So.2d 872 (1992).[17]

- Under a different name, Staples rented an apartment over a bank. He brought in power tools and equipment and, over a weekend when the bank was not open, drilled several holes through the floor into the ceiling of the bank. Nothing further was done, and at the end of the rental period, the landlord called in the police when he found the equipment and holes in the floor. Staples was arrested and stated that he had abandoned his criminal project. Because the crime of attempted burglary had already been committed, Staples was convicted of that crime. *People v. Staples,* 85 Cal.Rptr. 589 (1970).

Preliminary, Anticipatory (or Inchoate) Crimes

Crime	The Crime Consists of Evidence Showing:	Other Aspects of the Crime
Solicitation (the preparatory offense charged least often): The invitation or urging to commit a crime[a]	1. Requesting, encouraging, or commanding another person 2. To commit a crime (most states restrict general solicitation to felonies)	Because no requirement generally exists for an overt act, the crime is complete when the solicitation is made. If the request to commit the crime is accepted, a conspiracy could exist if the requirements for the crime of conspiracy in that state are met.
Conspiracy (the oldest of the preparatory offenses): The criminal partnership	1. An agreement between two or more persons (more than half the states now follow the Model Penal Code and do not require two or more guilty people. In these states, proof of guilt of one person is sufficient.) 2. Specific intent to commit a crime, or to obtain a legal goal by criminal acts 3. Most states now require an overt act in furtherance of the plan be proved for all.	A conspiracy is punishable whether or not it succeeds in its objective (*United States v. Rabinowich,* 238 U.S. 78). In federal courts and some states, convictions for both conspiracy and the completed crime are held not to violate double jeopardy. *Iannelli v. United States,* 420 U.S. 770, 95 S.Ct. 1284 (1975). The Federal Drug Conspiracy Law does not require proof of an overt act. *United States v. Shabani,* 115 S.Ct. 382 (1994).
Attempt (the inchoate crime charged most often): An attempt often puts a possible victim in fear and apprehension. Many near victims can and do appear as witnesses in criminal trials.	1. That the defendant intended to commit the crime of which he or she is charged, and 2. That he or she did acts that (a) came within "dangerous proximity" of the criminal end or (b) amount to a "substantial step" (§ 5.01 Model Penal Code)	The American Law Institute Model Penal Code recommends the broadening of criminal liability for the crime of attempt. See § 5.01(2) for a discussion of these proposals.

[a]The English call this crime *incitement* and use the term *solicitation* in the crime of solicitation for prostitution.

Parties to the Principal Crime

Under the Common Law

At the time of the American Revolution, more than two hundred crimes were punished by death in England. The death penalty was applied depending upon the degree of criminal participation in the completed crime. The following four common law categories were used to determine the penalty that would be applied after conviction:

1. *Principal in the first degree* was the person (or persons) who actually committed the crime and would receive the death penalty if applicable.

2. *Principal in the second degree* was a person who was present at the commission of the crime, was not involved in the planning of the crime, but aided and abetted in the actual commission of the crime. This offender could not be tried under the common law until the actual perpetrator had been apprehended and convicted of the offense.

3. *Accessory before the fact* was a person who, knowing that a crime was to be committed, aided in the preparation for the crime but was not present at the time the crime was committed.

4. *Accessory after the fact* was a person who knew that the crime had been committed and gave aid or comfort to the person who committed the crime. Neither the accessory before the fact nor after the fact could be tried until after the conviction of the principal in the first degree.

Criminal Liability in the United States Today

Today, most states have done away with the four common law categories. The majority of jurisdictions have statutes that create the following two categories of criminal liability and make all principals or parties to the crime liable to the same punishment.

1. All people who knowingly are involved in or connected with the commission of a crime either before or during its commission are known as principals or parties to the crime, regardless of their connection. This category is a combination of the common law principal in the first and second degree and the accessory before the fact.

2. The person or people who render aid to the criminal after the crime has been committed. Legislative bodies have statutorized criminal offenses in this category that were previously known to the common law as accessory after the fact. This category will be discussed in the section on *post-crime offenses* in this chapter.

The rule that neither the principal in the second degree nor the accessories before or after the fact could be forced to trial before the trial of the principal in the first degree has been abolished. Any participant in a crime may be tried and convicted, even though the person who actually committed the crime has not been apprehended and tried or even identified.[18]

Theories of Criminal Liability

Criminal Liability as an Aider and Abettor and/or a Conspirator

A person could be criminally liable for the conduct of another if he or she is a party to a conspiracy to commit a crime and hires, urges, counsels, or plans with another to commit a crime. A person is also liable for the conduct of another if he or she is an *aider* and *abettor* to a person who committed a crime.

Aiders and abettors to a crime are usually at the scene of a crime rendering aid and assistance to the person committing the crime. The aid and assistance could also be rendered miles from the crime scene. Or the aider and abettor could also have been involved in the planning of the crime and therefore would also be a *conspirator*. Or a conspirator could live in London, England (or elsewhere), hire the killing of a person in Los Angeles, and never go near the scene of the crime.

Fact finders (jury or judge) may draw reasonable inferences from the conduct of the offenders and make conclusions as to whether the people were *aiders and abettors or conspirators* to the crime, or both. Or in states using the common design rule, fact finders could infer from the facts of the case whether the defendants in a criminal case committed the crime (or crimes) under a *common design or plan.*

Criminal Liability Under the Common Design or Common Plan Rule

Under the "common design" rule, when people have a common plan to do an unlawful act, whatever is done in furtherance of the common design or common plan is the act of all and they can all be punished for that act.

If one of the parties to an armed robbery wore a mask, then all the parties to the robbery wore a mask and all are subject to the penalties of committing the crime of armed robbery while concealed. (See *Curl v. State,* 162 N.W.2d 77 [Sup. Wis. 1968].) If one of the parties to a drug trafficking offense carried a gun, then all the parties are subject to the penalties of carrying a loaded gun while trafficking marijuana. (See *United States v. Martinez,* 958 F.2d 217 [8th Cir. 1992].)

A common design is a spoken or unspoken conspiracy to commit an unlawful act. Any member of the conspiracy (plan) could be held liable as a principal for any offense committed in the furtherance of the plan or conspiracy while he or she is a member of it. Latecomers cannot be convicted as principals for offenses that were committed before they joined the conspiracy or after they withdrew from the conspiracy.[19]

Cases Illustrating Criminal or Civil Liability Under Theories That Hold "What One Did, They All Did"

In most cases, prosecutors are going to charge and juries are going to find criminal liability under the concept that what one of the parties to a criminal conspiracy did, all of the parties to the conspiracy did. The following cases illustrate:

- As a deputy sheriff was walking up to a car he had stopped for a minor vehicle license problem, one of the three men in the car pulled out a gun and killed the officer. The other two men in the car were surprised at what happened, but they too pulled out revolvers and began shooting at the remaining deputy sheriff in the squad car. The men fled after wounding the officer but were apprehended the next day. All three of the men were convicted of the murder of the officer and also of attempted murder of the wounded officer. The Wisconsin Supreme Court affirmed the convictions.[20]

- In the 1894 case of *State v. Tally,*[21] a group of men in one town set out to kill a particular person who lived in another town. The friends of the victim, hearing of the plot against him, attempted to warn him by sending him a telegram. Another person, a judge, who also disliked the potential victim, directed the telegraph operator to destroy the message, telling him that it was unimportant. The man was killed and the judge was held liable for the murder under the complicity theory because, although he was not involved in the plans to murder the victim, he did render aid and assistance. The perpetrators of the crime were not aware of the assistance given by the judge until after they had committed the crime.

■ Defendant Watts guarded the parents of a teenage girl while his two friends raped the girl. Watts was convicted of two counts of rape in concert because he aided and abetted both rapes. In affirming the California convictions for these and other crimes, the Federal Court of Appeals held:

> We hold that no violation of due process has occurred in this case. . . . The ancient and universally accepted principle of accomplice liability holds a defendant legally responsible for the unlawful conduct of others that he aids and abets.[22]

■ The California Supreme Court held in 1991 that because the crime of robbery is ongoing through the getaway, a getaway driver who has no prior knowledge of a robbery, but who forms the intent to aid (during the getaway), may properly be found liable as an aider and abettor of the robbery.[23]

■ The fact that the defendants provided the following lawful goods and services to drug traffickers—fueled their plane, rented hangar space, stored ammunition and guns, falsely identified conspirators to outsiders, and offered to pay a security guard $20,000 to disappear while the plane was being loaded—was sufficient to affirm their conviction for aiding and abetting.[24]

■ The defendant had not physically assisted in a battery but gave verbal encouragement to the assailant by yelling, "Kill him" and "Hit him more." In a *civil* action, the court found that liability did not require a finding of action in concert, nor even that the injury had directly resulted from the encouragement. Citing Restatement, section 876(b), the Court held:

> It is clear, however, that in the United States, civil liability for assault and battery is not limited to the direct perpetrator, but extends to any person who by any means aids or encourages the act. *Hargis v. Horrine,* 230 Ark. 502, 323 S.W.2d 917 (1959); *Ayer v. Robinson,* 163 Cal.App.2d 424, 329 P.2d 546 (1958); *Guilbeau v. Guilbeau,* 326 So.2d 654 (La.App. 1976); *Duke v. Feldman,* 245 Md. 454, 266 A.2d 345 (1967); *Brink v. Purnell,* 162 Mich. 147, 127 N.W. 322 (1910); 6 Am.Jur.2d Assault and Battery, section 128 (1963); 6A C.J.S. *Assault and Battery,* section 11 (1975); Annot., 72 A.L.R.2d 1229 (1960). According to the Restatement: "For harm resulting to a third person from the tortious conduct of another, one is subject to liability if he
>
> * * *
>
> (b) knows that the other's conduct constitutes a breach of duty and gives substantial assistance or encouragement to the other so to conduct himself."— Restatement (Second) of Torts, section 876 (1979).[25]

■ Four months after her husband kidnapped their child, a Colorado woman learned that her husband had appeared on television on the *Phil Donahue Show* to talk about parental kidnapping and why and how he had kidnapped their child. The show provided a babysitting service, and when the mother of the child requested information and help from the show, the television company stood on its pledge of confidentiality to a news source. In a civil lawsuit against the company for aiding and abetting parental kidnapping, the mother of the child was awarded $5.9 million. The father was arrested in Tulsa, Oklahoma, on a fugitive warrant in 1983, and the child was returned to the mother.

The following were held to be accomplices for their acts:

- A woman who unlocked the door to another woman's apartment with intent to allow accomplices in was convicted of home invasion, robbery, and burglary. *People v. Brown,* 197 Ill.App.3d 907, 145 Ill.Dec. 429, 557 N.E.2d 199 (1990).

- After his car struck another vehicle, injuring the other driver, the passenger got behind the steering wheel and drove away and was convicted of hit-and-run with injury. *People v. Lewis,* 162 Misc.2d 954, 418 N.Y.S. 737 (1994).

- The defendant forced two persons to have sexual intercourse with one another and was convicted of first-degree unlawful sexual intercourse. *Morrisey v. State,* 620 A.2d 207 (Del. 1993).

- A woman defendant who told a friend that she was attacked the previous night and to bring his gun, because she wanted her attacker hurt, but was not present at time of the shooting in which a man other than the intended victim was killed was convicted of manslaughter. *Herring v. State,* 540 So.2d 795 (Ala.Cr.App. 1988).

- A U.S. Customs agent who received $20,000 for allowing a marijuana shipment to pass through customs was held criminally liable for the entire conspiracy of four shipping operations. But a rental car employee who provided an untraceable car in return for an ounce of marijuana was not held liable for the entire smuggling operation. *United States v. Umagat et al.,* 998 F.2d 770 (9th Cir. 1993).

- *Soldier of Fortune* magazine was found liable for $12.4 million in a civil lawsuit for publishing a "gun for hire" advertisement. The advertisement was blamed for the killing of a businessman. (See the *New York Times* article, "Magazine Is Liable for Ad Run by 'Gun for Hire,'" December 9, 1990.)

Unindicted Co-Conspirators

The U.S. Supreme Court wrote:

> Secrecy and concealment are essential features of successful conspiracy. The more completely they are achieved, the more successful the crime. Hence the law rightly gives room for allowing the conviction of those discovered upon showing sufficiently the essential nature of the plan and their connections with it, without requiring evidence of knowledge of all its details or of the participation of others. Otherwise the difficulties, not only of discovery, but of certainty of proof . . . would become unsuperable, and conspirators would go free by their very ingenuity."[26]

Newspapers used the term *unindicted co-conspirator* in the Watergate scandal of the early 1970s. At that time, President Richard Nixon was listed as an "unindicted co-conspirator" (that is, prosecutors were stating they could have indicted him, but did not). By listing President Nixon as an unindicted co-conspirator, prosecutors were able to introduce statements made by Nixon as evidence. If prosecutors conclude that the evidence (such as statements) of an unindicted co-conspirator is more important than charging the person with a criminal charge, they might use this tactic to make a stronger case.

In 1996, former White House adviser Bruce Lindsey was listed as an unindicted co-conspirator in a Whitewater-related trial. Lindsey was called "one of (President Clinton's) closest confidants." (See the *Detroit News* article, "Whitewater Snags Close Clinton Aide," June 20, 1996.)

Liability for Crimes Other Than the Planned and Intended Offense

When the evidence demonstrates a common design or conspiracy to commit an unlawful act to which all the defendants agreed, whatever is done in the furtherance of the criminal plan is the act of all if it is a natural and probable consequence of the intended crime. If guns are carried and a shot is fired by one member of the group, that shot is fired by all the defendants, and all of them must answer for the results.[27]

In *People v. Jones,* the California courts held that an accused who knew that his co-defendants were armed was responsible for all the consequences when a night watchman was killed in a robbery.[28] The defendant in the *Jones* case was unarmed.

The definition of the natural and probable consequences of the intended crime will vary somewhat from jury to jury and court to court. The following example illustrates the problem:

EXAMPLE: X and Y conspire to burglarize a residence. X is the lookout and getaway driver while Y is in the house committing the burglary. Y commits the following additional crimes. Which of the following should X be charged with?

1. Y is surprised by the homeowner and, in an attempt to get away, kills the man.
2. Y is surprised by an 11-year-old boy who lives in the house and needlessly kills the boy.
3. In addition to stealing, Y comes upon a woman in bed and rapes the woman.
4. After stealing from the house, Y sees a gallon of gasoline in the back hall of the house, spills the gasoline around the house, and burns it down.

Prosecutors could charge X with all the additional crimes, but whether X would be convicted would depend on whether the finder of fact determined that the additional acts were a natural and probable consequence of the burglary. It certainly could be argued in this case that X aided and assisted in all the crimes while acting as the lookout and getaway driver. If X had hired Y to commit the burglary and X was not at the scene of the crime, X's liability would be the same.

X's defense could be that some of the offenses are not the natural or probable consequence of the intended crime of burglary, and therefore X would not be criminally liable for those offenses. In all cases, X would be charged with and convicted of the crime of burglary.[29]

Post-Crime Offenses

Today, all states and the federal government have enacted many statutes meant to assist law enforcement officers in performing their duty of investigating crimes and apprehending criminals. Some statutes punish people who knowingly give police false information with the intent to mislead them. Other statutes are designed to permit the proper

---

If the State Can Prove One of the Following Beyond Reasonable Doubt, a Person Can Be Held Criminally Liable

For a preliminary or anticipatory crime

- Solicitation
- Conspiracy
- Attempt

For the planned and intended crime (if completed)

- As the person who committed the crime, or
- As a person who intentionally aids and abets the person who committed the crime, or
- As a conspirator who advises, hires, counsels, or otherwise procures another to commit a crime

For a post-crime offense relating to the planned and intended crime.

States use one of the following theories of liabilities:

- *Party to a crime,* in which the state would have to prove each person participated in one of the preceding categories
- *Common design or plan*
- *Criminal liability* under the complicity, accountability, or accomplice rules

---

and efficient functioning of the courts and the criminal justice system. Some of these offenses existed under the common law, whereas others have been created in modern times. Examples are:

- Refusing to aid an officer while such officer is doing any act in his or her official capacity
- Obstructing or resisting an officer while such officer is doing any act in his or her official capacity (interfering with an officer)[30]
- Obstructing justice
- Compounding a crime: the making of an agreement (for a consideration) to withhold evidence of, or to abstain from prosecuting a crime of which the accused has knowledge[31]
- False reports to an officer or law agency[32]
- Misprision of a felony (failure to report or prosecute a known felon)[33]
- Harboring or aiding felons
- Committing perjury
- Escaping from custody
- Bribing witnesses
- Jumping bail
- Communicating with jurors with the intent to influence them

Stages of Crimes

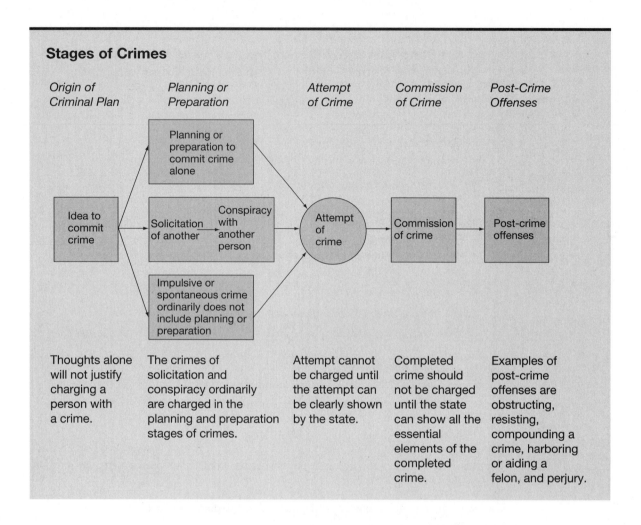

Origin of Criminal Plan	Planning or Preparation	Attempt of Crime	Commission of Crime	Post-Crime Offenses
Thoughts alone will not justify charging a person with a crime.	The crimes of solicitation and conspiracy ordinarily are charged in the planning and preparation stages of crimes.	Attempt cannot be charged until the attempt can be clearly shown by the state.	Completed crime should not be charged until the state can show all the essential elements of the completed crime.	Examples of post-crime offenses are obstructing, resisting, compounding a crime, harboring or aiding a felon, and perjury.

When Material Witnesses Can Be Criminally Liable

A *material witness* is a witness who has material information regarding a crime. A person who was in a business place at the time of an armed robbery and observed the robbers and the crime would be a material witness.

If the state cannot show probable cause that a material witness was a party to a crime, the material witness may not then be arrested. However, material witnesses may be reasonably detained to obtain their identity and to question them, because law enforcement officers have a legal duty and obligation to investigate criminal incidents.[34]

Most material witnesses are cooperative and will honestly provide information that they have regarding a criminal incident. If material witnesses are shown to have intentionally provided false material information regarding a criminal incident to an investigating officer, the witness could be charged with obstructing and hindering a law enforcement officer in the performance of his or her duty. The following is an example of a cooperative witness:

EXAMPLE: After the assassination of the Rev. Martin Luther King Jr., a witness was able to identify James Earl Ray as the man rushing down the steps of the hotel from which

Vicarious Liability Distinguished from Strict Liability

Strict liability   When a criminal statute imposes liability without requiring proof of mental fault, the offense is called a strict liability offense. If a statute requires proof of a mental element, the offense is not a strict liability offense.

To prove a strict liability offense, the state need only prove the defendant did the forbidden act. The state does not have to prove a mental fault (*mens rea*). *Minnesota v. White* (see Chapter 3) came before the U.S. Supreme Court in 1991 and is an example of strict liability. The state proved that White hired a minor to dance nude in her bookstore. After the state proved the forbidden act and the age of the girl, White could not use the defense of mistake of age or consent by the minor.

Vicarious liability   When a person becomes liable for the criminal act (or acts) of another, the liability is vicarious. Section 2.06 of the Model Penal Code lists the following categories of vicarious liability:

- Causing innocent or irresponsible persons to do a criminal act
- Becoming a criminal accomplice of another person by:
  a) soliciting the person to do a criminal act
  b) aiding the other person in planning or committing the act
  c) having a legal duty to prevent the act and fails to take reasonable steps to prevent the act
  d) a statute expressly establishes his complicity for the crime

the shots came. Because Ray was not apprehended until many months after the shooting, police were concerned for the safety of the witness, who was an older man living on a small pension. The man was cooperative and moved into the county jail in Memphis to ensure his safety. He was free to come and go but was accompanied by officers when he left the jail for a walk or to have a beer. Because of the inconvenience of providing guards every day, the State of Tennessee went to court and asked that bail be set to ensure the appearance of this cooperative witness at the trial of James Earl Ray (if and when he was apprehended). Bail was set at $10,000 cash, but because the witness did not have this amount of cash, he could not meet bail. He was then held in jail without any freedom to leave. Lawyers challenged this procedure and the statute authorizing it as a violation of due process. As a result, an apartment was rented, and the witness lived there with 24-hour-a-day police protection until Ray was apprehended and went to trial.

This example illustrates that unless probable cause is shown that a witness has committed a crime, he or she cannot be held. If a witness is uncooperative, he or she may be brought before a grand jury, coroner's inquest, "John Doe" proceedings, or court and questioned under oath. Under such circumstances, a witness could be compelled to answer questions. If the witness takes the Fifth Amendment, she or he could be granted witness immunity and then would face jail or contempt for failure to answer.

SUMMARY

One may be charged under the criminal laws even though the intended, underlying crime is not completed. These are called preliminary, anticipated, or inchoate crimes. They include solicitation, conspiracy, and attempt. Solicitation requires only that the defendant urge another to commit a crime, even if that other person refuses to do so. Conspiracy and attempt require that the defendant take some act in furtherance of the underlying crime. In attempt cases, such act or acts must be substantial enough to move the crime forward toward completion. In conspiracy cases, virtually any act will suffice.

Where the underlying crime is completed, a defendant can be charged with commission of the underlying crime if he or she is (1) the person who committed the criminal acts, (2) a person who intentionally aided and abetted the person who committed the criminal act, or (3) a person who conspires with or otherwise procures another person to commit the criminal act. A person who does not participate in the criminal acts under any of the above, but does act subsequently to assist the perpetrator of the crime or obstruct law enforcement officials investigating the crime, may be charged with a variety of post-crime offences.

A person can be shown by the prosecution to fit one of the above party categories by proof that the person was a party to the commission of the crime, was part of a common design or plan, or was liable under the conspiracy, accountability, or accomplice rules.

QUESTIONS AND PROBLEMS

1. The defendant owned and operated the Head Shop in Manchester, New Hampshire. A 14-year-old girl walked into the shop and purchased for 25 cents a button inscribed "Copulation Not Masturbation." When the girl's parents saw the button, they became angry and called the police. The defendant was convicted of contributing to the delinquency of a minor, which is a statutory offense in New Hampshire: "Anyone . . . who shall knowingly or willfully encourage, aid, cause or abet or connive at, or who has knowingly or willfully done any act to produce, promote or contribute to the delinquency of (a) child may be punished" (Sec. 169.32, N.H. Rev. Stat. Ann.).

The defendant was convicted in a trial at which the girl was the only witness for the state. The 14-year-old girl did not testify that the defendant sold her the button or that she even saw him in the store at the time of the sale. She testified that she could not identify the person who sold her the button. The defendant admitted that he "controlled the premises on July 26 [the date of the sale]." Should the defendant's conviction be affirmed by the U.S. Supreme Court? Explain. *Vachon v. New Hampshire,* 414 U.S. 478, 94 S.Ct. 664 (1974).

2. Parks was the president of a retail food chain with 36,000 employees, 874 stores, and 16 warehouses.

In 1970, federal inspectors advised officers of the corporation that unsanitary conditions were found in a warehouse. Twice in 1971, further unsanitary conditions were reported. In March 1972, continued evidence of rodent activity and "rodent-contaminated lots of food items" was found. Despite the repeated warnings by the federal inspectors, the violations were not corrected. When the food corporation and Parks were charged with violations of the Federal Food, Drug and Cosmetic Act, the corporation pleaded guilty and Parks pleaded not guilty before a jury. The jury convicted Parks of a misdemeanor. Should the U.S. Supreme Court affirm Parks's conviction? Explain. *United States v. Parks,* 421 U.S. 658, 95 S.Ct. 1903 (1975).

3. The following situation occurred in Milwaukee: Two teenage girls were walking toward a shopping center when a car containing two men in their twenties stopped. The men offered to give the girls a ride. When the girls refused, one of the men (the passenger) got out of the car and continued attempting to persuade the girls to ride with the men. When the man held one of the girls by her arm, she pulled away from him. The man then hit the girl in the face, sending her sprawling on the ground. The man immediately got back into the car and the driver quickly drove away. The other

girl, however, observed the license of the vehicle and provided this information to the police when reporting the incident. When the investigating officers obtained the name and address of the owner of the vehicle, they went to that residence. The vehicle was parked in the driveway and a young man matching the description of the driver was identified as the owner of the vehicle. The man at first denied being at the scene of the crime. But after he realized that the girls could identify him, he told the following story. The owner and driver of the car said that he picked up a hitchhiker about his age and that the two men had stopped to pick up the girls. After the battery occurred, the driver said he drove his passenger a short distance and then dropped him off. He stated that he did not know the man's name and had never seen him before. The police did not believe the man's story but what, if anything, can they do to obtain the identity of the man who sent the teenage girl to a hospital with a badly bruised face? Explain.

4. A man in a Nevada casino walked into a woman's bathroom and assaulted a 7-year-old girl in a toilet stall. The man's friend followed the first man into the woman's bathroom and tried to get the first man to leave as he was assaulting the little girl. When this failed, the second man quickly left the woman's bathroom and waited outside for his friend without seeking aid for the little girl. The first man was in the bathroom for nearly 25 minutes and was charged with raping and murdering the little girl.

If this incident occurred in your state what criminal charges, if any, could be brought against the second man who waited outside the woman's bathroom? (See the article, "Mother Rages Against Indifference: Charges Sought Against Bystander in Rape and Murder of Girl" in the August 24, 1998 *New York Times*.)

5. Defendant A agrees with another person, B, to murder C. Before any act is done by either A or B in furtherance of this agreement, B dies. A subsequently kills C. May A be convicted of the crime of conspiracy to commit murder? What act will satisfy the "overt act" requirement? See *Alleyne v. California*, 98 Cal.Rptr. 2d 737 (2000), cert den. 69 USLW 3642 (2001).

INFOTRAC COLLEGE EDITION EXERCISES

1. Go to InfoTrac College Edition and, using the keyword search term *conspiracy*, find the February 2002 article discussing the most famous conspiracy theory of the 20th century, the assassination of President Kennedy, and the role of New Orleans District Attorney Jim Garrison in that conspiracy theory.

2. Go to InfoTrac College Edition and, using the keyword search term *criminal attempt*, find the May 2000 article by Katz on the "successful assassin." What are his reasons for concluding that successful assassination attempts are morally worse than unsuccessful attempts?

NOTES

1. In the United States the crime is generally called *solicitation*, while in England the crime is called *incitement*, with the term *solicitation* being used in solicitation for prostitution. See the English *Moriarty's Police Law* (Law and Regulations for the Use of Police Officers), 21st ed. (Butterworths, 1972).

2. The English Parliament enacted the Incitement to Mutiny Act (English armed forces) in 1797. See *Moriarty's Police Law*, p. 12.

3. The general solicitation statute of many states limits the crime of solicitation to felonies. Therefore, cases that appear in court are solicitation

to commit murder, arson, robbery, and other felonies.

4. The prosecutor obviously charged the defendant with the wrong crime in this case. Court decision in Virginia would establish some precedent for charging (or not charging) this type of offense. Disorderly conduct (or disorderly person) would be commonly used elsewhere if the requirements of the *fighting words doctrine* can be shown. See Chapter 10 for the *Chaplinsky* fighting words doctrine.

5. In 1925, Judge Learned Hand called conspiracy the "darling of the prosecutor's nursery," as prosecutors were using conspiracy as a weapon against organized crime and illegal business practices. *Harrison v. United States,* 7 F.2d 259, 263 2d Cir.). Today, the federal and state RICO statutes are much more effective in this type of criminal prosecutions. See Chapter 22 for a discussion of the RICO statutes.

6. 336 U.S. 440, 445, 69 S.Ct. 716, 719 (1949).

7. *Commonwealth v. Hunt,* 45 Mass. (4 Metc.) 111, 123 (1842). .

8. Under the old common law, a husband and wife were one person, with the wife being subject to the control and discipline of the husband (see the discussion on the defense of duress and coercion in Chapter 7). Because of this relationship, the common law rule held that *because* the husband and wife were one person, they could not conspire together and be charged as the two persons to a conspiracy.

This old common law rule was rejected by the U.S. Supreme Court in the 1960 case of *United States v. Dege,* 80 S.Ct. 1589, in which the Court held that a wife is a person like anyone else and therefore is capable of entering into a criminal conspiracy with her husband or another person. Today, all states would follow this reasoning if the question were before a state court.

9. See *United States v. Delutis,* 722 F. 2d 902 (1st Cir. 1983). The *Wharton* Rule was held not to apply to the crime of possession with intent to distribute illegal drugs as one person alone can commit this crime. *Johnson v. State,* 587 A. 2d 444 (Del. 1991)

10. Section 110.00, McKinney's Consolidated Laws of New York, Annotated, Book 39.

11. Examples of conduct that was mere preparation and did not amount to conduct to attempt to commit the crime charged include:

- Police officers watching a bank night depository saw two young men park near the depository and remove something from the trunk of their car. The men then walked up near the depository and back. When a car approached, the men hid in nearby bushes. Because no crime occurred, the court held the police had no probable cause to arrest the men. *People v. Cradle,* 160 A.D.2d 891, 554 N.Y.S.2d 323 (1990).

- The defendant armed himself and then drove to a nearby city in a stolen cab that he intended to use as a getaway vehicle. The defendant stated he was looking for a jewelry store to rob. The defendant did not find the store he intended to rob. The Supreme Court of Illinois affirmed the defendant's convictions for a number of crimes but reversed the conviction for attempted robbery of the jewelry store, holding that the defendant did not commit a substantial step toward the robbery of the store. *People v. Smith,* 593 N.E.2d 533 (1992).

12. In the 1992 case of *Commonwealth v. Banfill,* 597 N.E.2d 47, the defendant stopped his truck and asked directions from a 13-year-old girl walking on the street. When the girl could not give the defendant information about a street, the defendant told the girl through the open truck window to "get in." The defendant was convicted of attempted kidnapping and appealed. The Supreme Judicial Court of Massachusetts reversed the conviction, holding there was insufficient evidence to support the conviction because no overt act is required by the statute. The Court pointed out that the defendant did not "make a move toward" the girl in any way, that he did not open the truck door or display a weapon, and that he did not "try to grab out" at the girl.

13. *United States v. Duran,* 884 F.Supp. 577 (D.D.C., 1995). Duran continued to fire his automatic weapon until the clip was empty. While Duran was replacing the empty clip, bystanders seized Duran on the sidewalk outside the White House and disarmed him.

14. *State v. Curtis,* 603 A.2d 356 (Sup.Ct.Vt. 1991).

15. See page 38 of LaFave and Scott, *Criminal Law,* 2d ed. (Belmont, Calif.: West/Wadsworth, 1986). Legal writers distinguish between legal and factual impossibility. However, the Supreme Court of Pennsylvania states that no American court has recognized factual impossibility as a defense to an attempt charge (*Commonwealth v. Henley,* 474 A.2d at 1116).

In addition to legal and factual impossibility, some courts write of *inherent impossibility.* The committee drafting the revised Illinois Criminal Code in 1961 wrote this comment on the defenses of impossibility (Chapter 38, p. 513):

> It is the intent of section 8-4(b) to exclude both factual and legal impossibilities as defenses to prosecution for attempt. However, inherent impossibility (attempts to kill by witchcraft such as repeatedly stabbing a cloth dummy made to represent the person intended to be killed) is not intended to be excluded as a defense. [Emphasis in original.]

16. The *Henley* case held that the fact the goods were not stolen provided no defense to an attempt charge. However, if the goods were not stolen, or lost their identity as stolen goods, the defendant could not be convicted of the charge of possession of stolen property. See Chapter 17 for material on the crime of possession of stolen goods.

17. In cases such as this, defendants can be charged with other criminal offenses depending on the criminal code of that state. Possible charges could be home invasion (or burglary), battery or assault, pointing a firearm at another person, and disorderly person (or disorderly conduct).

18. In the 1980 case of *Standefer v. United States,* 447 U.S. 10, 100 S.Ct. 1999, 27 CrL 3143, the U.S. Supreme Court held that a defendant may be convicted of aiding and abetting the commission of a federal crime, even though the person who actually committed the crime had been acquitted of the offense.

19. The New Jersey accountability and accomplice liability law is presented in the 1992 case of *State v. Bryant,* 607 A.2d 1343, as follows:

> N.J.S.A. 2C:2-6a provides that a person is guilty of an offense "if it is committed by his own conduct or the conduct of another person for which he is legally accountable, or both." N.J.S.A. 2C:2-6b provides in part: b. A person is legally accountable for the conduct of another person when:
>
> * * *
>
> (3) He is an accomplice of such other person in the commission of an offense; or
> (4) He is engaged in a conspiracy with such other person.
> c. A person is an accomplice of another person in the commission of an offense if:
> (1) With the purpose of promoting or facilitating the commission of the offense, he
> (a) Solicits such other person to commit it;
> (b) Aids or agrees or attempts to aid such other person in planning or committing it; or
> (c) Having a legal duty to prevent the commission of the offense, fails to make proper effort so to do; or
> (d) His conduct is expressly declared by law to establish his complicity.

20. *State v. Nutley,* 24 Wis.2d 527, 129 N.W.2d 155 (1964).

21. 102 Ala. 25, 15 So.2d 722 (1894).

22. *Watts v. Bonneville,* 879 F.2d 685 (9th Cir. 1989).

23. *People v. Cooper,* 53 Cal.3d 1158, 282 Cal.Rptr. 450, 49 CrL 1362 (1991).

24. *United States v. O'Neil,* 729 F.2d 1440 (2d Cir. 1983), review denied 104 S.Ct. 135 (1983).

25. *Rael v. Cadena,* 93 N.M. 684, 604 P.2d 822 (1979).

26. U.S. Supreme Court in *Blumenthal v. United States,* 332 U.S. at 557, 68 S.Ct. at 256 (1947).

27. *People v. Bracey,* 249 N.E.2d 224 (1969).

28. 29 P.2d 902 (1934).

29. In the 1991 case of *Ward v. State,* 567 N.E.2d 85, no evidence showed that the defendant knew anything about the planned robbery. The defendant drove three men to the store they planned to rob and then left the area. Another car arrived carrying the weapons and ski masks used. During the robbery, a store clerk was killed. The Supreme Court of Indiana reversed the

defendant's conviction of felony murder, pointing out that the defendant was not shown to have participated in either the planning or carrying out of the robbery, that he did not remain as a lookout but left the area, that he did not return to aid in the escape, and that he did not receive any proceeds of the robbery.

In the case of *Mumford v. Maryland,* 19 Md.App. 640, 313 A.2d 563 (1974), a rape and murder occurred during a burglary. The defendant (a 15-year-old girl) stated that she was elsewhere on the premises when the rape and murder occurred and that she did not know these crimes were being committed. In reversing her conviction for first-degree murder (felony murder) and ordering a new trial, the Court stated: "There must be a direct causal connection between the homicide and the felony. Something more than mere coincidence in time and place between the two must be shown; otherwise, the felony-murder rule will not be applicable. (See Chapter 13 for material on the felony murder rule.)

30. Obstructing or interfering with an officer sometimes occurs during an accident or public disaster. Newspaper photographers were convicted in the following cases for seeking to obtain photographs of accidents after being repeatedly told to stay in the area where the general public was permitted. In both disasters, police had cleared the area so that emergency fire and medical vehicles could enter the area, control fire and explosions, and render aid to the injured and dying.

In the case of *State v. Peruta,* 24 Conn.App. 598, 591 A.2d 140 (Conn.App. 1991), a fatal car accident had occurred. The photographer was convicted of "interfering with an officer" because he repeatedly interfered with rescue efforts. In the case of *City of Oak Creek v. King,* 436 N.W.2d 285 (1989), a commercial airline had crashed, causing many deaths and injuries. King was convicted of disorderly conduct because he would not stay behind police lines. The Supreme Court of Wisconsin pointed out that reporters do not have special rights that the general public does not have and must obey reasonable police orders at the scene of a public emergency.

31. The South Dakota statute of compounding a crime is as follows:

- Any person who *accepts or offers or agrees to accept* any pecuniary benefit as consideration for

  1. Refraining from seeking prosecution of an offender; or

  2. Refraining from reporting to law enforcement authorities the commission or suspected commission of any crime or information relating to a crime;

  is guilty of compounding. Compounding a felony is a Class 6 felony. Compounding a misdemeanor is a Class 1 misdemeanor.

32. For a false report case that went to the U.S. Supreme Court, see Questions and Problems 1 at the end of Chapter 10.

33. The drafters of the Model Penal Code state, "In general, our society does not use penal sanctions to compel reporting of crime." § 242.5, Comment at pp. 251–52, 1980.

34. Consider the following additional example: Police officers respond to an armed robbery call (tavern, bank, hotel, or other business place). The armed robbers have fled, and radio bulletins are sent out describing the men and their vehicle. Police officers then seek to obtain identification of witnesses and further information. However, a customer who had a good look at the robbers will not identify himself, stating he does not want to get involved. If the officers do not get name, address, and other information from the person, their superiors, the prosecutor, and the defense lawyer are going to be upset. The witness could be arrested and charged with interfering or obstructing a law officer or a criminal investigation. The threat to arrest or to bring the person to the police station usually is sufficient to obtain the name and address of the person.

5

Criminal Responsibility and the Capacity to Commit a Crime

CONTENTS

KEY TERMS

trial by ordeal

infant (child)

insanity tests:
    M'Naghten test
    substantial capacity test

"guilty but mentally ill"

diminished capacity defense

competency to stand trial

faking insanity or incompetency

criminal liability of corporations

Ancient Concepts of Criminal Responsibility

The law has undergone many changes over the centuries as to how criminal responsibility is determined and who has the capacity to commit a crime. At the time of the Norman Conquest of England (1066), for example, *trial by ordeal* and trial by battle were commonly used in the determination of criminal responsibility. A person who was of noble birth or titled could demand trial by battle if accused of a crime. If, in trial by battle, the suspect or accused came out second, it was then determined that he was guilty of the offense with which he was charged. However, the question of guilt or innocence could become moot, because the accused might be killed or badly injured.

In determining criminal responsibility in a trial by ordeal, the accused often would be required to take a pound weight of red-hot iron into his hands or to plunge his hand, up to the wrist, into boiling water. Ordeal by fire and ordeal by water were also used. Sir James Stephen described trial by ordeal in his *History of the Criminal Law of England,* published in 1883:

> It is unnecessary to give a minute account of the ceremonial of the ordeals. They were of various kinds. The general nature of all was the same. They were appeals to God to work a miracle in attestation of the innocence of the accused person. The handling of hot iron, plunging the hand or arm into boiling water unhurt, were the commonest. The ordeal of water was a very singular institution. Sinking was the sign of innocence, floating the sign of guilt. As any one would sink unless he understood how to float, and intentionally did so, it is difficult to see how anyone could ever be convicted by this means. Is it possible that this ordeal may have been an honourable form of suicide, like the Japanese happy despatch? In nearly every case the accused would sink. This would prove his innocence, indeed, but there would be no need to take him out. He would thus die honourably. If by accident he floated, he would be put to death disgracefully.[1]

Another form of superstition involved the concept that individuals deliberately became witches or practiced witchcraft, and were thought to be able to cause great social harm, such as crop failure, and to be able to cause serious injuries or bring illness and death to others. Witchcraft first became a crime under the Roman Empire. During the sixteenth, seventeenth, and eighteenth centuries, thousands of people were tried and put to death because it was believed that they were either witches or practiced witchcraft. For example, Joan of Arc was charged as being a witch and condemned to death. She was burned at a stake in France in 1431.

Prosecution of such people in the American colonies occurred in Massachusetts, Connecticut, and Virginia. These trials reached a high point in 1692, in Salem, Massachusetts, where 19 persons were executed as witches and 150 more were sent to prison. The Salem trials were the last American witchcraft trials; the last English witchcraft trial took place in 1712. In 1735, Scotland repealed all laws that made witchcraft a crime in that country.

Other Medieval Concepts

In the Middle Ages and later, animals were held criminally responsible for harm that they had done. They were tried in the same manner as human beings, except that domestic animals were taken before secular courts, whereas wild animals were required to face ecclesiastical (religious) courts. At many animal trials, horses, pigs, dogs, rats, and even roosters were accused of such crimes as murder, battery, and destruction of crops. Some people believed that animals who committed such offenses were possessed by demons; others believed that the devil himself took the form of an animal.

In 1499, a bear that had been killing people in a German village was captured and brought to trial. The attorney appointed to defend the bear was allowed to argue for days that the animal had the right to be judged by a jury of its peers (that is, other bears). However, the animal was tried and convicted by human beings. It was sentenced to dangle from the public gallows until relatives of its victims stoned the animal to death. In 1694, a mare was convicted of criminal homicide in France and was burned to death. The court found that the horse was possessed by demons. As late as 1712, an Austrian court sentenced a dog to a year in the marketplace pillory, where humans were also confined. The dog had bitten a man in the leg.

Today, no industrial nation would hold that an animal had the mental capacity to formulate criminal intent. An animal that killed or seriously injured a human being would probably be destroyed in recognition of the possibility that it might again attack humans. Criminal responsibility, if any exists, would attach not to the vicious animal but to its owner.

Infancy and Criminal Responsibility

Under the civil law, an *infant (child)* is a person who has not yet reached the age of majority, whether that age is 18, 19, 20, or 21 as determined by the law of each jurisdiction. Although infants, with some exceptions, are not able to enter into contracts, make wills, or vote, the law as to children's criminal responsibility for their acts differs from the law governing the children's civil capacity.

The question of the criminal responsibility of children came before the courts in the Middle Ages, and by the fourteenth century, the common law had determined that children under the age of 7 did not have the capacity to commit a crime. By that time, 7 was established as the "age of reason" under ecclesiastical law and also as the age of responsibility under Roman civil law. In establishing the age of 7 as the lowest age of criminal responsibility, the common law reasoned that a child under the age of 7 did not have the mental capacity to formulate the intent to commit a crime and that, therefore, for children under 7, the threat of punishment would not serve as a deterrent against crime.

Most states continue to maintain this common law rule in the form of a conclusive presumption.[2] The presumption is that children under the age of 7 do not have the capacity to commit a crime. As the presumption is conclusive, evidence to the contrary may not be presented. Persons over the age of 14 are inferred to be sane and capable of formulating the necessary mental frame of mind to commit a crime. Evidence showing otherwise, however, can be used to show incapacity.

A rebuttable presumption exists under the common law that children between the ages of 7 and 14 are presumed to be without criminal capacity to commit a crime. This presumption, however, may be overcome by the presentation of evidence by the state showing that the child has the mental capacity and the ability to formulate the necessary criminal intent.[3] British and American courts have held that the younger the child, the stronger must be the evidence of mental capacity. Testimony of doctors, psychiatrists, and others plus school records and reports are usually used to show that children have physically, mentally, and emotionally reached an age of capacity at which they should be held responsible for their acts. The common law reasoning was that failure to punish particularly atrocious crimes committed by children between the ages of 7 and 14 would encourage other children to commit similar acts with no fear of punishment.

California is one of the states that has by statute codified the rebuttable presumption of incapacity for children under the age of 14 in the California Criminal Code (Section 26). Under such statutes and under the common law, the state must carry the burden of proving that the child understood the wrongful nature of his or her conduct in not only cases of criminal charges but also charges of delinquency.

Adults, on the other hand, are presumed to be competent, sane, and responsible for their intentional, deliberate acts. In most states and under federal law, it is the adult defendant who must carry the burden of overcoming the presumption of sanity.

The Liability of Children Under State Statutes

All states have enacted statutes governing the jurisdiction of children's (juvenile) courts. These courts deal with children who are delinquent and in need of supervision or with children who are neglected and dependent. Delinquency is usually defined by statute as conduct by a child that, if committed by an adult, would be a violation of the criminal code of that state.

In the majority of states, children's courts have jurisdiction over anyone under the age of 18. However, other states set the children's court jurisdiction at an age above or below 18.

State statutes also generally provide that juvenile courts may waive jurisdiction to the adult courts of children at an age set by state statutes (14, 15, 16, or even younger). Such statutes often state that the waiver is to be made when public protection requires it and when the waiver is in the best interest of the child.

Many debates have arisen over the years about what should be done with children who commit serious crimes. Should they remain in the juvenile system for treatment and be released at age 18 or 19? Or should state statutes provide for some type of supervision until age 21, or even as high as age 25? Or should a child who has committed a serious crime be turned over to the adult system and sent to adult prison facilities?

The Insanity Defense

No subject in criminal law has received as much attention and debate as the insanity defense. The questions of what degree of insanity, mental defect, or mental disease renders a person blameless for acts or omissions and what tests should be used in determining legal and moral liability have been debated for years.

The insanity defense is seldom used by defense lawyers for minor criminal charges.[4] It is most often used in murder cases and for other serious felony charges in which the evidence against a defendant is sometimes so strong that no other defense is available.

Studies have shown that the insanity plea is usually not an easy way out for criminal defendants and that only about 2 percent of defendants charged with serious crimes use the insanity plea.[5] The success rate among defendants using the insanity plea is not high when medical doctors differ as to the sanity of a defendant. Terrible and gross crimes by a defendant are not likely to cause a jury to make a finding of not guilty because of insanity, as was demonstrated in the 1992 Jeffrey Dahlmer case, in which a Wisconsin jury quickly found Dahlmer sane and criminally liable despite his following acts:

> The murder of fifteen young men after drugging some of his victims and performing crude lobotomies on them in an attempt to have zombie-like creatures. Dahlmer had sex with some of the corpses and dismembered bodies. He stored hands in a kettle and had a severed head in his refrigerator. A heart from a victim was also saved to be eaten later.

Insanity at the Time of the Criminal Incident

The question of insanity (mental disease or defect) may be raised at specific stages during the criminal proceedings. If a defendant is found insane at the time the crime occurred, a judgment of not guilty because of insanity is then entered by the court and the defendant may never again be tried for that offense.

A defendant who is found not guilty because of insanity is almost always committed to a mental institution under the laws of that state (or the federal government). Such state and federal laws provide for the length of stay and the conditions under which the person may be eligible for release.[6]

In the 1992 case of *Foucha v. Louisiana,*[7] the defendant was found not guilty of burglary by reason of insanity. After four years in a state psychiatric hospital, a doctor at the hospital stated that Foucha was no longer mentally ill, but declined to certify that the defendant was no longer a danger to himself or others. Under Louisiana law at that time, Foucha had the burden of proving that he was no longer dangerous in order to earn his release from the hospital.

The U.S. Supreme Court held that the Louisiana law violated due process, holding that "the State must establish insanity and dangerousness by clear and convincing evidence in order to confine an insane convict beyond his criminal sentence, when the basis for his original confinement no longer exists."

Tests Used to Determine Insanity

The *M'Naghten* Case and the "Right and Wrong" Test

It was not until the 1800s that English and American courts considered the question of whether insanity, mental disease, and mental defect should be factors in determining the criminal responsibilities of people charged with crimes. The right and wrong test, which became the most widely used test to determine the question of legal insanity in the United States, was developed in 1843 in the aftermath of the famous English murder case of *Rex v. M'Naghten,* House of Lords, 1843.[8]

Daniel M'Naghten lived in London in the 1840s and believed that the British Home Secretary, Sir Robert Peel, was the head of a conspiracy to kill him. (Peel was the widely recognized founder of the British police, who thus received the nickname "bobbies.") In 1843, M'Naghten shot and killed Edward Drummond, private secretary to Peel, because he mistook Drummond for Peel. At his trial, the defense argued that M'Naghten was insane at the time of the shooting and that he should not be held responsible because his mental delusions had caused him to act as he did. The British jury agreed, and M'Naghten was found not guilty because of insanity.

The right and wrong test that emerged from the *M'Naghten* case became the prevailing standard and test for insanity in U.S. courts. Under this test, defendants are not legally responsible for their acts if at the time they were "laboring under such a defect of reason, from diseases of the mind, as not to know the nature and quality of the act he was doing, or, if he did know it, that he did not know that what he was doing was wrong." The *M'Naghten* Rule established the burden of proof as follows:

> Every man is presumed to be sane and to possess a sufficient degree of reason to be responsible for his crimes, until the contrary be proved to (the jury's) satisfaction; and that to establish a defense on the ground of insanity, it must be clearly proved.

Other Tests in the United States

Over the years, a few U.S. jurisdictions adopted tests other than the *M'Naghten* right and wrong test. In 1871, the New Hampshire courts rejected the *M'Naghten* test and adopted the New Hampshire test, but no other state has ever followed New Hampshire's lead. In 1886, Alabama adopted the *irresistible impulse test* in *Parsons v. State*.[9] This test extended the *M'Naghten* Rule and held that, if the defendant is found to have had a mental disease that prevented control of personal conduct, even when knowing the difference between right and wrong, the defendant should be found not guilty because of insanity. In practice, the irresistible impulse test often had the effect of freeing people who had committed crimes of passion. An example of this is found in the novel *Anatomy of a Murder* by John Donaldson Voelker (under the alias Robert Traver). Voelker was a retired Supreme Court Justice of the state of Michigan when he wrote the story. People who have read the book or seen the movie know that in most states, the issue before the court would have been that of self-defense or heat-of-passion manslaughter. Instead, the army officer in Voelker's story (based on an actual case) went free on the irresistible impulse defense.[10]

According to its critics, the principal fault of the *M'Naghten* test lies in its narrowness and its restricted application to only a small percentage of people who are mentally ill. In 1954, the *Durham product test* was adopted by the U.S. Court of Appeals for the District of Columbia in the case of *Durham v. United States*.[11] The Court stated that "an accused is not criminally responsible if his unlawful act was the product of mental disease or defect." The *Durham* case established a test for insanity based on a substantial lack of mental capacity rather than a complete lack of capacity. It has been criticized on the grounds that it is too broad and places too much discretion in psychiatrists, rather than in the jury, for determining the legal issue of insanity. "Criminal responsibility is a legal not a medical question."[12]

The Model Penal Code Substantial Capacity Test

About a year after the adoption of the *Durham* Rule by a few jurisdictions, the American Law Institute proposed still another test for determining criminal responsibility. In proposing the new rule, the following comment was made:

No problem in the drafting of a penal code presents larger intrinsic difficulty than that of determining when individuals whose conduct would otherwise be criminal ought to be exculpated (freed of guilt) on the grounds that they were suffering from mental disease or defect when they acted as they did. What is involved specifically is the drawing of a line between the use of public agencies and public force to condemn the offender by conviction. . . . [T]he problem is to discriminate between the cases where a punitive-correctional disposition is appropriate and those in which a medical-custodial disposition is the only kind that the law should allow. (Commentary to Section 4.01, Model Penal Code)

The final draft of the American Law Institute (ALI) *substantial capacity test* is found in Section 4.01 of the Model Penal Code and states:

1. A person is not responsible for criminal conduct if at the time of such conduct as a result of mental disease or defect he lacks substantial capacity either to appreciate the criminality (wrongfulness) of his conduct or to conform his conduct to the requirement of law.

2. As used in the Article, the terms *mental disease* or *defect* do not include an abnormality manifested only by repeated criminal or otherwise antisocial conduct.

The Model Penal Code test (or the ALI substantial capacity test) is now reported to have been adopted by about half the states.

While the *M'Naghten* test requires a defendant to show total mental impairment, the substantial capacity test puts less of a burden on defendants. Under the substantial capacity test, even if defendants "knew" what they had done, the defendants are permitted to attempt to show that they did not have the "substantial capacity to conform his or her conduct to the requirements of law" (lack of self-control).

EXAMPLE: In March 2002, Andrea Yates was found sane and guilty of the murder of her five young children in Houston, Texas. Texas uses the stricter *M'Naghten* test. Had Ms. Yates been tried in a state using the substantial capacity test, she would have had a much better chance of being found not guilty by reason of insanity.

States That Have Abolished the Insanity Defense

Some states that have used the Model Penal Code substantial capacity test have returned to the stricter standards of the *M'Naghten* test. Three states—Idaho, Montana, and Utah—have abolished the insanity plea altogether and have no insanity defense.

In 1994, the U.S. Supreme Court left states free to not use an insanity defense should they enact such legislation. In the case of *Montana v. Cowan*,[13] the U.S. Supreme Court left untouched the Supreme Court of Montana's holding that Montana was not constitutionally obligated to have an insanity defense.[14]

However, with or without an insanity defense, the state must prove mental fault (*mens rea*) in crimes such as first-degree murder. If mental illness or mental defect prevents a defendant from forming the required *mens rea*, a conviction for that crime could not be obtained and the defendant could be found not guilty.

In 2001 Andrea Yates (above) confessed to the crime of filicide (the murder of a child by a parent). Despite the testimony of doctors that she was psychotic when she drowned her five children, a jury in Houston, Texas, found her sane under the *M'Naghten* test. In March 2002 she was sentenced to serve a long prison term.   AP/Wide World Photos

The Plea and Verdict of "Guilty But Mentally Ill"[15]

The incidence of people who are found not guilty because of insanity and then go on to commit other violent crimes after release from mental hospitals has caused twelve states to adopt the plea and verdict of *guilty but mentally ill*.[16] The legislature of the state of Michigan passed such legislation after several defendants committed additional murders after being found not guilty because of insanity on earlier murders.

In Illinois, Thomas Vanda killed a girl when he was 18 years old. While undergoing psychiatric treatment in Chicago, he was released and killed another girl. He was found not guilty because of insanity. When doctors concluded that his psychosis had disappeared, he was again released over objections from the trial judge and his own defense attorney. In 1978, when he was 25 years old, Thomas Vanda was again charged with murder. The third victim was a 25-year-old woman.

Illinois enacted a guilty but mentally ill statute in 1981. Former Illinois Governor James R. Thompson described the new statutory procedure as follows:

Under this procedure, when an insanity defense is raised, the court, if the evidence permits, may instruct the jury on the alternative verdict of guilty but mentally ill. When a person is not legally insane, he or she may be found guilty but mentally ill if, at the time of the offense, he or she suffered from a disorder of thought or mood that does not represent a condition amounting to insanity in the legal sense.

When a guilty but mentally ill verdict is returned, the court may impose any sentence that could have been ordered for a conviction on the crime charged. However, the prison authorities must provide necessary psychiatric or psychological treatment to restore the offender to full capacity in an appropriate treatment setting. If the mental illness is cured, the offender must be returned to prison to serve out his or her sentence.

Insanity determinations under existing law deal in absolutes; a defendant must be found totally sane or totally insane. This fails to reflect reality. It does not allow the jury to consider the degree of an individual's mental impairment, the quality of the impairment, or the context in which the impairment is operative. A mental impairment does not necessarily eradicate the state of mind required to make a person guilty of a crime, and the jury should be permitted to consider the gradations of a defendant's mental state.

The guilty but mentally ill verdict does not abolish the insanity defense. It simply recognizes that there are gradations in the degree of mental impairment; it provides accountability, promotes treatment, and eliminates the need to manipulate the system. Most importantly, it is designed to protect the public from violence inflicted by persons with mental ailments who previously slipped through the cracks in the criminal justice system.[17]

Opponents of the guilty but mentally ill verdict argue that it is nothing but a nice name for "guilty and going to prison." The Alliance for Mentally Ill opposes such legislation "because it would stigmatize insane offenders with a criminal conviction, compounding the handicaps already faced by those persons in obtaining employment and social acceptance."[18]

Should a Compulsive Gambler Be Found Not Guilty Because of Insanity?[19]

Defendants sometimes use the compulsive gambling defense against criminal charges such as theft, bank robbery, and embezzlement. They argue they would not have committed such crimes but were compelled to do so because of their gambling urges. For example, in the case of *United States v. Lynch,* the defendant stole $7.5 million and unsuccessfully used compulsive gambling in an attempt to be found not guilty on his insanity plea.[20]

Prosecutors argue that accepting compulsive gambling as an insanity defense could set a dangerous precedent. In any state that would allow such a defense, thieves could claim kleptomania as a defense, arsonists could claim pyromania, perjurers could claim pathologic lying, drunk drivers could claim alcoholism, and prostitutes could claim nymphomania.

In all the reported cases, defendants using compulsive gambling as a defense have failed to be found not guilty because of insanity. There is no showing of acceptance in the mental health field that a compulsive gambler is unable to resist the impulse to steal or to commit other crimes

The Defense of Diminished Capacity

Some states and the federal government permit the *diminished capacity defense.* This defense was defined in the case of *United States v. Fishman* as follows:

Individuals Incapable of Committing Crimes

The following people are legally incapable of committing crimes and are therefore not responsible for their criminal acts in most states:

1. Children under the age of 7 are presumed under the common law to be incapable of committing crimes because they have not reached the "age of reason."

2. People found to be insane (mentally diseased or defective) under the test used in that state. A person found not guilty because of insanity cannot be tried again for that crime should they become sane. (See the section on double jeopardy in Chapter 7.)

Such persons could be institutionalized (or committed) under the laws of the state in which they reside.

The defense of "diminished capacity" is simply a label that identifies evidence introduced by a defendant to support a claim that he did not commit the crime charged because he did not possess the requisite *mens rea*. A diminished capacity defense varies from a legal insanity defense in several important respects. Whereas following a successful legal insanity defense the court retains control of the defendant and may order involuntary commitment, a successful diminished capacity defense results in a complete acquittal.[21]

The following cases illustrate conditions under which courts would not submit the issue of diminished capacity to a jury:

- The Supreme Court of California held that the drinking of three beers, which did not affect defendant's behavior other than causing him to speak slower and to shuffle his feet when he walked, was not sufficient to conclude that defendant lacked the ability to form the intent to kill by stabbing. *People v. Payton,* 839 P.2d 1035 (1992). In the 1986 case of *People v. Rodriquez,* 726 P.2d 113, the court held that the following statement did not justify a jury instruction on diminished capacity: "Defendant had been drinking and had a lot of cocaine . . . [and] was talkative and really hyper."

- Some organic brain dysfunction that resulted in a lowered intellectual function and capacity, and some antisocial behavior, were held insufficient to instruct the jury on diminished capacity. *State v. Friberg,* 252 Kan. 141, 843 P.2d 218 (1992).

- Emotions such as jealousy, fear, anger, and hatred are not mental disorders under the diminished capacity defense. *State v. Davis,* 64 Wash.App. 511, 827 P.2d 298 (1992).

- The fact that the defendant was below average in intelligence did not justify a jury instruction of diminished capacity in a first-degree sexual abuse case. *State v. Gill,* 806 S.W.2d 48 (Mo.App. 1991).

- The highest courts in these states held that the following circumstances did not bring the doctrine of diminished capacity into play: Husband stated he killed wife because of repeated humiliations in New York, *People v. White,* 590 N.E.2d 236 (1992); voluntary intoxication and/or mental disorder in California, *People v. Saille,* 820 P.2d 588

Defendants Who Were Found Not Guilty Because of Insanity

John Hinckley   In 1981, John Hinckley attempted to kill President Reagan. In a wild shooting spree in downtown Washington, Hinckley wounded the president and other people. Hinckley entered a not guilty plea and a not guilty because of insanity plea.

At that time, the federal courts had broken away from the majority rule in the United States and the government had the burden of showing that people such as Hinckley were sane and normal. Because of Hinckley's wild, bizarre behavior, the government was not able to carry the burden of showing that Hinckley was sane and normal, and Hinckley was found not guilty because of insanity. Within a short time, Congress passed a law changing the procedure, and now defendants pleading insanity have the burden of coming forward with evidence proving mental disease or defectiveness.[a]

Lorena Bobbitt   Lorena Bobbitt was charged with malicious wounding in 1993. She testified to repeated rapes, beatings, and sodomizing by her husband. On the night of the crime, she testified that her husband came home drunk, tore off her clothes, and forced himself on her. She said that her mind went blank and that it was only later that she realized that she had sexually mutilated her husband by cutting off his penis, which she threw in a field.

A Virginia jury found Mrs. Bobbitt not guilty under Virginia's *insanity test*, which holds that a defendant may be held blameless for an act he or she knows is wrong if "his [or her] mind has become so impaired by disease that he [or she] totally is deprived of mental power to control or restrain his [or her] act."

Mrs. Bobbitt was released from a Virginia mental hospital after a four-week stay on the condition that she get therapy. Her husband, John, had been acquitted earlier of marital sexual abuse.

[a]John Hinckley continues to be held in a Washington, D.C., hospital. Federal prosecutors stated that they have evidence that Hinckley has a "continued interest in violently themed books and music." (See *Washington Post* article, "Unsupervised Hinckley Visits Bad Idea, Hospital Says," June 29, 2000.)

(1991); mere personality changes including short temper and so on in Kansas, *State v. Wilburn*, 822 P.2d 609 (1991).

- The defendant in the 1991 case of *State v. Breakiron*, 532 A.2d 199, confessed that he killed the young woman with whom he lived, took her child, stole a car and money from the woman's parents, and fled to Florida. The defendant entered an insanity plea to charges of murder, kidnapping, and burglary. At his trial, he offered evidence that he suffered from schizophrenic tendencies, was hyperactive, disruptive, and had been abused as a child. The Supreme Court of New Jersey held that in New Jersey the defendant was entitled to have this evidence presented to a jury to be considered either with respect to the insanity defense or as part of defendant's defense of diminished capacity.

The Requirement of Competency to Stand Trial

A defendant must be competent (mentally fit) before the government can force him or her to go to trial on criminal charges. This means that defendants must have the ability to cooperate with their attorney and the ability to understand the charges and proceedings against them.[22]

Tests or Procedures Used to Determine Criminal Responsibility[a]

Test or Procedure	Year When First Used	Type of Test	Current Extent of Use
M'Naghten "right and wrong" test	1843	Based on ability of defendant to know the difference between right and wrong.	Used by practically all U.S. courts until the 1970s. Now used by fewer than half of the states.
Model Penal Code substantial capacity test	1955	Did defendant have the "substantial capacity" to (1) distinguish between right and wrong, or (2) conform his conduct to the requirements of law?	Used by many states, but California and the federal government returned to the M'Naghten test after using this test. See U.S. v. Carmel, 801 F.2d 997 (1986); and People v. Skinner, 39 Cal.3d 765, 217 Cal.Rptr. 685, 704 P.2d 752, 38 CrL 2002 (1985).
Abolishment of the insanity defense (Idaho, Utah, and Montana)	In 1994, the U.S. Supreme Court left states free not to use an insanity defense (Montana v. Cowan, 861 P.2d 884, review denied, 114 S.Ct. 1371).	However, if mental illness prevents a defendant from forming the required mens rea (specific intent for murder one or other homicide), a conviction could not be obtained for that offense.	
Guilty but mentally ill alternative verdict and plea	1975	Defendant may be found guilty but mentally ill if all the following are found beyond a reasonable doubt: (1) defendant is guilty of offense; (2) defendant was mentally ill at time offense was committed; (3) defendant was not legally insane at time offense was committed.	Used in twelve states with either the M'Naghten test or the substantial capacity test.
Diminished capacity defense	1957	Defense seeks to introduce evidence showing that because of mental or emotional conditions, the defendant did not possess the required mens rea for conviction of crime charged.	A finding that the state failed to prove the mens rea for the crime charged could result in a finding of not guilty.

[a]Civil commitments and plea bargains are also used when it is apparent that a defendant has serious mental problems. For example, a civil commitment was agreed upon where a minister set fire to his own church. Members of the church were relied that the matter was handled in this manner instead of a contested public trial for arson.

The test for competency originated in the common law and now has been statutorized in state and federal statutes. The U.S. Supreme Court has repeatedly held that it is a violation of due process to try to convict a mentally incompetent person. Because most states place the burden on the party challenging the presumption of competency, the standard of proof on defendants to prove incompetency is that of "preponderance of the evidence."[23]

A translator or an attorney who can speak the language of a defendant would solve the problem of a defendant who does not understand English. People skilled in sign language could communicate for a deaf-mute. But what about a defendant with an IQ (mental ability) of a 5-year-old child, or a defendant who is spaced out and in a semi-stupor because of excessive use of drugs or alcohol? If they do not understand the charges and proceedings against them, and cannot cooperate with the defense lawyers, they would be determined to be incompetent at that time.

A person could be incompetent (and unfit) to stand trial for a short time (a few weeks or months). Or a defendant could be permanently incompetent and a state could never force the person to go to trial on criminal charges. When a court makes a finding that a defendant lacks competency (is incompetent), the criminal proceedings must then be suspended. The defendant, in accordance with the statutes of that state, is placed in an institution.

If after a few weeks or months the defendant is found to be competent and fit to go to trial, criminal proceedings may again continue. But if a defendant is never going to become competent, can this person be held indefinitely in a mental institution by the state?

In the 1972 case of *Jackson v. Indiana,* the U.S. Supreme Court held that such defendants could not be held for longer than a "reasonable period of time" to determine whether they will regain their competence and capacity to stand trial.[24] Some courts have held that a *reasonable period of time* is a period no longer than the maximum sentence for the crime charged or, at the longest, eighteen months. After this period of time, the state may either

- try the defendant, if he or she is found competent and capable of standing trial or
- dismiss the charges or
- commence civil proceedings against the person for the purpose of committing him or her to a mental institution if he or she remains incompetent and cannot be tried criminally.[25]

Can Amnesia Be the Grounds for a Finding of Incompetency?

Amnesia is the total or partial loss of memory regarding past experiences. Brain injury, disease, mental disorder, shock, and the excessive use of alcohol or drugs are some of the many factors that can cause amnesia.[26] Although amnesia victims ordinarily have no difficulty comprehending the nature of the criminal proceedings against them, they would not necessarily remember the facts that occurred at the time of the alleged crime.

In the case of *Ex parte Thompson,* the defendant could understand the crime charged and factual proceedings against her and could assist counsel in her defense.[27] The court held that she was not rendered incompetent to stand trial by her alleged amnesia with respect to the commission of the alleged crime.

Courts generally have held that partial amnesia does not render a defendant incompetent to stand trial nor does it deny a defendant a fair trial. In the case of *Morrow v. State,* the defendant was the driver of one of the vehicles in a bad two-car accident.[28]

The defendant's passenger was killed. The court held the defendant to be competent to stand trial, pointing out that the defendant was aware of the trial events and was able to consult with and assist his lawyer. However, the defendant claimed not to remember the automobile accident because of head injuries. The court wrote:

> The practical effects of expanding the definition of incompetency to include amnesia must be considered. Several courts have indicated that they were unwilling to hold that limited amnesia was an adequate ground for a determination of incompetency because the effect of such a holding would be to free, without trial, persons against whom prima facie criminal cases had been established. See, *State v. Johnson,* 536 P.2d 1035, 1036 (Ariz. 1975); *Commonwealth v. Price,* 218 A.2d 758, 763 (Pa. 1966). It has been noted that, if amnesia were held to render an accused incompetent then, if the amnesia were permanent, the accused would never be competent and could never be tried; at the same time, because limited amnesia cannot be considered a mental defect or disease, an amnesic accused could not be hospitalized or institutionalized. See, *Commonwealth v. Price,* 218 A.2d at 763. Thus permanent amnesia as to the circumstances of the crime charged would be a permanent bar to the imposition of criminal responsibility. This is especially significant in light of "the extreme difficulty—often impossibility—of distinguishing real from feigned amnesia." 71 Yale L.J. at 123. It has been noted that "an attempt to verify all but the most patently phony claims of amnesia is at best a difficult and time-consuming task; at worst it is a hopeless one." Id. at 124.[29]

Faking Insanity or Incompetency

Every large U.S. city has had criminal cases in which the defendant has successfully faked either incompetency or insanity. The court in the case of *United States v. Carter* stated that the defendant had "bamboozled the U.S. Attorney."[30] Doctors later determined that the defendant was "without mental disorder." In the case of *Thompson v. Crawford,* the defendant fooled psychiatrists and was later discovered.[31] The Florida court vacated the judgment of acquittal and permitted the state of Florida to proceed again with criminal charges.

In the 1991 case of *United States v. Prince,* 938 F.2d 1092 (10th Cir.), the defendant was convicted of bank robbery and unlawful use of a firearm during the robbery, later admitting that he "acted out" the following conduct in the courtroom:

> The defendant exposed himself and began to urinate in the courtroom. A few minutes later, the defendant was brought back into the courtroom and while the trial judge was sternly warning him as to his conduct, the defendant began moaning loudly. This was followed by moans with screams. Five marshals were needed to take the struggling defendant from the courtroom.

Arguments were made that this conduct showed that the defendant was incompetent to stand trial, but the Federal Court of Appeals affirmed the defendant's conviction, holding that the trial court correctly continued with the trial.

In 1997, Vincent Gigante (the "Chin" or the "Robe") was convicted in a New York City federal court of conspiracy to kill other gangland figures (including his archrival, John Gotti) and of running lucrative rackets as the head of one of the most powerful Mafia families, the Genovese family.

Civil Laws Used by States for Public Safety and Health

Type of Law	*Examples*
Sexual violent predator laws used to detain persons likely to be sexually violent	The U.S. Supreme Court has twice affirmed state sexual violent predator laws that permit a state to hold for an indefinite period of time anyone "who has been convicted or charged with a sexual violent offense and who suffers from a mental abnormality or personality disorder which makes the person likely to engage in predatory acts of sexual violence." *Kansas v. Hendricks,* 117 S.Ct. 2072 (1997).
	If such laws are civil and not criminal, and not punitive in nature, they do not violate due process, ex post facto, or double jeopardy. As treatment is not a constitutional requirement for civil commitment, such laws do not have to provide for treatment. (See also *Allen v. Illinois,* 106 S.Ct. 2988, 1986.)
Emergency mental detention laws and civil commitment to mental hospital laws	States have emergency mental detention laws under which persons who appear dangerous to themselves or others or are unable to care for themselves may be detained for mental observation for a short period of time, as provided by the statutes of that state. For example, a person who has attempted to commit suicide could be detained for medical observation for a time as provided by the statute of that state.
	Involuntary civil commitment laws establish the procedure by which a person may be committed to a mental institution. In the case of *State v. Johnson,* 843 P. 2d 985, 1992, a 21-year-old pregnant, homeless woman with a history of drug and alcohol abuse was found on a cold day, naked, in front of a bus station. The involuntary commitment order by the trial court was affirmed, holding that the woman was unable to meet her basic needs for food and shelter due to her mental disorder, despite the findings by two examiners that the woman was not mentally ill.

For years, Mr. Gigante presented himself as mentally ill and not competent to stand trial. His lawyers argued that Gigante had a tested IQ of 70. Gigante was often seen walking on the streets of New York wearing pajamas and a bathrobe and mumbling incoherently. To heighten the effect, Mr. Gigante was brought into the courtroom every day in a wheelchair attended by a cardiologist.

Prosecutors successfully argued to the jury that Gigante was faking his condition. They put six former mobsters on the witness stand who testified that Gigante was the active boss of the Genovese family. Surveillance tapes were introduced in which the crimes charged were discussed by Mafia members (no tapes of Gigante were available). Mr. Gigante, who was 69 in 1997, was convicted by the jury. (See the *Milwaukee Journal Sentinel* article, "Mafia's 'Oddfather' Gets 12-Year Term in Prison," December 12, 1997.)

The Criminal Liability of Corporations

A corporation is a legal entity created under the laws of a state or the federal government. Because a corporation is not a living person and must act through human beings, any crime committed in the corporate name must be committed by a person or people in control of the corporation's affairs or in the employment of the corporation.

Defenses Sometimes Attempted by Defense Lawyers[a]

Defense	Description of Defense	Present Status
The Twinkie defense (hypoglycemia—too much sugar)	Because he lost his job as a San Francisco supervisor, Dan White gorged on junk food—Twinkies, Coca-Cola, candy. Depressed, he sneaked a gun into City Hall. After killing Mayor Moscone, he reloaded the gun and killed Supervisor Milk, who was a leader of the gay community, in 1978.	White used the defense of diminished capacity. A jury found him guilty of manslaughter instead of murder. After serving a short sentence, White was released. The jury verdict caused the gay community to riot, seizing downtown San Francisco, burning cars, and breaking windows.
Defendants or victims with multiple personalities	Many psychiatric experts agree that the disorder of multiple personalities exists but disagree on how common it is. If a woman with multiple personalities complains of rape, the defendant might argue that consent to sex was given by one of the personalities. A defendant with multiple personalities might argue that he or she could not control the bad personality.	People with multiple personalities are generally held competent to be tried and to testify, and are held responsible for their acts. See *State v. Badger,* 1988 WL 138308 (N.J.Super. 1988) and *State v. Donnelly,* 1990 WL 127412 (Mont. 1990).
Sleepwalking and other forms of automatism (unconsciousness)	Automatism is a state in which a person is capable of action but is not conscious of what he or she is doing. This defense is statutorized in some states, including California, and held to be an affirmative defense separate from insanity defense. *Fulcher v. State,* 633 P.2d 142, 29 CrL 2556 (Wyo. 1981).	States adopting or statutorizing Model Penal Code § 2.01 would hold as in *People v. Wilson,* 66 Cal.2d 749, 59 Cal.Rptr. 156, 427 P.2d 820 (1967): "Unconsciousness is a complete, not a partial defense to a criminal charge." See LaFave and Scott, *Criminal Law,* 2d ed. (Belmont Calif.: West/Wadsworth, 1986).
Cultural disorientation	Some immigrants to the United States bring with them cultural practices that are in conflict with our criminal codes. For example, some continue the ancient traditions of the medicinal use	The defendant in the 1986 case of *People v. Aphaylath,* 68 N.Y.2d 945, 510 N.Y.S.2d 83, 502 N.E.2d 998, killed his wife when she showed interest in an ex-boyfriend. The highest court

(continued)

Defenses Sometimes Attempted by Defense Lawyers (continued)

Defense	Description of Defense	Present Status
Cultural disorientation (continued)	of opium, "capturing young brides," and the ritual slaughtering of animals. In 1985 when a young Japanese mother of two children learned that her husband was having an affair with another woman, she walked into the Pacific Ocean with her children to commit suicide (*oy ako shinju*). She was saved but the children drowned.	in New York held that the trial court erred in not permitting testimony concerning the stress and disorientation the Laotian refugee of two years encountered. The defendant was permitted to attempt to establish the affirmative defense of extreme emotional disturbance for consideration by a judge or jury of conviction of a lesser degree of homicide.

[a]Other defenses that have been tried and failed are premenstrual syndrome (PMS) (no known American appellate case), television intoxication (see *Zamora v. State,* 361 So. 776 [Fla.1978], and the XYY chromosome defense, which argues a chromosome abnormality. (See LaFave and Scott, *Criminal Law,* 2d ed., for cases and material.)

Sir William Blackstone wrote in his eighteenth-century *Commentaries* that "a corporation cannot commit treason or felony or other crime in its corporate capacity, though its members may in their distinct individual capacities."[32] Blackstone's statement reflected the early common law thinking that because a corporation had no mind of its own, it could not formulate a criminal intent, and because it had no body, it could not be imprisoned or executed. The early common law view was understandable because relatively few corporations existed in those days, and other ways were available to handle crimes that were committed in the names of corporations. The corporate officers (or employees) who committed the act (or acts) could be criminally charged. The corporation was civilly liable for the acts of its officers and employees, and therefore civil suits for damages could be brought. And a corporation that had committed *ultra vires* acts (acts that are beyond the scope of the corporate charter or that violate the laws of the state) could have its corporate charter revoked by the state.

This common law view changed as corporations became more numerous and as it became apparent that corporations should be made criminally responsible for some types of criminal acts. Today, corporations may be charged with many but not all crimes. It would be hard to imagine, for example, how a corporation could be charged and successfully convicted of rape. If a corporate employee, however, stole trade secrets from another corporation, and the corporation, knowing of such theft, nevertheless used the stolen information for its benefit, the justification for charging the corporation with a criminal offense would be apparent.

Crimes Committed by Corporations[33]

Over the years, corporations have been charged with many different crimes. Corporations and people can conspire in restraint of trade. For example, if all the bakers and car manufacturers were to meet and agree upon prices for which bread and cars would be

Examples of Some of the Many Criminal Charges Against Corporations

Corporation	Charge	Disposition
Arthur Andersen, LLP (2002)	Charged with the felony of obstructing justice for allegedly destroying thousands of documents concerning the criminal investigation of the Enron Corporation. The records were destroyed by some of the 85,000 employees of the certified public accounting firm in Andersen's offices located in Houston, Texas, Chicago, Illinois, London, England, and Portland, Oregon.	Criminal charges are expected to be made against Enron.
Sara Lee Corp. (one of the largest makers of hot dogs and deli meat) (2001)	Misdemeanor of producing and distributing tainted meat linked to fifteen deaths and hundreds of sick people (not charged with felony, as there was no evidence that the company knew and intended to ship adulterated food).	Paid $4.4 million in civil and criminal fines (company was also liable to victims in civil lawsuits).
General Electric Corporation (1990)	Defrauding U.S. Army (overcharging).	Paid $16.1 million in criminal and civil penalties.
Northrop Corporation (1990)	Military fraud (cruise missile and Harrier jet).	Paid $17 million in penalties.
Eastern Airlines (1990)	Falsifying maintenance records.	Large money fines.
Ford Motor Corporation (1978)	Three counts of reckless homicide (deaths of three teenage girls in a Ford Pinto when Ford failed to recall and fix a gas tank problem in the Pinto).	Found not guilty by an Indiana jury but paid civil settlements of civil lawsuits.
Exxon Corporation (1990–91)	The worst oil spill occurring in the United States (11 million gallons of oil into Alaska's Prince William Sound in 1989).	Agreed to pay $100 million in criminal fines and $1 billion more in civil damages. (See Chapter 22 for more on environmental crimes.)
Art dealers, including Sotheby's and Christie's (2001)	Criminal charges under the 1890 Sherman Anti-Trust Law (for "bid pooling," "bid rigging," "knockout sales," "price fixing").	A sentence of one year and a day plus a fine of $7.5 million was imposed on the owner of Sotheby's in 2002.
Archer Daniels (1996)	For price fixing of agricultural products.	Paid $100 million in fines.

(continued)

Examples of Some of the Many Criminal Charges Against Corporations (continued)

Corporation	Charge	Disposition
Lazard Freres and Merrill Lynch & Company (1996)	Illegal kickback agreement in municipal bonds.	One partner went to jail for thirty-three months and was fined $1 million. The trial judge complained that Merrill Lynch "bought their way out for $12 million and none are going to jail."[a]

Also see Chapters 16 and 22 for crimes by business corporations.

[a]See the *New York Times* article "Former Lazard Partner Gets 33-Month Prison Term" (December 30, 1996).

sold in the United States, such agreements would be conspiracies in restraint of trade and violations of the Sherman Antitrust Act enacted by the U.S. Congress more than one hundred years ago. The Sherman Act (15 U.S.C.A. § 1) provides in part:

> Every contract, combination in the form of trust or otherwise, or conspiracy, in restraint of trade or commerce among the several States, or with foreign nations, is hereby declared to be illegal. Every person who shall make any contract or engage in any combination or conspiracy hereby declared to be illegal shall be deemed guilty of a felony, and, on conviction thereof, shall be punished by a fine not exceeding one million dollars if a corporation, or if any other person, one hundred thousand dollars, or by imprisonment not exceeding three years, or by both said punishments, in the discretion of the court.

SUMMARY

Many changes have been made since the days when guilt or innocence was determined by trials by an ordeal and people were executed for being a witch or practicing witchcraft.

Today, the U.S. Constitution provides the accused with the right of a jury of their peers and the right to be confronted by the evidence against them.

The two groups of persons incapable of committing crimes are (1) children under the age of 7 who are presumed to be incapable of committing crimes because they have not reached the age of reason and (2) persons found to be insane (mentally diseased or defective) under the test used in that state.

Juries use the test of their state to determine insanity. Fewer than half of the states use the stricter *M'Naghten* right or wrong test and other states use the broader substantial capacity test (A.L.I. test). Three states have abolished the insanity defense and more than ten states use the additional "guilty but mentally ill" alternative verdict and plea. Many states permit the defense of diminished capacity.

A defendant must be competent (have the ability to cooperate with the defense lawyer and also the ability to understand the criminal charges and procedures against him or her) before the defendant can be forced to go to trial.

Corporations can be charged with most but not all crimes.

BOOK-SPECIFIC WEB SITE

For chapter-related Web links, quizzing activities, and case and news updates, go to the *Criminal Law,* Eighth Edition, book-specific Web site at **http://info.wadsworth.com/gardner.**

QUESTIONS AND PROBLEMS

1. In the 1998 trial of Theodore Kaczynski, who was charged in a California federal court of being the Unabomber, a federal judge ordered Kaczynski to undergo mental evaluation to determine whether Kaczynski was competent to stand trial for the criminal charges. In such cases, what does incompetency mean? Is incompetency the same as not guilty because of insanity? What procedure is used if a defendant is found incompetent to stand trial?

2. A New York City cab driver took a passenger to a bank and, after waiting for the passenger for a short time, took the passenger to a second bank. After the stops at the two banks, the cab driver learned that the man committed four robberies at the two banks. A few days later, the cab driver saw the man on the street and held him until the police arrived.

   Why shouldn't the cab driver be charged as a party to the robberies? How could four robberies occur with only stops at two different banks? Explain.

INFOTRAC COLLEGE EDITION EXERCISES

1. Go to InfoTrac College Edition, and using the keyword search term *insanity defense*, find the 1998 article "One Flew Into the Cookoo's Nest" concerning problems with the insanity defense. Are many insane criminals being set free? If so, what does the author think should be done about it?

2. Using the keyword search term *juvenile crime*, find the May 2001 article "Juvenile Girl Crime Swells in U.S." What are some reasons girls appear to be the fastest growing segment of juvenile crime? What can be done to reverse this trend? Are the reasons girls get involved in crime different from the reasons boys do?

NOTES

1. Sir James FitzJames Stephen, *A History of the Criminal Law of England* (Macmillan & Co., 1883), vol. 1, p. 73.

2. In 1996, a 6-year-old boy was charged with attempted murder for the brutal beating of a month-old baby in Oakland, California. The beating occurred during a break-in to an apartment to steal a tricycle. Criminal charges, however, were dropped. (See the *New York Times* article, "Charges of Attempted Murder Lifted for 6-Year-Old in Beating," July 14, 1996.)

In the 1987 case of *In re Register,* 84 N.C.App. 336, 352 S.E.2d 889 (1987), a finding that a 6-year-old girl was delinquent was set aside by the majority of the North Carolina Court of Appeals, as the child was under the age of 7. The 6-year-old took part in a burglary and the ransacking of a home. The majority of the court held that "[a]t common law (the child could not be found guilty) because of irrebuttable presumption that she was doli incapax (incapable of criminal intent)." A dissenting judge, however, wrote that the common law presumption "only shields a child from indictment and punishment for criminal offenses. . . . While the 6-year-old in the instant case had an absolute defense to criminal prosecution, she could nevertheless be adjudicated delinquent in juvenile proceedings."

3. In 1994, a 10-year-old boy became the youngest child in a maximum-security juvenile prison when he and an 11-year-old were found to have thrown a 5-year-old out of a fourteenth-story Chicago housing project building. The 5-year-old, who died in the fall, had refused to steal candy for the older boys.

See the 1991 case of *In re Devon T.,* 85 Md.App. 674, 584 A.2d 1287, for a discussion of this law. Devon T. was almost 14 years old and a middle school student in Baltimore when twenty plastic bags of heroin were found on his person. The Maryland courts held that the state produced sufficient evidence permitting a reasonable inference that Devon knew the difference between right and wrong and knew the wrongfulness of his acts.

In the 1992 case of *State v. K.R.L.,* 840 P.2d 210, a Washington State Court of Appeals held that the state failed to overcome the presumption of incapacity and failed to show that an 8-year-old boy was capable of committing a residential burglary.

4. A defense lawyer who entered an insanity plea for a client in a minor charge could find the client committed to an institution for a much longer time than if the client were found guilty of the offense charged.

In *Lynch v. Overholser,* 369 U.S. 705, 82 S.Ct. 1063 (1962), a municipal court refused to accept a former mental patient's plea of guilty to a minor check forgery charge. Instead, the court found the defendant not guilty by reason of insanity. As the defendant was a first offender, he would probably have not received a jail sentence. After the defendant served two years in a mental institution, the U.S. Supreme Court reversed the trial court's decision, holding that the trial court was not justified in committing the defendant to a mental institution on bare reasonable doubt concerning past sanity.

Also note that prosecutors sometimes find that it is in the state's best interest to seek a civil commitment of a person when evidence shows that the individuals are dangerous to themselves or others and in need of treatment.

5. The 1990 study done by Policy Research Associates of Delmar, New York, is one such study.

6. The federal Insanity Defense Reform Act of 1984 requires that a federal criminal defendant found not guilty by reason of insanity may not be released onto the streets. Justice Stevens of the U.S. Supreme

Court summarized the Act as follows in *Frank v. United States,* 113 S.Ct. 363 (1992):

It (the federal Act) provides that "the Attorney General shall hospitalize the person [found not guilty by reason of insanity] in a suitable facility" until a State assumes responsibility for his care and treatment or the Attorney General finds that his release would not create a risk of harm to people or property. 18 U.S.C. § 4243(e). The question presented by the petition for certiorari is whether a defendant who has pleaded not guilty by reason of insanity is entitled to a jury instruction explaining the effect of this statute. If such an instruction is not given, there is a strong possibility that the jury will be reluctant to accept a meritorious defense because of fear that a dangerous, mentally ill person will go free.

7. 112 S.Ct. 1780 (U.S. Sup. Ct. 1992).

8. 10 Cl. & F. 200, 8 Eng.Rep. 718.

9. 81 Ala. 577, 2 So. 854 (1886).

10. It is unethical for either a prosecutor or a defense lawyer to fabricate a situation in which a defendant appears to be insane and suffering from a mental disease or defect. In the novel *Anatomy of a Murder,* the defense lawyer delivers the famous "lecture" that lets his client (the defendant) become aware that the only way that he could avoid a murder conviction would be by faking "irresistible impulse," which defense was permitted in Michigan at that time. The defense lawyer (played by James Stewart in the movie) won his case by manipulating the system but lost his legal fee. In the movie and book, loss of the legal fee seems to have been a just punishment for the improper conduct of the defense lawyer.

11. 94 U.S. App. D.C. 228, 214 F.2d 862 (1954).

12. *Sauer v. United States,* 241 F.2d 640, 648 (9th Cir. 1957).

13. 260 Mont. 510, 861 P.2d 884 (Sup. Ct. Mont. 1993).

14. 114 S.Ct. 1371 (U.S. Sup. Ct. 1994).

15. The heir to the du Pont fortune, John E. du Pont, was found guilty of third-degree murder but mentally ill. World-class wrestlers were using the du Pont Pennsylvania estate for training. John du Pont shot Olympic gold medalist David Schulz three times at point-blank range without any apparent provocation. The defendant was found to be "actively psychotic" and was ordered to be treated in a mental hospital until cured, after which he will be sent to a prison for the remainder of his sentence.

With du Pont's huge fortune, he is the wealthiest murder defendant in the history of the United States.

16. In 1998, the Federal Court of Appeals for the Tenth Circuit upheld the guilty but mentally ill law of New Mexico in the case of *Neely v. Newton,* 1998 WL 33423. The Court held that in clarifying the distinction between those not guilty by reason of insanity and those mentally ill yet criminally liable, the law serves a legitimate state interest. State court decisions upholding the constitutionality of guilty but mentally ill laws are found in *State v. Neely,* 819 P.2d 249 (New Mex. Sup. Ct. 1991).

However, in 1997 an Illinois appellate court held that the Illinois guilty but mentally ill law encouraged compromised verdicts in violation of due process and that the law seduced juries into settling on a middle ground between guilty and not guilty when in fact there is no middle ground. *People v. Robles,* 1997 WL 342483 (Ill. App. 2 Dist. 1997).

17. *The Journal of Criminal Law and Criminology* 73 (1982): 867–74 contains the entire text of former Governor Thompson's remarks as co-chair of the National Violent Crime Task Force. Governor Thompson stated that "the insanity defense has been described as the chronic scandal of American criminal law."

18. "The Insanity Defense: Ready for Reform?" *Wisconsin Bar Bulletin,* December 1982.

19. A 1997 study conducted by the Harvard Medical School and financed by the gambling industry concluded that 1.29 percent of adults in Canada and the United States have compulsive gambling disorders. However, the percentage of problem gamblers among people with alcohol or drug abuse problems or mental disorders was found to be 14.29 percent.

The need for money to gamble could cause compulsive gamblers to steal from employers, family, friends, and others. Compulsive gamblers also borrow money from other people, including loan sharks. Children of compulsive gamblers are often deprived of necessities needed for their well-being and education. (See the *New York Times* article "Compulsion to Gamble Seen Growing: Study Finds Legality Spreads the Problem," December 7, 1997.)

20. 699 F.2d 839 (7th Cir. 1982).

21. 743 F.Supp. 713 (N.D.Cal. 1990).

22. See *Drope v. Missouri,* 420 U.S. at 171, 95 S.Ct. at 903–04 (1975); and *Pate v. Robinson,* 383 U.S. at 378, 86 S.Ct. at 838 (1966).

23. See the 1996 U.S. Supreme Court case of *Cooper v. Oklahoma,* 34 L.Ed.2d 498, in which the Supreme Court invalidated laws in Oklahoma, Connecticut, Rhode Island, and Pennsylvania and required these states to use the burden on defendants of "preponderance of the evidence" in proving incompetency. Laws in these states had previously used the higher burden of "clear and convincing evidence."

24. 406 U.S. 715, 92 S.Ct. 1845 (1972).

25. A television movie was presented in 1979 of Donald Lang, an 18-year-old black, totally illiterate deaf-mute. Lang could not talk, write, read lips, or understand sign language. In 1965, he was charged with the murder of a Chicago prostitute (Cook County criminal case #65-3421). Because he could not hear, speak, read, or write, he was declared incompetent to stand trial and was placed in a state mental hospital. After Lang was held for five years, the Illinois Supreme Court ordered him tried or released. Because witnesses were no longer available, he was released. In 1973, Lang was charged with killing another woman. After a conviction for the second murder, he was held to be incompetent and was committed in 1979 to a mental hospital. In 1992, Lang again was found unfit to stand trial and was denied release from the Illinois institution to which he was committed. *People v. Lang,* 587 N.E.2d 490 (Ill.App. 1992).

26. The only survivor of the automobile crash in 1997 that killed England's Princess Diana and two others has been reported to have a loss of memory of most of the events that occurred. Doctors believe that his memory of all of the events that occurred is not likely to return.

27. 364 So.2d 687 (1978), review denied 441 U.S. 906, 25 CrL 4018 (Ala. 1978).

28. 47 Md.App. 296, 423 A.2d 251, 28 CrL 2335 (Md.Ct.SpecialApp., 1980).

29. Ibid.

30. 415 F.Supp. 15 (D.D.C. 1975).

31. 479 So.2d 169 (Fla. 1985).

32. C. 18, sec. 12.

33. See Section 2.07 of the Model Penal Code on "Liability of Corporations, Unincorporated Associations, and Persons Acting, or Under a Duty to Act, in Their Behalf." See *State v. Christy Pontiac-GMC Inc.,* 354 N.W.2d 17 (Minn. 1984), for case citations on criminal charging of corporations.

The Law Governing the Use of Force

CONTENTS

KEY TERMS

self-defense

battered women

defense of another

"Good Samaritan" laws

defense of property

defense of dwellings

booby traps

physical restraints

in loco parentis

No person, whether a law enforcement officer or a private person, may use force against another unless lawful authority exists justifying the use of force. If force is used, the person using the force should be able to come up with facts and reasons that legally justify the use of such force. The explanation of why force was used might be required by a law enforcement officer, a supervisor, or a prosecutor. If the matter goes before a prosecutor (as serious matters generally do), the prosecutor has to be provided with facts that justify the use of force, or he or she may issue charges.[1] This chapter presents the law having to do with the use of force as it is generally applied in the United States.

Self-Defense and the Defense of Others

Less Than Deadly Force in Self-Protection

Section 3.04 of the Model Penal Code provides that force can be used in self-protection "when the actor believes that such force is immediately necessary for the purpose of protecting himself against the use of unlawful force by such other person on the present occasion."

All states and the federal government have rules for the use of force in their criminal codes and in their court decisions. The state of New York, for example, provides in Public Law 35.15 that "one may use physical force upon another when and to the extent he reasonably believes necessary to defend himself or a third person from what he reasonably believes to be the imminent use of unlawful physical force by such other persons."

The key points in determining the lawfulness of force in *self-defense* or the *defense of another* are:

- *Unlawfulness.* Is what the other person doing unlawful? If it is not unlawful, force is not justified.
- *Necessity.* Force must be immediately *necessary* to protect the person or another from the use of *unlawful* force or interference by another.
- *Reasonableness.* The amount of force used in self-defense or defense of another must be *reasonable* under the circumstances that exist.

In determining what force is reasonable in self-defense, a court or a jury will take into account the size and age of the parties in relation to one another, the instruments or weapons used, and the aggressiveness of the assault made. Ordinarily, if fists were used in the attack and the parties were about the same size and strength, then fists and the strength of arms and body would be the maximum force that could be used in defense.

EXAMPLE: A 70-year-old, 100-pound woman becomes angry at a 25-year-old, 200-pound man and begins to hit him with an umbrella. The man may defend himself by taking the umbrella away from the woman, but because he has such physical control of the situation, the amount of force that he would be justified in using would end there.

Coming to the Aid of Another

A person may come to the aid of another and use necessary and reasonable force to defend the other person against unlawful force or interference. The person coming to the assis-

The Three Provisions of the U.S. Constitution That Are Relevant to the Use of Force by Law Enforcement Officers

Fourth Amendment: The Fourth Amendment specifically prohibits "unreasonable searches and seizures" (which includes the use of force). The U.S. Supreme Court held that the use of deadly force by law enforcement officers must be "objectively reasonable in light of the facts and circumstances confronting (the officers) . . . judged from the prospective of a reasonable officer on the scene . . . rather than the 20/20 vision of hindsight." *Graham v. Connor,* 490 U.S. at 396–97 (1989)

Eighth Amendment: The Eighth Amendment specifically prohibits "cruel and unusual punishment." This explicit language of the Eighth Amendment governs the use of force used to maintain control of convicted prisoners. The question before courts is "whether force was applied in a good faith effort to maintain or restore discipline or maliciously and sadistically for the very purpose of causing harm." *Whitley v. Albers,* 475 U.S. at 320–21 (1986)

Due Process Clause: The Due Process Clause of the Fifth and Fourteenth Amendments prohibits the federal and state governments from depriving any person of "life, liberty, or property without due process of law." Because of the generalized nature of the due process guarantee, the U.S. Supreme Court has limited its application to those circumstances in which there is no other "explicit textual source of constitutional protection against a particular sort of intrusive governmental conduct." *Graham v. Connor,* 490 U.S. at 395 (1989)

tance or defense of another must reasonably believe that the facts are such that the third person would be privileged to act in self-defense, and must reasonably believe that his or her intervention is necessary for the protection against unlawful force or interference.

In the case of *People v. Young,* Young intervened in a street struggle between three men.[2] Young argued that he came to the assistance of the younger man, believing in good faith that the two older men were unlawfully assaulting the younger man. Young injured the kneecap of one of the men and struck the other about the head with his fist.

The two injured men were police officers in plain clothes making an arrest of the younger man. In affirming Young's conviction for battery, the New York Court of Appeals rejected the argument that Young was privileged to use such force under the circumstances, holding: "The weight of authority holds . . . that one who goes to the aid of a third person does so at his own peril."[3]

In the 1982 case of *Alexander v. State,* the defendant, who was a prisoner, saw two guards subduing another prisoner.[4] The defendant intervened, arguing that the two guards were violently attacking his friend and that the defendant acted to prevent injury.

At the defendant's trial for assaulting the guards, the judge instructed the jury that the defendant's right to defend the other prisoner was no greater than the prisoner's own right of self-defense. The defendant was therefore convicted.

A new trial was ordered by the Court of Appeals because Maryland had passed a "Good Samaritan" statute that changed the common law and encouraged persons to "get involved." This statute applied to all persons in Maryland and required that the jury determine whether the defendant believed that an unlawful assault was occurring and whether the defendant made a good faith attempt to defend his friend, the other prisoner.

Good Samaritan Laws

Broadly defined, *Good Samaritan laws* include statutes that fall into the following categories:

- Practically all states have enacted Good Samaritan laws that encourage doctors and other health practitioners to aid injured or ill strangers. Such statutes do not encourage acts of heroism or impose a duty to aid, but rather they eliminate fear of malpractice suits that had discouraged doctors and others from rendering assistance to those who had been injured or were ill.

- In 1983, a young woman entered a crowded New Bedford, Massachusetts, tavern to purchase cigarettes. Men in the bar grabbed her and commenced gang-raping her. Other tavern patrons watched and some cheered. No one came to her aid or called the police. This incident caused some states to enact Good Samaritan statutes requiring persons to come to the aid of a victim if they can do so without endangering themselves. This could be simply calling the police. Violations of such laws are generally punished by a small fine. Many European countries have similar statutes that include possible jail sentences.

- Another form of a Good Samaritan law is a statute passed by Maryland in 1982: "Any person witnessing a violent assault upon the person of another may lawfully aid the person being assaulted by assisting in that person's defense" (Art. 27, § 12A). This statute and others authorizing force in self-defense or the defense of another *do not impose a duty* to come to the assistance of another. See the 1982 case of *Alexander v. State* in this chapter, in which a prisoner in a Maryland penitentiary saw two guards subduing another prisoner and was charged with assaulting the guards when he physically intervened. The prisoner used this Maryland statute in his defense, arguing that his conduct was lawful.

The Use of Deadly Force in Self-Defense or the Defense of Others

Deadly force is force that is likely to cause or is capable of causing death or serious bodily injury. Firing a weapon at a person is the use of deadly force, whether the intent is to kill or to wound.

All people, including law enforcement officers, may use deadly force, if necessary, to prevent imminent death or great bodily harm to themselves or others. The following civil case illustrates this rule of law:

Mullins v. Pence

Court of Appeals of Louisiana (1974) 290 So.2d 803

When a belligerent customer in a bar refused to leave, the bartender called the police. Before the police arrived, the customer told the bartender that he was going to tear his arm off and beat him over the head with it. When the customer began climbing over the bar toward the bartender, the bartender pulled out a pistol and fired one shot into the customer (Mullins). When Mullins still did not retreat, the bartender (Pence) rapidly fired four more shots into Mullins. Mullins was six feet tall and weighed 215 pounds, whereas the bartender, who was physically disabled, was five feet four inches tall and weighed 145 pounds. Mullins recovered and sued the bartender. In ruling in favor of the defendant bartender, the Court quoted other Louisiana decisions, holding:

Of course, resort to the use of a dangerous weapon in order to repel a supposed attack upon defendant's person . . . cannot be countenanced as justifiable save in exceptional cases where the actor's fear of the danger is not only genuine but is founded on facts which would be likely to produce similar emotions in men of reasonable prudence.

* * *

The trial court in the case seemed especially impressed with the belligerence of the plaintiff, the large difference in size and strength of the two parties confronting each other, an overt act made by the plaintiff toward Pence coupled with threats of serious bodily harm against the defendant, and the impossibility of retreat by Pence. Regarding the fact that five shots were actually fired into appellant, the trial court believed that Pence was reasonable in his fear following the first shot that the appellant was continuing in his act of aggression against him. Therefore, like the firing of the first shot, the appellee's action in firing the next series of shots was reasonable. We find no error in the trial court's application of the law to the facts in this case. For the above reasons, the trial court's judgment is affirmed, all costs to be paid by plaintiff-appellant.

Affirmed.

Loss of Self-Defense Privilege for a Wrongdoer or an Aggressor

Wrongdoers who use unlawful force against another have no privilege of self-defense. The victims of wrongdoers have the privilege of self-defense because of the wrongful conduct of the wrongdoers. State statutes and court decisions, however, recognize two situations in which the aggressor or wrongdoer could regain the right and privilege of self-defense.

1. A wrongdoer (X) begins an encounter with the unlawful use of his fists or some non-deadly weapon. The victim, however, unlawfully uses deadly force, which, under the circumstances, is unnecessary and unreasonable. Now, X may use force in self-defense but is not privileged to resort to the use of force intended or likely to cause death unless he has exhausted

   - every means of escape (under the duty to retreat), and
   - every means of avoiding death or great bodily harm to himself.

2. A wrongdoer may regain the right of self-defense if he or she withdraws in good faith from the fight and gives adequate notice to the victim as to the withdrawal. The wrongdoer has a duty to retreat, and his or her right to self-defense could be restored by giving notice (or attempting to) and by retreating.

The Castle Doctrine and the Duty to Retreat as an Exception to the Castle Doctrine

People who have been assaulted in their homes by a trespasser have no duty to retreat or flee but may stand their ground and use such force as is necessary and reasonable to defend themselves.[5] Because a person's home is his or her "castle," the privilege not to retreat in one's home is known as the *castle doctrine.*

The castle doctrine does not require a lawful occupant of a home to retreat when confronted by a trespasser or a person who does not reside in the home. However, state laws vary when the wrongdoer is also a co-occupant of the home (such as a spouse, live-in, or family member). A minority of states have an exception to the castle doctrine, which requires a co-occupant of a home to retreat (if safely possible) before using deadly force in self-defense.

The Supreme Court of New Jersey pointed out in the 1997 case of *State v. Gartland*[6] that New Jersey is now among the minority of states that require a lawful co-occupant to retreat (if possible) before using deadly force against another co-occupant. In the *Gartland* case, a wife was convicted of the crime of manslaughter because she failed to retreat before shooting her husband, who was assaulting her in a bedroom of their home.

The Supreme Court of New Jersey reversed the conviction and ordered a new trial because the question of whether the wife could have safely retreated was not presented to the jury. The New Jersey Supreme Court stated:

> Exactly where could she retreat? As we understand the record, there was no other way out of the bedroom other than the doorway where her assailant stood. The (jury) charge should have asked whether, armed with a weapon, she could have safely made her way out of the bedroom door without threat of serious bodily injury to herself.

In a similar Ohio case, a woman was trapped in her mobile home. Unable to escape but able to obtain a gun, she fired two warning shots before shooting her assailant. The Ohio Supreme Court held in the 1997 case of *State v. Thomas* that a domestic partner assaulted in her own home has no duty to retreat before using deadly force in self-defense.[7]

Battered Women and Domestic Homicides

The National Clearinghouse of the Defense of Battered Women states that every year 500 to 750 women kill men who abused them and "that our prisons are filled with women with long histories of abuse, linked to the crimes they're in prison for."[8] The Clearinghouse also estimates that a woman is abused in the United States every thirteen seconds.

These estimates indicate the high levels of anger, fear, hatred, and humiliation that exist in the households where such conditions prevail. Abused women (and those who allege they were abused) can be found in the prisons of every state serving sentences ranging from assault and battery to voluntary manslaughter and first-degree murder.

To lawfully use deadly force in self-defense, a real or reasonable fear of imminent death or great bodily harm must exist. If no immediate threat is present, then other alternatives are available to abused women, such as going to a shelter for *battered women* or going to their family for help. The following examples illustrate:

EXAMPLE: A wife or girlfriend is terrified as her husband or boyfriend comes toward her in a rage, screaming that he will use the knife in his hand to kill her. Witnesses state the woman had no opportunity to retreat but that she was able to grab a gun, which she used to kill the man. Held to be lawful use of force in self-defense. (See Chapter 13 on "perfect" self-defense.)

EXAMPLE: After years of beatings and many other abuses, Mrs. Norman killed her husband with a handgun as he was taking a nap. Her husband had been drinking for two days, and Mrs. Norman believed he would beat her again when he finished his nap and resumed drinking. The killing was held to be "imperfect self-defense," and Mrs. Norman went to prison for voluntary manslaughter. (See the case of *State v. Norman* in Chapter 13.)

Defense of Dwellings

Probably all of us have heard noises in our home and have gone to check the source of the noise with the thought in mind that we might have an unwelcome stranger in our home. Because half the burglaries in the United States occur during daylight hours, you could be a victim of one of the four million burglaries that occur every year in the United States in the middle of a day or night. What could you do if you were to come upon an intruder? Most burglars would attempt to flee. But maybe this burglar has been trapped, or maybe this person has violence in mind. What are the rules of law governing these situations?

Because the intruder's conduct is illegal, you may use the amount of force that is necessary and reasonable in self-defense, in defense of another, or in defense of property. These rules are defined by the statutes of your state and have been discussed in this chapter. You have no legal obligation to retreat from an intruder in your residence, but this may be a wise way out if it is possible. This is a national problem, and responses to it are occurring throughout the country. A few of the responses are described in the following material:

- **The Colorado "Make My Day Law"** Sections 18-1-704(3) of the Colorado Statutes became effective in 1986. It immediately became known as the Make My Day Law (Clint Eastwood's taunt to a felon in a movie). The backers of the law want it to be known as the Homeowner's Protection Law and point out that it is not a "license to kill" law. The law provides homeowners with immunity from prosecution for force used against a person making an unlawful entry into the home.[a]

- **The California "Home Protection Bill of Rights"** Section 198.5 of the California Penal Code permits a presumption that a person using deadly force on an intruder acted in reasonable fear of death or great bodily harm to himself or herself or a member of the household. (However, the presumption could be overcome with evidence showing otherwise.)

- **Shootings Receiving National Attention** A young Japanese exchange student dressed for a Halloween party was told to "freeze" as he approached the wrong house. The young student did not understand and was shot to death in Baton Rouge, Louisiana. A criminal jury found the homeowner innocent, but in 1994, a civil court awarded $650,000 for the killing.

- **Mistaken-for-a-Burglar Shootings** occur every year in the United States. In 1994, a young Scottish businessperson who was out on the town in Houston, Texas, became lost and pounded on the door of the wrong house at 4:00 A.M. The homeowner mistook the Scot for a burglar and shot and killed him.

Force Used in the Defense of a Home

An occupant of a home may use necessary and reasonable force in self-defense, defense of others, and defense of property. An occupant cannot use unnecessary or unreasonable force.

In the 1997 case of *Commonwealth v. Cyr,* 679 N.E.2d 550, the female occupant used excessive force against the trespasser (Cyr). In defending himself, Cyr killed the woman. The highest court in Massachusetts held, on retrial, that the jury should be instructed to consider manslaughter in addition to murder in determining Cyr's guilt.

[a]See the 1992 case of *People v. Young,* 825 P.2d 1004 (Colo.App.), in which the Colorado courts held that immunity from criminal prosecutions would not be granted under the Colorado law for shootings of people on a porch of a home.

The problem of domestic homicides has existed for many years. It could involve the killing of a spouse or other member of a household. When credible witnesses are available who provide information showing that the killing was necessary in self-defense, criminal charges should not be issued.

If, however, no one witnessed the killing and the only person alive to describe what occurred is the person who caused the killing, there may be reasons to believe that the killing was not in self-defense.

Women charged with the killing of their spouses or live-ins often use the *battered woman syndrome* as a form of self-defense. If they and other witnesses testify to a history of beatings and abuses inflicted on the woman by the deceased, expert witnesses can then generally testify to the syndrome associated with prolonged beatings and abuses on victims. In 1985, the Supreme Court of Kansas commented as follows on the problem:

> [T]here is no easy answer to why battered women stay with their abusive husbands. Quite likely emotional and financial dependency and fear are the primary reasons for remaining in the household. They feel incapable of reaching out for help and justifiably fear reprisals from their angry husbands if they leave or call the police. The abuse is so severe, for so long a time, and the threat of great bodily harm so constant, it creates a standard mental attitude in its victims. Battered women are terror-stricken people whose mental state is distorted and bears a marked resemblance to that of a hostage or a prisoner of war. The horrible beatings they are subjected to brainwash them into believing there is nothing they can do. They live in constant fear of another eruption of violence. They become disturbed persons from the torture.[9]

Many states now permit abused women charged with violence against their abusers to introduce evidence of their abuse and its psychological effects as part of their claim of self-defense. Women in prisons who were abused or who claim they were abused have appealed to state governors for clemency.

Governors in all states receive many requests for pardons and clemency each year. Parole boards and governors review the records of women requesting clemency because they were abused. Further material on battered women who kill can be found in Chapter 13 on homicide.

The Use of Force in the Defense of Property

Less Than Deadly Force in the Defense of Property

A person is privileged to threaten to or intentionally use force to protect property that is lawfully in his or her custody or care. In some instances, a verbal request is all that is needed to stop the interference with the property.

The interference with the property must be unlawful. Force may be used only when necessary to terminate the interference, and the amount of force must be reasonable under the circumstances.

EXAMPLE: Y, a store employee, observes X snatch merchandise and run out of the store. Y may use *necessary* and *reasonable* force to prevent the *unlawful* taking of merchandise by X.

EXAMPLE: X snatches W's purse and runs off. Y, who observed the crime, would be justified in using necessary and reasonable force to recover the purse. Theft from the person (or robbery, if force is used) is a felony in most, if not all, states, which would

When Force *Cannot* Be Used

Force in self-defense or in the defense of another person cannot be used if under the following circumstances:

- The force is not immediately necessary, or
- The amount of force is unreasonable, or
- If what the other person is doing is lawful. (Force in self-defense or the defense of another must be immediately necessary to protect against unlawful force.)[a]

Force cannot be used based on a fear that another person means to do harm sometime in the future if there is no immediate fear of harm. *State v. Buggs,* 806 P.2d 1381 (Ariz.App. 1990).

Force cannot be used to punish or to retaliate for past harm or past injury, such as a sexual assault in the past. *State v. Reid,* 747 P.2d 560 (Ariz. 1987).

A shoot-on-sight order would be unlawful unless the order was within the guidelines established by the U.S. Supreme Court and state courts for the use of force in self-defense, in the defense of another, or when force can lawfully be used to stop a fleeing felon. In the Ruby Ridge siege, deadly force was used to kill a fleeing 14-year-old boy and an unarmed woman.

[a]A minority of states hold that a duty to retreat exists before deadly force can be used against another co-occupant of a home (such as a spouse, live-in, or family member).

authorize Y, in most states, to make a citizen's arrest. Force could also be used under these circumstances under the state law governing the use of force in making an arrest.

Deadly Force in the Defense of Property

Under the old common law used on the American frontier, deadly force was often used to protect property. A farmer who sought to prevent the theft of his horse, cattle, or farm equipment might use deadly force, if necessary, because law enforcement officers were seldom readily available.

Today, most, if not all, states forbid the use of deadly force in the *defense of property.* The reasons for the change in the law can be summarized as follows:

1. On the frontier, a horse and many other items of property were important for survival. Today, few items of property are vital to survival because they can be replaced within a few days.

2. Today, many items of personal property (such as a car) are ordinarily insured against loss by theft. On the frontier, insurance was unknown, and the loss of major or personal items could be a tragedy to a frontier family.

3. Today, thanks to modern communication and transportation, law enforcement agencies are readily available to assist individuals confronted with theft.

The Use of Booby Traps to Protect Property

One cannot use deadly force to protect one's property. This rule applies whether the owner is present or uses a remote control device. Some jurisdictions, such as Oregon, Wisconsin, and England, go so far as to punish separately the mere setting of a spring gun.

EXAMPLE: A farmer who becomes exasperated because melons are being stolen from his melon patch is not justified in shooting the thieves with a shotgun. Neither can he set up a shotgun that is discharged when a thief brushes a wire attached to the trigger mechanism.

The common law in probably all states makes the user of such devices civilly liable for the wrongs that occur. The Restatement of Torts, Section 85, p. 180, states:

> The value of human life and limb, not only to the individual concerned but also to society, so outweighs the interest of a possessor of land in excluding from it those whom he is not willing to admit thereto that a possessor of land has, as is stated in Section 79, no privilege to use force intended or likely to cause death or serious harm against another whom the possessor sees about to enter his premises or meddle with his chattel, unless the intrusion threatens death or serious bodily harm to the occupiers or users of the premises. . . . A possessor of land cannot do indirectly and by a mechanical device that which, were he present, he could not do immediately and in person. Therefore, he cannot gain a privilege to install, for the purpose of protecting his land from intrusions harmless to the lives and limbs of the occupiers or users of it, a mechanical device whose only purpose is to inflict death or serious harm upon such as may intrude, by giving notice of his intention to inflict, by mechanical means and indirectly, harm which he could not, even after request, inflict directly were he present.

In 1990, the owner of a small machine shop in Denver, Colorado, rigged a shotgun booby trap after his business had been burglarized eight times in two years. A teenage burglar was killed by the booby trap. The business owner was convicted of manslaughter. Although the owner received probation, he was held civilly liable in a lawsuit. As the result of a damage award, he could lose his business, his home, and all his assets.[10]

After the Denver shooting, other Denver businesses put up signs on buildings stating that their premises were also booby-trapped. Police officers and firefighters became concerned for their safety and stated they would not enter such buildings until the buildings were determined to be safe. One building having such a sign (but no booby trap) was destroyed by fire when firefighters refused to enter.

The Use of Force in Making an Arrest

Less Than Deadly Force in Making an Arrest

Force may not be used legally in making an arrest unless the arrest is a lawful, custodial arrest made in good faith. This does not mean that the arrested person must be found guilty of the charge; however, it does mean that probable cause (reasonable grounds to believe) must exist to authorize the arrest.

Trainers and police officers try to restrain Mike Tyson after a boxing match that ended with Tyson biting off part of the ear of his opponent. While participants in body contact sports consent to physical contacts within the rules of the sport, would biting an adversary's ear be lawful in any legitimate sporting event?   © Michael Brennan/CORBIS

In most arrests, force is unnecessary because the person arrested complies with instructions and offers no resistance. If force should be necessary because of resistance or an attempt to escape, the officer may use only such force as is reasonably believed necessary to

1. detain the offender, make the arrest, and conduct lawful searches

2. overcome any resistance by the offender

3. prevent an escape and retake the person if an escape occurs

4. protect the officer, others, and the prisoner, if necessary

The tests used in determining whether excessive force was used by a law enforcement officer in making an arrest were established by the U.S. Supreme Court in the 1989 case of *Graham v. Connor,* 490 U.S. 386, 109 S.Ct. 1865. The U.S. Supreme Court held:

> Today we make explicit what was implicit in *Garner*'s analysis, and hold that *all* claims that law enforcement officers have used excessive force—deadly or not—in the course of an arrest, investigatory stop, or other "seizure" of a free citizen should be analyzed under the Fourth Amendment and its "reasonableness" standard, rather than under a "substantive due process" approach. Because the Fourth Amendment provides an explicit textual source of constitutional protection against this sort of physically intrusive governmental conduct, that Amendment, not the more generalized notion of "substantive due process," must be the guide for analyzing these claims.

Determining whether the force used to effect a particular seizure is "reasonable" under the Fourth Amendment requires a careful balancing of "the nature and quality of the intrusion on the individual's Fourth Amendment interests" against the countervailing governmental interests at stake. *Id.,* at 8, 105 S.Ct., at 1699, quoting *United State v. Place,* 462 U.S. 696, 703, (1983). Our Fourth Amendment jurisprudence has long recognized that the right to make an arrest or investigatory stop necessarily carries with it the right to use some degree of physical coercion or threat thereof to effect it. Because "[t]he test of reasonableness under the Fourth Amendment is not capable of precise definition or mechanical application," *Bell v. Wolfish,* 441 U.S. 520, 559, (1979), however, its proper application requires careful attention to the facts and circumstances of each particular case, including the severity of the crime at issue, whether the suspect poses an immediate threat to the safety of the officers or others, and whether he is actively resisting arrest or attempting to evade arrest by flight. See *Tennessee v. Garner,* 471 U.S., at 8–9, 105 S.Ct., at 1699–1700 (the question is "whether the totality of the circumstances justifie[s] a particular sort of . . . seizure").

The "reasonableness" of a particular use of force must be judged from the perspective of a reasonable officer on the scene, rather than with the 20/20 vision of hindsight. The Fourth Amendment is not violated by an arrest based on probable cause, even though the wrong person is arrested, *Hill v. California,* 401 U.S. 797, (1971); nor by the mistaken execution of a valid search warrant on the wrong premises, *Maryland v. Garrison,* 480 U.S. 79 (1987). With respect to a claim of excessive force, the same standard of reasonableness at the moment applies: "Not every push or shove, even if it may later seem unnecessary in the peace of a judge's chambers," *Johnson v. Glick,* 481 F.2d, at 1033, violates the Fourth Amendment. The calculus of reasonableness must embody allowance for the fact that police officers are often forced to make split-second judgments—in circumstances that are tense, uncertain, and rapidly evolving—about the amount of force that is necessary in a particular situation.

Standards for the Use of Deadly Force Established by the U.S. Supreme Court

Deadly force is force that is likely to cause death or serious bodily injury. The law regarding the use of deadly force in making an arrest varies somewhat from state to state. Police department regulations also vary in the language used to regulate and instruct officers as to the use of deadly force. State laws and police regulations must conform, however, to the requirements established by the U.S. Supreme Court in the 1985 case of *Tennessee v. Garner* (which follows) and the 1989 case of *Graham v. Connor,* 109 S.Ct. 1865.

Tennessee v. Garner

Supreme Court of the United States (1985) 471 U.S. 1, 105 S.Ct. 1694

At about 10:45 P.M. on October 3, 1974, Memphis Police Officers Elton Hymon and Leslie Wright were dispatched to answer a "prowler inside call." Upon arriving at the scene, they saw a woman standing on her porch and gesturing toward the adjacent house. She told them she had heard glass breaking and that "they" or "someone" was breaking in next door. While Wright radioed the dispatcher to say that they were on the scene, Hymon went behind the house. He heard a door slam and saw someone run across the backyard. The fleeing suspect, Edward Garner, stopped at a six-foot-high chain-link fence at the edge of the yard. With the aid of a flashlight, Hymon was able to see Garner's face and hands. He saw no sign of a weapon and, though not certain, was "reasonably sure" and "figured" that Garner was unarmed. . . . He thought Garner was 17 or 18 years old and about five feet five inches or five feet seven inches tall. While Garner was crouched at the base of the fence, Hymon called out "police, halt" and took a few steps toward him. Garner then began to climb over the fence. Convinced that if Garner made it over the fence he would elude capture, Hymon shot him. The bullet hit Garner in the back of the head. Garner was taken by ambulance to a hospital, where he died on the operating table. Ten dollars and a purse from the house were found on his body.

In using deadly force to prevent the escape, Hymon was acting under the authority of a Tennessee statute and pursuant to police department policy. The statute provides that "[i]f, after notice of the intention to arrest the defendant, he either flee or forcibly resist, the officer may use all the necessary means to effect the arrest." Tenn. Code Ann. § 40-7-108 (1982). The department policy was slightly more restrictive than the statute, but still allowed the use of deadly force in cases of burglary. The incident was reviewed by the Memphis Police Firearm's Review Board and presented to a grand jury. Neither took any action.

Garner's father then brought this action in the Federal District Court for the Western District of Tennessee, seeking damages under 42 U.S.C. § 1983 for asserted violations of Garner's constitutional rights. The complaint alleged that the shooting violated the Fourth, Fifth, Sixth, Eighth, and Fourteenth Amendments of the U.S. Constitution.[11]

The federal Court of Appeals held:

> [T]he killing of a fleeing suspect is a "seizure" under the Fourth Amendment, and is therefore constitutional only if "reasonable." The Tennessee statute failed as applied to this case because it did not adequately limit the use of deadly force by distinguishing between felonies of different magnitudes—"the facts, as found, did not justify the use of deadly force under the Fourth Amendment." Officers cannot resort to deadly force unless they "have probable cause . . . to believe that the suspect [has committed a felony and] poses a threat to the safety of the officers or a danger to the community if left at large."

The U.S. Supreme Court affirmed the Court of Appeals' conclusion that "the facts, as found, did not justify the use of deadly force" and further held:

> While we agree that burglary is a serious crime, we cannot agree that it is so dangerous as automatically to justify the use of deadly force. The FBI classifies burglary as a "property" rather than a "violent" crime. See Federal Bureau of Investigation, *Uniform Crime Reports, Crime in the United States* 1 (1984). Although the armed burglar would present a different situation, the fact that an unarmed suspect has broken into a dwelling at night does not automatically mean he is physically dangerous. This case demonstrates as much. . . . In fact, the available statistics demonstrate that burglaries only rarely involve physical violence. During the 10-year period from 1973–1982, only 3.8% of all burglaries involved violent crime.

Other Examples of the Use of Force by Police

Following are a few of the many civil cases applying the U.S. Supreme Court guidelines on the use of force:

Joos v. Ratliff

U.S. Court of Appeals, 8th Circuit (1996) 97 F.3d 1175

Joos repeatedly resisted fingerprinting after he was lawfully arrested. Finally, force was used to compel Joos to open his hand to complete the booking. The Court held that an officer pressing his thumb against Joos's mandibular nerve junction below Joos's jaw and repeatedly pushing the thumb forward toward Joos's nose were "both de minimis and a reasonable response when Joos resisted (the) officer's attempts to effect his arrest and booking."

Stroik v. Ponseti

U.S. Court of Appeals, 5th Circuit (1994) 35 F.3d 115, 57 CrL 3013 Review Denied, U.S. Supreme Court (1995) 115 S.Ct. 1692

New Orleans officers responded to a radio broadcast stating that four people suspected of committing a series of armed robberies were driving a blue van and that two of the suspects were white and two were black.

The officers chased the van in a high-speed chase until the van crashed. After one black suspect ran from the scene, a second black male and a white female exited the van. The black male was behind the white female with his left hand around her waist with a handgun in his right hand. An officer immediately fired seven to nine times, killing the black male and wounding the white female.

The radio dispatch was in error, as the woman was a hostage whose van had been carjacked by the two robbers. The Court dismissed this civil action by the woman, holding that the officer had probable cause and "could have reasonably believed that the suspects posed an imminent, deadly threat," justifying the officer's use of "deadly force."

Chew v. Gates

U.S. Court of Appeals, 9th Circuit (1994) 27 F.3d 1432

The defendant in this case was stopped for a routine traffic violation, and while police ran a computer check, Chew bolted and disappeared in a nearby scrap metal yard. After he could not be found, a police dog was brought in and turned loose. The dog found Chew, and the defendant almost lost his right arm before police called the dog off.

The trial court granted summary judgment to the police and dismissed Chew's civil lawsuit. However, the Court of Appeals reversed and sent the case back for reconsideration as to whether the force was excessive under *Tennessee v. Garner* and *Graham v. Connor*.

Factors that would be considered were (1) Was turning a "find and bite" dog loose excessive force, and was a "find and bark" dog available? (2) Was there any immediate threat to the police officers? (3) Because the officers did not know the seriousness of the defendant's two outstanding felony warrants disclosed by the computer check, this factor would have to be considered in view of the higher level of force used.

Definition of an Unreasonable Seizure Today

An *unreasonable seizure* would occur if deadly force were used by law enforcement officers or private people under any of the following circumstances:

1. *Deadly force may never be used to make the arrest of or to prevent the escape of a person who has committed a misdemeanor.*

EXAMPLE: Deadly force should not be used to catch a "prowler" seen in someone's backyard in the middle of the night or to halt a shoplifter who has taken a $75 item and cannot be apprehended in any other way.

2. *Deadly force may never be used on mere suspicion.*

EXAMPLE: In 1965, two New Orleans Police Officers fired at an automobile they were chasing because they suspected that the vehicle had been stolen. Mere suspicion does not justify the use of deadly force, and although "fleeing from an officer" is a felony in many instances, it would not justify the use of deadly force, as it ordinarily is a nonviolent offense.[12]

EXAMPLE: Late on a hot summer night, a woman is heard screaming, and a man runs out from between two houses and down the street. The man does not stop when ordered to stop by a police officer. The "rookie" officer (who later retired as a high-ranking officer with the Milwaukee Police Department) had the good sense not to shoot. When the man did stop, the officer found that the man was a boyfriend of the woman who had made advances on his girlfriend, causing her to scream. The officer stated that he woke up in a cold sweat a number of nights thinking what would have happened had he used his revolver in this situation.

3. *Deadly force may never be used by law enforcement officers to arrest or prevent the escape of a person who has committed a nonviolent felony.*

EXAMPLE: A burglar is fleeing from the scene as in *Tennessee v. Garner.* The burglar does not appear to be armed, and there is no threat of danger to the homeowner or law enforcement officer. As the burglary was a nonviolent felony, the use of deadly force is not justified.

The *FBI Law Enforcement Bulletin* article "Use of Deadly Force to Prevent Escape" (March 1994) states that the U.S. Supreme Court held in *Tennessee v. Garner*:

> [D]eadly force may be used when "necessary to prevent escape and the officer has *probable cause* to believe that the suspect poses a *significant threat* of death or serious physical injury to the officer or others" (emphasis added).
>
> The Court explained the standard as follows: "[I]f the suspect threatens the officer with a weapon *or* there is probable cause to believe that he has committed a crime involving the infliction or threatened infliction of serious physical harm, deadly force may be used *if necessary to prevent escape,* and if, where feasible, some warning has been given" (emphasis added).
>
> The *Garner* decision explicitly recognizes constitutional authority for the use of deadly force to prevent escape and provides a two-prong test to guide the exercise of that authority. First, an officer must have probable cause to believe that the fleeing suspect is *dangerous,* and second, the use of deadly force must be necessary to effect the seizure.

Use of Force in Resisting an Unlawful Arrest

Under the common law, a person had a legal right to forcibly resist an unlawful arrest. This rule developed hundreds of years ago in England, when safeguards did not exist to protect a person from unlawful arrest. Today, many safeguards exist, and the old rule has been changed by court decisions and statutes in most states. California Penal Code, Section 834a, and Connecticut Statutes, Sections 53a-23, are examples of such statutes. The Connecticut statute is as follows: "A person is not justified in using physical force to resist an arrest by a reasonably identifiable police officer, whether such arrest is legal or illegal." A few states, however, retain the old rule.[13]

What Is the Nature of the Contact Between Police and the People in the United States?

The U.S. Congress ordered a study of the nature of the day-to-day contacts between the police and the people in the United States. The results of this 1999 national survey were published by the U.S. Department of Justice in the NCJ 184957 document, reporting that in 1999

- 21 percent of U.S. residents had a contact with police
- 52 percent of these contacts were traffic stops
- 19 percent of the contacts were to report a crime
- Under 1 percent of the contacts involved police use of force
- 10 percent of white drivers were stopped
- 12 percent of black drivers were stopped
- 9 percent of Hispanic drivers were stopped
- 84 percent of drivers considered their stop legitimate, and 90 percent stated that the police acted properly during the traffic stop

About 1 percent of the 45 million people who had any face-to-face contact with police had been threatened with the use of force or had force used against them (this included being pushed, hit, choked, threatened with a flashlight, restrained by a dog, or threatened with a gun).

The survey concluded that in the United States, the use of force by police is quite uncommon and very low.

Cases in Which Force Was Not Legally Justified

The following cases illustrate situations in which the use of force is not legally justified:

- Words alone never justify the use of force (see the fighting words doctrine in Chapter 10). In the 1994 case of *State v. Escamilla*, 245 Neb. 13, 511 N.W.2d 58, the defendant claimed he killed the victim because the victim made a homosexual proposition to him. The trial court would not permit evidence of this defense.

- In the 1991 case of *People v. Miller*, 211 Ill.App.3d 572, 570 N.E.2d 515, the defendant claimed the victim beat her the night before. The Illinois courts held that this was not legal justification for the shooting the following day, and the conviction of attempted murder was affirmed.

- The father of a high school girl who had been sexually abused by the former high school basketball coach shot the man five times as he left court in Mound City, Illinois. ("Coach in Abuse Case Is Shot by Girl's Father," *New York Times*, October 17, 1993.)

- The mother of a 12-year-old boy who had been sexually abused fired five bullets into the head and neck of the male abuser as he sat in a Sonora, California, courtroom. The mother was sentenced to ten years in state prison. ("Mother in a Courtroom Slaying Calls Jail Term Fair," *New York Times*, January 9, 1994.)

- When a 19-year-old man broke into the cockpit of a commercial aircraft, seven passengers wrestled the man to the floor and continued to beat and pound the senseless man, causing his death. A Salt Lake City prosecutor did not seek an indictment, stating that he did not believe he could obtain a homicide conviction. ("U.S. Declines to Prosecute in Case of Man Beaten to Death on Jet," *New York Times*, September 21, 2000.)

Does this 1997 pepper spraying of demonstrators appear to be necessary use of force by Oregon police? Is there an apparent need of the police to defend themselves or to compel the demonstrators to comply with lawful police orders? The demonstrators were protesting the removal of trees. What other courses of action (other than pepper spraying) were available to the police in this situation?   AP/Wide World Photos

- A purse snatcher did not offer resistance after he was apprehended by witnesses to the crime. However, the purse snatcher was beaten and choked until he had no pulse and was taken to a hospital in critical condition. ("Purse Snatching Leads to a Severe Beating," *New York Times,* July 1, 1995.)

Disciplining Children

Use of Force by Parents

Under common law, parents and people who take the place of parents (*in loco parentis*) have a natural right to the custody, care, and control of their children. They have a duty to provide food, clothing, shelter, and medical care to the children and to educate and discipline them. Under the common law, a parent or a person *in loco* may use a reasonable amount of force in disciplining a child.

A 2001 study[14] reported that the majority of American families discipline their preschool children by using occasional mild to moderate spanking. The study reported that results showed no negative effects on children.

However, the study also showed that 4 percent to 7 percent of parents fell into the "red zone" (danger zone) because they disciplined their children frequently and impulsively by such means as verbal punishment, using a paddle, hitting their children in the face or body, or by throwing or shaking their child. These children were found more likely to have behavioral problems or experience anxiety or depression.

All states have laws requiring school officials, health professionals (nurses, doctors, therapists), and law enforcement officials to report suspected child abuse.

In determining what is a crime of child abuse, the following factors would have to be considered:

- The age, size and health of the child, as force used on a baby or a sick or helpless child is much different than the same force used on a healthy 14-year-old boy

- The reason for the discipline, because spanking a child for unintentional bed-wetting or becoming sick and throwing up could lead to the conclusion that the parent was out of control and not rational

The question of what amount of force is reasonable was presented to the Texas Court of Appeals (Houston) in the 1987 case of *Teubner v. State*.[15] The Court held:

Texas Penal Code section 9.61 permits the use of force against a child under a "reasonable belief" standard. However, force going beyond that which is necessary for discipline is prohibited. The question in this case is whether the appellants reasonably believed their use of force was necessary to discipline their child.

From the evidence presented, no reasonable person could possibly believe the conduct was justifiable. The child was subjected to a savage beating with a leather belt on two successive nights. On the first night, Victoria Teubner took over the whipping when her husband tired himself. On the second night, they gagged their daughter to stifle her crying. The photographs admitted into evidence offer a grim record of the effects of the beating. The appellants could not have reasonably believed that the degree of force used was necessary for disciplinary purposes. Appellants' second point of error is overruled.

Others Who May Discipline Children

Besides the parents, any person taking the place of the parents and thus classified as *in loco parentis* may reasonably discipline a child in his or her care. This category includes legal guardians, foster parents, and public school teachers.

Because of the threats of lawsuits and pressure from anti-paddling groups, many states have forbidden corporal punishment in public schools within those states. In the states that continue to permit corporal punishment, many school boards forbid or limit the use of corporal punishment of students within the school district. In 1977, the U.S. Supreme Court held in the case of *Ingraham v. Wright* that in common law, "a teacher may impose reasonable but not excessive force to discipline a child."[16] The U.S. Supreme Court noted:

Where the legislatures have not acted, the state courts have uniformly preserved the common law rule permitting teachers to use reasonable force in disciplining children in their charge.

Law enforcement officers, neighbors, and other adults who see children misbehave may not discipline a child (or children), although they may use reasonable force to prevent damage to property or injury to other persons or themselves. In Chapter 10, reference is made to an actual incident in which a 65-year-old man spanked an 8-year-old boy who

Use of Physical Restraints

Use of neck choke holds	Could be held to be unreasonable and excessive use of force[a]	The *FBI Law Enforcement Bulletin* article "Physiological Effects Resulting from Use of Neck Holds" (July 1983) states:[b] Because of the organs involved, neck holds must be considered potentially lethal whenever applied. Officers using this hold should have proper training in its use and effects. Police officers should have continual inservice training and practice in the use of the carotid sleeper. They should not use or be instructed in the use of the choke hold other than to demonstrate its potential lethal effect. Officers should recognize that death can result if the carotid sleeper is incorrectly applied.
Use of handcuffs	When an arrest is made	Generally upheld as reasonable; see *Healy v. City of Brentwood,* 649 S.W.2d 916 (Mo.App. 1983)
Use of handcuffs	When an investigative stop is made	Would be held reasonable if circumstances justified use; see *People v. Johnson,* 199 Colo. 68, 605 P.2d 46 (1980), in which suspects were believed to be armed robbers and murderers. See also *Rhodes v. State,* 945 S.W.2d 115 (Tex.Ct.App. 1997), which lists cases in which handcuffing was held reasonable during investigative stops.
Use of handcuffs	In transporting mental patients	Would be unreasonable if no need to handcuff, but would be justified when there was a reasonable concern for safety

[a]See the *New York Times* article "Police Officer Is Dismissed in Choke Hold Case" (November 10, 1997) (the victim died).
[b]See also the *FBI Law Enforcement Bulletin* article "Suspect Restraint and Sudden Death" (May 1996), where the risk to prisoners who are hog-tied is discussed.

made an obscene gesture to the man after the man reprimanded the boy for using vulgar language on a public street. The prosecutor did not charge the man with battery, as the boy's mother demanded, but the man was told that he had no right or privilege to discipline other people's children.

Reasonable force to maintain order (as distinguished from discipline) may be used by personnel on airplanes, ships, trains, or buses and by ushers for theaters, sporting events, and other public gatherings. A disorderly child or adult may be ordered to leave if he or she is disturbing other people or has failed to pay the fare or admission fee. The test, again, is that of reasonability. Did the provocation justify the action taken? Was the force reasonable under the circumstances? The Supreme Court of Minnesota held in 1885 that it was not reasonable to force a passenger off a moving train because he had not paid his fare.[17]

Products Used in Attempts to Avoid Violence

Device	Description
Stun gun, stun shields, stun belts and Tasers	Like mini cattle prods, these products seek to keep attackers at bay. The federal court in the case of *Michenfelder v. Sumer,* 624 S. Supp. at 463–64, held that Tasers and stun guns are more suitable than batons for use in prisons and inflict less discomfort than tear gas.
Chemical sprays such as pepper spray, mace, tear gas	Like stun guns, mace and other chemical sprays are marketed as defensive devices. Such devices seek to repel but not kill an attacker. Most if not all states permit persons 18 years and older to possess and use a variety of pocket-size chemical sprays that repel but do not kill.
Crowd control devices	Water cannons and tear gas have been used for years in the United States for crowd control purposes. American law enforcement agencies have been very reluctant to use rubber bullets and other "nonlethal projectiles" because they "can be lethal under certain circumstances." *FBI Law Enforcement Bulletin* article, "Controlling Subjects" (February, 1997).

Many new devices are being developed or are entering the market. For example, the military are developing ADS (active denial system), which uses electromagnetic waves to disperse crowds without injuring anyone. The device causes an intense burning sensation on the skin that causes people to flee or avoid the source of the pain.

Federal Guidelines for the Use of Deadly Force by Federal Agents (Issued 1996)

A. **Defense of Life:** Agents may use deadly force only when *necessary,* that is, when the agents have probable cause to believe that the subject of such force poses an imminent danger of death or serious physical injury to the agents or other persons.

B. **Fleeing Subject:** Deadly force may be used to prevent the escape of a fleeing subject if there is probable cause to believe (1) The subject has committed a felony involving the infliction or threatened infliction of serious physical injury or death and (2) the subject's escape would pose an imminent danger of death or serious physical injury to the agents or other persons.

C. **Verbal Warnings:** *If feasible,* and if to do so would not increase the danger to the agent or others, a verbal warning to submit to the authority of the agent shall be given prior to the use of deadly force.

D. **Warning Shots:** No warning shots are to be fired by agents.

E. **Vehicles:** Weapons may not be fired solely to disable moving vehicles. Weapons may be fired at the driver or other occupant of a moving motor vehicle only when the agents have probable cause to believe that the subject poses an imminent danger of death or serious physical injury to the agents or others and the use of deadly force does not create a danger to the public that outweighs the likely benefits of its use.

Application of Deadly Force

A. When the decision is made to use deadly force, agents may continue its application until the subject surrenders or no longer poses an imminent danger.

B. When deadly force is permitted under this policy, attempts to shoot to cause minor injury are unrealistic and can prove dangerous to agents and others because they are unlikely to achieve the intended purpose of bringing an imminent danger to a timely halt.

C. Even when deadly force is permitted, agents should assess whether its use creates a danger to third parties that outweighs the likely benefits of its use.

Summary of the Law on the Use of Force

Situation	Less Than Deadly Force	Deadly Force
In self-defense or in the defense of others	"The use of (reasonable) force upon or toward another person is justified when the actor (reasonably) believes that such force is immediately necessary for the purpose of protecting himself or herself (or another) against the use of unlawful force by such other person on the present occasion."[a]	"The use of deadly force is not justified . . . unless such force is necessary to protect . . . against death, serious bodily harm, kidnapping, or sexual intercourse compelled by force or threat."[b]
In the defense of property	"Only such degree of force or threat thereof may intentionally be used as the actor reasonably believes is necessary to prevent or terminate the interference."[c]	Under the old common law, deadly force could be used in the defense of property. All states now forbid the use of intentional deadly force in the defense of property.
To apprehend a person who has committed a crime	"When an officer is making or attempting to make an arrest for a criminal offense, he is acting for the protection of public interest and is permitted even a greater latitude than when he acts in self-defense, and he is not liable unless the means which he uses are clearly excessive."[d]	*Misdemeanor:* NEVER *Fleeing Felon:* Deadly force could be used when officers "have probable cause . . . to believe that the suspect (has committed a felony and) poses a threat to the safety of the officers or a danger to the community if left at large." *Tennessee v. Garner*
To stop a person for investigative purposes when only "reasonable suspicion" exists	Only such force that is reasonable and necessary under the circumstances that then exist	NEVER
Disciplining children (corporal punishment)	Only parents and other people having a status of *in loco parentis* to a child may use reasonable force "reasonably believed to be necessary for (the child's) proper control, training, or education."[e] Other persons (such as strangers or neighbors) may not discipline a child.	NEVER

[a]Sections 3.04(1) and 3.05(1) of the Model Penal Code.
[b]Section 3.04(2)(b) of the Model Penal Code.
[c]Section 939.49(1) of the Wisconsin Statutes.
[d]Restatement of Torts, Section 132(a).
[e]Restatement of Torts, Section 147(2), as quoted by the U.S. Supreme Court in *Ingraham v. Wright,* 429 U.S. 975, 97 S.Ct. 481 (1976).

SUMMARY

Force cannot lawfully be used against another person unless the other person's actions are unlawful and the force used is necessary for self-defense or the defense of another. The amount of force must be reasonable under the circumstances.

Deadly force cannot be used unless such force is immediately necessary to protect against serious bodily harm or death. There is no duty to retreat (flee) unless the person is the aggressor in the incident or the castle doctrine is applicable.

Reasonable force may be used to protect property against shoplifting, purse-snatching, and other crimes. Deadly force, however, cannot be used.

Parents and other persons *in loco parentis* may use reasonable amounts of force in disciplining children. Most parents will use occasional mild spanking to discipline preschool children. However, some parents will not. A very small percentage of parents use excessive force, which is unlawful and is criminal.

www BOOK-SPECIFIC WEB SITE

For chapter-related Web links, quizzing activities, and case and news updates, go to the *Criminal Law,* Eighth Edition, book-specific Web site at **http://info.wadsworth.com/ gardner.**

QUESTIONS AND PROBLEMS

In the following true incidents, was the use of force lawful?

1. In Long Beach, California, a 19-year-old woman who was raped by two men invited them to a return date, at which time she killed one with a shotgun while the other man fled. The men had released the woman after raping her when she promised not to call the police and she agreed to another meeting.

2. In Alexandria, Virginia, a 62-year-old retired army colonel was awakened just after midnight by someone rattling the chain lock on his bedroom door. When the noise stopped, the colonel took a pistol and went into the hall to investigate. In the dim light, he saw two men coming toward him from another room. He fired at them and fatally wounded two burglars. When police officers arrived, they found that the burglars were not armed and had in their possession only a large screwdriver and money taken from the house.

3. Occasionally, citizens take the law into their own hands and use force against public violators. A Los Angeles man who took frequent late-night walks came upon two young men spraying graffiti beneath the overpass of the Hollywood Freeway. He confronted them, argued with them, and then shot and killed one of them.

   The police accepted the man's assertion that the men had threatened him with a screwdriver and had tried to rob him, and released the shooter from custody without charges. Many callers to local talk shows praised the shooter for his actions. ("A Shooter as Vigilante, and Avenging

Angel," *New York Times,* February 12, 1995.) Should the shooter be charged with a crime even though it would be unlikely that a jury in Los Angeles would convict him?

4. In Tennessee, a man caught a window peeper looking into his sister's window at night. The window peeper ran away although he was ordered by the man to stay where he was. The man shot and killed the fleeing window peeper, who was also an adult male.

5. In Minnesota, the owner of a car chased a 28-year-old man who broke into his car and stole $150 in goods. The car owner shot the burglar in the foot, causing him to walk with a limp for the rest of his life. In Denver, Colorado, a store owner shot a fleeing burglar in the back, paralyzing him for life. The burglar, who was 14 years old, was on a beer-drinking spree with other boys and broke into the store to obtain more beer to continue the party.

6. When a speeder would not stop, a high-speed chase took place. The motorist was clocked at 103 mph. Police lights and sirens did not stop the speeder, and she was forced off the highway. One of the officers opened the car door and repeatedly re-

quested her to get out of the car. The woman was forcibly pulled from the car when she refused the repeated requests. In a civil lawsuit, she asks for monetary relief because of alleged neck and back injuries received when she was "yanked" out of the car. What are the tests to determine whether the police used lawful force in removing the woman from the car? *Clark v. Department of Public Safety,* 431 So.2d 83 (La.App. 1983).

7. After the 1991 Gulf War, General Norman Schwarzkopf ("Stormin' Norman") was interviewed at his Saudi Arabian headquarters for the ABC program *20/20.* During the interview, Barbara Walters asked the general about returning Vietnam soldiers being spit upon by civilians and whether he had ever been spit upon. General Schwarzkopf, who had served three tours of duty in the Vietnam theater, acknowledged that he had heard stories of returning military personnel being spit upon but emphatically stated that nobody had or was ever going to spit upon him.

If force can be used to prevent being spit upon, what legal limits of force could be used? Could force be used to punish a person who attempted to spit on you?

INFOTRAC COLLEGE EDITION EXERCISES

1. Go to InfoTrac College Edition and, using the subject search term *battered wife syndrome,* find the 2001 article about a recent Florida case involving this issue. Was the case discussed in that article really about "battered wife syndrome" or some other use of force issue? If so, what issue?

2. Go to InfoTrac College Edition and use the subject search term *deadly force by police;* click on the link

next to the article that appears and then click the "periodical references." Find the FBI article that discusses the reluctance of police to use deadly force. What is the cause of this reluctance, what training is used to overcome it, and what are the potential consequences of that training?

NOTES

1. When cases go before a criminal court, most states place the burden of proving there was no justification for the force (such as self-defense) upon the state. The U.S. Supreme Court pointed out in the

1987 case of *Martin v. Ohio,* 480 U.S. 228, 107 S.Ct. 1098, that only two states continue to follow the common law "that affirmative defenses, including self-defense, were matters for the defendant to prove."

Forty-eight states require "the prosecution to prove the absence of self-defense when it is properly raised by the defendant." Ohio and South Carolina continue to follow the common law rule. The Supreme Court held that the rule used in Ohio and South Carolina is constitutional. The Court pointed out that "the Constitution (does not) require the prosecution to prove the sanity of a defendant who pleads not guilty by reason of insanity."

2. 11 N.Y.2d 274, 229 N.Y.S.2d 1, 183 N.E.2d 319 (1962).

3. Two dissenting judges urged that the case be sent back to the trial court for a determination as to whether the degree of force used by Young was reasonable under the circumstances.

4. 52 Md.App. 171, 447 A.2d 880, 31 CrL 2371 (1982).

5. Although there is no legal duty to retreat (flee) from a person who is larger and stronger, in most instances, retreat (if possible) would be practical and sensible.

6. 694 A.2d 564 (N.J. 1997).

7. *State v. Thomas,* 673 N.E.2d 1339 (Ohio 1997).

8. See the *New York Times* article "More States Study Clemency for Women Who Killed Abusers," February 2, 1991.

9. *State v. Hundley,* 236 Kan. 461, 693 P.2d 475 (1985).

10. See the *New York Times* articles "Denver Machine Shop Owner Gets Probation in Booby Trap Slaying," August 22, 1990, and "Intruder Killed by Trap in House in Burglary-Prone Area of Mobile (Alabama)," December 29, 1989. Similar incidents have occurred in cities throughout the United States. See the 1971 case of *Katko v. Briney,* 183 N.W.2d 657 (Iowa), for a further discussion of civil liability and case citations on booby traps.

After his cabin in northern Wisconsin was burglarized three times in eight months, a man rigged a booby trap with a 12-gauge shotgun to the door of a shed housing an ATV (all-terrain vehicle). When a burglar opened the door days later, he received a load of buckshot in his leg. As Wisconsin makes setting a deadly booby trap a misdemeanor, both the cabin owner and the burglar were charged and convicted. (See "Cabin Owner Jailed for Setting Booby Trap Seeks Pardon From Governor," *Milwaukee Journal Sentinel,* February 3, 2000.)

11. The police officers in the U.S. Supreme Court case of *Tennessee v. Garner* could use the defense known as "qualified immunity." Under this defense, police officers or other public officials who are sued for violating someone's constitutional rights cannot be held liable if either the law at the time of the incident was unclear or if they (the police officers) reasonably believed at the time that their conduct was lawful.

12. *Sauls v. Hutto and Rupert,* 304 F.Supp. 124 (E.D.La. 1969).

13. *Commonwealth v. Moreira,* 388 Mass. 96, 447 N.E.2d 1224 (1983). In the 1998 case of *State v. Hobson,* No. 96-0914, the Supreme Court of Wisconsin also changed the old common law, holding:

> We agree that there should be no right to forcibly resist an unlawful arrest in the absence of unreasonable force. When persons resist arrest, they endanger themselves, the arresting officers, and bystanders. . . . Justice can and must be had in the courts, not in the streets.

The uniform rule throughout the United States is that force cannot be used to prevent a lawful or unlawful frisk, or a search under either a search warrant or some other lawful authority. To use force to or otherwise resist or obstruct a law enforcement officer in the performance of his or her lawful duties could be charged as a criminal offense in all states.

14. See "Finding Gives Some Support to Advocates of Spanking: Adding Fuel to Bitter Debate on Child Care," *New York Times,* August 25, 2001.

15. 742 S.W.2d 57 (Tex.App. 1987).

16. 430 U.S. 651, 97 S.Ct. 1401 (1977).

17. *State v. Kinney,* 34 Minn. 311, 25 N.W. 705 (1885).

7

Other Criminal Defenses

CONTENTS

KEY TERMS

affirmative defense

diplomatic immunity

mistake of law

general intent

duress

necessity

coercion

alibi

double jeopardy

res judicata

collateral estoppel

entrapment

statute of limitations

Affirmative Defenses

To prove the guilt of a person charged with a crime, the state must present evidence (1) that a crime was committed (corpus delicti) and (2) that the defendant committed or was a party to the crime charged. The U.S. Supreme Court has repeatedly held that "the requirement that guilt of a criminal charge be established by proof beyond a reasonable doubt dates at least from our early years as a Nation" (*In re Winship,* 90 S.Ct. at 1071, 1970).

Defendants in criminal cases may choose to sit quietly if they wish and place the burden on the government of coming forward with evidence proving guilt beyond a reasonable doubt. If the government does carry this burden, a defendant can then assert and come forward with evidence showing *actual innocence* or other justification. (See the 1993 U.S. Supreme Court case of *Herrera v. Collins,* 506 U.S. 390.)

Some of the many defenses to criminal charges have been presented in Chapter 1 (ex post facto, void for vagueness, equal protection of the laws), Chapter 3 (failure to prove all of the essential elements of the crime charged), Chapter 5 (infancy defense, insanity defense, and lack of competency to proceed), and Chapter 6 (defenses to the use of force).

Many of the defenses presented in this chapter are affirmative defenses, which were defined by the Supreme Court of Florida in the 1990 case of *State v. Cohen,* 568 So.2d 49, as follows:

> An **affirmative defense** is any defense that assumes the complaint or charges to be correct but raises other facts that, if true, would establish a valid excuse or justification or a right to engage in the conduct in question. An affirmative defense does not concern itself with the elements of the offense at all; it concedes them. In effect, an affirmative defense says, "Yes, I did it, but I had a good reason."

Immunity as a Defense

Diplomatic Immunity

By reason of their positions, foreign diplomats stationed in the United States are immune from arrest and criminal prosecution. Most foreign diplomats are located in Washington, D.C., or in New York (United Nations), whereas consular officials may be found in Chicago, San Francisco, and other cities. The *FBI Law Enforcement Bulletin* published an article entitled "Procedures and Policies Relating to Diplomatic and Consular Officials" (August 1973), which stated:

> *Diplomatic immunity,* a principle of international law, is broadly defined as the freedom from local jurisdiction accorded to duly accredited diplomatic officers, their families, and servants. Diplomatic officers should not be arrested or detained for any offense, and foreign career consular officers should not be arrested or detained except for the commission of a grave crime. Family members of diplomatic officers, their servants, and employees of a diplomatic mission are entitled to the same immunities under current U.S. law (22 U.S.C.A. § 252), if they are not nationals of or permanently resident in the receiving state.

Diplomatic immunity may be waived by the diplomat's home country, and in the case of serious crimes, the U.S. government frequently requests that waiver. An example of this waiver can be seen in *Van Den Borre v. State,*[1] in which Belgium waived immunity for a diplomat who was then convicted of a double murder.

Immunity for consular officers is not absolute, as it is for diplomats. Article 43 of the Vienna Convention, to which the United States and more than one hundred other countries are parties, provides that "[c]onsular officers . . . shall not be amenable to the jurisdiction of [the host nation] in respect to acts performed in the exercise of consular functions." Criminal acts not so performed expose the consular offices to prosecution. For example, in *United States v. Cole,*[2] a consular officer was successfully prosecuted for smuggling money out of the United States in a diplomatic pouch. The court said the officer was not exercising consular functions.

Legislative Immunity

Article I, Section 6, of the U.S. Constitution provides that U.S. senators and representatives "shall in all cases except treason, felony and breach of the peace, be privileged from arrest during their attendance at the sessions of their respective houses, and in going to and returning from the same." Most state constitutions extend the same or similar privileges to state legislators while the state legislature is in session. Representatives, senators, and state legislators thus have a limited degree of temporary immunity while their legislative bodies are in session. Charges, however, could be held until the legislative body adjourns. Also, state legislators enjoy no immunity from prosecution for federal crimes.[3]

Witness Immunity

Both the federal and state governments have enacted statutes that provide for the granting of immunity under specific circumstances. For instance, the Uniform Act for the Extradition of Witnesses provides that a person from another state who is summoned to testify under compulsion may be granted immunity from arrest for any pending criminal or civil wrong while in the state in response to such summons.

Many grants of immunity occur when witnesses claim the Fifth Amendment privilege against self-incrimination. When this privilege is claimed, the court may be asked to grant witnesses immunity. Witnesses can then be compelled to testify after immunity is granted, as their statements cannot be used against them. Because the element of self-incrimination is removed, no Fifth Amendment violation can occur.

A grant of immunity by one level of government also bars any other level from prosecuting witnesses and from using their answers as the basis for criminal proceedings. Such grants of immunity apply only to the extent allowed by state or federal law. If the law of the jurisdiction provides *transactional immunity,* the persons granted immunity may not be prosecuted for the offense about which they were compelled to testify. If the jurisdiction provides *use immunity,* only the testimony that was compelled may not be used against the witnesses. Any information that the authorities obtain through other means may be used to prosecute for the offense about which the witnesses were compelled to testify.

Immunity as a Defense[a]

Type of Immunity	Source	Extent	Public Purpose
Diplomatic	Historically, diplomats in a foreign country are not subject to the civil or criminal laws of that country. Therefore, foreign diplomats in the United States are not subject to federal or state civil or criminal laws.	Total	Diplomatic immunity, it is hoped, guarantees that American diplomats in foreign countries will not be arrested.
Legislative	Many states have similar constitutional provisions to that found in Art. I, Section 6, of the U.S. Constitution, which provides that U.S. senators and members of Congress "shall in all cases except treason, felony and breach of the peace, be privileged from arrest . . . at the sessions of their respective houses, and in going to and returning from the same."	Partial	Legislative immunity has existed since the birth of our republic. Its purpose was to prevent unnecessary harassment of legislators. As the question of legislative immunity seldom comes up, it is highly unlikely that the U.S. Constitution will be amended to change this form of immunity.
Witness	Federal and state statutes authorize courts and legislative bodies to grant immunity in order to obtain testimony.	Specific crimes	This is sometimes the only way in which certain evidence and information can be obtained. A witness who has been granted immunity can no longer take the Fifth Amendment in refusing to answer, because his or her answers can no longer be used to incriminate him or her.

[a]State and federal laws sometimes contain grants of immunity. The Federal Clean Water Act of 1972 grants immunity to anyone who reports oil spills to the authorities. Until 1992, operators of small vessels that spilled oil out at sea where they might not otherwise have been discovered were granted immunity.

In 1989, the Exxon *Valdez* spilled nearly eleven million gallons of crude oil when it hit a reef in Prince William Sound, Alaska. Because the captain called the Coast Guard to report the spill within twenty minutes of the accident, he claimed immunity under the Clean Water Act. The Supreme Court of Alaska held that the immunity grant in the Clean Water Act was meant for small spills and that this oil spill was so big that the doctrine of inevitable discovery applied. In the 1993 case of *State v. Hazelwood,* 866 P.2d 827 (Alaska), the defendant's conviction of the misdemeanor charge of negligent discharge of oil was affirmed.

Mistake or Ignorance of Fact or Law as a Defense

Mistake or Ignorance of Fact[4]

A man walking out of a restaurant takes the wrong coat from the coat rack. A few minutes later, the true owner of the coat angrily complains to a police officer. The officer stops the man with the wrong coat blocks away and brings him back to the restaurant. Investigation shows that the man does have a coat similar to the coat that he walked away in. Is this a theft, or has an honest mistake of fact been made?

The common law rule is that an honest mistake or ignorance of fact is a defense if it negates the existence of a state of mind essential to the crime. Did the man take the coat with intent to deprive the owner of possession of his coat? The following cases also illustrate this rule.

Morissette v. United States

Supreme Court of the United States (1952) 342 U.S. 246, 72 S.Ct. 240

The defendant had been deer hunting in northern Michigan on government property that had been used as a bombing range and was marked "Danger—Keep Out." However, the property was used extensively for hunting by people in the area. When the defendant failed to get a deer, he decided to salvage some of the spent bomb casings that had been lying around on the property for years. In broad daylight, he hauled out three truckloads and with much work realized a profit of $84. He was charged with and convicted of knowingly stealing and converting property of the United States. The trial judge would not allow the defense that the defendant believed that the property was abandoned, unwanted, and considered of no value to the government. After the trial court ruled that "this particular offense requires no element of criminal intent," the U.S. Supreme Court reversed the conviction, pointing out that criminal liability generally requires an "evil-meaning mind (and) an evil-doing hand," and held:

> Had the jury convicted on proper instructions it would be the end of the matter. But juries are not bound by what seems inescapable logic to judges. They might have concluded that the heaps of spent casings left in the hinterland to rust away presented an appearance of unwanted and abandoned junk, and that lack of any conscious deprivation of property or intentional injury was indicated by Morissette's good character, the openness of the taking, crushing and transporting of the casings, and the candor with which it was all admitted. They might have refused to brand Morissette as a thief. Had they done so, that too would have been the end of the matter.
>
> Reversed.

Crown v. Tolson

Queen's Bench Division (1889) 23 Q.B.D. 168

After the defendant was deserted by her husband, she was informed by people she considered reliable that her husband had been lost at sea while on a ship bound from England to America. After waiting more than five years, during which time she believed herself a widow, she married again. Her first husband then reappeared, and she was charged with bigamy.

The Court held that she was not guilty of bigamy because she had believed, in good faith and on reasonable grounds, that her first husband was dead. The Court stated:

> At common law an honest and reasonable belief in the existence of circumstances, which, if true, would make the act for which a prisoner is indicted an innocent act has always been held to be a good defense.

Therefore, the question of whether the defendant made an honest mistake of fact or was ignorant of the true facts and conditions is a question that must be determined by the trier of fact, whether a jury or a judge. The accused must show that he or she was honestly mistaken and that his or her conduct was prompted by this mistake or ignorance. In the following cases, defendants who could show some basis for their defenses were entitled to present their defense to the fact finder:

- Honest belief that the property he purchased was not stolen property. *Willis v. State,* 802 S.W.2d 337 (Tex.App. 1991).

- Defendant found the hat he was charged with shoplifting, *Binnie v. State.* 1991 WL 1251 (Md.).

- Defendant was given the baby by a friend and she believed that the baby was lawfully turned over to her as a defense to a charge of kidnapping of the child, *Miller v. State.* 815 S.W.2d 582 (Tex.App. 1991).

- In cases where defendants were charged with inflicting fatal blows to victims already seriously injured, defendants argue they were forced to do so and honestly but mistakenly believed the victims were already dead. *People v. Beardslee,* 806 P.2d 1311 (Calif. 1991); and *People v. Crane,* 585 N.E.2d 99 (Ill. 1991).

- In a rape charge, a reasonable but mistaken belief that consent to sex was given. *People v. Mayberry,* 542 P.2d 1337 (Calif. 1975); and *People v. Williams,* 52 CrL 1350 (Calif. 1993).

During the 1992 Mike Tyson trial on charges of rape, conflicting testimony between the complaining witness and Mike Tyson was presented as to the events that occurred. Tyson and his attorney requested a jury instruction that Tyson made an honest mistake of fact in believing the woman consented to sex. The Court held that an honest and reasonable belief that the woman would consent to sex at some time in the future is not a defense to a charge of rape and that the honest and mistaken belief must have been present at the time of the alleged offense. Tyson's rape conviction was affirmed. *Tyson v. Indiana,* 619 N.E.2d 276 (Ind.App. 1993), review denied 114 S.Ct. 1216, 54 CrL 3185 (1994).

Strict Liability Crimes and the Defense of Mistake

When a state legislature or the Congress of the United States creates a strict liability crime, the defense of mistake of fact cannot be used, because criminal liability comes from simply doing the forbidden act without any requirement for the state or government to prove any mental fault (see Chapter 3). The following cases illustrate:

- Statutory rape in which the defendant had sex with an underage child and could not use the defense of honest but mistaken belief as to the age of the child: *Jenkins v. State,* 110 Nev. 865, 1994 WL 389178 (1994); *State v. Stiffler,* 117 Idaho 405, 1990 WL 25145 (1990); *United States v. Ransom,* 942 F.2d 775 (10th Cir. 1991); *Commonwealth v. Knap,* 592 N.E.2d 747 (Mass. 1992); *Garnett v. State,* 322 Md. 571, 632 A.2d 797 (1993).[5]

- In assaulting a federal officer, the defendant cannot use the honest but mistaken belief that he or she did not know the victim was a federal officer: *United States v. Feola,* 420 U.S. 671; 95 S.Ct. 1255 (1975); and *United States v. Goldson,* 954 F.2d 51 (2d Cir. 1992).

- In use of employment of a minor in Minnesota for nude dancing, the honest but mistaken belief as to the age of the child cannot be used: *State v. Fan,* 445 N.W.2d 243 (Minn.App. 1989); and *Minnesota v. White,* 464 N.W.2d 585 (Minn.App. 1990), review denied 502 U.S. 819, 112 S.Ct. 77 (1991).

Mistake or Ignorance of Criminal Law

The Latin maxim *Ignorantia legis neminem excusat* (Ignorance of the law excuses no one) may have caused Blackstone to change the phrase in his *Commentaries* (4 Bl. Comm. 27) to "Ignorance of the law which every one is bound to know, excuses no man." Blackstone's statement is a far better expression of the law, because courts will not allow a defendant who has committed an offense that is generally well known to the public to argue ignorance or mistake of that law. Serious offenses, such as murder, rape, robbery, and theft, are violations not only of the statutory law but also of moral and ethical laws. Courts would not consider seriously a defense of mistake or ignorance of such laws. Nor would courts ordinarily permit a person charged with a traffic violation in the state in which he or she is licensed to drive to argue ignorance of the traffic laws of that state. It is presumed that the holder of a license knows the traffic laws when the license is received or renewed.

But what of the hundreds of criminal laws that are not well known? The President's Commission on Law Enforcement and Administration of Justice reported in 1966 in *The Challenge of Crime in a Free Society* (p. 18) that the federal government alone has defined more than 2,800 crimes and has observed that the offenses that state and local governments have defined are even more numerous. The following U.S. Supreme Court cases illustrate the complexity and great numbers of laws that exist today:

Cheek v. United States
Supreme Court of the United States (1991) 498 U.S. 192, 111 S.Ct. 604

Mr. Cheek is an airline pilot who did not file federal income tax returns for six years. Cheek argued that he did not "willfully" fail to file income tax returns and that he honestly believed his failure to file returns was lawful.

Because of the complexity of the U.S. tax laws, the Supreme Court held that the "willfully" requirement of the criminal charge against Cheek could not be met if the alleged violator was honestly confused about the meaning of the law.

Other courts now view this case as an exception to the general rule that ignorance of the law is no excuse. (See the 1993 case of *Sanford v. State,* 499 N.W.2d 496, reviewing court decisions.)

Lambert v. California
Supreme Court of the United States (1957) 355 U.S. 225, 78 S.Ct. 240

The defendant was charged with and convicted of failing to register as required under a Los Angeles municipal ordinance that requires "any convicted person" who was in the city for longer than five days to register with local authorities. The defendant had been convicted of forgery and had lived in Los Angeles for longer than seven years without registering. In a 5–4 decision, the U.S. Supreme Court held that the registration provision of the ordinance violated the due process requirement of the Fourteenth Amendment.

Justice William O. Douglas for the majority stated:

The rule that "ignorance of the law will not excuse". . . is deep in our law, as is the principle that of all the powers of local government, the police power is "one of the least limitable.". . . On the other hand, due process places some limits on its exercise. Engrained in our concept of due process is the requirement of notice. Notice is sometimes essential so that the citizen has the chance to defend charges. Notice is required before property interests are disturbed, before assessments are made, before penalties are assessed. Notice is required in a myriad of situations where a penalty or forfeiture might be suffered for mere failure to act . . . .

This appellant on first becoming aware of her duty to register was given no opportunity to comply with the law and avoid its penalty, even though her default was entirely innocent. . . . Where a person did not know of the duty to register and where there was no proof of the probability of such knowledge, he may not be convicted consistently with due process. Were it otherwise, the evil would be as great as it is when the law is written too fine or in a language foreign to the community.

(Author's note: The better practice with laws or ordinances that are not generally known to the public is to notify persons of the law or ordinance and of their obligation to comply with the law or ordinance.)

Sometimes what appears to be a *mistake of law* may nonetheless provide a defense. For example, in *United States v. Smith*,[6] a government employer was charged with violating the federal Espionage Act. That act makes it a crime to reveal classified information with the intent to cause injury to the United States. The defendant revealed classified information to two individuals the defendant believed were CIA officials. The defendant claimed he believed he was authorized by law to reveal the information to CIA officials, though in fact he was not authorized to do so. The court said his defense, if believed, negated the "intent to harm the United States" element of the crime, and could be raised.

Intoxication or Drugged Condition as a Defense

Voluntary intoxication or drugged condition as a defense to the commission of criminal acts is frequently raised unsuccessfully. Crimes that require only a *general intent*, that is, only the intent to do the act, do not permit an intoxication defense. For example, in the 2001 case of *United States v. Sewell*,[7] a defendant charged with robbery attempted to defend by offering evidence that he was high on crack cocaine when he committed the robbery. The court concluded that robbery was a general intent crime and rejected the defense.

Crimes that require a **specific intent** as to one or more elements of the crime do permit a defense based on voluntary intoxication or drugged condition. To assert the intoxication defense, the defendant must be charged with a specific intent crime, such as intentional murder, kidnapping, or arson. The degree of intoxication must be so great "as to render (the defendant) incapable of purposeful or knowing conduct."[8]

Even if the intoxication defense successfully negates a specific intent, the defendant may still be convicted of a lesser offense requiring only general intent. Thus, although defendants may lack the specific intent to commit murder, they could be convicted of a lesser, general intent crime such as second-degree murder or manslaughter.[9]

A few states have eliminated the defense of voluntary intoxication entirely. The State of Montana not only did away with the defense of intoxication but also prohibited any consideration of the defense of intoxication by a fact finder (judge or jury). The Montana law was challenged before the U.S. Supreme Court in 1996. In the case of *Montana v.*

Egelhoff, the Supreme Court found that the Montana law did not violate due process protections of the U.S. Constitution.[10]

Involuntary Intoxication or Drugged Condition

Involuntary intoxication or drugged condition is a defense if the trier of fact (the jury or judge) believes the defendant's story, supported by credible evidence, that (1) he or she did not voluntarily take the drug or intoxicant and was tricked or forced into taking such substance and (2) the defendant became so intoxicated or drugged that he or she was not able to mentally form the specific intent necessary for the crime charged but was physically able to commit the crime.

Insanity or Abnormality of Mind Caused by Alcohol or Drugs

Mere addiction to drugs or alcohol does not in itself constitute insanity. However, the prolonged or excessive use of alcohol and drugs can cause insanity and such conditions as delirium tremens. The insanity rules of the jurisdiction, whether the *M'Naghten* Rule or the American Law Institute Rule, would be used to determine the defendant's plea of not guilty because of insanity. If a jury or judge found that the facts were such as to constitute temporary insanity, the defendant could be found not guilty because of insanity, but if the defendant were merely drunk or drugged, he or she should then be convicted.

In the 1978 case of *Commonwealth v. Sheehan,* the Massachusetts Supreme Judicial Court held that the "normal consequences of drug consumption" provide no basis for a claim that the defendant lacked criminal responsibility.[11] The court noted that Massachusetts differs from most states because it does not recognize voluntary drunkenness as a factor negating specific intent.

Although the standards for determining insanity can vary somewhat from state to state, jury to jury, and court to court, alcohol and drugs affect different people in different ways. Weight, physical condition, and individual factors can make a difference in the effect of the drug or alcohol. The strength and potency of drugs purchased on the street vary considerably, and simply knowing the quantity consumed is not sufficient to measure its effect.

Use of Alcohol or Drugs to Build Up Courage to Commit a Crime

If it were found that a person used alcohol or drugs to build up courage to commit a crime, the defense of intoxication could not be used successfully. In the 1963 English case of *Rex v. Gallagher,* A.C. 349 (House of Lords), Lord Denning stated:

> If a man, whilst sane and sober, forms an intention to kill . . . and then gets himself drunk so as to give himself Dutch courage to do the killing, . . . he cannot rely on this self-induced drunkenness as a defense to a charge of murder, nor even as reducing it to manslaughter. . . . The wickedness of his mind before he got drunk is enough to condemn him, coupled with the act which he intended to do and did do.

A finding that an intent to commit a crime was formed before the requisite degree of intoxication was reached would defeat the defense of voluntary or involuntary intoxication or drugged condition. If it could be shown that the defendant was a habitual user of that particular drug or type of alcohol, it could then be argued that the defendant was well aware of the effect the drug or alcohol would ordinarily have on him or her.

Duress, Coercion, or Compulsion as a Defense

In attempting to use the defense of **duress** or *coercion*, defendants must admit that they committed the offense charged but assert that they were forced to do so to avoid death or serious bodily injury to themselves or others. Defining duress and coercion in *People v. Sanders,* the Court stated:

> In order for duress or fear produced by threats or menace to be a valid, legal excuse for doing anything, which otherwise would be criminal, the act must have been done under such threats or menaces as show that the life of the person threatened or menaced was in danger, or that there was reasonable cause to believe and actual belief that there was such danger. The danger must not be one of future violence, but of present and immediate violence at the time of the commission of the forbidden act. The danger of death at some future time in the absence of danger of death at the time of the commission of the offense will not excuse. A person who aids and assists in the commission of the crime, or who commits a crime, is not relieved from criminality on account of fears excited by threats or menaces unless the danger be to life, nor unless that danger be present and immediate.[12]

A well-known case involving the defense of duress was that of Patricia Hearst. Hearst claimed that she was kidnapped, brainwashed, and then forced to participate in the robbery of a California bank.[13] The question before the California jury was whether Hearst was forced to participate in the robbery (duress and coercion) or whether she freely and willingly took part in the robbery. After listening to the many witnesses who were in the bank, and viewing the bank videotape showing Hearst pointing a submachine gun at bank customers and employees, the jury found Patty Hearst guilty of bank robbery.

Duress or Coercion as Justification to Escape from Prison

In 1977, the Supreme Court of Delaware held that "intolerable conditions" were not justification for escape from prison, because the defendants failed to give sufficient proof that such justification existed.[14] The court held that the tests used by California courts could be employed in determining justification. The California tests, established in *People v. Lovercamp,* hold that justification is available as a defense to the charge of escape from prison only when

1. the prisoner is faced with a specific threat of death, forcible sexual attack or substantial bodily injury in the immediate future,

2. there is no time for a complaint to the authorities or there exists a history of futile complaints which make any result from such complaints illusory,

3. there is no time or opportunity to resort to the courts,

4. there is no evidence of force or violence used towards prison personnel or other "innocent" persons in the escape, and

5. the prisoner immediately reports to the proper authorities when he or she has attained a position of safety from the immediate threat.[15]

In 1980, the U.S. Supreme Court ruled as follows in the escape case of *United States v. Bailey:*

> We therefore hold that, where a criminal defendant is charged with escape and claims that he is entitled to an instruction on the theory of duress or **necessity,** he must proffer evidence of a bona fide effort to surrender or return to custody as soon as the claimed duress or necessity had lost its coercive force. We have reviewed the evidence examined elaborately in the majority and dissenting opinions below, and find the case not even close, even under respondents' versions of the facts, as to whether they either surrendered or offered to surrender at their earliest possible opportunity. Since we have determined that this is an indispensable element of the defense of duress or necessity, respondents were not entitled to any instruction on such a theory. Vague and necessarily self-serving statements of defendants or witnesses as to future good intentions or ambiguous conduct simply do not support a finding of this element of the defense.[16]

The Defense of Duress in a Charge of Murder

Under the common law, the defense of duress was not available to a defendant in a murder or treason charge. Blackstone stated that the reason for this was that a man under duress "ought rather to die himself than escape by the murder of an innocent."[17] This apparently is the common law today in more than half the states and in England. About twenty states define the defense of duress by statute, and most do not allow the defense in murder cases (or sometimes in other serious crimes). In a few states, however, if a jury (or court) believes the defense of duress in a murder charge, they may reduce the charge of first-degree murder to manslaughter.[18]

The Crime of Coercion

A person who forces (coerces) another to commit a crime can be charged and convicted of the crime committed in addition to other offenses. For example, a person who forced another to commit a murder could be charged and convicted of that murder.

But what can be done regarding a situation in which a person is forced to commit an act that is not a crime? Some states have addressed this problem and have created the crime of coercion. For example, the State of New York has two degrees of coercion. Public Law 135.60 defines coercion as compelling a person to engage in conduct "which the latter has a legal right to abstain from engaging in." First-degree coercion is punished as a class D felony, whereas second-degree coercion is a class A misdemeanor.

In 1990, a former New York school board president pleaded guilty to first-degree coercion when evidence was obtained showing that he illegally pressured school administrators into giving jobs to his friends (cronyism) (*New York Times,* April 27, 1990, p. A13).

Necessity or Choice of Evils Defense[19]

A person who, because of necessity, performs an act that otherwise would constitute a crime may use the justification of necessity as a defense if the "harm or evil sought to be avoided by such conduct is greater than that sought to be prevented by the law defining the offense charged."[20]

EXAMPLE: An airplane crashes at night in an isolated area. It is very cold and rescue is not likely until daylight, so the survivors break into a summer cottage and use the food and blankets in the cottage to comfort the injured and sustain themselves until help arrives.

In the example given, the necessity of breaking into the cottage is obvious. In 1986, the Eighth Circuit Federal Court of Appeals held regarding the defense of necessity:

> A vital element of any necessity defense is the lack of a reasonable alternative to violating the law; that is, the harm to be avoided must be so imminent that, absent the defendant's criminal acts, the harm is certain to occur. *United States v. Bailey,* 444 U.S. 394, 410, 100 S.Ct. 624, 634, 62 L.Ed.2d 575 (1980). As the Tenth Circuit has emphasized: "The defense of necessity does not arise from a 'choice' of several courses of action, it is instead based on a real emergency. It can be asserted only by a defendant who was confronted with such a crisis as a personal danger, a crisis which did not permit a selection from among several solutions, some of which did not involve criminal acts. It is obviously not a defense to charges arising from a typical protest."

In the above example, the survivors would openly admit what they had done. The owner of the cottage would be assured of compensation for the damages. Law enforcement officers and the prosecutor would not consider criminal charges, and the matter would not receive further attention.

Cases in which defendants unsuccessfully used the necessity defense include the following:

- Defendant forced his way into a mobile home because he said he had to use the telephone (other telephones were available nearby), *People v. Haynes,* 223 Ill.App.3d 126, 584 N.E.2d 1041 (1991).

- A street person broke into a car because he said he had not eaten for a day, *Lightner v. State,* 843 S.W.2d 161 (Tex.App. 1992).

- Traffic violations cases: Drove while intoxicated because he believed his friend was having a heart attack, *State v. Brodie,* 529 N.W.2d 395 (Minn.App. 1995); speeding so that police car behind him could pass more easily, *State v. Messler,* 19 Conn.App. 432, 562 A.2d 1138 (1989); driving while intoxicated because driver dove into back seat and passenger had to take control, *Toops v. State,* 643 N.E.2d 387 (Ind.App. 1994); driving with suspended license because of belief that friend had overdosed on cocaine, *State v. Harr,* 81 Ohio App.3d 244, 610 N.E.2d 1049 (1992).

- Unlawful trespass on a naval installation by a protestor who claimed he was attempting to cause the dispersion of nuclear submarines from the naval base and surrounding waters. The protestor unsuccessfully argued that such deployment was the "greater evil," and that his decision to trespass the lesser evil.[21]

Can One Kill to Save Oneself?

The question of whether a person can kill to save his or her life came before courts many years ago in the following cases.

United States v. Holmes

U.S. Court of Appeals (1842) 26 Fed.Cas. 360

The defendant was a member of the crew of a ship that sank, leaving him and many others in an overcrowded lifeboat. Because the ship's mate feared that the boat would sink, he ordered the male passengers thrown overboard, leaving the women and the ship's crew. The defendant assisted in throwing sixteen of the men out of the boat to their deaths. A grand jury refused to indict him for murder, so he was charged with and convicted of manslaughter.

Rex v. Dudley and Stephens

Queen's Bench Division (1884) 14 Q.B.D. 273

The defendants and another man and a boy were shipwrecked and adrift in an open boat for eighteen days. After seven days without food or water, the defendants suggested that the men kill the boy, who was then very weak. When the other man refused, the defendants killed the boy and all the men fed on the boy's body. Four days later, they were rescued. The jury, by a special verdict, found that the men would probably have died within the four days had they not fed on the boy's body. The jury also found that the boy would probably have died before being rescued. However, the defendants were convicted of murder, with the sentence commuted to six months' imprisonment.

These two cases have been debated by judges, lawyers, and law students throughout the English-speaking world for years. Few people urge that the doctrine of necessity be expanded to full forgiveness instead of the partial forgiveness of manslaughter used in both the cases given. In commenting on the problem, former U.S. Supreme Court Justice Benjamin N. Cardozo observed: "Where two or more are overtaken by a common disaster, there is no right on the part of one to save the lives of some, by killing of another. There is no rule of human jettison."[22]

The attitude of the British courts today is probably reflected by the 1971 case of *Southwark London Borough v. Williams:*

> [T]he law regards with the deepest suspicion any remedies of self-help, and permits these remedies to be resorted to only in very special circumstances. The reason for such circumspection is clear—necessity can very easily become simply a mask for anarchy.[23]

Other Uses of the Defense of Necessity

Many different types of genuine emergencies can be justification for minor violations of the law. A man rushing a badly bleeding child to a hospital twenty miles away could, if the road conditions were good, exceed the speed limit. He would not be justified, however, in running down a pedestrian.

Arguments over whether extreme hunger justifies theft of food have to be resolved by looking at each incident separately. The man who had just spent all his money on gambling or whiskey would not be justified in stealing food. Nor would the man who broke into a fine restaurant because he did not like the food available to him at the Salvation Army or the Rescue Mission. The person who was directly responsible for creating an emergency would not be in as good a position to use the defense of necessity as would a person who had done nothing to cause the emergency.

The *New York Times* article "Trespassing to Survive: Is It Justified?" (March 6, 1990) asked if, on a bitter cold night, a homeless person would be justified in gaining access to a warm building when the windchill was below zero? This is a common problem confronting police and building managers in large cities. Should trespass charges be issued, or should other solutions be sought?

Alibi as a Criminal Defense

In using the defense of *alibi*, the defendant is asserting that he or she physically could not have committed the crime, because at the time the crime was committed, he or she was at another place.

EXAMPLE: X is charged with robbery and has been identified by two witnesses and the victim as the man who robbed a liquor store. X uses the defense of alibi and argues that it was physically impossible for him to rob the store because he was at his mother's home one hundred miles away at the time of the robbery. His mother and his wife corroborate X's story, stating that they were there also.

Because an alibi can be easily fabricated, it must be carefully investigated. Many states have statutes requiring defendants who plan to use an alibi defense to serve notice on the prosecutor before trial. These statutes are meant to safeguard against the wrongful use of alibis, as they give law enforcement agencies and prosecutors necessary notice and time to investigate the merits of the proposed alibi.

Alibi Notice Statutes

Alibi notice statutes require that defendants make disclosures regarding their cases. Such disclosure includes the place where the defendant claimed to have been at the time the crime was committed and the names and addresses of witnesses to the alibi, if known. In the 1973 case of *Wardius v. Oregon*, the U.S. Supreme Court held that when a defendant is compelled to disclose information regarding his or her case, the state must also make similar disclosures. The U.S. Supreme Court held:

> [In] the absence of a strong showing of state interests to the contrary, discovery must be a two-way street. The State may not insist that trials be run as a "search for truth" so far as defense witnesses are concerned, while maintaining "poker game" secrecy for its own witnesses. It is fundamentally unfair to require a defendant to divulge the details of his own case while at the same time subjecting him to the hazard of surprise concerning refutation of the very pieces of evidence which he disclosed to the State.[24]

Alibi notice statutes now require disclosure by prosecutors as well as defendants.

Determining the Validity of Alibi Defenses

An alibi presented to and believed by a jury constitutes a complete defense to the crime charged. Even if the alibi raises only a reasonable doubt in the mind of a jury, it becomes a good defense because the jury cannot convict if a reasonable doubt exists. If only two or three of the jurors believe the alibi, a hung jury may result. The burden is not on the defendant to show that he or she was not at the scene of the crime, but is on the state to show beyond reasonable doubt that the defendant was at the scene and did commit the crime. Charges of perjury, solicitation to commit perjury, or subornation of perjury have resulted when it has been shown that alibi witnesses testified falsely or that attempts were made to persuade people to testify falsely.

The Defense That the Defendant Was Acting Under the Authority, Direction, or Advice of Another

A person who commits an act that is obviously criminal, such as arson or murder, and then attempts to use as a defense the fact that he or she was acting under the direction of a superior officer or on the advice of an attorney or another person would ordinarily be held fully liable for such an offense. The general rule is that one who performs a criminal act under the advice, direction, or order of another cannot use such a defense.

However, because hundreds of crimes are not well known to the general public, the U.S. Supreme Court, in 1908, quoted with approval a jury instruction stating that when a person

> fully and honestly lays all the facts before his counsel, and in good faith and honestly follows such advice, relying upon it and believing it to be correct, and only intends that his acts shall be lawful, he could not be convicted of crime which involves willful and unlawful intent; even if such advice were an inaccurate construction of the law. But, on the other hand, no man can willfully and knowingly violate the law, and excuse himself from consequences thereof by pleading that he followed the advice of counsel.[25]

In the 1975 case of *Toomey v. Tolin,* the Court held that following the advice of a legal adviser was a complete defense for law enforcement officers involved in a civil suit for false arrest and malicious prosecution.[26] Other cases are:

Cox v. Louisiana
Supreme Court of the United States (1965) 379 U.S. 559, 85 S.Ct. 476

Among other charges, the defendant was convicted of demonstrating "in or near" a courthouse in violation of a Louisiana law modeled after a 1949 federal statute. The U.S. Supreme Court reversed the conviction, stating:

> The highest police officials of the city, in the presence of the Sheriff and Mayor, in effect, told the demonstrators that they could meet where they did, 101 feet from the courthouse steps, but could not meet closer to the courthouse. In effect, appellant was advised that a demonstration at the place it was held would not be one "near" the courthouse within the terms of the statute.[27]

Raley v. Ohio
Supreme Court of the United States (1959) 360 U.S. 423, 79 S.Ct. 1257

The U.S. Supreme Court held "that the Due Process Clause prevented conviction of persons for refusing to answer questions of a state investigating commission when they relied upon assurance of the commission, either express or implied, that they had a privilege under state law to refuse to answer, though in fact this privilege was not available to them." The Court stated that this "would be to sanction an indefensible sort of **entrapment** by the State—convicting a citizen for exercising a privilege which the State had clearly told him was available to him."

The Defense of "I Acted on the Orders of My Boss"

In the following highly publicized situations, defendants used the defense that "I acted on the orders of others."

- In 1972, U.S. Army Lt. William Calley Jr. was charged with the murder of twenty-two infants, children, women, and old men in the village of My Lai, Vietnam. Calley used the defense that he acted under orders of his superiors in conducting the search-and-destroy operation in the manner he did. More than four hundred Vietnamese women, children, and old men were killed in the operation. *United States v. Calley,* 48 C.M.R. 19, 22 U.S.C.M.A. 534 (1973).[28]

- Some of the high-ranking Nazi officers and officials tried for criminal offenses after World War II used the defense that they were following orders from their superiors. The Nuremberg Court, composed of judges from the Allied nations, held that this defense was not available when the orders given violated commonly accepted standards of humanity. (See Chapter 9 of this text for more material on the Nuremberg trials.)

- As a result of the Watergate burglary in 1972, criminal charges were issued. Some of the people involved argued that they acted on the authority of others. In the case of *United States v. Ehrlichman,* 546 F.2d 910 (D.C.C. 1976), Mr. Ehrlichman failed in his attempt to persuade the court to permit him to use the mistake of law defense.

The Defense of Double Jeopardy

The Fifth Amendment of the U.S. Constitution provides that "no person . . . shall . . . for the same offense . . . be twice put in jeopardy of life or limb." In the 1978 case of *United States v. Scott,* the U.S. Supreme Court, quoting other Supreme Court cases, held that the **double jeopardy** clause ensures

> that the State with all its resources and power should not be allowed to make repeated attempts to convict an individual for an alleged offense, thereby subjecting him to embarrassment, expense and ordeal and compelling him to live in a continuing state of anxiety and insecurity, as well as enhancing the possibility that even though innocent he may be found guilty.[29]

Therefore, a person who has been acquitted by a judge or a jury may not be tried again, even if subsequent investigation reveals evidence that proves conclusively that the defendant is guilty. If a defendant is found not guilty because of insanity, the person may not be tried again for the same crime even if the person is later found sane and normal.

The Times When Jeopardy Attaches

In the 1984 case of *Press-Enterprise Co. v. Superior Court of California, Riverside County,*[30] the U.S. Supreme Court pointed out that jeopardy attaches when a jury is sworn.[31] In a non-jury trial, the Court pointed out that jeopardy attaches when the first witness is sworn.[32]

Prosecution by Both State and Federal Governments

Since most crimes are crimes only against a state, only the state may prosecute. Some crimes, however, are offenses not only against the state but also the federal government. The robbery of a federally insured bank or savings and loan association is an example.

The question of whether the state and federal governments may both prosecute for such offenses has come before the U.S. Supreme Court more than a dozen times. Justice Oliver Wendell Holmes, repeating the rule that both state and federal prosecution in such cases is not in violation of the Fifth Amendment, stated that the rule "is too plain to need more than a statement."[33] The reasoning is presented in the 1959 case of *Bartkus v. Illinois* as follows:

> Every citizen of the United States is also a citizen of a State or territory. He may be said to owe allegiance to two sovereigns, and may be liable to punishment for an infraction of the laws of either. The same act may be an offense or transgression of the law of both. That either or both may (if they see fit) punish such an offender cannot be doubted. Yet it cannot be truly averted that the offender has been twice punished for the same offense; but only that by one act he has committed two offenses, for each of which he is justly punishable. He could not plead the punishment by one in bar to a conviction by the other.[34]

In *Bartkus v. Illinois,* the defendant was tried in a federal court and acquitted of robbing a federally insured bank. He was then indicted by an Illinois grand jury and convicted on substantially the same evidence used in the federal court. The Illinois court sentenced him to life imprisonment under the Illinois Habitual Criminal Statute. The U.S. Supreme Court affirmed the conviction, holding that the second trial did not violate the Fifth Amendment of the U.S. Constitution.

However, since *Bartkus v. Illinois,* many states, including Illinois, have passed legislation that forbids prosecution after another jurisdiction has prosecuted the defendant for the same crime. In such states, the law of the state, and not the double jeopardy clause, forbids prosecution after prosecution in another jurisdiction.[35]

The Meaning of Separate Offense

Double jeopardy does not bar successive prosecutions of a defendant convicted of one offense if the subsequent prosecution involves a different or separate offense. The meaning of "separate" adopted by the U.S. Supreme Court has changed over time. In early cases, the Court adopted the following "different offense" rule:

> The applicable rule is that where the same acts or transaction constitutes a violation of two distinct statutory provisions, the test to be applied to determine whether there are two offenses or only one, is whether each provision requires proof of an additional fact which the other does not.[36]

This rule prevented, among other things, prosecutions for so-called "lesser included" offenses, that is, offenses whose elements were included in the greater offense.

In 1990, in *Grady v. Corbin,* the Supreme Court modified the *Blockburger* "same element" test, and held successive prosecutions arising out of the "same conduct" were barred by the double jeopardy clause.[37] If the same conduct violated two criminal statutes, successive prosecutions were barred, even though the statutes had different elements. For example, prosecution of a defendant for driving while intoxicated would bar a later prosecution for manslaughter, because, as part of the proof on the manslaughter charge, the prosecution would prove the "same conduct," driving while intoxicated, that constituted the first offense. The *Blockburger* rule would not bar the second prosecution because the manslaughter charge had different elements, that is, recklessness and death of another.[38]

In 1993, the Supreme Court reversed *Grady v. Corbin* and the "same conduct" rule.[39] It held that the *Blockburger* "same element" test determined double jeopardy questions.

Other Times When the Defense of Double Jeopardy Could Not Be Used Successfully

The defense of double jeopardy could not be used successfully in the following situations:

When one legal action is civil and the other is a criminal action.

The O. J. Simpson case illustrates this principle of law. O. J. Simpson was acquitted of murder charges in a Los Angeles criminal case, but the families of the victims then commenced civil lawsuits against Simpson and won jury awards of more than $34 million.

When a hung jury occurs or in most cases in which a mistrial is declared before jeopardy is attached.

After two all-white juries were unable to reach verdicts (hung juries), Byron De La Beckwith, a white supremacist, was convicted in a third trial for the murder of Medgar Evers, a civil rights activist. The third murder trial was thirty-one years after the first trial, but neither federal nor state laws have a *statute of limitations* for murder.

If there is serious fraud in the first trial, a defendant has not been placed at risk, so the defendant cannot claim double jeopardy.

It was shown in the 1997 U.S. Supreme Court case of *Illinois v. Aleman,* 136 L.Ed.2d 868, that an Illinois judge accepted a $10,000 bribe to acquit Aleman of murder. In the first such case in American legal history, the second Illinois trial judge held that Aleman had never been placed in jeopardy and that "absent such risk, the claim of double jeopardy is more imagined than real."

If the prior legal action is an in rem civil forfeiture, the following criminal action is not barred (stopped) by double jeopardy.

The U.S. Supreme Court has held repeatedly that *in rem* (against a thing, a car, a house, and so on) civil forfeiture actions are neither "punishment" nor criminal for the purposes of the double jeopardy clause if Congress or the state legislative body meant such actions to be civil and not punitive in form and effect. *United States v. Ursery,* 1996 WL 340815 (1996).

Under the dual sovereignty doctrine, different governments may each file separate criminal actions for the same criminal act.

Unless a state statute forbids it, a state may charge and convict a person who has already been charged in a federal court, in another state, or in a foreign country because the dual sovereignty doctrine permits different governments to each file separate criminal actions for the same criminal act committed against sovereign governments. In the 1996 case of *United States v. Guzman,* 1996 WL 294401, Guzman violated the drug laws of both the Netherlands and the United States and could be convicted for the same criminal acts by both countries.

Res Judicata and Collateral Estoppel as Part of the Double Jeopardy Guarantee

If Smith has a lawsuit against Jones, Smith is entitled to her day in court. However, if Smith loses her case, the controversy between the two people has then been adjudicated and Smith cannot continue to commence new lawsuits based on the same issue. Should Smith commence a new lawsuit on the same issue against Jones, the lawyer for Jones could use *res judicata* (the issue has been decided) as a defense.

Collateral estoppel, an extension of the doctrine of *res judicata,* forbids retrying of factual issues that have already been determined. The doctrines of *res judicata* and collateral estoppel apply not only to civil cases, but as early as 1916 were also made applicable to criminal cases by the U.S. Supreme Court.[40] The following cases illustrate the application of *res judicata* and collateral estoppel in criminal cases.

Ashe v. Swenson

Supreme Court of the United States (1970) 397 U.S. 436, 90 S.Ct. 1189

In 1960, six men playing poker in the basement of a house were surprised and robbed by three or four masked gunmen. The defendant was arrested and charged with six counts of robbery but was first brought to trial on the charge of robbing only one of the poker players. The jury found Ashe not guilty, after being instructed that the theft of "any money" would sustain a conviction. Six weeks later, Ashe was tried for the robbery of another of the poker players and this time convicted. The appeal was from the conviction. In reversing the conviction, the U.S. Supreme Court stated:

> The question is not whether Missouri could validly charge the petitioner with six separate offenses for the robbery of the six poker players. It is not whether he could have received a total of six punishments if he had been convicted in a single trial of robbing the six victims. It is simply whether, after a jury determined by its verdict that the petitioner was not one of the robbers, the State could constitutionally (bring) him before a new jury to litigate that issue again. . . .
>
> In this case the State in its brief has frankly conceded that following the petitioner's acquittal, it treated the first trial as no more than a dry run for the second prosecution: "No doubt the prosecutor felt the state had a provable case on the first charge and, when he lost, he did what every good attorney would do—he refined his presentation in light of the turn of events at the first trial." But this is precisely what the constitutional guarantee forbids.

State v. Proulx

Supreme Court of New Hampshire (1970) 110 N.H. 187, 263 A.2d 673

The defendant was charged with incest, based on allegations that he had sexual intercourse with his daughter on four different specific days in 1967 and 1968. His entire defense was that no act of intercourse had taken place. After he was acquitted of these charges, the state then charged him with the rape of his daughter on four days different from those that figured in the first trial. The defendant argued that double jeopardy bars the second trial.

The Court held that the doctrine of collateral estoppel, not double jeopardy, barred the second prosecution:

> Collateral estoppel which is an extension of the doctrine of res judicata bars relitigation of factual issues which have already been determined and, like the doctrine of double jeopardy, is designed to eliminate the expense, vexation, waste and possible inconsistent results of duplicatory litigation.

People v. Allee

Supreme Court of Colorado (1987) 740 P.2d 1

The defendant and his son were charged with assault on a police officer following a fight in the parking lot of a tavern. The defendant's son was tried first and was found not guilty (acquitted). At the defendant's trial, the defendant used the defense of collateral estoppel against the criminal charges of assault and resisting arrest. The Supreme Court of Colorado held:

> The doctrine of collateral estoppel "means simply that when an issue of ultimate fact has once been determined by a valid and final judgment, that issue cannot again be litigated between the same parties in any future lawsuit.". . . The doctrine was first developed in the context of civil litigation in order to promote judicial economy, conserve private resources, and protect parties from the prospect of vexatious litigation.

> * * *

> We conclude that the acquittal of one defendant in a separate proceeding does not collaterally estop the People from prosecuting another defendant in a separate trial. The jury's acquittal of Ronnie Allee does not mean that the People will necessarily be unable to prove Dale Allee's guilt beyond a reasonable doubt. We see no persuasive reason to forbid the People from attempting to do so.

Entrapment, Frame-Up, and Outrageous Government Conduct as Defenses

Entrapment

The defense of entrapment was created by the U.S. Supreme Court in the 1932 case of *Sorrells v. United States.*[41] In the *Sorrells* case, the Supreme Court ruled that entrapment occurs "when the criminal design originates with the officials of the government, and they implant in the mind of an innocent person the disposition to commit the alleged offense and induce its commission in order that they (the Government) may prosecute."

The defense of entrapment has two elements: (1) improper government inducement of the crime and (2) lack of predisposition on the part of the defendant to engage in the criminal conduct.

Defendants seeking to use the defense of entrapment carry the initial burden of coming forward with evidence of both the government's improper inducement and the de-

Other Important U.S. Supreme Court Cases on Double Jeopardy

Heath v. Alabama

Supreme Court of the United States (1985) 474 U.S. 82, 106 S.Ct. 433 (1985)

Heath hired two men in Georgia to kidnap his pregnant wife from their Alabama home and kill her. The murder then took place in Georgia. Both states convicted the defendant of murder. The Supreme Court affirmed both convictions under the dual sovereignty doctrine, holding that it would be shocking to "deny a State its power to enforce its criminal laws because another State has won the race to the courthouse."

Ball v. United States

Supreme Court of the United States (1896) 163 U.S. 662, 672, 16 S.Ct. 1192

The Court held:

> It is elementary in our law that a person can be tried a second time for an offense when his prior conviction for that same offense has been set aside by his appeal.

Missouri v. Hunter

Supreme Court of the United States (1983) 459 U.S. 359, 103 S.Ct. 673

Although the double jeopardy clause forbids multiple punishments for the same offense, it does not forbid the imposition, at the same trial, of convictions and punishments for two or more offenses that are specifically intended by the legislature to carry separate punishments. In the *Hunter* case, the defendant's conviction and punishment for robbery and armed criminal action was affirmed even though the offenses constituted the same crime.

Therefore, a defendant may be charged and convicted of multiple crimes arising out of one criminal act if the state legislature intends it.

Green v. United States

Supreme Court of the United States (1957) 355 U.S. 184, 78 S.Ct. 221

The law attaches particular significance to an acquittal. To permit a second trial after an acquittal, however mistaken the acquittal may have been, would present an unacceptably high risk that the government, with its vastly superior resources, might wear down the defendant so that "even though innocent he may be found guilty."

Smalis v. Pennsylvania

Supreme Court of the United States (1986) 476 U.S. 140, 106 S.Ct. 1745

The Supreme Court held that the granting of a "demurrer was an acquittal under the Double Jeopardy Clause." A *demurrer* is a finding that as a matter of law, the prosecution's evidence is insufficient to establish the factual guilt of a defendant. Further prosecution is forbidden.

Ball v. United States

Supreme Court of the United States (1985) 105 S.Ct. 1668

When there is a double jeopardy violation, the U.S. Supreme Court ruled that the remedy is to vacate (drop) one conviction and retain the conviction with the "most serious punishment."

North Carolina v. Pearce

Supreme Court of the United States (1969) 395 U.S. 711, 89 S.Ct. 2072

The Supreme Court held:

> [T]he double jeopardy clause affords three distinct constitutional protections: (1) protection against a second prosecution for the same offense after acquittal; (2) protection against a second prosecution for the same offense after conviction; (3) protection against multiple punishments for the same offense.

Lockhart v. Nelson

Supreme Court of the United States (1988) 488 U.S. 33, 109 S.Ct. 285, 44 CrL 3031

> It has long been settled . . . that the Double Jeopardy Clause's general prohibition against successive prosecutions does not prevent the government from retrying a defendant who succeeds in getting his first conviction set aside, through direct appeal or collateral attack, because of some error in the proceedings leading to conviction.
>
> . . . This rule, which is a well-established part of our constitutional jurisprudence, . . . is necessary in order to ensure the "sound administration of justice."

The double jeopardy clause does not forbid retrial so long as the sum of the evidence, erroneously admitted or not, would have been sufficient to sustain a guilty verdict.

Single Offense or Multiple Offenses?

A defendant, seeking to kill, fires a handgun three times at the victim, missing each time. Should the defendant be charged with one count of attempted murder or three? In a "drugstore" drug case where a defendant had large and small amounts of ten different illegal substances, what criminal charges should be issued? In a sexual assault case that went on for an hour with a variety of conduct, should multiple charges be issued?

Is a prosecutor justified in issuing (or seeking) multiple criminal charges in order to obtain a guilty plea in return for dropping one or two of the charges? Victims like this practice. Court calendars are kept smaller, and it saves time.

The following U.S. Supreme Court cases illustrate rulings on whether multiple charges or a single charge are justified. The specific wording of the criminal statute and the legislative intent in your state would generally govern.

Conduct	Ruling	Case
"Whether one who, in the same transaction, tears or cuts successively mail bags of the United States used in conveyance of the mails, with intent to rob or steal any such mail, is guilty of a single offense, or of additional offenses?"	"[I]t was the intent of the lawmakers to protect each and every bag. . . . Whenever any one mail bag is thus torn, cut, or injured, the offense is complete."	*Ebeling v. Morgan,* 237 U.S. 625, 35 S.Ct. 710 (1915)
Illegal sale of ten grains of morphine on a specific day, followed by a sale of eight grains on the following day, and additional morphine at a still later date.	"[T]he first transaction resulting in a sale, had come to an end. The next sale was not the result of the original impulse, but of a fresh one—that is to say, of a new bargain."	*Blockburger v. United States,* 284 U.S. 299, 52 S.Ct. 180 (1932)
Cohabiting with more than one woman (old crime of bigamy or adultery).	"It is inherently, a continuous offense, having duration; and not an offense consisting of an isolated act."	*In re Snow,* 120 U.S. 274, 7 S.Ct. 556 (1887)

In the following cases of the 1990s, courts held that the following were multiple and separate offenses that did not violate the double jeopardy clause (one act–one crime):

- Presentation of each bad check was a separate offense. *State v. Pomper,* 620 So.2d 1098 (Fla.App. 1993).

- Separate convictions for different sex acts upon the same victim are affirmed in many cases throughout the United States.

- Defendant, who sat next to three young girls in a movie theater and masturbated, could be convicted of multiple charges arising out of the single act. *State v. Jannamon,* 169 Ariz. 435, 819 P.2d 1021 (1991), and also *Bergen v. State,* 552 So.2d 262 (Fla.App. 1989).[a]

- Burning three separate apartments in the same building were separate arson offenses. *Richardson v. State,* 326 Md. 257, 604 A.2d 483 (1992).

- Possession of three different drugs with intent to distribute were held to be three separate crimes. *State v. Jordan,* 235 N.J.Super. 517, 563 A.2d 463 (1990).

[a]However, in the 1991 case of *Hawkins v. State,* 413 S.E.2d 525, the Georgia Court of Appeals held that a lewd act witnessed by two adults was only one crime, because the adult witnesses were not victims of the crime but witnesses to the crime.

fendant's lack of predisposition to commit the alleged offense. If a defendant makes a showing of improper inducement by the government and lack of predisposition by the defendant, the burden then shifts to the government. The government must then show "readiness" on the part of the defendant and that the "defendant was poised, was likely, to engage in criminal activity."[42]

The U.S. Supreme Court ruled in the 1988 case of *Mathews v. United States*[43] that a defendant "is entitled to an entrapment instruction (to a jury) whenever there is sufficient evidence from which a reasonable jury could find entrapment."

Inducements That Are Not Entrapment

Courts throughout the United States have long recognized that law enforcement officers (or their agents) can properly create ordinary opportunities for a person to commit an offense if the criminal intent or willingness originated in the mind of the defendant. The fact that the officer afforded the opportunity or the facility for the defendant to commit the crime in order to obtain evidence does not constitute entrapment. For example, a mere offer to purchase narcotics or other contraband without further inducement is not entrapment.

A sting operation is not improper inducement to commit a crime if it merely provides an opportunity to commit a crime. But proof of such a sting plus additional conduct by police may amount to sufficient evidence to meet a defendant's burden. Courts have found that police threats, forceful solicitation and dogged insistence, and repeated suggestions by police were sufficient to raise the defense of entrapment to present to a judge or jury.

Inducements That Are Improper and Constitute Entrapment

Although law enforcement officers may create and present the usual and ordinary opportunities for a person to commit a crime, they may not use excessive urging, inducement, temptations, or solicitations to commit a crime. The 1932 *Sorrells* case and the 1958 *Sherman* case illustrate misconduct by people representing the government. The Supreme Court quoted another court as follows in the *Sorrells* case:

> It is well settled that decoys may be used to entrap criminals, and to present opportunity to one intending or willing to commit crime. But decoys are not permissible to ensnare the innocent and law-abiding into the commission of crime. When the criminal design originates, not with the accused, but is conceived in the mind of the government officers, and the accused is by persuasion, deceitful representation, or inducement lured into the commission of a criminal act, the government is estopped by sound public policy from prosecution therefore.

States Are Free to Write Their Own Rules for Entrapment

The U.S. Supreme Court has held that the defense of entrapment is not of constitutional dimension. Therefore, the U.S. Congress and state legislative bodies may "adopt any substantive definition of the defense that [they] may desire."[44]

Some states have enacted statutes that define entrapment. Most states, however, use common law definitions created by their courts as the entrapment rules to be used within that state.

Most states and the federal courts use the "origin-of-intent" test in determining whether the defendant was predisposed to commit the crime charged. The test seeks to determine whether the defendant had the willingness and readiness to commit the crime and did the police or a government agent only provide what appeared to be a favorable opportunity.

FBI Guidelines on Entrapment

In the April 1993 issue of the *FBI Law Enforcement Bulletin,* the following guidelines were presented in the article "Undercover Investigations and the Entrapment Defense":

To ensure that undercover investigations do not give rise to successful claims of entrapment or related defenses, all law enforcement officers should consider the following three points before conducting undercover investigations. First, while reasonable suspicion is not legally necessary to initiate an undercover investigation, officers should nonetheless be prepared to articulate a legitimate law enforcement purpose for beginning such an investigation. Second, law enforcement officers should, to the extent possible, avoid using persistent or coercive techniques, and instead, merely create an opportunity or provide the facilities for the target to commit a crime. Third, officers should document and be prepared to articulate the factors demonstrating a defendant was disposed to commit the criminal act prior to Government contact.

Such factors include a prior arrest record, evidence of prior criminal activity, a defendant's familiarity with the terminology surrounding a particular criminal venture, and a defendant's eagerness to engage in the criminal activity. The most convincing evidence of predisposition will typically occur during the initial Government contacts, which officers should carefully document to successfully defeat the entrapment defense.

Determining Whether Police Have "Cast Their Nets in Permissible Waters"

The question of whether the police have cast their nets in permissible waters was raised in the *Sherman* case (Justice Frankfurter asking this question). The answer in that case and also in the *Sorrells* case was no. The police were held to be using excessive inducements to tempt otherwise innocent people. The question of whether the police were fishing in "permissible waters" was also raised in the following 1985 Florida case:

Cruz v. State

Supreme Court of Florida (1985) 465 So.2d 516, review denied 473 U.S. 905, 105 S.Ct. 3527

Police set up a "drunken bum decoy" in which an undercover police officer pretended to be drunk and smelled of alcohol. As the officer leaned against a building near an alleyway, $150 in currency could be seen sticking out of his rear pants pocket. Cruz came by with a woman, may have said something to the "bum," and continued down the street. Ten minutes later, Cruz came back and took the money without harming the decoy. Cruz was then arrested and convicted of grand theft.

The Supreme Court of Florida quashed (threw out) Cruz's conviction and established a two-part test to be used in the State of Florida. The Court held:

The decoy situation did not involve the same modus operandi as any of the unsolved crimes that had occurred in the area. Police were not seeking a particular individual, nor were they aware of any prior criminal acts by the defendant.

* * *

[T]he police activity . . . constituted entrapment as a matter of law under the threshold test adopted here.

In a similar Nevada drunken bum decoy case, the Supreme Court of Nevada also ruled that the defendant was entrapped. To target a specific person in Nevada, law enforcement officers must have reasonable suspicion to believe the person is predisposed to commit the crime. (See *Washoe County Sheriff v. Hawkins,* 43 CrL 2053 (1988); and *Shrader v. State,* 38 CrL 2069, 1985.)

Denying the Criminal Act While at the Same Time Using the Defense of Entrapment
Until 1988, most states would not permit defendants to plead innocence, while at the same time use an affirmative defense such as entrapment. The "innocent" plea generally means "I didn't commit the crime," whereas in the entrapment defense, the defendant is pleading "I wouldn't have committed the crime if it had not been for the improper conduct of the police."

In the 1988 case of *Mathews v. United States,*[45] the U.S. Supreme Court pointed out that such inconsistent defenses have historically been permitted in federal prosecutions. But because it is not a constitutional issue, the Supreme Court held that it is up to each state to determine whether inconsistent defenses would be permitted.

In response to the *Mathews* decision, many states now permit inconsistent defenses (such as entrapment and denying the criminal act), while other states continue to require that criminal defenses be consistent.

Frame-Up as Distinguished from Entrapment

Entrapment permits a defense based on unacceptable government persuasion even though the defendant admittedly chose to commit the crime. Frame-up is a related defense and arises when the government itself does the acts amounting to the crime and attributes those acts to the defendant. Frame-up differs from entrapment in that defendants deny they took the actions attributed to them by the government.

One must distinguish a frame-up from nongovernment entrapment. For example, assume a jilted lover wishes to exact revenge from her boyfriend by persuading him to commit a burglary. She tells the police about the crime, and they arrest the boyfriend in the act. Although the boyfriend was set up, he was not framed by the police, nor did the police entrap the defendant. He can be convicted for the burglary.

Other frame-up cases include the following:

■ A kilogram of cocaine was found in the defendant's truck, and at his trial, the defendant alleged that a police officer planted the cocaine in the truck. In affirming the defendant's conviction, the Court stated it was clear that the defendant's trial strategy was to put the police officer on trial and that such "a strategy is often used and sometimes successful." *United States v. McNatt,* 931 F.2d 251 (4th Cir., 1991).

■ The defendant was charged with carrying a concealed weapon and alleged that a police officer "planted" the gun on him when he was stopped and searched by the police. The court permitted the defendant to raise the frame-up defense. *Moore v. United States,* 468 A.2d 1342 (D.C. App. 1983).

Outrageous Government Conduct

A defendant who cannot claim entrapment may still be able to invoke the defense of *outrageous government conduct.* The U.S. Supreme Court first raised the concept of outrageous

The Five U.S. Supreme Court Cases Defining Entrapment

Sorrells v. United States

Supreme Court of the United States (1932) 287 U.S. 435, 53 S.Ct. 210

This is the first entrapment case to appear before the Supreme Court. A federal prohibition officer passed himself off as a tourist and became acquainted with Sorrells. After talking about the same army division they were in, the officer repeatedly asked the defendant to get him some illegal liquor. When Sorrells did, he was arrested and convicted. The Supreme Court reversed the conviction, holding:

> [T]he Government cannot be permitted to contend that [a defendant] is guilty of a crime where government officials are the instigators of his conduct." *Id.* at 452.

Sherman v. United States

Supreme Court of the United States (1958) 356 U.S. 369, 78 S.Ct. 819

A government informant and the defendant met in a doctor's office where they were both being treated for narcotics addiction. After several accidental meetings, the informant asked the defendant for a source of narcotics, stating that he was not responding to treatments. The defendant tried to avoid the issue, but the informant continued to ask for narcotics, stating that he was suffering. In holding that the informant "not only enticed the defendant into carrying out an illegal sale but also to returning to the habit of use" and that this was entrapment, the Court reversed the conviction of the defendant.

United States v. Russell

Supreme Court of the United States (1973) 411 U.S. 423, 93 S.Ct. 1637

An undercover narcotics agent worked his way into a group manufacturing the illegal drug speed by offering to supply them with an essential ingredient that was difficult to obtain but necessary. After seeing the drug lab, the undercover agent was told the defendants had been producing the illegal drug for seven months. After the agent supplied the essential ingredient, the agent received half of the finished batch of speed in payment. A month later, another batch of speed was made, and the agent obtained a search warrant. Defendant Russell's sole defense was en-

trapment. In holding that the participation of the narcotics agent was not entrapment, the Supreme Court stated:

> The illicit manufacture of drugs is not a sporadic, isolated criminal incident, but a continuing, though illegal, business enterprise. In order to obtain convictions for illegally manufacturing drugs, the gathering of evidence of past unlawful conduct frequently proves to be an all but impossible task. Thus in drug-related offenses law enforcement personnel have turned to one of the only practicable means of detection: the infiltration of drug rings and a limited participation in their unlawful present practices. Such infiltration is a recognized and permissible means of apprehension; if that be so, then the supply of some item of value that the drug ring requires must, as a general rule, also be permissible. For an agent will not be taken into the confidence of the illegal entrepreneurs unless he has something of value to offer them. Law enforcement tactics such as this can hardly be said to violate "fundamental fairness" or be "shocking to the universal sense of justice."

Hampton v. United States

Supreme Court of the United States (1976) 425 U.S. 484, 96 S.Ct. 1646

An informer arranged two separate unlawful heroin sales by the defendant to undercover law enforcement officers. A government witness testified at the trial that the defendant supplied the heroin, but the defendant testified that he received the heroin that he sold to the agents from the informer. The defendant also claimed that he believed the substance to be a "non-narcotic counterfeit drug which would give the same reaction as heroin." The defendant requested that the jury be instructed that he be found not guilty if they found that the informer, acting as a government agent, supplied the heroin. However, the trial court would not give the instruction, and the jury convicted the defendant despite his claims. On appeal to the U.S. Supreme Court, the defendant argued that the jury instruction should have been given, because when the government itself supplies narcotics, the defendant is a victim of illegal government entrapment. In affirming the defendant's conviction, the Court held that a successful entrapment defense re-

The Five U.S. Supreme Court Cases Defining Entrapment *continued*

quired that the defendant not have the criminal intention until implanted by the government agent.

Jacobson v. United States

Supreme Court of the United States (1992) 112 S.Ct. 1535

A 56-year-old Nebraska farmer with no criminal record legally ordered two magazines entitled *Bare Boys I and II* from a California adult bookstore. When the law changed three months later, an elaborate federal sting operation began to have the farmer order child pornography through the U.S. mail.

For two-and-a-half years, postal inspectors, posing as private organizations such as the American Hedonist Society, the Far Eastern Trading Co., and others, repeatedly contacted the farmer. Jacobson finally ordered through the mail a magazine called *Boys Who Love Boys,* which was in violation of the newly enacted Federal Child Protection Act of 1984.

The U.S. Supreme Court reversed Jacobson's conviction, holding that entrapment occurs "when the Government quest for convictions leads to the apprehension of an otherwise law abiding citizen who, if left to his own devices, likely would have never run afoul of the law."

The Court held that to convict, the government must show "readiness"—that "the defendant was poised, was likely, to engage in criminal activity."

police conduct in the 1973 case of *United States v. Russell* (presented in this chapter), in which the Court stated:

> [W]e may some day be presented with a situation in which the conduct of law enforcement agents is so outrageous that due process principles would absolutely bar the government from invoking judicial processes to obtain a conviction. . . . *Id.* at 431-32, 93 S.Ct. at 1642-43.

In the 1976 case of *Hampton v. United States,* Justice Powell stated that "police overinvolvement in crime would have to reach a demonstrable level of outrageousness before it could bar conviction."[46]

Outrageous Government Conduct That Violated the Due Process Rights of Defendants

The following conduct was held to fall within the *shock-the-conscience* or *outrageous conduct* exception so as to cause dismissal of the criminal charge:

- Using a defendant's attorney to gather information against him was held to violate not only due process but also the defendant's Sixth Amendment right to an attorney. *United States v. Marshank,* 50 CrL 1205 (N.D.Cal. 1991).

- False statements by law enforcement officers as to lineups in a murder case were held to be "outrageous conduct," but because the government case was strong, the charges were not dismissed. *People v. Montgomery,* 1994 WL 642376 (N.Y.A.D. 1994).

- Manufacture of crack cocaine by the police for use in a reverse sting[47] operation caused dismissal of charges by the Supreme Court of Florida. *Metcalf v. State,* 635 So.2d 11 (Fla. 1994).

- For two-and-a-half years, government agents supplied many materials and showed defendants how to manufacture illegal alcohol, which the agents said they would buy. *Greene v. United States,* 454 F.2d 783 (9th Cir. 1971).

- Intense and extensive police involvement in the manufacture of illegal drugs. *Commonwealth v. Mathews*, 347 Pa.Super. 320, 500 A.2d 853 (1985), and *United States v. Twigg*, 588 F.2d 373 (3rd Cir. 1978).

Police Conduct Held Not to Be Outrageous Government Conduct

In the following cases, courts have held that the conduct was not outrageous conduct:

- In the case of *United States v. Russell*, the U.S. Supreme Court held that supplying a necessary ingredient to an illegal drug lab manufacturing "speed" and also supplying a buyer for the finished product were not outrageous government conduct.

- A civilian working with a police department had sex with a woman to obtain evidence necessary to convict her of prostitution. The Supreme Court of Hawaii affirmed the conviction, holding that it was not outrageous conduct but it was not the "ethical standards which law enforcement officials should be guided by." *State v. Tookes*, 699 P. 2d 983 (1985).

- Using a defendant's former girlfriend and paying her living expenses while she assisted in building a criminal case against the defendant were held not to be outrageous conduct. *United States v. Miller*, 891 F.2d 1265 (7th Cir. 1989).

- Because underage decoys were used to determine whether merchants were selling alcoholic beverages to minors, claims of entrapment and outrageous conduct were made by defendants charged with such violations. The California Supreme Court held that sellers could not escape liability because of the mature-looking decoys and that neither of the defenses could stand. *Provigo Corp. v. Alcoholic Beverage Control Appeals Board*, 1994 WL 115921 (Cal. 1994).

The Right to a Speedy Trial as a Defense

The Sixth Amendment of the U.S. Constitution provides that "in all criminal prosecutions, the accused shall enjoy the right to a speedy and public trial."[48] Most defendants charged with a serious crime do not ordinarily wish either a speedy or a public trial, but unless the right to a speedy trial is waived with the consent of the trial court, the constitutional mandate of a speedy trial must be complied with.

The *four-factor balancing test* used to determine whether a speedy trial violation has occurred was established by the U.S. Supreme Court in the 1972 case of *Barker v. Wingo*.[49] The factors that are weighed are (1) the length of the delay, (2) the reason for the delay, (3) the defendant's assertion of his or her right, and (4) the prejudice resulting from the delay.

In holding that the right to a speedy trial commences when a person "is indicted, arrested, or otherwise officially accused," the U.S. Supreme Court held in *United States v. Marion* that:

> The protection of the Amendment is activated only when a criminal prosecution has begun and extends only to those persons who have been "accused" in the course of that prosecution. These provisions would seem to afford no protection to those not yet accused, nor would they seem to require the Government to discover, investigate, and accuse any person within any particular period of time.[50]

The Court stated that the purpose and "interests served by the Speedy Trial Clause" are as follows:

> Inordinate delay between an arrest, indictment, and trial may impair a defendant's ability to present an effective defense. But the major evils protected against by the speedy trial guarantee exist quite apart from actual or possible prejudice to an accused's defense. To legally arrest and detain, the Government must assert probable cause to believe the arrestee has committed a crime. Arrest is a public act that may seriously interfere with the defendant's liberty, whether he is free on bail or not, and that may disrupt his employment, drain his financial resources, curtail his associations, subject him to public obloquy, and create anxiety in him, his family and his friends.[51]

Cases Where No Speedy Trial Violation Occurred

The U.S. Constitution does not identify a specific number of days necessary to satisfy the speedy trial requirement. Therefore, the federal government and states have enacted statutes establishing their own standards. For example, the federal government requires that a person indicted for a felony be tried within seventy days unless the defendant waived his or her right to a speedy trial. Failure to try the person within that time could cause dismissal of the criminal charge if it were shown that the delay prejudiced the defendant under the *Barker v. Wingo* factors.

Because of the danger that a defendant charged with a serious crime might walk free because of a speedy trial violation, great attention is given to time on the speedy trial calendar. If necessary, civil trial or retired judges are brought in to try criminal cases that must be tried because of the speedy trial requirement. The following are a few speedy trial cases that received national attention:

- After a U.S. Army investigation of three murders, charges against a medical doctor were dropped. The doctor left the Army and practiced medicine for five years until he was indicted for the murders and convicted by a federal jury. In holding that no speedy trial violation occurred, the U.S. Supreme Court held:

  > Once the charges instituted by the Army were dismissed, MacDonald was legally and constitutionally in the same posture as though no charges had been made. He was free to go about his affairs, to practice his profession, and to continue with his life. *United States v. MacDonald*, 456 U.S. 1 (1982).

- After a thirteen-year delay, new evidence was obtained against a man who had been charged with felony murder and released after a preliminary hearing found that insufficient evidence existed at that time. The man was then charged and convicted. The Supreme Court of Georgia held that during the thirteen years, the defendant was free to go about his business, and affirmed the murder conviction. *Wooten v. State*, 426 S. E. 2d 852 (1993).

- As mentioned earlier, Byron De La Beckwith was tried twice for the 1964 murder of the civil rights leader, Medgar Evers. Both trials before all-white juries ended up with hung juries. In 1994, Beckwith was tried for the third time and was convicted. It was held that no violation of speedy trial had occurred. *State v. Beckwith*, 707 So.2d 547 (1997).

Stings and Scam Operations

The U.S. Supreme Court observed in *United States v. Sorrells* that American "courts have uniformly held that in waging (war against crime), . . . traps, decoys and deception (may be used) to obtain evidence of the commission of crime." 53 S.Ct. 210. Generally, law enforcement agencies receive information on illegal activities before they conduct one of the following types of stings or scams:

- "Storefront stings" in an effort to recover property taken in thefts, burglaries, shoplifting and robberies and to apprehend persons dealing in stolen property. Offenders bring stolen property to such fronts to exchange the property for money or drugs.

- "Open air drug dealing" set up on a street, in an alley, or shopping mall generally in areas known for drug dealing. See *State v. J.D.W.,* 56 CrL 1542 (1995), in which the Supreme Court of Utah affirmed proceedings against a juvenile who purchased marijuana from the police.

- Tavern, grocery store, and liquor store stings are conducted to determine whether food stamp laws are violated, liquor and cigarettes are being sold to minors, and whether stolen merchandise is being exchanged or other laws violated.

- Money laundering stings to determine whether automobile dealers, real estate brokers, financial institutions or other businesspeople are violating money laundering laws.

- "Hot car stings" in attempts to recover some of the more than a million cars stolen every year in the United States.

- Federal stings to determine whether local, state, or federal employees are accepting illegal bribes or favors.

- "Fugitive felon scams" used to apprehend some of the thousands of fugitive felons wanted on arrest warrants. Messages are sent out by letters and telephone calls that the wanted person has won a free trip or tickets to a game or has an income tax refund waiting or other prize. Such scams are sometimes very successful in causing many wanted persons to show up for their prize and instead are arrested.

- Because illegal drug trafficking offers quick and easy large amounts of illegal money, many sting operations have been run to apprehend law enforcement officers involved in illegal activities.

- Medicare and other insurance stings in the health field or false accident claims from phony automobile accidents.

Two Sting Operations Receiving National Attention

Operation Abscam
Abscam began as an FBI attempt in 1983 to catch art thieves. FBI agents dressed as Arab sheiks and let it be known that they would spend big money for stolen art items. However, U.S. Congresspeople walked into the net attracted by the money. Videos were made of the Congresspeople accepting bribes. Seven members of the U.S. Congress, including one senator, were indicted and convicted for a series of offenses.

Operation Greylord[a]
Because of information that for "the right price, bagmen can fix the outcome of court cases in Chicago ranging from theft to divorce to traffic violations to murder,"[b] a massive Abscam-type probe was commenced. The purpose was to uncover crooked attorneys, judges, and court personnel. With the assistance of a judge from southern Illinois, convictions of sixty-nine people, including twelve sitting or former judges, were obtained through 1988.

[a]"Greylord" is a reference to the wigs worn by British judges.
[b]Statement by Illinois Judge Lockwood, who worked with the FBI to uncover corrupt lawyers and judges.

Speedy Trial, Double Jeopardy, and Statutes of Limitation as Defenses

Double jeopardy and the requirement of a speedy trial are both mandated by the U.S. Constitution and must be complied with.

Speedy trial	As the U.S. Constitution does not specify the time period in which a defendant must be tried, federal law and the law of each state establishes this time period. Defendants, however, often waive their right to a speedy trial. This is done in open court and most often in writing signed by the defendant and the defense lawyer
Double jeopardy	A criminal defendant cannot be retried if jeopardy has attached to the crime with which the defendant has been charged. The U.S. Supreme Court has held that jeopardy attaches when a jury is sworn and, in a nonjury case, when the first witness is sworn.
Statutes of limitation	are not required by the U.S. Constitution and are optional state legislative enactments. The states of South Carolina and Wyoming have no criminal statutes of limitation.[a]

[a]"The Statute of Limitations in Criminal Law," 102 U.Pa.L.Rev. 630.

The Statute of Limitations as a Defense

The old English common law adopted the doctrine that "no lapse bars the King"; therefore, statutes limiting the time for criminal prosecutions are rare in England.

However, criminal statutes of limitations appeared in America as early as 1652. The federal government adopted time limits for the prosecution of most federal crimes in 1790, and the majority of the states have enacted statutes of limitations for most crimes.

The speedy trial requirements are constitutional mandates and therefore are imposed on all states. Statutes of limitations on criminal prosecutions are optional legislative enactments. Reasons given for limitations on criminal prosecutions are as follows:

A limitation statute is designed to protect individuals from having to defend themselves against charges when the basic facts may have become obscured by the passage of time and to minimize the danger of official punishment because of acts in the far-distant past.[52]

* * *

The Speedy Trial Clause and the limitations statutes work in tandem to prevent pretrial delay: the statutory period insures against pre-accusation delays and the Sixth Amendment controls the post-indictment time span. . . . Both provisions shield defendants from endless anxiety about possible prosecution and from impairment of the ability to mount a defense. By encouraging speedy prosecution, they also afford society protection from unincarcerated offenders, and insure against a diminution of

Other Defenses and Defensive Tactics

"Blame the victim" defense In rape, assault, and battery cases, defense lawyers sometimes seek to blame the victim. The defense is also sometimes used in murder cases, because the victim is not available to appear as a witness to present his or her story. In his 1994 book *The Abuse Excuse,* defense lawyer Alan Dershowitz lists fifty-three abuse excuses and points out that the Menendez brothers, who admitted killing their wealthy parents, obtained a hung jury by accusing their parents of sexually abusing them. Lorena Bobbitt was acquitted of cutting off her husband's penis by blaming her husband for sexually abusing her.

Other "blame the victim" tactics are as follows: Would a decent woman dress like that? She didn't wear a bra. (Rape) Why didn't you lock your windows? (Burglary) What were you doing alone in that part of town? (Mugging or assault) Why did you leave valuables in plain view on the seat of your car? (Theft from vehicle)

Defense of selective prosecution In traffic court, defendants sometimes argue that other cars were going faster than they were. The U.S. Supreme Court has held that to prevail in the defense of selective enforcement, a defendant must show that he or she has been singled out from others and that "it must be shown that 'the selection was deliberately based upon an unjustifiable standard such as race, religion, or other arbitrary classification,'" *Oyler v. Boles,* 82 S.Ct. at 506 (1962).

Someone else committed the crime as a defense This defense can be used if the defendant "can present evidence that directly connects a third party to the crime with which the defendant has been charged. . . . It is not enough to show that another had the motive to commit the crime . . . nor is it enough to raise a bare suspicion that some other person may have committed the crime." Supreme Court of Connecticut in the 1992 case of *State v. Hernandez,* 618 A.2d 494.

No personal gain and no profit defense In showing that the defendant did not personally benefit or profit from the crime, defendants sometimes argue that the offense was done to benefit another person or the community. This defense is also called the "Robin Hood" defense if it is used as a variation of "rob the rich and give to the poor." This defense is rarely successful and is used primarily as a plea for a light sentence.

Misidentification as a defense The defendant could acknowledge that a crime was committed but argue that the state has accused the wrong person. *Misidentification* as a defense differs from a corpus delicti defense, in which a defendant argues that no crime has been committed. The corpus delicti defense is used often in acquaintance rape cases in which the defendant argues that the woman consented to sex and therefore no crime has been committed. (See Chapter 18.)

The "groupie" defense Male celebrities, who attract female fans, sometimes use the "groupie" defense to rape charges. Not only will they emphasize clothing the victim wore ("sleazy" pants, midriff blouses, miniskirts), but also they will "blame the victim."

Truth as a defense Truth can always be used as a defense to criminal or civil charges. In 1986, a San Diego man used truth as a defense to criminal tax fraud charges. He admitted in court to receiving $400,000 in unreported income from drug dealing. The jury believed his statements that he got out of the narcotics business in 1976 because of his fears of being caught. The defendant was acquitted because the five-year statute of limitations had run.

Patriotism as a defense Patriotism has always been used as a defense. It was used by Lt. Col. Oliver L. North, who stated, "Everything I did was done in the best interests of the United States of America." Not only do prosecutors have great amounts of discretion, but juries can, and do, acquit defendants in disregard of instructions given them. As mentioned earlier, during the Vietnam War, Lt. William Calley Jr. was convicted of offenses relating to the My Lai massacre. He was originally sentenced to life in prison at hard labor. This was cut to twenty years, then to ten years, and eventually he served three years of house arrest.

The alcohol defense Some people call blaming the booze the equivalent of the insanity plea. A defendant who gets into trouble blames a drinking problem and agrees to a treatment program.

Using news conferences and talk shows as defensive tactics Defense lawyers seek to help their clients with statements that the charges against their clients are utter nonsense.

the deterrent value of immediate convictions, as well as the reduced capacity of the government to prove its case.[53]

Statutes of limitations generally permit a longer period for the prosecution of felonies than for the prosecution of misdemeanors. No time limit is generally placed on prosecution for murder. As discovery of some theft offenses could occur years after the theft, extensions of time are generally given based on the time of discovery of the offense. The running of time under a criminal statute of limitation could be halted by

- issuance of an arrest warrant or summons, an indictment, filing of information, or the commencement of prosecution

- statute requirement that the person must be a public resident of that state for the time to toll

- acts by the suspect to avoid or to frustrate legal proceedings against him or her

SUMMARY

This chapter presents the many defenses that are used in defending persons charged with crimes. Many of these defenses are affirmative defenses that the Supreme Court of Florida defined as "any defense that assumes the complaint or charges to be correct but raises other facts that, if true, would establish a valid excuse . . ."

Mistake of fact, duress or coercion, and necessity all depend upon proof that the defendant acted reasonably under the facts as he or she reasonably believed them, or was forced by circumstances or another to commit the crime, or had no real choice but to commit the crime, given other unacceptable alternatives. If successful, these defenses excuse or justify the criminal acts.

Intoxication or drugged condition rarely provide a complete defense to criminal acts. Acts requiring only general intent are not excused under these defenses, though the defenses may negate any specific intent as an element of an offense.

Entrapment, frame-up, and outrageous government conduct are defenses that not so much justify the criminal act as punish the government for acting in a manner unacceptable to our society. In a related way, double jeopardy exists to prevent the government from unfairly harassing its citizens.

 **BOOK-SPECIFIC WEB SITE**

For chapter-related Web links, quizzing activities, and case and news updates, go to the *Criminal Law,* Eighth Edition, book-specific Web site at **http://info.wadsworth.com/ gardner.**

QUESTIONS AND PROBLEMS

1. A friend of yours, C, received a speeding ticket for doing sixty in a 30-mph zone. The only defense that C has is that the officer was in an unmarked vehicle. Can C successfully argue entrapment, frame-up, or outrageous government conduct? Explain.

2. N.S., a juvenile, was charged with rape in the third degree. The prosecution was commenced within the three-year statute of limitations for rape in the third degree. The prosecution was unable to prove penetration, an essential element of rape; however, the trial court convicted N.S. of attempted rape, a lesser included offense of rape. Attempted rape has a two-year statute of limitations, which period had expired before prosecution commenced on the rape charge. Was the conviction of N.S. proper? See *State v. N.S.,* 991 P.2d 133 (Wash. App. 2000).

3. Police officers responded to a fight in a parking lot outside a restaurant where a wedding reception had just occurred. Six police officers arrived to stop the fight and to control the crowd gathered around the fight. One of the participants in the fight resisted arrest, and physical force had to be used to restrain him. Fogarty had been at the wedding reception and was in the crowd of bystanders but had not participated in the fight.

   Fogarty objected loudly to the force the police were using to restrain his friend who had been in the fight, and a police officer told Fogarty to leave the area. When Fogarty did not leave, the officer, who

had a nightstick in his hand, again told him to get in his truck "and get out of here or you're going [to the police station] too." Fogarty got in the truck, put it in reverse, and backed into a parked police car. Fogarty was arrested and charged with DWI (driving while under the influence). A test revealed a 0.12 blood alcohol level.

   Fogarty was convicted of drunk driving in the lower court and appealed his conviction to the Supreme Court of New Jersey, arguing entrapment and also that he was coerced (duress) into driving the vehicle by the police officer. Should either or both of his defenses apply? Or would any other defense be available to Fogarty? *State v. Fogarty,* 607 A.2d 624 (1992).

4. A salesperson, Herbert North, arrived at the Seattle airport and stopped to make a telephone call. At the telephone, North found a wallet with $10 inside but no identification. North put the $10 in his pocket and, after finishing his telephone call, walked toward the airport parking lot. North was arrested at the front door of the airport, handcuffed, and held in jail until the next day. North was one of the twenty people who had been caught in a police sting operation designed to curtail theft at the airport. In this sting operation, did the police "cast their nets in permissible waters"? *North v. Port of Seattle,* Circuit Court, King County (Wash. 1983).

INFOTRAC COLLEGE EDITION EXERCISES

1. Go to InfoTrac College Edition and use the subject search term *double jeopardy;* click on "periodical references" and find the July 1998 article on the Fourth Circuit's opinion on the consequences of payment of "tax penalties for failure to report income from sales of illegal drugs on subsequent prosecutions for violation of federal antidrug laws."

2. Go to InfoTrac College Edition and, using the keyword search term *entrapment,* find the 2000 article "Editorial Entrapment" on a newspaper's cooperation in a police sting operation. Is it ethical for the news-

paper to cooperate with the police by publishing false information designed to trick a suspect into revealing his or her identity? What public or social policies are relevant to that ethical question?

3. Go to InfoTrac College Edition and, using the keyword search term *coercion,* find the 2001 review of a recent book written by Thornhill and Palmer titled *A Natural History of Rape* on the biological bases for sexual coercion. What are the authors' theses? Do you agree? What do the authors suggest as a method or strategy to prevent sexual coercion?

NOTES

1. 596 So.2d 687 (Fla.App. 1992).

2. 717 F. Supp. 309 (E.D.Pa. 1989).

3. *U.S. v. Gonzalez De Modesti,* 145 F. Supp.2d 771 (D.P.R. 2001).

4. The fact that a law enforcement officer made an honest mistake as to an important fact in making an arrest would not necessarily invalidate the arrest. In the 1971 U.S. Supreme Court case of *Hill v. California,* 401 U.S. 797, 91 S.Ct. 1106, police made an "honest mistake" in arresting the wrong man. In the 1980 case of *United States v. Allen,* 629 F.2d 51, 27 CrL 2307 (D.C.Cir.), the appellate court held that "the case law establishes that an arrest based on actual assumptions later found erroneous may be valid if there is adequate basis in the record to determine the reasonableness of the officer's conduct in making the arrest."

The U.S. Supreme Court heard another honest mistake case in 1987. In the case of *Maryland v. Garrison,* 480 U.S. 79, 107 S.Ct. 1013, police officers obtained a search warrant for a search on the third floor of a building, believing that there was only one apartment on that floor. Before they discovered that there were two apartments on that floor, police found heroin and drug paraphernalia in the apartment of another man (Garrison). The Supreme Court held that the evidence was lawfully obtained, adding another case to what is known as the honest mistake exception.

The following three examples are found in the New York Criminal Code Annotated Practice Commentary to Section 15.20, Effect of Ignorance or Mistake Upon Liability.

- A police officer having a warrant for the arrest of A mistakenly arrests B, who resembles A, and holds him in a police station for an hour before ascertaining his mistake and releasing him. The officer is not guilty of "unlawful imprisonment" (Section 135.05) because his mistake of fact "negatives a culpable mental state necessary for the commission of the offense," namely, "knowledge that the restriction is unlawful" (Section 135.00(1)).

- M has sexual intercourse with F, a mentally ill woman whose condition is not always apparent and is not known to or realized by M. Although M would be guilty of third degree rape if he had realized F's condition, . . . his unawareness thereof is, by statute, expressly made a defense to the charge (Section 130.10).

- During a heated argument between A and B, B, a man with a reputation for violence and rumored to carry a pistol on occasion, suddenly places his hand in his bulging pocket, and A strikes him in the face, breaking his nose. Although B did not have a pistol and was merely reaching for a cigarette, A is not guilty of assault . . . because his factual mistake was of a kind that supports a defense of justification (Section 35.15 (1)).

5. In the case of *Garnett v. State,* the Maryland Court pointed out in 1993 that seventeen states have laws that permit a mistake of age defense in some form in cases of sexual offenses with underage children. 632 A.2d at 802.

6. 592 F. Supp. 424 (E.D. Va. 1984).

7. 252 F.3d 647 (2d Cir. 2001).

8. *State v. Cameron,* 514 A.2d 1302 (1986).

9. State v. Souza, 72 Haw. 246, 813 P.2d 1384 (1991).

10. 116 S.Ct. 2013, 59 CrL 2153 (1996).

11. 376 Mass. 765, 383, N.E.2d 1115 (1978).

12. 82 Cal.App. 778, 785, 256 P. 251, 254 (1927).

13. The Hearst family is a wealthy and prominent California family. The kidnapping of their college-age daughter received a great amount of national attention. Patricia Hearst was not seen or heard of until the bank robbery, when she was recognized as one of the robbers. In 1988, a movie about Patty Hearst was produced and released.

14. *Johnson v. State,* 379 A.2d 1129 (Del. 1977).

15. 43 Cal.App.3d 823, 118 Cal.Rptr. 110 (1974).

16. 444 U.S. 394, 100 S.Ct. 624 (1980).

17. Blackstone, *Commentaries,* iv, 30.

18. See Wisconsin Statute 939.46.

19. In the 1980 case of *United States v. Bailey,* 444 U.S. 394, 100 S.Ct. 624, the U.S. Supreme Court pointed out the distinctions between the defenses of duress and ne-

cessity as follows: "Common law historically distinguished between the defenses of duress and necessity. Duress was said to excuse criminal conduct where the actor was under an unlawful threat of imminent death or serious bodily injury, which threat caused the actor to engage in conduct violating the literal terms of the criminal law. While the defense of duress covered the situation where the coercion had its source in the actions of other human beings, the defense of necessity, or choice of evils, traditionally covered the situation where physical forces beyond the actor's control rendered illegal conduct the lesser of two evils. Thus, where A destroyed a dike because B threatened to kill him if he did not, A would argue that he acted under duress, whereas if A destroyed the dike in order to protect more valuable property from flooding, A could claim a defense of necessity. See generally LaFave & Scott, *Criminal Law, 2d ed.* (Belmont, Calif.: West/Wadsworth, 1986), pp. 374–384.

20. Model Penal Code, § 3.02 (Justification Generally).

21. *U.S. v. Maxwell*, 254 F.3d 21 (1st Cir. 2001). Protestors violating criminal law frequently argue that the law they are protesting is the "greater evil." Examples of such unsuccessful claims are *Cyr v. State*, 887 S.W.2d 203 (Tex. App. 1994) (abortion); *Troen v. Oregon*, 501 U.S. 1232 (1991) (nuclear power plants); *State v. Marley,* 509 P.2d 1095 (Haw. 1973) (the Vietnam War). One court in *United States v. Schoon,* 955 F.2d 1238 (9th Cir. 1991), has held that necessity can never be a defense in so-called "indirect civil disobedience" cases. These are cases in which the law violated is not the law being protested. The "greater harm" is thus not caused by the law violated but some other law or governmental policy. Direct civil disobedience, where the defense of necessity might be available, occurs when the protestors violate the very law they are protesting. For example, if a law required citizens to use lead paint in painting their houses, the harm caused by lead paint would likely exceed the harm caused by violating the law.

22. *Selected Writings of Justice Cardozo*, 390.

23. 2 All E.R. at p. 181 (1971).

24. 412 U.S. 470, 93 S.Ct. 2208 (1973).

25. *Williamson v. U.S.,* 207 U.S. 425, 453, 28 S.Ct. 163, 173 (1908).

26. 311 So.2d 678 (Fla.App. 1975).

27. The defense lawyer missed the boat on this case. He or she could have also had the statute declared invalid as being "void for vagueness." Everybody has to guess about what is meant by "near." Modern statutes now forbid demonstrations "in" a courthouse or within two hundred or three hundred feet of a courthouse. Such statutes do not violate "void for vagueness" (see Chapter 1).

28. In affirming Lt. Calley's criminal convictions, the Military Court of Appeals held:

[There is] ample evidence from which to find that Calley directed and personally participated in the intentional killing of men, women and children who were unarmed and in the custody of soldiers. . . . [T]he uncontradicted evidence is that . . . they were offering no resistance. In his testimony, Calley admitted he was aware of the requirement that prisoners be treated with respect. . . . [H]e knew that the normal practice was to interrogate villagers, release those who could satisfactorily account for themselves and evacuate the suspect among them for further examination. . . .

29. 437 U.S. 82, 98 S.Ct. 2187 (1978).

30. 464 U.S. 501, 104 S.Ct. 819, 34 CrL 3019 (1984).

31. *Downum v. U.S.,* 372 U.S. 734, 83 S.Ct. 1033 (1963).

32. *Wade v. Hunter,* 336 U.S. 684, 69 S.Ct. 834 (1949).

33. *Westfall v. U.S.,* 274 U.S. 256, 47 S.Ct. 629 (1927).

34. 359 U.S. 121, 79 S.Ct. 676 (1959).

35. In 1993, the United States prosecuted several Los Angeles police officers for civil rights violations arising out of a beating they gave Rodney King. In a previous, very controversial state prosecution, the same officers were acquitted of state criminal charges. Two of the officers, Koon and Powell, were convicted, and two were acquitted. The double jeopardy clause did not prevent those convictions because of the dual sovereignty rule.

The famous videotape of the King beating, which showed that beating in great detail, was extensively used by the federal court in its sentencing decision. See

U.S. v. Koon, 833 F.Supp. 769 (C.D. Cal. 1993). Koon and Powell were sentenced to thirty months in prison, based on various sentencing guidelines which indicated a downward departure from the eighty- to eighty-seven-month sentence guidelines for their convictions. The Ninth Circuit Court of Appeals reversed the downward departure made by the federal district court (see 34 F.3d 1416), but the U.S. Supreme Court essentially restored the original sentences. See Koon v. United States, 518 U.S. 81 (1996).

36. *Blockburger v. United States*, 284 U.S. 299, 304 (1932). Thus, a prosecution for auto theft barred prosecution for the lesser offense of joyriding, and vice versa. *Brown v. Ohio*, 432 U.S. 161 (1977).

37. *Grady v. Corbin*, 495 U.S. 508 (1990).

38. *Id.*

39. *United States v. Dixon*, 509 U.S. 688 (1993).

40. See *United States v. Oppenheimer*, 242 U.S. 85, 37 S.Ct. 68 (1916).

41. 287 U.S. 435, 454, 53 S.Ct. 210, 217 (1932), separate opinion.

42. *Jacobson v. United States*, 503 U.S. 540 (1992).

43. *Mathews v. United States*, 485 U.S. 58 (1988).

44. *U.S. v. Russell*, 411 U.S. 423 (1973).

45. 485 U.S. 58, 108 S.Ct. 883 (1988). Examples of inconsistent defenses that were permitted when the evidence justified it are:

- In an 1896 murder case arising out of a gunfight in Indian Territory, the defense of self-defense was used along with an instruction on manslaughter. Killing in the heat of passion is inconsistent with self-defense. *Stevenson v. United States*, 162 U.S. 313, 16 S.Ct. 839 (1896).

- In a 1970 rape case, the defendant was permitted to argue that the act did not take place and that

the victim consented. *Johnson v. United States*, 426 F.2d 651 (D.C.Cir. 1970), cert. granted 400 U.S. 864, 91 S.Ct. 107 (1970).

46. 425 U.S. at 495 n. 7.

47. A reverse buy or reverse sting scheme is one in which the government sells or attempts to sell an illegal drug rather than buy it. Because this conduct by the police could cause defense lawyers to use the entrapment or outrageous government conduct defenses, great caution should be used by law enforcement officers.

In the 1992 case of *State v. James*, 484 N.W.2d 799, an undercover officer was standing in an area known for high drug activity and "sold" crack only to persons who approached him. Eight such locations were used in Minneapolis to discourage buyers who came into high drug activity areas to buy drugs. The Minnesota Court of Appeals affirmed the defendant's conviction, pointing out that the state carried the burden of showing predisposition by the defendant and that the officer did not solicit or encourage the defendant in any way. See also the case of *United States v. Cea*, 963 F.2d 1027 (7th Cir. 1992).

48. The Federal Speedy Trial Act, 18 U.S.C.A. 3161, sets a seventy-day limit, which begins to run with the date of indictment. Sec. 3161(c)(1). See *Henderson v. United States*, 476 U.S. 321, 106 S.Ct. 1871 (1986).

49. 407 U.S. 514 (1972).

50. 404 U.S. 307, 92 S.Ct. 455 (1971).

51. *Id.* at 320, 92 S.Ct. at 463.

52. See *Toussie v. U.S.*, 397 U.S. 112, 114–115, 90 S.Ct. 858, 859–60 (1970).

53. *United States v. Levine*, 658 F.2d 113 (3d Cir. 1981).

8

Criminal Punishment

CONTENTS

KEY TERMS

benefit of clergy

sanctuary

cruel and unusual
punishment

proportionality

corporal punishment

capital punishment

procedural due process

substantive due process

aggravating
circumstances

mitigating circumstances

forfeiture

recidivist

three strikes law

Punishments Used in Early England

The criminal punishments used hundreds of years ago in England and Europe were very severe. In England alone, more than two hundred offenses were punishable by death. Condemned criminals were usually hanged, although occasionally they were beheaded, quartered, or drawn (dragged along the ground by the tail of a horse). Burning continued until 1790 to be the punishment inflicted on women for treason, high or petty (which later included not only the murder by a wife of her husband and the murder of a master or mistress by a servant, but also several offenses against the king). In practice, women were strangled before they were burned; this however, depended on the executioner. In one notorious case, a woman was actually burned alive for murdering her husband, the executioner being afraid to strangle her because he was caught by the fire.[1]

For lesser offenses, various forms of mutilations, such as cropping (clipping of the ears), blinding, amputation of the hand, and branding, were common. The whipping post and the pillory were often used, as were fines and imprisonment. The pillory is a frame erected on a post. The offender's head and hands are placed in the open holes, and the top board is then moved into place, immobilizing the offender in a standing position.

Practices Used in England to Avoid Severe Penalties

Probably because of the severity of penalties, England developed procedures to avoid severe penalties. By usage and custom, the following came into practice:

Benefit of Clergy [2]

In the twelfth century, a controversy arose about whether priests accused of felonies should be tried by the royal courts or the ecclesiastical courts. It was decided that the royal courts could try priests but could not put them to death for the first felony conviction. This privilege was known as the *benefit of clergy,* and by the end of the Middle Ages, it was extended to all laypeople who could read.

The test to determine which laypeople could claim the privilege of benefit of clergy was their ability to recite the first verse of Psalm 51: "Have mercy upon me, O God, after Thy great goodness." This came to be known as the "neck verse" because it saved the accused from hanging. The only punishment that could then be inflicted was imprisonment for one year and having an "M" branded on the brawn of the left thumb to prevent claiming of the privilege again. For many years, only three crimes were excluded from benefit of clergy (high treason, highway robbery, and the willful burning of a house), but in 1769, Blackstone noted that "among the variety of actions which men are daily liable to commit no less than 160 have been declared by Act of Parliament to be felonies without benefit of clergy."[3]

The Law of Sanctuary and the Right of Asylum

Sanctuary was common in the Middle Ages. The place of sanctuary was generally a church or some other religious place. Criminals who were permitted to take refuge in a church or monastery could not be removed from it. A system developed in England in which the refugee would take an oath of abjuration before a coroner, admit his or her guilt, and swear to leave the country for life to an agreed-upon place (often the American colonies or Australia).

Sanctuary was abolished in England in 1623; however, a modified form reportedly continued in England for another century.[4] Sanctuary never became part of the legal system of the American colonies nor of the newly formed United States of America.

The United States, however, recognizes and grants a right of asylum to refugees from other countries when a "well-founded fear of persecution" can be shown.[5] Over the last fifty years, the United States has granted asylum to thousands of refugees under various refugee acts of the federal government. Two famous refugee cases illustrate this practice:

1. After the Soviet invasion of Hungary in 1956, the United States gave asylum to Joszef Cardinal Mindszenty in the American embassy in Budapest for fifteen years until the Soviets permitted the cardinal to leave Hungary.

2. In 1989, the U.S. embassy in Beijing, China, sheltered for months China's most prominent dissident, Fang Lizhi, and his wife, until China permitted them to leave China.

Unlike the United States, Latin American countries have a long tradition of granting political sanctuary to people within their countries. The *New York Times* (December 26, 1989) quoted Otto Reich, a former American ambassador to Venezuela, who explained this tradition as follows: "Politics had been so unstable in Latin America that all politicians have feared they'd have to use the right of asylum, so they all allowed their political enemies to use it."

General Manuel Noriega requested asylum in the Vatican's embassy in Panama City in 1989. Asylum was granted in keeping with the Catholic Church's long tradition. Weeks later, Noriega became fearful that mobs of Panamanian citizens would storm the Papal Nunciature (as the Vatican embassy is called). General Noriega walked out of the Vatican embassy of his own free will and surrendered to U.S. troops.

Transportation

People convicted of crimes in England could be pardoned if they agreed to be transported to a colony to do hard labor for a number of years. The first convicts were sent abroad to America in 1655. By the time of the American Revolution, some two thousand convicts a year were being sent overseas.

After the American Revolution, Australia became the principal place to which prisoners were sent under the condition of the pardon. Over the years, approximately one hundred thousand prisoners were sent to America and an equal number sent to Australia.[6] Australia and other British colonies objected strongly to the practice of transporting convicts, which was gradually abolished between 1853 and 1864. Imprisonment in England and hard labor on public works were then substituted as punishment.[7]

Punishment Used in Early America

Blackstone points out that English criminal law and punishments, before the American Revolution, were fairly civilized when compared with those of the rest of Europe. U.S. Supreme Court Justice Thurgood Marshall made the following observations in comparing **capital punishment** in the American colonies with its use in England:

Capital punishment was not as common a penalty in the American Colonies. "The Capitall Lawes of New-England," dating from 1636, were drawn by the Massachusetts Bay Colony and are the first written expression of capital offenses known to exist in this country. These laws make the following crimes capital offenses: idolatry, witchcraft, blasphemy, murder, assault in sudden anger, sodomy, buggery, adultery, statutory rape, rape, man stealing, perjury in a capital trial, and rebellion. Each crime is accompanied by a reference to the Old Testament to indicate its source. It is not known with any certainty exactly when, or even if, these laws were enacted as drafted; and, if so, just how vigorously these laws were enforced. We do know that the other Colonies had a variety of laws that spanned the spectrum of severity.

By the 18th century, the list of crimes became much less theocratic and much more secular. In the average colony, there were 12 capital crimes. This was far fewer than existed in England, and part of the reason was that there was a scarcity of labor in the Colonies.[8]

The Constitutional Limitation on Punishment

The Eighth Amendment of the U.S. Constitution, ratified in 1791 as part of the Bill of Rights, provides that "excessive bail shall not be required, nor excessive fines imposed, nor cruel and unusual punishments inflicted." Two members of Congress opposed passage of this amendment. One stated, "What is meant by the term excessive bail? Who are to be the judges? What is understood by excessive fines? It lies with the court to determine. No *cruel and unusual punishment* is to be inflicted; it is sometimes necessary to hang a man, villains often deserve whipping, and perhaps having their ears cut off; but are we in the future to be prevented from inflicting these punishments because they are cruel? If a more lenient mode of correcting vice and deterring others from the commission of it could be invented, it would be very prudent in the Legislature to adopt it; but until we have some security that this will be done, we ought not be restrained from making necessary laws by any declaration of this kind."[9]

Justice William J. Brennan stated in 1972 that "the Cruel and Unusual Punishments Clause, like the other great clauses of the Constitution, is not susceptible of precise definition. Yet we know that the values and ideals it embodies are basic to our scheme of government. And we know also that the Clause imposes upon this Court the duty, when the issue is properly presented, to determine the constitutional validity of a challenged punishment, whatever that punishment may be."[10]

The Proportionality Test for Determining Appropriate Punishment

In the 1984 case of *Pulley v. Harris,* the U.S. Supreme Court defined the manner of evaluating the appropriateness of a punishment for a particular crime:

Traditionally, *proportionality* has been used with reference to an abstract evaluation of the appropriateness of a sentence for a particular crime. Looking to the gravity of the offense and the severity of the penalty, to sentences imposed for other crimes,

U.S. Supreme Court Cases Stating the Constitutional Limitations on Punishment

Coker v. Georgia

Supreme Court of the United States (1977) 433 U.S. 584, 97 S.Ct. 2861

The defendant escaped from a Georgia prison where he had been serving sentences for murder, rape, kidnapping, and aggravated assault. While committing an armed robbery and another offense, he raped an adult woman. The defendant was convicted of rape, armed robbery, and other offenses and was sentenced to death on the rape charge. The U.S. Supreme Court reversed the sentence of death, holding:

> That question, with respect to rape of an adult woman, is now before us. We have concluded that a sentence of death is grossly disproportionate and excessive punishment for the crime of rape and is therefore forbidden by the Eighth Amendment as cruel and unusual punishment.

State of Louisiana ex rel. Francis v. Resweber

Supreme Court of the United States (1947) 329 U.S. 459, 67 S.Ct. 374

Because of an accidental failure of equipment, the defendant was not executed in the first attempt. The Court held that there was no intention to inflict unnecessary pain, and even though the defendant had been subjected to a current of electricity, this did not prevent the state from executing him in the second attempt. In the 1972 case of *Furman v. Georgia,* the U.S. Supreme Court stated that "had the failure been intentional, however, the punishment would have been, like torture, so degrading and indecent as to amount to a refusal to accord the criminal human status."

Robinson v. California

Supreme Court of the United States (1962) 370 U.S. 660, 82 S.Ct. 1417

California enacted a law making narcotics addiction in itself a crime. The defendant received a ninety-day sentence for being a narcotics addict. The Court held that a state may not punish a person for being "mentally ill, or a leper, or . . . afflicted with a venereal dis-

ease" or for being addicted to narcotics. "Even one day in prison would be a cruel and unusual punishment for the 'crime' of having a common cold."

Wilkerson v. Utah

Supreme Court of the United States (1878) 99 U.S. 130, 25 L.Ed. 345

In this case, the Court upheld death by shooting on the grounds that it was a common method of execution in the 1870s.

Roberts v. Louisiana

Supreme Court of the United (1977) 431 U.S. 633, 97 S.Ct. 1993

The Supreme Court held that the fact that the murder victim was a police officer performing his regular duties may be regarded as an aggravating circumstance. The Court held that there is a special interest in affording protection to those public servants who regularly risk their lives in order to safeguard other persons and property. However, a Louisiana statute that provided for a mandatory sentence of death for the crime of first-degree murder of a police officer and that did not allow consideration for particularized mitigating factors was held unconstitutional. The Supreme Court held that such a statute invites "jurors to disregard their oaths and choose a verdict for a lesser offense whenever they feel the death penalty is inappropriate."

Woodson v. North Carolina

Supreme Court of the United States (1976) 428 U.S. 280, 96 S.Ct. 2978

In holding a North Carolina death penalty statute unconstitutional because it provided for an automatic death penalty in all first-degree murder cases, the Court held that "the Eighth Amendment draws much of its meaning from 'the evolving standards of decency that mark the progress of a maturing society.'" The Court concluded that North Carolina's mandatory death penalty statute varied "markedly from contemporary standards."

and to sentencing practices in other jurisdictions, this Court has occasionally struck down punishments as inherently disproportionate, and therefore cruel and unusual, when imposed for a particular crime or category of crime. See, e.g., *Solem v. Helm,* 463 U.S. 277 (1983); *Enmund v. Florida,* 458 U.S. 782 (1982); *Coker v. Georgia,* 433 U.S. 584 (1977). The death penalty is not in all cases a disproportionate penalty in this sense.[11]

Corporal Punishment

Corporal Punishment as Criminal Punishment

Corporal punishment was used as criminal punishment in the early history of the United States. Mutilations, such as cutting off ears and various types of branding, were discontinued many decades ago. Whipping, however, continued in some states into the early 1900s. The Eighth Circuit Court of Appeals observed that in 1968 only two states permitted the use of the strap as punishment. As a result of the Eighth Circuit Court's decision in the 1968 case of *Jackson v. Bishop,* whipping as a form of punishment was discontinued in the remaining two states. In the *Jackson* case, the Court held:

> We have no difficulty in reaching the conclusion that the use of the strap in the penitentiaries of Arkansas is punishment which, in this last third of the 20th century, runs afoul of the Eighth Amendment; that the strap's use, irrespective of any precautionary conditions which may be imposed, offends contemporary concepts of decency and human dignity and precepts of civilization which we profess to possess; and that it also violates those standards of good conscience and fundamental fairness enunciated by this court in the *Carey* and *Lee* cases.[12]

The Use of Corporal Punishment in Schools

In the 1977 case of *Ingraham v. Wright,* the U.S. Supreme Court considered the relationship between the cruel and unusual punishment clause and the use of corporal punishment in public schools. The Court first observed that there existed no general rule prohibiting corporal punishment in schools: "The prevalent rule in this country today privileges such force as a teacher or administrator 'reasonably' believes to be necessary for [the child's] proper control, training or education."[13]

In holding that the Eighth Amendment cruel and unusual punishment clause is not applicable to the use of corporal punishment for disciplinary purposes in the public schools, the Court held:

> The schoolchild has little need for the protection of the Eighth Amendment. Though attendance may not always be voluntary, the public school remains an open institution. Except perhaps when very young, the child is not physically restrained from leaving school during school hours; and at the end of the school day, the child is invariably free to return home. Even while at school, the child brings with him the support of family and friends and is rarely apart from teachers and other pupils who may witness and protest any instances of mistreatment.

> The openness of the public school and its supervision by the community afford significant safeguards against the kinds of abuses from which the Eighth Amendment protects the prisoner. In virtually every community where corporal punishment is permitted in the schools, these safeguards are reinforced by the legal constraints of the common law. Public school teachers and administrators are privileged at common law to inflict only such corporal punishment as is reasonably necessary for the proper education and discipline of the child; any punishment going beyond the privilege may result in both civil and criminal liability. . . . As long as the schools are open to public scrutiny, there is no reason to believe that the common law constraints will not effectively remedy and deter excesses such as those alleged in this case.
>
> We conclude that when public school teachers or administrators impose disciplinary corporal punishment, the Eighth Amendment is inapplicable.

Ingraham continues to be the law today. However, some lower federal courts have interpreted the decision as applying only to Eighth Amendment cruel and unusual punishment claims. Other claims based upon Fourteenth Amendment procedural and substantive due process may be possible, these courts hold.

Procedural due process claims under the Fourteenth Amendment are based on the absence of fair procedures regulating state conduct. For example, if a school district permitted corporal punishment without a prior determination of some violation of school rules by the student, the student's procedural due process rights would be violated.[14] Moreover, even if the school had fair procedures regulating such punishment, procedural due process could be violated if the state had no adequate means for a student to seek redress from a school or teacher that violated those procedures.[15]

Substantive due process claims under the 14th Amendment are based on state conduct that is so brutal, demeaning, and harmful as to shock the conscience.[16] Almost all the federal courts of appeal have concluded that excessive corporal punishment by a school official can give rise to a Fourteenth Amendment substantive due process claim.[17]

An example of a substantive due process claim can be found in *Neal v. Fulton County Board of Education,* a 2000 decision of the Federal Eleventh Circuit Court of Appeals. In *Neal,* a student was seriously injured when the varsity football coach struck him in the eye with a metal weight lock as punishment for fighting with another student. The court concluded that the coach intentionally used an excessive amount of force that presented a reasonably foreseeable risk of serious bodily injury.[18]

In *Garcia v. Miera,* the Federal Tenth Circuit Court of Appeals summarized the law concerning school punishments:

> We thus envision three categories of corporal punishment. Punishments that do not exceed the traditional common law standard of reasonableness are not actionable; punishments that exceed the common law standard without adequate state remedies violate procedural due process rights; and finally, punishments that are so grossly excessive as to be shocking to the conscience violate substantive due process rights, without regard to the adequacy of state remedies.[19]

The Use of Corporal Punishment in Prisons

The use of corporal punishment against inmates of prisons is subject to Eighth Amendment cruel and unusual punishment claims. Unlike school students, prison inmates have none of the "community and legal constraints" that provide safeguards against the sort of abuses the Eighth Amendment prohibits.[20]

Eighth Amendment claims by prison inmates have both an objective and subjective requirement. The inmate must show that the punishment failed the Eighth Amendment's proportionality test (the objective test) and also that the official administering the punishment possessed the requisite mental intent (the subjective test).[21] An example of such a punishment can be found in *Austin v. Hopper,* 15 F. Supp. 1210 (M.D. Ala. 1998).

In *Austin,* an Alabama prison inmate was chained to a "hitching post" for several hours as punishment for violation of a prison regulation. He was denied food and water, and was not permitted to use a bathroom. The federal court held that his punishment constituted cruel and unusual punishment. It was excessive and not necessary to enforce the prison regulation and thus failed the objective, proportionality test. Also, the official administering the punishment did so with "deliberate indifference to the inmate's health and safety," thus failing the subjective, mental intent test.[22]

Capital Punishment

The death penalty was widely accepted at the time the U.S. Constitution and the Bill of Rights were ratified. The only reference to capital punishment in the Constitution is found in the Fifth Amendment, which reads: "No person shall be held to answer for a capital, or otherwise infamous crime, unless . . . "

In the 1972 case of *Furman v. Georgia,* the death penalty laws in all the states using the death penalty were struck down as "arbitrary and capricious" by the U.S. Supreme Court.[23] The Court required all states wishing to use the death penalty to adhere to the following requirements:

- The issue of whether the death penalty will be used in the state must be submitted to the people of the state in a referendum.

- If a substantial majority of the voters approve the use of the death penalty, the state legislature must enact laws permitting the use of the death penalty.

- The new state statute must determine which crime (or crimes) could be punished by the death penalty, whether it will be the trial judge or jury who will make the decision to impose it, in what method it will be inflicted, and the appellate process used to review the sentence.

- The new statute must require that juries or judges considering the death penalty make findings of statutory *aggravating circumstances* to justify the imposition of the death penalty and also make findings of the *mitigating circumstances* that existed that would weigh against the imposition of the death penalty.

Death Penalty Laws After *Furman v. Georgia* in 1972

The 1972 case of *Furman v. Georgia* invalidated death penalty statutes in forty-one states as well as federal crimes for which the death penalty could be imposed. In 1984, the U.S. Supreme Court observed that

In responding to (*Furman v. Georgia*), roughly two-thirds of the States promptly redrafted their capital sentencing statutes in an effort to limit jury discretion and

After spending sixteen years on death row, Anthony Porter was released and embraces his mother in Chicago. His murder conviction and death sentence was overturned in 1999 after another man confessed to the murder. Attention had been focused on the case by Northwestern University students who concluded that Porter was not guilty.
AP/Wide World Photos

avoid arbitrary and inconsistent results. All of the new statutes provide for automatic appeal of death sentences. Most, such as Georgia's, require the reviewing court, to some extent at least, to determine whether, considering both the crime and the defendant, the sentence is disproportionate to that imposed in similar cases. Not every State has adopted such a procedure. In some States, such as Florida, the appellate court performs proportionality review despite the absence of a statutory requirement; in others, such as California and Texas, it does not.[24]

In 1976, the U.S. Supreme Court reviewed the new death penalty statutes of Georgia,[25] Florida,[26] and Texas.[27] In the 1984 California death penalty case of *Pulley v. Harris*,[28] the U.S. Supreme Court quoted from its 1976 *Jurek v. Texas* decision in affirming the death penalty procedure used by California:

Texas' capital sentencing procedures, like those of Georgia and Florida, do not violate the Eighth and Fourteenth Amendments. By narrowing its definition of capital murder, Texas has essentially said that there must be at least one statutory aggravating circumstance in a first-degree murder case before a death sentence may even be considered. By authorizing the defense to bring before the jury at the separate sentencing

Death Penalty for Juveniles and the Mentally Retarded

The young age of one convicted of a capital crime such as murder can be an issue in death penalty cases. Defense counsel will contend that young people lack the ability to understand the true nature of their actions, and thus cannot possess the malicious mental state necessary for the death penalty. The U.S. Supreme Court has not stated any absolute rule on this issue but has held the death penalty appropriate when given to defendants 16 or 17 years old when they committed the crime.[a] The young age of a defendant is always relevant as a mitigating factor in imposing the death penalty.

The U.S. Supreme Court has held that there is no absolute prohibition under the Eighth Amendment against executing the mentally retarded.[b] Like the young age of the defendant, mental retardation is relevant as a mitigating factor. The Court has recently required courts to carefully instruct sentencing juries on the effect of mental retardation of the defendant and its relationship to the jury's decision to impose the death penalty.[c] The Court has frequently held that the Eighth Amendment prohibits the execution of a prisoner who is insane.[d] However, if the prisoner regains sanity, he or she may then be executed.

In early 2002, the U.S. Supreme Court heard arguments in the case of *Atkins v. Virginia,* 122 S.Ct. 29 (2001), which involved imposition of the death penalty on a mentally retarded defendant. The Court granted review of the sentence expressly to consider whether imposition of the death penalty to mentally retarded individuals violates the Eighth Amendment. At the oral arguments the Court seemed most interested in whether or not society generally was moving in a direction against application of the death penalty to mentally retarded defendants. In Eighth Amendment cases the concept of "cruel and unusual" has a strong tie to prevailing public sentiment. Opponents of the death penalty noted a growing number of states that permit capital punishment, prohibit its application to mentally retarded defendants. Proponents responded that a majority of states using the death penalty don't prohibit its application to mentally retarded defendants. The Court's decision should be announced in the Fall of 2002.

[a] *Wilkins v. Missouri,* 492 U.S. 361 (1989).
[b] *Penry v. Lynaugh,* 492 U.S. 302 (1989). In *McCarver v. North Carolina,* 462 S.E.2d 25 (N.C. 1995), a defendant with an IQ of around 70 was convicted of murder and sentenced to death. The U.S. Supreme Court stayed his execution and granted his petition for certiorari in March of 2001. The question the Court agreed to hear was whether the Eighth Amendment prohibits sentencing a mentally impaired defendant to the death sentence. However, on September 25, 2001, the Supreme Court dismissed the certiorari petition as "improvidently granted." *McCarver v. North Carolina,* 122 S. Ct. 22 (2001). At the date of this writing, McCarver had not been executed.
[c] *Penry v. Johnson,* 532 U.S. 782 (2001).
[d] *Ford v. Wainwright,* 477 U.S. 399 (1986).

hearing whatever mitigating circumstances relating to the individual defendant can be adduced, Texas has ensured that the sentencing jury will have adequate guidance to enable it to perform its sentencing function. By providing prompt judicial review of the jury's decision in a court with statewide jurisdiction, Texas has provided a means to promote the evenhanded, rational, and consistent imposition of death sentences under law. Because this system serves to assure that sentences of death will not be "wantonly" or "freakishly" imposed, it does not violate the Constitution.

Aggravating and Mitigating Factors in the Oklahoma City Bombing Case of Timothy McVeigh

Before sentencing Timothy McVeigh to death in 1997, federal jurors had to consider aggravating factors, any one of which could have served as grounds for the death penalty.

Federal Crimes for Which the Death Penalty Can Now Be Applied

When President Clinton signed the 1994 Violent Crime Control and Law Enforcement Act, the number of federal crimes for which the death penalty could be applied increased significantly. The following is the 1994 list of federal death penalty crimes:

Assassination of the president, vice president, member of Congress, cabinet member, or Supreme Court Justice

Drug trafficking of large amount of drugs

First-degree murder on federal land or property

Genocide

Gun murders during federal crimes of violence and during drug trafficking crimes

Killing a person in a federal witness protection program

Killing (or attempted murder) by a drug kingpin of a public officer or a juror to obstruct justice

Murder at a U.S. international airport

Murder by a federal prisoner or escaped prisoner who is (or was) serving a life sentence

Murder for hire (when federal crime)

Murder in aid of racketeering activity (federal)

Murder in federal facility involving a firearm

Murder of federal witness, victim, or informant

Murder of state correctional officer by inmate

Murder of U.S. citizen abroad by another U.S. citizen

Murder of court officer or juror

Murder of federal law enforcement official

Murder of foreign official or internationally protected person on U.S. soil

Murder of state or local official assisting federal law officers

Murder within special maritime and territorial jurisdiction of United States

Treason and espionage

Where death results:

aircraft hijacking (domestic or international)

alien smuggling

carjacking (federal)

destroying federal property with explosives

destruction of aircraft, motor vehicles, or their facilities (federal)

drive-by shooting (federal)

hostage taking (federal)

kidnapping (federal)

mailing injurious articles (such as explosives)

robbery of a federally insured bank

sexual abuse (federal)

sexual exploitation of children (federal)

torture (federal)

train sabotage (federal)

transporting explosives with intent to kill

use of weapons of mass destruction (poison gas or biological, and so on)

violating federally protected rights based on race, religion, or national origin

Mitigating factors, presented by McVeigh's defense lawyers, also had to be considered by the jury in determining whether McVeigh should live.

Aggravating and mitigating factors presented to the McVeigh jury were:

Aggravating Factors Presented by the Government	Mitigating Factors Presented by the Defense Team
The offenses resulted in the deaths of 168 people.	McVeigh believed deeply in the ideals upon which the United States was founded.
The defendant also caused serious physical and emotional injury, including maiming, disfigurement, and permanent disability.	McVeigh believed the Bureau of Alcohol, Tobacco and Firearms was responsible for the Branch Davidian deaths at Waco in 1993.
The defendant also caused severe injuries and losses suffered by the victims' families.	He believed federal agents murdered a wife and a 14-year-old boy at Ruby Ridge in 1992.
	He believed that tactics and acts of federal agents were leading to a police state in the United States.
	He believed the federal government failed to take responsibility for their actions at Ruby Ridge and Waco.
	He served "honorably and with great distinction" in the Army and received the Bronze Star for heroic service in the Gulf War.
	He had had no prior criminal record.

In considering the cruelty of the acts and the vulnerability of the victims killed or wounded as the federal building was destroyed, the jury unanimously voted for the death penalty. McVeigh's alleged statement that he wanted a high body count when he set off the bomb was not permitted to be used as evidence.

Imprisonment as Punishment

Under early Roman law, imprisonment was illegal as punishment and was used for detention only.[29] Imprisonment is as old as the law of England, but only rarely did statutes in early England provide for imprisonment as punishment for crime. Nearly every English court had its own particular prison, and the right of keeping a gaol (jail) in and for a particular district was a franchise the king granted to certain people, just as he granted other rights connected with the administration of justice in England. In addition to the franchise prisons, there was the Fleet, the prison of the Star Chamber, and the prison of the Court of Chancery.[30]

Because of the filthy, unsanitary conditions of the early English prisons and the corruption and brutality that arose from the franchise system, reform movements began in England as early as 1773. In that year, John Howard became sheriff of Bedfordshire. When he saw the disgraceful conditions in his jail, he proposed that salaried gaolers replace the franchise system. The condition of U.S. prisons has also been the subject of many reform movements, and the use of prisons for the purpose of punishment has been subject to much debate.

Can Indigents Be Held in Jail to Work Off Their Money Fines?

In the 1970 case of *Williams v. Illinois*,[31] the question of whether a person who was indigent (without money) could be imprisoned for the inability to pay a fine was presented to the U.S. Supreme Court. In the *Williams* case, the Illinois courts ruled that Williams would be held in prison and work off his fine at the rate of $5 per day. Williams asked to be released so he could get a job and pay the fine and court costs.

In the case of *Tate v. Short*,[32] the indigent defendant owed fines of $425 on nine traffic offenses and was ordered to serve eighty-five days in a Texas prison farm and work off the fines at the rate of $5 per day.

The U.S. Supreme Court held that other ways of collecting fines are available and that the equal protection clause of the U.S. Constitution is violated by permitting a person with money to pay fines, whereas a person without money would work off a fine in jail or prison.[33]

Fines as Punishment

Money fines payable by the convicted criminal are frequently used as an alternative to incarceration, or together with incarceration. In most states, the maximum fine for any designated criminal act is set by statute. Also, it is common to limit the amount of a fine each level of court within a state may assess against a defendant. A municipal court that handles minor offenses has a lower fine limit than a district court with the jurisdiction to hear major crimes.

Fines must not be excessive. The Eighth Amendment to the U.S. Constitution prohibits "excessive fines imposed" as punishment. Generally, analysis of punishment under the cruel and unusual punishment clause requires application of the proportionality test. In excessive fines cases, that means comparing the fine assessed to the nature of the offense charged. (For a more detailed examination of proportionality in this context, see Questions and Problems 2 at the end of this chapter.)

Fines can be difficult to collect if the offender is unemployed or has a low-paying job. To improve the rate of collection of fines, some or all of the following methods are being used:

- Allowing offenders to pay their fines on an installment plan, which is usually worked out by a clerk taking into account the income of an offender and the amount due

- Accepting credit cards for payment

- Computerizing record-keeping systems

- Telemarketing (use of the telephone to contact people and remind them of payments due)

- Turning collection over to private collection agencies that can pursue debtors across state lines and often have access to databases that allow them to track the movements of an offender. Collection agencies often routinely notify credit bureaus of delinquent accounts, a practice that is reported to be an important factor in recovering overdue fines.

Forfeiture as Punishment

The concept and use of *forfeiture* go back to early English law. Seizing the property that was used to commit a crime is a strong deterrent to crime. Seizing the profits of crime is also a deterrent in crimes committed for profit.

Forfeiture was first used in customs violations such as smuggling. In addition to the traditional criminal punishments of death and fines, the economic sanction of forfeiture was imposed with seizure of ships, implements, and the goods being smuggled.

Forfeiture not only punished the wrongdoers by depriving them of ships (or boats), implements, and goods, but it also rewarded the king and government, who benefited from the use and sale of these items.

The concept of forfeiture came to America with English common law. It was used over the years in various forms. During Prohibition, forfeiture was used extensively to deter and discourage the manufacture, sale, and use of illegal alcohol.

Federal statutes today authorize the forfeiture not only of contraband property but also of instrumentalities used in narcotics, gambling, and untaxed alcohol and tobacco. For example, Section 55 of the Uniform Controlled Substance Act, which has been adopted by many states and the federal government, provides for forfeiture not only of controlled substances in violation of the law but also of all raw material, all vehicles— "used, or intended for use," weapons, records and books, and all property, "including money" and profits. Section 55.5 of the Act details forfeiture proceedings.[34]

Important recent U.S. Supreme Court cases regarding civil forfeitures are as follows:

- *United States v. Ursery,* 116 S.Ct. 2134 (1996). The Supreme Court held that "in rem civil forfeitures are neither 'punishment' nor criminal for the purposes of the Double Jeopardy Clause"; therefore, the government can commence both a criminal action and a civil forfeiture action without violating double jeopardy.

- *Bennis v. Michigan,* 116 S.Ct. 994 (1996). In this case, the Supreme Court held that a state forfeiture law could provide for forfeiture (seizure) of property from an owner who was unaware of the illegal use of the property. (Bennis was convicted of a sex act with a prostitute in a car owned by Bennis and his wife, who was unaware of the illegal use of the car.) The U.S. Supreme Court held that under such a state statute, "the innocence of an owner (Bennis's wife) has almost uniformly been rejected as a defense to forfeiture."

- *United States v. 785 Nicholas Ave.,* 983 F.2d 396, review denied U.S. Supreme Court 113 S.Ct. 2349 (1993). Under 21 U.S.C.A. § 881(a)(7), the federal government may seize real estate being used for illegal activity such as drug dealing. To defend against such a forfeiture action, the owner must demonstrate a lack of consent to the illegal activities and that he or she did all that reasonably could be expected to prevent the illegal activities once he or she learned of the illegal activities.

Under federal law today and under the provisions of the forfeiture statutes of many states, the following can now be seized under court order:

- Instrumentalities of the crime (vehicles, watercraft, and so on used in the commission of the crimes)
- Profits of the crime (money from drug dealing, stolen goods, and so on)
- Proceeds of the illegal acts (farms, yachts, cars, homes, and other luxury goods purchased from profits of illegal acts)

The Internal Revenue Service can also seize under court order property of people charged with or convicted of crimes. Because people involved in the sale of marijuana, cocaine, and other narcotics often make huge profits without paying proper taxes, tax liens may be filed against them. Property belonging to such people may be seized. Such property could include homes, furniture, cars, stereo equipment, video games, gems, and real estate.

Career Criminals and the Repeat Offender

Priority as to law enforcement is most often determined by the crime itself. High priority is most often given when crimes involve injury or death or when important aspects of public interest are involved.

Attention is focused on the person committing the crime rather than on the crime when it is determined that the person is a career criminal or a repeater (or habitual criminal). The career criminal or repeater has received special attention and priority since studies done between 1975 and 1978 showed that in Washington, D.C., 7 percent of the criminals committed 24 percent of the crimes. By taking such offenders off the street, the incidence of crimes can be considerably lessened.

Many cities and states have created career-criminal programs. Such programs ordinarily

- operate under statutes providing additional and longer sentences for repeat offenders
- establish special career-criminal units in the offices of police and prosecutors that vigorously investigate frequently committed crimes or crimes following patterns
- speed up prosecution of career criminals
- discourage plea bargaining, which could lessen prison terms, unless the suspect incriminates associates

Two repeater (**recidivist**) cases have come before the U.S. Supreme Court in recent years. The 1980 Texas case of *Rummel v. Estelle* involved a defendant who received a life sentence under the Texas repeater statutes for three nonviolent crimes that netted the defendant a total of $230. The Court affirmed the conviction and sentence, holding that the sentence did not violate the Eighth Amendment. The following case was also decided by the U.S. Supreme Court:

Alternatives to Prisons for Offenders Believed to Be Nonviolent

Alternative Punishment	Description	Probable Use
Boot camp—shock incarceration	Young, nonviolent offenders spend from 90 to 180 days in a military-style boot camp subject to discipline, physical training, and hard labor. The young person agrees to the program to avoid serving a longer prison term for an offense such as burglary.	Looked upon as "a constructive approach to offender rehabilitation. . . . Boot camp teaches young people how to become productive citizens." *National District Attorney's Magazine,* April 1994.
House arrest or confinement with electronic monitoring	The monitoring could be done with an ankle or wrist bracelet, or a telephone device that monitors the detainee's presence in the house.	Used as a mixture of penalties tailored to the offender. Person must agree as condition of parole, probation, or work release program.
Agreement to take a drug such as Antibuse, or to commit to a drug treatment program	When the problem and cause of the criminal conduct is alcohol abuse, drugs are available to suppress or eliminate the urge to drink. Drug and alcohol treatment programs are available in all states.	Person agrees to take suppressant medication "voluntarily" as condition of probation or parole, usually to avoid imprisonment.
"Intensive sanctions" or "shock" probation or parole	Usually used for nonviolent, nondrug user. Can be sentenced by court, or enter program from a correctional institution. Used in overcrowded jails or prisons to free space for new inmates.	The overcrowding of jails and prisons causes use of this type of program. Because of lack of adequate home facilities, house arrest is not used.
Voluntary commitment to drug or alcohol treatment	Many crimes are related to serious drug or alcohol problems. Treatment programs are not effective unless participant cooperates fully.	Could be used in a mixture of punishments believed to achieve the best results. Defendants would voluntarily commit themselves as a condition of probation or parole.
Mandatory deportation	Under stricter immigration laws enacted by the U.S. Congress, immigrants who have been convicted of a broad range of felonies (from murder to drug possession) are required to be deported back to the country of their origin.	In 1997, more than forty thousand people were deported to free up prison space in the United States and to lower crime rates. The eventual success of the program is discussed in the *New York Times* article, "U.S. Deports Felons but Can't Keep Them Out" (August 11, 1997).
Banishment to another city or state	Giving an unwanted person the choice to "get out of town" or go to jail was not an uncommon practice forty years ago. Some cities would even provide bus fare to such people. Another practice was to suspend a criminal sentence if the defendant joined the military. It was much easier to get into the military in those days.	Today, the banishment order must be reasonably related to the offense and to rehabilitation. In the 1991 rape case of *McCreary v. State,* 582 So.2d 425, the Supreme Court of Mississippi reviewed cases from other states where banishment was part of a punishment package that the defendant agreed to (usually in a plea bargain agreement).

Sentence Enhancement Statutes

All states and the federal government use sentence enhancement statutes that increase criminal penalties. The following are some of the usual conditions that cause enhancement:

- The crime is a hate crime, or the victim is elderly or handicapped.
- The person is a repeat offender (habitual criminal statute).
- A dangerous weapon is used committing the crime.
- A bulletproof garment is used in committing the crime.
- Concealment of identity (such as a mask) is used.
- Drugs or a weapon is used or sold within one thousand feet of a school.

Another form of enhancement used to protect people having duties within the criminal justice system increases a misdemeanor battery to a felony battery if committed against:

- a law enforcement or fire fighting officer if the officer is acting in an official capacity
- a witness or juror
- a public official or officer
- a prison guard, another prisoner, visitor, and so on by a prisoner

In the 1997 case of *United States v. Gonzales,* 1997 WL 525410 (C.A.5, Tex.), the defendant carried a machine gun during a drug transaction. The 30-year additional sentence enhancement under the federal enhancement statute (18 U.S.C.A. § 924[c]) was held not to violate the Eighth Amendment because machine guns are uniquely associated with drug trafficking and crimes of violence and present a grave danger to the public.

Solem v. Helm

Supreme Court of the United States (1983) 463 U.S. 277, 103 S.Ct. 3001

Helm lived in South Dakota and had a serious problem with alcohol. By 1975, he had committed six nonviolent felonies. In 1979, he pleaded guilty to uttering (passing) a "no account" check for $100 (his seventh felony). Under the South Dakota recidivist statute, he was sentenced to life imprisonment. Unlike Texas statutes, South Dakota statutes forbade parole in such cases. Murderers and rapists were eligible for parole in South Dakota, but Helm would never be eligible for parole. The Supreme Court held that the sentence violated the Eighth Amendment as follows:

> The Constitution requires us to examine Helm's sentence to determine if it is proportionate to his crime. Applying objective criteria, we find that Helm has received the penultimate sentence for relatively minor criminal conduct. He has been treated more harshly than other criminals in the State who have committed more serious crimes. He has been treated more harshly than he would have been in any other jurisdiction, with the possible exception of a single State. We conclude that his sentence is significantly disproportionate to his crime, and is therefore prohibited by the Eighth Amendment.

Three Strikes Laws

For many years, most states and the federal government have had laws that provided for increased punishment for multiple felony convictions. In the mid-1990s these laws,

Review of Sentencing

Sentencing authority is granted to the trial judge by the law defining the crime and by other statutes in the state or federal criminal code. The sentencing judge could be further guided by sentencing guidelines enacted by that state's legislature. Reviews of imposed sentences may be made by the following:

- *Trial judge* On motion by the defense attorney, the trial judge will review his or her sentence of a particular defendant and may modify the sentence after hearing arguments presented by both the defense lawyer and the prosecutor.

- *Appellate courts* (including the U.S. Supreme Court and state supreme courts) On appeal, an appellate court could find that a particular sentence was not within the statutory authority of the trial judge to impose, or that the sentence violated the Eighth Amendment's cruel and unusual clause. (See the 1910 case of *Weems v. United States,* in which the U.S. Supreme Court held that fifteen years at hard labor in ankle chains was excessive punishment for the crime of falsifying government records.)

- A state prisoner would ordinarily use a writ of habeas corpus in attempting to get his or her case into the federal courts. To do this, a violation of a right under the U.S. Constitution must be shown. Because there are very few violations (or errors) of this type, few habeas corpus hearings are granted.

- *State parole board or parole authorities* (The federal government is phasing out the use of parole.) Parole authority is granted by a statute of that state. State statutes might provide that parole eligibility for murder does not commence until after sixteen years—or after twenty or twenty-five years. Whether the convicted person would be released on parole (and the conditions of parole) would then be determined by the parole board.

- *Pardoning power of the president of the United States and state governors* The power to pardon, grant amnesty, or commute a sentence by the president or a state governor is generally broad. Such authority is constitutional with additional statutory power often also provided. Article II of the U.S. Constitution provides that the president "shall have Power to grant Reprieves and Pardons for Offenses against the United States, except in Cases of Impeachment."[a]

[a]See the case of *Murphy v. Ford,* 390 F.Supp. 1372 (W.D.Mich. 1975), in which a federal district court found that President Gerald R. Ford had the constitutional authority to grant a pardon to former President Richard M. Nixon before Nixon was charged with a crime.

popularly called "three strikes and you're out" laws, gained prominence when the U.S. Congress incorporated a three strikes provision into the Violent Crime Control and Law Enforcement Act of 1994. Many states followed suit.[35]

In November of 1994, California voters adopted Proposition 184, a three strikes law, in part as a response to the murder of Kimberly Reynolds, an 18-year-old fashion student, by a paroled drug dealer with a long history of violent crime. California's law is among the harshest *three strikes laws* for three reasons: (1) the third or "trigger" conviction may be any felony, not necessarily one for a violent crime, (2) the first two strikes may be convictions for any "serious" felony, though not necessarily a violent crime, and (3) a sentence of twenty-five years to life must be assessed on each count, with multiple counts served consecutively. Parole may not be considered until the entire mandatory sentence is served.[36]

Three strikes laws have come under frequent attack on Eighth Amendment grounds. While no court has held that a three strikes law is in principal unconstitutional under the Eighth Amendment's cruel and unusual punishment provision,[37] such laws have been found unconstitutional as applied in certain factual situations. A recent example of this is the 2001 case of *Andrade v. California.*[38]

In 1996, Andrade, a heroin addict, was charged with two counts of stealing videotapes from a Kmart store. The videotapes had values of $84 and $68. These offenses would normally be petty theft under California law. However, because Andrade had a prior misdemeanor theft conviction, California law permitted the prosecutor to charge Andrade with two counts of "petty theft with a prior," a felony charge. The jury convicted Andrade of the two counts charged. Andrade had been convicted of three counts of burglary in 1983; the sentencing judge therefore sentenced Andrade to two twenty-five-years-to-life sentences, to run consecutively, meaning Andrade would not be eligible for parole until 2046.

The California appellate courts affirmed Andrade's sentence,[39] but on a petition for habeas corpus, the Federal Ninth Circuit Court of Appeals reversed Andrade's conviction.

The *Andrade* court concluded that Andrade's conviction constituted cruel and unusual punishment because (1) all of his prior offenses were nonviolent offenses, (2) the triggering offense was a misdemeanor made into a felony because of his past criminal conduct, thus making his recidivism count double, (3) he would serve at least fifty years in prison for stealing goods worth $153, whereas under California law a convicted murderer could receive fifteen years to life and a convicted rapist eight years imprisonment, and (4) no other state's three strikes law would have resulted in as severe a sentence.[40]

SUMMARY

The primary limitation on the power of the states or federal government to punish convicted criminals is the Eighth Amendment. Both the excessive fines clause and the cruel and unusual punishment clause require courts to examine the punishment to determine if it is proportional to the crime. Proportionality is generally determined by comparing the gravity of the offense with the severity of the crime.

Corporal punishment by a public school of a student is not judged under the cruel and unusual punishment clause but can run afoul of both procedural and substantive due process.

Capital punishment is permitted, but sentencing juries must consider both mitigating and aggravating circumstances before imposing the death sentence. Both mentally impaired and teenage defendants may be given the death sentence, though their mental condition and young age must be considered in imposing that sentence.

BOOK-SPECIFIC WEB SITE

For chapter-related Web links, quizzing activities, and case and news updates, go to the *Criminal Law,* Eighth Edition, book-specific Web site at **http://info.wadsworth.com/ gardner.**

QUESTIONS AND PROBLEMS

1. Were the sentences in the following well-publicized cases appropriate in achieving the goals of the criminal justice system?

Person	Offense Convicted of	Sentence
Pete Rose (baseball player and manager)	Failed to report and pay income taxes on $354,968	Five months in jail, three months at a halfway house, 11,000 hours of community service, $50,000 fine
Joseph Hazelwood (former captain of the oil tanker Exxon *Valdez*)	Was drinking the night his ship caused the biggest oil spill in the history of Alaska	Sentenced to scrub oil-soaked beaches in Alaska for 1,000 hours (25 weeks)
Leona Helmsley (hotel owner)	Failed to report and pay taxes on $1.8 million	Four years in prison and a fine of $7.1 million
Zsa Zsa Garbor (actress)	Slapped a motorcycle officer during a valid traffic stop in Beverly Hills, California	Three days in jail, 120 hours of community service in a homeless shelter for women, $13,000 fine
Lawrence Singleton (raped a 15-year-old California hitchhiker and then hacked her forearms off in 1978; released after serving eight years of a fourteen-year sentence)	Moved to Florida after being run out of several California towns; convicted in 1991 in Florida of petty theft and obstruction (lying to police as to his identification)	The *Singleton* case caused California and other states to increase mandatory sentences for violent crimes. In 1997, Singleton was convicted of the murder of a Tampa, Florida, prostitute and sentenced to death. He was 69 years old at the time. (Singleton died of cancer in 2001 while on death row in Florida.)
John du Pont (the wealthiest murder defendant in the history of the United States)	Without provocation, he shot and killed Olympic gold medalist Dave Schultz	Found guilty of third-degree murder but mentally ill in 1997. After receiving the mental treatment he needs, du Pont will serve the balance of his sentence of five to ten years.
Daniel Rostenkowski (as Chairman of the House Ways and Means Committee was one of the most influential members of the U.S. Congress)	Federal charges of mail fraud in a scandal in the House Post Office and using federal money for personal expenses	Lost his reelection bid after his conviction in 1994 and served a 15-month sentence followed by two years of probation. Will keep his federal pension of $104,000 a year for serving 36 years in the U.S. Congress.

2. Bajakajean ("B") was convicted of the federal crime of willful transportation of U.S. currency in excess of $10,000 outside U.S. borders. B had $357,144 in his possession and was about to board a plane for Italy when arrested. He was sentenced to three years' probation and fined $15,000.

The United States sought forfeiture of the $357,144 under a law which stated that the sentencing court "shall order that the person forfeit . . . any property . . . involved in the offense "

a. If the sentencing court orders forfeiture of the $357,144, is it a "fine"?

b. If so, would it violate the no excessive fines clause of the Eighth Amendment? How is "excessive" to be determined in such cases? See *United States v. Bajakajean,* 524 U.S. 321 (1998).

INFOTRAC COLLEGE EDITION EXERCISES

1. Go to InfoTrac College Edition and, using the keyword search term *cruel and unusual punishment,* find the December 2000 article titled "Torture Bearers." What role, if any, should international opinion play in punishment decisions reached by U.S. courts? What should the United States do in response to such criticism?

2. Could it be possible for anyone to actually impersonate Tiger Woods and use forged credit cards to purchase merchandise in his name? Click on InfoTrac College Edition and, using the subject term *Three Strikes Law,* find the article on Bilking Tiger Woods. Do you think the sentence was appropriate?

NOTES

1. A History of the Criminal Law of England (three volumes) by Sir James FitzJames Stephens, Judge of High Court of Justice, Queen's Bench Division (England, 1883), I: 477.

2. In 1996, John Silber, president of Boston University, wrote an op-ed article for the New York Times titled, "Students Should Not Be Above the Law: Judging Crimes Is a Job for Courts, Not Colleges" (May 9, 1996). In his article, Mr. Silber pointed out that colleges and universities are "circumventing the courts (to) bury serious criminal cases in their own judicial systems." By talking crime victims out of reporting their cases to the police, Mr. Silber points out that students are receiving special treatment, just as persons did who qualified under the "benefit of clergy" exception centuries ago. Mr. Silber cited as an example a man who graduated in 1996 from Miami University in Ohio, a private university. After the man was accused of sexually assaulting an 18-year-old freshman as she was sleeping, the man was allowed to graduate on "student conduct probation" instead of having Ohio police and prosecutors handle the matter.

3. Blackstone's *Commentaries,* 4 Comm. 18.

4. *A History of the Criminal Law of England,* Chapter 13, pp. 491–92.

5. Refugees from Cuba, Haiti, Mexico, Central America, and other parts of the world have been a continuing problem in the United States. The Immigration and Naturalization Service (INS) most often concludes that the refugees are fleeing from poverty in their countries and thus are not eligible for legal entry into the United States.

Transporting, smuggling, or harboring aliens in violation of the Refugee Act of 1980 (Public Law 96-212) is a criminal offense. The defendants in the case of *United States v. Aguilar et al.,* 871 F.2d 1436 (9th Cir. 1989), opinion amended and suspended 883 F.2d 662 (9th Cir. 1989), ran a "modern-day underground railroad" that smuggled Central American natives across the border between Mexico and Arizona. The defendants in the *Aguilar* case were convicted of violations of the immigration laws (smuggling, transporting, and harboring aliens) arising from their participation in a "sanctuary movement."

6. *A History of English Criminal Law and Its Administration,* Radzinowicz (London: Stevens, 1948), and

Crime, Courts, and Probation, Chute and Bell (New York: Macmillan, 1956).

7. "Transportation" was used by a number of countries. The Roman Empire transported prisoners to Rumania; Russia transported hundreds of thousands of political prisoners to Siberia. In addition, the frontiers of the world have always been used as a refuge by people fleeing from the law or in political trouble.

8. *Furman v. Georgia,* 408 U.S. 238, 92 S.Ct. 2726 (1972).

9. Annals of Congress, 782 (1789).

10. *Furman v. Georgia,* 408 U.S. 238 at 258, 92 S.Ct. 2726 at 2736.

11. *Pulley v. Harris,* 465 U.S. 37, 104 S.Ct. 871, 34 CrL 3027 (1984).

12. 404 F.2d 571 (8th Cir. 1968), where the Court presents reasons why whipping is unconstitutional as a punishment.

13. 429 U.S. 975, 97 S.Ct. 481 (1977).

14. Most school districts permitting corporal punishment require such punishment to be administered only after the principal approved it, administered in the presence of another adult, and not with an instrument that could cause physical injury to the student.

15. See *Garcia v. Miera,* 817 F.2d 650, 656 (10th Cir. 1987).

16. *County of Sacramento v. Lewis,* 523 U.S. 833 (1998).

17. *Neal v. Fulton County Board of Education,* 229 F.3d 1069, 1075 (11th Cir. 2000).

18. *Id.,* at 1076.

19. 817 F.2d 650, 656.

20. *Ingraham,* 429 U.S. 975 (1977).

21. Because of state and federal sentencing guidelines, it is very unlikely that a convicted defendant would be sentenced by a court to receive corporal punishment. If such a sentence was given, it would be judged solely by the objective, proportionality test of the Eighth Amendment. Other unusual sentences can run afoul of the Eighth Amendment. For example, in *Williams v. State,* 505 S.E.2d 816 (Ga. App. 1998), a convicted sex offender was required to walk in the area where he committed his crime, wearing a sign that said, "BEWARE HIGH CRIME AREA." The appellate court said this sentence constituted cruel and unusual punishment because the defendant was put in harm's way from other criminals frequenting the designated area.

22. This is the test established by *Farmer v. Brennan,* 511 U.S. 825 (1994). Had the prison official administered the corporal punishment in order to quell a riot, the test would have been, Was the official acting in a "good faith effort to restore discipline or order." See *Whitley v. Albers,* 475 U.S. 312 (1986).

23. 408 U.S. 238, 92 S.Ct. 2726 (1972).

24. In the 1984 case of *Pulley v. Harris,* the Supreme Court defined and explained the use of proportionality.

25. *Gregg v. Georgia,* 428 U.S. 153, 96 S.Ct. 2909 (1976).

26. *Proffitt v. Florida,* 428 U.S. 242, 96 S.Ct. 2960 (1976).

27. *Jurek v. Texas,* 428 U.S. 262, 96 S.Ct. 2950 (1976).

28. 465 U.S. 37, 104 S.Ct. 871, 34 CrL 3027 (1984).

29. *The Law of Criminal Corrections,* Rubin (St. Paul, Minn.: West, 1963).

30. England also had debtors' prisons in which people who owed civil debts could be imprisoned until the civil debt was paid. England abolished the practice of debtors' prisons in 1869. Such imprisonment would not be lawful under the U.S. Constitution, and some state constitutions specifically forbid this form of imprisonment. Most of the democratic world has abolished the practice.

31. *Williams v. Illinois,* 90 S.Ct. 2018 (1970).

32. 915 S.Ct. 668 (1971).

33. In footnote 19 of the *Williams* case, the Court stated: "We wish to make clear that nothing in our decision today precludes imprisonment for willful refusal to pay a fine or court costs. See *Ex parte Smith,* 97 Utah 280, 92 P.2d 1098 (1939)." Therefore, a person who has money or an income may be imprisoned for refusal to pay either a fine or court costs.

34. Other federal statutes having forfeiture provisions are the Controlled Substance Act, 21 U.S.C.A. § 881, Organized Crime Control Act of 1970, 18 U.S.C.A. §§ 1963 and 1955(d), Copyrights Act, 17 U.S.C.A. §§ 506(b) and 509(a), and Child Protection Act of 1984, 18 U.S.C.A. §§ 2253 and 2254.

A driver's license may be revoked (or suspended) not only for traffic violations but also, depending on state law, for sex crimes, failure to pay child support, failure to pay nontraffic fines, underage drinking, truancy, or other reasons specified by the law of the state.

35. Between 1993 and 1995, twenty-four states enacted three strikes laws. See *State v. Oliver*, 745 A.2d 1165, 1169 (N.J. 2000).

36. California Penal Code § 1170.12.

37. See *State v. Oliver*, 745 A.2d 1165 (2000). In *Harmelin v. Michigan*, 501 U.S. 957 (1991), the Supreme Court upheld a life sentence without possibility of parole for possession of cocaine; the case generated five separate opinions on the cruel and unusual punishment question.

38. 2001 WL 1346065 (9th Cir. 2001).

39. 2001 WL 1346065, *3.

40. 2001 WL 1346065, *13–17.

Authors' note
The Death Penalty

On June 20, 2002 the U.S. Supreme court decided *Atkins v. Virginia*, 2002 WL 1338045, discussed in the box on page 173 of this chapter. In *Atkins* the Court held that the Cruel and Unusual Punishment clause of the Eighth Amendment to the U.S. Constitution prohibited states from imposing the death penalty on mentally retarded defendants. The Court concluded that the prevailing consensus in the United States today was against applying the death penalty to the mentally retarded. Historically, the Court said, the Cruel and Unusual Punishment clause had derived its meaning from the evolving standards of permissible punishment shared by the American public. Because, in the Court's view, most Americans did not subscribe to imposition of the death penalty for the mentally retarded, the Cruel and Unusual Punishment clause prohibited any state from imposing that punishment.

In *Ring v. Arizona*, 2002 WL 1357257, decided June 24, 2002, the U.S. Supreme Court held that the Sixth Amendment's right to a trial by jury applied to the sentencing stage in capital cases. In Arizona, as is the case in four other states that have the death penalty, after the jury has convicted the defendant of murder, a judge or judge panel determines if the necessary aggravating circumstances are present justifying imposition of the death penalty.

The Supreme court held that since these aggravating circumstances are fact questions that determine the nature of the punishment the defendant will receive, the Sixth Amendment requires that a jury rather than a judge make the determination that the aggravating circumstances were present. Thus, while a judge may technically impose the death sentence, a jury must first find that the circumstances exist that warrant such a sentence.

For many defendants currently on death row in the states with procedures like those thrown out in *Ring*, the ruling will result in either a new trial on the aggravating circumstances issue, or a commuted sentence of life imprisonment. As Chief Justice Rhenquist noted in his dissent, for some of these defendants the "harmless error" doctrine may prevent them from using the *Ring* decision to seek a new trial. If a jury did in fact find that aggravating circumstances were present, a defendant may not have been harmed by putting the sentencing decision in the judge's hands. Also, under federal procedural rules, it is possible some death row defendants may have exhausted their appeals, and may not be permitted to raise the *Ring* issue in federal courts. This last point is unclear, and may depend upon how the Supreme Court applies such exhaustion rules.

9

Jurisdiction

KEY TERMS

venue

jurisdiction

dual sovereignty

long-arm statutes

extradition

territorial waters

federal enclave

retrocession

martial law

Jurisdiction to Create Criminal Laws

States have broad authority to regulate conduct through the use of criminal laws because they have the primary responsibility to provide for safety and public order within their borders. Most criminal violations in the United States are against the state or local government, whereas a small percentage of crimes are against the federal government.

The federal government, however, has the narrow authority to enact criminal laws given to it by the U.S. Constitution. The following example illustrates a federal law declared invalid because the U.S. Congress did not have constitutional authority to enact the law:

EXAMPLE: More than forty states make the carrying of a gun in a local school yard or building a crime. But does the federal government have *jurisdiction* over local school yards to make such conduct a federal crime?

In the 1995 case of *United States v. Lopez,* 115 S.Ct. 1624, 57 CrL 2031, the U.S. Supreme Court held that local school yards are not a part of interstate commerce so as to give the federal government authority to regulate conduct on local school property under the commerce clause of the U.S. Constitution. Therefore, the federal criminal conviction of a twelfth-grade student in Texas was held invalid. The state and the school could discipline Lopez, but the federal government did not have such authority under the federal Gun-Free School Zones Act of 1990.

Jurisdiction Over the Offense and the Person Charged

Jurisdiction Over the Offense Charged

When a state or the federal government issues a criminal complaint and seeks to commence a criminal action, it must allege and prove that the court has jurisdiction not only over the offense (or offenses) charged, but also over the defendant's person. The Sixth Amendment of the U.S. Constitution provides that "in all criminal prosecutions, the accused shall enjoy the right to a speedy and public trial, by an impartial jury of the State and district wherein the crime shall have been committed, which district shall have been previously ascertained by law."

Therefore, a defendant charged with a crime has a right to demand that the criminal trial occur in the county where the crime is alleged to have occurred (**venue**). A court in the county where the offense occurred would have jurisdiction to try the case. Venue refers to the locality, particularly the county, in which the criminal act or acts charged are alleged to have occurred. In 22 Corpus Juris Secundum (Criminal Law), Section 173, the following statement is made: "Venue is not an element of the offense, and it has been said that persons obviously guilty of criminal acts cannot escape punishment through technical questions of venue."

The following cases illustrate venue:

- *Murder cases.* Murder charges against O. J. Simpson had to be filed in Los Angeles County because the two murders with which he was charged occurred there (venue) and a Los Angeles court would have jurisdiction to try the case against Simpson.[1]

The U.S. Supreme Court Building in Washington, D.C. Over the entrance to the building are the words "Equal Justice Under Law." Most issues of national importance end up before the U.S. Supreme Court.   © Bettmann/CORBIS

- *Burglary and arson cases.* Venue for these crimes would be in the county where the buildings burglarized or burned were located.

- *Rape and sexual assault cases.* In most rapes, the victim would testify to the location where the offense occurred. However, in the following case, rape occurred in a moving vehicle that traveled through different counties and states. Venue could be the pickup location of the victim or any other county or state where the vehicle traveled during the commission of the crime. The Supreme Court of Arkansas held in *Garner v. State:*[2]

> It is not essential to a prosecution in this state that all the elements of the crime charged take place in Arkansas. It has been said that it is generally accepted that if the requisite elements of the crime are committed in different jurisdictions, any state in which an essential part of the crime is committed may take jurisdiction.

Because a moving vehicle can travel through two or more counties (or states) within a short time, most states' statutes provide that if some acts material and essential to a crime occur in one county (or state) and some acts in another, the accused may be tried in either county (or state).

In the 1992 case of *State v. Rose,*[3] the defendant was convicted of rape and sexual abuse. The Oregon courts upheld the validity of an Oregon statute that allowed a criminal trial to be held in the county in which the defendant resided when the county in which the crime had occurred could not readily be determined.

Venue and Jurisdiction

Venue. A defendant has a right to be tried in the place (venue) where the crime is alleged to have occurred.

Jurisdiction. Courts and police must show that they have the authority and power (jurisdiction) to act. Florida courts and police do not have jurisdiction over a burglary that occurred in Seattle. The venue to try a defendant for a Seattle burglary would be Seattle, Washington. The statutes of the State of Washington would determine which Seattle court would have jurisdiction, depending on whether the offender was an adult or a 10-year-old child.

Jurisdiction Over the Person Charged With a Crime

Not only must the state show that the court has jurisdiction over the offense charged, but it must also show that jurisdiction over the person exists. The fact that the accused is physically present in the court is usually sufficient to show jurisdiction over the person.[4]

If a defendant does not appear as ordered in a criminal court, the criminal trial will not commence, and a bench warrant could be issued for the person's arrest if it appears that the failure to appear was deliberate and without good reason.[5] In very minor offenses (when permitted by the statutes of the state and with the permission of the court), a defendant may request and be granted the privilege of not appearing personally. Under these circumstances, the defendant is generally represented by an attorney and usually enters a plea of guilty or no contest.

As a general rule, once a court has acquired jurisdiction of the accused and the charge against him or her, this jurisdiction continues until final disposition or determination of the case is made in the manner prescribed by law. If the defendant jumps bail or fails to appear as ordered, the jurisdiction of the court continues and the defendant is then liable for other charges.

In 1973, the case of *Taylor v. United States*[6] came before the U.S. Supreme Court. The defendant, who was charged with selling cocaine, failed to return to court after a luncheon recess during his trial. After waiting that day for the defendant to appear, the trial judge continued with the case. The jury found the defendant guilty after being instructed that they were to draw no inference from the defendant's absence. The U.S. Supreme Court affirmed the conviction of the defendant.

Dual Sovereignty and "Long-Arm" Statutes

Dual Sovereignty

The federal government and each of the states are distinct, separate sovereign governments. The great majority of all the crimes committed in the United States are committed against only one government. But a small percentage of crimes consist of one act that violates the criminal laws of two or more sovereign governments. The following cases illustrate:

- In the 1959 case of *Bartkus v. Illinois,* 79 S.Ct. 676, the defendant robbed a federally insured bank in Illinois, which was not only a crime against the state of Illinois but also a federal crime. The U.S. Supreme Court held that both sovereign governments could criminally try Bartkus:

  > Every citizen of the United States is also a citizen of a State or territory. He may be said to owe allegiance to two sovereigns, and may be liable to punishment for an infraction of the law of either. The same act may be an offense or transgression of both.

- Heath hired two men in Georgia to kidnap his pregnant wife from their Alabama home and kill her. The murder then took place in Georgia. Both states then convicted Heath of murder. The U.S. Supreme Court affirmed both murder convictions under the *dual sovereignty* doctrine, holding that it would be shocking to "deny a State its power to enforce its criminal laws because another State has won the race to the courthouse." *Heath v. Alabama,* 106 S.Ct. 433 (1985).

In the 1970s and the 1980s, some states—including Illinois and Wisconsin—enacted legislation that forbids prosecution in that state if another state or federal government has already prosecuted for the same offense. The state law in such states would then govern and control as to second prosecutions for the same offense.

Long-Arm Statutes

In 1911, the U.S. Supreme Court ruled as follows in regard to *long-arm statutes:*

> Acts done outside a jurisdiction, but intended to produce and producing detrimental effects within it, justify a State in punishing the cause of the harm as if he had been present at the effect, if the State should succeed in getting him within its powers." *Strassheim v. Daily,* 221 U.S. 280 (1911).

All states have long-arm statutes within their criminal codes, which could be used in the following example:

EXAMPLE: X lives in New York and hires B, who lives in another city, to kill C, who lives in California. B is taken into custody after killing C and agrees to testify against X. Under the California long-arm statute, X could be extradited to stand trial for murder in California.

Rights of an Accused

An accused has a right to be
- charged under a valid statute or ordinance
- tried in a court having jurisdiction
- tried in the district (venue) where the crime was committed
- present at his or her trial (unless right is waived)

Use of Extradition and Forcible Abduction to Bring Fugitives Before Courts

Ordinarily, jurisdiction over a person who has fled from the United States is obtained by means of *extradition*. The United States has more than eighty extradition treaties in force with foreign countries. A compilation of these treaties can be found in 18 U.S.C.A. § 3181.

Fugitives who flee to another state can also be extradited back for trial under the Uniform Criminal Extradition Act.[a] In the following cases, forcible abduction was used to bring fugitives back for trial on criminal charges:

Case	Year	Facts	Ruling
Ker v. Illinois, 119 U.S. 43	1886	The defendant was forcibly abducted from Peru, South America, to face trial for robbery in Illinois.	The U.S. Superior Court affirmed the robbery conviction, holding that the forcible abduction was "no sufficient reason why the defendant should not answer" for the robbery charges.
United States v. Rauscher, 119 U.S. 407	1886	The defendant was forcibly abducted from Mexico.	Case is similar to *Ker* case except that an extradition treaty existed between the countries, but the treaty did not expressly forbid forcible abduction.
Frisbie v. Collins, 342 U.S. 519	1952	Michigan police went to Chicago, Illinois, and forcibly abducted the defendant back to Michigan.	The U.S. Supreme Court held that the *Ker* doctrine continued to be valid. Such conduct, however, would cause civil lawsuits.
United States v. Alvarez-Machain, 112 S.Ct. 2188	1992	Because the defendant was believed to be involved in the torture and murder of a U.S. Drug Enforcement Administration (DEA) agent, Dr. Alvarez was snatched from his office in Mexico and flown to Texas, where he was arrested.	The U.S. Supreme Court held that while the kidnapping may be "shocking," it did not violate the Mexican–U.S. treaty. A federal court acquitted Dr. Alvarez, holding that the evidence against him was insufficient.
United States v. Noriega, 746 F.Supp. 1506 and 752 F.Supp. 1037	1990	In what critics called the "biggest drug bust in history," the United States invaded Panama in 1989. Several hundred Panamanians and two dozen Americans were killed. More than $1 billion in property damage occurred.	When Gen. Manuel Noriega feared death from citizens in his country, he surrendered to U.S. forces. With the consent of the new government of Panama, Noriega was taken to Miami, Florida, where he was tried and convicted of drug charges. He was sentenced to forty years in federal prison.

[a] Courts in the United States have held that the Uniform Criminal Extradition Act has changed the common law. Bail bond agents and law enforcement officers can now be sued civilly for violations in failing to comply with the Uniform Criminal Extradition Act in forcing a person to return to another state without that person's consent. For cases involving bail bond agents, see *State v. Lopez,* 105 N.M. 538, 734 P.2d 778 (App. 1986), review denied 107 S.Ct. 1305, 40 CrL 4173 (1987), and *Loftice v. Colorado* (Colo.Ct.App.1988), review denied 490 U.S. 1047, 109 S.Ct. 1957, 45 CrL 4025 (1989). However, in many states bail bondsmen continue to have greater arrest power than private citizens. See *Shifflett v. State,* 319 Md. 275, 572 A.2d 167 (1990).

In a 1998 unanimous decision, the U.S. Supreme Court held that states have essentially no discretion and must extradite as long as proper procedures are followed and the wanted person's identity and fugitive status are confirmed. See *New Mexico v. Reed,* 118 S.Ct. 1860 (1998).

An example of a federal long-arm statute is the following case:

United States v. Layton

U.S. District Court, District of Northern California (1981) 509 F.Supp. 212

A U.S. congressperson and staff members were murdered in South America in 1978 while they were investigating reports that Americans were being held against their will by a California-based cult. Following these murders, nine hundred murders and suicides of cult members occurred.

Although the murder of Congressman Leo Ryan occurred in South America, Layton was apprehended and tried for the murder in California. Layton was charged and convicted of the following crimes: (1) conspiracy to murder a U.S. congressperson, (2) aiding and abetting his murder, (3) conspiracy to murder an internationally protected person, and (4) aiding and abetting in this murder (these charges are under 18 U.S.C. §§ 351 and 1117). The Court held that an "attack upon a member of Congress, wherever it occurs, equally threatens the free and proper functioning of government."

Nation-to-Nation Jurisdiction

Nations long ago realized that the world could not afford criminal jurisdictional gaps between nations. An alarming situation would exist, for example, if a person could commit a murder in the middle of the Atlantic or Pacific Ocean and no nation would have criminal jurisdiction. Because of this, the jurisdiction of each nation was extended to follow its ships over the high seas. The English common law gave jurisdiction to English courts over crimes committed on British ships and over crimes committed by British subjects on foreign ships.

Today, statutes in both England and the United States give each country jurisdiction over crimes committed not only on ships but on aircraft controlled by each country. By virtue of the international convention ratified by the Tokyo Convention Act of 1967, the courts of any country in the world may try piracy (armed violence at sea committed on a surface ship or an aircraft), even though the piracy was not committed within that country's *territorial waters*.[7] In addition to piracy, international conventions of nations have sought the elimination of slave trading, war crimes, hijacking and sabotage of civil aircraft, genocide, and terrorism.

Because of the statutes giving many nations jurisdictions over crimes, situations could exist in which a number of nations have concurrent jurisdiction (that is, the same crime could be tried in the courts of another nation).

EXAMPLE: A Romanian man was on an American airliner flying from Europe to New York City. While in the air, the man placed his hand on the genitals of a 9-year-old Norwegian girl. It was held that jurisdiction existed to try the man for sexual assault in a New York federal court under the federal "special aircraft jurisdiction." *United States v. Georgescu,* 723 F.Supp. 912 (1989).

The Law of the Seas: Territorial Waters

Each nation has established territorial jurisdiction in the waters and airspace around it. In 1983, the United States claimed sovereignty over waters extending two hundred

Crimes Against Ships and Aircraft

Piracy or Highjacking	The seizure of a ship or aircraft while it is underway. This is a federal crime and also a crime against the law of nations. (See *United States v. Palmer*, 3 Wheat. 610, 4 L. Ed. 57)
Mutiny	When the crew (or some of the crew) seize an aircraft or ship and revolt against lawful authority, the crime of mutiny is committed. In military law, the crime also includes an insurrection of soldiers against lawful authority.
Barratry or Barretry	Unlawful acts committed by the captain or officers of a ship that are contrary to their duties. The term is also used for the offense of frequently exciting and stirring up quarrels or lawsuits.

nautical miles from the United States and its possessions.[8] Vessels within these waters or on the high seas may be stopped under any of the following circumstances:

1. When there is reasonable suspicion or probable cause to believe that contraband such as illegal drugs exists or other criminal activity is occurring,[9] or

2. If a ship or vessel is without nationality (stateless) or "a vessel on the high seas whose nationality (is) unclear," *Singleton v. United States,* 789 F.Supp. 492 (D. Puerto Rico 1992), or

3. With consent or a statement of no objection from the foreign nation where the vessel is registered, *United States v. Pretel,* 939 F.2d 233 (5th Cir. 1991); *United States v. Robinson,* 843 F.2d 1 (1st Cir. 1988), review denied 488 U.S. 834, 109 U.S. 93 (1988), or

4. If the ship meets the statutory definition of a "hovering vessel," *United States v. Cariballo-Tamayo,* 44 CrL 2401 (1989); *United States v. Gonzalez,* 875 F.2d 875 (1989).

International Criminal Law

Article I, Section 8, of the U.S. Constitution provides that "The Congress shall have Power . . . To define and punish Piracies and Felonies committed on the high Seas, and Offenses against the Law of Nations."

Over the years, the United States has participated with the other nations of the world to define international criminal law—*offenses against the law of nations.* This was done by international treaties and international conventions. In 1928, sixty-three nations, including Germany and Japan, outlawed aggressive warfare by signing and agreeing to the Kellogg-Briand Pact. The brutalization of civilians and deportation of people from their homeland to slave labor camps were defined and forbidden by the Geneva Convention of 1897.

After the defeat of the Nazis and Japanese in 1945, the Allied Nations tried many of the surviving military and civilian leaders. The international tribunal at Nuremberg, Germany, tried many of the surviving Nazi leaders for offenses against the laws of nations.[10] The brutal and deliberate killings of millions of civilians, ethnic cleansing, and deportation of thousands of people to slave labor camps in German and Japanese war factories were just some of the many crimes against humanity that occurred during World War II.

In 1997, the United States appointed an Ambassador at Large for War Crimes. David J. Scheffer was confirmed as the ambassador by the U.S. Senate and worked with the United Nations and other democratic countries of the world in the investigation of war crimes. The U.S. Office for War Crimes issued reports on the following situations:[11]

- The massacres in Bosnia and what was formerly Yugoslavia of thousands of Bosnian Muslims, Croats, and Serbs. U.S. troops and military forces from other nations of the world are presently in Bosnia to maintain order and seek to prevent violence.[12]

- The slaughter of about half a million Tutsi and moderate Hutu in Rwanda and Tanzania, Africa, in the years since 1994.

- The "killing fields" where Pol Pot, the leader of the militant Khmer Rouge, ordered more than a million people killed in the effort to control Cambodia from 1975 to 1979. Pol Pot was taken into custody in 1997 and died in 1998. (See the *New York Times* article "World Justice System Lacks Means to Try Pol Pot," June 21, 1997.)

- Saddam Hussein's use of poison gas on Kurdish people in 1988 two years before the seizure of Kuwait, which triggered the Gulf War in 1990.

The war crimes courts that tried Nazi and Japanese leaders for war crimes at Nuremberg and Tokyo after World War II were special temporary courts. Other special temporary courts sat in The Hague in 1993 to try crimes committed during the civil war in the former Yugoslavia (Bosnia), and in Africa after the slaughter of half a million Tutsi and Hutu people. In 1998, a permanent war crimes court was established by the United Nations.

At present, most nations recognize the "universal principle" of international law. Under this principle, where an offender commits a crime so heinous and so widely condemned, "any state if it captures the offender may prosecute and punish that person on behalf of the world community regardless of the nationality of the offender or victim or where the crime was committed." M. Bassiouini, *II International Criminal Law*, p. 298 (1986).

Criminal Jurisdiction of the Federal Government

Federal crimes fall into the following three classes:[13]

1. Crimes in which interstate or international travel or communication occurs are covered by the following: the Travel Act (interstate travel or use of U.S. mail, telephone, and so on to facilitate a crime), the Wire Fraud Act (interstate transfer of stolen or illegal funds), the National Stolen Property Act (interstate transfer or possession of stolen property), the Fugitive Felon Act (fleeing across state lines to avoid prosecution), the Mann Act (interstate prostitution), the Hobbs Act (extortion), and the Lindbergh Act (interstate kidnapping).

2. Crimes committed in places beyond the jurisdiction of any state. These include crimes committed in the District of Columbia and crimes committed overseas by the military or on U.S.-controlled ships or aircraft.

3. Crimes that interfere with the activities of the federal government.[14] Because the scope of the activities of the federal government is broad, this category of federal crimes is broad. It includes fraud by use of the U.S. mails, robbery of federally insured banks or savings and loan associations, violation of the federal income tax laws, and attempt to overthrow the U.S. government.

Some of the situations in which the federal government would have jurisdiction over a criminal homicide include the following:[15]

- Within the special maritime and territorial jurisdiction
- When death results from terrorism, sabotage, or certain cases of reckless or negligent destruction of "federal" transportation facilities
- When the victim is the president of the United States, the vice president, or successors to the office[16]
- When the victim is engaged in performing federal functions
- When the victim is killed "on account of the performance of his official duties"
- When death occurs in connection with a federally punishable bank robbery
- When the homicide occurs during an offense defined by the Civil Rights Act of 1968 (18 U.S.C.A. § 245)

Federal Enclaves and the Assimilative Crimes Act

Federal enclaves are federally owned and controlled lands that can be found in all states. Military installations, such as army posts, naval yards, Air Force bases, Coast Guard stations, and marine bases, are enclaves if they are within the borders of states. National parks and forest lands and federal buildings, such as post offices, federal court buildings, and federal office buildings, could under certain circumstances also be enclaves. The federal government owns almost one-fourth of the land in the continental United States and has exclusive jurisdiction over much of this land.[17]

Before 1948, some of the enclaves had a degree of autonomy, which created some problems throughout the United States.

In 1948, Congress passed the Assimilative Crimes Act (18 U.S.C.A. § 13) to incorporate, by reference, the state criminal law of the surrounding state in force at the time of the defendant's conduct. In the case of *United States v. Sharpnack,* the U.S. Supreme Court held that the Assimilative Crimes Act was constitutional.[18] In that case, the defendant, who was a civilian, was convicted of committing sex crimes involving two boys at the Randolph Air Force Base, a federal enclave in Texas. In affirming the conviction, the Court stated:

> There is no doubt that Congress may validly adopt a criminal code for each federal enclave. It certainly may do so by drafting new laws or by copying laws defining the criminal offenses in force throughout the State in which the enclave is situated. As a practical matter, it has to proceed largely on a wholesale basis. Its reason for adopting local laws is not so much because Congress has examined them individually as it is because the laws are already in force throughout the State in which the enclave is situated. The basic legislative decision made by Congress is its decision to

conform the laws in the enclave to the local laws as to all offenses not punishable by any enactment of Congress. Whether Congress sets forth the assimilated laws in full or assimilates them by reference, the result is as definite and as ascertainable as are the state laws themselves.

Indian Tribes Within the United States

Of the almost one-and-a-half million Native American Indians in the United States, more than half live on reservations located mainly in seventeen states. The U.S. Supreme Court has pointed out that the 310 recognized Indian tribes in the United States "possess those aspects of sovereignty not withdrawn by treaty or statute, or by implication as a necessary result of their dependent status."[19]

In 1975 and again in 1977, the U.S. Supreme Court held that

Indian tribes are unique aggregations possessing attributes of sovereignty over both their members and their territory, *Worcester v. Georgia,* 31 U.S. 6 Pet. 515, 557 (1832), they are "a separate people" possessing the power of regulating their internal and social relations. *United States v. Mazurie,* 419 U.S. 544, 557, 95 S.Ct. 710, 717 (1975).[20]

The division of criminal jurisdiction among the tribal courts, the federal government, and states in which the Indian reservations are located is complex. Under current law, all three jurisdictions have some power to adjudicate crimes related to Indians. However, Congress has the final authority on how that jurisdiction is exercised.

After entering into treaties with many Indian tribes during the mid-nineteenth century, Congress passed the Indian Country Crimes Act, 18 U.S.C. Section 1152. This act extended federal criminal laws to "Indian country," mainly reservations where Indians resided, except for "offenses committed by one Indian against the person or property of another Indian." These offenses were then under the exclusive jurisdiction of tribal courts.

In 1885, Congress passed the Indian Major Crimes Act, 18 U.S.C. Section 1153, which lists fourteen serious crimes that, if committed by an Indian against another Indian or non-Indian, are subject to exclusive federal jurisdiction. Indian tribal courts lack jurisdiction to adjudicate such serious crimes.

Beginning in 1940, Congress enacted statutes that gave various designated states jurisdiction over "offenses committed by or against Indians on Indian reservations" within that state's borders.[21] Kansas, Iowa, and North Dakota were given that jurisdiction. In the 1993 case of *Negonsatt v. Samuels,* the United States Supreme Court held that the Kansas Act, as that 1940 act was called, conferred jurisdiction on Kansas to prosecute a Kickapoo Indian for the state law offense of aggravated battery against another Indian committed on an Indian reservation.[22]

Finally, beginning in 1953 and continuing through 1984, Congress passed various laws which gave states exclusive jurisdiction over crimes committed by Indians in Indian country, but within designated municipal boundaries. For example, in 1984, Congress passed a statute giving Colorado exclusive jurisdiction over crimes by Indians on the Southern Ute Reservation if they were committed within the boundaries of the town of Ignacio, Colorado, which is located on the reservation.[23] Thus, a federal court was held to lack jurisdiction under the Indian Major Crimes Act to prosecute an Indian for manslaughter committed within the Ignacio, Colorado, town borders.[24]

At the present time, tribal courts have exclusive jurisdiction only for crimes not falling within the above statutes, essentially less serious crimes such as petty misdemeanors. Moreover, that jurisdiction is limited to members of the tribe in question. Thus, a crime committed by an Indian on a reservation where the Indian resides is not subject to tribal courts' jurisdiction if the Indian is a member of another tribe.[25]

Crimes on Indian country involving only non-Indians are subject to the jurisdiction of the state in which the Indian country is located, just as are crimes committed by Indians outside Indian country.[26]

Self-Government by Indian Tribes

In various treaties between the U.S. government and many Indian tribes, some signed more than 150 years ago, the tribes relinquished their rights to vast amounts of land in exchange for a "special relationship" with the federal government. Among other obligations, the federal government was required to provide the tribes such services as health care and education. That special relationship exists today but is in the process of change.

The tribes are seeking, with the approval of the U.S. Congress, to eliminate their dependence on the Bureau of Indian Affairs (BIA), which together with the tribal councils has managed Indian affairs since 1824. Recent studies show that Indian reservations have received only about 11 cents out of every dollar appropriated to the BIA by Congress.

In 1988, the U.S. Congress enacted a federal law that permits Indian tribes to have profit-making gambling operations on their land. Under this law, Indians can run the same games of chance that the state allows charities and other groups to run.

Indian tribes now operate more than one hundred casinos and large-scale bingo halls in seventeen or more states. Agreements are generally negotiated with the local state and the federal government about the type of gambling and the location of the gambling facility. With the revenues from gaming, Indian tribes are able to finance community projects for their people and to move toward self-government.

The Military, Martial, and War Powers Jurisdiction of the Federal Government

Jurisdiction of Military Courts[27]

When a person enters U.S. military service, he or she becomes subject to the Uniform Code of Military Justice.[28] Over the years, hundreds of thousands of military personnel have been tried for many offenses, ranging from "military" crimes, such as desertion, unauthorized absences, willful disobedience of orders, and drunkenness on duty, to "civilian" crimes, such as rape, murder, and drug violations, that took place on leave.

From 1969 through 1987, U.S. military courts did not have jurisdiction over offenses that were not "service connected" and were committed off-base or off-post. In 1987, military courts were given back the authority and jurisdiction they lost in 1969. The

U.S. Supreme Court abandoned the "service connection" requirement that was established in the 1969 case of *O'Callahan v. Parker.*[29]

In the 1987 case of *Solorio v. United States,*[30] the U.S. Supreme Court held that the military justice system has jurisdiction to try a member of the armed service for *any* crimes committed (on- or off-base) as long as the accused was a member of the military service at the time of the alleged offense.

Terrorist Trials in Military Tribunals

Following the September 11, 2001, terrorist attacks on the World Trade Center and the Pentagon, President George W. Bush issued an executive order as commander in chief that suspected terrorists could be tried by military tribunals, rather than civilian courts. Many questioned the wisdom, if not the legality, of that order.

The U.S. Supreme Court has held that the federal government may not prosecute a U.S. citizen who is not a member of the armed forces in a court martial or other military tribunal.[31] That is because, as a U.S. citizen, the defendant is entitled to the constitutional guarantees of trial by jury, speedy trial, and the like, many of which are not used in military court trials.

Crimes committed by terrorists who are noncitizens present two questions: (1) Does the United States possess the jurisdiction to punish the criminal act and (2) if it has such jurisdiction, may it use military or similar courts to try those charged with the criminal act? These courts are called Article I courts, because they are formed as "necessary and proper" for the exercise of Congress's powers given it under Article I of the U.S. Constitution. Among others, those powers include the power "to define and punish piracies and felonies committed on the high seas, and offenses against the law of nations."[32]

The United States has the jurisdiction to punish terrorist attacks like those on September 11, 2001. Since part of the attack was against the Pentagon in Washington, D.C., the territorial jurisdiction principle confers jurisdiction on the United States.[33] In addition, international treaties like The Montreal Convention[34] authorize signature countries to establish jurisdiction over offenses where the offender is present in the country's territory. Finally, the universal principle, discussed earlier in this chapter, would also authorize jurisdiction of the United States to try terrorists associated with the September 11 attack, even if those terrorists are apprehended outside the territory of the United States.[35]

With the establishment of the new war tribunals, the United States now has three court systems to try persons who face criminal charges:

1. Civilian courts to try civilians charged with crimes

2. U.S. Armed Forces tribunals created under the uniform code of Military Justice

3. The new military tribunals to try persons for such crimes as terrorism, crimes of war, aiding the enemy and spying

The decision by President Bush to try noncitizen terrorists in military courts was made under his powers as commander in chief of the U.S. Armed Forces. Section 818 of Article 18 of the Uniform Code of Military Justice (UCMJ) gives authority to the president to create military courts to "try any person who by the law of war is subject to trial by a military tribunal and may adjudge any punishment permitted by the law of war." Section 836 of Article 36 of the UCMJ gives the president authority to prescribe procedures

Who Is Behind the Police Officer on the Street?

Officer Needs Help!!

The officer can call for help from his or her department.

→

Assistance from nearby departments can be requested under mutual assistance agreements.

→

The department can request assistance from the state governor, who can activate state guard units if needed.

→

Article IV, Section 4, of the U.S. Constitution provides "the United States shall . . . protect (every state) . . . against domestic violence. . . ."[a] Therefore, if needed, the U.S. Army, Marines, Navy, and Air Force stand behind the police officer on the street.[b]

[a]States may not maintain armed forces without the consent of the U.S. Congress: Article I, Section 10, of the U.S. Constitution provides that "No State shall, without the Consent of Congress . . . keep Troops, or Ships of War in time of Peace." (See Appendix A of this text for applicable sections of the U.S. Constitution.)

[b]During the Vietnam War, soldiers fired upon students at Kent State University in Ohio who were protesting the Vietnam War, killing and wounding a number of students. The Posse Comitatus Act was then amended by the U.S. Congress. This Act forbids the use of the military to enforce civilian law unless it is authorized by the U.S. Constitution ("protect against domestic violence"), or is authorized by the U.S. Congress. (See footnotes 43 and 44 of this chapter for more on the Posse Comitatus Act.)

and modes of proof in military tribunals that try cases subject to the UCMJ. Section 821 of Article 21 states that military tribunals that have jurisdiction over offenses because of the "law of war" have concurrent jurisdiction with court martials. These sections would appear to give the President the authority to convene military courts to try terrorists.

One or more American citizens may have served in the Taliban armed forces in the United States' actions against Afghanistan. Service by an American citizen in a foreign nation's armed forces may result in loss of such citizenship if the armed forces are engaged in hostile action against the United States and the citizen joined the foreign army with the intention of relinquishing U.S. nationality.[36] Moreover, such action might constitute treason under 18 U.S.C.A. Section 2381, for which the death penalty is a possible punishment. Since such American citizens "owed allegiance to the United States" when they joined the Taliban, even if they subsequently lost their citizenship, they most likely could only be tried for treason in civil courts.

When U.S. Citizens or Military Are in a Foreign Country

Americans who commit crimes in foreign countries are subject to prosecution before foreign courts, whether they are military personnel or tourists. U.S. civilians have been sentenced to serve long prison terms in Turkey, Mexico, and other countries for narcotics violations. This is a grim reminder that sentences in some countries are quite severe.

U.S. military personnel are stationed in many countries throughout the world. If a service person commits a crime while off-base, while off-duty, and in a foreign country, he or she is subject to the jurisdiction of the laws of that country. Under the status of forces agreement that many countries have with the United States, the military person could be tried by the courts in that foreign country.[37] However, in many instances the prosecutor in the foreign country will waive jurisdiction and turn the offender over to the U.S. military authorities for trial before a military court.

Examples of crimes that American service personnel were charged with are murder of a West German taxi driver and desertion, *Plaster v. United States;*[38] murder of a Mexican prostitute, *United States v. Newvine;*[39] and rape of a German woman, *Bell v. Clark.*[40]

Because foreign countries in the past generally want a continued U.S. military presence, they will often waive criminal prosecution. However, in November 1995, Japan did not waive jurisdiction to try three U.S. servicemen for the rape of a 12-year-old schoolgirl on the island of Okinawa. Before a Japanese court, one serviceman pleaded guilty and the other two admitted assisting in the rape. Thousands of Okinawans demonstrated, demanding the removal of U.S. military bases from Okinawa and removal of the 47,000 U.S. troops from Japan.[41]

Martial Law and the Use of Military Forces in the Continental United States

In attempting to define *martial law* in 1946, the U.S. Supreme Court made the following statements in the case of *Duncan v. Kahanamoku:*

The term "martial law" carries no precise meaning. The Constitution does not refer to "martial law" at all and no Act of Congress had defined the term. It has been employed in various ways by different people and at different times. By some it has

Jurisdiction of Law Enforcement Officers

The jurisdiction of law enforcement officers

- is limited to their municipality or county (in the case of deputy sheriffs) unless determined to be otherwise by state statute

- may extend into other states, counties, or municipalities if authorized by hot (or fresh) pursuit statutes or common law authority. If an arrest is made in another state, the officer must comply with the Uniform Criminal Extradition Act and take the suspect before a judge in that state to commence extradition proceedings

- may be extended to other counties or municipalities in their state under the authority of a state arrest or search warrant

- may be supplemented by the statutory or common law authority to make a citizen's arrest in their state

- Federal officers are not limited by city, county, and state borders

been identified as "military law" limited to members of, and those connected with, the armed forces. Others have said that the term does not imply a system of established rules but denotes simply some kind of day-to-day expression of a General's will dictated by what he considers the imperious necessity of the moment. . . . In 1857 the confusion as to the meaning of the phrase was so great that the Attorney General in an official opinion had this to say about it: "The Common Law authorities and commentators afford no clue to what martial law, as understood in England, really is. . . . In this Country it is still worse." . . . What was true in 1857 remains true today.[42]

Military forces have been used many times in the history of our country to maintain public order and to enforce laws. In 1787, the year in which the Constitution was formulated, the governor of the Massachusetts colony used the militia to cope with Shay's Rebellion. Federal troops were sent by President Washington into Pennsylvania to suppress the Whiskey Rebellion of 1794. Federal troops were used by President Lincoln to prevent the withdrawal of the southern states from the Union and to maintain public order. Federal troops remained in the South until the 1880s. During some of this time, martial law was in effect in the southern states in which federal troops remained.

Federal troops were used by President Eisenhower to secure compliance with Supreme Court school desegregation orders in Arkansas in 1957 and by President Kennedy in Mississippi in 1962 and in Alabama in 1963. In the twenty-nine-month period between January 1968 and the end of May 1970, National Guard troops were called upon 324 times to cope with urban riots and disorders and unrest on college campuses.[43] In all the incidents in the 1950s, 1960s, and 1970s, troops and National Guard units provided assistance to civilian law enforcement agencies that had the primary responsibility for preserving public order. People arrested or taken into custody were brought before federal and state courts, where they were advised of their constitutional rights.

General Jurisdiction Requirements

To charge a person with a crime, the state or federal government must

- charge under a statute or ordinance that is constitutional on its face,
- charge in the county or place in which the crime is alleged to have occurred, and
- produce the person to be charged before the court that will try him or her.

Native American Indians who commit crimes while *not* within their reservation or Indian country are subject to the jurisdiction of the state or government, just as non-Indians are. Indians who commit crimes while on their reservation or within Indian country can be tried (1) by their tribal court and punished by not more than six months' imprisonment and/or a $500 fine (25 U.S.C.A. § 1302[7]), or (2) before a U.S. federal court for the fourteen serious crimes under the federal Major Crimes Act (18 U.S.C.A. §§ 1153 and 3242).

Non-Indians charged with committing crimes against other non-Indians in Indian country are subject to prosecution under state law. *United States v. McBratney,* 104 U.S. (14 Otto) 621 (1881); *United States v. Antelope,* 430 U.S. 641, 97 S.Ct. 1395 (1977), footnote 2.

U.S. military personnel may be tried by a military court for all crimes they commit while they are in the military service, whether the offense was committed on or off a military base, ship, aircraft, and so on.

People who commit crimes on federal enclaves can be tried before

- a federal court, using the criminal code of the surrounding state under the Assimilative Crimes Act (18 U.S.C.A. § 13)
- a military court, if the person was a member of the U.S. armed services

Federal military forces can be used to support a request from a state to respond to civil disturbances, or they can be used to enforce federal authority or to protect constitutional rights. But unless the use of federal military forces is authorized by the U.S. Constitution or the U.S. Congress,[44] the federal Posse Comitatus Act of 1878[45] forbids the use of federal forces to enforce civil laws. Violations of the Posse Comitatus law may be punished as a felony.

SUMMARY

States have broad powers to define criminal conduct and prosecute those who commit crimes within the state. The federal government may pass criminal laws only where authorized by the Constitution, and only has jurisdiction to prosecute those who commit such crimes. The federal government also has jurisdiction to try those who commit crimes outside the United States under several treaties and conventions made among nations, as well as under the universal principle.

The federal government has jurisdiction over Indian tribes and may enact criminal laws governing Indians. However, the federal government has distributed some of this power to several states and to Indian tribunal courts.

Persons serving in the military are subject to the criminal laws contained in the Uniform Code of Military Justice. That Code permits trials by military courts. Non-American citizens charged with war crimes may also be tried by military tribunals, though American citizens may not.

 BOOK-SPECIFIC WEB SITE

For chapter-related Web links, quizzing activities, and case and news updates, go to the *Criminal Law,* Eighth Edition, book-specific Web site at **http://info.wadsworth.com/ gardner.**

QUESTIONS AND PROBLEMS

1. In the mid-nineteenth century, Congress created the Unitah Indian Reservation in Utah. In 1902, Congress passed a law allotting individual parcels of that reservation to members of Ute Indian tribes. Unallotted land was open to public settlement. Hagen, a Ute Indian, was convicted in Utah state court of distributing a controlled substance on a portion of the reservation opened to public settlement.

   Does Utah have jurisdiction over Hagen's actions?
   What are the ways Utah might acquire that jurisdiction? *See Hagen v. Utah,* 510 U.S. 399 (1994).

2. Wheeler, a Navajo tribal member, was convicted in tribal court of contributing to the delinquency of a minor. He was subsequently indicted in federal court for statutory rape arising out of the same incident.

   a. If the above occurred in the same jurisdiction, would it violate the double jeopardy clause?

   b. Should the indictment be dismissed? *See Wheeler v. United States,* 435 U.S. 313 (1978).

 INFOTRAC COLLEGE EDITION EXERCISES

1. The question of the legality of using military tribunals to try suspected terrorists has many facets. Using InfoTrac College Edition and the keyword search term *Military Tribunals and Terrorists,* find two articles discussing the relative advantages and disadvantages of using military tribunals to try suspected terrorists.

2. Go to InfoTrac College Edition. Using the keyword search term *International Criminal Law,* find an article discussing the International Criminal Court (ICC). What crimes are within the ICC's jurisdiction? Where do the substantive criminal laws come from? Are these crimes adequately defined?

NOTES

1. Venue will not ordinarily be presumed in criminal cases but may be inferred from the evidence available in the case. For example, the body of a man who was shot is found. There are no eyewitnesses to the crime, and there is no evidence showing that the body has been moved. From this evidence, probably all courts would conclude or infer that the crime occurred in the county and state in which the body was found. The accused has a right to be tried in the county or state in which the crime occurred. Thus, if prosecution has been in one venue but evidence is discovered that reveals the venue lies elsewhere, the venue must be changed.

2. 569 S.W.2d 74 (1978), review denied U.S. Supreme Court 99 S.Ct. 1224 (1978).

3. 117 Or.App. 270, 843 P.2d 1005 (1992).

4. The U.S. Supreme Court held in the 1993 case of *Crosby v. United States,* 113 S.Ct. 748, that under Rule 43 of the Federal Rules of Criminal Procedure, a defendant who is absent at the beginning of his or her criminal trial cannot be tried in absentia.

5. The problems encountered by the Milwaukee, Wisconsin, court system are similar to the problems of many cities in the United States. In 1997, Milwaukee County alone had more than 20,000 outstanding arrest warrants for failure of defendants to appear for misdemeanor trials. In addition, there were 1,539 arrest warrants for people who failed to appear for felony trials.

Moreover, because of crowded conditions in the jails, it is a common practice to tell people sentenced to a jail sentence to report at a future date (a week or ten days) to commence serving their jail sentences. Many of these people do not appear as instructed. (See the *Milwaukee Journal Sentinel* article "County Aims to Reduce Warrants," December 8, 1997.)

People who have warrants on file for their arrest are in most cases taken into custody when there is a name check following a traffic or street stop or when they are arrested for another offense. For years, the number of outstanding unserved warrants has remained very high in Milwaukee County.

6. 414 U.S. 17, 94 S.Ct. 194 (1973).

7. Article 19 of the Geneva Convention on the High Seas (1958) states: "On the high seas, or in any other place outside the jurisdiction of any State, every State may seize a pirate ship or aircraft, or a ship taken by piracy and under pirates, and arrest the persons and seize the property on board. The courts of the State which carried out the seizure may decide upon the penalties to be imposed, and may also determine the action to be taken with regard to the ships, aircraft or property, subject to the rights of third parties acting in good faith."

8. *Innocent passage* is defined by the Law of the Sea Treaty as follows: "Passage is innocent so long as it is not prejudiced to the peace, good order or security of the coastal state."

9. During Prohibition in the 1920s (when the consumption and sale of alcoholic beverages and beer were illegal in the United States), European ships would sell liquor to Americans in "Rum Row," international waters off the East Coast of the United States. The U.S. Supreme Court upheld a Coast Guard vessel coming alongside Lee's ship and observing illegal whiskey on the deck. Lee's conviction was affirmed in the case of *United States v. Lee,* 47 S.Ct. 746 (1927).

10. U.S. Supreme Court Justice Robert H. Jackson represented the United States at the Nuremberg trials. He wrote as follows:

No half-century ever witnessed slaughter on such a scale, such cruelties and inhumanities, such wholesale deportations of people into slavery, such annihilations of minorities. The terror of Torquemada pales before the Nazi inquisition. . . . Goaded by these facts, we have moved to redress the blight on the record on our era. . . . We should not overlook the unique and emergent character of this body as an International Military Tribunal. It is no part of the constitutional mechanism of internal justice of any of the Signatory nations. Germany has unconditionally surrendered, but no peace treaty has been signed or agreed upon. The Allies are still technically in a state of war with Germany, although the enemy's political and military institutions have collapsed. As a Military Tribunal, it is a continuation of the war effort of the Allied Nations. As an International Tribunal, it is not bound by the procedural and substantive refinements of our respective judicial or constitutional systems, nor will its rulings introduce precedents into any country's internal civil system of justice. As an International Military Tribunal, it rises above the provincial and transient and seeks guidance not only from International Law but also from the basic principles of jurisprudence which are assumptions of civilization and which long have found embodiment in the codes of all nations.

11. See the *New York Times* article "Trying to Make Sure That War Crimes Aren't Forgotten or Go Unpunished" (September 22, 1997).

12. The first person convicted for Balkan war crimes was a Croat. See the *New York Times* article "Croat Is First to Be Convicted (in The Hague) by Balkan War Crimes Panel" (June 1, 1997). The article points out that of seventy-six people charged with Balkan war crimes, only nine are in custody.

A Bosnian Serb who returned to live in Germany was sentenced to life imprisonment by a German court for war crimes committed in Bosnia. After the man was arrested in Germany, the German government agreed to try him under German law because the United Nations War Crimes tribunal in The Hague stated they were overburdened. See the *New York Times* article "Bosnian Serb Is Sentenced to Life Term for Genocide" (September 27, 1997).

13. In the 1995 case of *United States v. Lopez*, 115 S.Ct. 1624, 57 CrL 2031, the U.S. Supreme Court stated that

we have identified three broad categories of activity that Congress may regulate under its commerce power. . . . [First] '[T]he authority of Congress to keep the channels of interstate commerce free from immoral and injurious uses has been frequently sustained, and is no longer open to question.'

* * *

Second, Congress is empowered to regulate and protect the instrumentalities of interstate commerce, or persons or things in interstate commerce, even though the threat may come only from intrastate activities.
. . . [F]or example, the destruction of an aircraft (18 U.S.C. § 32), or . . . thefts from interstate shipments (18 U.S.C. § 659). Finally, Congress' commerce authority includes the power to regulate those activities having a substantial relation to interstate commerce, Jones & Laughlin Steel, 301 U.S., at 37, i.e., those activities that substantially affect interstate commerce.

14. If federal property is intentionally damaged or destroyed, the federal government ordinarily has jurisdiction over the matter. When state property is intentionally damaged or destroyed within that state, the state government has jurisdiction. What about a situation in which the property is internationally owned, such as the United Nations building in New York City? In the 1976 case of *People v. Weiner*, 85 Misc.2d 161, 378 N.Y.S.2d 966 (1976), the defendant was charged with criminal mischief for having sprayed red paint on the outside wall of the U.N. headquarters. The New York Criminal Court held that it had jurisdiction over the person of the defendant and the offense.

15. This material was presented in the Working Papers of the National Commission on Reform of Federal Criminal Laws, Vol. II, p. 832.

16. At the time of the assassination of President Kennedy, only the state of Texas had jurisdiction to try the homicide charges.

17. The *National Geographic* magazine article "To Use or To Save" (October 1996) states that the federal domain "covers a third of the nation, more than 700 million acres, a public trust unmatched in the world."

18. 355 U.S. 286, 78 S.Ct. 291 (1958).

19. *U.S. v. Wheeler*, 98 S.Ct. 1079 (1978).

20. 412 U.S. 205, 93 S.Ct. 1993 (1973).

21. 18 U.S.C. § 3243. This act is titled the Kansas Act.

22. 507 U.S. 99 (1993).

23. See *Burch v. U.S.*, 169 F.3d 666, 669 (10th Cir. 1999).

24. *Id.* The jurisdictional grants to states are not unalterable. Through a congressionally approved procedure called *retrocession*, a state may, by legislative vote and consent of affected Indian tribes, cede jurisdiction over crimes back to the federal government. When this happens, jurisdiction over crimes committed on Indian country will be regulated by federal statutes such as the original Indian Country Crimes Act, the Indian Major Crimes Act, and acts like the Kansas Act.

25. *Duro v. Reina*, 495 U.S. 676 (1990).

26. *New York ex rel. Ray v. Martin*, 326 U.S. 496 (1946).

27. Article I, Section 8, of the U.S. Constitution provides (in part) that

The Congress shall have Power . . . To define and punish Piracies and Felonies committed on the high Seas, and Offenses against the Law of Nations; To declare War . . . and make Rules concerning Captures on Land and Water; To raise and support Armies; . . . To provide and maintain a Navy; To make Rules for the Government and Regulation of the land and naval Forces; To provide for calling forth the Militia to execute the Laws of the Union, suppress Insurrections and repel Invasions; . . . To make all Laws which shall be necessary and proper for carrying into Execution the foregoing Powers, and all other Powers vested by this Constitution in the Government of the United States, or in any Department or Officer thereof.

Article II of the U.S. Constitution provides in part that

Section 1. The executive Power shall be vested in a President of the United States of America. . . . Section 2. The President shall be Commander in Chief of the Army and Navy of the United States, and of the Militia of the several States, when called into the actual Service of the United States.

28. 10 U.S.C.A. §§ 801–940 (Supp.V. 1970) amending 10 U.S.C.A. §§ 801–940 (1964).

29. 395 U.S. 258, 89 S.Ct. 1683 (1969).

30. 483 U.S. 435, 107 S.Ct. 2924 (1987).

31. *Reid v. Covert,* 354 U.S. 1 (1957).

32. U.S. Constitution, Art. I, § 8.

33. See W. Lafave and A. Scott, *Criminal Law,* p. 118 (2nd ed., 1986).

34. Convention for the Suppression of Unlawful Acts Against the Safety of Civil Aviation, Sept. 23, 1971. T.I.A.S. No. 7570.

35. See *U.S. v. Yunis,* 681 F. Supp. 896 (D.C. Dist. 1988). There, the universal principle was used to give jurisdiction to the United States to try a Lebanese terrorist who hijacked an airplane in Jordan that had American passengers on board. The terrorist was forcibly abducted from a foreign country and taken to the United States for trial.

36. 8 U.S.C.A § 1481(a)(3).

37. The best known SOFA (status of forces agreement) is that with the NATO countries. The largest U.S. military commitment has existed in these European countries since 1945 in a continuous effort to keep the peace.

38. 720 F.2d 340, 34 CrL 2154 (4th Cir. 1983).

39. 14 CrL 2387 (1974).

40. 437 F.2d 200 (4th Cir. 1971).

41. See the *New York Times* article "One Pleads Guilty to Okinawa Rape; 2 Others Admit Role" (November 8, 1995).

42. 327 U.S. 304, 66 S.Ct. 606 (1946).

43. From the testimony of Maj. Gen. Wilson, Chief of the National Guard Bureau, before the President's Commission on Campus Unrest, 116 Cong.Rec. 27, 339.

44. 10 U.S.C.A. § 331 also provides: "Whenever there is an insurrection in any State against its government, the President may, upon the request of its legislature or of its governor if the legislature cannot be convened, call into federal service such of the militia of the other States, in the number requested by that State, and use such of the armed forces, as he considers necessary to suppress the insurrections."

45. The Posse Comitatus Act, 18 U.S.C. §§ 1385 (1878), forbids the use of the military to enforce civilian laws. Federal law 10 U.S.C. 375 requires the Secretary of Defense to establish regulations to ensure against direct participation by members of the military in the enforcement of civilian laws. The Act provides:

Whoever, except in cases and under circumstances expressly authorized by the Constitution or Act of Congress, willfully uses any part of the Army or the Air Force as a posse comitatus or otherwise to execute the laws shall be fined not more than $10,000 or imprisoned not more than two years, or both.

For cases in which courts have held there was no violation of the Posse Comitatus Act, see *Applewhite v. U.S. Air Force,* 995 F.2d 997, review denied U.S. Supreme Court 54 CrL 3201 (1994) (military set up sting operation off-base to catch military drug violators rather than civilians); *Kim v. State,* 817 P.2d 467 (1991) (military conducted undercover investigation to determine whether soldiers were "a market" for illegal drugs); and *Fox v. State,* 1995 WL 757942 (Alaska 1995) (Army investigation of a soldier's drug source).

10

The Limits of Free Speech

CONTENTS

KEY TERMS

clear and present danger test

"fighting words"

obscene communications

inciting

defamation: libel and slander

symbolic speech

threats of violence

nuisance speech

Belief—Speech—Action

Belief

Because thought and belief are not subject to control by government, people may legally entertain any thoughts on any subject. Because thought and belief, by themselves, do not infringe on the rights of others, the right to believe is absolute. People may not be punished for what they think; thoughts about committing a crime are not, by themselves, punishable by the state.

Speech

Speech and other forms of communication, however, are not absolute rights, for they can seriously clash with the rights of others. For example, a man who calls another man's wife or mother the most vile and vulgar names he can think of may not assert that this is within his constitutional freedom of speech. The U.S. Supreme Court has stated that the right of freedom of speech and other forms of communication "implies the existence of an organized society maintaining public order without which liberty itself would be lost in the excess of unrestrained abuses."[1] The Court has also stated that "the line between speech unconditionally guaranteed and speech which may be regulated, suppressed or punished is finely drawn."[2]

Human communications take many forms. Pure speech includes words spoken on a face-to-face basis and through the various media. Written communication includes newspapers, books, and magazines as well as signs or symbols carried or displayed in public. A certain gesture with a finger, which would be interpreted by many as very insulting, vulgar, or obscene, is certainly a form of communication. Picketing, protest marches, boycotts, and the like are also forms of communication. (These are discussed in Chapter 11.)

Action

Speech is often the link between thought and action. Action, like speech, is not an absolute right, because it can interfere with the rights of others; people have a right to swing their arm, but that right ends where another person's nose begins. Each state and the federal government have enacted criminal statutes forbidding certain conduct and, in some instances, requiring other conduct.

The Clear and Present Danger Test

The First Amendment of the U.S. Constitution provides that "Congress shall make no law . . . abridging the freedom of speech, or of the press." Does this mean that people can say and communicate anything and everything without restriction by either state or local government?[3] The answer is no, because under the old English common law and under the laws of the United States, there have always been restrictions on speech and communications within constitutional limitations.

Free speech is essential to a democracy. The "freedom to speak one's mind is not only an aspect of individual liberty—and thus a good unto itself—but also is essential to the common quest for truth and the vitality of society as a whole."[4]

The test used for government restriction of speech is the **clear and present danger test.** Local, state, or federal governments in the United States cannot forbid or suppress speech and punish the speaker unless the connection between the speech and an illegal harm is so close that the speech presents a clear and present danger. Justice Oliver Wendell Holmes announced the clear and present danger doctrine in the 1919 case of *Schenck v. United States:*

> The most stringent protection of free speech would not protect a man in falsely shouting "Fire" in a crowded theater, causing panic. It would not even protect a man from an injunction against uttering words that may have all the effect of force. The question in every case is whether the words are used in such circumstances that are of such a nature as to create a clear and present danger that they will bring about the substantive evils that Congress has a right to protect. It is a question of proximity and degree. When a nation is at war many things that might be said in time of peace are such a hindrance to its efforts that their utterances will not be endured so long as men fight and that no court could regard them as protected by any constitutional right.[5]

Using Oliver Wendell Holmes's example, a person could go into a public park on a sunny day and stand in a large, open field and yell "Fire!" Bystanders might be curious or amused, but they would not panic and would not stampede, injuring one another. They would know that they were in no immediate danger because they could see and smell that there was no fire in the area. Therefore, no "clear and present" danger could come from the person's speech that would bring about a harm and a wrong that would concern society. Other examples of the use of the clear and present danger test follow:

EXAMPLE: A man may believe that a 55 mph speed limit "stinks." He may state this belief in any form of communication available to him, because this communication would not ordinarily present any clear and present danger to other people. However, when the man actually violates the speed limit by action, he may then be punished.

EXAMPLE: In an extreme case, a woman may believe that she has the right to kill the president of the United States because she disagrees with presidential policies. However, because of the clear and present danger that communication of this thought presents, the woman may be arrested and convicted under 18 U.S.C. § 871(a) of the Federal Code if she knowingly and willfully threatens the life of the president or encourages other people to do so.[6]

Clear and Present Danger Cases

In the following cases, the U.S. Supreme Court defined the clear and present danger standards that are used today in balancing rights under the First Amendment with the need for public safety:

Facts of the case	U.S. Supreme Court ruling as to whether a "clear and present danger" existed
In 1967, Cohen expressed his opposition to the Vietnam War with the words "Fuck the Draft" (instead of "The Heck With the Draft") on the back of his jacket. He was arrested and convicted of disorderly conduct.	As the words were not addressed to any specific person and did not create or tend to create a public disorder, Cohen's conviction was thrown out. *Cohen v. California,* 91 S.Ct. 1780 (1970).
During an anti-Vietnam demonstration, streets were blocked and traffic was stopped. As sheriffs were clearing the streets, Hess was heard to say, "We'll take the fucking street later." Hess was immediately arrested and convicted of disorderly conduct.	The U.S. Supreme Court held that Hess's words "were (not) intended to produce and likely to produce imminent (immediate) disorder." As it was held that there was no "clear and present danger," Hess's conviction was reversed. *Hess v. Indiana,* 94 S.Ct. 326 (1973).
A Ku Klux Klan leader addressing a meeting on an Ohio farm stated, "If our president, our Congress, our Supreme Court continues to suppress the white Caucasian race, it is possible that there might have to be some revenge taken." The speaker was charged and convicted of the crime of *inciting*.	In reversing the criminal conviction, the Supreme Court ruled that the language was not "directed to inciting or producing imminent (immediate) lawless action." *Brandenberg v. Ohio,* 89 S.Ct. 1827 (1969).
A group of American Nazis sought to march and demonstrate peacefully in the village of Skokie, Illinois, where more than half of the population were Jewish. A parade permit was refused on the grounds that the swastika and storm trooper uniforms amounted to fighting words to many of the residents. An injunction was issued forbidding "displaying the swastika . . . in the course of a demonstration, march or parade" in the village.	The Illinois Supreme Court reversed the lower court, holding that the swastika is symbolic political speech and not "fighting words." It was held that the village did not meet its "heavy burden" necessary to justify a prior restraint on speech. (Villagers who would become angry at the Nazis could stay home or go somewhere else the day of the parade). *Village of Skokie v. National Socialist Party of America,* 373 N.E. 2d 21 (1978), review denied U.S. Sup.Ct. S.Ct.
Hustler magazine published an article apparently intended for comic effect but also to ridicule the Rev. Jerry Falwell. In the article, it was stated that Rev. Falwell's "first time (sex)" was "during a drunken incestuous rendezvous with his mother in an outhouse." There was a small-print disclaimer at the bottom of the page.	Mr. Falwell sued *Hustler* magazine for civil damages. The U.S. Supreme Court held unanimously (8–0) that *Hustler* magazine could not be punished criminally or civilly because the "expressions involved in this case (are) not governed by any exceptions to the general First Amendment principle." *Falwell v. Hustler Magazine,* 108 S.Ct. 876 (1988) (Note: If the words that *Hustler* used were presented in a face-to-face confrontation, they could easily be found to be fighting words.)

Fighting Words

All states have enacted disorderly persons or disorderly conduct laws forbidding conduct that causes a public disorder or tends to cause a public disorder. The U.S. Supreme Court defined **fighting words** as "those words which by their very utterance . . . tend to incite an immediate breach of the peace."[7]

Using vulgar and insulting language toward another person on a face-to-face basis could be held to be a fighting word violation if the language did cause or tended to cause a violent response. Calling another man's child, niece, or wife vile and vulgar names could easily result in violence in many instances. The following incident is an example:

EXAMPLE: During an angry exchange of words in a restaurant in Washington, D.C., a 35-year-old man called 70-year-old Texas Congressman Henry Gonzalez a "Communist." The police report stated that Gonzalez "nailed (the man) with his fist," causing a black eye and a cut over his eyebrow. Citations for disorderly conduct were issued to both men, and after pleading guilty, they paid their fines. Congressman Gonzalez stated, "The word 'Communist' is a fighting word."

Calling a Texas Congressman a Communist during the height of the Cold War (as was done in the example) was very provocative, and most juries in those days would probably find that a fighting word violation had occurred.

But one wrong does not justify another wrong, and Gonzalez committed a misdemeanor battery when he struck the other man. The police properly issued citations to both men, as two crimes had occurred. To prove a fighting word violation, the city, county, or state would have to prove the following in most jurisdictions:

- That the defendant addressed very insulting and abusive language,

- To another person on a face-to-face basis,

- Causing a likelihood that "the person addressed will make an immediate violent response."[8]

- If the charge is a public disorder, then the statute or ordinance would probably require a showing that the offense occurred in a public place.

The Higher Fighting Word Standards That Many Courts Apply to Police

Many state courts have imposed higher standards for words directed at police officers, reasoning that police officers are expected to exercise greater restraint when foul, insulting language is directed toward them.

In October 2001. Mayor Rudolph W. Giuliani of New York City publicly criticized a New York judge for dismissing a case against a defendant who used vile, vulgar language and name-calling to a New York police officer. This incident reflects the controversy that exists in the United States about just how much verbal abuse law enforcement officers are required to take before the language becomes a fighting word violation.

After reviewing hundreds of state cases, the *FBI Law Enforcement Bulletin*[9] listed the following generally accepted concepts to assist law enforcement officers in deciding whether to arrest for speech directed at them:

1. *Direct threats to the safety of an officer* "generally constitute 'fighting words' unprotected by the first amendment."

"Fighting words" are insulting and abusive words said in a face-to-face situation causing a likelihood that "the person addressed will make an immediate violent response." Fighting words are not protected by the First Amendment.

EXAMPLE: A man became very angry because he did not think the police were doing anything about the vandalism to his car. He was immediately arrested when he said to officers, "You fucking son of a bitch, I'm going to go back into the house and get my shotgun and blow you bastards away." His lawyer appealed the case to the state supreme court, where the conviction was affirmed.[10]

However, if the speech falls short of a direct, outright threat and is only harassing and nasty, state courts have held that such communications do not fall under the threat exception.

2. When a crowd is present and the *speech is likely to incite the crowd* (or some of the people in the crowd) to violence, state courts will hold that such speech is not constitutionally protected. In the case of *State v. Dickey,*[11] the police were called because of a fight in an apartment. The defendant was in a crowd of onlookers and protested the arrest of a man yelling to the police, "What the fuck's going on? What are you doing, asshole pig? You going to arrest me?" After the man failed to heed police

Former vice president of the United States, Nelson Rockefeller, "responding in kind" (his words) to hecklers during an appearance for Senator Robert Dole (background). Could this gesture, under entirely different circumstances, ever amount to "fighting words"?   © Bettmann/CORBIS

warnings to desist, he was arrested and his conviction for disorderly conduct was affirmed.

3. Speech that *obstructs and hinders* police in the performance of their duty has generally been held to justify an arrest. Probably all states have statutorized the old common law crime of obstructing and hindering police officers in the performance of their public duty. However, state statutes vary considerably in defining the crime of obstruction. A few states limit the crime to "resisting." Other states use the words *resist, obstruct,* or *oppose,* and still other states use *resist, obstruct,* or *abuse.*

Some states hold that verbal acts alone cannot constitute obstruction and that physical acts are also required. However, other states hold that verbal communication can amount to obstruction.

Obstructing or hindering law enforcement officers in the performance of their duty could occur while the officers are making an arrest, while a roadside sobriety test is being conducted for drunk driving,[12] while the officers are investigating a major felony of violence,[13] while the officers are questioning witnesses, or in many other situations such as the failure of a material witness to a major crime or serious accident to properly identify himself or herself.

Fighting Words Violations

Words (or other communication) may be offensive, profane, and vulgar, but not be fighting words.

Words may be insulting and even outrageous but not be fighting words because they involved no face-to-face confrontation, as in *Falwell v. Hustler Magazine.*

Words may make a person or an audience angry and may be protected by the First Amendment and thus not be forbidden by government.

Words may be rude, impolite, and insulting but may fall short of the fighting words violation.

Speech or gestures may be vulgar, profane, and obscene, but may fall short of being a fighting words violation.

If the person to whom the words are addressed is not angered by the words, no fighting words violation has occurred.

If the person to whom the words are addressed is not likely to make an immediate violent response, no fighting words violation has occurred.

Many states apply a higher fighting words standard to law enforcement officers because they are expected to exercise a higher degree of restraint than the average citizen, but if direct threats to the safety of an officer occur, or if the speech clearly disrupts or hinders officers in the performance of their duty, or if the speech tends to incite unlawful conduct by bystanders, such speech is not constitutionally protected

Fighting Words and Obscenity

Obscenity is a concept different from fighting words. To be obscene, the state must show as a matter of law that (1) the work taken as a whole appeals to the prurient (lustful) interest in sex, (2) the work "portrays sexual conduct in a patently offensive way," (3) the work "taken as a whole does not have a serious literary, artistic, political or scientific value." *Miller v. California,* 413 U.S. 15, 93 S.Ct. 2607 (1973).

Fighting words and obscenity cause different reactions in people. Fighting words cause people to become angry, whereas obscenity appeals to the prurient (erotic) interest.

A movie, picture, words, dance, or other communication could be sexually explicit without being obscene if the communication has serious "literary, artistic, political, or scientific value" (U.S. Supreme Court in *Miller v. California*).

"Dirty words" by themselves are generally not obscene or fighting words.

Although it is absolutely disgusting, it is not necessarily obscene.

Nudity in itself is not obscene or lewd, but a state or community may regulate (1) when nudity is in a place where liquor is sold (see *California v. LaRue,* 409 U.S. 109, 93 S.Ct. 390 [1972]) and (2) when public nudity is forbidden by a specific ordinance or law.

Obscene Communications

Obscenity is not protected by the First Amendment and may be forbidden by government. Defining obscenity, however, has been the subject of many court rulings and debates. The U.S. Supreme Court established the following guidelines for American courts to define obscenity in the 1973 case of *Miller v. California,* 93 S.Ct. 2607:

The Tougher Standard for Radio and Television

Howard Stern has one of the largest radio audiences in the United States and earns a salary of more than $2 million per year. Mr. Stern is known for pushing the boundaries of acceptable language in broadcasting with talk of "masturbation," "defecation," "fantasy sex" with well-known actresses, and other subjects viewed as indecent.

The Federal Communications Commission (FCC), which regulates radio and television, defines indecency as programming that is "patently offensive." In 1992, the FCC fined Mr. Stern $600,000 for indecent broadcasts. Mr. Stern has an audience of 12 million listeners each day in the New York area and is the top-rated show in that area. In 1995, an additional penalty of almost $2 million was paid in settlement of additional charges against Mr. Stern.

- Whether "the average person applying contemporary community standards" would find that the work, taken as a whole, appeals to the prurient interest[14]
- Whether the work or communication depicts or describes, in a patently offensive way, sexual conduct specifically defined by the applicable state law
- Whether the work or communication, taken as a whole, lacks serious literary, artistic, political, or scientific value

Further material on obscenity can be found in Chapter 19.

Inciting and Urging Unlawful Acts

Inciting or urging other people to commit a crime or perform an unlawful act is a misdemeanor in common law. The offense of inciting is committed even though the other person does not commit the suggested crime. Speech or other forms of communication that urge unlawful conduct are not protected by the U.S. Constitution and may be forbidden by government. To be unlawful, however, the speech or other communication must be "directed to inciting or producing *imminent* lawless action and [must be] likely to incite or produce such action."[15]

The U.S. Supreme Court cases of *Hess v. Indiana* and *Brandenberg v. Ohio* were discussed earlier in this chapter. The U.S. Supreme Court held that the words of the defendants in both cases did not urge imminent (immediate) lawless action, and therefore neither defendant could be convicted either of disorderly conduct or inciting. In neither case did the words of the defendants present a clear and present danger.

Defamation: Libel and Slander

The crime and the civil offense of defamation goes back more than seven hundred years in the law. As early as 1275, the English Parliament enacted a libel statute that forbade false news and tales. The colonies and the original thirteen states undoubtedly all had laws concerning libel and slander. Over the years, the laws of England and the United States developed into the libel, slander, and defamation laws of today.

Defamation is the offense of injuring the character or reputation of another by oral or written communication of false statements. Defamation consists of the twin offenses of *libel* and *slander*. Libel is generally a written offense, whereas slander is generally an oral offense. Although most states probably have one or more criminal defamation statutes, charges under these statutes are infrequent. Most victims choose to rely primarily on the civil actions of libel and slander that are available to them. Money awards can be obtained through the civil suits to both compensate and punish. The burdens of proof are also lower in civil actions.

The crime of fighting words is limited to a face-to-face confrontation involving a communication that either causes violence or tends to cause a violent reaction by the person to whom the words are addressed. The law of defamation requires that the communication be made to people other than the victim and that the victim's reputation be lowered in the esteem of any substantial and respectable group. It is possible that words spoken could not only be fighting words but also the basis for civil libel and slander suits.

Law enforcement officers and other public officials carry a heavier burden if they file a lawsuit for defamation. After reviewing U.S. Supreme Court cases, an article in the *FBI Law Enforcement Bulletin* concludes:

> Under the current state of the law, a public official faces a far more difficult situation than a private citizen with regard to obtaining recompense for defamatory publications. A law enforcement officer has been defined by case law as a public official. To succeed as a party plaintiff in a defamation proceeding he must therefore plead and move that the person publishing the defamation did so with a reckless disregard as to the truth or falsity of his statements.[16]

Symbolic Speech and the First Amendment

Symbols, along with gestures, conduct, and speech, have always been used to communicate between human beings. The symbol can be used alone or with other forms of communication.

Uniforms and the manner in which people dress are forms of symbols. People often communicate by their dress who they are, what their lifestyles are, and, to some extent, what they think and believe. A *symbolic speech* case that has come before the Court:

During the Vietnam War, a group of Iowa students wished to communicate their opposition to the war by wearing black armbands in school. However, the high school principal forbade the armbands, which caused the filing of the lawsuit *Tinker v. Des Moines Independent Community School District,* 89 S.Ct. 733 (1969). Because the black armbands did not disrupt classes or school, the U.S. Supreme Court sustained the students' action, holding:

> The wearing of an armband . . . was closely akin to pure speech, which we have repeatedly held is entitled to comprehensive protection under the First Amendment. Students or teachers [do not] shed their constitutional rights of freedom of speech or expression at the schoolhouse gate.

The Former Crimes of Blasphemy, Profanity, and Indecent Language

Prior to the 1970s, most American cities and counties had ordinances that made it an offense to use profanity or vulgar language in a public place. The 1970 ruling of the U.S. Supreme Court in the case of *Cohen v. California* made major changes in this area of criminal law.

Cohen was arrested in the Los Angeles courthouse because he was wearing a jacket with the words "Fuck the Draft" printed on the back to protest the Vietnam War. Cohen would not have been arrested if he had voiced his opposition to the Vietnam War with the message "Darn the Draft" or "To Heck With the Draft." The U.S. Supreme Court reversed Cohn's conviction for disorderly conduct, ruling that a state "may not, consistent with the First and Fourteenth Amendments, make the simple public display here involved of this single four-letter expletive a criminal offense."

The *Cohen* case established the following two concepts regarding the public use of vulgar, profane, or indecent language:

1. The U.S. Supreme Court defended Cohen's use of the admittedly vulgar word "fuck." The Court refused to allow a state "to cleanse public debate to the point where it is grammatically palatable to the most squeamish among us," because the Court concluded that "one man's vulgarity is another's lyric." This ruling makes it difficult to define any vulgar, profane, impolite, or other type of curse as a crime, in and of itself.

2. The U.S. Supreme Court also held that people "in the Los Angeles courthouse could effectively avoid further bombardment of their sensibilities simply by averting their eyes." In the 1975 case of *Erznoznik v. City of Jacksonville,* the Supreme Court held that "the burden normally falls upon the viewer to avoid further bombardment of [his] sensibilities simply by averting his eyes."[a]

The following bumper sticker cases illustrate the efforts in a few states to regulate language seen on bumper stickers:

■ The State of Georgia attempted to stop the use of a bumper sticker stating "Shit Happens." The Georgia Supreme Court held that the statute used was overbroad, because it regulated protected speech as well as unprotected speech. The Court held that because people were not compelled to look at the bumper sticker and could turn their eyes away, there was no captive audience. And because the law was not written to protect children, the relaxed standard of review for the protection of children could not be used. *Cunningham v. State,* 400 S.E.2d 916 (1991).

■ The 1991 case of *Baker v. Glover,* 776 F.Supp. 1511 (M.D.Ala.), concerned an Alabama law forbidding obscene bumper stickers and signs. "Warning tickets" were issued for the first violation of the new obscenity statute. Baker was a truck driver and received a warning for a bumper sticker on his truck that read, "How's My Driving? Call 1-800-EAT Shit!"

After Baker was warned that he would be fined if he did not remove the bumper sticker, he commenced a lawsuit in a federal court alleging violation of his First Amendment right of freedom of expression.

The federal court held that because the message on the bumper sticker did not appeal to a "prurient interest," the state could not forbid the message as obscene. The bumper sticker also was held to have a serious literary or political value as a protest against the Big Brother mentality of urging the public to report bad driving by truck drivers.

[a]91 S.Ct. 1788.

Flag Burning and Cross Burning as Symbolic Speech

Flags are symbols. The American flag has symbolic meanings that are cherished by most Americans. This, however, has caused some protesters and demonstrators seeking to make a political statement to sometimes burn or otherwise defile an American flag in an attempt to communicate the message.

In past years, states had statutes that made this type of defilement of the American flag a crime. If the demonstrators burned their own flag as a means to communicate a political message, the symbolic act was held to have the protection of the First Amendment in the two U.S. Supreme Court cases of *Texas v. Johnson*, 109 S.Ct. 2533 (1989), and *United States v. Eichman*, 110 S.Ct. 2404 (1990).

Cross burning can also be a symbolic act that seeks to communicate a message and therefore can also have First Amendment protection. In the 1992 case of *R.A.V. v. St. Paul, Minn.*, 112 S. Ct. 2538, the U.S. Supreme Court held that a St. Paul ordinance making cross burning[17] a crime was invalid because the ordinance forbade the symbolic conduct "based on its hostility to the underlying (hate) message."

Threats of Violence as Crimes

A threat becomes a crime if it is explicit and likely to cause "imminent lawless action" (108 S.Ct. 876). Threats could be charged as disorderly conduct, or inciting, or under a state or the federal racketeering law if repeated threats are made. (See Chapter 21 for material on racketeering laws.)

Threats of violence are a constant problem in the American criminal justice system. The First Amendment protects most speech and communications, but it does not protect threats of violence or intimidation. Some of the types of threats that are of constant concern are the following:

- Threats against public officials, which are taken very seriously in view of the fact that four American presidents have been killed in our history and attempts have been made on the lives of five other presidents

- Some of the threats by teenagers in past years were sometimes viewed as idle statements, attempts at humor, or attempts to get attention. However, since the eight school shootings during the school year of 1997–98, threats or hints of violence by teenagers are treated much more seriously today. Sixteen students and teachers were killed in school shootings during the 1997–98 school year and forty-six others were wounded.

- Terrorist threats are of great concern in the United States since the events of September 11, 2001, and the deaths and illnesses caused by contamination of anthrax in the weeks that followed. The likelihood of additional terrorist violence is present in the minds of most Americans.

- Restraining orders are issued every working day by courts throughout the United States in attempts to prevent violence and intimidation by former spouses, boyfriends (or girlfriends), and sometimes family members or neighbors.

- In order to extort money or other valuables from people, threats of violence or threats to disclose embarrassing information are made. Such threats are made in committing the crime of extortion (blackmail), which is punished under both federal and state law.

Using the U.S. Mail, Telephones, or E-Mail to Threaten

Using the U.S. mail, a telephone, or e-mail to threaten violence is not only a state offense but could also be charged as a federal crime. The following cases illustrate:

- The defendant telephoned a bank employee and stated, "You all better have my personal items to me by five o'clock today or it's going to be a lot of hurt people there." The defendant was convicted of knowingly transmitting a threat in interstate commerce. *United States v. Cox,* 957 F.2d 264 (6th Cir. 1992).

- Using the mail to threaten or harass can be charged under the federal criminal code. 18 U.S.C. Section 1201(c) or 18 U.S.C. Section 1623 The defendants in the following cases were convicted: *United States v. Winn,* 948 F.2d 145 (5th Cir. 1991) (mail threat to kidnap and hold for ransom) and *United States v. Taylor,* 972 F.2d 1247 (11th Cir. 1992) (defendant used the mail for twenty years to harass his former high school girlfriend and her family, causing them to move several times. When a state restraining order did not stop the defendant, he was convicted of mailing threatening letters.)

- In using e-mail to discuss sexual fantasies, the defendant was convicted of expressing a sexual interest in violence against women and girls. Holding that the statement was not directed toward a specific person, the conviction was reversed. *United States v. Alkhabaz,* 1997 WL 30655 (6th Cir. 1997).

Unlawful Telephone Calls

In 1995, the Florida and U.S. Supreme Courts upheld the constitutionality of Florida Statute 365.16, which forbids telephone calls with intent to "abuse, threaten or harass."[18]

Abusive phone calls include the deliberate obscene call, threats, the cruel hoax, bomb scares and threats of bombs, and the "silent" call, in which the person answering the telephone hears nothing or hears just breathing on the other end of the line. Criminal charges may be issued in all the preceding cases if the call was deliberate and made with intent to harass, frighten, or abuse another person. However, charges should not be issued if it appears that the person has dialed the wrong number and simply does not explain the error. Other criminal uses of the telephone include situations in which the telephone is used to case the residence by people planning a burglary (in this way, they are able to determine whether anyone is in the residence).

Other unlawful uses of a telephone include using a telephone to facilitate a crime. For example, the federal Comprehensive Drug Abuse Prevention and Control Act of 1970 forbids the use of a telephone to facilitate narcotic transactions and money laundering.[19]

Loud Noise or Nuisance Speech

In 1989, the U.S. Supreme Court held that "it can no longer be doubted that government has a substantial interest in protecting its citizens from unwelcome noise." *Ward v. Rock Against Racism,* 109 S.Ct. at 2756.

In the *Ward* case, the Supreme Court upheld a New York City regulation that gave the city broad authority to regulate sounds from concerts and other performances at the Central Park band shell. In the case of *Kovacs v. Cooper,* the U.S. Supreme Court upheld a city ordinance that prohibited the use of sound trucks that emitted "loud and raucous" noise on city streets. The Supreme Court held:

Perjury, the Federal False Statement Act, and "Perjury Traps"

The crime of perjury consists of knowingly and materially testifying falsely while under oath. The crime of subornation of perjury is committed when a person induces, urges, or knowingly permits another to testify falsely. In 1968, the President's Commission on Crime stated that perjury has always been widespread and that there should be more effective deterrents against perjury to ensure the integrity of trials.

People who lie to a federal investigator can be charged with a crime under the Federal False Statement Act, even if they are not under oath. In the 1998 case of *Brogan v. United States*, 118 S.Ct. 805, federal investigators from the Labor Department and the Internal Revenue Service asked Brogan during an investigation whether he had received any illegal cash or gifts in the matter they were investigating. Brogan was not in custody, nor did the federal agents intend to take him into custody. But the federal agents did know and had evidence that Brogan had received illegal payments.

When Brogan denied receiving illegal payments and said "no" to the question of the federal investigators, his lie became the basis for federal prosecution under the Federal False Statement Act, which forbids "false, fictitious, or fraudulent statements or representations." Brogan's statement was found to be a deliberate falsehood, and he was convicted of violating the Act.

Was this a "perjury trap"? Defense lawyers commonly refer to such incidents as "perjury traps," even though Brogan was not under oath when he lied to federal investigators. In its decision, the U.S. Supreme Court pointed out that the "plain language" of the Federal False Statement Act clearly prohibited and punished statements such as the false statement made by Brogan to federal investigators.

Justice Ginsburg of the U.S. Supreme Court wrote in a separate concurring opinion that the question of whether the U.S. Congress should change the "extraordinary authority"[a] that Congress "has conferred on (federal) prosecutors to manufacture crimes" will be considered by Congress in the months and years to come.

[a]At the time of Brogan's conviction, the Federal False Statement Act punished lying in violation of the Act, with a maximum penalty of five years in prison and a $5,000 fine. In many federal investigations, this punishment would be greater than many of the punishments for the crimes that are under investigation.

City streets are recognized as a normal place for the exchange of ideas by speech or paper. But this does not mean the freedom is beyond all control. We think it is a permissible exercise of legislative discretion to bar sound trucks with broadcasts of public interest, amplified to a loud and raucous volume, from the public ways of municipalities. On the business streets of cities like Trenton, with its more than 125,000 people, such distractions would be dangerous to traffic at all hours useful for the dissemination of information, and in the residential thoroughfares the quiet and tranquility so desirable for city dwellers would likewise be at the mercy of advocates of particular religious, social or political persuasions. We cannot believe that rights of free speech compel a municipality to allow such mechanical voice amplification on any of its streets.[20]

Loud party noises in an apartment house or in a neighborhood could cause telephone calls to the police or could cause a fight between neighbors if it were the middle of the night. Such "noise" calls are common on weekends in the summer in all large cities. The noises under such circumstances are interfering with the rights of other people. Notice and cautions are generally given before a citation is issued by the police.[21]

Verbal Offenses

Type of verbal offense	To constitute the verbal offense, there must be
fighting words[a]	1. insulting or abusive language 2. addressed to a person on a face-to-face basis 3. causing a likelihood that "the person addressed will make an immediate violent response."
obscenity	1. a communication that, taken as a whole, appeals to the prurient (lustful) interest in sex, 2. and portrays sexual conduct in a patently offensive way, 3. and the communication, taken as a whole, does not have serious literary, artistic, political, or scientific value.
inciting or urging unlawful conduct	1. language or communication directed toward inciting, producing, or urging 2. *imminent* lawless action or conduct, or 3. language or communication likely to incite or produce such unlawful conduct.
obstruction of a law enforcement officer or of justice	1. deliberate and intentional language (or other communication) that hinders, obstructs, delays, or makes more difficult 2. a law enforcement officer's effort to perform his or her official duties (the scienter element of knowledge by the defendant that he or she knew the person obstructed was a law enforcement officer is required); 3. some states require that "the interference would have to be, in part at least, physical in nature" (see the New York case of *People v. Case*).
defamation (libel and slander)[b]	1. words or communication that are false and untrue 2. injury to the character and reputation of another person 3. defamation communicated to a third person
abusive, obscene, or harassing telephone calls	1. evidence showing that the telephone call was deliberate, 2. and made with intent to harass, frighten, or abuse another person, 3. and any other requirement of the particular statute or ordinance.
loud speech and loud noise	Cities and states may: 1. forbid speech and noises meant by the volume to disturb others, and 2. forbid noise and loud speech that create a clear and present danger of violence.

[a]Many state courts apply a higher fighting words standard to law enforcement officers. Consult your legal adviser for the standard used in your state.

[b]When a public official is the victim, it must also be shown that the words or communications were uttered or published with a reckless disregard as to the truth or falsity of the statement. (See also the case of *Falwell v. Hustler Magazine,* as Rev. Falwell is a public figure.)

In 1998, a Florida appellate court upheld a noise statute that made it an offense to play a radio so loudly in a motor vehicle that it is plainly audible at a distance of one hundred feet or more from the motor vehicle. In the case of *Davis v. State,* 1998 WL 150696, the Florida court held that the Florida law addresses noise, not speech; is content neutral; and permits people to listen to anything, although not as loudly as they may wish.

SUMMARY

The First Amendment of the U.S. Constitution protects "freedom of speech . . . [and] of the press " However, the First Amendment does not protect speech or other communications that tend to produce an imminent disorder or that is "directed to inciting or producing imminent lawless action." The test used to determine whether government may restrict speech and punish the speaker is the clear and present danger test.

This chapter presents examples of speech protected by the First Amendment and also "expressions" that the U.S. Supreme Court has held are not protected by the First Amendment of the U.S. Supreme Court.

BOOK-SPECIFIC WEB SITE

For chapter-related Web links, quizzing activities, and case and news updates, go to the *Criminal Law,* Eighth Edition, book-specific Web site at **http://info.wadsworth.com/ gardner.**

QUESTIONS AND PROBLEMS

1. On June 2, 1982, Larry Rodgers telephoned the Kansas City, Missouri, office of the FBI and reported that his wife had been kidnapped. The FBI spent more than one hundred agent hours investigating the alleged kidnapping, only to determine that Rodgers's wife had left him voluntarily. Two weeks later, Rodgers contacted the Kansas City office of the Secret Service and reported that his "estranged girl-friend" (actually his wife) was involved in a plot to assassinate the president. The Secret Service spent more than 150 hours of agent and clerical time investigating this threat and eventually located Rodgers's wife in Arizona. She stated that she left Kansas City to get away from her husband. Rodgers later confessed that he made the false reports to induce the federal agencies to locate his wife. *United States v. Rodgers,* 466 U.S. 475, 104 S.Ct. 1942 (1984). If Rodgers had made such false reports to law enforcement agencies in your state, would he be charged with one or more criminal offenses? If so, indicate the offense(s).

2. At about 10:45 P.M. on Christmas night 1971, the defendant was walking home from work in a high-crime neighborhood. A police officer approached the defendant because the officer had been notified of a "suspicious man" in the neighborhood. The defendant was 69 years old and had lived in the United

States for twenty years. When the officer asked him if he lived in the area, the defendant looked at him and walked away. The officer then stopped the defendant twice, but each time the defendant threw off the officer's arm and protested, "I don't tell you people anything." The defendant would not stay in the officer's presence nor answer any of the officer's questions. The defendant was charged and convicted of disorderly conduct, and his conviction was appealed to the U.S. Supreme Court. Was the conduct of the defendant disorderly so as to justify the conviction? *Norwell v. City of Cincinnati,* 414 U.S. 14, 94 S.Ct. 187 (1973).

INFOTRAC COLLEGE EDITION EXERCISES

1. Go to InfoTrac College Edition, and using the keyword search term *hate crimes,* find the August 2001 article, "Hate Beyond a Reasonable Doubt" by Bradley Chilton, that discusses the U.S. Supreme Court case of *Apprendi v. N.J.* What effect does the author think *Apprendi* will have on hate crimes?

2. Using the same search term, find the July 2001 *FBI Enforcement Bulletin,* giving hate crime statistics for 1999.

NOTES

1. *Cox v. New Hampshire,* 312 U.S. 569, 61 S.Ct. 762 (1941).

2. *Speiser v. Randall,* 357 U.S. 513, 78 S.Ct. 1332 (1958).

3. A small group of people, including the late U.S. Supreme Court Justice Hugo Black, have argued that government should not restrict speech or communication in any way. These "absolutists" (as they are called) argue that the First Amendment should be interpreted literally and that freedom of speech and communication be absolute rather than limited. However, most justices and people in democratic societies have believed otherwise.

4. The U.S. Supreme Court in the 1988 case of *Hustler Magazine v. Falwell,* 485 U.S. 46, 108 S.Ct. 876, quoting *Bose Corp. v. Consumers Union of the United States, Inc.,* 466 U.S. 485, 104 S.Ct. 1949 (1984).

5. 249 U.S. 47, 39 S.Ct. 247 (1919).

6. See *Watts v. United States,* 394 U.S. 705, 89 S.Ct. 1399 (1969).

7. *Chaplinsky v. New Hampshire,* 315 U.S. 568 (1942).

8. A Wisconsin police officer who was on radar duty and issued many speeding tickets told of the nasty verbal language that was often directed at him. He found that carrying a tape recorder was very effective in stopping profane verbal abuse.

When a speeder would began using inappropriate language, the officer said he would take the tape recorder out of his shirt pocket and would say, "Just a minute sir [or ma'am], I want to record this." He would then hold the tape recorder close to the driver and say, "Okay, go ahead with what you want to say." Drivers generally stop their offensive language, not knowing that most of the time there were no batteries in the tape recorder.

9. See the *FBI Law Enforcement Bulletin* article "The 'Fighting Word' Doctrine" (April 1992).

10. *City of Bismarck v. Nassif,* 449 N.W. 2d 127 (1989).

11. 600 N.E. 2d 365 (Sup.Ct. Ohio, 1991).

12. *State v. Manning,* 370 A.2d 499 (N.J., 1977).

13. *People v. Cooks,* 58 Cal.Rptr. 550 (Cal.App. 1967).

14. How the term "prurient interest" is defined in a criminal jury instruction could make a big difference in the outcome of the case. The term is ordinarily defined as that which would be appealing to the sexual interest,

causing a person to become sexually aroused. The Wisconsin Supreme Court held that the following definition given to a jury was an accurate statement of the law when a trial court defined prurient interest as material that "appeals to a shameful, unhealthy, unwholesome, degrading . . . interest in sex." See *County of Kenosha v. C&S Management Inc.,* 238 N.W.2d 428 (1999).

15. U.S. Supreme Court in *Brandenburg v. Ohio,* 89 S.Ct. 1827 (1969). See also *Terminiello v. City of Chicago,* 69 S.Ct. 894 (1949).

16. See the *FBI Law Enforcement Bulletin* article "A Law Enforcement Officer Sues for Defamation" (February 1974).

17. Many communities have ordinances regulating the manner and time that burning can occur. Some require a burning permit. Burning a flag or cross in violation of such ordinances could be cited as an ordinance violation.

18. *Gilbreath v. Florida,* 650 So.2d 10 (Fla. 1995), review denied 115 S.Ct. 1996, 57 CrL 3043 (1995).

19. Sec. 403 (b) 21 U.S.C.A. § 843 (b).

20. 336 U.S. 77, 69 S.Ct. 448 (1949).

21. Many city ordinances define in decibels what volume is "too loud." An interesting twist on this is that air conditioners, construction equipment, and farm machinery, among other things, often run afoul of the definitions.

Maintaining Public Order in Public and Private Places

KEY TERMS

"time, place, and manner" regulations

picketing, demonstrations, and parades

crimes of:

    unlawful assembly

    rioting

    stalking

    public nuisances

    aggressive panhandling

truancy

curfew violations

Regulating the Use of Public and Private Places

Most private property and some public property are closed to the public. Private homes and apartments, for example, are closed to the public. Private offices of most public officials are closed to the public.

Streets and parks are open to the public as are many government buildings. In determining the regulations and controls that may be used by government over public places, courts have pointed out that the following must be considered: (1) the character and normal use of the property, (2) the extent to which it is opened to the public, and (3) the number and type of people who use the facility.[1] In applying these factors, one can see that the waiting room of a mayor's or governor's office could ordinarily accommodate a small number of protesters, but a large number of protesters would interfere with the functioning of the office. Nor could sidewalks used by many people accommodate large numbers of protesters without interfering with pedestrian traffic.

"Time, Place, and Manner" Regulations by Government

Private individuals may absolutely deny demonstrators access to their property if the property is not generally open to the public.[2] Nor is there a general right to exercise First Amendment rights on public property and private property open to the public if this interferes with normal use of the property. As the U.S. Supreme Court pointed out (see footnote 1), making a speech in the reading room of a public library would interfere with the normal use of such a facility. However, students silently protesting the Vietnam War were held not to disrupt and disturb their high school classes by wearing black armbands.[3]

Therefore, both public and private places may be regulated for the normal use of the property. Libraries, hospitals, and schools would have different regulations than basketball arenas, taverns, and gyms because of the different uses of such facilities.

Public and private places must be regulated by the people in charge of such facilities, because failure to provide ordinary care in protecting employees, customers, and other people lawfully on their premises make such businesses or public places liable for accidental negligence or intentional acts of third parties. In 1972, the U.S. Supreme Court held:

> The right to use a public place for expressive activity may be restricted only for weighty reasons. Clearly, government has no power to restrict such activity because of its message. Our cases make equally clear, however, that reasonable *"time, place and manner" regulations* may be necessary to further significant governmental interests, and are permitted. For example, two parades cannot march on the same street simultaneously, and government may allow only one. A demonstration or parade on a large street during rush hour might put an intolerable burden on the essential flow of traffic, and for that reason could be prohibited. If overamplified loudspeakers assault the citizenry, government may turn them down. Subject to such reasonable regulation, however, peaceful demonstrations in public places are protected by the First Amendment. Of course, where demonstrations turn violent, they lose their protected quality as expression under the First Amendment.[4]

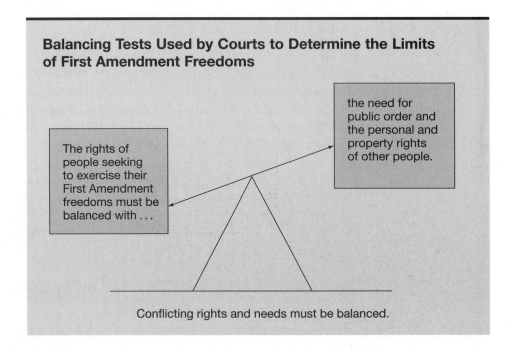

Balancing Tests Used by Courts to Determine the Limits of First Amendment Freedoms

the need for public order and the personal and property rights of other people.

The rights of people seeking to exercise their First Amendment freedoms must be balanced with . . .

Conflicting rights and needs must be balanced.

Anyone who is lawfully present in a public or private place may engage in peaceful and orderly conduct that does not disrupt or disturb the place. That place might be a school,[5] a library,[6] a private lunch counter,[7] the grounds of a statehouse,[8] the grounds of the U.S. Capitol,[9] a bus terminal,[10] an airport,[11] or a welfare center.[12]

Conduct that has First Amendment protection include:

- An orderly demonstration by 187 students on the grounds of the South Carolina Statehouse carrying signs that read "Down with segregation" and "I am proud to be a Negro." Convictions for disorderly conduct dismissed. *Edwards v. South Carolina,* 372 U.S. 229, 83 S.Ct. 680 (1963).

- Five blacks were convicted of breach of the peace for sitting or standing silently in a library that served whites only. Convictions vacated. *Brown v. Louisiana,* 383 U.S. 131, 86 S.Ct. 719 (1966).

- High school students wore black armbands to school to protest the Vietnam War. No disruption of classes or school functions occurred; therefore, their conduct was protected by the First Amendment. *Tinker v. Des Moines Independent Community School District,* 393 U.S. 503, 89 S.Ct. 733 (1969).

First Amendment freedoms and the rights of expression in public places, however, are not absolute. They may be limited or restricted, as illustrated by the U.S. Supreme Court cases in the following box titled, "Types of Public and Quasi-Public Property." When a city, state, or governmental agency restricts or limits conduct, it must show that

1. The government has significant interest (or good reason) based upon the nature of the property, or some other source.

2. However, the restriction or limitation can be no greater "than is essential to the furtherance of that (substantial) interest." *United States v. O'Brien.*

Types of Public and Quasi-Public Property

Property	Use by public for communicating and demonstrating	Restrictions that may be placed on use
Publicly owned streets, sidewalks, and parks	Such property "has been used for purposes of (public) assembly, communicating thoughts between citizens, and discussing public questions."[a]	Reasonable regulations may be imposed to assure public safety and order (for example, traffic regulations).
Government buildings, such as courthouses and city halls	Property used for the business of government during business hours is open to the public at these times so that the public may ordinarily come and go as they wish.	Greater restrictions may be imposed to ensure the functioning of government or the regular use of the facilities by the public. They can accommodate only limited expressions of social protest.
Public hospitals, schools, libraries, and so on	Use of these public facilities is ordinarily limited to the specific function for which they are designed.	Because these facilities need more order and tranquility than do other public buildings, they generally have more restrictions concerning use by the public.
Quasi-public facilities, such as shopping centers, stores, and other privately owned buildings or property to which the public has access	Many quasi-public facilities are as extensively used by the public as are public streets, sidewalks, and parks.	Private owners of quasi-public facilities have greater authority to regulate their property than does the government of public streets and parks (see the material in this chapter).
Public property to which access by the public is limited and restricted	Government may limit and restrict in a reasonable manner the access by the public to jails, executive offices (mayor, police chief, and others), and other facilities that must be restricted to permit government to function effectively.	Such restrictions must be made in a reasonable and nondiscriminating manner.

[a]U.S. Supreme Court in *Kunz v. New York,* 340 U.S. 290, 7 S.Ct. 312 (1951).

3. "The State, no less than a private owner of property, has the power to preserve the property under its control for the use to which it is lawfully dedicated." *Adderley v. Florida,* 385 U.S. 39.

4. Where there is communication (for example, yelling at a basketball game in a public arena as distinguished from yelling in a library or during a church service), the U.S. Supreme Court has said, "[T]he crucial question is whether the manner of expression is basically incompatible with the normal activity of a particular place at a particular time." *Grayned v. City of Rockford,* 408 U.S. 104, 92 S.Ct. 2294 (1972).

U.S. Supreme Court Cases Limiting Conduct[a]

No constitutional right to:	*Facts of the case*	*Ruling of U.S. Supreme Court*
Camp and sleep in national parks in downtown Washington, D.C. (the Mall and Lafayette Park)	Demonstrators argued that "without a permit to sleep, it would be difficult to get the poor and homeless to participate or to be present at all" in a demonstration to call attention to the plight of the homeless.	"[T]here is a substantial Governmental interest in conserving park property. . . . [We are not going to] assign to the judiciary the authority to replace the Park Services as the manager of the Nation's parks." *Clark v. Community for Creative Non-Violence,* 468 U.S. 288, 104 S.Ct. 3065 (1984).
Destroy government property (burn draft card issued to person)	As a protest against the Vietnam War, O'Brien burned his draft card in a public demonstration in violation of federal law. O'Brien wanted "to carry a message" of protest against the draft.	In affirming O'Brien's conviction, the Court noted that the draft card "furthers an important or substantial government interest . . . unrelated to the suppression of free expression." *U.S. v. O'Brien,* 391 U.S. 367, 88 S.Ct. 1673 (1968).
Trespass on government property in area closed to the general public	Demonstrators entered jail grounds through a driveway used only for purposes relating to jail business. They were arrested after they refused to leave after being requested to leave and warned.	"Nothing in the Constitution . . . prevents Florida from evenhanded enforcement of its general trespass statute. . . . The State, no less than a private owner of property, has power to preserve the property under its control for the use to which it is lawfully dedicated." *Adderley v. Florida,* 385 U.S. 39, 87 S.Ct. 242 (1966).
Sell or solicit funds at a fairground, airport, and so on in violation of rules limiting such conduct to fixed locations (such as booths or tables)	The Krishna religion challenged such a regulation, arguing that it violated its religious ritual of Sankirtan, which requires its members to go into public places to sell and distribute religious literature and to solicit donations for the support of the Krishna religion.	All exhibitors, including religious and political exhibitors, can be restricted to booths or tables at airports and state or county fairs. Solicitation for money at airports can be forbidden because of the interference with passengers and traffic. *Heffron v. International Society for Krishna Consciousness,* 101 S.Ct. 2559 (1989).
Distribute literature and solicit political contributions on the sidewalk in front of a post office in violation of a postal regulation	Defendants set up a table and distributed literature and asked for political contributions on a postal sidewalk used by postal customers. They would not leave when warned.	Convictions affirmed. "The Government's ownership of property does not automatically open that property to the public." *United States v. Kokinda,* 110 S.Ct. 3115 (1990).

(continued)

U.S. Supreme Court Cases Limiting Conduct *(continued)*

[a]In the following cases, the U.S. Supreme Court ruled that (1) all political speeches can be forbidden on military bases (*Greer v. Spock,* 96 S.Ct. 1211 (1976); (2) because of improper conduct, a person can be ordered not to enter a military base. (*U.S. v. Albertini,* 105 S.Ct. 2897 (1985); (3) a city may refuse to accept paid political advertising on city buses (*Lehman v. City of Shaker Heights,* 94 S.Ct. 2714 (1974), but a city cannot refuse advertising just because the city mayor did not like the message (*New York Magazine v. Metropolitan Transportation Authority,* 119 S.Ct. 68 (1998).

Picketing, Demonstrations, and Parades

The 1990s produced an increase in the number of protests and *demonstrations* in which civil disobedience occurred. Major issues that caused persons to demonstrate and protest included abortion, nuclear proliferation, environmental concerns, civil rights concerns, and incidents such as a police shooting.

Demonstrations can be orderly and peaceful and cause no disruption of traffic or movement of pedestrians. Or there can be civil disobedience, in which the entrances to buildings are blocked, vehicle and pedestrian traffic is interrupted, and shouting, yelling, chanting, and use of bullhorns, vehicle horns, and sound amplification can occur. The protest might then escalate into an *unlawful assembly* or a riot.

Abortion clinics throughout the United States have been the scenes of constant protests. Most are lawful, with antiabortion protesters expressing their views verbally or with signs. If protesters trespass or block the entrances to abortion clinics, police officers at the scene will react. If threats or intimidation are expressed, buffer zones and clear zones can be established by court injunctions.

In the 1994 case of *Madsen v. Women's Health Center, Inc.,*[13] the U.S. Supreme Court affirmed the establishment of a thirty-six-foot buffer zone ordered by Florida courts around abortion clinic entrances. Noise restrictions were also imposed upon the protesters similar to noise restrictions around hospitals and medical facilities.

In 1997, the U.S. Supreme Court upheld a lower court order in upstate New York that prohibited demonstrators from coming within fifteen feet of the doorways and driveways of abortion clinics. However, the Supreme Court in *Schenck v. Pro-Choice Network*[14] struck a provision in the same court order that prohibited demonstrators from coming within fifteen feet of people entering or leaving the clinics. The Supreme Court held that the "floating" and indefinite nature of the movable buffer zone made it difficult to administer, and raised the prospect that more speech than necessary would be suppressed.

Picketing

Picketing is a form of communication protected by the First Amendment. People may picket city hall or the state capitol with messages. Strikers may picket their place of employment with signs telling the public why they are striking. All public places may be picketed, but cities and states may place reasonable restrictions on picketing. People who are picketing cannot interfere with the rights of others (blocking traffic, interfering with the right to enter the place being picketed, creating a public disorder, and so on).

Cities and counties that enact ordinances forbidding the picketing of private homes (residential picketing) must tailor such ordinances to the guidelines established in the following U.S. Supreme Court case:

Frisby v. Schultz

Supreme Court of the United States (1988) 487 U.S. 474, 108 S.Ct. 2495

The town of Brookfield, Wisconsin (a suburb of Milwaukee), enacted an ordinance forbidding the picketing before or about any residence in the town. Sandra Schultz and others were strongly opposed to abortion and expressed their views on the subject by peaceful picketing on a public street outside the home of a doctor who performed abortions at two clinics in the area. The Supreme Court held that the ordinance was a valid limit of the First Amendment right to picket. Cities, towns, and villages may enact such ordinances if

1. "Alternative channels of communications" are left open. In this case, Ms. Schultz and other protesters could "enter such neighborhoods, alone or in groups, even marching. . . . They may go door-to-door to proselytize their views. They may distribute literature in this manner . . . or through the mails. They may contact residents by telephone, short of harassment."
2. The ordinance is "narrowly tailored to serve a significant government interest." The Court held:

   Because the picketing prohibited by the Brookfield ordinance is speech directed primarily at those who are preemptively unwilling to receive it, the State has a substantial and justifiable interest in banning it. The nature and scope of this interest make the ban narrowly tailored. The ordinance also leaves open ample alternative channels of communication and is content-neutral.

Parades and Demonstrations [15]

The First Amendment gives people the right to "peaceably . . . assemble"; therefore, *parades*, picketing, and demonstrations are a protected form of speech. People gather in such assemblies to express a message. Most municipalities require that groups obtain permits in advance for use of streets or parks. In this manner, municipalities can minimize those inconveniences that a parade or demonstration might cause other people. Parades and demonstrations can be scheduled at times other than rush-hour traffic periods so that sufficient law enforcement officers are in the area to handle traffic and other problems. The following cases illustrate situations that have come before the courts:

- A court held that the city properly refused a parade permit for a second group to conduct a nearby Fourth of July parade because of the possibility of violence. The Federal Court held: "If anything is clear in the area of freedom of expression, it is that two parades cannot march on the same street simultaneously and the city may allow only one." *We've Carried the Rich, Etc. v. City of Philadelphia*, 414 F.Supp. 611, 19 CrL 2273 (1976).

- The U.S. Supreme Court held that a permit had to be issued to a Nazi group to march in storm trooper uniforms and to display swastikas. *National Socialist Party of America v. Village of Skokie*, 434 U.S. 1327, 98 S.Ct. 14, 21 CrL 4088 (1977).

- Sponsors of the New York St. Patrick's Day parade were told that to get a parade permit, they had to include homosexual organizations as a condition of the parade permit. In holding that this violated the free speech of the sponsors of the parade, the Court held that "the message intended to be conveyed by a parade . . . is to be determined by the parade sponsors and not by the state or the city. . . . To hold otherwise would give local government the right of censorship over the thoughts and speech of the people." *Ancient Order of Hibernians v. David Dinkins, Mayor of New York*, 814 F.Supp. 358 (S.D.N.Y. 1993) (The U.S. Supreme Court unanimously ruled similarly in the 1995 Boston case of *Hurley v. American Gay, Lesbian and Bisexual Group of Boston*, 115 S.Ct. 2338.)

The Crimes of Unlawful Assembly[16] and Rioting

Under the old common law, an unlawful assembly was a gathering of three or more people for any unlawful purpose or under such circumstances as to endanger the public peace or cause alarm and apprehension.[17]

An unlawful assembly became a riot under the old common law when those assembled began to execute their enterprise by a breach of the peace. A riot was a tumultuous disturbance of the peace by three or more people assembled with a common purpose to do an unlawful act. Riot was a misdemeanor in common law, with all persons who encouraged, promoted, or took part in it being criminally liable.

States have statutorized one or both of these common law crimes. The state of New York, for example, has enacted the following offenses:[18]

- § 240.10 Unlawful assembly (class B misdemeanor)
- § 240.08 Inciting to riot (class A misdemeanor)
- § 240.06 Riot in the first degree (class E felony)
- § 240.05 Riot in the second degree (class A misdemeanor)

The present Federal Riot Control Statute, Section 2102, Title 18, United States Code Annotated, is as follows:

(a) As used in this chapter, the term "riot" means a public disturbance involving (1) an act or acts of violence by one or more persons part of an assemblage of three or more persons, which act or acts shall constitute a clear and present danger of, or shall result in, damage or injury to the property of any other person or to the person of any other individual or (2) a threat or threats of the commission of an act or acts of violence by one or more persons part of an assemblage of three or more persons having, individually or collectively, the ability of immediate execution of such threat or threats, where the performance of the threatened act or acts of violence would constitute a clear and present danger of, or would result in, damage or injury to the property of any other person or to the person of any other individual.

Obeying Lawful Police Orders[a]

Failure to obey a lawful, valid police order is probably punished as an offense in all states. For example, § 843.02 of the Florida Criminal Code forbids *resisting an officer*: "Whoever shall obstruct or oppose any such officer . . . in the execution of legal process or in the lawful execution of any legal duty . . . shall be guilty of a misdemeanor of the first degree."

A defense to the charge of refusal to obey a police order is an attack on the lawfulness of the order. If the order is not lawful, there would be no duty to obey. In the first two cases presented below, prosecutors issued the wrong criminal charge and the defendants were convicted of crimes they did not commit.

Case	Facts of case	Ruling
Gregory v. City of Chicago, U.S. Supreme Court, 89 S.Ct. 946 (1969)	Comedian Dick Gregory was leading a peaceful and orderly demonstration to the home of the Chicago mayor. Police officers accompanied the marchers, and things went very well until people in a large crowd near the mayor's home began throwing rocks and eggs at the demonstrators. Tough, foul language was directed toward them. Because the situation was dangerous and becoming riotous, the senior police officer asked and then ordered Gregory to discontinue the march and lead the demonstrators out of the area. After repeated refusals, Gregory and others were arrested for disorderly conduct (not the charge of refusal to obey a police officer) and fined $200. The U.S. Supreme Court reversed the convictions, holding:	"[Dick Gregory and others] were convicted not for the manner in which they conducted their march but rather for their refusal to disperse when requested to do so by Chicago police. However reasonable the police request may have been and however laudable the police motives, petitioners were charged and convicted for holding a demonstration, not for a refusal to obey a police officer. As we said in *Garner v. Louisiana,* 368 U.S. 157, 164, 82 S.Ct. 248 (1961): '[I]t is as much a denial of due process to send an accused to prison following conviction for a charge that was never made as it is to convict him upon a charge for which there is no evidence to support that conviction.'"
Norwell v. City of Cincinnati, U.S. Supreme Court, 94 S.Ct. 187 (1973)	The defendant, a 69-year-old man, was walking home from work about 10:45 P.M. on Christmas night in a high-crime neighborhood. A police officer approached the defendant because he had been notified of a "suspicious man" in the neighborhood. When the officer asked the defendant if he lived in the area, the defendant looked at him and walked on. The officer then stopped the defendant twice, but each time the defendant threw off the officer's arm and protested, "I don't tell you people anything." The defendant would not stay in the officer's presence and would not answer any of the officer's questions. The defendant was charged and convicted of disorderly conduct (not refusal to obey a police officer). The U.S. Supreme Court reversed the conviction, holding:	"Upon this record, we are convinced that petitioner was arrested and convicted merely because he verbally and negatively protested Officer Johnson's treatment of him. Surely, one is not to be punished for nonprovocatively voicing his objection to what he obviously felt was a highly questionable detention by a police officer. Regardless of what the motivation may have been behind the expression in this case, it is clear that there was no abusive language or fighting words. If there had been, we would have a different case. See *Chaplinsky v. New Hampshire,* 315 U.S. 568 (1942)."

(continued)

Obeying Lawful Police Orders[a] (continued)

Case	Facts of case	Ruling
City of Oak Creek v. King, Wisconsin Supreme Court, 436 N.W.2d 285 (1989)	When a commercial airline crashed near an airport, the site was sealed off so that emergency equipment and personnel could assist the injured and dying. The defendant and other employees of a newspaper were repeatedly ordered to leave the area, but the defendant wanted to take pictures of the crash site and stated that he would not leave unless he was arrested. The defendant was arrested and convicted of disorderly conduct (not the charge of refusal to obey the police order). The Wisconsin Supreme Court affirmed his conviction and $40 fine.	"We conclude that the appellant's repeated refusal to obey Detective White's reasonable order, combined with his continued penetration into a nonpublic restricted area in the presence of the general public, was conduct of a type which tends to cause or provoke a disturbance, under the circumstances as they then existed. Therefore, we affirm the decision of the circuit court finding the appellant guilty of disorderly conduct."
Georgia v. Storey, Court of Appeals of Georgia, 351 S.E.2d 502, review denied U.S.Sup.Ct., 41 CrL 4023 (1987)	The defendant and others disrupted the Georgia legislature by shouting opposition to the death penalty. They then refused to obey orders of police and security persons to leave the state capitol building.	Convictions for disrupting the legislature and refusal to obey orders were affirmed, and review was denied by the U.S. Supreme Court.
State v. Werstein, Wisconsin Supreme Court, 211 N.W.2d 437 (1973)	To protest the Vietnam War, three women and one man refused to leave the waiting area of an armed forces induction center. There was no evidence that they interfered with or disrupted the functioning of the center. The Court did not believe that the staff of the center feared for their safety because of the presence of the group. The conviction of disorderly conduct was reversed.	The defendants were merely present. Mere presence absent any conduct that tends to cause or provoke a disturbance does not constitute disorderly conduct.
State v. Jaramillo, New Mexico Supreme Court, 498 P.2d 687 (1972)	The defendants sat and lay on the floor in the governor's waiting room. They refused to leave when the office closed at 5:00 P.M. and refused to leave when the building closed at 6:00 P.M. They were convicted under the New Mexico "wrongful use of public property" statute.	The convictions were affirmed, and the statute was held to be constitutional. The Court stated: "There is no question but that a State may regulate the use and occupancy of public buildings."
Daniel v. Tampa, Florida, Federal Court of Appeals, 11th Cir., 38 F.3d 546, review denied U.S. Sup.Ct, 57 CrL 3065 (1995), 515 U.S. 1132.	Because of serious crime problems in public housing projects, canvassing was forbidden. Defendant was warned and refused to leave the building. Conviction for trespass was affirmed.	Florida's trespass-after-warning statute was sustained, and because this was a neutral restriction on speech, it was held to be a reasonable means of combating crime in the public housing project. No First Amendment violation occurred.

(continued)

Obeying Lawful Police Orders[a] (continued)

[a]Other cases in which defendants failed to obey the lawful orders of law enforcement officers include:

- The defendant refused to stay at the scene of a stabbing "until the officers made an assessment of the situation." *Commonwealth v. DeLuca,* 597 A.2d 1121 (Pa. 1991).

- The Maryland Court of Appeals held that police had a right and duty to obtain the identification of a tavern patron who indicated he had material information concerning a stabbing at the tavern, which the officers were investigating. Defendant refused to provide information. *Barnhard v. State,* 602 A.2d 701 (Md. 1992).

Disruption of Religious Services and Public or Private Meetings

Many types of meetings and religious services are conducted daily and weekly throughout the United States. Audiences have a right to hear a speaker, and people attending religious services have a right not to be disturbed. The U.S. Supreme Court has stated: "Hecklers may be expelled from assemblies and religious worship may not be disturbed by those anxious to preach a doctrine of atheism. The right to speak one's mind would often be an empty privilege in a place and at a time beyond the protecting hand of the guardians of public order."[19]

In the case of *State v. Smith,* the defendant was ordered to leave a city council meeting on urban redevelopment because of his disruptive conduct.[20] When the defendant resisted a police officer's efforts to remove him, he was arrested for disorderly conduct. In affirming the defendant's conviction, the Supreme Court of New Jersey held:

> Government could not govern if its vital processes could thus be brought to a halt. . . . The chair must have the power to suppress a disturbance or the threat of one, and the power to quell a disturbance would be empty if its exercise could be met by still another disturbance designed to test the officer's judgment. 46 N.J. at 517, 218 A.2d at 150.

During a Louisiana parish (county) meeting, the defendant refused to give up the floor and insisted on talking on a subject that was not on the agenda for the evening. The defendant and his group yelled, clapped, and sang, causing an uproar. They refused to permit the council to conduct its business, even after a number of recesses and many warnings. In affirming the convictions for disturbing the peace, the Louisiana Court of Appeals held:

> Defendants' First Amendment rights do not allow them to seize the rostrum at a public meeting and voice their opinions in violation of the rights of other citizens who have previously scheduled business. To allow defendants to disrupt a public meeting whenever and wherever they please would result in anarchy and a disintegration of our entire government by law. Defendants violated the disturbing the peace statute, and trial court properly convicted them.
>
> Accordingly, the convictions are affirmed. *State v. Encalade,* 505 S.2d 87, review denied U.S. Sup. Ct., 42 CrL 4057 (1987).

In the 1996 case of *State v. Berrill,* 474 S.E.2d 508, the West Virginia Supreme Court affirmed the defendant's conviction for disrupting a public meeting. The defendant wore a mask and a costume to a school board meeting, interrupted the meeting, and would not follow established procedures for addressing the board. The mask and costume frightened people attending the meeting.

Heckling Political Speakers

Some courts have held that more latitude and a greater opportunity to respond should be permitted at political meetings and demonstrations than would be allowed at religious services or other types of meetings. In the case of *City of Spokane v. McDonough,* the defendant shouted "Warmonger" once to the vice president of the United States during a political speech by the vice president. In reversing the defendant's conviction for disorderly conduct, the Court held:

> Shouting "Warmonger" but once—without more to indicate a further purpose or intention of breaking up the meeting or to deprive the speaker of his audience or to interfere with the rights of others to hear or the speaker to speak—did not amount to a disturbance of the peace, in fact or in law.[21]

The California Supreme Court set aside the defendants' convictions for disturbing a lawful meeting in the 1970 case of *In re Kay.*[22] The defendants clapped, shouted slogans, and waved a flag bearing the emblem of farm workers at an open-air meeting in a public park at which a congressman spoke. The Court held:

> After Congressman Tunney had given a portion of his speech, a comparatively small part of the total crowd, between 25 and 250 persons, engaged in rhythmical clapping and some shouting for about five or ten minutes. This demonstration did not affect the program. Congressman Tunney, who had been using a microphone, finished his speech despite the protest, pausing to assure those protesting that they had a right to do so and to urge them to be grateful that they live in a country whose Constitution protects their right to demonstrate in that manner. At no time did either the speaker or the police ask the protestors to be silent or to leave. Following the end of the protest and of the congressman's speech, the fireworks were shown. The police made no arrests during or immediately following the protest; the prosecution filed charges only some two weeks later.
>
> * * *
>
> Audience activities, such as heckling, interrupting, harsh questioning, and booing, even though they may be . . . discourteous, can nonetheless advance the goals of the First Amendment.

In the 1993 case of *State v. Hardin,*[23] Hardin paid $25 to attend a fund-raising rally at which President George H. W. Bush was the main speaker. Hardin and others opposed the Gulf War, and during Bush's speech continued to chant "No blood for oil" and "Bring the troops home." The chanters were repeatedly asked to be quiet, to sit down, and then to leave. When Hardin refused, he was arrested and convicted of disorderly conduct. A

In order to keep streets and public areas open and safe for the public, some regulations are needed. Here, a senior police officer is advising the leader of a demonstration of his limitations while the news media is filming and recording the conversation. AP/Wide World Photos

jury found that Hardin intentionally disrupted the meeting, and the Iowa Supreme Court affirmed the conviction.

In the case of *Morehead v. Texas,*[24] the defendant disrupted a speech by the Rev. Jesse Jackson, and then loudly called Rev. Jackson a liar. His conviction for obstructing a lawful meeting was affirmed.

Public Order in Business Places

Private places such as restaurants, theaters, sporting facilities, and taverns are regulated to a large extent by the managers and owners of such facilities. A person using coarse and indecent language in a loud voice in a restaurant, for example, might be asked to leave by the manager or the owner. If he or she failed to leave and continued the disruptive conduct, the police would likely be called. In most instances, the police would order the person to leave if he or she were not too intoxicated to drive. The person's disruptive language would not fall within the fighting words doctrine unless it were addressed to a specific person.

In 1977, the case of *Griego v. Wilson* came before the New Mexico Court of Appeals.[25] Evidence showed that Griego became angry, abusive, and profane and used obscene gestures toward John Wilson and other employees of a lumber store. The employees cautioned Griego to stop and offered to refund his money. When the employees became fearful that Griego was about to attack an employee, they restrained him. In ruling that the employees used reasonable force under the circumstances, the Court held:

> We hold that the proprietor of a business has the right to expel or restrain a person who by virtue of abusive conduct refuses to leave or persist in this abusive conduct after being cautioned, though that person was initially on the premises by express or implied invitation, so long as the expulsion or restraint is by reasonable force. See *Ramirez v. Chavez,* 71 Ariz. 239, 226 P.2d 143 (1951); *Penn v. Henderson,* 174 Or. 1, 146 P.2d 760 (1944); *Crouch v. Ringer,* 110 Wash. 612, 188 P. 782 (1920); *Austin v. Metropolitan Life Insurance Co. of New York,* 106 Wash. 371, 180 P. 134, 6 A.L.R. 1061 (1919); *Johanson v. Huntsman,* 60 Utah 402, 209 P. 197 (1922). Annot. Right to Eject Customer from Store, 9 A.L.R. 379.[26]

Civil Liability for Crimes Committed on Premises

Business firms and public organizations do not have an absolute obligation to prevent crimes on their premises, but they do have a duty to provide anyone lawfully on their premises with adequate security and safeguards against foreseeable risks.

The Restatement of Torts (2d) states that civil liability should be imposed

> for physical harm caused by the accidental, negligent, or intentionally harmful acts of third persons . . . and by the failure of the possessor (of premises or land) to exercise reasonable care to a) discover that such acts are being done or are likely to be done, or b) give (an adequate) warning.

Public Nuisances as Civil or Criminal Offenses

In common law, a *public nuisance* was a civil offense. More than two hundred years ago, Blackstone, the famous English lawyer, described nuisances as "anything that unlawfully worketh hurt, inconvenience, or damage." (3 Blackstone Comm., 216.)

Today, cities and states continue to use the civil law of public nuisances to correct problems. By going into a civil court and filing a civil lawsuit, cities can petition the court to declare a public problem to be a nuisance and urge civil remedies. Public nuisance laws have been used to

- Seize and tear down crack houses and property owned by slumlords who allow their properties to be used by gangs or drug dealers
- Seize and take title to the motor vehicle of people who commit offenses such as having sex with a prostitute on a public street[27]
- Obtain court orders against repeat offenders such as people who blocked the entrances to abortion clinics. After some people were arrested more than fifty times, a Wisconsin court issued a court order forbidding this conduct and made violations of the court order punishable by a fine of up to $5,000 and jailing up to one year.
- Obtain court orders against prostitutes with five or more convictions, ordering them not to loiter in specific areas of a city or to flag down cars. Violation of the court order is a much more serious offense than the conviction for prostitution or loitering for the purpose of prostitution and can be punished by a larger fine and longer jail sentences.

Freedom to Dress as You Wish

Like other freedoms, there are limitations upon the freedom to dress as you wish. Dressing as you wish is a liberty right of persons that the government may not restrict unless there are substantial reasons justifying the interference by government. Some of the limitations to dress as you wish are:

- States and cities may (and do) forbid nudity or the exposure of a sex organ in a public place.

- Many jobs, occupations, and professions have dress requirements that must be complied with if a person wants to keep his or her job. In 1986, the U.S. Supreme Court affirmed the uniform requirement of the U.S. Air Force when an officer would not comply and was dropped from the service. *Goldman v. Weinberger,* 475 U.S. 503, 106 S.Ct. 1310.

- Wearing a bulletproof garment or concealing identity while committing a crime is punishable in many (if not all) states in addition to the crime committed.

- The Georgia Supreme Court held in 1990 that wearing the mask and hood of the Ku Klux Klan can be punished as a crime. The Court held that the Klan's history of anonymous violence makes the mask a form of intimidation subject to government control. *State v. Miller,* 398 S.E.2d 547. (See also the case of *Hernandez v. Commonwealth,* 406 S.E.2d 399, in which the Virginia courts sustained a similar antimask statute in the State of Virginia.)

However, a Federal Court of Appeals held that the Town of Palm Beach, Florida, went too far when it made it an offense for male joggers to run without a shirt. *DeWeese v. Town of Palm Beach,* 812 F.2d 1365 (11th Cir. 1987). The Wisconsin Supreme Court also held that the City of Kenosha violated the personal rights of taxi drivers when they established a taxi driver dress code in that city (*Peppies Courtesy Cab Company v. City of Kenosha,* 475 N.W. 156 [1991]).

One of the many dangers in picking up a prostitute is the possibility that the person dressed as a woman may be a man dressed in women's clothing. To minimize this type of dangerous trap, the City of Chicago passed an ordinance forbidding cross-dressing by men (the ordinance did not forbid women from wearing men's clothing in public). The defendants who were arrested argued that they were male transsexuals "undergoing psychiatric therapy in preparation for a sex reassignment operation." The Illinois Supreme Court sustained the ordinance but held that as the ordinance applied to the defendants, it was "an unconstitutional infringement of their liberty interest." The Court did not respond to the defendants' arguments of violations of equal protection and vagueness. *City of Chicago v. Wilson,* 75 Ill.2d 525, 27 Ill.App. 458, 389 N.E.2d 522 (1978). See also the 1986 case of *D.C. v. City of St. Louis,* 795 F.2d 652 (8th Cir.), in which "D.C." was arrested for cross-dressing. In a civil suit for the arrest, he was awarded only nominal damages (a few dollars).

Handbills and Door-to-Door Canvassing as Forms of Communication

Handbills[28]

By standing on a sidewalk of a busy street, a person may communicate with a large number of people by passing out handbills or leaflets. Handbills are an inexpensive means of communication used for many years; their message may be political, religious, social, or commercial.[29] Like pure speech, written communications, such as handbills, cannot urge violence or unlawful acts. They may not contain libel or use clearly obscene communications. They may not direct insulting or fighting words to anyone receiving the handbills.

The U.S. Supreme Court observed that "the unwilling listener is not like the passerby who may be offered a pamphlet in the street but cannot be made to take it."[30] Many of

Other Problems of Cities

Graffiti	To gangs, it is the newspaper of the street. Some call it art. To property owners and to the police, it is crime and a constant problem. In courts, it is charged as criminal damage to property, or under an antigraffiti statute or ordinance.
Fake IDs	Stolen, counterfeited, or doctored ID cards have been called the multimillion-dollar migraine for police, merchants, and financial institutions. MasterCard alone puts its annual losses from false IDs at more than $100 million worldwide. Fake IDs are used by teenagers to gain admission to taverns and by professional criminals to commit forgery and other big-time crimes. Phony driver's licenses, fake state ID cards, phony employee cards, fake Social Security cards, and even fake hospital ID cards can be obtained in most cities.
Vehicle "Cruising"	Vehicle congestion on city streets has been aggravated in many cities by cruising vehicles. Businesses in cruising areas complain, emergency vehicles can be blocked and hampered, and other people using the roads can be delayed and become annoyed. Laws limiting or forbidding cruising have been enacted by some cities and counties. In 1990, the U.S. Court of Appeals for the Third Circuit upheld the cruising law in the case of *Lutz v. City of York, Pennsylvania,* 899 F.2d 255. The Court pointed out that neither the right to speak nor the right to travel is absolute. Public streets, like public forums, must be subject to reasonable regulations to avoid "chaos." It was held that the city's significant safety and congestion problems justified the law, which was held to be "narrowly tailored." Other courts, including the Wisconsin Supreme Court, have upheld cruising ordinances. Wisconsin held that cruising ordinances are a valid function of government in the 1996 case of *Brandmiller v. Chief of Police Arreola,* 544 N.W.2d 894.

the people who do accept handbills will only glance at them and then dispose of the material. This, of course, can create a litter problem.

Because of the litter problem, New York City passed an ordinance forbidding all handbills selling or promoting products (commercial handbills). The highest court in the New York state held that the ordinance violated constitutionally protected speech in the case of *People v. Remeny*:

> The City of course has a legitimate interest in seeing that the exercise of the right does not contribute to the litter on the streets or otherwise violate the law. Thus they may enact reasonable regulations governing the time, place and circumstances of the distribution. But in our view they cannot enact an ordinance absolutely prohibiting all distribution of commercial handbills on city streets and call it a reasonable regulation of the activity. Although we sympathize with the City's desire to eliminate litter from the streets, we have concluded that the ordinance, as presently worded, is unconstitutional.[31]

Door-to-Door Canvassing

Political candidates or individuals with a religious message are among those who frequently go from door-to-door. Door-to-door communication is also used by people selling a product or a service. Door-to-door calls may be limited to verbal communication alone, or they may be combined (as they are in most instances) with the use of handbills.

Many ordinances and statutes have been passed regulating door-to-door canvassing. These ordinances have been designed to prevent crime, to reduce residents' fears about strangers wandering door-to-door, and to avoid harassment of dwellers who find it annoying to answer such calls. The U.S. Supreme Court stated in *Martin v. City of Struthers*:

> Ordinances of the sort now before us may be aimed at the protection of the householders from annoyance, including intrusion upon the hours of rest, and at the prevention of crime. Constant callers, whether selling pots or distributing leaflets, may lessen the peaceful enjoyment of a home as much as a neighborhood glue factory or railroad yard which zoning ordinances may prohibit. . . . In addition, burglars frequently pose as canvassers, either in order that they may have a pretense to discover whether a house is empty and hence ripe for burglary, or for the purpose of spying out the premises in order that they may return later. Crime prevention may thus be the purpose of regulatory ordinances.[32]

In the *City of Struthers* case, the U.S. Supreme Court struck down a municipal ordinance that made it a crime for a solicitor or canvasser to knock on the front door of a resident's home or to ring the doorbell. The Court held that the manner in which the ordinance was written conflicted "with the freedoms of speech and press."

States and municipalities, however, do have the authority to regulate door-to-door canvassing. As door-to-door canvassing falls under the First Amendment, "government may regulate . . . only with narrow specificity."[33] The U.S. Supreme Court affirmed the right to regulate door-to-door canvassing in the 1976 case of *Hynes v. Mayor and Council of Borough of Oradell*, holding:

> There is, of course, no absolute right under the Federal Constitution to enter on the private premises of another and knock on a door for any purpose, and the police power permits reasonable regulation for public safety. We cannot say, and indeed appellants do not argue, that door-to-door canvassing and solicitation are immune from regulation under the State's police power, whether the purpose of the regulation is to protect from danger or to protect the peaceful enjoyment of the home.

Possible regulations of door-to-door canvassing could be (1) a requirement that payment and delivery of an item sold occur twenty-four or forty-eight hours after the initial call at the home or (2) a requirement that canvassers secure permits and be responsive to complaints or (3) an ordinance that forbids door-to-door sales without first obtaining an invitation to enter the premise.

The Crime of Stalking

Stalking has become a serious problem in the United States and in Europe.[34] Victims of stalkers have included women, well-known performers, athletes, government officials, and others. Stalkers have attacked John Lennon, tennis star Monica Seles, and former U.S. presidents. Governors, U.S. senators, and movie and television stars have complained of stalkers.

Waiting in a public place to see or to photograph a publicly known person is not a crime. However, entering onto private land or a private home or building is trespass. Blocking a sidewalk or a roadway and refusing to move are offenses, as are traffic violations. Grabbing, menacing, holding, or touching a person in a threatening manner could justify a criminal charge of assault.

Stalking could be charged under a state stalking statute, or it could be charged under a harassment, disorderly conduct, or disorderly person statute or ordinance. In 1996, interstate stalking and harassment was made a crime regardless of whether the stalker is a spouse or an intimate of the victim. The law, which was part of the 1997 Defense Spending Act, sets penalties of up to five years in prison for interstate stalking and harassment and up to life in prison for bodily injury.

Threatening behavior and harassment could justify criminal charges or could cause a court to issue a restraining order. For example, because photographers were causing Jacqueline Onassis (then widow of former President John F. Kennedy) to become concerned for her young children, a court issued an order requiring photographers to stay some distance away from the children. Such orders are issued when a particular photographer or a member of the paparazzi crosses the line between covering and harassing a celebrity.

In the 1997 California case of *People v. Grams*,[35] a court had issued a protective order against Grams. Grams was charged with violating the order by stalking his estranged girlfriend.

The California law provided that protective orders remained enforceable notwithstanding the acts of the parties until the order was changed by order of the court. Grams argued that he could be entrapped if his girlfriend invited him over and then called the police. The California appellate court held that the California legislature could reasonably provide that only the court could lift the order, as the victim's consent is often misguided. (For further material on harassment and protective orders, see Chapter 14.)

Other Public Order Aspects of U.S. Streets

The Homeless on U.S. Streets

A 1994 report to President Clinton estimated the number of homeless in the United States at about 600,000, stating that the emptying of mental hospitals and the rise of crack abuse have contributed to the problem.[36]

Every city and county in the United States has to deal with the problem of homelessness and poverty. Religious groups, community groups, the police, and government agencies provide assistance to and are in daily contact with the homeless and other people in extreme poverty.

Approximately one-third of all nontraffic tickets issued in the downtown areas of large American cities go to the homeless or persons with histories of moving in and out of homeless shelters.

The nontraffic offenses most often issued are jay-walking, public drinking, public urination, *aggressive panhandling,* and disorderly conduct. Libraries and other public

Homelessness is a serious problem in all large American cities. Most homeless people are adult males, but an increasing number of women and children are among those without homes.
AP/Wide World Photos

buildings generally enforce code violations forbidding sleeping, loitering, extreme body odors, and other misbehaviors.

Persons who are about to be issued a police citation are required to provide identification. In about half of such cases, record checks disclose that the person is wanted for other offenses or for failure to pay previous citations. Some persons have been found to be wanted for up to forty to sixty unpaid citations. Persons showing a false I.D. could be charged with obstruction.

People who are temporarily homeless and on the street are reported to be there primarily because of unemployment, eviction, loss of income, or a domestic fight or disagreement. Long-term homeless people are likely to be mentally ill or to have serious drug or alcohol problems. A national organization providing services for the homeless estimates that as many as half of the homeless people are mentally ill or have emotional problems.

Panhandling or Begging

Panhandling or begging has always occurred in large cities and elsewhere in the United States. The begging can be friendly and nonaggressive. It is usually an impersonal, brief, verbal request for money. Or the panhandling can be aggressive and not friendly. Aggressive panhandling can be menacing and threatening.

A belligerent, angry panhandler who follows a person who has refused to give money would be using aggressive tactics. The language addressed to the passerby could become foul and insulting. Touching, blocking, or shoving the person would be further aggressive acts that could cause the pedestrian to become concerned for his or her safety, to take protective action, or to react in anger.

Homeless people frequently panhandle for money. Most often the begging is done in a pathetic, impersonal manner, or sometimes a friendly appeal to generosity is used. College students are said to be the most likely group to make contributions. Older people are more likely to believe that any money given will be used for alcohol or drugs.

Old begging laws have repeatedly been held to be invalid, as courts have ruled that a simple request for money is speech that is protected by the First Amendment. However, new laws that forbid aggressive panhandling have been enacted and are generally sustained by courts. Laws or regulations that forbid begging in airports, subways, or public buildings have also been upheld.

New York City's law forbidding begging in its subway was upheld in the 1990 case of *Young v. New York City Transit Authority*, 903 F.2d 146 (2d Cir.). But a law forbidding begging throughout the entire city was held to violate the First Amendment, because peaceful begging was held to be a means of communicating with fellow citizens. *Loper v. New York City Police Department*, 999 F.2d 699 (2d Cir. 1993).

Urinating in a Public Place

Since the first century, when the Romans forbade the conduct, urinating in a public place has been an offense. Both European countries and municipalities throughout the United States also forbid such conduct.

However, the offense continues to be a problem. People use streets, sidewalks, public buildings, and subways as a toilet. Public officials point out that public urination creates a health hazard and is also offensive to the general public. Not only is the sight of an adult urinating in a public place offensive, but the smell of urine can linger for some time.

The unavailability of public rest rooms presents a problem in some areas. Private businesses (such as restaurants and gasoline stations) can reserve their facilities for their customers and employees. Vandalism and crime have caused the closing of some public toilets. Clogging of toilets is the biggest problem, while in other instances, fixtures are torn off the wall or otherwise damaged. Public facilities are sometimes closed due to a lack of maintenance and cleaning funds.

People charged with urinating in a public place sometimes complain that no toilet facilities were available in the area. An offender could be a person who has had too much to drink or is too lazy to seek out a toilet facility. The homeless are also sometimes cited as offenders.

Men, by far, are the principal offenders. Enforcement varies with the area of town. Conduct sometimes tolerated in run-down parts of town would not be tolerated in more fashionable areas with beautiful homes and nice shopping centers. In addition, homeowners may become belligerent if strangers enter their property to urinate. A Milwaukee homeowner was convicted of manslaughter in 1988 because of such a confrontation. He came out of his home in the late afternoon to find a stranger urinating on his flowers. The homeowner angrily scolded the stranger for his conduct. The man responded with ugly language, which was overheard by the homeowner's children. In an overwhelming rage, the homeowner obtained a handgun and shot the stranger, killing him.

Compulsory School Attendance Laws and Truancy

All states are reported to have laws requiring parents to send their children to school until the age required in that state. Failure to comply with the compulsory attendance statute could result in a civil or criminal conviction of the parents as provided by the statutes of that state.

A student who is not attending school as required can be classified as a truant if the state statutes so provide. *Truancy* laws vary considerably from state to state. The California Supreme Court stated that a minor (ages 6 to 18) "must be enrolled in a compulsory full-time education program and must be in school during school hours or else he is subject to a § 48264 arrest (truancy arrest)."[37]

Tough truancy laws that are enforced have been shown to cut down on crimes such as burglary, criminal damage to property, theft, and graffiti. Dropout rates in high schools have been reduced. School attendance rates have increased, and parental involvement with children is believed to have increased.

Another type of law that has been used to fight truancy is the daytime "curfew" law. Most of the two hundred largest cities in the United States have enacted daytime curfew ordinances, which require children of school age to be in schools and not on the streets during school hours.[38]

The 1996 report *Creating Safe and Drug-Free Schools*[39] points out that truancy is "a gateway to crime" and that many daytime burglaries and acts of vandalism are linked to truancy. Seventy-one percent of juveniles prosecuted for criminal violations in Miami, Florida, were shown to have serious truancy problems. After Minneapolis, Minnesota, police began citing truant students, daytime crime in that city dropped 68 percent. San Diego, California, reported that 44 percent of violent juvenile crime occurs between 8:30 A.M. and 1:30 P.M.

Curfews

The use of curfews goes back in history to the Middle Ages. William the Conqueror reportedly imposed a curfew on the English people after his invasion of England in 1066. Bells were rung in England at 8:00 P.M., at which time fires were to be put out and people were not to be on the street. This law appears to have been met with so much opposition that, in 1103, it was repealed. Both Blackstone and Shakespeare refer to the use of curfews in early England.

Today, many states and cities have emergency curfew laws, which could be put into effect in the event of an emergency (war, riots, snow emergency, or other widespread disaster such as an earthquake). However, a curfew law aimed at all citizens when no genuine emergency exists is not likely to be passed, because such a law would not be constitutional. The U.S. Supreme Court has repeatedly pointed out that the "freedom to leave one's house and move about at will is of the very essence of a scheme of ordered liberty."[40]

In addition to daytime curfew laws aimed at keeping children in school during school hours, many cities have evening curfews for school-age young people. These laws and ordinances require teenagers and younger children to be off the public streets after the curfew time. Such laws and ordinances were enacted after communities concluded that late-night activities led teens into drinking, drugs, sex, fighting, vandalism, gang activities, and theft. The *Associated Press* article "Clinton Proposes Curfews to Keep Minors off the Street" (May 30, 1996) reported that President Clinton urged all American cities to enact ordinances similar to the ordinances used in seven large cities. *Curfew violations* may be punished by criminal or civil penalties.

SUMMARY

Streets and public places have always been used by the public to express and communicate ideas necessary to a democracy. Government must balance these First Amendment rights with the need for public order and the need to protect property rights and freedoms of others.

The First Amendment protects the right to picket, demonstrate, and conduct parades, door-to-door canvassing, and the passing out of handbills.

Aspects of the crimes of disorderly conduct (disorderly person), obstructing (failure to obey lawful police orders), unlawful assembly, affray, rioting, trespass, public nuisance, stalking, aggressive panhandling, truancy, and curfew violations are presented in this chapter.

BOOK-SPECIFIC WEB SITE

For chapter-related Web links, quizzing activities, and case and news updates, go to the *Criminal Law,* Eighth Edition, book-specific Web site at **http://info.wadsworth.com/ gardner.**

QUESTIONS AND PROBLEMS

1. Cantwell stopped two men on the street. He received permission from them and played a phonograph record that attacked their religion and church. Both men became angry and threatened to strike Cantwell unless he went away. Cantwell immediately left. He was charged with and convicted of violating the breach of the peace statute. Did the U.S. Supreme Court affirm the conviction? *Cantwell v. Connecticut,* 310 U.S. 296, 60 S.Ct. 900 (1940).

2. The defendant addressed a group of blacks who had assembled to protest alleged police brutality. The defendant commended the crowd for their good conduct and restraint and stated that he believed in nonviolent behavior. He then stated to the crowd, "Do your own thing." Was this sufficient to justify a

conviction for the offense of inciting to riot? *State v. Douglas,* 278 So.2d 485 (La. 1973).

3. An off-duty police officer and his friend attended a city council meeting in their home city. They were both properly found to be out of order by the mayor, who was presiding over the meeting. When it appeared that they were going to continue to disrupt the meeting, they were ordered by the mayor to leave. Although the off-duty officer would not leave, his friend did and urged the officer to do the same. The mayor then ordered the off-duty officer removed from the meeting by other police officers. The off-duty officer physically resisted removal from the meeting and was then arrested. He argued that he had a constitutional right to attend the meeting and the mayor as chair of the meeting did not have the

right to eject him. Who is right and who is wrong in this situation? Explain. Should the conviction be affirmed by the Court of Appeals? *Gigler v. City of Klamath Falls*, 21 Or.App. 753, 537 P.2d 121 (1975).

4. Police were called to a reported fight between juveniles and arrived at 9:00 P.M. to observe about twenty juveniles (ranging from teenagers to children as young as 6 years old) heading west in or across a street. Cars traveling on the street had slowed down to go around the children.

The police were told that the fight had broken up and that some of the juveniles left at the sound of the approaching police sirens.

Other children could be seen leaving the group as the police approached.

The remaining juveniles were asked to leave the area. At this point, a 17-year-old boy who was standing just off the street shouted, "What the fuck are you gonna do about it? We can be here if we fucking want to!" The boy was arrested for disorderly conduct and placed in handcuffs in the rear of the squad car.

With about eight or ten juveniles remaining, a 15-year-old boy yelled, "This is bullshit! This whole thing is fucked up! We can do anything we fucking want to do." This boy was also arrested for disorderly conduct, handcuffed, and placed in a squad car. All of the remaining children then dispersed from the area.

Did the language and conduct of the two boys amount to fighting words violations? If these incidents had occurred in your state, could the unlawful assembly statute or the curfew law or ordinance be used to disperse the juveniles? *In re Welfare of M.A.H. and J.L.W.*, 572 N.W. 2d 752 (Minn.App. 1997).

INFOTRAC COLLEGE EDITION EXERCISES

1. Go to InfoTrac College Edition and, using the keyword search term *stalking,* find the March 2001 *Harvard Mental Health Letter* article titled "Stalking" describing the psychological makeup of stalkers. What are some steps prospective victims of stalkers can take to deal with the problem?

2. Go to InfoTrac College Edition and, using the keyword search term *nuisance,* find the 1999 *Stanford Law Review* article discussing the use of public nuisance injunctions to curb urban street gangs. What are some constitutional problems with such a use?

NOTES

1. In the case of *Grayned v. City of Rockford,* 408 U.S. 104, 92 S.Ct. 2294 (1972), the U.S. Supreme Court held: "The nature of a place, 'the pattern of its normal activities, dictates the kinds of regulations of time, place, and manner that are reasonable.' Although a silent vigil may not unduly interfere with a public library, making a speech in the reading room almost certainly would. That same speech should be perfectly appropriate in a park. The crucial question is whether the manner of expression is basically incompatible with the normal activity of a particular place at a particular time. Our cases make clear that in assessing the reasonableness of regulation, we must weigh heavily the fact that communication is involved; the regulation must be narrowly tailored to further the State's legitimate interest. 'Access to [the streets, sidewalks, parks, and other similar public places] for the purpose of exercising [First Amendment rights] cannot constitutionally be denied broadly.' Free expression 'must not, in the guise of regulation, be abridged or denied.'"

2. See *Breard v. Alexandria,* 341 U.S. 622, 71 S.Ct. 920 (1951); *Hall v. Commonwealth,* 188 Va. 72, 49 S.E.2d 369 (1948); appeal dismissed 335 U.S. 875, 69 S.Ct. 240.

3. *Tinker v. Des Moines Independent Community School District,* 393 U.S. 503, 89 S.Ct. 733 (1969). See this case in Chapter 10.

4. *Grayned v. City of Rockford,* 408 U.S. 104, 92 S.Ct. 2294 (1972).

5. *Tinker v. Des Moines Independent Community School District,* 393 U.S. 503, 512–513, 89 S.Ct. 733, 739–740 (1969). This paragraph is a modified version

of a paragraph presented by U.S. Justice Marshall in his concurring and dissenting opinion in the case of *U.S. v. Grace,* 461 U.S. at 185.

6. *Brown v. Louisiana,* 383 U.S. 131, 142, 86 S.Ct. 719, 724 (1966); *id.,* at 146, and n. 5 (Brennan, J., concurring in judgment).

7. *Garner v. Louisiana,* 368 U.S. 157, 201–202, 82 S.Ct. 248, 271–272 (1961) (Harlan, J., concurring in judgment).

8. *Edwards v. South Carolina,* 372 U.S. 229, 83 S.Ct. 680 (1963).

9. *Jeannette Rankin Brigade v. Chief of Capitol Police,* 342 F.Supp. 575 (D.D.C. 1972), summarily affirmed 409 U.S. 972, 93 S.Ct. 311 (1972).

10. *Wolin v. Port of New York Authority,* 392 F.2d 83 (2d Cir. 1968), cert. denied 393 U.S. 940, 89 S.Ct. 290 (1968).

11. *Chicago Area Military Project v. City of Chicago,* 508 F.2d 921 (7th Cir. 1975), cert. denied 421 U.S. 992, 95 S.Ct. 1999 (1975); *Kuszynski v. City of Oakland,* 479 F.2d 1130 (9th Cir. 1973).

12. *Albany Welfare Rights Organization v. Wyman,* 493 F.2d 1319 (2d Cir. 1974), cert. denied 419 U.S. 838, 95 S.Ct. 66 (1974).

13. 114 S.Ct. 2516 (1994).

14. *Schenck v. Pro-Choice Network of Western New York,* 117 S.Ct. 855 (1977).

15. Ku Klux Klan demonstrations and parades cost local communities a lot of money. There generally are less than two dozen Ku Kluxers who will show up, but the number of people who will appear to protest against the Ku Klux Klan will be many more. The likelihood of violence and disorderly conduct is very great. Therefore, adequate police protection must be provided, which means providing sufficient money for the necessary extra law enforcement and other costs.

Because of such additional expenses, some communities passed laws and ordinances permitting the imposition of a fee based upon anticipated costs. This would mean that a local administrator would have to estimate the costs depending upon who the group was. The U.S. Supreme Court struck down an ordinance that provided for a fee in the case of *Forsyth County v. Nationalist Movement* (a Ku Klux Klan group), 112 S.Ct. 2395 (1992). The U.S. Supreme Court pointed out that to estimate the fee, the local official had to consider who the group was and the contents of the message they were communicating.

Requiring the prepayment of an $85 fee for the processing of a parade permit application and the cost of traffic control was upheld by the courts in the case of *Stonewell Union v. City of Columbus,* 931 F.2d 1130 (6th Cir. 1991), review denied U.S. Supreme Court 112 S.Ct. 275 (1991).

16. States generally statutorize the crime of unlawful assembly, as does Florida in § 870.03 of the Florida Criminal Code. But some states provide that the crime of unlawful assembly is committed when the person gathered in the unlawful assembly fails to leave the area after law enforcement declares the gathering to be an unlawful assembly and orders the group or crowd to disperse and leave the area.

17. Under the old common law, if a number of people met together and suddenly quarreled and fought among themselves, this would constitute an affray. An *affray* differs from a riot in that an affray is not premeditated. Under the old common law, a riot required three or more persons, while an affray could consist of two or more.

18. Under New York statutes, four or more people plus the person charged are needed for the crime of "unlawful assembly." To convict of any of the riot offenses, it must be shown that there were ten or more people plus the person charged.

19. *Kovacs v. Cooper,* 336 U.S. 77, 69 S.Ct. 448 (1949).

20. 46 N.J. 510, 218 A.2d 147 (1966). See also *Bennett v. Hansen,* 948 F.2d 397, review denied U.S. Sup. Ct., 50 CrL 3198 (1992).

21. 79 Wash.2d 351, 485 P.2d 449 (1971).

22. 83 Cal.Rptr. 686, 464 P.2d 142 (1970).

23. 498 N.W.2d. 677 (Iowa 1993).

24. 807 S.W.2d. 577 (Tex.App. 1991).

25. 91 N.M. 74, 570 P.2d 612 (1977).

26. *Griego v. Wilson* was a civil action for damages for injuries the plaintiff alleged he received at the hands of the store employees. The dismissal of the case by the trial court was affirmed by the Court of Appeals.

27. In the case of *Bennis v. Michigan,* 134 L.Ed.2d 68 (1996), the vehicle of Mr. Bennis was forfeited after he was convicted of this offense. But Mrs. Bennis was an

innocent co-owner of the car and appealed to the U.S. Supreme Court. The Supreme Court held that as the vehicle was an abatable nuisance, it could be forfeited without an offset for the innocent co-owner and without a showing that the innocent co-owner knew or consented to the public misuse of the vehicle.

28. Malls, shopping centers, and supermarkets are privately owned properties that are open to the public. Most shopping centers and supermarkets forbid demonstrations and the distribution of handbills on their property. Most states have held that the owners of shopping malls may forbid handbills and any demonstrations on their property if the regulations apply to all groups.

Six states—California, Oregon, Massachusetts, Colorado, Washington, and New Jersey—however, hold that shopping malls have replaced parks and downtown streets that in past years were the home of free speech. In these states, handbills, picketing, demonstrating, and other forms of First Amendment communications may be "reasonably exercised . . . even when the centers are privately owned." *PruneYard Shopping Center v. Robins*, 100 S.Ct. 2035 (1980).

29. Commercial messages include commercial advertising by firms or people seeking to promote sales of their products or services. In the 1942 case of *Valentine v. Chrestensen*, 316 U.S. 52, 62 S.Ct. 920, the U.S. Supreme Court held that cities and states could absolutely forbid the distribution of commercial handbills in public places. However, in 1976 the U.S. Supreme Court reversed itself in *Virginia State Board of Pharmacy v. Virginia Citizens Consumer Council, Inc.*, 425 U.S. 748, 96 S.Ct. 1817, in which the Court held that "commercial speech, like other varieties, is protected."

30. *Kovacs v. Cooper*, 336 U.S. 77, 69 S.Ct. 448 (1949).

31. 40 N.Y.2d 527, 387 N.Y.S.2d 415, 355 N.E.2d 375, 19 CrL 2366 (1976). In the 1994 case of *Miller v. City of Laramie*, 1994 WL 479065, the Wyoming Supreme Court reversed Miller's conviction for littering.

Miller had distributed free newspapers door-to-door. A few complaints were made to the police that newspapers ended up in streets, yards, and other places as litter. As there was no evidence that Miller had personally caused the litter, his conviction was reversed, with the Wyoming Supreme Court holding that the conviction violated Miller's First Amendment rights.

32. 319 U.S. 141, 63 S.Ct. 862 (1943).

33. *NAACP v. Button*, 371 U.S. 415, 433, 83 S.Ct. 328, 338 (1963).

34. The *New York Times* article "His Credo: Be Afraid. Be Very Afraid" (July 14, 1997) states that a federal study estimates that a million American women and 400,000 men are stalked each year. The article is about Gavin de Becker, who is the security adviser to many Hollywood stars.

35. 60 Cal.Rptr.2d 423 (Cal.App.2d 1997).

36. See the *New York Times* article "Report to Clinton Sees Vast Extent of Homelessness" (February 17, 1994).

37. *In re James D.*, 43 Cal.3d 903, 239 Cal.Rptr. 663, 741 P.2d 161 (1987), quoting *In re Miguel G.*, 111 Cal.App.3d 345, 168 Cal.Rptr. 688 (1980).

38. See *A Manual to Combat Truancy* published by the U.S. Office of Juvenile Justice and Delinquency Prevention in the United States. See also the *Milwaukee Journal Sentinel* article "Daytime Curfews May Come to Wisconsin" (September 10, 1997), which points out that a few smaller cities in Wisconsin have daytime loitering ordinances that are similar to daytime curfew laws. In one Wisconsin city, the forfeiture for loitering is $61.90, which can be levied against the student or the parent.

39. The report "Creating Safe and Drug-Free Schools" was published by a combined effort of the U.S. Department of Justice and the U.S. Department of Education.

40. *Palko v. Connecticut*, 302 U.S. 319, 325, 58 S.Ct. 149, 151 (1937).

12

The Limits of Other Freedoms

KEY TERMS

Second Amendment

regulating firearms:
federal laws, state laws

deadly weapons

crime of failure to
properly store a loaded
firearm

religious freedom to
believe

right of privacy

The Second Amendment

The twenty-seven words of the *Second Amendment* of the U.S. Constitution read as follows:

> "A well regulated Militia, being necessary to the security of a free State, the right of the people to keep and bear Arms, shall not be infringed."

When the Second Amendment of the U.S. Constitution was ratified in 1791 as part of the Bill of Rights, the newly formed United States was a frontier nation with its three million or so people isolated from one another to a degree that is hard for us to imagine. There were no telephones, radios, or motor vehicles by which public officials and law enforcement officers could be summoned in an emergency. The few law enforcement officers could be found only in the towns and cities that were hours and sometimes days away from the farms and homes of many of the settlers.

Firearms were essential for survival because most of the families depended on wild game as part of their subsistence. Guns were also needed for self-defense, because organized law enforcement agencies were not within immediate call of most of the population. The American colonies were fearful of standing armies, since they had just thrown off the military control of Great Britain. The American Revolution had been fought by citizen part-time soldiers. Under the new republic, the country had no need for a big army and looked on all able-bodied men as militia members who would be available in time of need, just as they had been in the 1770s. The "well regulated Militia" to which the Second Amendment refers was composed of the farmers and townspeople who had taken up arms against the British. Under those circumstances, the logic and meaning of the Second Amendment was apparent, because it stated a national need as basic as free speech and free religion to the newly formed democracy.

The Second Amendment Today

Today, the United States is composed of fifty states with more than 280 million people living primarily in crowded metropolitan areas. Instead of a militia made up principally of citizen part-time soldiers who bring their own weapons, it maintains huge federal military forces and National Guard units. Because the country no longer needs the private arms of its citizens for defense, what is the meaning of the Second Amendment today?

Nations such as England[1] and Japan strictly regulate the private possession and ownership of weapons. Other European countries have strict gun control laws. Compared with these nations, the United States exerts little control over the private ownership and possession of weapons. The United States has the highest per capita ownership of handguns in the world today and is the most lawless of the industrial nations of the world, with the highest homicide rate of that group.

The American Police Foundation estimates that there are more than 192 million privately owned firearms in the United States.[2] Forty-six percent of the gun owners stated they own the gun for protection against crime. The Police Foundation survey concluded that on any given day in the United States, 3 million adults carry a gun, either on their person (1 million) or in their car or truck (2 million).

The Political Battle as to Gun Control Laws in the United States

All states and the federal government have criminal laws concerning deadly weapons, and about 2 percent of arrests throughout the United States are reported as being for firearm violations.[3]

States may regulate firearms as they wish.[4] No federal court has ever struck down either a state or a federal gun control law of any kind as a violation of the Second Amendment. The U.S. Congress has the power to regulate all aspects of the international and interstate sales and shipments of firearms.

The National Rifle Association (NRA) has led the fight at federal and state levels of government against gun control laws. The NRA has about 2.8 million members and more than $70 million in annual revenues. It has skillfully pushed NRA programs with members of the U.S. Congress and members of state legislative bodies, obtaining support from members of both political parties. Positions of both sides of the gun control issue can be summarized as follows:

National Rifle Association	Advocates of Gun Control Laws
People in the United States have a constitutional right to own and carry arms.	The claim that gun control laws violate the Second Amendment has no legal or historic basis. Former U.S. Supreme Court Chief Justice Warren Burger called the NRA claim a "fraud on the American public."
If guns are outlawed, only outlaws will have guns.	Sensible gun control laws will help stem the gun violence that causes the deaths of more than 30,000 Americans a year, including more than 4,000 children.
Guns are not the problem; criminals are the problem. ("Guns don't kill; people kill.")	Guns "contribute . . . directly to the shocking number of murders in our country." (Retired U.S. Supreme Court Justice Lewis F. Powell before the American Bar Association)

Federal Laws Regulating Firearms

In the 1920s and 1930s, criminals began crossing state lines and using cars, automatic weapons, shotguns, and handguns to commit crimes. In reaction to this gang warfare and the assassination attempt against President-elect Franklin D. Roosevelt in 1933 (which resulted in the killing of the mayor of Chicago), federal legislation was enacted. The following is a summary of the present *federal laws regulating firearms*:

To convict a person of the crime of CCW (carrying a concealed weapon), the city or state must show

1. that the instrument was a "dangerous weapon," "deadly weapon," or "weapon," as described by the statute or ordinance,

2. that the weapon was concealed, and

3. that the weapon was within the defendant's "easy reach and under his control," and

4. the statute might also require that it be in a public place or that "going armed" would require that it be a place other than the home of the defendant.

Present Federal Firearm Law	Summary of the Law
The 1934 National Firearms Act	Requires FBI background checks of machine-gun buyers and registration of automatic weapons and sawed-off shotguns.
The 1938 Federal Firearms Act	Requires that dealers shipping firearms across state lines and importers be licensed by the federal government. But federal firearm dealer licenses are easy to obtain, and thousands of licensed dealers plus many private persons have fireams to sell to gun buyers.
The 1968 Gun Control Act is the primary gun law in the United States today. It was enacted after the murders of President Kennedy, Rev. Martin Luther King, Jr., and Senator Robert Kennedy.	Requires the registration of "destructive devices" (cannons, antitank guns, bazookas, and so on) and forbids the importation of cheap handguns such as the $6 "Saturday Night Special" that killed Senator Robert Kennedy. Critics point out, however, that although foreign junk guns and military firearms cannot be imported, gun parts may be imported and assembled in the United States.
The 1986 Firearms Owners' Protection Act	Allows gun dealers to sell at gun shows and restricts unannounced inspections by the federal Bureau of Alcohol, Tobacco and Firearms (BATF) to one per year.
The 1994 Brady Handgun Violence and Prevention Act	Establishes a national five-day waiting period to check the background of people seeking to purchase handguns. The U.S. Bureau of Justice Statistics reported that over twelve thousand people a month were rejected because of felony records or mental impairment and could not purchase handguns. The Brady Act does not cover the private sale of handguns between private individuals, so a person seeking a handgun can buy one from a private person or use a "straw buyer" to get around the Brady Act.

(continued)

Present Federal Firearm Law	Summary of the Law
The 1994 Violent Crime Control and Law Enforcement Act	Forbids the manufacture, sale, or possession of 19 kinds of assault weapons and also the manufacture and sale of semiautomatic weapons with military characteristics such as bayonet mounts, grenade launchers, and flash suppressors.[5]

Dangerous or Deadly Weapons[6]

All states and cities hold that operational revolvers, rifles, and shotguns are dangerous or *deadly weapons* within the meaning of their statutes or ordinances. Firearms (by themselves) have always been considered deadly and dangerous. In order to make rifles and shotguns concealable, people about to commit a crime will sometimes saw off the barrel. Many states and cities make sawed-off rifles and shotguns contraband in themselves and forbid possession of such objects.

State Laws Regulating the Carrying of a Concealed Weapon

Possession of weapons by private persons and the carrying of concealed weapons are matters regulated by each state. The following are the classes of laws regulating the carrying of concealed weapons:

Type of law	Requirement of law	States reported to have this law
Carrying a concealed weapon is a basic right of citizens. Permits are easily obtained.	Usual requirements include that the person has no criminal record and no mental illness, and many states require completion of classroom and range training course.	Most southern states including Texas and Florida; most western states (except California), Virginia, Alaska, Pennsylvania, and a few New England states
Permits to carry a concealed gun are limited.	The preceding restrictions and others are used.	California, Colorado, Iowa, Minnesota, Michigan, New York, South Carolina, Louisiana, Maryland, Delaware, New Jersey, Massachusetts, and Connecticut
Permits to carry a concealed weapon are not issued.	Only law enforcement officers may carry concealed weapons	Ohio, Kentucky, Illinois, Wisconsin, Missouri, Kansas, Nebraska, and New Mexico
Carrying a loaded gun out in the open technically is legal.	Guns can be carried in the open by hunters in towns, and private security people may carry guns in the open.	Many western states (except California), Kansas, Missouri, Wisconsin, Kentucky, Michigan, Virginia, Pennsylvania, North Carolina, New Hampshire, Maine, Alaska, and Nebraska
Permits are required to carry a loaded gun openly in a vehicle		Alabama, Michigan, and Pennsylvania

Other objects that could fall within the category of dangerous or deadly weapons include switchblade knives, folding knives with blades that lock open, brass knuckles, saps, and other specially designed objects with little or no other use than to cause injury to another person.

The question of whether an unloaded gun is a dangerous weapon was presented to the U.S. Supreme Court in the 1986 case of *McLaughlin v. United States*.[7] In following the majority rule used for years in the United States, the Supreme Court held:

> Three reasons, each independently sufficient, support the conclusion that an unloaded gun is a "dangerous weapon." First, a gun is an article that is typically and characteristically dangerous; the use for which it is manufactured and sold is a dangerous one, and the law reasonably may presume that such an article is always dangerous even though it may not be armed at a particular time or place. In addition, the display of a gun instills fear in the average citizen; as a consequence, it creates an immediate danger that a violent response will ensue. Finally, a gun can cause harm when used as a bludgeon.

Proving the Weapon Was Within the Defendant's "Easy Reach and Under His/Her Control"

Courts have held that, in the following cases, weapons were within a defendant's easy reach and under his or her control and sustained convictions for carrying concealed weapons:

- In a zippered canvas bag that the defendant put on a conveyor belt at an airport security checkpoint. *State v. Molins,* 424 So.2d 29 (Fla.App. 1982).

- In a suitcase or briefcase carried by the defendant. *People v. Dunn,* 132 Cal.Rptr. 921 (Cal.App. 1976), and *People v. Pugach,* 204 N.E.2d 176 (N.Y.App. 1964).

- In a satchel on the seat of his car or on the floor of the car next to the defendant's foot. *State v. Williams,* 636 P.2d 1092 (Utah 1981), and *State v. Morrison,* 549 P.2d 1295 (Ore.App. 1976).

- The pistol was found under the driver's seat of the car, and ammunition was under the passenger's seat. *Ridley v. State,* 621 So.2d 409 (Fla. 1993).

- The Illinois "armed violence" statute forbids a person from committing a felony while armed with a dangerous weapon. While committing a drug violation, the firearm was present at defendant's thigh, and a clip of ammunition was in his coat pocket. Defendant's conviction was affirmed. *People v. Orsby,* 675 N.E.2d 237 (Ill.App. 1996).

Concealed Weapons

The question of when a weapon is concealed has come before many courts in CCW cases. Does a weapon have to be so concealed that it gives absolutely no notice of its presence, or is a weapon concealed when it cannot be seen in ordinary observation? In the following 1981 decision, the Florida Supreme Court adopted the majority position in the United States that "a weapon need not be totally hidden from view to be 'concealed.'"

Does Your State Have Gun Control Laws Regulating the Following?

Statute #

Forbidding possession by

- a minor? (pistol only?)   _____
- a person convicted of a felony?   _____
- a person who is intoxicated?   _____
- a person who is committing a crime?   _____
- a person going into or who is
  in a public building?   _____
- other?   _____

Statutes providing "add-on" prison terms for

- committing a crime with use of
  (or threat of) a dangerous weapon:
      misdemeanor?   _____
      felony?   _____
- use of bulletproof garment while
  committing crime?   _____
- concealing identity while committing
  crime:
      misdemeanor?   _____
      felony?   _____
- repeater or habitual criminal statute
  for person who has previously
  committed:
      misdemeanors?   _____
      felonies?   _____
- other?   _____

*Forbidding possession, sale, use,
or transportation of*

- short-barreled ("sawed-off") rifle
  or shotgun?   _____
- machine gun?   _____
- bomb, hand grenade, shell,
  projectile?   _____
- switchblade knife?   _____
- silencer?   _____
- electric weapon (stun gun)?   _____
- mace, tear gas, and/or other
  chemical sprays?   _____
- other?   _____

Statute #

Forbidding the following conduct

- carrying a concealed weapon
  (CCW)?   _____
- pointing a firearm at or toward
  another person?   _____
- discharging a firearm on the land
  of another?   _____
- discharging a firearm within a
  municipality?   _____
- discharging a firearm into a vehicle
  or building?   _____
- setting a spring gun (trap)?   _____
- selling or giving a pistol to a minor?   _____
- reckless use of a weapon?   _____
- possession or transportation of
  firearm in:
      a watercraft (motorboat)?   _____
      an aircraft?   _____
      a motor vehicle?   _____
- brandishing a firearm?   _____
- possession of an unlicensed gun
  in a home or place of business?   _____
- other?   _____

Regulating purchase and use of firearms

- persons excluded (insane,
  convicted of felony, and so on)?   _____
- waiting period for purchase of?   _____
  waiting time?   _____
- instructional program on safe
  use of firearms?   _____
- other?   _____

Requiring firearm owners

- to store firearms in a place that
  is reasonably inaccessible to
  children or to use a gun lock that
  makes the gun inoperable:
      loaded firearms only?   _____
      loaded or unloaded?   _____
      ammunition also covered?   _____
- other?   _____

Ensor v. State

Florida Supreme Court (1981) 403 So.2d 349, 29 CrL 2304

After police officers made a lawful traffic stop, a derringer was observed protruding from a floor mat in the car. The gun was held to be "concealed" within the meaning of the state law, and the defendant was convicted of CCW. The court affirmed the conviction, holding:

> The majority of courts in other jurisdictions that have considered the issue have concluded that a weapon need not be totally hidden from view to be "concealed." See, e.g., *Mularkey v. State,* 230 N.W. 76 (Wis. 1930), *People v. Williams,* 39 Ill.App.3d 129, 350 N.E.2d 81 (1976), and *Driggers v. State,* 26 So. 512 (Ala. 1899).
>
> We agree with the majority view and find that absolute invisibility is not a necessary element to a finding of concealment under section 790.001. The operative language of that section establishes a two-fold test. For a firearm to be concealed, it must be (1) on or about the person and (2) hidden from the ordinary sight of another person. The term "on or about the person" means physically on the person or readily accessible to him. This generally includes the interior of an automobile and the vehicle's glove compartment, whether or not locked. The term "ordinary sight of another person" means that casual and ordinary observation of another in the normal associations of life. Ordinary observation by a person other than a police officer does not generally include the floorboard of a vehicle, whether or not the weapon is wholly or partially visible. Further, the fact that a firearm is encased in a holster does not remove it from the application of section 790.001. A firearm encased in a holster and hidden under an automobile seat is no different than a traditionally concealed firearm in a shoulder holster under one's coat. Both appear to be outside the "ordinary sight of another person."

Endangering Public Safety by Failure to Properly Store Loaded Firearms

If loaded firearms are carelessly stored in places where children and teenagers can easily obtain them, tragedy can occur. Deaths and injuries will happen if children play with loaded firearms. Children and teenagers could take firearms to school, and in one instance, a 4-year-old boy in a Cleveland day-care center was found to have a loaded revolver hidden in his clothing.

To address this problem, states in recent years began passing laws requiring adults to either store loaded firearms in a place that is reasonably inaccessible to children or to use a gun lock that makes the firearm inoperable. If a child obtains an improperly stored gun in a state that imposes the legal duty to properly store weapons, the owner is criminally liable under the law of that state. It is hoped that all gun owners will act responsibly to ensure public safety.

The Free Exercise of Religion

The Right to Believe or Not to Believe

In 1890, the U.S. Supreme Court defined the First Amendment freedom of religion as follows:

> The First Amendment was intended to allow every one under the jurisdiction of the United States to entertain such notions respecting his relations to his Maker and the duties they impose as may be approved by his judgment and conscience, and to ex-

hibit his sentiments in such form of worship, as he may think proper, not injurious to the equal rights of others." [8]

Freedom to believe is absolute; freedom to act is not. The U.S. Supreme Court stated, "We have never held that an individual's religious belief excuses him from compliance with an otherwise valid law prohibiting conduct that the state is free to regulate."

The U.S. Supreme Court and other courts have held that the conduct described in the following box is not protected by the First Amendment freedom of religion clause.

Conduct Not Protected by the Freedom of Religion Clause

Conduct not protected [9]	*Case*
Multiple marriages in violation of state polygamy laws (crime of bigamy)	*Reynolds v. United States,* U.S. Supreme Court (1879) 98 U.S. 145, 25 L.Ed. 244
Handling poisonous snakes in a public place in violation of the state law [10] as part of a religious ceremony	*State v. Massey,* North Carolina Supreme Court (1949) 229 N.C. 734, 51 S.E.2d 179
Requirements at airports, state fairs, and so on that religious, political, and other groups distribute or sell literature only from booths provided for that purpose. [11]	*Heffron v. International Society for Krishna Consciousness,* U.S. Supreme Court (1981) 452 U.S. 640, 101 S.Ct. 2559
Mailboxes are for mail only. Putting other literature (religious, political, and so on) into a mailbox can be a violation of a postal regulation that was upheld by the U.S. Supreme Court, which noted that a mailbox is not a "soapbox."	*Council of Greenburgh Civic Associations v. U.S. Postal Service,* U.S. Supreme Court (1981) 453 U.S. 917, 101 S.Ct. 3150
Violation of child labor laws	*Prince v. Massachusetts,* U.S. Supreme Court (1944) 321 U.S. 158, 64 S.Ct. 438
Failure to comply with compulsory military service by defendants who conscientiously objected only to the Vietnam War	*Gillette v. United States,* U.S. Supreme Court (1971) 401 U.S. 437, 91 S.Ct. 828
Air Force officer continued to wear his yarmulke (Jewish skullcap) after repeated orders to remove it. He was dropped from the service. Affirmed for Air Force.	*Goldman v. Weinberger,* U.S. Supreme Court (1986) 475 U.S. 503, 106 S.Ct. 1310
Illegal importation of aliens in violation of Immigration and Nationality Act 8 U.S.C.A. § 1324	*United States v. Merkt,* review denied U.S. Supreme Court (5th Cir. 1987) 794 F.2d 950, 41 CrL 4001 [12]
Members of the Old Order Amish who do not use motor vehicles but travel in horse-drawn buggies, would not obey a state law requiring reflecting triangles on the rear of all slow-moving vehicles. Held not exempt from complying with this highway safety law.	*Minnesota v. Hershberger,* U.S. Supreme Court (1990) 495 U.S. 901, 110 S.Ct. 1918, vacating 444 N.W.2d 282
There was also no exemption on religious grounds from complying with required vehicle liability insurance. South Dakota law makes it a crime not to carry the insurance.	*South Dakota v. Cosgrove,* South Dakota Supreme Court (1989) 439 N.W.2d 119, review denied 493 U.S. 846, 110 S.Ct. 140, 46 CrL 3008

Cults, Sects, and Nontraditional Churches in the United States[13]

More than 70 percent of Americans are members of an organized religion. Most religious organizations in the United States are old, traditional organizations, whereas some churches (primarily Evangelical Christians) are served by television ministers. Only a small percentage of the thousands of churches can be classified as cults.

Cults have received a great amount of worldwide attention because of events such as the following:

- In the 1960s, Charles Manson's "family" murdered eight people in Los Angeles, including actress Sharon Tate.

- In the 1970s, to end a standoff with a religious cult, Philadelphia police bombed the cult headquarters, killing eleven people and destroying buildings in two city blocks.

- In 1978, U.S. Congressman Leo Ryan and his staff traveled to South America to investigate reports that residents of California were being held against their will in the People's Temple located in Jonestown, Guyana. As Congressman Ryan and his staff were leaving Jonestown, they were slaughtered in a barrage of gunfire. This ambush was followed by murders and suicides of almost nine hundred cult members living in the People's Temple.

- In 1984, the followers of Bhagwan Shree Rajneesh deliberately contaminated restaurant salad bars in Oregon, causing about 751 cases of salmonella poisoning.

- In the 1993 federal assault on the Branch Davidian buildings at Waco, Texas, federal agents and more than eighty Branch Davidians were killed in the confrontation. Cult leader David Koresh, who predicted the world was coming to an end, was among the dead.

- In 1994, Swiss and Canadian police were investigating the deaths of fifty-two members of a cult operating in Canada and Switzerland.[14]

- In 1995, Japanese police were investigating the Aum Shinrikyo religious sect because of the poison gas attacks on the Tokyo subway system. The cult is believed to have ten thousand members in Japan and thirty thousand in Russia.

- In 1996, New York City police responded to a call reporting a crying child and found the headquarters of a heavily armed cult. The officers seized pistols, rifles, shotguns, and two Thompson submachine guns.[15]

- In 1997, thirty-nine members of the Heaven's Gate cult committed suicide in Rancho Santa Fe, California (near San Diego). A Web site owned by the cult stated that the members wished to leave earth and rendezvous with a spaceship behind Comet Hale-Bopp.[16]

The Right of Privacy

The Use and Distribution of Contraceptives

In the 1960s, some states had criminal laws regulating contraceptives. For example, in Wisconsin it was a criminal offense to sell or give a contraceptive, such as a condom, to an unmarried person. The fact that the law was generally ignored was demonstrated by a newspaper reporter who purchased condoms at more than a dozen drugstores, making it known that he was not married. Another man attempted to get arrested and challenge the law by handing out hundreds of condoms to students at the University of Wisconsin. However, no one would arrest him, and the Wisconsin law remained unused until it was repealed.

Prosecutors in Connecticut, however, decided to issue a charge using a statute that made it a crime for any person (married or unmarried) to use a contraceptive device or to counsel or advise in the use of such devices. The defendants were operators of a Planned Parenthood clinic and were convicted of providing information and medical advice to a married woman on methods to prevent conception. When the case of *Griswold v. Connecticut* was appealed to the U.S. Supreme Court, the Court recognized a constitutional right of privacy for the first time.[17] The Court held that the marital relationship was within the "zone of privacy" created by the Bill of Rights. It was held that the Connecticut statute invaded the protected right of privacy and was therefore invalid.

The concept that the Bill of Rights creates a fundamental right of privacy was again stated by the U.S. Supreme Court a few years after *Griswold* in the 1969 case of *Stanley v. Georgia.*[18] In *Stanley,* the Court held that the *right of privacy* protects the right to possess and look at obscene films in one's home. In the 1972 case of *Eisenstadt v. Baird,* the U.S. Supreme Court upheld the right of unmarried people to use contraceptives.[19]

Today, because of AIDS, some public and private agencies are distributing free condoms. The need for protected sex and safe sex is being taught to children in some public and private schools.

The Abortion Question

Until 1973, abortion was a crime in most states, with only four states permitting abortion on demand by women. In 1973, the cases of *Roe v. Wade,* 93 S.Ct. 705, and *Doe v. Bolton,* 93 S.Ct. 739, came before the U.S. Supreme Court. The rulings in these cases found that the abortion laws in thirty-one states were unconstitutional and made changes necessary in the abortion laws of fifteen other states.

The issue of abortion continues to remain highly controversial, and laws differ from state to state. Abortion practices are generally governed by the following:

1. Because only a licensed physician may perform a legal abortion, any other person who engages in such acts may be charged with the crime of practicing medicine without a license.[20]

2. Licensed physicians (who do abortions) generally limit abortions to early in the pregnancy, because of the increased possibilities of
   a) a civil malpractice suit
   b) criminal charges if the fetus is "born alive"[21] and then destroyed
   c) disciplinary measures taken by the medical licensing board (such as loss of license)
   d) loss of hospital privileges for violating hospital rules and thereby making the hospital vulnerable to civil suit
   e) increased malpractice insurance premiums because of increased liability

SUMMARY

States may regulate firearms as they wish, and all states have criminal laws regulating firearms. Some states, such as the New York, have very strict gun laws. In other states, permits to carry a canceled weapon are easily obtained. Review the firearm laws of your state to determine whether your state has a firearm law regulating conduct listed in this chapter.

Freedom to believe as to religion or politics is absolute, but freedom to act may be regulated to protect other persons or for the needs of society.

 ## BOOK-SPECIFIC WEB SITE

For chapter-related Web links, quizzing activities, and case and news updates, go to the *Criminal Law*, Eighth Edition, book-specific Web site at **http://info.wadsworth.com/ gardner**.

QUESTIONS AND PROBLEMS

Illegal "possession" of a firearm is a different crime from that of illegal "use" of a firearm. Chapters 3 and 20 define the legal concepts of "possession."

To convict a person of "using" a firearm in connection with a drug offense or other felony, the government must prove that the defendant fired, brandished, threatened someone with, or in some other way actively deployed a weapon to commit the crime.

Should the U.S. Supreme Court affirm or reverse the convictions of the persons charged with using a firearm in connection with the following drug offenses?

1. A man who was found to have a loaded pistol in the trunk of his car after police officers lawfully stopped him and discovered twenty-seven bags of cocaine in the passenger compartment of the car

2. A woman who was found to have an unloaded derringer in a locked trunk in a closet in her apartment, where she had sold crack to an undercover agent. See the case of *Bailey v. United States,* 116 S.Ct. 501 (1995).

 ## INFOTRAC COLLEGE EDITION EXERCISES

1. Go to InfoTrac College Edition and, using the subject search term *abortion* and the subdivision *litigation*, find an article analyzing the *Stenberg-Cathhart* case. Why was the Nebraska partial birth law held unconstitutional? What must a state criminal statute prohibiting partial birth abortions provide in order to pass constitutional muster?

2. Go to InfoTrac College Edition and, using the subject search term *gun control* and the subdivision *analysis*, find the 2001 Wheeler article in support of the right to bear arms. Why does the author argue there is a "right" to bear arms? What does his chief critic, LaFollette, contend? Who do you think is right?

NOTES

1. The right to carry arms was regulated in England as early as 1328 in the Statute of Northampton. The English Bill of Rights of 1688 denounced the discriminatory arming of people and seemed to acknowledge the legislature's power to regulate. Carrying weapons was not an absolute right under the old common law. See *Burton v. Sills,* 53 N.J. 86, 248 A.2d 521 (1968).

2. The 1997 American Police Foundation survey reported that of the 192 million privately owned firearms in the United States, 65 million are handguns, 70 million are rifles, and 49 million are shotguns.

3. See the U.S. Department of Justice publication *Weapon Offenses and Offenders* (November 1995).

4. The question of the power of states to regulate weapons was settled in the 1982 case of *Quilici v. Village of Morton Grove,* 695 F.2d 863, review denied U.S. Supreme Court 104 S.Ct. 194 (1983). The Village of Morton Grove, Illinois, passed an ordinance forbidding the possession of all operative handguns within the village. All the courts hearing the challenge to the ordinance upheld the ordinance as valid.

The National Rifle Association then went to state capitals and was successful in getting state legislatures to enact state laws in many states that restricted the power of cities and villages in those states from enacting ordinances such as the one enacted by the Village of Morton Grove.

Citizens in the Village of Shorewood, Wisconsin, gathered enough votes in 1994 to pass an ordinance similar to the ordinance passed by the Village of Morton Grove. On the evening of the public hearing on the bill, the first speaker in opposition to the ordinance was a highly respected 40-year-old woman who was a long-time resident of the village. She dramatically told how she was brutally raped and assaulted for over an hour and then produced pictures of her taken immediately after the assault.

The woman stated that she had a handgun in her home and that she had every intention of using it to prevent a recurrence of her rape and assault. The woman stated that if the ordinance was enacted in Shorewood, she would sell her home and move to an area where she could lawfully keep a handgun in her home.

The woman was applauded for her courage in publicly presenting her traumatic experience, and the efforts to pass an antigun ordinance stopped that evening.

5. In a 1997 editorial, the *New York Times* criticized the BATF for granting permission to an Israeli-owned company to import and sell the Uzi American and Galil Sporter (both semiautomatic weapons) under this law. The editorial argues that the 1968 Gun Control Act, which allows the import of only those guns that are suitable or are readily adaptable for "sporting purposes," should be the controlling federal law. The editorial states that the two Israeli guns are not intended for hunting or target shooting.

The *Chicago Tribune* stated on its front page that this federal law "has done nothing to keep assault weapons . . . off the street. With gaping loopholes, the law is easily skirted."

See the *Chicago Tribune* article "Assault Gun 'Ban' Designed to Backfire" (December 31, 1997). In another article in this series, the *Chicago Tribune* wrote that the federal government has sold more than 500,000 military rifles and handguns to private individuals. Background checks are made on these people, but the buyer is free to dispose of the guns "according to his or her personal desires." See "Built for the Battlefield, Bound for the Streets" (December 29, 1997).

6. A *firearm* has been defined as "any weapon from which a shot is discharged by force of an explosive or a weapon which acts by force of gunpowder." Under this definition, a New York court held that a Very pistol, designed to fire warning flares, is a firearm within the meaning of the New York Penal Code. People on Complaint of *Altomari v. Evergood,* 74 N.Y.S.2d 12 (Mag.Ct. 1947).

It has been held that when a broken spring does not totally impair the use of a revolver and the hammer can be operated manually, the instrument is a firearm within the meaning of the New York Penal Code. *People v. Tardibuono,* 174 Misc. 305, 20 N.Y.S.12d 633 (1940).

7. 476 U.S. 16, 106 S.Ct. 1677 (1986).

8. *Davis v. Beason,* 133 U.S. 333, 10 S.Ct. 299 (1890).

9. The Freedom of Religion Clause could not be used as a defense for destroying government property

(760 F.2d 447), extortion and blackmail (515 F.2d 112), racketeering (695 F.2d 765, review denied 460 U.S. 1092), refusal to testify before a grand jury (465 F.2d 802, see 409 U.S. 944), refusal to be photographed after being arrested (848 F. 2d 113), putting a logging road through an area sacred to Indian tribes (108 S.Ct. 1319), refusal to have children vaccinated (25 S.Ct. 358), and refusal to participate in the Social Security system (102 S.Ct. 1051).

10. According to the New Testament in Mark 16:16–18, "He that believeth and is baptized shall be saved. . . . [T]hey shall speak with new tongues; they shall take up serpents; and if they drink any deadly thing, it shall not hurt them." In *State v. Massey,* the defendant was convicted of handling poisonous snakes in a religious ceremony, taking literally these words from the New Testament. The Court ruled that the state law forbidding the handling of poisonous snakes was a valid use of the police power of the state of North Carolina and held that the public safety factor outweighed the right to religious freedom.

However, the practice of handling poisonous snakes continues to a limited extent in some southern Appalachian churches. In 1972, two young men who had successfully handled such snakes as copperheads further testified to their belief in Mark 16:16–18 by drinking a mixture of strychnine and water at an evening service. Both were dead by the next morning.

11. The Minnesota State Fair made distribution or sale of literature or merchandise away from a booth rented on the fairgrounds a misdemeanor, subject to arrest and expulsion from the fairgrounds. Booths were rented on a nondiscriminatory first-come, first-served basis. The Krishna religion argued that this regulation suppresses their religious practice of Sankirtan, which requires its members to go into public places to distribute or sell religious literature and to solicit donations for the support of their sect.

The U.S. Supreme Court held that the rule of the Minnesota State Fair did not violate First Amendment rights of the Hare Krishna sect. The fairgrounds consists of a relatively small area in view of the massive crowds of people and the enormous variety of goods, services, entertainment, and so forth that are exhibited. The Court held that the state's interest in maintaining the orderly movement of the crowd is sufficient to impose the time, place, and manner restriction not only on the Hare Krishna sect but also on the many other groups seeking to exercise their First Amendment rights.

12. See also the case of *U.S. v. Aguilar et al.,* 871 F.2d 1436 (9th Cir. 1989), opinion amended and superseded 883 F.2d 662 (9th Cir. 1989), in which the defendants ran an "underground railroad" smuggling Central Americans into the United States in violation of federal law. It was held that the defendants were not entitled to defenses of "mistake of law" or First Amendment religious belief.

13. See the *FBI Law Enforcement Bulletin* three-part article "Cults: A Conflict Between Religious Liberty and Involuntary Servitude?" (1982). The article tells of continuing problems "of coercive acts of some cults in recruitment and proselytizing" of young people that would cause their parents to hire deprogrammers to snatch the young adult away from the cult. Investigators had to determine whether the crimes of involuntary detention, shoplifting, and drug use were being committed by the cults, on one hand, and on the other hand, whether parents committed the crime of kidnapping of their young adult child.

14. See the *New York Times* article "Swiss Examine Conflicting Signs in Cult Deaths" (October 17, 1994).

15. See the *New York Times* article "Child's Cries Lead Police to Arsenal in Brooklyn" (November 13, 1996).

16. See the *Mobile Register* article "They Planned to Meet UFO" (March 28, 1997).

17. 381 U.S. 479, 85 S.Ct. 1678 (1965).

18. 394 U.S. 557, 89 S.Ct. 1243 (1969).

19. 405 U.S. 438, 92 S.Ct. 1029 (1972).

20. In the case of *Connecticut v. Menillo,* 423 U.S. 9, 96 S.Ct. 170 (1975), the U.S. Supreme Court held that a state may prohibit abortions by nonphysicians.

21. A "viable" fetus is defined by the U.S. Supreme Court in *Colautti v. Franklin,* 439 U.S. 379, 99 S.Ct. 675 (1979), as follows: "In *Roe v. Wade,* the Court defined the term 'viability' to signify the stage at which a fetus is 'potentially able to live outside the mother's womb, albeit with artificial aid.' This is the point at which the State's interest in protecting fetal life becomes sufficiently strong to permit it to 'go so far as to proscribe abortion during that period, except when it is necessary to preserve the life or health of the mother. 410 U.S. at 163–164, 93 S.Ct. at 732.'"

13

Homicide

CONTENTS

KEY TERMS

corpus delicti

"no body" cases

"born alive" requirement

crimes of:

    feticide

    murder

    felony murder

    manslaughter

    assisting suicide

    euthanasia

perfect and imperfect self-defense

Homicide in General

Homicide, the killing of one human being by another, is not always criminal. Sir William Blackstone wrote in the eighteenth century that there were three kinds of homicide—justifiable, excusable, and felonious. He wrote that the first involved no guilt, the second involved little guilt, and the third was the highest crime that humans were capable of committing against the law of nature.

Justifiable homicide is defined in the common law as an intentional homicide committed under circumstances of necessity or duty without any evil intent and without any fault or blame on the person who commits the homicide. Justifiable homicide includes state executions, homicides by police officers in the performance of their legal duty, and self-defense when the person committing the homicide is not at fault.

Excusable homicide is the killing of a human being, either by misadventure or in self-defense, when there is some civil fault, error, or omission on the part of the person who commits the homicide. The degree of fault, however, is not enough to constitute a crime.

Criminal (or *felonious*) *homicide* occurs when a person unlawfully and knowingly, recklessly, or negligently causes the death of another human being. The common law and the states have divided criminal homicide into the crimes of murder, manslaughter, and negligent homicide.

This chapter deals with criminal homicide and the circumstances that give rise to specific charges. Criminal homicide encompasses a wide variety of acts. The acts and the intent with which they were committed determine whether the homicide is intentional or unintentional. Such determination is relevant, because penalties are more severe when the killing was intentional rather than as a result of recklessness, negligence, or carelessness.

The Corpus Delicti Requirement

Corpus delicti means the body or substance of the crime (proof that a crime has been committed). Corpus delicti must be proved in all criminal charges. The state must show that a crime actually has been committed before it may convict a person of committing the crime. If the state cannot show that a crime was committed, it may not charge a person with a criminal offense.

Corpus delicti cannot be presumed but must be established by legal evidence. Mere hearsay or the showing that the defendant had a motive to commit a crime is not sufficient to prove corpus delicti. As a general rule, corpus delicti must be established beyond a reasonable doubt.[1] It may be established not only by direct and positive evidence but also by circumstantial evidence. When corpus delicti is established by circumstantial evidence, the general rule is that the evidence must be so conclusive as to eliminate all reasonable doubt in showing that a crime was actually committed. If no evidence of the corpus delicti is shown, the court may so properly hold. But whether the corpus delicti has been proved is a question of fact for a jury.[2]

The Pennsylvania Supreme Court stated in the case of *Commonwealth v. Leslie* that in order to prove corpus delicti in a criminal homicide case, the state must show "that the person for whose death the prosecution was instituted is in fact dead and that the death occurred under circumstances indicating that it was criminally caused by someone."[3]

In the *Leslie* case, the state police officer who investigated a fire that destroyed a summer cottage found no evidence that the fire was a deliberate burning. However, he had a hunch that it was not accidental. Because Leslie's description was similar to the description of a person seen in the area at the time of the fire, the officer interviewed Leslie in prison when he heard that Leslie had been arrested on other charges. Leslie confessed that he had started the fire, and the officer went back to the scene of the fire but could not uncover any evidence that the fire was not started accidentally. Because no corroborating evidence supported the confession, the Pennsylvania Supreme Court reversed Leslie's conviction for arson.

Proving Corpus Delicti in "No Body" Cases

Every large American city has active cases of persons reported missing. In April 2001, when Washington, D.C., intern Chandra Levy, 24, was reported missing, the city of Washington had an active list of 140 missing persons.

Most missing persons are missing for a short period of time, or they are living elsewhere and are not communicating with their families and friends. Some, however, are victims of murders and other crimes.

Usually, if there is *no body*, there is no criminal case to prosecute. Extraordinary efforts were made in the Chandra Levy case to find her whereabouts or to find evidence of wrongdoing. Despite the efforts of thousands of people, no evidence was uncovered.

Corpus delicti is ordinarily proved in homicide cases by evidence obtained from the body of the victim or witnesses to the crime. Corpus delicti can also be proved by circumstantial evidence or by confessions that have been corroborated and affirmed by other evidence. In cases in which a body is never found, the state must carry the burden of proving corpus delicti (that the crime alleged by the state has occurred). The following two cases illustrate the rules:

People v. Lipsky

Court of Appeals of New York (1982) 57 N.Y.2d 560, 457 N.Y.S.2d 451, 443 N.E.2d 925

While the defendant was in custody on an assault charge in Utah, he confessed that he had murdered a prostitute in Rochester, New York. The victim, Mary Robinson, had been reported missing, but her body had not been found. To corroborate the confession, the state showed that the victim's purse, sandals, wallet, glasses, identification card, and other personal effects were found in an apartment that the defendant had rented in New York within a week of her disappearance. Although the defendant had registered to go to college in New York, he left the state a week after the victim's disappearance and appeared emotionally overwrought. Then, while he was in prison in Utah, he wrote a poem indicating that he had killed another person. In affirming the defendant's conviction and holding that sufficient evidence justified the jury's verdict of guilty, the Court held:

> The evidence reviewed above, when read with defendant's confession, the poem he composed and his admissions to his two Provo co-workers, sufficiently establishes both Mary Robinson's death and defendant's strangulation of her as the cause of it to take the issues to the jury. More is not required.

Confessions and the Corpus Delicti Rule

A confession alone will not sustain a conviction. A mentally unstable person might confess to a crime that never happened. Or improper police conduct could cause a person to confess to a crime that had not occurred.

The Supreme Court of California stated the corpus delicti rule in the following case of *People v. Jennings* as follows: "[S]o long as there is some indication that the charged crime actually happened, we are satisfied that the accused is not admitting to a crime that never occurred."

People v. Jennings

California Supreme Court (1991), 807 P.2d 1009

The police heard that Jennings was bragging that he picked up prostitutes, paid them for sex, then killed them and took their money before burying the bodies. Sufficient evidence was presented at Jennings's trial to corroborate the confession (his bragging). The California Supreme Court affirmed his convictions for three murders, kidnapping, and robberies of the women.

In re Flodstrom

California Supreme Court, 288 P.2d 859 (1955)

The California Supreme Court ordered the release of a mother despite the fact that she had confessed to smothering her baby. The mother's confession could not be corroborated, and corpus delicti could not be proved because doctors could not determine whether the baby died of the mother's alleged criminal act or of natural causes. Charges against the mother were dropped.

Epperly v. Commonwealth

Virginia Supreme Court (1982) 224 Va. 214, 294 S.E.2d 882

The victim was last seen leaving a dance with the defendant. Her body was never found, but her blood-soaked clothes and car were found, and there was evidence of a violent struggle at a house on Claytor Lake, where the defendant was seen after the dance. Dog-tracking evidence corroborating some of the allegations made by the state was permitted to be used at the defendant's trial. The defendant also made incriminating statements. In affirming the defendant's convictions, the Court held:

> We think the evidence was sufficient to warrant the jury in finding, to the full assurance of moral certainty, that Gina Hall was dead as the result of the criminal act of another person. The jury was entitled to take into account, in this connection, her sudden disappearance, her character and personal relationships, her physical and mental health, the evidence of a violent struggle at the house on Claytor Lake, her hidden, blood-soaked clothing, and the defendant's incriminating statements—particularly his reference to "the body" before it was generally thought she was dead.

Body Without Proof of the Cause of Death Cases

The body of the deceased is available in most criminal homicide cases. But if doctors are not able to testify specifically that the cause of death was due to an unlawful act, corpus delicti has not been proved. Unexplained deaths are unusual but not rare in medical history. If doctors are unable to determine the cause of death, or if they are uncertain and unable to state whether the death resulted from criminal acts or from natural causes, then a reasonable doubt may have been created.

Corpus delicti has historically been difficult to prove in SIDS (sudden infant death syndrome) deaths of babies between 2 months and 1 year old because doctors did not know the reason for the cause of death in many of the cases.

Today, with more medical knowledge, physicians and medical journals have called into question the SIDS explanation for the deaths of some infants, particularly when multiple deaths occurred in one family. Prosecutors in many states reopened the death investigations of some infants that earlier had been classified as SIDS. For example, a woman in New York was convicted of the murder of five babies, which earlier had been classified as SIDS deaths, and in Philadelphia a woman was charged with the deaths of eight babies, which had earlier been thought to be SIDS deaths.[4]

The testimony of doctors that they "suspected" or had a "hunch" that a criminal act was the cause of death is not sufficient to prove corpus delicti. The following case illustrates the corpus delicti requirement that proof of the cause of death must be established:

People v. Archerd

California Supreme Court (1970) 3 Cal.3d 615, 91 Cal.Rptr. 397, 477 P.2d 421

During the period from 1947 to 1966, the defendant married a series of women. After each woman took out a large life insurance policy, she would die after being in a coma for a number of hours. It was suspected in each case that a massive injection of insulin was the cause of death. But it was not until 1967 that doctors were able to testify with certainty that the brain tissues of the victims showed this was true. The defendant was suspected of killing six women but was charged and convicted of three deaths. A movie was made of the trial and conviction of the defendant, and a detailed account of the investigation can be found in the *FBI Law Enforcement Bulletin* article by Sheriff Pitchess, "Proof of Murder by Insulin—A Medico-Legal First" (January 1969).

The "Born Alive" Requirement

Under the common law, the killing of a fetus (unborn baby) was not a homicide. Because a fetus is not by law a "person" or a "human being," and because most criminal homicide statutes forbid only the killing of a person or a human being, these statutes do not include the killing of a fetus.

Most states follow the common law, which requires that if the state is charging the homicide of a newborn baby, it must show that the child was "born alive" and was living at the time it was killed. The testimony of a competent witness that he or she saw the living child or heard the baby cry would ordinarily be sufficient to prove "born alive." The 1989 case of *State v. Cornelius*, 448 N.W.2d 434, and the 1980 case of *People v. Greer*, 402 N.E.2d 203, illustrate the rule.

However, in civil law, most states recognize unborn viable (quickened) children as persons for the purposes of commencing civil lawsuits for wrongs. Noting this inconsistency, the South Carolina Supreme Court in the case of *State v. Horne* also recognized a quickened fetus as a person in criminal cases, ruling:

It would be grossly inconsistent for us to construe a viable fetus as a "person" for the purposes of imposing civil liability while refusing to give it a similar classification in the criminal context.

From the date of this decision henceforth, the law of feticide shall apply in this state.[5]

Before effective birth control and legal abortion, many more infant homicide cases occurred than do today. Because of the difficulty of obtaining proof that the child was born alive and then killed, many states long ago enacted statutes making the concealing of the death of an infant a crime.

The following case illustrates the *"born alive" requirement:*

A pregnant woman was injured in an automobile accident. The woman's 6-month-old fetus was taken from her in a hospital because the fetal heartbeat was low. Unfortunately, the baby died shortly after being taken off a respirator. The defendant who caused the automobile accident was charged with and convicted of negligent homicide. It was held that the baby was "born alive" and thus a "person" under Michigan's negligent homicide statute because the baby showed signs of "spontaneous breathing." *State v. Silvia,* 543 N.W.2d 321 (Mich. App. 1996).

The Crime of Feticide

Whereas South Carolina created the crime of *feticide*—the murder of a fetus—by a court ruling changing the common law, many states created the crime of feticide by legislation.

Section 16-5-80(a) of the Georgia statutes provides that "a person commits the offense of feticide if he willfully kills an unborn child so far developed as to be ordinarily called 'quick' by any injury to the mother of such child that would be murder if it resulted in the death of such mother." The Georgia Supreme Court defined "quick" as that "time when the fetus is able to move in its mother's womb."[6]

California statutes now define *murder* as the "unlawful killing of a human being, or a fetus, with malice aforethought" (Title 8, Section 187). This statute makes the killing of a fetus in California "with malice aforethought" murder and changes the common law. This statute, however, does not make abortion murder in California, because Section 187 does not apply when the "act was solicited, aided, abetted, or consented to by the mother of the fetus." In 1994, the California Supreme Court held that the state could punish fetal murder without regard to the viability of the fetus.

Proof That the Victim Was Alive at the Time of the Defendant's Unlawful Act

Because criminal homicide is the unlawful killing of a living human being, the state has the burden of showing that the victim was alive at the time of the unlawful act. All people have a right to life, and whether they have ten minutes or ten years left to live makes no difference in the eyes of the law.

Child Death Review Teams

The United States (all fifty states), Australia, and Canada now have child death review teams to review deaths of children from violence, child abuse or neglect, motor vehicle accidents, child suicide, and from natural or undetermined causes.

The National Center on Child Fatality Review reports that approximately fifty thousand children die each year in the United States. Of these deaths, an estimated two thousand children in the United States die of child abuse and/or neglect. Forty percent of the two thousand children are younger than 1 year, and the majority of the children are younger than 5 years.

The New "Safe Haven" Laws for Unwanted Babies

For years, tragic stories of illegally abandoned babies found dead or in unsafe places have appeared in the news. Because of the continuing, sad, attention-getting cases, states began to enact safe haven laws to save the lives of babies. These laws allow a person (usually the mother) to leave an unwanted baby (anonymously and without fear of prosecution) at a hospital, a fire station, or other designated place.

Most states (if not all) have now enacted safe haven laws. It is hoped that as the laws become more widely known, the safe haven law will be a safety net for all (or most) unwanted babies. This will save the lives of many infants and will avoid felony prosecutions against young mothers (and sometimes fathers) for illegally abandoning infants.

However, if the victim had already died of illness or other injuries at the time of the defendant's unlawful act, the crime of criminal homicide was not committed. In the 1973 murder trial of a New York doctor, the doctor was charged with causing the death of a dying cancer patient by injecting a lethal dose of potassium chloride. The patient was in a coma and was not expected to live longer than two days. During the twelve-day trial in New York City, the defense attorney argued that the deceased was already dead of natural causes when the injection was made. The state failed to show conclusively that the deceased was still alive at the time of the injection, and the jury acquitted the doctor of homicide.

Motive is no defense in a murder charge. Nor is it a defense to show that the victim wanted to die. The crime of murder has been committed if it is shown that the unlawful act that caused the death was done deliberately and with premeditation. Motive and consent by the victim may be considered by the judge in sentencing the defendant in those states in which the sentence is not mandatory.

Many *euthanasia* (mercy-killing) cases have taken place in the United States and in Europe over the years. The author of an article entitled "Euthanasia: None Dare Call It Murder" points out that the victims of this type of homicide usually fall into three groups: (1) people with painful and terminal diseases, such as cancer, who have only a short time to live, (2) mentally defective or retarded people and old people suffering from senility (some of whom are kept alive by artificial medical means), and (3) infants and young children with gross mental or physical defects.[7]

When Is a Person Legally Dead?

Until the 1950s and 1960s, the heart was considered the body's most vital organ, and therefore death was defined in terms of cessation of heart and respiratory functions. When doctors became able to keep the heart and other organs alive for transplanting to other patients, medical science recognized that the body's real seat of life is the brain.

Court and state legislative bodies followed the medical profession in defining death in terms of "brain death." For example, the Indiana Supreme Court in 1981 defined death as the "permanent cessation of all brain function" and joined other states in holding that "for the purposes of the law of homicide proof of the death of the victim may be established by proof of the irreversible cessation of the victim's total brain function."[8]

End-of-Life Decisions

On an average day in the United States, more than six thousand people die. Doctors estimate that at least several hundred of these deaths occur after doctors, patients, and family members agree to withhold life-sustaining treatment and allow the inevitable to occur.

To stay within the law and to avoid criminal prosecution, the decision to withhold treatment or to "pull the plug" should only be made when the following can be shown:

1. Terminally ill patients who are mentally competent can instruct that treatment or life-support systems be withdrawn. Courts have held that the individual's right to refuse treatment must come before the interests of the state in keeping the individual alive.

2. Life-support systems or treatment may be withheld from patients who are comatose or are in a persistent vegetative state if one of the following is clearly shown:
   a) That the patient left prior explicit written instructions that this be done, or
   b) That the patient had legally appointed another adult to make such health care decisions should the patient be unable to do so, or
   c) Clear and convincing evidence is presented to a court showing that the withdrawal of treatment or of a life-support system is in accordance with the patient's own wishes or best interests.[9]

The Causation Requirement

Causation and Proximate Cause

Causation and proximate cause are discussed in Chapter 3 of this text. *Causation* is an essential element of all crimes. The state must show that what the defendant did (or failed to do) was the direct and proximate cause of the harm that occurred. The following two examples illustrate the law of causation:

EXAMPLE 1: After loading a gun with live ammunition, X points the gun at Y and pulls the trigger. The firing pin comes down hard on the back of the live cartridge that X has placed in the chamber of the gun. The blow of the hammer detonates the primer in the cartridge, and the primer detonates the powder in the cartridge. The powder burns so rapidly that hot gases immediately build up tremendous pressure in the chamber of the gun. This pressure forces the propellant (the bullet) out of the muzzle of the gun at a high rate of speed. Because of rifling in the barrel of the gun and the direction in which X is pointing the gun, the bullet travels through the air and strikes Y in the head, killing Y immediately.

EXAMPLE 2: After being shocked by seeing the defendant smash her door open and then rip her telephone cord out of the phone, an elderly woman died of a heart attack. The defendant argued that he wanted to burglarize the woman's home but had no intention of harming her.

A jury can easily conclude in Example 1 that X intended the natural and probable consequences of the deliberate act; it would then find that X intended to kill Y. In Example 1, X's acts were the direct and proximate cause of Y's death. The chain of events that occurred after X pulled the trigger was expected and desired by X. Therefore, X can be held criminally responsible for Y's death.

In Example 2, the Nebraska Supreme Court affirmed the defendant's conviction for felony murder in the case of *State v. Dixon,* 387 N.W.2d 682 (1986), holding:

> Dixon admitted to Detectives Circo and Wade that Jourdan was alive when he entered the house. The implosion of window glass and part of the wooden kitchen door would startle the most imperturbable individual. Seeing Dixon coming through the doorway into the kitchen probably would stir one to "stare" at him, visual fixation founded in fear intensified by Dixon's ripping the "cord out of the phone." All that unfolded before Susan Jourdan, 76 years old and living alone. What total terror likely seized and constricted Susan Jourdan's heart may be beyond another's comprehension. What the jury did understand was Dr. Roffman's explanation of the cause of Susan Jourdan's death, "emotional trauma of having her door kicked in and stimulating her heart to beat abnormally, causing her collapse and ultimate death."

The Year-and-a-Day Rule

The *year-and-a-day rule* is also discussed in Chapter 3. The old common law rule stated that a person could not be convicted of a murder unless the victim died within a year and a day from the time of the wrongful act.

The Michigan Supreme Court pointed out in 1982 that the year-and-a-day rule dates back to 1278 and that the "original rationale for the rule was probably tied to the inability of 13th century medicine to prove the cause of death beyond a reasonable doubt after a prolonged period of time."[10]

The Michigan Supreme Court and other courts have abolished this rule. However, some courts continue to use it. The California legislature extended the time limits in amending the California Penal Code in 1969, providing that "[t]o make the killing either murder or manslaughter, it is requisite the party die within three years and a day after the stroke received or the cause of death administered" (Title 8, Section 194).

Murder

The first murder to be reported in the American colonies occurred ten years after the Pilgrims landed at Plymouth Rock. In 1630, John Billington, one of the original band of 102 Pilgrims to come over on the *Mayflower*, fired his blunderbuss at a neighbor and killed the man at close range. John Billington was charged with the common law offense of murder under the English law and, after a prompt trial and conviction, was hanged.[11]

Only one degree of murder existed under the common law, and it was punishable by death. After the American Revolution, some state legislative bodies began creating other degrees of murder. They were probably motivated by a desire to separate murder to be punished by death from murder that they did not want to be punished by death.

By the year 1900, virtually all the states had more than one degree of murder, with most states having two degrees and some having three degrees. At that time, the degree system was a useful and meaningful method of distinguishing murder that was punished by capital punishment and that which was not. With the decline in the use of the death penalty in this century and its virtual nonuse in the 1960s and 1970s, the utility of the degree system declined considerably.

The degree system is still meaningful today when first-degree murder carries a mandatory life imprisonment sentence or the death penalty. The degree system is also used as part of plea bargaining when the state finds advantage in allowing the defendant to plead guilty to second-degree murder or to some other lesser offense if a reduction is appropriate.

Intent-to-Kill Murder

The unlawful, intentional killing of another human being is considered the most serious criminal offense. These killings range from cold and careful killings by a paid assassin to those that are the culmination of one spouse's rage and frustration toward the other. The weapon used to implement the murder can be anything from a firearm to one's bare hands. The type of weapon used or the manner in which the fatal blow is delivered is not necessarily significant. Rather, the specific intent to take the life of another human being separates this crime from all other degrees of homicide. The type of weapon and the manner in which it is used, however, may give rise to the legal inference that a person intends the natural and probable consequences of his or her deliberate acts.

Murder in common law and as enacted by the statutes of many states as first-degree murder is defined as unlawful homicide with malice aforethought. The phrase "malice aforethought" signifies the mental state of a person who voluntarily, without legal excuse or justification, does an act that ordinarily will cause death or serious injury to another. Although the word "malice" ordinarily conveys the meaning of hatred, ill will, or malevolence, it is not limited to those meanings in malice aforethought but can include such motives as a mercy killing, in which the homicide is committed to end the suffering of a loved one. "Aforethought" has been interpreted to mean that the malice must exist at the time of the homicidal act. Courts have held that if the design and intent to kill precede the killing for even a moment, the person can be convicted of first-degree murder.[12]

Other states have defined first-degree murder as causing "the death of another human being with intent to kill that person." The American Law Institute Model Penal Code

Classifications of Common Law Murder

Intent-to-Kill Murder The most common murder, the intentional unlawful killing of another human being, is considered the most serious criminal offense. (The most frequent criminal homicide is that caused by drunk driving.)

Intent-to-Do-Serious-Bodily-Harm Murder In this type of murder, it is found that the defendant intended to do serious bodily injury short of death, but his or her acts resulted in a killing.

Depraved-Mind or Depraved-Heart Murder When a death results from conduct that shows a wanton disregard for human life and when there is a high probability that the conduct will result in death, the homicide can be classified as this type of murder.

Felony Murder In common law, one who caused another's death while committing or attempting to commit a felony was guilty of felony murder. However, when the felony murder doctrine was created, there were only eight felonies and all were punishable by death. Because all states now have many felonies, they generally limit the felony murder doctrine to felonies of violence.

uses the words "purposely" and "knowingly," whereas the proposed Federal Criminal Code uses the wording "intentionally or knowingly causes the death of another human being."

The Deadly Weapon Doctrine

Although intentional killings are the most common of all murders, rarely is direct evidence of the intent available. The evidence most often available to the state is objective observations of the cause of death—for example, the defendant pointed a gun at the deceased and pulled the trigger, or the defendant plunged a knife into the body of the deceased. Witnesses who have heard the defendant express intention to kill the deceased are seldom available. The questions that then arise are whether such evidence is sufficient to support a finding that malice existed and whether the defendant showed an intent to kill.

The *deadly weapon doctrine* is related to and is part of the inference that a person intends the natural and probable consequences of his or her deliberate acts. A loaded revolver is certainly a deadly weapon when aimed and fired at close range. Under such circumstances, a jury can easily infer an intent to kill, because the natural and probable consequences of this act would be death or serious bodily harm.

Determining what is a deadly weapon would depend on the object used and the circumstances that existed at the time of the homicide. A strong man who struck a year-old infant in the head several times with his fists could easily be found to have an intent to kill, and his fists, under these circumstances, would be considered deadly weapons. However, a man who was in a fistfight with another man just as strong and agile as he would not ordinarily be considered to have used a deadly weapon when he used his fists.

Therefore, in determining what a deadly weapon is, a jury would consider the instrument used, who used it, and how it was used. Some items are almost always considered deadly weapons because of the potential harm they can cause. Other instruments, such as automobiles, would have to be viewed in light of their uses. The U.S. Supreme Court ruled in the 1895 case of *Allen v. United States* that a lower court erred when it withdrew the question of self-defense from a jury on the ground that sticks and clubs were not deadly weapons.[13] Sticks and clubs can be deadly weapons, depending on their size, who is using them, and how they are used.

Juries and judges have held the following unusual objects to be deadly weapons under the circumstances in which they were used:

- Cowboy boots used to "stomp" a grown man's girlfriend's head into the pavement. *People v. Carter,* 423 N.E.2d 30 (1981).

- A floor against which the defendant struck an infant's head, causing fatal injuries. *Stanul v. State,* 870 S.W.2d 329 (Texas 1994).

- An automobile used to run down a victim of a robbery attempt. *Jackson v. State,* 662 So.2d 1369 (Fla. 1995).

- Bare hands, when used by a strong adult against a weaker person. *People v. Ross,* 831 P.2d 1310 (Colo. 1992).

- A nail gun, when used to threaten robbery victims. *Toy v. State,* 855 S.W.2d 153 (Texas 1993).

Transferred Intent

If a killer is a poor shot and misses the intended victim but hits and kills another person, he or she could argue that there was no intent to kill that person. Or if there was a mistake of identity and the killer kills the wrong person, the same argument could be made. Defense lawyers have used these arguments for hundreds of years, arguing that because there was no ill will and malice toward the victim killed by accident, the defendant should not be convicted of intent-to-kill murder but, at the most, negligent or reckless homicide.

To accept such arguments would allow killers to benefit because of their poor marksmanship or because they killed the wrong person in a mix-up. The *doctrine of transferred intent* became part of the common law before the American Revolution and was stated in 1766 by Blackstone in 4 *Commentaries* 200–201. The following case states the rules:

Gladden v. Maryland

Maryland Court of Special Appeals (1974) 20 Md.App. 492, 316 A.2d 319

In a dispute over a bad batch of heroin, Gladden emptied a revolver, firing wildly at the heroin pusher. He did not hit the man he was shooting at, but instead hit and killed an innocent 12-year-old boy. The defendant appealed his conviction of intent-to-kill murder. In affirming the conviction, the Court held:

The doctrine of "transferred intent" has long been recognized at common law. Sir Matthew Hale, in 1 History of the Pleas of the Crown (published posthumously in 1736), said, at 466: "To these may be added the cases abovementioned, *viz.* if A. by malice forethought strikes at

B. and missing him strikes C. whereof he dies, tho he never bore any malice to C. yet it is murder, and the law transfers the malice to the party slain; the like of poisoning."

Forty years later, Sir William Blackstone, in 4 *Commentaries* on the Laws of England, reiterated the common law rule according to Hale; at 200–201: "Thus if one shoots at A. and misses him, but kills B., this is murder; because of the previous felonious intent, which the law transfers from one to the other. The same is the case where one lays poison for A.; and B., against whom the prisoner had no malicious intent, takes it, and it kills him; this is likewise murder."

* * *

The appellant contends that he should not have been convicted of murder, since he bore no malice toward the victim. He urges upon us that the common law doctrine of "transferred intent" should not be received into Maryland, although he acknowledges that this is the law in the overwhelming majority of common law jurisdictions. We have no difficulty in deciding that "transferred intent" is, and should be, a part of the common law of this State.

Intent-to-Do-Serious-Bodily-Harm Murder

The courts long ago decided that a death at the hands of one who intended to do only serious bodily harm was nevertheless murder. Under modern homicide statutes, such killing is not intent-to-kill murder but is usually considered a lesser degree of murder. The following English cases illustrate this type of offense:

Rex v. Errington
2 Lew.C.C. 148, 217 (1838)

The defendants covered a drunken man, who was sleeping, with straw, on which they threw a shovel of hot cinders. The man burned to death in the fire that resulted. The court instructed the jury that if they found that the defendants intended to do any serious harm to the deceased, the crime was murder under the common law; if the defendants' only intent was to play a joke or frighten the deceased, the crime was manslaughter.

Holloway Case
79 Eng.Rep. 715 (K.B. 1628)

The defendant tied a boy to a horse's tail and hit the horse to make it run. The boy was killed. The defendant was convicted of murder even though it was found that there was no intent to kill.

Depraved-Mind or Depraved-Heart Murder

This classification, in some states called second-degree murder, is similar in some aspects to the intent-to-do-serious-bodily-harm murder. The primary difference is that the *depraved-mind murder* includes no specific intent to injure or harm. However, if the conduct of the defendant was so reckless as to create a high degree of risk of death, he or she would, in many instances, be found guilty of depraved-heart or reckless-conduct murder.

The California Supreme Court pointed out in the following case that malice may be implied when a person, knowing that his or her conduct endangers the life of another, deliberately continues to act in a manner that shows a conscious disregard for life:

Firearms Used to Kill U.S. Presidents

President	Firearm used	Assassin
Abraham Lincoln, killed 1865	A cheap, single-shot derringer	John Wilkes Booth
James A. Garfield, killed 1881	A .44 caliber British bulldog	Charles Guiteau
William McKinley, killed 1901	An inexpensive .32 caliber revolver	Leon Czolgosz
John F. Kennedy, killed 1963	An inexpensive imported rifle	Lee Harvey Oswald

Presidents who were targets of unsuccessful assassination attempts	Details of the failed attempt
Theodore Roosevelt, in 1912	Bullet was stopped by papers in the president's pocket.
Franklin Roosevelt, in 1933	Mayor Cermak of Chicago was killed by the bullet meant for Roosevelt.
Gerald Ford, two attempts in 1975	In the first attempt, a bystander pushed the woman's arm up, causing the bullet to go into the air.
Ronald Reagan, in 1981	In a wild shooting spree in downtown Washington, D.C., President Reagan was wounded.
Bill Clinton, in 1994	A man walking on the sidewalk outside the White House pulled an assault rifle from under his trench coat and showered the White House with bullets until he was wrestled to the ground by two passersby on Pennsylvania Avenue. The man was found sane and convicted of attempted assassination of the president.

Six bullets that killed three young Americans within a five-year period (1963–1968)   President John F. Kennedy, age 46, the Rev. Martin Luther King Jr., age 39, and Attorney General Robert Kennedy, age 43, were killed by six bullets.

People v. Watson

California Supreme Court (1981) 30 Cal.3d 290, 179 Cal.Rptr. 43, 637 P.2d 279

After drinking a large volume of beer in a bar, the defendant drove through a red light and avoided a collision with another car, late at night, only by skidding to a halt in the middle of the intersection. After the near collision, the defendant drove off at a high rate of speed (twice the 35 mph speed limit). On approaching another intersection, the defendant again applied his brakes, but he struck a Toyota sedan, killing the driver and her 6-year-old daughter. Defendant's blood-alcohol content one-half hour after the collision was 0.23 percent, which was twice the 0.10 percent then necessary to find a person legally intoxicated.

The issue before the California Supreme Court was whether the defendant could be charged and forced to go to trial on two counts of second-degree murder instead of the usual charges of homicide by intoxicated use of a vehicle or of vehicular manslaughter. In holding that the conduct of the defendant was sufficient to support a probable cause finding of implied malice to justify charging and trying the defendant for second-degree murder, the Court stated:

We have said that second degree murder based on implied malice has been committed when a person does "an act, the natural consequences of which are dangerous to life, which act was deliberately performed by a person who knows that his conduct endangers the life of another and who acts with conscious disregard for life." *People v. Sedeno.* . . . Phrased in a different way, malice may be implied when defendant does an act with a high probability that it will result in death and does it with a base antisocial motive and with a wanton disregard for human life. . . .

Based upon our independent review of the record, we believe that there exists a rational ground for concluding that defendant's conduct was sufficiently wanton to hold him on a second degree murder charge.

State v. Ibn Omar-Muhammad

New Mexico Supreme Court (1985) 102 N.M. 274, 694 P.2d 922

In fleeing from arrest by law enforcement officers (a crime in itself), the defendant tried to run police officers off the road. He ran roadblocks at high rates of speed. He was charged with depraved-mind murder when he killed a man while fleeing from the police. The Court held that he was properly convicted of depraved-mind murder instead of the lesser offense of vehicular homicide because the defendant knew the risk involved in his conduct.

Felony Murder

The **felony murder** rule came into existence in England many years ago. The rule states that if a death occurs while a defendant is committing or attempting to commit a felony, the defendant could be convicted of felony murder even if the death was unintended and accidental.

The Supreme Judicial Court of Massachusetts and the drafters of the Model Penal Code point out that U.S. courts have narrowed the scope of the felony murder rule by imposing one or more of the following limitations:

1. The felony that was attempted or committed must be one that is dangerous to life (or the state lists the felonies or requires the felony be *malum in se,* or a common law felony).
2. A direct causal connection must be established between the felony and the death that occurred.
3. The act that caused the death must have occurred while the felony was in progress.

Most states use the felony murder rule. However, courts in some states have abolished the rule. Many of the prisoners on death row are there because of felony murder. The following cases illustrate the rule:

Conduct	Finding	Case
Defendant kicked in door of elderly woman's home, tore telephone from wall, and burglarized home.	"[E]motional trauma of having door kicked in and stimulating her heart to beat abnormally, causing her collapse and ultimate death."	*State v. Dixon,* previously presented to illustrate proximate cause

(continued)

Conduct	Finding	Case
Defendant tied up his victim during a robbery.	Medical testimony established the cause of victim's death as a heart attack "brought on by the emotional stress resulting from the action of the defendant."	*State v. Spates,* Connecticut Supreme Court, 176 Conn. 227, 405 A.2d 656 (1978)
Armed robberies (and one burglary) of victims who died of heart attacks after crimes (in burglary, victim exchanged gunfire with burglar).	Medical testimony that victims died of "cardiac arrest caused by . . . the stress of events before the victim's death."	*Durden v. State,* 250 Ga. 325, 297 S.E.2d 237 (1982); *People v. Stamp,* 2 Cal.App.3d 203, 82 Cal.Rptr. 598 (1969); *Booker v. State,* 386 N.E.2d 1198 (Ind. 1979); *State v. Atkinson,* 298 N.C. 673, 259 S.E.2d 858 (1979)
Death of firefighters while fighting blazes started by defendants (deliberate arsons).	Felony murder convictions affirmed.	*State v. Leech,* 114 Wash.2d 700, 790 P.2d 160 (1990); *People v. Zane,* 152 A.D.2d 976, 543 N.Y.S. 2d 777 (1989); *Bethea v. Scully,* 834 F.2d 257 (2d Cir. 1987)
State could not show whether sexual assault victim was killed before or after rape.	Court held that state did have to show that victim was alive at the time of rape and affirmed convictions for both first-degree felony murder and second-degree intentional murder of a single victim.	Minnesota Supreme Court in *State v. Nielsen,* 467 N.W.2d 615 (1991)
Felons fleeing at high speed killed innocent people in traffic fatalities in their attempt to get away after robberies.	Because fleeing from a crime scene is part of the crime, felony murder convictions were affirmed.	*People v. Jonson,* 1992 WL 73337 (Cal.App. 1992); *Whitman v. People,* 420 P.2d 416 (Sup.Ct. Col. 1966); *People v. Fuller,* 150 Cal.Rptr. 515 (Cal.App. 1978)
During an armed robbery, the victim shot and killed one of the robbers. Defendant was convicted of killing the other robber.	*Conviction reversed:* "It is clearly the majority view (that) the doctrine of felony murder does not extend to a killing . . . (by one other than) those associated with him in the unlawful enterprise."	*State v. Canola,* New Jersey Supreme Court, 73 N.J. 206, 374 A.2d 20 (1977)

Manslaughter

Definition

Manslaughter was defined by common law as a classification of criminal homicide that is less than murder. The common law divided manslaughter into two categories: voluntary and involuntary. Most U.S. jurisdictions follow the common law classifications, but a few states have created three categories. For example, Section 192 of the California Penal Code creates the three classifications of voluntary, involuntary, and vehicular manslaughter. A few states have only one degree of manslaughter. A form of classification other than voluntary and involuntary manslaughter is that of identifying manslaughter by degrees (first, second, and so on).[14]

Reasons given for a manslaughter conviction rather than a murder conviction are as follows:

1. The victim may have provoked the killing, or his or her unlawful conduct set into motion a chain of events that resulted in the killing.
2. The killings are not bad enough to be charged as murder, but the criminal conduct should be punished.
3. In some cases, the jury cannot unanimously agree on a finding of murder and compromise on a manslaughter conviction.

Manslaughter is a crime that is generally considered to be separate and distinct from murder. Because the penalties are less severe than for murder, defense lawyers who are unable to obtain an acquittal for clients seek a conviction of manslaughter rather than murder.

Voluntary Manslaughter

The following example is used to illustrate voluntary manslaughter:

EXAMPLE: When Robert Lee Moody was 18 years old, he killed his father with a shotgun and then went to a California police station to turn himself in, stating what he had done. The prosecutor charged Moody with voluntary manslaughter because of the following reported conduct of the father: he had seduced his two teenage daughters, had begun fondling his 11-year-old daughter, had forced his wife into prostitution to help pay for a pleasure boat, was a child and wife beater, and had opened his older son's head with a screwdriver (the son was committed to a mental hospital). After the trial court convicted Moody of voluntary manslaughter, the court received more than seven hundred letters, most of which urged a lenient sentence for Moody. The sentence handed down in 1984 was five years of probation, with two of the years served in "Peace Corps-like" missionary work.[15]

In such cases as the *Moody* case, spouse beating, and other cases of shocking conduct, judges and juries have used manslaughter as an alternative to the more severe penalties of murder. Although state criminal codes permit six to fifteen years' imprisonment for voluntary manslaughter, the judge in the *Moody* case imposed a lenient sentence because of the facts in the case.

Heat of Passion Requirement

Many voluntary manslaughter cases are cases in which the defendant intentionally kills another person while the defendant has temporarily lost his or her normal self-control because of the conduct of the victim. To reduce murder to manslaughter, courts hold that the following four requirements must exist:

1. There must be adequate provocation.

2. The killing must have been in a heat of passion (anger, rage, or emotional disturbance).

3. There must have been no opportunity to cool off.

4. There must be a causal connection between the provocation, the rage or anger, and the fatal act.

Sufficient and Adequate Provocation

Sufficient provocation is the provocation that naturally and instantly produces in the mind of an ordinary person the highest degree of exasperation, rage, anger, sudden resentment, or terror. The provocation must be of such a nature and be so great as to overcome or suspend an ordinary person's exercise of good judgment. The provocation must be such as to cause the person to act uncontrollably. The killing must occur immediately during or after the provocation and during the intense heat of passion. Only a few categories of provocation have been recognized by the law as legally sufficient and adequate to justify reduction of a murder charge to that of manslaughter.

In the United States, there is an almost uniform rule that words and gestures are never sufficient provocation to reduce a charge of murder to that of manslaughter. The U.S. Supreme Court stated in the 1895 case of *Allen v. United States* that "mere words alone do not excuse even a simple assault. Any words offered at the time [of the killing] do not reduce the grade of the killing from murder to manslaughter."[16]

In the 1991 case of *State v. Girouard,* 583 A.2d 718, the defendant got into an argument with his wife. She used taunting, angry words, and he murdered her. The Maryland Court of Appeals held that words alone are not adequate provocation to reduce murder to manslaughter. The Court cited decisions from other states, pointing out that other "jurisdictions overwhelmingly agree . . . and hold that words alone are not adequate provocation."

Just as insulting words are not sufficient provocation, neither is failure to pay a debt. In the California case of *Morse v. People,* the fact that the deceased victim welshed on a gambling debt to the defendant and then had the audacity to try to "bum" cigarettes from him was held to be insufficient provocation.[17]

In the 1998 case of *Powers v. State,* 696 N.E.2d 865, the Indiana Supreme Court held that the crying of a 5-month-old baby did not constitute sufficient provocation to allow a jury to consider lowering a murder charge to voluntary manslaughter. The defendant argued that the baby's crying provoked the vicious assault that killed the baby.

The U.S. rule that words and gestures are never sufficient provocation has been criticized as bringing about harsh results in some cases. However, if other provocation, such as a battery, accompanies the verbal provocation, then it might be held to be sufficient. In *People v. Rice,* the deceased slapped the defendant's child and a quarrel resulted.[18] This was held to be sufficient provocation. A minor and technical battery accompanied with words was held in the 1928 Georgia case of *Lamp v. State* to amount to a sufficient provocation to justify reducing the conviction from murder to manslaughter.[19] But in *Commonwealth v. Cisneros,* the Pennsylvania Supreme Court arrived at an opposite conclusion.[20]

The Illinois court in *People v. Williams* held that "it is the defendant's state of mind at the time of the incident that is the critical element."[21] The following batteries were held to be sufficient provocations: a severe beating with a nightstick that fractured the defendant's jaw in *People v. Sain,* 384 Ill. 394, 51 N.E.2d 557 (1943); throwing hot water into the defendant's face and partially blinding him in *People v. Rice,* 351 Ill. 604, 184 N.E. 894 (1933); an attack with a knife in a fight in which several people were involved in *People v. Ortiz,* 320 Ill. 205, 150 N.E. 708 (1926); and shoving and knocking the defendant into a rock pile in *State v. Ponce,* 124 W.Va. 126, 19 S.E.2d 221 (1942).

Many U.S. courts have held that when a married person finds his or her spouse in an act of adultery, this amounts to sufficient provocation if it causes a genuine heat of passion.[22] However, this rule may not apply if a girlfriend is caught cheating on her boyfriend (or vice versa).[23]

Trespass, like battery, depends on the facts and circumstances in each particular case. A homeowner certainly would not have sufficient and adequate provocation to kill someone who walked across a lawn, yard, farm, or field in the middle of an afternoon. But snowmobilers who broke onto a farmer's land in Wisconsin and were circling the farmhouse at midnight caused a Wisconsin prosecutor to charge manslaughter when the farmer, in a terrible anger and rage, shot and killed one of the trespassers.

Heat of Passion and the Test of the Reasonable Person

The test of sufficiency or adequacy of provocation must be made in view of how the average or reasonable person would react to such provocation. Some people have extraordinary self-control and could endure much provocation before an uncontrollable rage would cause them to use deadly force. Others have short tempers and fly into a rage with little provocation.

A jury cannot give any special considerations to a defendant who has an extraordinarily bad temper. If the provocation is such that it would not cause the average reasonable person to explode in a sudden outburst of rage, it is not adequate or sufficient provocation to reduce murder to manslaughter. California courts have quoted the 1917 case of *People v. Logan* as follows:

> The fundamental . . . inquiry is whether or not the defendant's reason was, at the time of his act, so disturbed or obscured by some passion—not necessarily fear and never of course the passion of revenge—to such an extent as would render *ordinary men of average disposition* liable to act rashly or without due deliberation and reflection, and from this passion rather than from judgment.[24] [Emphasis added.]

The defendant in the 1971 case of *Bateman v. State* was convicted of two counts of murder in the second degree.[25] He had found his wife being warmly hugged by a man whom the defendant had told to stay away from his wife. This occurred at a party of ten adults to which the defendant had not been invited. The Maryland Court of Special Appeals affirmed the trial court's refusal to give the "heat of passion" instruction to the jury. With respect to the question of the use of intoxicants, the Court stated:

Furthermore, it is still the well-settled law in Maryland that "voluntary intoxication will not reduce murder to manslaughter," *Chisley v. State,* 202 Md. 87, 106, 95 A.2d 577, but will be considered simply for purposes of lowering first-degree murder to second-degree murder.

The case of *Bedder v. Director of Public Prosecutions* received considerable attention throughout the English-speaking world.[26] The defendant, who knew that he was impotent, attempted to have sexual intercourse with a London prostitute in a quiet courtyard. She jeered when he was unsuccessful and attempted to get away from him. He tried to hold her, and she slapped him in the face and punched him in the stomach. When he grabbed her shoulders, she kicked him in the groin. He took a knife from his pocket and stabbed her twice, killing her. The House of Lords affirmed both the finding of the jury that there was not sufficient or adequate provocation and the following jury instruction given by the trial court:

> The reasonable person, the ordinary person, is the person you must consider when you are considering the effect which any acts, any conduct, any words, might have to justify the steps which were taken in response thereto, so that an unusually excitable or pugnacious individual, or a drunken one or a man who is sexually impotent is not entitled to rely on provocation which would not have led an ordinary person to have acted in the way which was in fact carried out.

Cooling of the Blood

Cooling of the blood, also known as *cooling time* or *reasonable time to cool off,* is a factor that must be considered if an interval takes place between the provocation and the killing. Assume that after Y provokes X into a heat of passion, X, who has lost his self-control, runs to get his gun. If it took X two minutes to get his gun, was this sufficient time for X to cool off? If it took X a half hour or an hour to obtain his gun, was this sufficient time for the heat of passion to cool off? These questions would have to be answered by a court and jury that would consider the type and degree of the provocation that caused the heat of passion.

Imperfect or Unlawful Force in Self-Defense Charged as Manslaughter

Homicide in *perfect self-defense* is either justifiable or excusable, and carries no criminal liability. Perfect self-defense requires that the killer not only subjectively believes that his or her conduct was necessary and reasonable, but that, by objective standards, it was lawful and complied with the requirements of the law.

To use deadly force in self-defense, a person must be in fear of *imminent* (right now) death or great bodily harm. If the threat is not *imminent* and the person has other options available, deadly force is not legally justified.

In *imperfect self-defense,* the killer subjectively believes that his or her conduct was necessary. But if the killing was done with excessive or unnecessary force in self-defense, it is unlawful. An unnecessary killing in self-defense, in defense of another, or to prevent or terminate a felony of violence could be imperfect.

The fact that a killing was imperfect would cause it to be reduced from murder to manslaughter because

1. The deceased victim provoked the killing by his or her conduct (however, the killing was not legally justified) or

2. The killer believed that his or her conduct was lawful, and therefore possessed no "malice."

The following case received national attention and is used to illustrate imperfect self-defense (voluntary manslaughter):

State v. Norman

North Carolina Supreme Court (1989) 324 N.C. 253, 378 S.E.2d 8

John Norman and his wife had been married for twenty-five years and had five children. John seldom worked and forced his wife to prostitute herself to support him. Norman beat his wife "most every day," especially when he was drunk and when other people were around, to "show off." If his wife made less than the minimum of $100 per day in prostitution, he would beat her.

Norman made numerous threats on his wife's life. He would call her names and seek to humiliate her in many ways. An expert witness testified that after years of such treatment, Norman's wife "fits and exceeds the profile of an abused or battered spouse" and that Norman through "torture, degradation" had reduced her "to an animal level of existence, where all [her] behavior was marked purely by survival."

After a particularly horrible two days of drinking, beating, name-calling, and acts seeking to humiliate his wife, Norman lay down to take a nap. His wife obtained a handgun and shot Norman three times in the head. The jury convicted Mrs. Norman of voluntary manslaughter after the trial judge refused to give the jury an instruction on perfect self-defense. Mrs. Norman appealed, arguing that the trial judge erred in failing to give the perfect self-defense instruction to the jury.

The North Carolina Supreme Court affirmed the conviction for voluntary manslaughter and the six-year sentence of imprisonment, holding:

> Our law has recognized that self-preservation under such circumstances springs from a primal impulse and is an inherent right of natural law. . . .
>
> The right to kill in self-defense is based on the necessity, real or reasonably apparent, of killing an unlawful aggressor to save oneself from *imminent* death or great bodily harm at his hands.
>
> * * *
>
> In North Carolina, a defendant is entitled to have the jury consider acquittal by reason of *perfect* self-defense when the evidence, viewed in the light most favorable to the defendant, tends to show that at the time of the killing it appeared to the defendant and she believed it to be necessary to kill the decedent to save herself from imminent death or great bodily harm. . . .
>
> That belief must be reasonable, however, in that the circumstances as they appeared to the defendant would create such a belief in the mind of a person of ordinary firmness. *Id.* Further, the defendant must not have been the initial aggressor provoking the fatal confrontation. *Id.* A killing in the proper exercise of the right of *perfect* self-defense is always completely justified in law and constitutes no legal wrong.
>
> * * *
>
> The defendant in the present case was not entitled to a jury instruction on either perfect or imperfect self-defense. The trial court was not required to instruct on *either* form of self-defense unless evidence was introduced tending to show that at the time of the killing the defendant reasonably believed herself to be confronted by circumstances which necessitated her killing her husband to save herself from *imminent* death or great bodily harm. *Id.* No such evidence was introduced in this case, and it would have been error for the trial court to instruct the jury on *either* perfect or imperfect self-defense.

Involuntary Manslaughter

Involuntary manslaughter—sometimes called *unintentional* or *unlawful act manslaughter*—was discussed in Chapter 3 in relation to proximate cause or causation.

Conduct of Defendant	Resulting Harm	Case
Repeated incidents of allowing horses to escape because of rotted fences	Horses ran on public highway, and motorist was killed in collision with a horse.	*Sea Horse Ranch, Inc. v. Superior Court,* 30 Cal.Rptr. 681 (Cal.App. 1994)
Furnishing heroin or cocaine to victim, who dies of an overdose	Could also be charged under the *Len Bias* laws of some states or as felony murder if supplying the drug was a felony.	*Commonwealth v. Perry,* 1993 WL 28569 (Mass.App. 1993); *People v. Patterson,* 46 CrL 1007 (Sup.Ct.Calif. 1991)
Both men were intoxicated in a bar when defendant struck victim once in the face. Victim fell straight back, struck his head, and died.[27]	Defendant's felony murder conviction was reversed because defendant was entitled to a jury instruction on involuntary manslaughter. Jury could find defendant did not intend to kill or do great bodily harm. The fall rather than the blow killed the victim.	*People v. Taylor,* 570 N.E.2d 1180 (Ill.App. 1991)
A San Francisco husband and wife kept two large dogs that repeatedly threatened and frightened neighbors. The husband wrote in a letter, "Neighbors be damned. . . . They can move."	The dogs killed a woman at the door to her apartment in a prolonged attack. After thirty witnesses testified to the increased threatening behavior of the dogs, the jury found that implied malice existed and convicted the defendant-wife of second-degree murder. Because the defendant-husband was not present during the attack, he was convicted of involuntary manslaughter and other charges.	See the *New York Times* articles "Dog Mauling Prosecution Ends With Bold Letter on Neighbors" and "Couple Convicted of All Charges in Dog Mauling Fatal to Neighbor" (March 15, 2002, and March 22, 2002). (A Superior Court judge later threw out the murder conviction citing lack of evidence that the defendant-wife knew her dog would kill someone that day. Both defendants are now sentenced to prison for involuntary manslaughter.)

Involuntary manslaughter is often charged when extreme negligence or wanton or reckless conduct by the defendant brings about an unintended or accidental death. In some of these instances, the defendant is committing a misdemeanor or other minor offense. Examples of cases in which defendants were charged and convicted of involuntary manslaughter are summarized in the table above. For further cases on involuntary manslaughter, see Chapter 3.[28]

Suicide, Assisting Suicide, and Euthanasia

In common law, suicide was considered to be self-murder and was a felony. Because the person who committed such a crime was beyond the reach of the law, the punishment was forfeiture of the deceased person's estate to the king and burial off the highway.

Examples of Manslaughter

Example of heat of passion manslaughter
Defendant and his wife were separated. Defendant went to the home where the wife and child lived and found his wife having sexual intercourse with another man. Defendant shot and killed the other man and was convicted of first-degree murder. *Reversed to voluntary manslaughter.*

Heat of passion manslaughter was the finding in this case because:

1. there was adequate provocation, that caused

2. extreme anger and rage ("In our opinion, the passions of any reasonable person would have been inflamed and intensely aroused by this sort of discovery."),

3. there was no opportunity to cool off, and

4. there was a causal connection between the provocation, anger, and the fatal act.

State v. Thornton, Tennessee Supreme Court, 730 S.W.2d 309 (1987)

Example of involuntary manslaughter (also called unintended manslaughter) Defendant repeatedly allowed vicious dogs to run loose. The dogs killed a jogger. *State v. Powell,* 426 S.E. 91 (N.C.App. 1993). (See this chapter and Chapter 3 for material on involuntary manslaughter.)

Example of imperfect self-defense manslaughter Defendant and his brother became involved in a fight outside a Baltimore bar. When the defendant believed the other man had a knife, he pulled out a handgun and fired, killing the other man. The victim did not have a knife. The trial court did not submit the imperfect self-defense issue to jury. *Reversed for new trial.*

In a long decision tracing the history and cases on manslaughter, the Court used the honest but unreasonable belief rule. Faulkner produced evidence sufficient to generate a jury issue as to whether he had a subjectively honest but objectively unreasonable belief that he was in imminent danger of death or serious bodily injury, and the trial court should have granted his requested instruction on imperfect self-defense. *State v. Faulkner,* Court of Appeals of Maryland, 301 Md. 482, 483 A.2d 759 (1984).

Manslaughter convictions that caused a riot After losing his job, Dan White sneaked a gun into City Hall in San Francisco, where he shot Mayor Moscone four times. He then reloaded the gun and shot Supervisor Harvey Milk, a leader of the gay community, six times. Both victims died, and Dan White used the Twinkie defense. (See Chapter 5.) White was convicted of two counts of voluntary manslaughter, causing San Francisco gays to riot, taking over the downtown area, burning cars, and breaking windows. *People v. White,* California Court of Appeals, 117 Cal.App.3d 270, 172 Cal.Rptr. 612 (1981).

Assisting a suicide is a crime in most states. A person could assist another to commit suicide by conduct (or words) that a trial judge or a jury find to amount to "assisting."

Euthanasia—or mercy killing—is murder. But the motive for the murder is love, or concern for the suffering of the victim. In the 1987 case of *State v. Forrest,* 362 S.E.2d 252, the defendant was convicted of first-degree murder and sentenced to life imprisonment for the mercy killing of his terminally ill father, who was suffering from a number of untreatable illnesses. In such cases, appeals are made to the governor of the state for clemency, which is frequently granted after a number of years.[29]

Murder, Assisted Suicide, or Neither?

When one person participates in the death of another, that participation may constitute the crime of murder or assisted suicide. It may not be a crime at all, depending on the degree of participation and the laws of the state having jurisdiction over the acts.

The difference between murder and *assisting suicide* was explained by the California Supreme Court in *In re Joseph G.,* 667 P.2d 1176 (1983), as follows:

> The key to distinguishing between the crimes of murder and of assisting suicide is the active or passive role of the defendant in the suicide. If the defendant merely furnishes the means, he is guilty of aiding a suicide; if he actively participates in the death of the suicide victim, he is guilty of murder.[30]

The difference between participation that constitutes the crime of assisting suicide and participation that is not criminal is harder to draw. A doctor who, at the patient's or family's request, removes a life-support machine obviously hastens death but does not furnish the means of that death. On the other hand, a doctor who, like Dr. Jack Kevorkian, furnishes a person with a "suicide machine" clearly has furnished the means. Kevorkian admitted in 1997 to "being present" at more than one hundred deaths.[31]

So-called "passive euthanasia" in hospitals does not fall easily into either category. A doctor who "sends a patient home" with a morphine drip, and stops all other treatment, is in one sense only letting nature take its course. On the other hand, the doctor knows that the morphine will shorten the patient's life, so that in prescribing large doses of the morphine he or she is providing the means for death.

Because of the ambiguities surrounding physician-assisted suicide, and because many patients asserted a "right" to choose physician-assisted suicide, various constitutional attacks on state-assisted suicide statutes have been made. In *Washington v. Glucksberg,* 117 S.Ct. 2258 (1997), and *Vacco v. Quill,* 117 S.Ct. 2293 (1997), the U.S. Supreme Court upheld the constitutionality of statutes in New York and Washington making physician-assisted suicides criminal. The Court rejected the contention that the Fourteenth Amendment prohibited states from making such conduct criminal. The concept of "liberty" in the Constitution, which spawned the right to marry, to have children, or to an abortion, does not, the Court held, include a right to assistance in choosing the time and manner of one's death.

The Oregon "Death with Dignity" Law

Most states make assisting a suicide a crime. Oregon, however, enacted the Oregon death with dignity law, which became effective in November 1997. The controversial law, which permits assisted suicides, is the first of its kind in the United States.

To qualify under the Oregon law, a patient must be found to be terminally ill and have less than six months to live. Patients must have the mental capacity to fully understand the situation that confronts them. There is a fifteen-day waiting period after the patient applies and is found to have qualified for physician-assisted suicide. Medication is then provided by a physician to end the life of the patient.

The Clinton administration decided not to challenge the Oregon death with dignity law, but the Bush administration moved to overturn it. In November 2001, Attorney General John Ashcroft authorized federal drug agents to revoke the license of any doctor acting under the Oregon law who prescribed lethal drugs for a patient.

SUMMARY

When *no legal justification* exists,

- To knowingly or intentionally kill another human being is *murder.*

- A death that occurs while the defendant is committing or attempting a felony of violence is *felony murder.*

- To kill while acting under a sudden heat of passion (rage) caused by the victim is *voluntary manslaughter.*

- To kill when the killer actually but unreasonably believes his or her conduct is necessary in self-defense (*imperfect self-defense*) is *voluntary manslaughter*

- An unintended death that occurs because the defendant is committing a misdemeanor or other minor offense (see Chapter 3) is *involuntary manslaughter.*

- An unintended death that occurs because of "wanton or reckless conduct," as defined in that state, could be charged as *involuntary manslaughter* or under a somewhat similar statute.

When *legal justification* exists,

- *perfect self-defense* is *justifiable homicide.*

- if some civil fault exists (but no criminal fault), it is *excusable homicide.*

 ## BOOK-SPECIFIC WEB SITE

For chapter-related Web links, quizzing activities, and case and news updates, go to the *Criminal Law,* Eighth Edition, book-specific Web site at **http://info.wadsworth.com/ gardner.**

QUESTIONS AND PROBLEMS

1. An elderly woman resisted a purse snatching near her home and was knocked to the pavement. The two purse-snatchers escaped with $15 to $20 in the purse. The woman was taken to a hospital with a cut on the back of her head. Because a blood clot developed in her brain, surgery was performed. The woman remained in a coma, into which she had lapsed within hours of the purse snatching, and died six weeks after the incident. What criminal charges could be issued against the two men, and what defenses to these charges would be used by a defense lawyer?

2. In 1984, a St. Paul, Minnesota, man admitted to police that he had murdered his wife and buried her body in the snow. His defense attorney then advised him not to provide any further information. The man was arrested, and for weeks the police attempted to find the body of the woman. In order to obtain information on the location of the body, the district attorney agreed to accept a plea to second-degree murder. Based on the plea bargain, the man disclosed the location of the body. The court, upon receiving the guilty plea, imposed a sentence of

twenty-five years in prison, with parole eligibility in seventeen years.

- What are the factors that would cause a prosecuting attorney to make a plea bargain offer of second-degree murder instead of going for a conviction of first-degree murder in this case?
- What bargaining leverage does a defense attorney have in a situation such as this?
- Are the interests of the public and of justice served by the outcome in this case?

3. In New York City in 1988, police officers were making what they called "a routine drug arrest" of three men. They had one man in custody when he suddenly broke loose, knocking the arm of one of the police officers, who had his revolver in his hand. The gun discharged, killing one of the other officers. Should the man, Joseph Barker, who attempted to escape, be charged with a criminal homicide? If so, what would be the charge in your state? Explain.

4. A Wisconsin woman heard noises in her backyard one morning. She looked out a window and saw two men hooking up the family boat and trailer to their car. The trailer and boat were worth more than $5,000. Instead of immediately calling the police, she got her husband's handgun and commenced firing, killing one of the men.

    Was this a lawful use of force in the defense of property? (See Chapter 6.) If the woman is charged with a crime, what should the criminal charge be? Could the woman be sued in a civil court for her conduct?

5. Should the defendants in the following cases be charged with murder, manslaughter, a lesser offense, or no crime at all?

- During a domestic argument, a wife taunted her husband with words that enraged the man. He killed his wife. *Girouard v. State,* 321 Md. 532, 583 A.2d 718 (1991). ~~manslaughter~~ *murder*
- The victim threw a glass of beer at the defendant and swore at him. The defendant knocked the victim to the ground and kicked her repeatedly until she died. *Commonwealth v. Vanderpool,* 367 Mass. 743, 328 N.E.2d 833 (1985). *murder*
- The victim threw a glass figurine at the defendant and then began to stab at the defendant with a knife. In the struggle, the victim was stabbed and died. *State v. Rhodes,* 63 Ohio St.3d 613, 590 N.E.2d 261 (1992). *self-defense / predatory*
- The defendant forced his way into his girlfriend's apartment and threatened to kill the woman if she did not get out of his way. As he opened the door to the bedroom, he began shooting into the dark room, killing her male guest. *State v. Tatum,* 824 S.W.2d 22 (Mo.App. 1991). *murder*
- The defendant was angry because of past abuses of his sister by the victim and killed the man. *State v. Hanson,* 286 Minn. 317, 176 N.W.2d 607 (1970). *murder*
- A 13-year-old girl jumped from a moving car when the defendant attempted to sexually assault her. The victim died the next day of multiple injuries. *State v. Statum,* 390 So.2d 886 (La. 1980), review denied 450 U.S. 969, 101 S.Ct. 1489. *murder*

INFOTRAC COLLEGE EDITION EXERCISES

1. Go to InfoTrac College Edition and, using the subject search term *homicide* and subdivision *cases,* find the article discussing the York, Pennsylvania, case where suspects in a thirty-year-old murder case were arrested and charged in the summer of 2001. The case involved over a hundred white men who allegedly shot a black woman thirty years ago. Can they still be tried after thirty years? (See Chapter 7). If so, what problems do you see for the prosecution?

2. Go to InfoTrac College Edition and, using the subject search term *manslaughter,* find the November 2000 article in the *British Medical Journal* reviewing the number of physicians charged with manslaughter when patients died because of the physicians' carelessness. Although it is a review of English prosecutions, it seems likely that similar cases have occurred in the United States. What should the standard be for such prosecutions?

NOTES

1. 23 Corpus Juris Secundum Criminal Law 917.

2. 23A Corpus Juris Secundum Criminal Law 1124.

3. 424 Pa. 331, 227 A.2d 900 (1967).

4. See the *Newsweek* article "Death of the Innocent" (August 17, 1998), the *New York Times* article "Mother Goes from Martyr to Defendant in Infanticides" (August 7, 1998), and the *Chicago Tribune,* p. 20 (September 25, 1997).

5. *State v. Horne,* 282 S.C. 444, 319 S.E.2d 703 (1984).

6. *Brinkley v. State,* 253 Ga. 541, 322 S.E.2d 49 (1984). See also *Minnesota v. Merrill,* 274 N.W.2d 99 (Minn. 1978), review denied U.S. Supreme Court, in which the defendant was charged with first-degree murder of his girlfriend and second-degree murder of a 28-day-old embryo (no premeditation).

Many states require in a charge of murder of a fetus that the fetus be "quick." Minnesota does not, and the killing of any age fetus is covered by the Minnesota statute.

7. *The Journal of Criminal Law, Criminology and Police Science* (1974) 60:351.

8. *Swafford v. State,* 421 N.E.2d 596 (Ind. 1981).

9. Of the many court cases of brain-dead victims, two young women received a great amount of public attention. Nancy Cruzan received severe injuries in an auto accident, and Karen Ann Quinlan was brain-dead because of a drug overdose. After years in vegetative states, the parents of both young women went into courts to obtain permission to withdraw life-support systems. In both cases, the parents carried the burden of showing that their incompetent daughters would not have wanted to go on living in vegetative states. *In re Quinlan,* 70 N.J. 10, 355 A.2d 647 (1976), review denied 429 U.S. 922, 97 S.Ct. 319 (1976), and *In re Cruzan,* 497 U.S. 261, 110 S.Ct. 2841 (1990).

In the 1990 *Cruzan* case, the U.S. Supreme Court held that states could establish standards such as the Missouri "clear and convincing" evidence requirement showing that Nancy Cruzan would have wanted to die. The state of Missouri, which was paying about $112,000 per year to keep Cruzan alive in a "persistent

vegetative state," had opposed efforts by her parents to have life-support systems withdrawn. In a hearing after the Supreme Court's decision, a Missouri court heard new evidence presented by three of Cruzan's co-workers, who testified that Nancy had stated she would never have wanted to live "like a vegetable." Cruzan's doctor testified that her existence was a "living hell." After eight years on life-support systems, the feeding tube was removed and Nancy Cruzan died.

10. *People v. Stevenson,* 416 Mich. 383, 331 N.W.2d 143 (1982). See also *State v. Hefler,* 60 N.C.App. 466, 299 S.E.2d 456 (1983), affirmed 310 N.C. 135, 310 S.E.2d 310, 34 CrL 2374 (1984), in which the North Carolina court stated: "For the courts to remain judicially oblivious of these advances [in medical science] when considering whether to extend an ancient common law rule would be folly."

11. See *Bloodletters and Badmen: A Narrative Encyclopedia of American Criminals from the Pilgrims to the Present,* by Jay Robert Nash (New York: M. Evans & Co., 1974).

12. In a case in which the defendant shot a 15-year-old gasoline service station attendant in the head, neck, and back six times, the Minnesota Supreme Court held: "Extensive planning and calculated deliberation need not be shown by the prosecution.

"The requisite 'plan' to commit a first-degree murder can be formulated virtually instantaneously by a killer. . . . Moreover . . . premeditation can be inferred from either the number of gunshots fired into the victim . . . or the fact that a killer arms himself with a loaded gun in preparation." *State v. Neumann,* 262 N.W.2d 426, 22 CrL 2465 (Minn. 1978).

13. 157 U.S. 675, 15 S.Ct. 720 (1895).

14. See the New York Penal Code, Section 125.20.

15. See the *Newsweek* article "Sentence by Public Opinion?" (March 5, 1984).

16. 157 U.S. 675, 15 S.Ct. 720 (1895).

17. 70 Cal.2d 711, 76 Cal.Rptr. 391, 452 P.2d 607 (1969).

18. 351 Ill. 604, 184 N.E. 894 (1933).

19. 38 Ga.App. 36, 142 S.E. 202 (1928). In this case, the deceased used profane and insulting language, with threats to cut the defendant's throat.

20. 381 Pa. 447, 113 A.2d 293 (1955).

21. 56 Ill.App.2d 159, 205 N.E.2d 749 (1965).

22. Years ago, Texas, New Mexico, and Utah enacted laws that provided that if a husband killed a man caught in an act of adultery with his wife, the killing was a justifiable homicide.

Critics of these statutes argued that this permitted an "open shooting season" on paramours if they were caught by husbands in the act of adultery. Women's groups in these states angrily demanded that the statutes be either repealed or amended so as to give wives the same rights. It is reported that all three states have repealed these statutes and probably have gone back to the common law rule.

23. In a case where a fiancée was killed after she admitted infidelity, and in another case where a spouse was killed after confessing to adultery, the question before two state supreme courts was whether "mere words" justified reducing murder charges to voluntary manslaughter.

Neither the Ohio Supreme Court nor the Michigan Supreme Court would reduce the murder charges to manslaughter because of mere words. *State v. Shane,* 590 N.E. 2d 272 (Ohio), and *State v. Pouncey,* 471 N.W. 2d 346 (Michigan).

24. 175 Cal. 45, 164 P. 1121 (1917).

25. 10 Md.App. 630, 272 A.2d 64 (1971).

26. House of Lords, 2, All Eng. R 801 (1954).

27. The blow to the face would ordinarily be charged as a battery or simple assault (or disorderly conduct). Unless there was an intent to kill or do great bodily harm, it would not be a felony so as to justify the felony murder conviction.

28. A man was killed playing Russian roulette with two other men. The survivors were charged with and convicted of involuntary manslaughter. The court held that the game involved an unreasonable and high degree of risk of death. *Commonwealth v. Atencio,* 345 Mass. 627, 189 N.E.2d 223 (1963).

29. The *Roswell Gilbert* case caused a national debate on euthanasia in 1985. Mr. Gilbert killed his wife, who was suffering from terminal debilitating diseases. He was 76 years of age at the time and received a sentence of twenty-five years imprisonment without parole. After serving five years, he was granted clemency by the Florida governor and returned to Fort Lauderdale.

30. In the case of *In re Joseph G.,* a minor (Joseph G.) and his friend made a mutual suicide pact. The two males drove a car over a cliff to carry out the suicides. Joseph G. survived, but his passenger was killed. The California Supreme Court reversed the first-degree murder conviction, holding that Joseph G. should be charged with assisting a suicide.

31. In April 1999, Dr. Kevorkian was convicted of the crime of murder by a Michigan jury and sentenced to ten to twenty-five years in prison, with the possibility of parole after six years and eight months. Dr. Kevorkian was 70 years old in 1999.

14

Assault, Battery, and Other Crimes Against the Person

KEY TERMS

assault

battery

offensive touching

menacing

mayhem and malicious disfigurement

kidnapping

false imprisonment

Missing Children Act

violation of a court order

road rage

The Crime of Assault

Under common law, **assault** and **battery** were two separate crimes. Today, however, the term *assault and battery* is sometimes used to indicate one offense. Because an assault is often an attempt to commit a battery, the California courts point out that an assault is an attempt to strike, whereas a battery is the successful attempt. A battery cannot be committed without assaulting a victim, but an assault can occur without committing a battery.

Most states have statutorized the old common law crime of assault. Included in the crime of assault are (1) an attempt to commit a battery in which no actual battery or physical injury resulted, and/or (2) an intentional frightening (such as pointing a loaded gun at a person or **menacing** with a fist or knife). Generally, in an assault, the state must show apprehension or fear on the part of the victim if no blow, touching, or injury occurred.

In many states, the crime of assault also includes batteries. The state of New York does not have a crime of battery.[1] Therefore, in New York, a person who swings a knife at another with intent to cause serious physical injury is guilty of first-degree assault if successful but is guilty only of attempted assault if no injury occurs. (See New York Commentaries, Art. 120, p. 331.)

Section 240 of the California Penal Code (enacted in 1872) defines assault as "an unlawful attempt, coupled with a present ability, to commit a violent injury on the person of another." Chapter 38, Section 12-1, of the Illinois Statutes provides that "a person commits an assault when, without lawful authority, he engages in conduct which places another in reasonable apprehension of receiving a battery."

One need not be the size of a football linebacker to commit an assault. A well-known 70-year-old television evangelist was charged with assault while on an airplane, a federal offense, when he entered the airplane's galley, argued with a flight attendant about the quality of service, and shook the attendant by his shoulders.[2]

In some states (including California), the lack of "present ability" to commit the injury or battery is a defense to an assault charge.[3] The defendant in the 1983 case of *People v. Fain* used this defense.[4] He argued that the rifle he pointed at three men was not loaded. However, one of the victims (Steen) testified that the defendant fired a shot from the gun during the incident and that the defendant struck two of the victims with the gun. In affirming the defendant's conviction, the California Supreme Court held:

> Defendant testified that the gun was unloaded. . . . The jury, however, may not have believed defendant's testimony in this regard, as Steen had testified that at one point defendant had fired a round from the rifle.
>
> In any case, even an unloaded gun can be used as a club or bludgeon. . . . Defendant struck both Maestas and Steen with the gun, and approached sufficiently near Watkins to have the present ability to injure Watkins in the same manner.

Instead of requiring a showing of present ability, other states require a showing of "apparent ability." In an assault with a dangerous weapon (gun), testimony of the victim that he or she reasonably believed the gun was loaded is sufficient to show apparent ability to discharge the weapon. Apparent ability is easier for the state to prove than present ability, for which the state has to have specific proof that the gun was loaded. Florida is one of the states requiring only apparent ability (§ 784.011).

Assault Under the Present Federal Criminal Code

Under the present Federal Criminal Code, the crime of assault also includes an actual battery; 18 U.S.C.A. Section 113(c) forbids "assault by striking, beating, or wounding." Therefore, the two common law aspects of assault are used, as well as a third aspect in which the crime of assault is committed by inflicting injury on another person. The following federal case illustrates:

United States v. Masel [5]

U.S. Court of Appeals, 7th Circuit (1977) 563 F.2d 322, 22 CrL 2065

During a campaign for the presidency of the United States, defendant Masel became angry at U.S. Senator Henry Jackson and spat in his face. The defendant was charged with assaulting a member of the U.S. Congress and was convicted in a jury trial. The Federal Court of Appeals affirmed the conviction, holding:

> [I]t is clear that Congress intended to include "battery" within the term "assault." Accordingly, the district court instructed, in effect, that if the jury found a battery had been committed, defendant should be convicted of the charge of assault. . . . We also note that every battery must include or be the culmination of an assault (in the sense of attempt).

Assault with a Deadly or Dangerous Weapon

A simple assault is a misdemeanor or ordinance charge. The criminal charge of assault with a deadly or dangerous weapon is a felony charge. A gun or a dangerous knife is certainly a deadly weapon if it is used to threaten or harm.

As pointed out in Chapter 12, the issue of what is a dangerous or deadly weapon is a question of fact for the fact finder (jury or judge). Just as it was held in New York that a common handkerchief can, under certain circumstances, be a deadly weapon, many courts have also held that hands can be dangerous or deadly weapons, even if the assailant has no training in martial arts or boxing.

The relative size and strength of the assailant as compared with the victim, the manner and duration of the assault, and the severity of the injuries are all facts that must be taken into consideration in determining whether hands are dangerous or deadly weapons. Fact finders would surely find the hands of an adult man who punched a baby to be dangerous or deadly weapons under the circumstances.[6]

The defendant in *State v. Zangrilli* broke his ex-wife's jaw in two places, grabbed her by the throat and strangled her until she could feel her "eyes bulge," dragged her through several rooms in her house, punched her several times in the face and neck, and shoved her into a bathtub.[7] The Rhode Island Supreme Court affirmed his conviction of assault with a dangerous weapon, quoting the trial judge's holdings:

> The manner in which he used his hands on her throat constituted use of his hands in such a way that it could easily have led to her death.
>
> For that reason, I have concluded that his assault upon her was done with a dangerous weapon. As I say, hands are not per se dangerous weapons, but they are a means to produce death. And they were used, even though briefly, in a manner and in such circumstances as could be reasonably calculated to produce death.

A rubber-soled tennis shoe was held to be a dangerous weapon in the 1991 case of *State v. Munoz,* 575 So.2d 848 (La.App.). An eyewitness testified that the defendant kicked the victim so hard in the head that the victim's body was lifted off the ground. The attending physician also characterized the attack by the defendant as brutal.

The Crime of Armed Violence

Some states have created a separate crime of committing a felony while armed with a dangerous weapon, whereas other states enhance (increase) penalties of people committing a felony while armed. What constitutes "armed" is most often a question of law. A person who actually carries a pistol on his or her person is "armed." But it is less clear if one who commits a felony with a pistol in his or her vicinity is armed. The following two Illinois cases illustrate this problem.

In *People v. Board,*[8] an appeals court upheld a conviction for armed violence in which the defendant was sitting on a sofa that had a gun under one of the cushions. Although the defendant made no attempt to get the gun, the Court held that its accessibility sufficed to support the armed violence conviction. Conversely, in *People v. Shelato,*[9] the Court reversed a conviction for armed violence when the defendant's gun was in the same room with the defendant but hidden in a zippered bag underneath sixty bags of marijuana. The Court stated that it "defied common sense" to believe the defendant could have gotten this gun under the "watchful eyes of several police officers," and vacated the conviction.

Battery

In order for an offense to constitute assault, the victim must ordinarily be apprehensive of the impending harm or danger. This is not necessary in a battery. A blow from behind is a battery whether or not the victim is aware that it is coming. Battery is a crime that, like murder and manslaughter, is defined in terms of the conduct of the offender and also in terms of the harm done.

A battery is an unlawful striking; in many states, even a touching could be charged as a battery. Batteries can be committed with fists, feet, sticks, stones, or other objects used to inflict injury. Under some circumstances, dogs or other animals could be used to commit a battery if they are used to injure another person illegally.[10]

All states that make battery a crime require that the act to commit a battery must be intentional (or must be done knowingly), because an accidental physical contact or injury is not a battery.

The term "medical battery" is used to describe an unauthorized or illegal medical procedure. Most medical batteries are civil wrongs in which the victim could obtain civil damages. An example of a medical battery that was both a criminal and a civil violation occurred in New York City when a doctor after performing a cesarean section carved his initials into the stomach of his patient. Both criminal and civil proceedings were brought against the doctor.

Bill Gates, the chairman of Microsoft Corporation, had a pie thrown in his face as he arrived at a meeting with business and government leaders in Brussels, Belgium, in February 1998. Pranksters also hit the mayor of San Francisco, Willie Brown, with a pie in 1998. In the United States, charges against the perpetrators would vary somewhat from state to state but generally would be disorderly conduct or simple assault.   AP/Wide World Photos

Street Fights and Public Brawls

Under the old common law, an affray was the offense of two or more people fighting in a public place. Many street fights, tavern fights, and public brawls are matters of mutual combat in which both parties want to settle a dispute by use of force. If a prosecutor concludes it was mutual combat, both parties are likely to be charged with disorderly conduct (or as disorderly persons). If the parties are charged with assault or battery, a long jury trial might then result if one or both of the parties uses either the defense that the other party consented to the fight (mutual combat) or self-defense.

If one of the parties is the aggressor and wrongfully attacks the other party, who then uses force in self-defense, it is not then mutual combat. In such a situation, the wrongdoer is the party who should be charged with either assault, battery, disorderly conduct, or a combination of these offenses.

Affrays differ from assaults and batteries in that the old offense of affray had to be committed in a public place. Assaults and batteries can be committed in either a private or a public place. Affrays also required two or more people engaged in mutual combat, whereas an assault or a battery may be committed by one person on another.

A victim of an assault or battery can claim the privilege of self-defense, as necessary and reasonable force may be used to defend against an unlawful attack (see Chapter 6 on defenses to the use of force). In an affray (fight in a public place), the combat generally is mutual, which would make it more difficult to assert self-defense or the defense of another.

Offensive Touching Under Sexual Assault and Sexual Battery Statutes

Many states have enacted sexual assault statutes to replace or add to their old rape statutes. These statutes generally provide for three or four degrees of sexual assault. In addition to defining sexual intercourse broadly, these statutes also forbid and punish *offensive touching*.

Before the enactment of the sexual assault statutes, offensive touching was ordinarily charged under the general assault statute or as a battery or as disorderly conduct. Although offensive touching may continue to be charged under the old statutes, the sexual assault statute is now available. However, under the sexual assault statutes, the offensive touching generally must be of an "intimate part" or "private part" of the body and for the purpose "of arousing or gratifying sexual desire of either party" (§ 213.4 Model Penal Code).

The rape charge in the case of *People v. Margiolas* was dropped because of lack of evidence of resistance. However, the defendant admitted that he unbuttoned the victim's blouse, despite her verbal as well as physical objections. The defendant was convicted of sexual battery in forcibly unbuttoning the blouse.[11] Under such a statute, a prosecutor with a weak case might also issue a sexual battery charge when it is apparent that the rape charge has defects that might be insurmountable. (See Chapter 18 for more material on sexual assault and sexual battery statutes.)

The Crime of Genital Mutilation

In 1996, the U.S. Congress outlawed the practice of female genital cutting, a rite of passage prevalent among African and Middle Eastern immigrants. In this practice, a young girl's genitalia is cut or altered. Under this law, those who perform such a procedure on a female under the age of 18 face imprisonment for a term of up to five years. Several states have also made genital mutilation a crime.

Sports Injuries When Force Exceeds the Rules of the Game

A hard tackle in football or a blow to the jaw in boxing would be within the rules of the sport being played. Players in body contact sports consent to such conduct as part of the game.

But if the conduct is beyond the rules of the game, such as a deliberate elbow to the face or a knee to the groin in basketball, the deliberate use of spikes by a runner in baseball, eye gouging in football, or other violence that causes unnecessary injuries, is it a battery or an assault? In one recent case, the Washington Court of Appeals held that an assault was committed when, during a game, one basketball player intentionally punched another player.[12]

Spectator violence and sometimes parental rage can occasionally be a problem at sporting events. Angry words between two fathers at a kids' pickup hockey game led to blows and the death of one of the men. A Massachusetts prosecutor charged the other man with manslaughter.

Because of parental rage and disruptions, a midwest city arranged to have active duty police officers act as umpires and referees at games between schools having a history of excessive verbal abuses and other inappropriate parental conduct.

Other Physical Contact Without Consent[13]

Pushing, pinching, biting, scratching, touching, kissing, punching, spitting, tackling, and so on are all forms of physical contact in which the person initiating the contact could be acting in a friendly, joking, or loving manner, or the contact could be hostile, angry, or belligerent.

If such contact were intentional (not accidental) and done without any legal justification, it could cause a great amount of anger or concern by the person not consenting to such physical contact. If the physical contact were made in an obviously hostile or belligerent manner, the physical contact could provoke a verbal or physical reaction.

If it is shown that the conduct provoked or tended to provoke a disturbance or a disorder, the offender could be charged with disorderly conduct.

EXAMPLE: A strange man roughly grabs a woman or a girl in a public place and kisses or touches her in the presence of her husband, boyfriend, or other member of her family or friends. Because such conduct is highly likely to cause a public disturbance or disorder, it can be charged as disorderly conduct (or disorderly person).

Defenses to a charge of touching or physical contact could be that the touching was accidental. Implied consent could also easily be inferred if the touching was done to pull a victim away from danger or if mouth-to-mouth resuscitation was necessary to restore breathing to a victim of an accident, fire, and so on. The defense of necessity could also be used if the physical contact was necessary to prevent and avoid a greater harm.

Menacing, Intentional Scaring, and Jostling

Some states have enacted the crime of *menacing,* which is defined as follows in Public Law 120.15 of New York:

> By physically menacing, intentionally placing or attempting to place another person in fear of imminent serious physical injury. (New York class B misdemeanor)

Other states have extended the scope of the crime of assault to also include intentional scaring or menacing if a victim is apprehensive of immediate bodily harm.

A fierce look with intent to frighten would not amount to menacing or intentional scaring. Section 211.1 of the Model Penal Code provides:

(1) Simple Assault . . .
  (c) attempts by physical menace to put another in fear of imminent serious bodily injury.

The crimes of jostling and menacing are both listed in W. J. Wlliams's *Moriarty's Police Law,* 21st ed. (London: Butterworths, 1972), the handbook of British police officers.

Defenses to an Assault or Battery Charge

The aggressor defense

That the other party was the aggressor, and the defendant acted in self-defense

Perfect or imperfect self-defense can then be argued by attempting to show that force was necessary and the amount of force used was reasonable.

The mutual combat defense

That mutual combat occurred (mutual combat was defined as a "fight or struggle in which both parties enter willingly, or two parties engage in sudden quarrel, in hot blood, and mutually fight on equal terms."[a])

When seeking to avoid the defenses that the other party was the aggressor or that mutual combat occurred, police and prosecutors are likely to charge disorderly conduct. This usually avoids long trials and long arguments that the other party consented to fight in mutual combat or that because the other party was the aggressor, self-defense was justified.

Other defenses

That the other party consented within the rules of the sport being played

That it was reasonable discipline of a child by a parent, guardian, or a person acting in place of the parent

That in an "offensive touching" battery, the touching was accidental, or consented to, or necessary under the circumstances

That the conduct was necessary and lawful:

- in the accomplishment of a lawful arrest
- when necessary to lawfully detain or hold a person in custody
- when necessary to prevent an escape of a person lawfully in custody
- when necessary to prevent a suicide
- for any other reason when the conduct is privileged by the statutory or common law of that state

[a]See *People v. Dower*, 578 N.E.2d 1153 (Ill.App. 1991), in which the defendant used the defense of mutual combat. The defendant (a big man) shot a woman (5′2″ and 120 pounds) in the head from less than two feet away. The woman was unarmed, and defendant admitted she never threatened him. The defense was rejected.

Jostling is listed under obstruction of public ways and means pushing and shoving in a way that obstructs and blocks the use of a public street, building, sidewalk, and so on. Victims whose passage is blocked are likely to react in anger and violence, which causes the conduct to be charged as disorderly conduct (or disorderly person) in the United States.

Most cities and states have not passed jostling statutes. However, New York City has done so in response to the pickpocketing problem that exists in crowded public places such as subways. The procedure used by most pickpockets is to bump or shove (or have a partner distract by bumping and shoving) to permit entry into a pocket or purse for the theft. Jostling is defined by Public Law 165.25 in New York as follows:

In a public place, intentionally and unnecessarily:
1. Placing one's hand in the proximity of a person's pocket or handbag, OR
2. Jostling or crowding another person at a time when a third person's hand is in the proximity of such person's pocket or handbag.

Felonious and Aggravated Assaults and Batteries

Misdemeanor assault and misdemeanor batteries are classified as class A or B misdemeanors in most states. The degree of these crimes and the penalties are increased with aggravating factors used by state legislatures. The Oregon Supreme Court pointed out that the three factors used in Oregon are (1) the severity of the injury, (2) the use of a deadly or dangerous weapon, and (3) a culpable mental state.[14] The presence of one or more of these aggravating factors could result in a felonious assault or battery. For example, if only minor injury occurred when hands were used, a misdemeanor assault or battery could be charged. However, in the 1982 *Zangrilli* case, the defendant almost caused the death of his ex-wife by strangling her with his hands. The Rhode Island Supreme Court held that hands in the *Zangrilli* case were dangerous weapons and affirmed the felony conviction.

Mayhem and Malicious Disfigurement

Mayhem and malicious disfigurement (or malicious wounding) have been distinguished by federal courts as follows: "[M]ayhem involves disablement of normal functioning of a human body, by contrast with malicious disfigurement which focuses on willful permanent disfigurement."[15]

Lorena Bobbitt was convicted of malicious wounding in Virginia when, in a rage, she cut off her husband's penis and threw it in a field. Believing Mrs. Bobbitt to be a battered woman, a Virginia jury found her not guilty under Virginia's insanity test. She spent four weeks in a Virginia mental hospital and was released on the condition that she receive therapy.

States also follow the common law definition of mayhem, which is the unlawful and violent depriving of the victim of full use of any functional member of the body (hand, arms, feet, eyes, legs, and so on) that would make the victim less able to defend himself or herself.

Article 1166 of the Texas Penal Code provides that "whoever shall willfully and maliciously cut off or otherwise deprive a person of the hand, arm, finger, toe, foot, leg, nose, or ear, or put out an eye or in any way deprive a person of any other member of his body shall be confined in the penitentiary not less than two nor more than ten years."[16]

Mental Culpability Increasing the Degree of the Crime

All states have statutes making assaults and batteries felonies because of the seriousness of injuries or because dangerous or deadly weapons were used to commit the offense.

State statutes also increase penalties and also increase the degree of crimes because of mental culpability.

The Oregon assault statute raises the offense from third- to second-degree assault if the crime is committed "under circumstances manifesting extreme indifference to the value of human life."[17] In holding that a jury must find not only recklessness but also conduct that shows extreme indifference, the Oregon Supreme Court affirmed the defendant's conviction of assault in the second degree in the case of *State v. Boone,* holding:

> Witnesses testified that prior to the accident defendant was swerving across the road, tailgating so closely he almost hit the car in front of him and passing on a curve. The overwhelming weight of the evidence indicated that the accident occurred because defendant was across the center line in the oncoming lane of traffic. He sideswiped the first oncoming vehicle, bounced or swerved into his own lane and then swerved back across the center line into the second oncoming vehicle, causing serious injury to the passenger. Defendant had a blood alcohol content of .24 percent two hours after the accident. He was belligerent at the scene of the accident, threatening to hit the passenger of the first car he sideswiped. Because of his intoxication he was not only unable to assist the victim, but at one point interfered with the assistance. The degree of intoxication, defendant's erratic driving and his conduct at the scene of the accident are circumstances the jury could properly consider in determining whether defendant was extremely indifferent to the value of human life.
>
> We hold that the circumstances which exist in this case suffice to establish defendant's extreme indifference to the value of human life.[18]

Hate Crime Laws

The U.S. Supreme Court has repeatedly held that states may not silence "speech on the basis of its contents,"[19] as was done in the flag-burning and cross-burning U.S. Supreme Court cases (see Chapter 10).

But states may enact "hate crime" laws that enhance and increase penalties for crimes if it is proved that the defendant intentionally selected the victim because of the victim's race, religion, color, disability, sexual orientation, national origin, or ancestry. The Wisconsin "hate crime" was challenged before the U.S. Supreme Court in the following case:

Wisconsin v. Mitchell
Supreme Court of the United States, 508 U.S.476, 124 L.Ed. 2d 436 (1993)

A group of young black youths including Mitchell viewed a scene from the motion picture *Mississippi Burning,* in which a white man beat a young black boy who was praying. The group then moved outside and Mitchell asked if they were "hyped up to move on some white people." When a white boy was seen, Mitchell said "There goes a white boy; go get him." The group ran after the boy, beat him severely, and stole his tennis shoes. The victim was in a coma for four days.

Mitchell was convicted of aggravated battery in a trial before a jury. The maximum penalty for the crime of aggravated battery was two years. But because the jury found that the defendant had intentionally selected his victim because of the victim's race, the trial judge imposed a sentence of four years of imprisonment under the Wisconsin penalty-enhancement statute, known as the hate crime statute.

The U.S. Supreme Court affirmed the conviction and defendant's sentence upholding the Wisconsin hate crime statute. The Court pointed out that the ordinance struck down in the hate

Hate Crime 1997–1999

Why? (motivation)	Where? (place of crime)	Type of Hate (crime committed)	Offenders' Characteristics
Race 61%	Residence 32%	Violent offense 60%	White male 62%
Religion 14%	Open area 28%	Property offense 38%	Black male 20%
Sexual orientation 11%	Retail store 19%	Other 2%	White female 11%
Ethnicity 11%	School/College 12%		Black female 5%
Victim disability 1%	Church/synagogue 3%		

Age of Offenders

Under 24 62%

25–44 years 30%

45 or older 9%

Source is U.S. Dept. of Justice, Sept. 2001, NCJ 186765

crime case of *R.A.V. v. St. Paul,* 112 S. Ct. 2538, was "explicitly directed at expression (i.e., speech or message) . . . where the statute in this case is aimed at conduct unprotected by the First Amendment."

Finally, the Supreme Court held that in the *Mitchell* case, there was no First Amendment violation on the basis of a "chilling effect" on protected speech (overbreath).

Child Abuse and Neglect

Child abuse, child neglect, and sexual abuse are serious problems throughout the United States. Estimates of the number of children who die every year as the result of child abuse in the United States range from two thousand to five thousand. New York City reports that about one hundred children die from child abuse each year.

Thousands of children in the United States suffer head injuries; broken bones from beatings; burns from cigarettes, stoves, and hot liquids; ruptured internal organs (such as liver, spleen, kidneys, and bowels) from blows to the abdomen; missing teeth; multiple scars; knife and gunshot wounds; and bruises and lacerations.

People who inflict such injuries on children may be charged with assault, battery, assault with a dangerous weapon, aggravated battery, and other offenses in the criminal code of the state in which the offense occurred. Criminal codes also have child abuse statutes and statutes forbidding the neglect of children. These statutes seek to protect children from injury and trauma inflicted on them by parents, stepparents, paramours, relatives, baby-sitters, and other adults.

Parents and others responsible for children have a duty to protect children and provide food, clothing, shelter, medical care, education, and a reasonable physical and moral environment for them. Child neglect is the failure to provide adequate food, clothing, shelter, sanitation, medical care, or supervision for a child.

The child abuse that generally appears in courts is physical abuse, such as deliberate injuries inflicted on children. Such injuries could result from excessive and unreasonable force used in disciplining children. The U.S. Supreme Court pointed out in *Ingraham v. Wright* that parents and people taking the place of parents may use force "reasonably believed to be necessary for [the child's] proper control, training, or education."[20] What is reasonable is determined in view of the child's age and sex; the physical, emotional, and mental health of the child; and the conduct that prompted the punishment. Unfortunately, most children who are victims of abuse are under age 5 and are helpless in protecting themselves.

"Child abuse" as a crime has both an active and a passive element. Physical abuse—hitting, burning, cutting, kicking—of children is obviously the active part of child abuse crimes. But action is not always required for child abuse convictions. Most states have statutes making it a crime for one responsible for a child's welfare to endanger the life of the child. This can be done by failing to adequately feed or clothe a child, by leaving a child unattended at home, by leaving a child in an automobile on a hot day, or by failing to intervene when it is known that the child is being sexually molested.[21]

In response to the national problem of child abuse, the following have occurred:

- *Mandatory reporting laws* have been enacted by all states requiring doctors, nurses, teachers, day care workers, and other people coming in contact with children to report suspected child abuse. But experts say there is still a tremendous amount of underreporting of abuse.

- *Increased authority to social workers* by some states to permit social workers to interview children without notifying their parents. Increased numbers of trained social workers are needed to handle growing caseloads.

- As domestic violence and child maltreatment often go hand-in-hand, more efforts are being made to address them together instead of as separate, unrelated problems.

- *New criminal laws* such as the homicide by abuse statute enacted by the state of Washington, which makes child abuse resulting in death the equivalent of first-degree murder. Under this statute, prosecutors no longer have to prove premeditation or intent to kill for a conviction. Instead, the state must show that the defendant displayed "extreme indifference to human life." The writer of the bill stated, "Premeditation in child abuse cases is almost impossible to prove. This [law] gets around that oft-heard defense—'I didn't mean to kill the boy; I just wanted to discipline him.'"

Sexual abuse and sexual exploitation of children are discussed in Chapter 18. Sexual abuse may be combined with physical abuse or child neglect. Abuse or neglect in any form may have a severe emotional and psychological effect on a child, causing behavioral problems that could have great impact on the child's life.

Offenses Against the Liberty of a Person

Kidnapping

Kidnapping was a crime in common law, punishable by life imprisonment. All states and the federal government with some variations have enacted statutes making kidnapping a crime. Section 212.1 of the Model Penal Code defines kidnapping in part as follows:

Child Abuse

Child abuse is a crime that cuts across all walks of life and all social classes

Types of child abuse

Physical abuse	The possible sources of physical abuse of children

- may be parents who are unable to distinguish between discipline and cruelty (or be unable to determine when one becomes the other),
- may be the result of intoxication (drug or alcohol, or both),
- may reflect severe stress because of such problems as unemployment, financial problems, and so on,
- may be any or all of the above combined. Reports indicate that the abused child often becomes an abusive parent.

Neglect	Children can be neglected

- if adequate, proper food is not provided,
- if they are left alone or unsupervised for long periods of time,
- if clothing is dirty or not adequate for the weather,
- if medical, dental, or other physical needs are ignored,
- if a child is not kept clean (poor hygiene, odors).

Sexual abuse (See Chapters 18 and 19)	Under the law, children cannot consent to sexual acts. Sexual abuse occurs when a child is used for the sexual stimulation of an adult (or older child). The sexual abuse could include fondling, prolonged kissing, exhibitionism, and sex acts. Sexual abuse is estimated to be the least reported of the abuses that are criminally prosecuted.
Emotional abuse and neglect (psychological)	Parents have a duty to love and emotionally care for their children. Constantly belittling, treating a child unequally, blaming the child for problems, emotionally neglecting the child, and failing to give children love and affection are forms of emotional abuse and neglect. Emotional abuse, alone or when combined with one or more of the other abuses, can have a devastating effect on a child.

A person is guilty of kidnapping if he unlawfully removes another from his place of residence or business, or a substantial distance from the vicinity where he is found.

The most common motive for kidnapping is to obtain money ransom, as occurred in 1976 when an entire school bus with twenty-six children in Chowchilla, California, was taken. Other kidnappings occur as part of crimes of rape, robbery, murder, and other felonies. Kidnappings have also occurred to terrorize, blackmail, or obtain a hostage for escape.

The question that has come before many courts is whether movements of short distances incident to the commission of such crimes as rape or robbery constitute kidnapping. According to California Jury Instruction 652:

Criminal and Civil Laws That Seek to Protect Children

Under early Roman law, children were considered to be the property of their father, who could discipline them as he saw fit: he could sell them, or even condemn them to death. This law changed slowly over the years, and by the early 1800s, mothers were the primary custodians of their children when a divorce occurred. The concept of the *tender years presumption* held that only a mother has the nurturing qualities needed to love and care for a child through the early part of the child's life, or the tender years. The tender years presumption also changed, and today more than thirty states offer joint custody and shared parenting arrangements with parents who are divorced or have never married. Most criminal laws seek to protect all parties (children and adults alike). States seek to provide additional protection to children by the enactment of most (if not all) of the following statutes:

Laws forbidding	*Statute # in your state*
■ child abuse	_____
■ child neglect	_____
■ abandonment of a child	_____
■ contributing to the delinquency of a child	_____
■ child snatching from the lawful custody of a guardian of the child	_____
■ child endangerment	_____
■ child enticement	_____
■ exposing children to sexually harmful material	_____
■ sexual exploitation of a child	_____
■ statutory rape (children cannot consent to sexual intercourse or sexual contact) under age _____ is (crime) _____	_____
■ other	_____

Compulsory school attendance laws:

■ imposing duty on parents until age _____	_____
■ making student offense of skipping school truancy	_____
■ authorizing police to take truant into custody	_____

To constitute the crime of simple kidnapping, . . . there must be a carrying, or otherwise forceful moving, for some distance of the person who, against his will, is stolen or taken into custody or control of another person, but the law does not require that the one thus stolen or taken be carried or moved a long distance or any particular distance.

In interpreting "some distance," the California courts have held that "movement across a room or from one room to another" is not sufficient movement to justify a kidnapping conviction.[22] The general rule seems to be that movement "merely incident to the commission of the robbery [or rape]" is not kidnapping.[23]

In 1982, the Florida Supreme Court stated that there is a "definite trend" toward allowing a kidnapping conviction "where the purpose in confining or moving another person is to use that person as a hostage." In *Mobley v. State,* the defendants were inmates in a jail.[24] They took two guards and an attorney captive in the course of an escape attempt. In affirming the convictions of the defendants for kidnapping and other offenses, the Florida Supreme Court held that the "confinement was not incidental to the attempted escape once [defendants] began using [the victims] as hostages and threatening physical harm."

In the case of *State v. Masino,* the defendant dragged his victim from her car and down an embankment, out of sight from passersby, before sexually assaulting her.[25] The New Jersey Supreme Court affirmed the convictions of sexual assault and kidnapping.

In the 1990 case of *State v. La France,* 117 N.J. 583, 569 A.2d 1308, the defendant was burglarizing a home in the early morning hours when he was confronted by the husband and wife. La France pretended to have a gun and tied up the husband. After finishing his search for valuables, he then sexually assaulted the wife, who was seven months pregnant. After thirty minutes, the husband freed himself and overpowered the defendant. The New Jersey Supreme Court affirmed the convictions of kidnapping, robbery, assault, sexual assault, and resisting arrest, stating:

> There are two basic kidnapping patterns. In one, the criminal seizes the victim and removes him or her to another place; in the other, the criminal confines the victim in the place where he or she is found. Were the latter not regarded as the moral equivalent of a kidnapping, the criminal might safely isolate a victim in the victim's "summer home in the mountains" and demand ransom with impunity. See *Commonwealth v. Hook,* 512 A.2d 718.
>
> Just as obviously, however, not every movement or confinement of a victim is a kidnapping. The easiest illustrations are situations in which "the burglar puts the householder in the closet while he fills his sack with the silver," see *State v. Estes,* 418 A.2d 1108, 1113 (Me. 1980), or in which the victim of a robbery is forced to open a safe in the home or go to the back of the store. See *State v. Dix,* 282 N.C. 490, 499, 193 S.E.2d 897, 902 (1973). Because courts sensed that these crimes should not be considered kidnapping, the problem became one of definition. In the absence of more precise statutes, courts supplied the necessary content.
>
> * * *
>
> We repeat, as we did in *Masino,* that one is confined for a substantial period if that confinement "is criminally significant in the sense of being more than merely incidental to the underlying crime," and that determination is made with reference not only to the duration of the confinement, but also to the "enhanced risk of harm resulting from the [confinement] and isolation of the victim [or others]. That enhanced risk must not be trivial." 94 N.J. at 447, 466 A.2d 955.

Hostage Taking

Because kidnapping requires a forcible movement of the victim "some distance" or a "substantial distance," some states have created the crime of "taking hostage." A movement of the victim is not required to prove this offense. In creating this new offense, the

Offenses Against the Liberty of a Person

Offense	Usual definition	Usual motivation and use of offense
False imprisonment	False imprisonment is the unlawful restraint of another and is committed when a person is detained unlawfully.	False imprisonment most often occurs when a retail store employee makes an improper detention for shoplifting or an improper arrest is made by a law officer. These incidents are brought in civil courts and often are called "false arrest" lawsuits
Kidnapping	Kidnapping is a false imprisonment that is aggravated by the movement of the victim to another place.	Motives could be to obtain ransom, or as part of rape, robbery, or murder, to terrorize, blackmail, and so on. Kidnapping is punished severely, as it is one of the most serious crimes against a person.
Hostage-taking	Used to gain an advantage and compel others to comply with demands.	"Taking hostage" is often a tactic used as part of an escape attempt. The crime does not require forcible movement of the victim "some distance."
Parental kidnapping or child snatching (includes former live-ins, lovers, and family)	This crime is often a kidnapping by a parent who has lost (or will lose) custody of the kidnapped child.	This serious crime is committed to retaliate, to harass, to use as leverage in determining support payments and to control and maintain custody of the child. Some children are never seen again by the other parent.
Abduction	The English enacted the first abduction statute in 1488. For many years, the crime forbade taking a female for any sexual purposes.	States using abduction as a crime generally limit it to a natural parent taking a child from a person having lawful custody.
Slavery and involuntary servitude	The Thirteenth Amendment forbids "slavery . . . [and] involuntary servitude, except as a punishment for crime."	Slavery, serfage, peonage, debt bondage, and exploitation of children still exists in parts of the world. In 1988, the U.S. Supreme Court affirmed the convictions of Michigan men for the crime of involuntary servitude of two mentally retarded men who were held slaves for at least eleven years. *United States v. Kozminski,* 487 U.S. 43.

state legislature can require all the elements of the serious felony of kidnapping, except movement of the victim. They can require the state to prove "intent to use the person as a hostage."[26] Because "taking hostage" is a serious offense, it can be made a class A or B felony. To encourage offenders to release victims unharmed, the offense can be reduced to a class B or C felony under such conditions.

False Imprisonment[27]

Under the old common law, *false imprisonment* was also a crime that, like kidnapping, was punishable by life imprisonment. Many states have enacted statutes making false imprisonment a crime. The usual elements are as follows:

1. The defendant must have confined or restrained the liberty or freedom of movement of another.

2. Such act must have been intentional and without the consent of the victim.

3. The defendant had no lawful authority to confine or restrain the movement of the victim.

False imprisonment differs from kidnapping in that, in kidnapping, the victim must be moved to another place. In false imprisonment, the confinement or restraint may be at the place of the false arrest or unlawful detention of the victim. Under the old common law, it was also required that kidnapping be done secretly; this was not required for false imprisonment. However, the requirement of secretness for kidnapping has probably been eliminated by most state statutes.

Many false imprisonment actions today are civil actions alleging false arrest or the improper detention of a person. Law enforcement officers and retail store employees should not interfere with the liberty of a person unless authority exists that justifies the restraint of a person. Many civil false imprisonment lawsuits concern detention of people believed to be shoplifters. Chapter 16 presents the law governing detentions and arrests in shoplifting cases.

Parental Kidnapping or Child Snatching

Child snatching is the abduction of a child by one parent without the consent of the other parent. It could occur before the parents had commenced a divorce action, during the time in which a divorce action was pending, or after divorce judgment had been granted. Child snatching is also known as parental kidnapping, child abduction, or child stealing.

Thousands of children disappear each year as a result of parental kidnapping. Although the offending parent may state that he or she seeks to protect the child's welfare, other motives for child snatching are

- retaliation against and harassment of the other spouse
- as a means to bargain for reduced child support or reduced division of property in the divorce settlement
- an attempt to bring about a reconciliation of the marriage

Children who are kidnapped by a parent experience changes that may lead to emotional damage. First, the child will probably be told that the parent who had custody is either dead or no longer loves the child. Second, in most instances, the child begins a lifestyle in which he or she grows up with only one parent. Third, the child is frequently exposed to life on the run, because parental kidnapping is a felony in most states. The

Every large city in the United States has problems with missing persons who are never found or whose remains are found long after the person is reported missing. Chandra Levy was working as a government intern in 2001 when she suddenly disappeared. Her skeletal remains were found nearly 13 months later in a park in the Washington, D.C., area.   AP/Wide World Photos

pain, fear, guilt, anger, and anxiety from these experiences can cause severe, irreparable psychological harm.

Most states are generally prepared to extradite the offending parent back to the state in which the offense was committed, if he or she can be located. Before the passage of the Uniform Child Custody Jurisdiction Act (UCCJA), a fleeing child snatcher could run to another state, where residence would be established and a custody order would be sought from the courts of the new state. Under UCCJA, the home or resident state would continue to have jurisdiction.

Because the federal kidnapping statute (the "Lindbergh Act")[28] specifically excludes parents from its scope, a federal Parental Kidnapping Prevention Act was passed by Congress in 1981. This Act facilitates interstate enforcement of custody and visitation determinations. The Act also declares that the Fugitive Felon Act applies in state felony parental kidnapping cases, giving the FBI jurisdiction when the child snatcher crosses state lines.[29]

The Missing Children Act[30]

Because of increasing concern about child kidnapping by strangers, voluntary programs to fingerprint children for identification exist throughout the nation. The parents or legal guardians retain the fingerprint cards for use if the child, at a later date, gets lost or is missing.

The *Missing Children Act* of 1984 requires the U.S. Attorney General to "acquire, collect and preserve any information which would assist in the location of any missing person (including children, unemancipated persons as defined by the laws of the place of residence) and provide confirmation as to any entry [into FBI records] for such a person to the parent, legal guardian or next of kin." The Act thus gives parents, legal guardians, or next of kin access to the information in the FBI National Crime Information Center's (NCIC) missing person file.

The Act does not confer on the FBI any new investigative jurisdiction. The FBI can enter parental kidnapping cases through the Fugitive Felon Act if the following conditions exist:

1. A state arrest warrant has been issued charging the parent with a felony violation.

2. Law enforcement officers have evidence of interstate flight.

3. A specific request for FBI assistance must be made by state authorities, who agree to extradite and prosecute.

4. A U.S. attorney must authorize issuance of an unlawful flight warrant.

The National Center for Missing and Exploited Children coordinates efforts to recover missing children. A telephone hot line and other facilities are available to aid in these efforts.

Family Violence and Disturbances

A study conducted for the National Institute of Mental Health concluded that "physical violence occurs between family members more often than it occurs between other individuals or in any other setting except wars and riots."

The disturbance is often a quarrel between family members. It may start with a few angry words, or it could be a simmering dispute that explodes into violence. Destruction or damaging or taking of property may occur. One or both (or all) the parties may be under the influence of alcohol or drugs. Job stress or unemployment may contribute to the situation.

Hitting, pushing, choking, or wrestling combined with other abusive behavior may occur. Insulting and offending language is almost always used. Injuries range in severity from minor to critical and life threatening.

Both parties could be at fault, or one party could be the agitator and the offender. The offender may have a prior record of violence and may be under a court order (divorce) or restraining order (criminal) forbidding such conduct. Or the offender may be on probation or parole, and his or her domestic conduct may violate the terms of that probation or parole. The offender's presence on the premises may be in *violation of a court order* or a condition of probation or parole. In addition to these violations, the offender may also be a trespasser.

Family units include not only the traditional family relationships but also homosexuals and unwed heterosexual couples. The disturbance or violence could include not only adults but also children within the family unit.

Past experience has demonstrated that family-trouble calls can be dangerous for law enforcement officers. Approximately one-fifth of police deaths and almost one-third of

Missing Children in the United States

The U.S. Department of Health and Human Services estimates that more than 1.5 million children disappear from their homes each year. Studies done as required by the Missing Children Act enacted by the U.S. Congress in 1984 show that the missing children problem is really "a set of at least five very different, distinct problems."[a] These problems, which are reported to law enforcement agencies, are identified as follows:

Family Abductions in which a family member took (or failed to return) a child in violation of custody rights or an agreement. More than 150,000 family abductions are reported each year in which a child was absent at least one night. Most of the missing children were under 11 years of age. About half of the abductions involved an unauthorized taking, whereas half were a failure to return a child after an authorized visit. Sexual abuse was reported in 1 percent of the cases, whereas neglect or abandonment of the child was a greater concern. The motive for taking the children was generally not love and concern for the children but revenge and retaliation. Family abductors were not limited to parents but also included other family members, lovers, and former live-ins. To deal with this growing problem, the Parental Kidnapping Prevention Act was passed by Congress in 1980.

Runaways Runaway age does not commence until 9 or 10. Physical or sexual abuse in the home could cause the runaway. Home conditions could be deplorable, or the child could have become involved in crimes, drugs, sexual relations, or a gang (sometimes all). Most of the reported runaways return home after being missing for one night or more. Runaways from juvenile facilities tend to be more serious than household cases. More than half leave the state, one-third are picked up by the police, and 10 percent are placed in jail.

Thrownaway Children are abandoned, deserted, told to leave the home, or not allowed to return to the house, or no effort is made to locate them. These children experience more violence within the family and more sexual and physical abuse away from the home. Shelters for runaway and thrownaway children report a high rate of exposure to AIDS and other diseases.

Lost Children are generally children so young that they cannot identify themselves or give a home address. However, older children could be lost in a rural or wooded area, causing extensive searches for the lost child. A "lost" child could be a runaway, a thrownaway child, or the victim of an abduction. Lost children in most cases are found and returned home.

A survey conducted by the U.S. Senate Subcommittee on Investigations shows that more than 85,000 children were missing in twenty-five of the largest American cities in 1981. Tragically, at the end of the year at least 7,000 of the cases remained unsolved. Law enforcement officers report that few stranger-abducted children are recovered alive. (See the *Prosecutor,* "Plight of the Children," vol. 16, no. 5, 1983. The entire issue is devoted to this subject.)

Abduction by Strangers or the Victims of Other Crimes Two hundred to three hundred children are kidnapped by strangers every year in the United States. Criminal homicides of children average up to 147 per year. But it is also estimated that two thousand to five thousand unidentified bodies are buried each year in the United States in John or Jane Doe graves, with approximately half of the unidentified being children. Strangers who steal children are broadly categorized by the Behavioral Science Department of the FBI Academy as follows:

- *The Pedophile.* The pedophile abducts a child primarily for sexual purposes. The Center for Child Advocacy and Protection states that such people are generally young and middle-aged men who seek to control children rather than injure them. They will, however, murder children and perhaps make up the largest group in this category.

- *The "Serial" Killer.* The killings of twenty-nine young blacks in Atlanta, after abduction, shocked the nation. Wayne Williams was convicted for the murders of two of the older victims.

- *The Psychotic.* The psychotic is usually a woman who has lost a baby or cannot conceive. To solve her problem, she abducts another family's child.

- *The Profiteer.* This person seeks to make money by stealing children. The child may be used by a baby adoption ring, pornographers, or, in rare instances, as a kidnapping for ransom.

[a]See the *National Incidence Studies on Missing, Abducted, Runaway, and Thrownaway Children in America; The Parental Abduction Prosecutor's Handbook,* available at the National Center for Prosecution of Child Abuse, 1033 N. Fairfax Street, Alexandria, VA 22314; and see the May 2000 report, "Children as Victims" by the U.S. Department of Justice (NCJ 180753).

assaults on officers occur when they respond to family quarrels and domestic disputes in which a weapon is used.

In past years, unless serious injury occurred or a clear violation of a court order or probation (or parole) existed, an arrest would ordinarily not be made. Police officers would attempt to mediate the dispute. In counseling women, officers would sometimes ask, "Who will support you if he's locked up? Do you realize he could lose his job? Do you want to spend days in court? Why don't you kiss and make up? Why did you get him so worked up that he slugged you? Why do you want to make trouble? Think of what he'll do to you the next time."

Studies by the Police Foundation have shown that police arrests sharply reduce violence in the home. The police commissioner of New York City stated that because of this study and because of his own experience as a "cop on the street," he concluded that past police efforts to mediate have done little to stop what has been a growing problem. The commissioner stated that arresting violent members of a household would be more effective in protecting other family members and would help to safeguard police officers who are called to intervene in situations in which violence could occur.

Criminal charges could be, for example, assault, battery, disorderly conduct, trespass, criminal damage to property (if another person's property was damaged or destroyed), or reckless use of a weapon. In addition to spending time in jail, the offender could be placed under a restraining order or injunction in an attempt to prevent repeated violence or disturbances.

In past years, it was not uncommon for police departments to receive calls from women asking for protection from men who had threatened them or from wives who expected to be beaten by their husbands when they came home from a tavern. Threats to injure can be the basis of a criminal charge. If the threat was made over a telephone, the charge of unlawful use of a telephone may be made.

Because of the battered woman problem, crisis counseling centers and shelters have been established throughout the United States to assist victims and their families. These centers provide shelter when needed, counseling, support, and emergency food and clothing. Location of the shelters are generally not disclosed to the public to avoid further confrontation of the victim by the offender.

Domestic Violence and Women

Physical abuse of women, usually by husbands, ex-husbands, or boyfriends, is a crime that is likely to go unreported, and if reported, not prosecuted. Frequently, the victim refuses to press charges against the abuser. Although in theory the prosecutor may continue to prosecute a case even after the complainant wants charges dropped, in practice such cases become hard to prove and are usually dismissed.

FBI studies show that refusals by the battered spouse to cooperate with prosecutors rarely lead to better relations with the abusive spouse. This is because domestic abuse follows a familiar cycle of violence. In the first phase, the tension-building phase, the abusive spouse becomes hostile and belligerent and heaps verbal abuse on the partner. This phase almost always leads to the next phase, the acute-battering phase. Injury and death can be the result in this phase. Following a severe battering, the abusive spouse will shower the partner with flowers, affection, and contrite behavior. This is called the

Responses to Domestic Violence

The following are some of the responses available to violent family situations:

- Arrest of the offending person (or people)
  if the state or city has a mandatory arrest law
  or at the discretion of the officer (or under the policy of the officer's department)
- Obtain a protective court order under the statutes of that state
- Seek shelter for the victim (spouse, children, parent, or others) under the shelter program available in that community
- Divorce action and obtaining immediate (and also permanent) court orders that could:
  protect
  remove offending spouse from premise
  forbid communication or contact by offending spouse
  restrict visitation rights with children, and enforce other restrictions
- Issue (or threaten to issue) a civil citation with a substantial money fine
- Use of the emergency detention section of the state mental health act (if applicable) to place the offending party into custody for observation
- Revocation of probation or parole if the offender has violated terms of a probation or parole agreement
- In 1996, the U.S. Congress enacted a law that forbids anyone convicted of domestic violence from possessing a firearm. This little-known law could put a violator in a federal prison for up to ten years.

honeymoon phase, but like all honeymoons, it always ends. The next phase in the cycle is the tension-building phase, and the cycle continues from there.[31]

In 1994, Congress passed the Violence Against Women Act (VAWA).[32] This law creates new federal domestic violence crimes and also provides millions of dollars for battered women shelters and child care. The following cases illustrate prosecutions under VAWA:

- *United States v. Bailey:*[33] Bailey beat his wife, placed her in the trunk of his car, and drove back and forth between West Virginia, Kentucky, and Ohio for several days. He was convicted under VAWA and sentenced to life imprisonment.
- *United States v. Steele:*[34] Steele beat his girlfriend in Oregon, then forced her to drive with him to California. While she was attempting to escape, Steele dragged her dangling from the car door. Steele was convicted of interstate domestic violence and sentenced to eighty-seven months in prison.

Abuse of the Elderly

In 1990, the House Subcommittee on Health and Long-Term Care on Aging reported that an estimated 1.5 million elderly Americans (5 percent of all older Americans) are abused each year, often by their own children. The report points out that older people

Slavery in the Twenty-First Century

Slavery, defined as "involuntary subjection to another person," has been present throughout recorded history. As the world is now in the twenty-first century, what is the status of this ancient evil, and what forms does it take?

Internationally Traditional slavery, that is, outright ownership of another human being, still exists in some countries in the world, most located in Africa and South Asia. Sudan, Gabon, and Nigeria are some of the countries where slavery is still practiced.

Debt-bondage, indentured servitude, domestic servitude, and prostitution all have many of the same qualities as classic slavery. To the extent a person is physically or legally compelled to stay in one place, work for only one employer, or sell his or her sexual favors, that person is enslaved under United Nations conventions and other international laws. The Indian child of the lowest caste, called an "untouchable," who is mutilated and shipped to Saudi Arabia to beg outside mosques is a slave, even if his or her "wages" are used to repay a family debt.

United States Classical slavery is made a crime under federal law by the "antislavery law," 18 U.S.C. § 1584. Slavery, or "involuntary servitude," requires a showing that one was held in bondage by physical force or threats of legal coercion. Thus, brainwashing a person to stay in a religious cult and work only for the cult is not slavery, but confining an illegal immigrant to work in a sweatshop under threats of physical force or of deportation would be.

In a recent case, eighteen people were indicted under the federal involuntary servitude law when they forced several deaf illegal Mexican immigrants to sell trinkets on the streets of New York, Chicago, and other cities. The defendants physically abused the immigrants and threatened them with deportation. See the *New York Times* article "Eighteen People Indicted for Involuntary Servitude of Deaf Mexican Immigrants" (August 21, 1997).

often are ashamed to admit that their families abuse them, or they fear reprisals if they complain. The report also states that "elder abuse has been virtually ignored by the federal government." However, with the increase in the number of elderly people in the United States, the number of cases of elder abuse reported has increased. An *FBI Law Enforcement Bulletin* article entitled "Elder Abuse" (February 1994) called elder abuse a "national tragedy" and quoted the congressional subcommittee on aging as stating, "1 out of every 25 Americans over the age of 65 (is suffering) from some form of abuse, neglect, or exploitation."

A July 2001 report of federal and state inspections of the nation's seventeen thousand nursing homes showed that 30 percent of nursing homes in the United States were cited over a two-year period for physical, sexual, or verbal abuse of residents. About one in ten of the citations was a serious incident that either put the victim at great risk of harm or killed the patient. The report contained examples of nursing home residents being punched, choked, or kicked by staff members or by other residents. (See the *Milwaukee Journal Sentinel* article "30% of Nursing Homes Cited for Abuse," July 31, 2001).

Many states have passed laws making failure to care for a dependent elderly person a crime. California's law states that it is a crime, a misdemeanor, or a felony, depending on the dangerousness of the situation, for any person charged with the duty of caring for an elder person to "willfully cause or permit the elder or dependent adult to be placed in a situation such that his or her person or health is endangered."[35]

In *People v. Heitzmann*,[36] a daughter was convicted under this statute when her 68-year-old father died from neglect. Although the father lived with the defendant's brothers, the Court held that she knew the brothers were not caring for her father, but did nothing about it.

The Crime of Violation of a Court Order (or Court Injunction)

Many court orders or injunctions are issued every year in the United States. They are issued in divorce cases in which one of the parties requests such an order (or orders). They are issued when serious harassment causes the victim to go to a court for protection. The injunction could order a husband (or wife) or a boyfriend not to contact or harass a former spouse or live-in partner. The order could forbid the person against whom it is issued from going into or near the residence or the place of employment of the person the order seeks to protect. The order may forbid harassment, violence, or contact with a person or people.

An increasing number of states are making the violation of such court orders crimes in themselves, because so many of these orders have been violated, because tragedies sometimes occur, and because there is no other practical way of enforcing such orders. Other statutes could also make a person who violates a court order subject to immediate arrest without the necessity of an arrest warrant or another court hearing.

When a court order is issued under these new laws, the person against whom it is issued is informed in the court order that any violation of the order could result in immediate arrest.[37]

If a violation does occur, law enforcement officers are generally called by the person the court order seeks to protect. The person should be able to produce a copy of the order for the law enforcement officers. The order will generally show that it has been personally served on the defendant.

EXAMPLE: A court order is issued against a former live-in boyfriend, ordering him (among other things) not to go near or into the place of employment of his former girlfriend. The police are called when the man enters the store or office that the order forbids him to enter. The police detain the man until they have viewed and read the copy of the court order. When it is clear that he has violated the order, the police then arrest the man and charge him with the crime of violation of the court order.

The Violence Against Women Act discussed earlier has a provision that makes criminal the "interstate violation of a protection order."[38] If a wife travels to another state from her home state and obtains a protection order against her husband, any violation of the order by the husband will be a crime under the federal law and the state that issued the order.

Violence in the Workplace

The U.S. Department of Justice reports that each year one million people become victims of violent crimes while at work. Most of such victims are robbed, are victims of felonious assault, or are raped.[39]

While newspapers and television depict scenes of crazed co-workers or fired employees coming back to wreak carnage, statistics show that about one thousand people are killed by violence in the workplace each year.

Is the workplace violent? Should we fear our fellow workers? Statistics show that we have little to fear. For example, in 1993, 1,063 people were killed at work, but only 59 of those killings were committed by fellow workers. Thus, out of a national workforce in 1993 of 120.8 million, only 1 in 2.1 million was killed by a co-worker. The odds of getting hit by lightning each year are about 600,000 to 1.

Road Rage: Violent Aggressive Driving

In any recent ten-year period, vehicle traffic on American roads has increased almost one-third during the ten-year period. New roads and additional traffic lanes, however, have only increased about 1 percent. In many areas, traffic enforcement by law enforcement officers could be down.

The National Highway Traffic Safety Administration reported to the U.S. Congress that "violent aggressive driving" had increased 7 percent a year during the late 1990s.

Violent aggressive driving (also called *"road rage"*) was described as aggressive behavior like tailgating, weaving through busy traffic lanes, honking, screaming at other drivers, exchanges of insults, and even gunfire. The National Highway Safety Chief told members of Congress that road rage was present in two-thirds of the 1996 highway deaths of 41,907 and in one-third of the nonfatal crashes that resulted in three million injuries.

The U.S. House Transportation Committee also heard the testimony of other highway safety experts, including a California psychologist who has studied the "road rage disorder" and has treated "road ragers." "It is curable," stated Dr. Arnold Nerenberg, "but first, 'road ragers' must acknowledge that they have a problem" and then "say to themselves, it's just not worth it."

SUMMARY

The crimes of simple assault and simple battery will be increased to serious felonies depending upon the following factors, which would be considered by a jury or judge in determining guilt or innocence of the crime charged (or of a lesser-degree crime):

1. The harm done to the victim (For example, a push would be at most a simple assault or simple battery. But if the victim is deliberately pushed off a cliff or down a long

flight of stairs and seriously injured, a felon will charged. If the victim is killed, a criminal homicide will be charged.)

2. A weapon is present or is used to commit the assault or battery (was the weapon dangerous or deadly? Was it displayed? Brandished? Pointed? Waved about? Pointed directly at the victim? Pointed with verbal threats? Discharged?)

3. The mental culpability of the offender, which in many cases is demonstrated by the harm done and whether a weapon was used by the offender. Was the harm done the result of deliberate acts of the offender? Reckless acts? Extreme indifference? High degree of negligence? Or ordinary negligence?

Possession or display of weapons, whether deadly or not deadly, could demonstrate mental culpability. Mental culpability could also be demonstrated by the language and possible threats of the offender coupled with the offender's conduct at the time.

 BOOK-SPECIFIC WEB SITE

For chapter-related Web links, quizzing activities, and case and news updates, go to the *Criminal Law,* Eighth Edition, book-specific Web site at **http://info.wadsworth.com/ gardner.**

QUESTIONS AND PROBLEMS

1. When the doors of a subway train opened at Grand Central Station in New York, a young woman dragged a man off the train. As the 27-year-old woman punched the man and beat his head against a concrete wall, she accused him of fondling her body while on the crowded subway train. He apologized while calling for the police. Both complained of the conduct of the other. The 31-year-old man was charged with third-degree sexual abuse, and the woman was issued a criminal summons for harassment (*New York Times* news article). Assuming the accusations of the woman are correct, what amount and degree of force could she legally use against him? (State the test used to determine how much force she could use.) Are the criminal charge and the citation that were issued appropriate? (Third-degree sexual abuse is "offensive touching" or "sexual contact" in New York under Public Law 130.55 and a class B misdemeanor.) What would be appropriate (if any) charges in your state?

2. Former baseball star Reggie Jackson was having lunch in a Milwaukee restaurant when he was spotted by a man at the bar who had been drinking. The man immediately went to Jackson's table, interrupted the conversation at the table, and insisted on an autograph. After an exchange of words, with the parties and witnesses differing as to what occurred, the man ended up on the floor with a broken jaw. Who is at fault? Which of the parties should be charged? Or should both of the parties be charged? With what offenses? Explain.

3. As basketball star Charles Barkley was escorting a woman to her car at night in the parking lot of a restaurant, a bystander yelled an obscenity at the woman. Barkley angrily hit the young man in the face, breaking his nose. Should charges be issued against either or both men after the incident was reported to the police? What should the charge or charges be?

INFOTRAC COLLEGE EDITION EXERCISES

1. Go to InfoTrac College Edition and, using the key-word search term *kidnapping* and the subdivision *prevention*, find the article discussing the incidence of infant kidnapping in hospitals. What preventative steps should hospitals be taking to avoid this kind of kidnapping?

2. Go to InfoTrac College Edition and, using the key-word search term *assault* and the subdivision *laws*,

find the article discussing an assault with a chair. Should you receive the same punishment for throwing a chair at another person in a bar altercation as you would if you used a gun in an assault and actually struck the victim with the gun? What does the author think? Do you agree?

NOTES

1. A few states (including Wisconsin) have not statutorized the common law crime of assault. Disorderly conduct and attempt to commit a battery are substituted for assault in charging.

2. See the *New York Times* article "Television Evangelist Schuller Agrees to Counseling in Airline Assault Case" (August 14, 1997).

3. Probably all states have passed statutes that criminalize the conduct of pointing an unloaded gun at a victim who does not know if the gun is loaded or unloaded and becomes apprehensive and frightened. The New York crime of menacing (Section 120.15) by placing "or attempting to place another in fear of imminent serious physical injury" is an example of such criminal statutes.

4. 34 Cal.3d 350, 193 Cal.Rptr. 890, 667 P.2d 694 (1983).

5. See also *U.S. v. Frizzi*, 491 F.2d 1231 (1st Cir. 1974), in which the defendant spat in the face of a mail carrier and then hit the carrier in the face when he demanded an apology. The Court affirmed the defendant's conviction of assaulting a federal officer in the performance of his duties.

6. In the 1991 case of *Ray v. State*, 580 So.2d 103, the Alabama Court of Appeals quoted another court as to an adult man's fists being used to beat a baby:

Certainly the use of an adult man's fists to beat a seventeen month [old] child may appropriately allow

those fists to be classified as a deadly weapon or a dangerous instrument.

7. 440 A.2d 710 (R.I. 1982).

8. 534 N.E.2d 312 (Ill.App. 1989).

9. 592 N.E.2d 585 (Ill.App. 1992).

10. Other batteries and assaults include a running leap onto a woman's back as assault in *Russell v. State*, 814 S.W. 2d 871 (Tex.App. 1991); poking a teacher in the chest as assault in *People v. Dunker*, 577 N.E.2d 499 (Ill.App. 1991); a profane threat of physical violence as assault in *Wells v. State*, 418 S.W.2d 437 (Ga.App. 1992); grabbing the victim by his coat and punching him in the face as assault in *State v. Waltrip*, 484 N.W.2d 831 (Neb. 1992); held the victim against her will as battery in *Barnette v. State*, 217 S.W.2d 20 (1949); head butt into victim as disorderly conduct and assault in *State v. McKenzie*, 605 A.2d 72 (Maine 1992); attempting to film under victim's dress with camcorder as simple battery in *Fitzgerald v. State*, 411 S.E.2d 102 (Ga.App. 1991); and throwing rocks at moving cars on highway as several counts of assault, battery, and malicious destruction in *Ford v. State*, 603 A.2d 883 (Md. 1992).

11. 117 Ill. App.3d 363, 73 Ill.Dec. 17, 453 N.E.2d 842. The Illinois Appellate Court cited the following:

Other instances of conduct held to be simple battery based solely on insulting or provoking physical contact [include]: *People v. Hamilton*, . . . 401 N.E.2d

318 . . . (where defendant reached around the female complainant and placed his hand over her mouth); *People v. Siler*, . . . 406 N.E.2d 891 . . . (where defendant lifted up complainant's dress during a confrontation having sexual overtones).

12. *State v. Shelly*, 929 P.2d 489 (Wash. 1997).

13. The Federal Aviation Act of 1958 (49 U.S.C.A. § 1472[j]) forbids assault, intimidation, or threatening of a flight crew member, and punishes such conduct by imprisonment for up to twenty years.

In the 1991 case of *U.S. v. Tabacca*, 924 F.2d 906 (9th Cir.), the defendant continued to smoke a cigarette after airline flight attendants requested that he extinguish the cigarette. After vulgar language to the attendant, Tabacca grabbed her arm "and jerked and twisted her arm, causing her to strike the bulkhead of the seat across the aisle." The defendant's conviction was affirmed.

14. *State v. Boone*, 294 Or. 630, 661 P.2d 917 (1983).

15. *Whitaker v. U.S.*, 616 A.2d 843 (D.C.App. 1992).

16. Vernon's Penal Code of the State of Texas Annotated.

17. Oregon Stat. 163.175 (1)(c). Also, sentences for firearms and other dangerous weapons are increased if the weapon is brandished (pointed, waved about or displayed), pointed directly at a victim, pointed with verbal threats to use the weapon, or discharged. See 2A2.2(b)(b) of the federal sentencing guidelines and the sentencing guidelines used in your state.

18. 294 Or. 630, 661 P.2d 917 (1983).

19. 124 L.Ed.2d 4376 (1993).

20. 429 U.S. 975, 97 S.Ct. 481 (1976). The 1997 U.S. Department of Justice publication *In the Wake of Child Abuse and Childhood Maltreatment* states that more than three million children are reported to Child Protective Services each year as being abused. Of these three million reported cases, one million of the children are found to be abused children.

The majority of abused children (85 percent) are under age 5, and nearly half of the victims (45 percent) have not reached their first birthday. More than three children die each day as a result of parental maltreatment. Abuse is the most common cause of death (48 percent), followed by neglect (37 percent), and a combination of abuse and neglect (15 percent). Child abuse is a crime that cuts across all walks of life and all social classes.

21. In *Commonwealth v. Miller*, 600 A.2d 988 (Pa. Super. 1992), the Court discussed the endangerment statutes requirement that the defendant "knowingly" endangered a child's welfare. The Court said the defendant must know he or she has a duty to care for the child, is aware the child is in a dangerous situation, and has either failed to act or has acted in so meager a way that it could not reasonably be believed actions would be effective. Thus, a mother who leaves her child unattended while she goes out to a nightclub can be convicted of endangerment of a child, but a mother who believes, wrongly and perhaps unreasonably, her boyfriend's statement that another person is watching her child probably would not.

22. See *People v. Daniels*, 71 Cal.2d 1119, 80 Cal. Rptr. 897, 459 P.2d 225 (1969).

23. See *People v. Williams*, 2 Cal.3d 894, 88 Cal.Rptr. 208, 471 P.2d 1008 (1970).

24. 409 So.2d 1031 (Fla. 1982).

25. 94 N.J. 436, 466 A.2d 955 (1983).

26. Section 940.305 Wisconsin "taking hostage" felony.

27. The tort of false imprisonment is sometimes called "false arrest." False arrest is a wrongful arrest made either by a law enforcement officer or a private person. Arresting, detaining, and holding a person in custody without authority is false imprisonment and gives the victim the basis for a civil lawsuit to recover for the false arrest and false imprisonment. In a civil lawsuit (tort action) for false arrest, the plaintiff alleges that there was no authority or legal justification for the defendant to interfere with the plaintiff's freedom of movement.

28. 18 U.S.C.A. § 1201.

29. 18 U.S.C.A. § 1073.

30. In October 1984, President Ronald Reagan of the United States signed the Missing Children's Assistance Act (36 CrL 3063), which provides for the operation of a national toll-free telephone line for exchanging information on missing children through a national resource center and clearinghouse. The administrator of the program will "facilitate effective coordination among

all federally funded programs relating to missing children." Section 406(a) of the Act provides that "The Administrator is authorized to make grants to and enter into contracts with public agencies or nonprofit private organizations, or combination thereof, for research, demonstration projects, or service programs designed—

(1) to educate parents, children, and community agencies and organizations in ways to prevent the abduction and sexual exploitation of children;

(2) to provide information to assist in the locating and return of missing children;

(3) to aid communities in the collection of materials which would be useful to parents in assisting others in the identification of missing children;

(4) to increase knowledge of and develop effective treatment pertaining to the psychological consequences, on both parents and children.

31. *FBI Law Enforcement Bulletin*, July 1, 1996, p. 15.

32. 18 U.S.C.A. § 2261–2266. In the May 2000 case of *U.S. v. Morrison,* the U.S. Supreme Court declared the civil remedy provisions of the Violence Against Women Act unconstitutional. Just as in the Gun Free School Zones Act case of *U.S. v. Lopez,* 115 S. Ct. 1624, violence against women and firearms in a school zone do not affect interstate commerce, and therefore the federal government has limited authority to enact such criminal laws. All states have criminal laws forbidding violence against women, and most states have gun-free school zone laws.

33. *U.S. v. Bailey,* cited in the *Prosecutor,* June 1996, p. 23.

34. *U.S. v. Steele, id.*

35. California Penal Code § 368(a).

36. *People v. Heitzmann,* 54 CrL 1019 (1993).

37. A Texas Court of Appeals held that prior actual knowledge of the protective order is an essential element of the crime of violating a court order. *Small v. State,* 809 S.W.2d 253 (Tex.App. 1991). In the 1993 case of *State v. Haley,* 629 A.2d 605 (Me. 1993), the highest court in Maine held that a former husband's repeated telephoning of his former wife, asking her to take him back and threatening to kill himself if she did not, did not violate the protective order forbidding him from "abusing" his former wife and minor children.

38. 18 U.S.C. § 2262.

39. NCJ 148199, U.S. Department of Justice, July 1994.

15

Theft, Robbery, and Burglary

CONTENTS

KEY TERMS

theft/larceny

fraud

embezzlement

robbery

carjacking

home invasion robberies

extortion

bribery

burglary

General Property Concepts

Understanding the criminal law as it relates to property or interests in property requires some understanding of property law concepts. The following paragraphs illustrate some of these concepts.

- "Property" is divided into two types, real property and personal property. Real estate is real property; everything else is personal property.

- Two important rights to property are (1) the right of ownership and (2) the right of possession of the property. A person may have the lawful possession of property but not necessarily be its owner. Possession of personal property is presumptive evidence of ownership if no evidence to the contrary is shown. Possession accompanied by the exercise of the complete acts of ownership for a considerable period is strong evidence of the ownership of property.[1]

- Property ownership may be in the form of sole ownership. It may be in the form of joint ownership, as between husband and wife, business partners, or friends or relatives. The property may be owned by a corporation or a business partnership. Property ownership may be vested in a governmental unit, such as a city, a county, a state, or the national government.

- Lawful possession of property takes many forms. The owner may have the possession of property or may permit another person to have lawful possession and use of the property. An employee or agent of the owner of the property may have possession. Bailees and pledges also have the lawful possession of property that belongs to others. A bailment would exist, for example, when people take their car into a garage for repairs. The owner of the car retains title and ownership to the vehicle but gives possession to the garage so the repair work may be done on the vehicle. State statutes give the garage a right to a lien on the vehicle in the amount of the work that was done on the car. The garage then has a superior right of possession of the vehicle until the owner satisfies the amount lawfully due the garage. In many states, the owners of the property could be charged with theft if they intentionally and unlawfully took possession of such property from a pledgee or bailee who had a superior right of possession.[2]

- A thief has neither the lawful right to possession nor ownership of stolen property. Therefore, in almost all situations, a thief cannot convey lawful title to stolen property to another person, even if that person is an innocent good-faith purchaser of the property. Known by the Latin phrase *nemo dat quod non habet* (one cannot give what one does not have), this principle requires the innocent purchaser to be very wary of buying from strangers, as the following case illustrates:

Greek Orthodox Church of Cyprus v. Goldberg et al.

U.S. Court of Appeals, 7th Circuit (1990) 917 F.2d 278

Peg Goldberg, an art dealer, was in Europe on a buying trip. She "fell in love" with four early Christian mosaics that she was told were "found" in the rubble of an "extinct" church in northern Cyprus and were exported to Germany with the permission of the Cyprus government. Goldberg made some inquiries about the mosaics and then borrowed money to purchase them for U.S.

$1,080,000. After she shipped the mosaics to the United States, she was informed that the sixth-century mosaics had been stolen from the Greek Orthodox Church. Possession of the mosaics was awarded to the church, with the Court concluding:

> [W]hen circumstances are as suspicious as those that faced Peg Goldberg, prospective pur-chasers would do best to do more than make a few last-minute phone calls. As testified to at trial, in a transaction like this, "All the red flags are up, all the red lights are on, all the sirens are blaring.". . . (quoting testimony of Dr. Vikan). In such cases, dealers can (and probably should) take steps such as a formal IFAR search; a documented authenticity check by disinterested experts; a full background search of the seller and his claim of title; insurance protection and a contingency sales contract; and the like. If Goldberg would have pursued such methods, perhaps she would have discovered in time what she has now discovered too late: the Church has a valid, superior and enforceable claim to these Byzantine treasures, which there-fore must be returned to it.

■ One exception to the *nemo dat* rule involves the transfer by a thief of stolen money or negotiable securities, such as bearer bonds, which are securities payable to any person in possession of the bonds. Called the "money rule," it provides that a person who receives money in good faith and for value given takes title to the money. For example, in *City of Portland v. Berry*,[3] a thief stole nine $1000 bills and eighteen $500 bills from her employer and took them to her bank, where she converted the large bills to bills of smaller denomination. When the theft was discovered, the bank still had possession of the large bills, and the owners sought their return. The court said no, because the bank had given value for the bills in good faith, that is, it had no reason to suspect the bills were stolen.

The justification for the money rule has been stated as follows:

> It is absolutely necessary for commerce and business to continue that one who receives money, cashier's checks or money orders is not put on inquiry as to the source from which the funds have been derived. It is generally impossible or im-practical to discover the source of money, and for this reason one who receives money in good faith for valuable consideration prevails over the victim.[4]

Larceny or Theft[5]

Historically, the common law recognized a broad and often confusing number of theft of property crimes. Today, virtually all states have consolidated these many crimes under the heading of larceny or theft.[6] A great number of these crimes remain, however. The federal government alone has more than one hundred separate statutes in Title 18 of the United States Code that deal with theft or theft-related activity.[7]

A typical *theft* or *larceny* statute today would require an unlawful (1) taking of (2) property of another with (3) the intent to deprive the owner of possession thereof. In this section, these requirements are discussed in detail.

The Taking

Taking refers to the act of obtaining physical possession or control of another's property. A taking can occur by acts of a stranger, by a trusted employee, or even a spouse. It can

Phrases of Children

An inaccurate statement of law	*An accurate statement of law*
"Finders keepers, losers weepers."	"Sticks and stones will break my bones, but names will never hurt me." (Neither battery nor homicide are ordinarily justified because of name-calling or insulting language.)

be by one having no right to possess the property or by one with limited rights to that possession. The key to taking is that the thief exercise unauthorized dominion over the property.

Direct Taking

The most easily understood taking is direct taking, where the thief directly takes physical possession of another person's property. Examples of this include purse snatching, pickpocketing, shoplifting, or car theft. This kind of taking requires that the thief obtain actual physical possession of the property, even if for a short time.

EXAMPLE: A stranger walks into your backyard and up to your locked bike. He attempts to break the lock, but before he can do so, is stopped by a passing police officer. He has not yet taken the bike, and is not guilty of theft.

EXAMPLE: The same facts, except that the stranger breaks the lock. While turning to wheel the bike out of your yard, the police stop him. Even if he has moved only a few feet, he has taken the bike and is guilty of theft.

The common law and some states today require both a taking ("caption") and carrying away ("asportation") of the stolen property. Carrying away requires that the property be moved in some manner. However, even the slightest change of position of the property satisfies this requirement. Thus, in the example above, in a state that retains a carrying away requirement, the smallest movement of the bike would be sufficient. (See note 21 of this chapter for cases illustrating this rule and Chapter 16 for carrying away-related problems in the crime of shoplifting.)

The Taking of Lost and Mislaid Goods or Goods Delivered by Mistake

A taking may also occur where the initial physical possession of the property of another is not unlawful, but where the person in possession acts in a manner showing an intent to deprive the owner of ownership rights.

EXAMPLE: A woman finds a purse under a bush near a walking path. Inside the purse she finds $500 in cash. The woman puts the cash in her pocket. At this point, she has not taken the cash, because her possession is not yet unlawful. Later, she uses the cash to buy herself a new coat. At this point, she has taken the cash.

EXAMPLE: A man deposited a federal income tax return check in the amount of $1,907 into his checking account. His bank mistakenly credited his account in the amount of $10,907. When he discovered the mistake, the man withdrew over $7,000 of the money. He was convicted of theft.[8]

EXAMPLE: A man leaving the U.S. Army was to receive a severance check for $183, but to his surprise, the check he received was for $836,728.19. The man immediately deposited the money and began spending it. After the error was discovered, action was taken against the man.[9]

Sometimes in situations like the examples above, the person in possession of lost or misdirected property does nothing about it. For example, the owner of a checking account does nothing when he discovers that his bank has credited his account with too much money. Proving a taking in those cases may be difficult, even though the account's owner plans to wait and see if the bank discovers the mistake, and if not, keep the money. Some states have followed the Model Penal Code's approach to this problem. Section 223.5 makes one guilty of theft if "with purpose to deceive the owner thereof, he fails to take reasonable measures to restore the property to a person entitled to it."

Taking by Trick, Deception, or Fraud

Taking has been achieved by the use of many tricks, *frauds*, and deceptions. The owner of the property may be deceived by false representations that cause the owner to give up possession of the property. Con games would fall into this category. Modern theft and larceny statutes specifically define these forms of taking as elements of the crimes of theft and larceny.

Confidence games and schemes (con games) have been used for hundreds of years. The *pigeon drop* was reportedly used more than a thousand years ago in China. The deception has always been the same. The con man or woman wins the confidence of the victim, talking fast enough to keep the victim confused while enough temptation is dangled to appeal to the victim. Unfortunately, a large percentage of the victims are elderly. Information on specific con games and schemes is presented in Chapter 17.

Phone call thefts are also common in the United States. The Federal Trade Commission (FTC), which monitors and investigates interstate telemarketing scams, reported that Americans lose nearly $1 billion each year in phony telemarketing schemes. The FTC reported that telephone swindlers are increasingly defrauding the elderly in telephone frauds. The chance of victims recovering their money in con games and phone call thefts, unfortunately, is low.

The following cases illustrate only two of the many ways used to commit theft by fraud:

People v. Rohlfs
Illinois Court of Appeal, 752 N.E.2d 499 (2001)

While in jail on similar charges, the defendant made telephone calls to elderly women, telling them he was a relative in need of cash. One of these women sent the defendant a $1,500 money order made out to his name. Western Union delivered the money order to the defendant in jail, where he endorsed it. Before he could cash the money order, jail officials seized it. The court held that he "obtained" money by deception, and convicted him of that crime.

Lambert v. State

Supreme Court of Wisconsin (1976) 73 Wis.2d 590, 243 N.W.2d 524

The defendant obtained substantial amounts of money from different women by promising to marry them. The Supreme Court of Wisconsin affirmed the convictions of the defendant for six charges of theft by fraud. (Broken promises are punished in only a minority of the states as theft by fraud.)

The Wisconsin jury found in this case that Lambert made false promises meant to deceive so that he could obtain money from his victims by fraud (in breach of promise cases, promises are genuine and are then broken).

Embezzlement[10]

Many employees have money and property that belong to their employer. Lawyers, stockbrokers, business partners, and bailees also have money or property that belongs to clients and business associates. Because bank clerks and cashiers in restaurants and stores already have possession of money belonging to their employers, they do not have to *take* the money in the legal sense in order to steal.

To fill in this large gap left in the criminal codes, the crime of *embezzlement* was created by statutes in England and the United States. It forbids a person already in lawful possession of money or property from fraudulently converting the money or property to his or her own use.

Many states have solved this problem by expanding the "taking" in their theft or larceny statutes to also include "uses, transfers, conceals or retains possession." Under such a statute, a stockbroker, lawyer, or cashier who stole money could be charged with theft or larceny.

Defining What Property Can Be Stolen

Under the old common law, only tangible personal property could be stolen. Real estate and items attached to the land could not be stolen. Documents such as stocks, bonds, checks, or promissory notes were not subject to theft, because they are intangible personal property.

All states and the federal government have broadened the original common law definition of property that can be stolen. Some modern criminal codes include any sort of property of value that can be moved. Illinois defines property subject to theft as "anything of value," including real estate, money, commercial instruments, tickets, written documents, and so forth.[11] Minnesota defines *property* to include documents and things growing on or affixed to land.[12] Section 223.2 of the Model Penal Code defines "Theft by Unlawful Taking or Disposition" as

1. *Movable Property.* A person is guilty of theft if he takes, or exercises unlawful control over, movable property of another with purpose to deprive him thereof.

2. *Immovable Property.* A person is guilty of theft if he unlawfully transfers immovable property of another or any interest therein with purpose to benefit himself or another not entitled thereto.

Forms of Taking and Types of Theft

Shoplifting (retail theft) or price altering
- Shoplifting—the most common form of theft in retail stores—is the taking by concealment to avoid payment for goods.
- Price altering avoids payment of the full price of an object by lowering the amount on the price tag.

Taking by employee, bailee, or trustee
- Employee theft of money and other objects causes large losses in business places.
- Embezzlement of funds or negotiable securities that are in the custody of employees, bailees, or trustees

Snatch and run
- The taking is observed, and the offender flees to avoid apprehension.

Till tap
- Thief opens cash register unobserved and takes cash and coins.
- While store employee has cash drawer open, money is grabbed and the thief flees (snatch and run).

Taking by trick, deception, or fraud (stings, scams, or swindles)
- Con games and operations
- Deceptions and tricks to obtain property illegally
- Obtaining property by false pretense

Taking by force, or the threat of the use of force (robbery)

Taking during a burglary (trespass with intent to steal or commit a felony)

Taking by extortion (threats of future violence or threats to reveal embarrassing information—blackmail)

Taking from a person
- Purse snatching (a form of snatch and run)
- Pickpocketing
- Rolling a drunk (taking from a person incapacitated by alcohol, drugs, or other means)
- Taking from a corpse

Taking of lost or mislaid goods or money

Taking of objects or money delivered by mistake
- Example: a check for too much money is mailed to a person by mistake.

Looting
- Taking property from or near a building damaged, destroyed, or left unoccupied by tornado, fire, physical disaster, riot, bombing, earthquake, and so on.

Taking by failure to return a leased or rented object
- Example: failure to return a rented car or videotape within the time specified by state statutes or city ordinance

Taking by illegal entry into locked coin box
- Vending machine, pay telephone, parking meter, and so on.

Smash and run
- A store or other window is broken, and after snatching objects, the thief runs to avoid apprehension.
- Women drivers waiting at stoplights are sometimes subjected to this tactic. The thief breaks the car window, takes the woman's purse from the front seat, and runs.[a]

Taking by illegally obtaining or using information
- Such as the "inside trading" scandals
  See the 1987 U.S. Supreme Court case of *Carpenter v. United States,* 108 S.Ct. 316. One of the defendants in the case was the co-author of a *Wall Street Journal* column.

Taking by illegal use of a credit card or credit card number

Taking from a person with a superior right of possession
- People may acquire a superior right of possession over the owner of property because of a bailment, pledge, or contract. State criminal codes may make taking from a person with a superior right of possession a crime.

Theft by possession of stolen property
- See 832 P.2d 337 (Idaho, 1992), 473 N.W.2d 84 (Nebraska, 1991), and 419 S.E.2d 759 (Georgia, 1992).

Ordinary theft
- Taking occurs observed or unobserved by owner or other people.

[a]The "bump" technique is also used. An expensive car with only a driver occupant is usually picked as the victim. While the victim is waiting at a stoplight, the victim's car is bumped intentionally. When the victim gets out of the car to view damages, one of the thieves distracts him or her while the other thief sneaks around to get into the victim's car. Because the victim generally leaves the keys in the ignition, the thief drives off in the victim's car. The other thief jumps in his or her car and also speeds away, leaving the victim stranded.

Under modern statutes, not only personal property can be stolen but also real estate and fixtures. Trees, crops, minerals, electricity, gas, and documents are all subject to theft. In the 1966 case of *United States v. Bottone,* the Court pointed out that the content of a document is often much more important and valuable than the paper on which it is written.[13]

Not only may documents be stolen, but information from computers, files, and other places may be stolen.[14] Under fraud statutes and other specific statutes, telephone and computer services may be stolen.[15] Contraband, such as illegal drugs, can be stolen even though people losing such property are not likely to report such thefts to the police.

Value of Property

If the property has no intrinsic value, a prosecution for theft or larceny would be hard to sustain. A single sheet of paper worth a penny or less would have little intrinsic value. But if a signed promissory note for $1,000 were on the sheet of paper, the value of the paper would increase considerably. In charging theft or larceny, the state must introduce evidence showing the value of the property alleged to have been stolen.

The value of the property stolen, in most instances, determines whether the charge is a misdemeanor or a felony. The value of the property must be determined by the court or jury. Statements by the owner concerning what he or she paid for the property, how long it was possessed, its replacement cost, and its condition are admissible in determining value. Evidence of the value of comparable property in comparable condition is admissible to show the value of the property at issue. Experts and appraisers may, in some instances, be called into court to testify as to value (sentimental value can generally not be considered).

In the New York case of *People v. Harold,* the defendant was convicted of grand larceny for the theft of a water pump that had been purchased five days before the theft. However, the pump had been damaged before the theft by two men, Crego and Terpening, who had attempted to install the pump. In ordering a new trial, the Court stated:

> The question presented by this appeal pertains to the value of the stolen pump. . . . [T]he market value of a stolen item is to be measured by what the thief would have had to pay had he purchased the item instead of stealing it. . . . In the instant case, the value of the pump must be reduced to reflect the mechanical prowess of Crego and Terpening. Additionally, an allowance must be made for the fact that the pump, when taken, was no longer new.
>
> Many state statutes provide that "value" means the market value at the time of the theft or the cost to the victim of replacing the property within a reasonable time after the theft. The replacement value to a retail store would be the replacement cost to the store, and not the retail price of the item.[16]

As the New York court pointed out in the *Harold* case, the value in New York would be "market value" or "what the thief would have to pay had he purchased the item instead of stealing it." Colorado[17] and many other states also follow this rule in determining value. Other states would use the replacement value rule, which would be the replacement cost to a retail store to replace a stolen item.

Property of Another

In order to prove theft or larceny, the state must show that the property belonged to another. A showing that the property belonged to the city, a school, a corporation, or an individual would suffice. Because the consent of the owner would constitute a total defense in a theft or larceny charge, the owner (or a representative of the owner) must testify that the taking was without his or her consent. A showing that the owner did not consent to the conduct of the defendant is also necessary in criminal damage to property, in trespass, and in arson of either real property or personal property.

Under modern law, a husband and wife are not treated as a single entity for many purposes, including the criminal law of theft. As a result, one spouse can be guilty of theft of the other spouse's property, since that property qualifies as property "of another." However, the property must belong to the spouse from whom it is taken, and it cannot be the kind of property that is "normally accessible" to both spouses. A refrigerator, for example, even if bought by one spouse, cannot be stolen by the other spouse if the couple is still living together.

An example of theft by a spouse is *State v. Krinitt,*[18] a 1991 decision of the Supreme Court of Montana. In *Krinitt,* a husband was convicted of stealing his wife's trust fund check. The husband had a history of wasting the couple's finances, so the wife instructed the trust fund to send the check to her attorney. When the check was delivered to their home by mistake, the husband cashed it and spent the money. He was convicted of theft because the trust fund check was not "accessible" to both spouses.

Many people hold property jointly with others. Suppose a business partner steals $1,000 out of the partnership checking account and uses it for his personal needs. Or suppose a wife runs off with another man and takes $500 out of a savings and loan account that is in the name of her husband and herself. Is this stealing the property of another? Whether this constitutes theft or larceny would be determined by the statutes of that jurisdiction in defining the property of another.

The question of property of another came up in the Michigan case of *People v. Young.* In that case, the defendant took back from a prostitute the $10 he had paid the woman for her sexual services. In affirming the conviction for the crime of larceny from the person, the Court stated:

> On appeal defendant Young's only argument is that his actions did not constitute a crime since the agreement he made to purchase sexual services was illegal and so his forcefully taking back the $10 was not a crime.
>
> We are not persuaded by that argument. The trial court did not enforce any contract legal or otherwise. The agreement had been completed and both parties had received the agreed-upon consideration. Defendant Young then forcefully took back the $10 which by that time belonged to the woman. Such action constituted the crime of larceny from a person. "Public policy requires that courts should lend active aid in punishing persons who obtain money or property from others by criminal means, and it is no defense that the complaining witness was himself engaged in an illegal transaction." 1 Gillespie, *Michigan Criminal Law and Procedure* (2d Ed.), § 29, p. 49.[19]

Difficulties in Identifying Property

Some property is difficult for owners to identify. Diamonds and other valuable stones are an example. Valuable stones may be easily identified by their settings, but once they are removed, it is difficult to distinguish them. The four C's of the diamond business—cut, clarity, carat, and color—provide only the roughest means of identification. An owner's testimony, "That looks like my property, but I am not sure," is not sufficient identification. Because of the difficulty of identification, in some situations the police have been forced to return property to a known thief because of lack of evidence that the property was stolen.

The stolen property must be identified by the introduction of evidence showing no reasonable doubt as to its identity. For this reason, law enforcement agencies urge the marking of property in such ways that the identification marks cannot be easily removed or obliterated.

Abandoned Property

If the property has been abandoned or if the owner of the property cannot be located, then theft or larceny cannot be proved.

Abandonment has been defined as the relinquishment or surrender of property or the rights to property. In 1952, the U.S. Supreme Court considered the case of *Morissette v. United States*.[20] Morissette was charged with the theft of scrap metal from an old bombing range. His defense was that he honestly thought that the property had been abandoned. Because the trial court would not allow the jury to determine whether the property had been abandoned or whether Morissette honestly, but mistakenly, believed that the property was abandoned, the conviction was reversed.

Intent to Steal

Proving Intent to Steal

Theft or larceny requires a specific intent to deprive the owner of possession of the property. The intent to steal may be proved by direct evidence or by circumstantial evidence. Generally, the fact finder (jury or judge) concludes and infers an intent to steal from the conduct and acts of the defendant. In the following shoplifting case, the California Court of Appeals directed that the described California jury instructions on intent to steal be given to the jury:

People v. Jaso

Court of Appeals of California (1970) 4 Cal.App.3d 767, 84 Cal.Rptr. 567

The defendant was walking toward the parking lot and his car when he was stopped with unpaid merchandise in a shopping bag from a Sears store. The defendant stated that he left his wallet in the glove compartment of his car because he was wearing tight Levi's. He stated that he was going to get his wallet and would pay for the merchandise, but when the security officer held him and would not let him go, he struggled with the security officer. Defendant was subdued and placed in handcuffs. A new trial was ordered after the defendant was convicted at the first trial. The Court of Appeals held that the trial court had failed to give the following California jury instruction:

In the crime of [theft], there must exist in the mind of the perpetrator the specific intent to [take the property of another], and unless such intent so exists that crime is not committed. (CALJIC Instruction 71.11)

The specific intent with which an act is done may be manifested by the circumstances surrounding its commission. But you may not find the defendant guilty of the offense charged in

Count [II] unless the proved circumstances not only are consistent with the hypothesis that he had the specific intent to [take the property of another] but are irreconcilable with any other rational conclusion. (CALJIC Instruction 27-A)

Frequently, defendants attempt to defeat the intent to steal requirement by contending that they only intended to borrow the property. In many cases, the jury will give little credence to this defense, sensibly concluding that the defendants' actions show a different intent. But, if true, an intent to return the property negates guilt of theft, unless the return date is unusually far in the future. For example, taking a neighbor's lawn mower in April and intending to return it in November may be enough to prove theft, unless the theft statute of that state requires a showing that the taker intended "to permanently deprive the owner of possession."

In some cases, even short-term borrowing can be a crime. Many states have statutes that make it a crime to use or operate another person's automobile, motorcycle, or other motor-propelled vehicle without permission of the owner, even if the person intends to return the vehicle after a short joy-ride.

Robbery

Robbery is forcible stealing. It is one of the most frequent crimes of violence in the United States. The common law crime of robbery was defined before the early English courts had defined larceny. The usual elements incorporated into the modern statutory definition of robbery are as follows:

- A taking and carrying away (only a slight movement of the property is needed)[21]
- of the property of another
- with intent to steal
- from the person or from the presence of the victim
- by the use of force against the person, or
- with the threat of the use of imminent force, to compel the victim to acquiesce in the taking and carrying away of the property.

Strong-armed robbery, such as mugging and yoking (or simple robbery), is distinguished in probably all state statutes from the aggravated form of robbery, commonly called "armed robbery." Armed robbery carries penalties that are more severe than those for simple robbery. Some of the statutory distinctions used by various states in distinguishing between armed robbery and simple robbery are the following:

- That the perpetrator was armed with a "dangerous" or "deadly" weapon
- That the perpetrator intended to kill or wound if the victim resisted
- That the perpetrator did actually inflict a bodily injury[22]

Robbery, then, is the taking of property from a person or from the presence of a victim by the use of force or the threat of force. The crime of robbery creates a great deal of anxiety, because the victim is threatened not only with the use of force and violence but with the loss of property.

Car and Vehicle Theft in the United States

What happens to stolen cars and vehicles?
More than 1.5 million vehicles are stolen and more than 3 million vehicles are illegally entered every year for valuables or accessories.

Chop-shop operations, in which professionals cut up the vehicle for parts. Because nothing is left of the vehicle, the criminals are called "buzzards." Chop-shop operations are generally believed to be under the control of organized criminal groups.
Strippers, who "strip" cars for some of the easily resalable parts, such as tires, wheels, doors, fenders, hoods, radios, stereos, and spark plugs. Strippers are considered semi-professional; some are drug addicts who sell car parts to finance their habits. Stripped cars are generally recovered by owners.

Exported from the United States
The National Automobile Theft Bureau estimates that 200,000 vehicles are exported to other countries, where the vehicles or the parts sell at prices much higher than in the United States. (See "Motor Vehicle Theft Investigations" in the September 1990 *FBI Law Enforcement Bulletin.*)

Abandoned or Returned or Recovered
- after use by a joyrider (once the biggest offender but now estimated to be responsible for 10 percent of missing cars)
- after being used for a crime
- after being abandoned by strippers
- after a breakdown or being damaged

Phony Car Thefts
Car owners hide or abandon their vehicles and then falsely report them stolen in hopes of collecting insurance. Estimates range that from 15 percent to as high as 30 percent of reported thefts are phony.

Used on Streets and Highways of the United States
- with original VINs and different plates
- with identification numbers salvaged from similar make and model cars in junkyards ("salvage and switch" operations)

Car theft and vehicle looting cost the American public an estimated $8 billion a year in out-of-pocket expenses, plus the costs of higher insurance and the additional cost of law enforcement expenses.

If your motor vehicle is stolen, you can speed the search for your vehicle by immediately providing the following information to the police: year, make, and model of the vehicle, license plate number, VIN, and color. Carrying a copy of your certificate of registration in your purse or wallet would provide this information.

The FBI called this bank robber "The Shootist." He is seen leaving one of the 56 banks that he confessed to robbing. He and his wife were arrested after robbing a Seattle bank in 1994.   AP/Wide World Photos

The *Chicago Police Department Training Bulletin* lists the following factors that favor a robber:

- He or she can carry out the crime swiftly.
- He or she will usually leave few clues that would lead to his or her arrest.
- The robbery is committed in such a short period that the victim and witnesses sometimes do not have sufficient time and composure to view the offender so as to furnish an accurate description to the police.
- The probability of interruption is limited because of the short time.[23]

Distinguishing Robbery from Theft or Larceny

Robbery differs from theft or larceny because, in charging the crime of robbery, it must be shown that

- property was taken from the victim or taken from the presence of the victim, and
- the use of force or the threat of the use of force was used in the taking.

If no force or threat of force is used, the crime of robbery has not been committed, and a lesser crime such as theft or larceny should be considered.

Where State Courts Differ on What Constitutes Robbery

In ruling whether the crime of robbery has occurred, state courts differ in the following areas:

1. When force is not used in the taking of property, but is used to keep the property and to escape.

Majority View[24]	Minority View
Held that a robbery occurred even though the bottle of wine was taken without the use of force. Force was then used to prevent the store owner from recovering the wine, and a knife was waved to make the escape. *People v. Hovenec,* 596 N.E.2d 749 (Ill.App. 1992). Also *People v. Pham,* 1993 WL 128504 (Cal.App. 1993), and *State v. Handburgh,* 830 P.2d 641 (1992), in which the Supreme Court of Washington called this view the majority view in the United States.	Held that to be robbery, force must be used at the time of taking and concurrent with the taking. After the victim discovered his money was taken, he attempted to get it back. The defendant then pulled a gun and threatened. The Court held that the crime was not that of robbery. *State v. Lewis,* 1993 WL 564208 (N.M.App. 1993). Also *Royal v. State,* 490 So.2d 44 (Fla.Sup.Ct. 1986).

2. In the U.S. Supreme Court case of *Ashe v. Swenson,* 90 S.Ct. 1189 (1970), masked gunmen robbed six men playing poker and took money from all six of the men. The defendant in that case was charged with six counts of robbery. (See Chapter 7 for the case.)

    However, courts differ when a business is robbed and employees of the business place are also robbed.

Holding That Robbery Is an Offense Against the Person Assaulted	Holding That Robbery Is an Aggravated Form of Theft
The defendant robbed a Cumberland Farms store and took store money from two different store employees. Two counts of masked, armed robbery were affirmed. *Commonwealth v. Levia,* 431 N.E.2d 928 (Mass. 1982). Also see *State v. Green,* 833 P.2d 311 (Or.App. 1992).	The Supreme Court of Hawaii held that only one count of robbery could be used for a conviction, even though money was taken from five different Ramada Inn employees. *State v. Faatea,* 648 P.2d 197 (1982). Also held to be single robbery when money belonging to both a restaurant and the manager was taken. *Harris v. State,* 399 S.E.2d 284 (Ga.App. 1990).[25]

Carjacking: A New Name for an Old Crime

Thieves have been stealing cars from their owners or occupants by force or fear of force for years. These cases did not fit easily into theft or robbery criminal statutes because the thief often did not intend to keep the car permanently. As the October 1993 issue of the *FBI Law Enforcement Bulletin* stated, over 90 per cent of the vehicles taken in carjacks were returned.

To remedy this, most states and the federal government passed statutes making *carjacking* a separate offense. The Anti-Car Theft Act of 1992, 18 U.S.C. 2119, was passed by Congress in response to the more than thirty-five thousand carjackings completed or attempted each year in the United States. An example of a carjacking statute is the following California law:

> Carjacking is the felonious taking of a motor vehicle in the possession of another, from his or her person or in the immediate presence . . . against his or her will and with the intent to either permanently or temporarily deprive the person . . . of his or her possession, accomplished by force or fear.[26]

Carjacking statutes have presented several problems concerning the requisite elements of the offense. Some of these are the following:

- A taking occurs even if the true owner of the car remains in the car during the carjacking. *People v. Duran,* 106 Cal.Rptr.2d 812 (2001).

- The true owner is in "possession" of the car even if he is alighting from the car when the carjacking occurs. *State v. Mobley,* 681 A.2d 1186 (Md.App. 1996).

- The carjacker need not move the car to be guilty of the offense. *People v. Montero,* 56 Cal.Rptr.2d 303 (1996).[27]

- At least one state, Maryland, has interpreted its carjacking statute as requiring no specific intent to deprive the owner of possession. This means intoxication or drugged condition, which can be a defense to specific intent crimes (see Chapter 7) is not a defense to carjacking. *State v. Harris,* 728 A.2d 180 (Md.App. 1999).

Home Invasion Robberies

Home invasion robbery has also been around as a crime for many years. It could occur when the occupant of a home or apartment opens the door in response to a ring or knock. It also could occur when a robber follows the victim's car to the home and confronts the victim in the garage or as the victim is opening an outer door with a key.

Weapons and violence are often threatened in *home invasion robberies.* The victim might be alone or with family members or with children. Victims under such circumstances are vulnerable, and other crimes could also be committed.

A few precautions ordinarily can prevent home invasion robberies from occurring. Caution in opening outer doors and remaining alert as to whether your vehicle is being followed or whether people are lurking near your garage or entrances to your home are safeguards that should be kept in mind.

Purse Snatching, Pickpocketing, and Other Thefts from a Person

The Supreme Court of New Jersey quoted other courts in pointing out that the majority rule in the United States is that the force used in the usual purse snatching is not sufficient force to constitute robbery. There are purse snatchings, however, in which the amount of force used does make the crime robbery (for example, when a victim resists a purse snatching, and force is used to overcome the resistance).

In the 1991 case of *State v. Sein*,[28] the Supreme Court of New Jersey stated the majority rule as follows:

> [A] simple snatching or sudden taking of property from the person of another does not of itself involve sufficient force to constitute robbery, though the act may be robbery where a struggle ensues, the victim is injured in the taking, or the property is so attached to the victim's person or clothing as to create resistance to the taking.

A few courts, however, have adopted the rule that the snatching of a purse without the use of any other force is sufficient to permit a jury verdict on the charge of robbery. The Supreme Judicial Court of Massachusetts adopted this rule in the 1972 case of *Commonwealth v. Jones*.[29] In affirming the defendant's conviction of unarmed robbery for a purse snatching, the Court stated:

> The question whether the snatching or sudden taking of property constitutes robbery has arisen in other jurisdictions although not in Massachusetts. In Kentucky, the rule is that snatching, without more, involves the requisite element of force to permit a jury verdict on a charge of robbery. See *Jones v. Commonwealth*, 112 Ky. 689, 692–695, 66 S.W. 633; *Brown v. Commonwealth*, 135 Ky. 635, 640, 117 S.W. 281. According to the rule prevailing in most jurisdictions, however, snatching does not involve sufficient force to constitute robbery, unless the victim resists the taking or sustains physical injury, or unless the article taken is so attached to the victim's clothing as to afford resistance. . . .
>
> We prefer the Kentucky rule on purse snatching. The majority jurisdiction rule, in looking to whether or not the victim resists, we think, wrongly emphasizes the victim's opportunity to defend himself over the willingness of the purse snatcher to use violence if necessary.

Theft from the person is punished more severely than ordinary theft and is a felony in most states, whether the amount taken is very small or very large. State legislative bodies and courts are well aware that injury can easily occur to a victim who is often startled by the theft and may seek to protect his or her property.

Common forms of theft from a person are pickpocketing and purse snatching. However, theft of a purse from a shopping cart was also held to be theft from the person when the victim's hand was on the cart.[30]

Distinguishing Robbery from Extortion

Robbery and **extortion** (blackmail) are methods used to obtain money or property illegally. Extortion differs from robbery in these ways:

- There is a threat to inflict a future harm (extortion) rather than an immediate harm (robbery).
- In robbery, the victim must immediately comply with the criminal demand or violence will immediately occur. In extortion, future compliance is demanded to avoid future harm to a third party or to the victim.

- Robbery must be committed in the presence of the victim, whereas extortion can be committed over the telephone or by use of the mail (such conduct, however, immediately makes the offense also a federal violation).

The harm that is threatened differs also. In robbery, immediate force is threatened or used against the owner or victim to compel the victim to acquiesce in the taking of the property. In extortion, the victim must pay the amount demanded to avoid

- destruction of property (bombing a restaurant or business place has been a standard practice of organized crime that could result in a serious loss of life and injuries if the restaurant or business place were open for business)
- kidnapping or injuries to the victim or his or her family or friends
- accusations of crime, and so forth
- damaging the good name or business reputation of the victim or his or her family
- exposing a secret or failing of the victim or family

English textbooks point out that the term "blackmail" originated to describe the tribute paid Scottish chieftains by landowners to secure immunity from raids on their lands. In the early days of common law, blackmail seems to have been an offense included within the crime of robbery. Cases illustrating the crime of extortion are as follows:

- Threats to tamper with soft drinks unless money was paid. *United States v. Hummer,* 916 F.2d 186 (4th Cir. 1990).
- To drive a service station out of business by illegal means. *United States v. Penn,* 966 F.2d 55 (2d Cir. 1992).
- Threats to collect a legitimate debt by illegal means. *United States v. Goode,* 945 F.2d 1168, 50 CrL 1060 (10th Cir. 1991).
- Threats to kill unless hospital administrator had criminal charges against defendant dropped. *People v. Discala,* 379 N.E.2d 187 (N.Y. 1978).
- Strong-arm tactics and threats used by a wholesale meat distributor to collect money owed by customers for products. *United States v. Lima et al.,* 914 F.2d 967 (7th Cir. 1989).

When the Hobbs Act was enacted by the U.S. Congress, the statute was aimed primarily at gangsters who were extorting protection money from businesses. That is, the business would not be bombed or other violence occur if the protection money was paid.

The Hobbs Act defines extortion as "the obtaining of property of another, with his consent, induced by wrongful use of actual or threatened force, violence, or fear." 18 U.S.C.A. 1951(b)(2).

Actor Bill Cosby as a Victim in a 1997 Extortion Case

A young woman, Autumn Jackson, was convicted of seeking to criminally extort $40 million from actor Bill Cosby in 1997. Cosby admitted that he had had a brief affair with the young woman's mother but denied that he was the father of the 22-year-old woman.

Cosby stated at the trial that he had paid more than $100,000 over the years to the young woman's mother, and that he had agreed to pay college and living expenses for the young woman. But Jackson demanded $40 million or she would sell her story that she was Bill Cosby's daughter to the supermarket tabloids. After she began writing letters to companies whose products Cosby endorsed, he went to the FBI and began tape recording telephone conversations. A New York jury found Jackson guilty of extortion.[31]

The Crime of Bribery

Bribery is also a crime in which money or valuables are exchanged. But instead of force or threat of the use of force, a gift, favor, or contribution is voluntary made "coupled with a particular criminal intent."[32] Most bribery cases involve a public official, as in the following 1997 U.S. Supreme Court case:

> A jail prisoner paid a sheriff and his deputy a series of bribes for private "contact" visits twice a week, in which he remained alone with his wife (and occasionally his girlfriend). The officers were paid $6,000 per month and $1,000 per contact visit. The U.S. Supreme Court affirmed the convictions of both officers under the federal bribery statute (18 U.S.C.A. Section 666) and for RICO violations (see Chapter 22). *United States v. Salinas*, 522 U.S., 139 L.Ed.2d 352 (1997).

Bribery, occasionally, does not involve a government official, as in the basketball "point-shaving" scandals that occur from time to time over the years. The *New York Times* article "Ex-Northwestern Players Charged in Point-Shaving" (March 27, 1998) reported that two former Northwestern University basketball players were criminally charged with taking bribes to fix Big Ten games.

Other recent basketball bribery charges for point-shaving occurred at Columbia University (1998) and Arizona University (1997). See Chapter 21 for material on the federal Professional and Amateur Sports Protection Act.

Burglary

Burglary is among the most frequently committed major crimes in the United States, with more than 3.5 million burglaries committed every year. Because burglary is a crime of stealth and opportunity, the national clearance rate, as reported by the Uniform Crime Report, is low at approximately 15 percent. (That is, arrests are made in only approximately 15 percent of the burglaries reported.)

Burglary is a crime committed by both amateurs and professionals. It is committed against residences (homes and apartments) and nonresidences (offices, business places, and so on). It is committed not only at nighttime but also during the day.

Under the old common law, burglary was punished by death. Because of the severe penalty, burglary required a breaking under the common law. It was also limited to the dwelling house of another, in the nighttime, and with intent to commit a felony.

All states have modified and changed the definition of burglary in their jurisdictions, resulting in differences in the definitions of burglary in the United States.[33] The Uni-

Burglaries, Robberies, and Extortions That Received National Attention

Watergate: The burglary that brought down a president

Information became public that the White House attempted to cover up a bungled burglary of the Democratic National Committee headquarters in the Watergate office building in 1972. Because of the cover-up of the crime:

- President Richard Nixon resigned and was saved from criminal prosecution by a pardon from President Ford.
- Attorney General John Mitchell served nineteen months in prison for conspiracy, obstruction of justice, and perjury.
- Other prosecuted officials: John Ehrlichman (18 months), Chief of Staff H. R. Haldeman (18 months), G. Gordon Liddy (52 months), E. Howard Hunt, Jr. (33 months).

Extortion and downfall of New York state's chief justice

Pleading serious mental problems, the highest justice in New York state, Sol Wachtler, entered a plea of guilty to extortion (blackmail) and harassment of his former lover and her daughter.

Reformed bank robber of the 1950s

Asked why he robbed banks, Willie Sutton replied, "Because that's where the money is."

Bank robberies by heavily armed and heavily armored men

Men in body armor carrying assault rifles opened deadly fire in similar 1997 robberies in Los Angeles and St. Louis within weeks of one another. Police at the scene of both robberies were outgunned because of the heavy fire from the assault rifles. Police stated that the St. Louis robbery could have been a copycat crime of the earlier Los Angeles robbery, which received a great amount of national attention.

Million-dollar robberies during the 1990s

Street robberies and robberies of small convenience stores result in losses that average less than $200 each. The largest art robbery occurred in the Boston Stewart Gardner Museum when men dressed as police officers seized eleven paintings now valued at $300 million. A San Francisco street robbery of a jewelry salesman resulted in a $2 million loss of gems, gold, and black pearls. Robbery of a Loomis armored car resulted in a $17 million loss in Charlotte, North Carolina, but seventeen persons were taken into custody and all but about $4 million was recovered. A New York bank was robbed during a currency transfer, and $1.6 million was stolen.

form Crime Reporting Program defines burglary as "the unlawful entry of a structure to commit a felony or theft. The use of force to gain entry is not required to classify an offense as burglary."

Breaking

Under common law, a "breaking" or a "breach" was required to constitute the crime of burglary. An entry through an open door or window without the consent of the person living in or controlling the building was not a breaking. All states have abolished the re-

Examples of Different Theft Crimes

Theft: A man lays his ring on the edge of a sink while washing his hands. Another man takes the ring and runs off while the owner is not looking (felony if value is more than amount determined by state statute).

Theft from person: A ring is taken from a pocket by a pickpocket or taken in a purse by a purse-snatcher (felony in most or all states regardless of value of ring).

Simple robbery (mugging): A woman is accosted in an alley by a menacing robber who threatens to beat her if she does not give the thief the ring on her finger (felony regardless of value of ring if she gave up the ring out of fear).

Armed robbery: A woman is held at gunpoint by a robber who demands that she give him the ring on her finger (higher felony than "mugging").

quirement of breaking in their simple burglary statutes. Today, a good percentage of burglaries occur when someone leaves a window or door unlocked or open.

Some states, however, continue to use breaking as an aggravated form of burglary in addition to their regular or simple burglary statutes.

Unlawful Entry Into Premises

Because burglary is a form of trespass, an unlawful entry into the premises must take place. An entry could be made by inserting a hand or arm (or even the tip of a screwdriver) into the premises. For example, suppose X threw a brick through a jewelry store window and then inserted his hand and arm through the broken window to obtain watches and rings that were in the window display. This would be an unlawful entry that would justify a conviction of X for burglary of the jewelry store.

Suppose that instead of using his arm, X inserted a cane and began removing watches and rings by hooking them with the cane. Would this be an entry so as to justify a conviction of burglary? Most courts would hold that this was an entry, because the cane was an extension of X's body inserted into the store to carry out his criminal purpose.[34]

In the 1983 case of *People v. Tingue*, the defendant entered a New York church that was open at all hours so that the public could pray and meditate.[35] However, instead of praying, the defendant stole the amplifier system from behind the altar rail and entered a room of the church not open to the public, where he attempted to force the lock of a safe. The defendant was charged with burglary. In his first trial, the state failed to "muster sufficient evidence" to prove unlawful entry, and the case was dismissed. The state tried again and in the second trial obtained a conviction for burglary. (The appellate court reversed the conviction, because double jeopardy forbade the second trial and conviction.)

Any element of a crime may be proved by circumstantial evidence. In the U.S. Supreme Court case of *United States v. Edwards,* someone had burglarized a U.S. post office using a pry bar on a window.[36] The defendant had stolen property taken from the post office in his possession. Direct evidence of the break-in could not be shown, because no witnesses were available. However, crime lab tests showed paint and wood fragments on the defendant's clothing similar to the paint and wood on the post office window. A jury held that this evidence proved unlawful entry, and the defendant's conviction was affirmed.

In the case of *State v. Tixier,* police officers responded to a triggered burglar alarm within a minute.[37] They found a small hole near the door-opening mechanism of a garage. The defendant was found hiding among tires stacked near the door. The piece of the door that had been removed was found near the defendant. It was concluded that the defendant had used an instrument to penetrate the building. In affirming the defendant's burglary conviction, the Court held:

> Evidence of a break-in by use of an instrument which penetrates into the building is, in our opinion, evidence of entry into the building. The sufficiency of this evidence is not destroyed by a failure to prove that the instrument was used to steal something from the building or to commit another felony. Such proof is unnecessary because burglary does not depend upon actions after the entry; the crime is complete when there is an unauthorized entry with the requisite intent.

In the case of *Champlin v. State,* the defendant entered a hotel lobby open to the general public twenty-four hours a day and removed a television set and a cash register.[38] Instead of charging the defendant with theft, a prosecutor charged the defendant with burglary. In reversing the conviction for burglary, the Court pointed out that the defendant's conduct, although illegal, was not burglary, because the premises were open to the general public.

The Dwelling House of Another

A "dwelling house" is a place where people live and sleep. Under the common law, unlawful entry into and theft from a business place would not be a burglary, because a business place is not a dwelling house. Hotel rooms and apartments are dwelling houses, because people live and sleep in such places. A new building into which no one has yet moved has been held not to be a dwelling house.[39]

All the states and the federal government have changed the common law restricting burglary to only dwelling houses. Today, virtually all buildings are contained within the scope of the crime of burglary (and some states, such as California, also include vehicles). Many states punish the burglary of an inhabited building more severely than that of an uninhabited building. In the case of *People v. Lewis,* the Court held that the question of "inhabited" or "uninhabited" turns not on the immediate presence or absence of people in the building but rather on the character of the use of the building.[40]

Nighttime

The common law required that burglary be committed at night, which was defined as the time between sunset and sunrise. An entry into a dwelling house with an accompanying theft during the day could not be charged as a burglary under this definition. The defendant, however, could be charged with the separate crimes of trespass, stealing, and, depending on the circumstances, criminal damage to property. Today, about half the burglaries in the United States are committed during the day, and all jurisdictions recognize daylight burglaries. Some states impose more severe penalties for nighttime burglaries.

Intent to Commit a Felony

Old common law burglary required proof of "intent to commit a felony." All states and the federal government have broadened this element of burglary. Some states now require that the state prove an intent to steal or commit a felony. Others provide that the intent must be to commit a crime (misdemeanor or felony). Other state statutes specify crimes, whereas still others require that an intent to commit a larceny or theft or other felony be shown.

A defendant who is apprehended in a warehouse in the middle of the night with an armful of merchandise leaves little question concerning intent in that particular situation. With respect to proving intent for burglary when there is no evidence of stealing or of any other crime, the Supreme Court of Illinois stated in the case of *People v. Johnson* that

> Intent must ordinarily be proved circumstantially, by inferences drawn from conduct appraised in its factual environment. We are of the opinion that in the absence of inconsistent circumstances, proof of unlawful breaking and entry into a building which contains personal property that could be the subject of larceny gives rise to an inference that will sustain a conviction of burglary. Like other inferences, this one is grounded in human experience, which justifies the assumption that the unlawful entry was not purposeless, and, in the absence of other proof, indicates theft as the most likely purpose. This conclusion is supported by the decisions of other courts.

In the 1973 Pennsylvania case of *Commonwealth v. Muniem*, the defendant, who had been found in an empty warehouse about noon, was convicted of burglary.[41] The door was half open and the defendant was walking out when the police arrived. He was cooperative, did not run, and had nothing in his possession. The owner testified that

---

Intent to Steal in a Burglary Charge

The general rule of law is that intent to steal cannot be inferred from the single fact of an unlawful entry into a building. Additional circumstances must be considered, such as:

- Type of entry—was it forcible?
- Manner of entry—was there a breaking or splintering?
- Place of entry—was it the rear or side of the building?
- Type of building—did the building contain items that a thief would be interested in stealing?
- Time of entry—was it the middle of the night or the middle of the day?
- Conduct of the defendant when interrupted—did he or she attempt to hide or escape?

Source: This material is adapted from a chart originated by the Supreme Court of Wisconsin in the case of *State v. Barclay,* 54 Wis.2d 651, 196 N.W.2d 745 (1972).

What Is the State Obligated to Prove?

In addition to the "intent" or mental element of each crime

In order to charge	That there was a stealing (taking and carrying away)?	The value of the property taken?	Elements other than the crime of stealing?
Theft/Larceny	Yes	Yes	No
Robbery	Yes	Not necessary as long as the property was something of value	Yes, (1) that the taking was by force or threat of force and (2) that the taking was from the victim's person or presence
Burglary	No, only an intent to steal or to commit a felony as required by the statutes of that state	Not necessary as long as the property was something of value (or there was an intent to steal)	Yes, requires a showing of an unlawful entry into a dwelling or building (or an unlawful remaining after closing)

nothing was missing. The defendant stated that he had to go to the toilet and had looked for a lavatory in the empty building. The defendant was 33 years old, employed, married, and had no prior record. In reversing the conviction and ordering the defendant discharged, the Court stated:

> In the instant case, the only evidence produced against the appellant is his presence, perhaps as a trespasser, in a vacant building in daylight at about noontime. When found by the police, he was walking to the open door by which he testified he entered the building. The owner of the building testified that nothing was missing and there was no evidence of a forcible entry, or possession of any burglary tools, other tools or anything else.
>
> Each case must stand on its own facts in determining whether the Commonwealth has sustained its burden of proof. At best, the evidence of the Commonwealth may give rise to suspicion and conjecture of guilt but most certainly does not have such volume and quality capable of reasonably and naturally justifying an inference of a willful and malicious entry into a building with the intent to commit a felony so as to overcome the presumption of innocence and establish guilt beyond a reasonable doubt of the crime of burglary.

Proof of Burglary When Other Crimes Are Committed

As a trespass offense, burglary is most often committed by a defendant who steals or who has an intent to steal. Criminals, however, enter private premises for criminal purposes other than to steal. Offenders have entered the premises of others with intent to commit rape, arson, or other serious felonies. The charge of burglary is sometimes one

Forms of Theft

Theft/larceny	Theft from the person	Robbery[a] (theft[b] by force or threat of force)	Burglary[a] (trespass with intent to steal or to commit a felony)
▪ ordinary theft (usually done secretly)	▪ purse snatching	▪ mugging or yoking (strong-armed robbery)	▪ ordinary burglary (some states punish burglary committed at night more severely)
▪ "snatch and run" theft	▪ pickpocketing	▪ armed robbery (weapon shown or not shown)	▪ armed burglary
▪ shoplifting	▪ "rolling a drunk" (taking valuables from an intoxicated person or person in a stupor)	▪ carjacking	▪ burglary in which an occupant of the building is injured
▪ theft from autos	▪ taking valuables from injured, dead, or disabled people	▪ burglaries that turn into robberies	▪ "break and run" burglary (breaking store window and running off with property)
▪ theft from buildings		▪ purse snatching and pickpocketing in which such force is used against the person that it constitutes strong-armed robbery	▪ newspapers use the term "car burglary." Some states do have this crime. See *State v. Subin,* 536 A.2d 758 (N.J. 1988), and *State v. Martinez,* 832 P.2d 331 (Idaho App. 1992).
▪ theft by fraud (con game)		▪ home invasion robbery	
▪ embezzlement			
▪ theft by bailee			
▪ fraud on innkeeper, restaurant			
▪ looting—taking property from building that has been destroyed by disaster, riot, bombing, fire, tornado, and so on			

[a]Depending on the laws of your state, sentences could be enhanced (increased) when there is concealment of identity (mask), or a bulletproof garment is used, or a police scanner radio is used during the commission of the crime.
[b]In robberies of banks and stores, the terms "counter-jumpers" and "take-over robberies" (as distinguished from "single teller" or "single clerk" robberies) are sometimes used to describe the methods used by the robbers.

of multiple serious charges against a defendant who went on a criminal rampage in a private home or business place. The charge of burglary also offers prosecutors an alternative charge when doubt exists as to whether the state can prove attempted rape, murder, arson, or other crime. If X broke into W's apartment with the intent to rape her but found that she was not home, X could be charged with burglary if the state could prove his intent to commit a felony. The following case illustrates:

Mitchell v. State
Court of Criminal Appeals of Oklahoma (1971) 489 P.2d 499

Evidence showed that at approximately 1:30 A.M., the defendant drove his fist through the screen door of a house and unlatched it after he tore the screen door off the facing. After gaining entry, he choked the 79-year-old woman who lived in the house. He demanded $25 from her and struck her in the face. He then discharged a firearm into the floor of the house. He left after an hour, demanding that the woman give him $100 by the following morning or he would come back and kill her. He received no money from the woman, who called the sheriff as soon as the defendant left. The conviction for first-degree burglary and the sentence of fifteen years' imprisonment were affirmed by the Court of Criminal Appeals of Oklahoma.

SUMMARY

The criminal code of some states uses the term "larceny," while in other states the crime is called "theft." The terms are identical and have no legal differences.

The criminal code of your state defines the many types of theft/larceny and establishes the essential elements necessary to convict a person of theft/larceny, burglary, robbery, and extortion. This chapter presents material on these crimes, including historic development.

Members of the armed forces and persons under the jurisdiction of the federal government will use the Code of Military Justice and the Federal Criminal Code for definitions of the crimes presented in this chapter.

 ## BOOK-SPECIFIC WEB SITE

For chapter-related Web links, quizzing activities, and case and news updates, go to the *Criminal Law,* Eighth Edition, book-specific Web site at **http://info.wadsworth.com/ gardner.**

QUESTIONS AND PROBLEMS

The following situations actually occurred. What, if any, crime should be charged in each incident?

1. A witness and the victim stated that Harrison kicked the victim while the victim was on a bike, told the victim to get off the bike, and then took the bike and pedaled off. *State v. Harrison,* 598 So.2d 1211 (La.App. 1992).

2. The defendant ordered gas pumped into his car, which he refused to pay for. He then threatened the gas station owner and drove off. *State v. Dean,* 824 P.2d 978 (Kan.Sup.Ct. 1992).

3. The defendant took a bucket of coins left unattended in a gambling casino and walked away. The owner chased after the defendant, shouting an alarm. In running from the area, the defendant collided with three women, knocking one down. The defendant was then apprehended. *State v. Sewell,* 603 A.2d 21 (N.J.Sup.Ct. 1992).

4. After giving an automobile dealer a false address, the defendant took a car for a test-drive and did not return the car. The car was worth $13,900. *State v. DeVries,* 780 P.2d 1118 (Kan.App. 1989).

5. The defendant stole civil service exams for police promotions and sold copies of the exams with the answers. *United States v. Keohane,* 918 F.2d 273 (1st Cir. 1990).

6. After the victim had his shoes shined, he gave the defendant a $20 bill, which the defendant took and would not make change for or return. The defen-

dant was convicted of simple robbery. *State v. Florant,* 602 So.2d 338 (La.App. 1992).

7. The defendant was present when a pickpocketing occurred. No evidence showed that he knew the thief or was working with the thief, but the defendant ran when the police arrived. He was convicted of theft by pickpocketing. *People v. Ceasar,* 596 N.E.2d 89 (Ill.App. 1992).

8. Because of robberies at an ATM cash machine, police set up a surveillance. Two young males were seen parking a car near the ATM; they removed something from the trunk of their car; they approached the ATM and then retreated from the ATM. When a car was heard approaching the area, the men hid in nearby bushes. Based on this conduct, have the men committed a crime that would authorize a police arrest of the men? *People v. Cradle,* 554 N.Y.S. 2d 323 (1990).

9. The defendant grabbed a woman and transported her to an ATM at a bank, where he forced her to withdraw money and turn the money over to the defendant. *State v. Tweedy,* 594 A.2d 906 (Conn. Sup.Ct. 1991).

10. A man walked into a Milwaukee fast-food restaurant and handed a note to the 17-year-old clerk at the counter. The note read, "Hurry up. Give me the money." The man was carrying a paper bag. No other customers were in the restaurant, and the clerk was very nervous. The man looked at her and said, "Hurry up." The clerk then scooped up $80 from the cash register. The man took the money and ran out of the restaurant.

11. X threw a brick through a jewelry store window and with a long stick was able to hook watches and rings worth more than $500.

12. A $10,000 check endorsed for deposit to a Miami bank disappeared in the mail. The defendant obtained possession of the check and deposited it to an account that he had opened at the bank. To make the deposit, the defendant had to alter the account number on the check to show the defendant's new account number at the bank. After the 20-day hold on the funds in his account, the defendant withdrew all the funds and closed the account. Has the defendant committed a crime? If so, what should he be charged with? *Bell v. United States,* 462 U.S. 356, 103 S.Ct. 2398 (1983).

INFOTRAC COLLEGE EDITION EXERCISES

Got to InfoTrac College Edition and, using the keyword search term *larceny,* find articles relating to the following areas:

1. How do employees steal cash from their employers? What can be done about it?

2. What are the causes of the "crime bust" of the 1990s?

3. What are the elements of the crime called "bank larceny"?

NOTES

1. A 22A Corpus Juris Secundum (Criminal Law), Section 597.

2. For cases in which the owners of cars were convicted of theft when they took their car from a person with a superior right of possession, see *State v. Pike,* 826 P.2d 152 (Sup.Ct.Wash. 1992) (car taken from mechanic without paying for repairs, but the conviction was reversed when it was shown that a written repair estimate was not provided as required by state law); and *Courtney v. Rice,* 546 N.E.2d 461 (Ohio App. 1989) (car towed to police lot after a parking violation. Defendant was convicted of theft and the parking violation, but both convictions were reversed on appeal).

3. 739 P.2d 1041 (1987).

4. *Transamerica Ins. Co. v. Long,* 318 F.Supp. 156 (W.D.Pa. 1970).

5. "Theft" and "larceny" are interchangeable terms for the crime of stealing. Some states use the term "theft," while other states use "larceny." The Model Penal Code uses "theft" (Article 223).

6. Neb.Rev.Stat. section 28-510.

7. "Working Papers of the National Commission on Reform of Federal Criminal Laws," 2:913.

8. *People v. Schlicht*, 709 P.2d 94 (Colo. App. 1985).

9. See the *Chicago Tribune* article "$836,000 Check for GI Triggers Row" (October 23, 1993). For criminal cases on the taking of mislaid or lost property, see *State v. Evans*, 807 P.2d (Idaho App. 1991); and *State v. Getz*, 830 P.2d 5 (Kan. 1992).

10. *Criminal Law* by LaFave and Scott, 2d ed. (Belmont, Calif.: West/Wadsworth, 1986), discusses the following on pp. 729–739:

a) Embezzlement by a person in lawful possession of money or property (an employee; a person who found the money or property; or a person who obtained it by mistake),

b) what is called fraudulent embezzlement, and

c) embezzlement by public officials.

The crime of "breaking bulk" is sometimes classified as an embezzlement crime. It is committed when a person takes a portion of goods that have been temporarily placed in his or her custody by the owner. This could be done by a warehouse employee or a common carrier in charge of transporting a shipment of goods. (For example, dockworkers loading cases of beer into a railroad car remove many bottles from cases for their own consumption.) Some states have statutorized the common law crime of breaking bulk (or breaking bale). Other states have made the offense that of larceny or embezzlement; still others include it as larceny by bailee.

11. Illinois Rev.Stat., Chapter 38, § 15-1.

12. Minnesota Statut. Ann. § 609.25.

13. 365 F.2d 389 (2d Cir. 1966).

14. See *U.S. v. Riggs*, 739 F.Supp. 414 (N.D., Ill. 1990).

15. *People v. Tansey*, 1992 WL 396786 (N.Y.App. 1993).

16. 22 N.Y.2d 443, 293 N.Y.S.2d 96, 239 N.E.2d 727 (1968).

17. See *People v. Schmidt*, 1996 WL 350878, in which the Colorado Court of Appeals pointed out that Colorado has a statute that makes price tags attached to a stolen item prima facie evidence of the item's value in a theft prosecution, unless the price is commonly subject to negotiation as a motor vehicle would be.

18. 823 P.2d 848 (1991). Also, in the case of *People v. Wallace*, 434 N.W.2d 423 (Mich. 1989), a Michigan court of appeal held that a chain given to a wife during the marriage was her property and not the jointly owned property of the husband and wife.

19. 25 Mich.App. 371, 181 N.W.2d 551 (1970). In the 1983 case of *U.S. v. Perez*, 707 F.2d 359 (8th Cir. 1983), the defendant stole an exhibit of the government that was being used in a criminal case against him and others for the distribution of cocaine. The exhibit consisted of fifteen $100 bills. The Court of Appeals affirmed the conviction, holding: "We have little difficulty holding that here the United States had sufficient possession and control, if not actual title, to the property." The property had been seized when the defendants were arrested.

20. 342 U.S. 246, 72 S.Ct. 240 (1952). This case is also discussed in Chapter 7.

21. The asportation or carrying away requirement in robbery is usually easily met. For example, in *State v. Johnson*, 432 So.2d 758 (Fla.App. 1983), the court found asportation complete when the defendant forced a store clerk to put money in a paper bag and set it on the counter near the defendant, even if the defendant never touched the bag. In *Lattimore v. U.S.*, 684 A.2d 357 (D.C. Court of Appeals), asportation was found when the defendant took a wallet from the victim, saw only a payroll check in the wallet, and threw the wallet back at the victim.

22. Many states also make concealing identity while committing a crime such as robbery conduct for which the degree of the crime and the penalty may be increased. The Supreme Court of Wisconsin has held that if one robber concealed his identity and the other did not, the second robber could be a party to the crime of concealing identity. *Vogel v. State*, 96 Wis.2d 372, 291 N.W.2d 838 (1980).

23. Volume IX, No. 27, July 1, 1968.

24. Other majority-view cases include the following: while the taking may be without force, the offense is robbery if the departure with the property is accomplished by use of force. *People v. Sanders,* 28 Mich.App. 274, 184 N.W.2d 269 (Ct.App. 1970); a woman who saw the defendant run from her house with her purse and bag of money called for help; her grandson, who pursued the defendant, gave up the chase when the defendant fired a gun. *Hermann v. State,* 239 Miss. 523, 123 So.2d 846 (1960); the defendant asked a service station attendant to fill up his gas tank, then displayed a rifle in a threatening manner and drove away without paying. *State v. Bell,* 194 Neb. 554, 233 N.W.2d 920 (1975).

25. See *State v. Canty,* 469 F.2d 114 (D.C. Cir. 1972), holding that the robbery of each of four bank tellers did not constitute a separate taking within the meaning of the federal bank robbery statute, and therefore the defendant could not be convicted on four counts of robbery based on a single incident; *Rogers v. State,* 272 Ind. 65, 396 N.E.2d 348 (1979), holding that the defendant was improperly convicted on two counts of robbery of a grocery store despite the fact that money was taken from two employees; *Williams v. State,* 271 Ind. 656, 395 N.E.2d 239 (1979), holding that an individual who robs a business establishment, taking that business's money from four employees, can be convicted of only one count of armed robbery; *State v. Potter,* 285 N.C. 238, 204 S.E.2d 649 (1974), holding that when the lives of all employees in a store are threatened and endangered by the use or threatened use of a firearm incident to the theft of their employer's money or property, a single robbery is committed; *State v. Whipple,* 156 N.J.Super. 46, 383 A.2d 445 (1978), holding that the defendant's robbery of a liquor store and its owner constituted but a single transaction, which could not be fractionalized to enhance the defendant's punishment for a single crime. See also the 1980 case of *State v. Perkins,* 45 Or.App. 91, 607 P.2d 1202.

26. West's Ann. Cal. Penal Code, § 215.

27. Courts facing the movement or asportation question under the general robbery statute have reached a different answer. In *State v. Johnson,* 558 N.W.2d 375

(Wis.1996), the Wisconsin Supreme Court held that the robber must move the car to be guilty.

28. 590 A.2d 665 (1991).

29. 362 Mass. 83, 283 N.E.2d 840 (1972).

30. See *Alfred v. State,* 659 S.W.2d 97 (Tex.App. 1983).

31. See the *New York Times* articles "Cosby Describes Requests for Money from 2 Women" (July 16, 1997) and "To Ask Is Not Always to Extort: In the Case Involving Bill Cosby, a Troubling Legal Issue" (July 18, 1997).

32. *U.S. v. Arthur,* 544 F.2d 730 (4th Cir. 1976). A longer definition of bribery from the *Arthur* case is presented in Chapter 22.

33. Florida's burglary statutes, adopted in 1975, provide that "burglary means entering or remaining in a structure or conveyance with the intent to commit an offense therein, unless the premises are at the time open to the public or the defendant is licensed or invited to enter or remain."

34. The New Mexico Court of Appeals held in the 1976 case of *State v. Tixier,* 89 N.M. 297, 551 P.2d 987, that "A one-half inch penetration into the building is sufficient. Any penetration, however slight, of the interior space is sufficient. The fact that the penetration is by an instrument is also sufficient. 2 *Wharton's Criminal Law and Procedure* (1957) § 421; Clark and Marshall, *Crimes,* 6th ed., § 13.04."

35. 91 A.D.2d 166, 458 N.Y.S.2d 429 (1983).

36. 415 U.S. 800, 94 S.Ct. 1234 (1974).

37. See footnote 34.

38. 84 Wis.2d 621, 267 N.W.2d 295 (1978).

39. *Woods v. State,* 186 Miss. 463, 191 So. 283 (1939).

40. 274 Cal.App.2d 912, 79 Cal.Rptr. 650 (1969).

41. 225 Pa.Super. 311, 303 A.2d 528 (1973).

16

Shoplifting and Other Crimes Against Businesses and Corporations

CONTENTS

KEY TERMS

shoplifting

probable cause

false imprisonment

defamation

malicious prosecution

under ringing

uttering

forgery

kiting

computer access

Shoplifting

Theft is generally the single biggest crime problem of any retail business. **Shoplifting** is the form of theft that occurs most frequently and probably causes the greatest losses. *U.S. News & World Report* reported that shoplifting losses amounted to at least $23 billion in 1999. On the basis of this figure, shoplifting costs consumers more than a nickel on every dollar they spend in retail stores.

The crime of shoplifting, or retail theft, is a form of theft and larceny. Shoplifting has the same essential elements as theft and larceny: (1) a taking and carrying away (2) of the property of another (3) without consent, and (4) with intent to steal and deprive the owner of possession of the property.

Taking and Carrying Away in Shoplifting

In modern self-service stores, customers are invited to examine merchandise on display. Garments may be taken to dressing rooms and tried on. Customers carry about merchandise either in their hands or in shopping carts provided by the store. The Court of Appeals of New York pointed out in the case of *People v. Olivo* that stores therefore consent "to the customer's possession of the goods" for limited purposes.[1]

Stores do not consent, however, to concealment of their merchandise by customers. The merchandise is offered for sale, and if customers are not going to purchase an object, they are obligated to return the merchandise to the display counter in good condition. If customers are going to take the merchandise, they have a legal obligation to pay the purchase price. The highest court in New York state held in the *Olivo* case:

> If the customer exercises dominion and control wholly inconsistent with the continued rights of the owner, and the other elements of the crime are present, a larceny has occurred. Such conduct on the part of a customer satisfies the "taking" element of the crime.
>
> * * *
>
> A taking of property in the self-service store context can be established by evidence that a customer exercised control over merchandise wholly inconsistent with the store's continued rights. Quite simply, a customer who crosses the line between the limited right he or she has to deal with merchandise and the store owner's rights may be subject to prosecution for larceny. Such a rule should foster the legitimate interests and continued operation of self-service shops, a convenience which most members of the society enjoy.[2]

Proving the Crime of Shoplifting When the Suspect Has Not Left the Store

There is a common belief that shoplifting has not occurred until the merchandise has been taken from the store premises. The Criminal Court of the City of New York discussed this belief in *People v. Britto:*

> There are a number of myths about the criminal law, comfortably shared and nourished by those in the street, the business community and sometimes, the courts.

One of these is the belief that an observed shoplifter acts with impunity unless and until he or she leaves the store with the goods. So strong is this belief that the majority of store detectives are instructed to refrain from stopping the suspect anywhere inside the premises; although the likelihood of apprehension is thus enormously decreased.[3]

Courts are virtually unanimous in holding that goods need not leave the store for theft to occur. The New York Court of Appeals explained that result as follows:

> Case law from other jurisdictions seems unanimous in holding that a shoplifter need not leave the store to be guilty of larceny. . . . This is because a shopper may treat merchandise in a manner inconsistent with the owner's continued rights—and in a manner not in accord with that of a prospective purchaser—without actually walking out of the store.[4]

Inconsistent actions might include hiding the goods under the shopper's coat or other clothes. As the Maryland Court of Special Appeals held in *Lee v. State,* if merchandise is secreted under clothing, it meets the requirement of concealment, and it doesn't matter if the concealment was for a short time or if the shopper didn't leave the store.[5]

The Requirement of Probable Cause Based on Personal Knowledge

Private security officers and retail store employees are often told, "If you have not seen it, it has not happened." Customers are not to be treated like shoplifters until hard, first-

---

Self-Service Stores

Customers are impliedly invited to

- enter store
- view and handle merchandise
- try on clothing (if approved by store)
- carry merchandise in shopping cart, in basket, or by hand (customer possession of goods for the limited purpose of bringing goods to a checkout counter)

There is no invitation for customers to

- stay for long periods of time or to dress inappropriately ("no shoes—no shirt—no service" restrictions)
- intentionally conceal unpurchased merchandise
- engage in furtive and unusual behavior
- abandon their garments in exchange for property of store
- move toward one of store's exits with concealed merchandise
- possess known shoplifting device used to conceal merchandise (specially designed outer garment or a false-bottomed carrying case)

hand information demonstrates that a shoplifting has occurred. The Criminal Court of New York emphasized the **probable cause** requirement in *People v. Britto:*

> It must be emphasized that this court's holding in no way lessens the burden of proof on the People in shoplifting cases. On the contrary, there is, and should be, a higher standard of proof upon the People in self-service situations than in other larceny cases, because the mere fact of possession may not be used to demonstrate larceny. This remains true even when such possession is accompanied by suspicious or equivocal actions, such as placing unpaid goods directly into the defendant's shopping bag (see, *Durphy v. United States,* 235 A.2d 326 [D.C.App. 1967]). It is only when the trier of fact concludes, beyond a reasonable doubt, that defendant's actions were totally inconsistent with and clearly adverse to the owner's interests that a conviction may lie. If the facts are sufficient to support such a conclusion *before* the defendant leaves the store, the fact that he has not left is wholly irrelevant and should not absolve him from the consequences of his acts.[6]

The U.S. Supreme Court defined probable cause as "facts and circumstances within their knowledge and of which they had reasonable trustworthy information [that] were sufficient in themselves to warrant a man of reasonable caution in the belief" that the suspect had committed a crime.[7] The Supreme Judicial Court of Massachusetts held:

> Historically, the words "reasonable grounds" and "probable cause" have been given the same meaning by the courts.
>
> * * *
>
> The Oregon Supreme Court construed the meaning of the words "reasonable grounds" in its "shoplifting statute" as having the same meaning as they have in a statute authorizing arrest without a warrant and applied the probable cause standard to the facts before it.[8]

EXAMPLE: On a hot July day, a woman customer stated to a clerk in a large food store, "I suspect that young man of shoplifting." She pointed at a young black man wearing a jogging suit. The clerk relayed the statement to the assistant manager of the store, who confronted the young man, accusing him in a voice overheard by other people of shoplifting. The young man was detained, and the police were called. Did probable cause exist to justify this action?

When the police arrived, they questioned the store employees and the woman customer. The woman customer stated that she had not witnessed a shoplifting but had only "suspected" that a theft had occurred. The police then realized that probable cause did not exist from the facts known to the store employees, and they released the young man. In the civil lawsuit that followed, a jury awarded the young man money damages for *false imprisonment* and *defamation* (slander).

Merchants that detain or prosecute suspected shoplifters face the possibility of large damage awards if they are found to have acted unreasonably, as the following cases held:

- An employee who drank a soft drink in a damaged can was prosecuted for shoplifting by the employer; after acquittal, the employee sued the employer for *malicious prosecution* and won a $30,000 verdict. *Bi-Lo Inc. v. McConnell,* 404 S.E.2d 327 (Ga. App. 1991).

- The Court held there was a "total lack of probable cause," and the plaintiff in a civil lawsuit was awarded $83,500 in compensatory damages and $1 million in punitive damages. *Kroger Food Stores, Inc. v. Clark,* 598 N.E.2d 1084 (Ind.App. 1992).

- After a search disclosed no stolen merchandise, a security guard continued accusations of theft. The defendant was awarded $75,000 in actual damages and $100,000 in punitive damages. *Caldwell v. Kmart Corp.,* 410 S.E.2d 21 (S.C.App. 1991).

- The *New York Times* article "Woman Wins $1.56 Million in Department Store Bias Case" (December 11, 1997) tells of black shoppers who won large money awards in federal lawsuits when juries found that store security officers discriminated against black customers in shoplifting stops and searches without probable cause. An award of $1.56 million was rendered against Dillard's Department Store in Kansas City, Kansas, and $3 million was awarded against an Eddie Bauer store in Greenbelt, Maryland (a suburb of Washington, D.C.).

To give some protection to store owners in cases like the above, some states have enacted statutes called Shoplifting Detention Acts. An example of such an act is Indiana Code Section 35-33-6-2. That act grants immunity from civil prosecution if the detention is authorized by the Act. The Act permits a merchant with probable cause who believes shoplifting has occurred to detain the suspect, demand identification, search the suspect, and inform the suspect's parents of the detention.[9]

Criminal or Civil Prosecution of Shoplifters?

Shoplifting cases can be handled in a variety of different ways, depending on the circumstances of the case. Following are some of the alternative options in handling shoplifting cases:

- When the amount stolen is very small or the offender is very young or very old, a scolding and warning might be used. Parents of children could be called, or the police could take the child home and inform the parents of the problem. Many states have laws making parents liable in a civil action for goods damaged or taken by a minor in a theft.

- More than thirty states have passed laws giving merchants and retailers authority to extract payments and fines from thieves they catch in the act. The offender could sign an agreement under a Civil Settlement of Shoplifting Law acknowledging guilt and agreeing to make the payments to the merchant. In this way, the merchant can save time and expenses by bypassing the police and the courts. The advantages to the shoplifter are that a criminal record is avoided and the incident is taken care of without a court appearance.

- Because criminal courts are very crowded, shoplifting cases are not ordinarily charged criminally unless the amount taken is very large. Civil citations are issued in many cases, and offenders can pay the fine in the same way as parking tickets are paid. Or the offender can be ordered to appear in a municipal court, where the case is heard by a judge in the same way speeding and other traffic violations are heard.

- Criminal charges are likely to be issued in shoplifting cases when
  - ◆ the shoplifter commits a serious assault or battery in resisting detention or in attempting to escape. Assault on a law enforcement officer is a felony in probably all states.
  - ◆ escape is made from a law enforcement officer while in custody, which is a crime. Some states also forbid escape from a merchant who has lawfully detained a shoplifter. See *State v. Hughes,* 598 N.E.2d 916 (Ohio, 1992).
  - ◆ the shoplifter has a concealed weapon or has illegal drugs on his or her person. Or the shoplifter is in possession of a criminal tool or a shoplifting device. See the case of *State v. Lee,* 586 N.E.2d 190 (1990), in which the defendant had a girdle as a shoplifting tool.
  - ◆ the shoplifter causes considerable damage to the merchant's property in an effort to escape. Many states make criminal damage to property a crime if the damage is done either "intentionally" or "recklessly."
  - ◆ the shoplifter obstructs and hinders a law enforcement officer by giving the wrong name and date of birth, as in the case of *State v. Caldwell,* 454 N.W.2d 13 (Wis. App. 1990), or obstructs by refusing to obey a law enforcement officer. See the case of *Mathis v. State,* 391 S.E.2d 130 (Ga.App. 1990), in which the defendant refused to get into the patrol car and struggled with officers.
  - ◆ the shoplifter has a long prior record of theft and/or has a serious drug or alcohol problem, which the person is stealing to support. (Prosecutors can encourage such people to enter drug treatment programs by threatening jail sentences.)
  - ◆ other crimes are committed by the shoplifter. For example, in the case of *State v. Santilli,* 570 So.2d 400 (Fla.App. 1990), the defendant was convicted of robbery when, after shoplifting a greeting card, the defendant backed his car into a law enforcement officer in attempting to escape.

Other Retail Theft Crimes

- *Tag switching:* a lower price tag is placed on a store item. In the case of *State v. Nguyen,* 584 So.2d 256 (La.App. 1991), tags were switched on a dress and blouse. The state would have to show the switching was done by the defendant and was not a mistake by a store employee or done by another person.

- *Undercharging by checkout clerk* ("*under ringing*" schemes): the checkout clerk will undercharge a friend or co-conspirator. See *Wal-Mart v. Medina,* 814 S.W.2d 71 (Tex.App. 1991).

- *"Storming" or mass shoplifting:* two or many more people storm an all-night or late-night convenience store, take items, and then leave. If force is used or threatened, this could be charged as robbery.

Fraudulent Use of Credit Cards

Credit cards are a means of extending short-term credit. The three parties ordinarily involved in a credit card transaction are (1) the issuer of the credit card, which could be a bank or an organization, such as American Express or MasterCard; (2) the credit card

Handling a Shoplifting Incident

1. Make sure you have probable cause and a good solid case before you restrain the freedom of movement of a person for shoplifting. Probable cause (or "reasonable grounds to believe") must be based on personal knowledge (firsthand information) by you or another reliable adult employee. Remember: "If you did not see it, it did not happen. When in doubt, let them go."

2. Observing a person concealing "something" or putting "something" in his or her pocket or purse is not sufficient to establish probable cause. The person may be putting a handkerchief or glasses back in a pocket. You must have "reasonable grounds to believe" (probable cause) that the object is unpaid merchandise and that the item belongs to the store. If you do not have probable cause, you may:

   - keep the person under observation
   - engage in voluntary conversation ("May I help you?" "Are you looking for something?" and so on)
   - ask the person what they put in their pocket, or whether they have a receipt for merchandise in their possession under circumstances in which there is no restraint of their freedom of movement

3. After a person is observed shoplifting, the following options are available to store employees or a security officer:

   - Confront the person immediately, and ask that he or she produce the item. *Always* ask if the person has a receipt showing that he or she paid for the item. Under these circumstances, you may seek only recovery of the item and deterrence, rather than prosecution in court.
   - You may be under instructions to allow the person to go beyond the last pay station (or in some cases, even out of the store). Under these circumstances, the person should be kept under surveillance. If the person becomes aware of your surveillance, he or she may attempt to discard the shoplifted item or pass it onto another person. If you fail to observe the "discard" or "pass-on," you may then be unable to explain why the stolen property was not recovered. If it appears that the person may outrun you and other store employees, it may be wise to position yourself between the exit door and the person.

4. If your state has a Civil Settlement of Shoplifting Law, you should know the requirements of this law and also any guidelines that your employer has established for using the law.

5. Shoplifting cases are handled by your local law enforcement agency (police or sheriff), prosecutor, and judge. It is advisable to consult a knowledgeable official to determine whether any specific standards are required, such as

   - whether the local judge requires that the person observed shoplifting be allowed beyond the pay station (or out of the store) before being detained. (A young man in gym shoes who gets near a door or out of the store is going to outrun most store security people.)
   - whether cases will be prosecuted when:
     - the value of the merchandise stolen is small (what is the minimum for prosecution?)
     - the merchandise or item stolen has not been recovered
     - the offender is very young or very old
     - other factors are considered

6. Absolute defenses to civil suits are

   - that the person either voluntarily stayed in the area, or that the restraint of movement was made in good faith on probable cause based on personal knowledge
   - that if any force was used, it was necessary and reasonable either
     - in self-defense, or
     - to detain the person, and/or
     - to prevent the theft of the property.

Stay Within the Law While Preventing Shoplifting

In acting to prevent shoplifting and apprehend shoplifters, merchants and their employees must obey the law. Failure to do so could result in civil lawsuits such as the following:

- False imprisonment, false arrest, or malicious prosecution because of failure to have probable cause to make forcible detention. See *Lazarus Dept. Store v. Sutherlin,* 544 N.E.2d 513 (Ind.App. 1989).
- Slander and false imprisonment because after customer opened her purse to show that no merchandise was taken, guard continued to accuse her in a voice overheard by others in *Caldwell v. K-Mart Corp.,* 410 S.E.2d 21 (S.C.App. 1991); and *Wal-Mart Stores, Inc. v. Dolph,* 825 S.W.2d 810 (1992).
- Wrongful detention in *Taylor v. Dillards Dept. Stores, Inc.,* 971 F.2d 601 (10th Cir. 1992).

---

user, who is the holder of the card and the person purchasing the merchandise or service; and (3) the seller of the merchandise or provider of the services.

A person holding a valid credit card signs for the receipt of the goods and commits himself or herself to pay for the service or the property that has been received. The merchant or business organization supplying the goods or services is then reimbursed for the amount of the billing by the issuer of the credit card. The credit card issuer then bills the credit card holder.

Obtaining Credit Cards and Bank Cards for Fraudulent Use

The methods of obtaining credit cards for fraudulent use are many and varied. They can be stolen by burglars, pickpockets, or robbers. They can be retained by workers in gas stations or restaurants, or stolen from the mail. They can be counterfeited or altered. The credit card itself need not be stolen; if a thief uses the card number unlawfully it is credit card theft.[10] Many states have credit card abuse laws that make it a crime to use a revoked or cancelled credit card to fraudulently obtain property.[11]

Thieves obtain credit cards to commit crimes in the following ways: by counterfeiting cards (29 percent), by stealing credit cards (22.4 percent), by obtaining lost and mislaid credit cards (16.4 percent), by theft from the mail (13.7 percent), by making fraudulent applications for credit cards (3.2 percent), and by placing telephone and mail orders with false cards (9.3 percent).[12]

Criminal Use of Bank Cards and Credit Cards

More fraudulent charges are made during a Christmas season using stolen, counterfeit, and lost credit cards than at any other time of the year. Merchants and salesclerks are busy and probably don't take the precautions they would at other times of the year.

Purchasing goods and services is the principal type of credit card and bank card fraud in the United States. Automated teller machines also present another means of theft and fraud.

A large automated teller machine fraud occurred with one bank card in 1995. The machines are supposed to give no more than $200 per day to any single card. However, because of a program changeover, thieves were able to obtain $346,770 from a single card by making 724 withdrawals from many different machines. See *New York Times* article "Missing Bank Card Brings Overwithdrawal of $346,770" (February 12, 1995).

Check Violations

Worthless Checks, or Checks That Bounce

Most checks that bounce are the result of negligence, mistake, or bad bookkeeping. Persons writing NSF (nonsufficient funds) checks or ISF (insufficient funds) checks generally make the checks good within the period provided by the statutes of that state. For example, Florida statutes, Section 832.07, require that a bad check be made good within seven days or a criminal prosecution may be commenced and the writer of the check is liable in a civil action for triple the amount of the check.

Bad checks are a constant problem for retail businesses and banks, as the crime is easy to commit and the money losses are huge.[13] Not only are the money losses growing every year, but an *FBI Law Enforcement Bulletin* article of 1996 pointed out that one-half of all check fraud in the United States is committed by professional and organized groups.[14] The article pointed out that even street gangs are using sophisticated means to commit check fraud.

The problem of bad checks overwhelms most local law enforcement agencies. The sheer volume of bad checks limits the number that can be investigated and prosecuted.

The Crime of Uttering

When a person signs a false name in the presence of a bank clerk to a check that does not belong to him or her, the felony crime of *forgery* has been committed. The bank clerk can then testify in court that he or she witnessed the forgery. When a forged check is presented for payment, the felony of **uttering** has been committed. The Supreme Court of Virginia defined the crime of uttering as the following:

> Under our bad-check statute, the gravamen of the offense is the intent to defraud, and the offense is complete when, with the requisite intent, a person utters a check he knows to be worthless. . . . A check is uttered when it is put into circulation; for example, when it is presented for payment. . . . The presentment is more than a request for payment; it constitutes an implied representation that the check is good. The statute itself dispenses with proof of an extrinsic representation.
>
> * * *
>
> It need not be shown that the implied representation was relied upon or that anything was received in return for the check; indeed, the discovery by a payee that a check is worthless before a purchase transaction is completed does not preclude a conviction under the statute. . . . And, while we have stated that the statute is "specifically aimed to discourage the giving of bad checks for what purports to be

a cash purchase," . . . such a purchase is not the only transaction proscribed; the statute clearly encompasses a worthless check given to obtain cash.[15]

The crime of uttering a forged instrument is most often committed when a person presents a forged instrument for payment. In the case of *England v. State,* the defendant handed a forged check to a bank teller without saying anything.[16] In affirming the defendant's conviction for uttering a forged instrument, the Supreme Court of Indiana held: "We conclude the offering of the check to the teller with no instructions, when this act is generally construed in the banking industry as a request to exchange said check for cash, is sufficient conduct to warrant the jury to believe that the appellant intended to cash a forged instrument."

In the 1989 case of *State v. Tolliver,*[17] the defendant deposited a forged check into his own checking account through the use of an ATM. A Wisconsin Court of Appeals affirmed his conviction for uttering, holding that the defendant's act introduced the forged check "into the stream of financial commerce."

The crime of uttering can be committed with a forged check or with a bad check that is not forged but is known to be worthless.

The crime of uttering can also be committed with counterfeit money or "raised" bills. In the 1991 case of *United States v. Brown,*[18] the defendant was convicted of connecting parts of different money bills and uttering the altered bills (defendant "raised" $1 bills to $20 bills and would then utter them).

The Crime of Forgery

Documents and writing are important in the functioning of a modern society. The crimes of forgery and uttering are offenses created primarily to safeguard confidence in the genuineness of documents and writing. Forgery is committed when a person with an intent to defraud falsely makes or alters a writing or document. Forgery may be committed by

- Creating a wholly new false writing or document
- Altering an existing document (raising the amount of a check would be an example)
- Endorsing a check or other instrument with another person's name (example: X steals Y's check and cashes the check by endorsing Y's name on the back of the check)
- Filling in blanks over a signature of another, either without authority or with unauthorized terms

When a check is presented either for cash or in payment for goods, there is an implied representation that the check is good. A common business practice is to request people presenting a check to either endorse or sign the check in the presence of the person who is about to honor the document. If the presenters of the check (the bearers) know that the check is forged, they have committed the crime of uttering in presenting the forged document. If they sign a false name to the check, they have then committed the crime of forgery in the presence of the person who is about to honor the check.

The many types of forged documents include forged driver's licenses, forged identification cards, forged credit cards, forged passports, forged residency cards for people illegally in the United States, and so on.

Safeguards in Handling Checks

- Do not endorse checks in blank (with just your name), as the instrument then becomes a bearer instrument that can be cashed by any person obtaining possession.
- Do not sign blank checks, as any person obtaining possession of the checks could fill in the amount and cash the checks.
- In sending checks through the mail, make the checks payable to a specific person or corporation. Make bank deposits payable to "deposit only" or "for deposit to account number. . . ."

With checks, the forgery could be done by hand. But the many desktop computers have created a new industry. Forgery and counterfeiting of documents, including checks, is a fast-growing problem throughout the United States. The American Bankers Association states that desktop counterfeiting is the No. 1 crime problem facing banks.[19]

Operations of Check Forging Rings

Check forging rings operate in all large cities in the United States. Some of their blank checks are obtained as the result of burglaries or thefts from business firms. Other checks are the product of a desktop computer, which is a new tool for making false copies of checks and other documents.

The checks are often forged using names found on stolen identification cards and papers. Such identification can be obtained by purse snatching and pickpocketing. The thief looks for a victim with the same general appearance as the person who will utter (pass) the check. With a good set of identification cards and with checks that have all the appearance of payroll checks, the check-forging ring goes to work.

To minimize the possibilities of being apprehended, professional criminals will often recruit other people to commit the actual uttering and passing of the checks. This can be done by selling the checks made out in whatever amount and name the person wishes. Or the criminal transaction can be done under an agreement to share the criminal loot.

If a criminal is apprehended while attempting to pass a forged check, he or she is likely to attempt to destroy the evidence of the crime. This might be done by eating the check or destroying it in some other way. Should the offender be successful, he or she could then be charged with the offense of destroying (or attempting to destroy) evidence of a crime.

Passing Forged Checks and Other Counterfeit Securities in Interstate Commerce

In the 1930s, the U.S. Congress became concerned about the use of fraudulent securities in interstate commerce. The Congress amended the National Stolen Property Act (58 Stat. 1178) by also forbidding "falsely made, forged, altered or counterfeit securities" to be used and passed in interstate commerce. The U.S. Supreme Court recognized that the "general intent" and "broad purpose" of Congress was to "curb the type of trafficking in fraudulent securities that often depends for its success on the exploitation of interstate commerce." *Moskal v. United States,* 111 S.Ct. at 466 (1990).

The National Stolen Property Act, therefore, not only makes it unlawful to transport stolen property in interstate commerce but also fraudulent securities, which include forged or "falsely made" checks. The following U.S. Supreme Court cases illustrate the enforcement of law:

United States v. Sheridan

Supreme Court of the United States (1946) 329 U.S. 379, 67 S.Ct. 332

The defendant was convicted under the National Stolen Property Act for cashing checks at a Michigan bank, drawn on a Missouri account, with a forged signature. The Supreme Court held:

> Drawing the [forged] check upon an out-of-state bank, knowing it must be sent there for presentation, is an obviously facile way to delay and often defeat apprehension, conviction, and restoration of the ill-gotten gain. There are sound reasons therefore why Congress would wish not to exclude such persons (from the statute's reach), among them the very case with which they may escape the state's grasp.

McElroy v. United States

Supreme Court of the United States (1982) 455 U.S. 642, 102 S.Ct. 1332

The defendant used blank checks that had been stolen in Ohio to buy a car and a boat in Pennsylvania. The Supreme Court held that the defendant circulated fraudulent security in violation of the National Stolen Property Act and that Congress's general purpose was "to combat interstate fraud."

Check Kiting

Check *kiting* can be compared to a *shell game* at a carnival, in that manipulations are used in both to deceive. The most common reason for the deception in check kiting is to create a false bank balance from which to draw and run off with money that does not belong to the person. The U.S. Supreme Court used the following example to explain a check kiting scheme in the 1982 case of *Williams v. United States:*

> The check kiter opens an account at Bank A with a nominal deposit. He then writes a check on that account for a large sum, such as $50,000. The check kiter then opens an account at Bank B and deposits the $50,000 check from Bank A in that account. At the time of deposit, the check is not supported by sufficient funds in the account at Bank A. However, Bank B, unaware of this fact, gives the check kiter immediate credit on his account at Bank B. During the several-day period that the check on Bank A is being processed for collection . . . the check kiter writes a $50,000 check on his account at Bank B and deposits it into his account at Bank A. At the time of the deposit of that check, Bank A gives the check kiter immediate credit on his account there, and on the basis of that grant of credit pays the original $50,000 check when it is presented for collection.

By repeating this scheme, or some variation of it, the check kiter can use the $50,000 credit originally given by Bank B as an interest-free loan for an extended period of time. In effect, the check kiter can take advantage of the several-day period required for the transmittal, processing, and payment of checks from accounts in different banks.[20]

A check kiter can build up a big "float" using a number of bank accounts in different banks and then run off with all the money. In *United States v. Payne*,[21] used-car dealers exchanged checks for the sale of automobiles between themselves and used the immediate credit to operate their businesses. One nonexistent car was sold seven or eight times a week for a four-month period. The Court concluded that

> Payne and Fountain successfully managed a kite for four months with a float that rose to $178,000. They obtained that credit, advance, and loan only by falsely representing the worthless checks as worth their face value. 18 U.S.C. § 1014 makes their misrepresentation a federal offense when the injured bank is insured by the FDIC.

In 1985, the stock brokerage firm of E. F. Hutton & Co. pleaded guilty to two thousand felony counts of check kiting (federal mail and wire fraud). E. F. Hutton agreed to pay a $2 million fine and also to make restitution to the many banks cheated by their scheme. Investigations showed that three techniques were used by some of the top E. F. Hutton managers to obtain maximum illegal interests on huge sums of money.

After pleading guilty to massive check kiting charges in 1985, federal prosecutors sought criminal indictments against E. F. Hutton in 1987 for allegedly helping organized-crime figures launder hundreds of thousands of dollars illegally.[22] (See Chapter 22 for material on the crime of money laundering.)

Computer Crimes

In the 1950s, a reformed bank robber named Willie Sutton was asked on talk shows why he robbed banks. His response was, "That's where the money is."

Today, computers are where the money is. It is estimated that more than $400 billion is transferred every day through commercial and governmental computers. Our society is becoming increasingly cashless through credit cards and paperless through computers.

In 1977, a governmental committee estimated the average loss in a computer crime at $430,000, compared with a $19,000 average when accounting was done manually.[23] The average "take" in a street holdup is about $38, while the take in the average bank robbery is just over $300.

Computer crime is reported to be at a "staggering level."[24] Concern is increasing over computer crime that has been committed and remains undetected. Estimates of the risk of detection and risk of prosecution were given as only 1 in 22,000.[25] Computer crime has been called the "crime of the future" and home computers the "burglar tool of the electronic age." These accusations may be exaggerations, but they do reflect the concern for the rising rate of computer crime.

Law enforcement officials from eight countries met in 1997 to work out plans to fight computer crimes together. The British Home Secretary pointed out at the meeting that

Security of computers and computer networks is of great concern to governments and corporations throughout the world. The computer hacker above, Mudge, appeared before the U.S. Senate Governmental Affairs Committee to testify on computer security problems in 1998. Mudge works as a consultant to explore corporate computer networks and find weak spots.
AP/Wide World Photos

today "one person can . . . commit crimes in several countries without leaving his armchair (by use of a computer)."[26]

Computers as Crime Tools

Many of the unauthorized uses of computers that would constitute violations of computer crimes also would be violations of other criminal laws. Use of a computer could also be charged as theft, embezzlement, fraud, or other more traditional crimes. Illegal computer use can thus be both a crime and the tool to commit other crimes. Among the crimes computers could be used to commit are the following:

1. *Theft of funds*[27]
   a. By an outsider (or insider) who, by using a telephone and the necessary passwords from a remote terminal, could make the unauthorized transfer of millions of dollars to a designated account.
   b. By an insider who would falsify claims in an insurance company (such as medical insurance), and the computer would process and mail out checks paying such claims.
2. *Theft of information or data.* Computer data banks hold many different types of information worth billions of dollars (lists of customers, employees, banking information, consumer records, business plans, and so on). Two examples are theft of FBI investigative records[28] and the theft of the names of Drug Enforcement Administration informants and the status of drug investigation cases.[29]

3. *Theft of services.* If an authorized or unauthorized person uses a system for unauthorized purposes, such misuse could be charged as theft in many states.

4. *Electronic break-ins.* Break-ins into the computers of other people, businesses, or governmental agencies to steal, alter, or modify information.

Computers as Crime Targets

But what about the emerging crime trend that is unique to computers—in which the computer is the target? This type of crime occurs when a computer and the information it stores are the targets of a criminal act committed either internally by employees or externally by criminals. The external threat usually involves the use of telecommunications to gain unauthorized access to the computer system.

In its investigations, the FBI has determined three groups of individuals involved in the external threat. The first, and the largest, group consists of individuals who break into a computer just to see if they can do it—without stealing or destroying data. The next group breaks into computer systems to destroy, disrupt, alter, or interrupt the system. Their actions amount to malicious mischief because they do not attack the system for financial gain, which is the motive of the last group. This group constitutes a serious threat to businesses and national security, for these individuals are professionals who use specialized skills to steal information, manipulate data, or cause loss of service to the computer system.

Computer Crime Statutes

Virtually every state has passed laws making unauthorized use of a computer with the intent to obtain information, money, or other property a crime. The Maryland Court of Appeals in *Briggs v. State,* 704 A.2d 904(1998), noted that every state with the exception of Vermont had adopted some form of criminal computer use or access statute. In 1999, Vermont enacted an unauthorized *computer access* crime law.[30] In 18 U.S.C. Section 1030(a)(1), the U.S. Congress made it a crime to access a computer without authorization, or in excess of authorization to obtain or alter information without authority.

The definition of "unauthorized" use or access varies among these statutes. New York's statute requires that the computer use be without authority and that the computer be equipped with a coding system designed to limit access. Thus, a defendant who without authorization accessed a computer and copied a customer list with the purpose of selling the list could not be convicted of illegal computer use, because the state did not prove the computer had a coding system.[31]

In some states, the computer offence statute is applicable only if the person had no authority to access the computer.[32] Other states make it a crime to exceed the authority given to use the computer.[33]

A person can be convicted of unauthorized use of a computer if he or she uses a home computer and telephone modem to obtain long distance access codes from a telephone company computer and then uses those codes to make long distance calls charged against those codes.[34] On the other hand, courts have held that simply using a telephone to make a long distance call to commit a crime did not amount to "accessing" a computer under the computer crime statute.[35]

SUMMARY

Merchants, banks, credit card companies, and corporations that do business with the public run a risk of illegal activity directed at them. Shoplifting, for example, is a major concern of merchants. The retail theft laws make it possible to convict shoplifters once they have acted in a manner designed to deprive the merchant of the goods. At the same time, the law protects innocent shoppers by requiring the merchant to act only after obtaining probable cause that shoplifting has occurred.

Credit cards and checks are a vital part of our society. However, they can be used by the criminal to effectively steal goods, services, and money. The criminal law therefore not only punishes the underlying conduct, but it also punishes the use of the credit card or check in furtherance of that conduct. Forgery occurs when an instrument or check is signed or altered illegally, even if the instrument or check doesn't result in payment to the forger. Uttering is complete when a forged check or instrument is presented for payment, even if payment is refused.

All states and the federal government have statutes making unauthorized use of or access to computers a crime. As computers become more and more involved in everyday life, the kinds of criminal uses they may be put to increases. State, national, and international authorities will be used to curb those criminal uses.

BOOK-SPECIFIC WEB SITE

For chapter-related Web links, quizzing activities, and case and news updates, go to the *Criminal Law,* Eighth Edition, book-specific Web site at **http://info.wadsworth.com/ gardner.**

QUESTIONS AND PROBLEMS

Does probable cause exist in the following cases to restrain the movement of the person? Or should a voluntary conversation with the person be used?

1. A well-dressed woman was looking at merchandise in a drugstore. After she left the store without purchasing anything, a clerk observed that only six items were on the shelf of the seven previously observed on the shelf. *Crase v. Highland Village Value Plus Pharmacy,* 176 Ind.App. 47, 374 N.E.2d 58 (1978).

2. Would it make any difference in Problem 1 if the woman were poorly dressed or very young or very old?

3. A man was leaving a department store with a shopping bag. In the bag was a tie rack that he had not paid for. He was stopped at the door of the store by a security guard. The man immediately admitted that he had not paid for the tie rack. Stating that he would pay for it, he went to a checkout counter and tendered a $20 bill. *Mullen v. Sibley, Lindsay & Carr Co.,* 51 N.Y.2d 924, 434 N.Y.S.2d 982, 415 N.E.2d 971 (1980).

4. A man was observed walking briskly up and down the aisles of a Sears store. The man was then observed backing his car up to a portable building used to display merchandise. The man took a lawn mower from the building and put it in the trunk of his car. The man would not produce a sales receipt for the mower. When the man was asked to get out of his car, he broke and ran away. *Tinsley v. State,* 461 S.W.2d 605 (Texas Ct.App. 1970).

5. A woman was waiting in a checkout line in a drugstore. The cashier saw a wrapping bow on the counter in front of the woman. The bow had all the appearances of bows that were on sale in the store. A few minutes later, the bow was not on the counter. When the woman paid for other items, the cashier asked if she had anything else to pay for. The woman did not pay for the bow, and as she walked away from the store, she was asked if she had anything in her purse for which payment had not been made. The woman answered no. *Kon v. Skaggs Drug Center, Inc.,* 115 Ariz. 121, 563 P.2d 920 (App. 1977).

6. A man was seen leaving a men's clothing store with a bulge under his overcoat. A security officer who had arrested the man for shoplifting on two prior occasions followed the man to a barbershop. When the man sat down in the barbershop, the security officer returned to the clothing store, where he determined that a man's leather coat was missing. The security officer started back to the barbershop and saw the man on the street. The officer identified himself and asked for the coat. The man gave the officer the coat and then ran away. When the officer followed, the man threatened him with a knife. *State v. Gonzales,* 24 Wash.App. 437, 604 P.2d 168 (1979).

7. Police warned the manager of a Woolworth store to be on the lookout for three teenage girls believed to be shoplifting (two dark-haired and one blonde). When girls matching this description were observed in the store, it was determined that two hairpieces were missing. A clerk stated that the girls were near the hairpiece counter. *Meadows v. F.W. Woolworth Co.,* 254 F.Supp. 907 (N.D.Fla. 1966).

8. A store clerk saw a woman place a sticker on a tube of suntan lotion, reducing the price from $1.99 to $1.12. The woman then paid the lower price at the checkout counter and commenced to leave the store. *Duke v. Schwegmann Bros. Giant Super Markets,* 384 So.2d 1019 (La.App. 1980).

9. An assistant security manager identified herself to a woman leaving a Kmart store and asked the woman to show her a receipt for the scarf in the loop of the handle of the woman's purse. The woman stated, "Oh, I must have forgot to pay for it." The woman was then asked to go to the store office, where she was asked to show identification. When the guard asked, "You come all the way from North Riverside to steal at Kmart?" the woman responded, "Sure, why not?" The woman signed a report stating that she "was wandering around the store, took the price [tag] off the scarf and put the scarf on her purse." *People v. Raitano,* 81 Ill.App.3d 373, 36 Ill.Dec. 597, 401 N.E.2d 278 (Ill.Ct.App. 1980).

10. A woman was leaving a department store when an antishoplifting device sounded. *Sears, Roebuck & Co. v. Young,* 384 So.2d 69 (Miss. 1980), and *Clark v. Rubenstein, Inc.,* 326 So.2d 497 (La. 1976).

11. A security guard observed two women stuffing a pantsuit into a shopping bag. The women were not in the pantsuit department at the time. The women were then seen leaving the store. When the guard attempted to place the younger woman under arrest, a skirmish broke out. *Jones v. Montgomery Ward & Co., Inc.,* 49 Or.App. 231, 619 P.2d 907 (1980).

12. A security employee at a large shopping mall saw a man "carrying a large garbage bag" and "walking very fast" toward an exit.

> At that time I just seen [sic] how fast he was going, and I was curious that he was carrying a large garbage bag, so I followed him down, and right as he was going out the exit, I asked him, "I don't believe we sell any garbage bags in here, why do you have a garbage bag?" And he told me it wasn't his bag, it didn't belong to him. So I said, "Well, if it don't [sic] belong to you, I'll take the bag." At that time I asked him if he would come along and be checked out, and he said fine, and we went and I took him in to Richard Bennett's, asked him if I could look in the bag. He said fine. I seen [sic] tags and all that in—and notified Wauwatosa Police on it.

The garbage bag contained stolen clothing, but the security employee had not seen the man take any of the items. *State v. Lee,* 157 Wis.2d 126, 458 N.W.2d 562 (App. 1990).

13. In a 1998 case, Kmart employees suspected a black man of shoplifting. Based on suspicion, the man was followed out of the store, where he was seized and a struggle ensued. The man was handcuffed, and it was found that he had not shoplifted anything. Did "suspicion" authorize the action and conduct of the Kmart employees? *Jones v. Kmart Corp.,* 70 Cal.Rptr. 844, 949 P.2d 941 (Sup.Ct. Calif. 1998).

INFOTRAC COLLEGE EDITION EXERCISES

1. Go to InfoTrac College Edition and, using the subject search term *shoplifting,* find an article on new antitheft devices, called source tagging, to be installed on the factory floor. What impact on shoplifting will these new devices likely have, if manufacturers of retail products use them extensively?

2. Go to InfoTrac College Edition and, using the subject search term *forgery,* find an article on forging antiquities and an article on new scientific methods of determining the authenticity of old manuscripts. Will the methods help the other antiquities problem?

NOTES

1. 420 N.E.2d 40 (1981).

2. In affirming the convictions of three different defendants in the *Olivo* case, the New York Court held: "In *People v. Olivo,* defendant not only concealed goods in his clothing, but he did so in a particularly suspicious manner. And, when defendant was stopped, he was moving towards the door, just three feet short of exiting the store. It cannot be said as a matter of law that these circumstances failed to establish a taking."

In *People v. Gasparik,* defendant removed the price tag and sensor device from a jacket, abandoned his own garment, put the jacket on and ultimately headed for the main floor of the store. Removal of the price tag and sensor device, and careful concealment of those items, is highly unusual and suspicious conduct for a shopper. Coupled with defendant's abandonment of his own coat and his attempt to leave the floor, those factors were sufficient to make out a prima facie case of a taking.

In *People v. Spatzier,* defendant concealed a book in an attaché case. Unaware that he was being observed in an overhead mirror, defendant looked furtively up and down an aisle before secreting the book. In these circumstances, given the manner in which defendant concealed the book and his suspicious behavior, the evidence was not insufficient as a matter of law.

3. 93 Misc.2d 151, 402 N.Y.S.2d 546 (1978).

4. 438 N.Y.S. at 246 (1981).

5. 59 Md.App. 28, 474 A.2d 537 (1984).

6. 402 N.Y.S.2d at 548 (1978).

7. *Carroll v. United States,* 267 U.S. 132, 45 S.Ct. 280 (1925).

8. *Coblyn v. Kennedy's, Inc.,* 359 Mass. 319, 268 N.E.2d 860 (1971).

9. See *Wal-Mart Stores Inc. v. Bathe,* 715 N.E.2d 954 (Ind.App. 1999).

10. In *State v. Morgan,* 985 P.2d 1022 (Alaska App. 1999), a former boyfriend gave his girlfriend's credit card number to the defendant, who used it to place $3,669 worth of long distance calls. The court held his use of the card number was obtaining a credit card by fraudulent means.

11. See *Nolan v. State,* 629 S.W.2d 940 (Tex. App. 1982).

12. MasterCard International and the *New York Times* article "Guarding Credit Cards from the Latest Scams" (July 2, 1994).

13. Even the Congress of the United States had a "bad check" scandal in 1992. More than one hundred members of the House of Representatives had written bad checks in a year's time on the House Bank. One member of Congress wrote 996 bad checks in a three-year period. See the *New York Times* articles "Adding Up the Casualties in the House Bank Scandal" and "The House Is Getting Jittery Over Bad-Check Disclosures" (March 12, 1992). All the bad checks were made good, but at the time they were written there were insufficient funds to cover the checks.

14. See the *FBI Law Enforcement Bulletin* article "Check Fraud: A Sophisticated Criminal Enterprise" (August 1996).

15. *Warren v. Commonwealth,* 219 Va. 416, 247 S.E.2d 692 (1978).

16. 249 Ind. 446, 233 N.E.2d 168 (1968).

17. 149 Wis.2d 166, 440 N.W.2d 571 (Wis.App. 1989).

18. 938 F.2d 1482.

19. See the *New York Times* article "New Breed of Check Forgers Exploit Desktop Publishing" (August 15, 1994).

20. 458 U.S. 279, 102 S.Ct. 3088 (1982).

21. 602 F.2d 1215 (5th Cir. 1979), review denied 445 U.S. 903, 100 S.Ct. 1079, 26 CrL 4209 (1980).

22. See the *FBI Law Enforcement Bulletin* article "Check Kiting: Detection, Prosecution and Prevention" (November 1993).

23. Committee on Government Operations, "Staff Study of Computer Security in Federal Programs" (Washington, D.C.: Government Printing Office, 1977).

24. Committee Report, note 13, and LEAA Newsletter, January 1980.

25. Committee Report, note 13.

26. See the *New York Times* article "Eight Countries Worried by Computer Crime, Agree to Join Forces" (December 11, 1997). The article quoted British Home Secretary Straw, who also stated, "We're using 19th-Century tools to face a 21st-Century problem." The agreement signed by Britain, France, Russia, Germany, Japan, Italy, Canada, and the United States also agrees to work together to fight the crimes of industrial espionage, money laundering, child pornography, computer crimes, and other wrongdoings in cyberspace.

27. The Equity Funding fraud of the late 1970s, which resulted in losses of more than $100 million, was done with the use of computers. Also in a computer fraud, Jack Benny, Liza Minnelli, and another man lost $925,000.

28. *U.S. v. DiGilio,* 538 F.2d 972 (3d Cir. 1976).

29. 22 CrL 2478 (1986).

30. *Vt. St. T.* 13 § 4102 (1999).

31. *People v. Angeles,* 687 N.Y.S.2d 884 (Criminal Court of City of New York).

32. *Briggs v. State,* 704 A.2d 904 (Md. App. 1998).

33. See, e.g., *Ariz. Rev. Stat.* Section 132316(A).

34. See *State v. Riley,* 846 P.2d 1365 (Wash. 1993).

35. See *State v. Rowell,* 908 P.2d 1379 (N.M. 1995) and *State v. Allen,* 917 P.2d 848 (Kan. 1996).

17

Fraud and Other Property Crimes

KEY TERMS

fraud

consumer fraud

con game

pyramid scheme

Ponzi scheme

security

mail fraud

counterfeiting

fence

arson

trespass

defiant trespass

Fraud and Fraudulent Practices

Fraud consists of deceitful means or acts used to cheat a person, corporation, or governmental agency. Theft by fraud or larceny by fraud is often the criminal charge used, as fraud can be a form of theft and larceny. Fraud is always intentional, as distinguished from negligence. The following material illustrates the wide range of deception, fraud, and corruption that occurs at all levels of society.

Fraud and Corruption in Government

Fraud against government is as old as government itself. Reports of fraud and corruption date back to biblical times and throughout early civilizations. The U.S. government today is spending $1.4 trillion per year in its total budget, so it is not surprising that it has serious fraud and corruption problems.

Losses through fraud and corruption occur in many ways. Fraud can be charged criminally in federal courts as *mail fraud* (when the U.S. mails are used), wire fraud (when interstate or international communications are used), racketeering, bribery and theft of public funds, fraud and conspiracy to commit fraud, false entries or false statements, fraud in connection with government contracting, equity skimming, false statements and misappropriation of funds, conspiracy to defraud the United States, and interstate transportation of funds obtained by fraud. The following areas account for most of the fraud losses in the federal government:

- *Contract fraud:* In the procurement of arms and military supplies, the federal government spends more than $300 billion yearly. Fraud in military procurement contracts has been discovered in the selling of inside information on contract bids, bid rigging, bribes and kickbacks, double billing, falsifying test results or failure to conduct tests, and overcharging for materials and services.[1]

  Contract fraud has also been found in procurement and construction contracts issued by state and local governments and by corporations contracting for supplies and services.

- *Program frauds:* Billions of dollars are dispersed every year in programs such as Medicaid, Medicare,[2] food stamps,[3] small business loans, subsidy programs, HUD (U.S. Department of Housing and Urban Development), Social Security, and various aid programs. Programs at state and local government levels include welfare. Welfare frauds include "ghost eligibles" and also people taking welfare payments who are not entitled to the assistance.[4]

  Health care fraud on Medicare and Medicaid programs are particularly costly. The U.S. General Accounting Office estimates that health care fraud amounts to 10 per cent of annual health care expenditures, or about $100 billion dollars.[5] Moreover, the Health Care Financing Administration estimates that by the year 2008, health care spending will reach $2.2 trillion annually, which would equal 16.2 per cent of the U.S. Gross Domestic Product.[6]

  The federal government has passed many criminal laws directed at health care fraud, such as the Medicaid False Claims Statute and the Anti-Kickback Statute.[7] These laws provide for massive fines when corporations violate them. For example, in 2001, TAP Pharmaceutical Products Inc. was fined $875 million dollars, the largest fine ever for health care fraud, for fraudulent manipulation of Medicare and Medicaid programs.[8]

- *Fraud by public officials:* This category includes bribes, kickbacks, and other types of fraud. Fraud and corruption by public officials could be charged as theft or larceny, misconduct in public office, bribery, or other crimes. Sting operations have uncovered such dishonesty.

Consumer Fraud

Consumer fraud consists of fraudulent promotions, dishonest business practices, and fraudulent schemes directed at buyers of products and services. Consumer frauds range from small money losses to losses of hundreds of thousands of dollars. The elderly are often targets of consumer frauds because of their vulnerability and trust in statements made by people seeking to defraud them.

Among the most frequent consumer complaints are complaints of fraud in home improvement and repair, auto repairs, door-to-door sales, fraudulent insurance pitches, health and medical aids, land sales schemes, unlawful and deceptive charitable solicitations, and unsolicited merchandise.

Door-to-door selling can be deceptive if deceptive contract terms are used, if poor-quality merchandise is used deliberately, if nondelivery of goods ordered occurs, or if pressure selling and scare tactics are used. Generally, such victimizing occurs with uninvited sellers.

Deceptive selling practices include the "bait and switch" practice of deceptive advertising and sales.[9] The technique of "bushing" occurs when the selling price of an item is increased above that originally quoted to the purchaser. The increase occurs after the purchaser, in good faith, makes a down payment with money or a trade-in and before acceptance of a purchase order by the seller.

Charitable solicitations are fraudulent if the collectors plan to use the money for their own use or if there is no cause or organization.[10] Fraud to obtain money also occurs if the collector falsely asserts that he or she is associated with a charity or religious group. Misrepresentation as to the use of the contribution could also be fraudulent, depending on the representations.

Phony billing schemes include sending out invoices and billings for merchandise, supplies, or services that were never ordered or supplied. Substantial amounts of money have been lost through carelessness and failure to recognize the scheme. Other phony billing schemes include selling phony advertisements or directory advertising; the publication may not exist or the ad is not run.

Fraudulent Insurance Claims

Fraudulent insurance claims can occur with any type of insurance. The claim could be for a burglary loss of property when no burglary occurred or for property that was not stolen. It could be for a fraudulent damage claim or for the loss of property in a robbery that is a false claim. *Arson* for profit is the crime of arson committed to present a false insurance claim.

Insurance fraud costs the United States an estimated 80 billion dollars a year. Criminal convictions for all classes of insurance fraud rose from 961 in 1995 to 2,123 in 2000.

Automobile insurance fraud is a major area of fraudulent claims. The Coalition Against Insurance Fraud of Washington, D.C., estimated in 1995 that over $13 billion in fraudulent auto insurance claims were filed that year, causing a $250 increase in an American family's annual auto insurance premium.[11] Most of these claims were based on phony automobile accidents. In July 2001, New Jersey police arrested 192 people, including a lawyer and three doctors, who were engaged in a massive conspiracy to fake auto accidents and injuries.[12]

The Con Game as a Form of Fraud

Con games, or confidence games, obtain their names because the swindle depends on gaining the victim's confidence. Most con men or women believe that there is a little bit of larceny in everyone. By selecting the right victim and applying the right techniques to gain the confidence of the victim, the con artist goes to work.

The *short con* operation generally is limited to the money that the victim has at the time. Examples of short con games are card games in which fraud is used, handkerchief switch, and dropped pocketbook or wallet. The famous pigeon drop is a short con game that usually involves all or a good portion of someone's life savings.

The *big con* operation usually takes a considerable length of time to accomplish. The confidence of the intended victim must be gained. The stage must be set and the victim lured into believing that he or she can make a quick profit. The take in the big con operation is generally larger than the take in a small con operation.

An example of a pigeon drop con game can be seen in *Commonwealth v. Lawson*, a 1995 Pennsylvania court decision. There, a con woman approached the victim and showed her an envelope said to contain a large stack of $100 bills. The con woman suggested they split the money, but first talk to her "boss," the president of a nearby bank. They went to the bank to talk to the boss, who was waiting inside the bank lobby. He said the envelope contained $60,000 and that the con woman and the victim could split it if they placed some of their own money up as "*security.*" The victim gave $16,000 to the "boss" as security and agreed to come back the next day with an additional $9,500 more. Fortunately, the victim's daughter found about the scheme and informed the police, who arrested the con artists. They received two sentences of three-and-one-half to seven years in prison.[13]

Pyramid Schemes[14]

"Pay $105—Recruit two other investors—And you will make $46,700 profit."

More than 28,000 people in twenty-one states and Canada were cheated out of more than $1 million when they fell for this *pyramid scheme* in 1989 and 1990. FBI agents pointed out that the victims "were just ordinary people." Payments of $46,700 were made to some people throughout the scheme to keep enthusiasm up.

In recent years, a number of states have enacted statutes making pyramid promotional schemes illegal. Other states have older statutes in their criminal codes forbidding pyramid schemes.

Pyramid schemes or Ponzi swindles that have received national attention in the 1990s include the following:

- In what is called the largest pyramid scheme in the United States, the federal government indicted officials of the Bennett Funding Group in 1997 for selling "investments" to more than twelve thousand people and two hundred banks in forty-six states. Early investors were paid off from money from later investors, with losses estimated at over $700 million. The largest number of victims lived in New York, New Jersey, and Florida.[15]

- Big pyramid schemes have operated in Russia, Bulgaria, and Romania. In 1996 and 1997, over 200,000 people in the poorest country in Europe, Albania, were swindled of millions of dollars by a pyramid scheme, causing riots and calamities.[16]

- A former Detroit deputy police chief was convicted in 1991 of forty fraud and tax violations in running a pyramid scheme. The Internal Revenue Service stated that the three men running the pyramid scheme made no investments but did return $13 million to investors from 1983 through 1986, while pocketing $4 million in profits on which they paid no taxes. See the *New York Times* article "Ex-Deputy Police Chief in Detroit Is Convicted in a Pyramid Scheme" (January 6, 1991).

Stock Market and Financial Market Frauds

The stock markets and financial markets of the United States and other industrial democratic countries are important to their economic development in creating jobs and providing for economic security. Among the crimes created to protect these vital activities is the crime of inside trading. People obtaining inside information on the plans of large corporations can often make huge profits by inside trading on information that is often bought illegally.

Stock market fraud reached a new high in 1996, when Americans lost $6 billion through stock fraud. In 1997, nineteen people were indicted in New York City for stock fraud. Several of the indicted people were described as being senior members of two New York crime families. See the *New York Times* article "Investment Fraud Is Soaring Along With the Stock Market" (November 30, 1997).[17]

Financial experts point out that the costliest fraud scandal in the history of Wall Street is the 1994 Prudential Securities losses of $1.1 billion in limited partnerships in assets such as real estate and oil wells. See the *New York* Times article "Prudential Fraud Costs to Exceed $1.1 Billion" (July 13, 1994).

Internet Securities Fraud

The number of people using the Internet to buy and sell shares of stock has multiplied enormously over the past three years. With that increase has come a corresponding increase in Internet securities fraud schemes. Securities fraud can lead to civil or criminal action brought by the Securities and Exchange Commission (SEC) as well as prosecution under the Federal Securities Act of 1933 and state securities statutes.

Internet securities frauds can take many forms, but the most common are the "pump and dump" and "cyber smear" schemes. In pump and dump, a person buys shares of stock in a company at a low price and then makes misrepresentations about the company on Internet chat rooms and bulletin boards that convince others to buy the stock, thus driving up the price of the stock. The fraudulent investor then sells the stock at the inflated price.

In cyber smear, the person "shorts" a stock in a company by agreeing to sell the shares at a stated price on a future date, even though the person does not own any shares of the stock. If the price of the shorted stock goes down, the person may buy at the lower price and sell at the higher, agreed price. The cyber smearer puts out false information on the Internet about the company, leading people to sell shares, driving the price down. The fraudulent "short" seller then buys the stock at the artificially low price and makes a profit. Some recent examples of these schemes are as follows:

- Fifteen-year-old Jonathon Lebed used the pump and dump scheme to drive the price of a stock from $1.81 per share to $4.68 per share in a matter of hours. Lebed agreed to return $250,000 of illegal gains.[18]

- Three Washington, D.C.-area law students used a stock rating Internet company they ran to make over $345,000 in illegal profits. The students bought shares of a company in the morning, then went on the Internet and made the stock their pick of the week, causing persons using their service to go out and buy the stock. The law students then sold the stock at its inflated price.[19]

- Mark Jacob was losing thousands of dollars shorting a company called Emulex. Jacobs put out a fake press release on the Internet that said the CEO of Emulex left the company because of an SEC investigation. The Emulex stock dropped $2.2 billion of value in sixteen minutes, and Jacob made a profit of $241,000. He pleaded guilty to securities fraud in December 2000.[20]

- A 17-year-old boy tricked investors into sending him almost a million dollars by posting an Internet Web site that promised enormous returns based on the boy's ability to bet on sports. He paid large returns to early investors using money from later investors, but then stopped, a classic *Ponzi scheme*. See the *New York Times* article "Teenager's Money-Making Plan Drew 1,000 Investors and SEC" (January 8, 2002).

The Crime of Mail Fraud

Many criminal frauds use the U.S. mail to execute their fraudulent scheme. They are then likely to be charged as a mail fraud crime under 18 U.S.C.A. Section 1346. Information regarding a mail fraud can be reported to the nearest office of the Postal Inspector Service. The crime of mail fraud was defined as follows in *United States v. Bailey,* 123 F.3d 1381 (11th Cir. 1997):

> To prove mail fraud, the government must show that the defendant (1) intentionally participated in a scheme to defraud and (2) used the mails to execute the fraudulent scheme. . . . The government must establish only that the fraudulent scheme existed; conviction for mail fraud "need not rest on the success of the fraudulent scheme." *United States v. Wingate,* 997 F.2d 1429, 1433 (11th Cir. 1993).

What U.S. Consumers Complain of Most

High on the list of complaints from U.S. consumers are telemarketing schemes that use the telephone to sell travel and vacation trips, health spa memberships, home refinancing plans, and other "bargains" with the pitch "you must buy today" to get the bargain price. The Federal Trade Commission estimates that fraudulent telemarketers bilk

The Enron Scandal

In February 2001, energy giant Enron Corporation had a market value of over $60 billion based on a price of $90 per share of stock. On December 2, 2001, when Enron filed for bankruptcy protection, a share of Enron was worth less than $1. Thousands of investors, including Enron employees and retired employees, lost much of their retirement savings. Now Enron and Enron executives face possible criminal charges.

For several years prior to 2001, Enron set up shell companies that made partnerships with Enron to engage in various energy-related businesses. Losses sustained by these partnerships were put in the shell companies books, enabling Enron to show false profits for those years.

In the fall of 2001, Enron announced it was making an accounting change that resulted in a loss for the third quarter of 2001 of $618 million. This revelation caused the stock price to plummet, and also resulted in Enron losing its ability to borrow money. As a result of these and other financial problems becoming public in late 2001, Enron was forced into bankruptcy. The bankruptcy is the biggest in the history of the United States. Enron has listed assets of $49.8 billion and debts of $31.2 billion: if it were a nation it would be ranked the thirtieth largest financially in the world.

Congress and the Securities Exchange Commission began investigating the actions of Enron and its accounting firm, Arthur Andersen LLP. Criminal charges against Enron or its executives under the securities laws might result from those investigations. Some factors that may be relevant in potential violations are as follows:

- Enron executives sold personal stock holdings in Enron worth hundreds of millions of dollars during the months prior to the earnings restatement in October 2001

- Employees owning Enron stock in retirement accounts were not permitted to sell their stock during the same period, causing most of them to lose a major part of their retirement savings

- The president of Enron was telling others that the stock was worth $120 a share at the same time he was selling his own Enron shares

If these actions were taken with knowledge of the financial misrepresentations being made by Enron and with the intent to violate securities laws, Enron executives could face criminal charges under the securities laws. Some Arthur Andersen employees who were accountants and auditors for Enron had knowledge of Enron's true financial situation but permitted Enron to misstate its financial situation. When it became clear that Enron needed to reveal the true nature of its finances, Andersen destroyed thousands of Enron financial audit records, until an SEC subpoena was served on Andersen on November 8, 2001. It is possible that Andersen's actions in destroying these records could expose it to criminal and civil liability.

Sources: Time, January 21, 2002, p. 28; *Fortune,* January 7, 2002, p. 88; *Fortune,* December 24, 2001, p. 58.

Americans out of $40 billion a year. (See the *New York Times* article "Phone Swindlers Dangle Prizes to Cheat Elderly Out of Millions," June 29, 1997.)

Auto repairs and new and used vehicle sales are also high on the list of consumer complaints in the United States. Rolling back odometers and "title washing" schemes are just two of the frauds that could be costly to consumers.

A dishonest car or truck dealer who rolls back mileage on a vehicle often then fraudulently alters the title to reflect the new rolled-back mileage. The forged vehicle title is then sent to a state motor vehicle department to have a new title issued. The title has now been washed, and the fraud is more difficult to uncover. The following U.S. Supreme Court case concerned interstate title washing:

Moskal v. United States[21]

Supreme Court of the United States (1990) 111 S.Ct. 461

Odometers on two used cars were rolled back thirty thousand miles on each car. The titles for the cars were fraudulently altered to reflect the new mileage. The altered titles were then sent from Pennsylvania to Virginia, where an accomplice submitted them to Virginia authorities who, unaware of the false mileage figures, issued Virginia titles. The washed titles were then sent to Pennsylvania, where they were used in the sale of the vehicles to unsuspecting buyers. Defendant Moskal's role in this scheme was forwarding the altered titles to Virginia and receiving the washed titles when they returned. He was convicted under the National Stolen Property Act, 53 U.S.C.A. 1178, which also forbids the knowing transportation of falsely made, forged, altered, or counterfeited securities in interstate commerce. In affirming his conviction, the Supreme Court held:

> We think that "title washing" operations are a perfect example of the "further frauds" that Congress sought to halt in enacting § 2314. As Moskal concedes, his title-washing scheme is a clear instance of fraud involving securities. And as the facts of this case demonstrate, title washes involve precisely the sort of fraudulent activities that are dispersed among several States in order to elude state detection.

Identity Theft

The Federal Trade Commission has determined that identity theft is the top U.S. fraud. On the basis of a review of over two hundred thousand complaints received in 2001 by law enforcement and consumer groups, it was found that identity theft accounts for more than 40 per cent of consumer fraud complaints. The total number of identity thefts may be as high as 750,000 per year. Thefts and illegal use of credit card numbers, drivers licenses, and Social Security numbers has exploded in the past few years, according to the Privacy Rights Clearinghouse, a San Diego-based consumer group (*Denver Post*, January 24, 2002, p. 6A).

Counterfeiting of Money and Commercial Products

Counterfeiting of Currency

Counterfeiting of currency is a serious federal offense because it could have a severe economic impact on society. The history of counterfeiting in the United States can be summarized as follows:

- *Until and during the Civil War,* counterfeiting was a serious problem; thousands of different legal bills were being printed by more than fifteen hundred state banks. An estimated one-third of the currency used during the Civil War was counterfeit. Counterfeiting was easy during that period.

- *Establishment of a single national currency* in 1863 and creation of the U.S. Secret Service immediately made counterfeiting difficult. Counterfeiting the new currency required highly skilled people with highly sophisticated equipment. The diligent efforts of the Secret Service made the pooling of the necessary material and equipment plus the necessary highly trained skills difficult. Counterfeiting and alteration of currency were kept at a minimum over the years.

Identity Theft

Identity theft has grown rapidly to the point where the U.S. Federal Trade Commission reports that 500,000 to 700,000 people have pieces of their identity stolen every year. The crime occurs as follows:

To commit the crime a thief needs

Your name, date of birth, Social Security number, and an estimate of your annual income.

How *would a thief obtain this information?*

Steal (or find) a purse or wallet, steal your mail, or go through your trash looking for credit or bank card statements. Old or recent tax returns also have this information. Or it could be obtained from the database of some business.

A thief can then

Open a new credit card account or bank account in your name. Use the credit card (or cards) to obtain goods. Write bad checks on your bank account. Open charge accounts with retail stores. Establish telephone or wireless service in your name. Use your identity and credit to obtain many items of value.

To avoid immediate detection, the thief can

Use a change-of-address form and divert your mail and the bills to another address.

To protect your family and you, take the following precautions: (1) keep an eye open for missing mail, as a change of address filed by a clever thief will send bills and credit card statements to another address, (2) reveal only such personal information as is necessary, (3) check your credit file every year or two to make sure a thief is not borrowing money in your name.

In theft of identity, thieves seek to profit in the following ways:

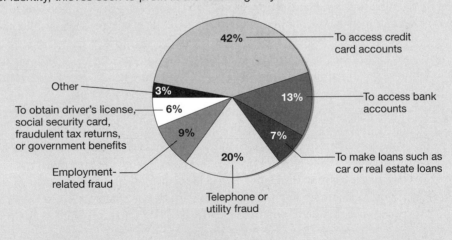

42% — To access credit card accounts

13% — To access bank accounts

7% — To make loans such as car or real estate loans

20% — Telephone or utility fraud

9% — Employment-related fraud

6% — To obtain driver's license, social security card, fraudulent tax returns, or government benefits

3% — Other

Victim has a relationship with suspect

10% Yes

90% — No

Average amount per victim obtained by suspect from financial institutions

$6,767

Average out-of-pocket expense for victim

$1,173

Source: Federal Trade Commission, Identity Theft Clearinghouse.

- *Today,* sophisticated color copiers allow what law enforcement officers call "casual counterfeiters" to print thousands of crude bills. But the principal problem is professional craftspeople, many of whom live in foreign countries and are producing counterfeit money that is difficult to detect.

In response to the growing problem of counterfeiting, the United States began issuing new folding money that is much harder to counterfeit. The introduction of new $100 bills began in 1996 and $50 bills in 1997. The $20 bill, which most Americans use in their daily lives, began being replaced in 1998. The $10 and $5 bills have been replaced, and a "more modestly redesigned" $1 bill is to follow.

Amateur counterfeiters such as high school students using school computers and color printers will continue to be a problem to merchants and people who do not look closely at paper money they are receiving. See the *New York Times* article "Teens Accused of Using Computers to Counterfeit" (February 17, 1997).

Continued efforts are being made to make counterfeiting difficult. This may require issuing new folding money in the coming years.

Other Counterfeiting Problems

Designer jeans, compact discs, videotapes of movies, electronic components, computers, books, circuit relays, and drugs are counterfeited and sold extensively in the United States. Many of the counterfeit products are manufactured in foreign countries, where they are also sold under the well-known label. Usually, the counterfeit product is a cheap or inferior copy of the real thing. However, the phony label deceives many dealers and consumers, who believe that they are buying the name-brand product.

Importation, manufacture, or sale of a counterfeit product in the United States could result in (1) prosecution under the criminal code of a state, which would probably treat the offense as a misdemeanor, (2) civil suit and sanctions in federal or state civil courts, or (3) federal prosecution under the mail fraud statute (18 U.S.C.A. Section 1341), the wire fraud statute (18 U.S.C.A. Section 1343), the Food, Drug and Cosmetic Act (21 U.S.C.A. Sections 301, 321, and so on), or other federal statutes.

Countries where most counterfeiting piracy occurs are China (which far exceeds all other countries), Russia, Italy, Mexico, and Brazil. See the *New York Times* article "With Piracy Blooming in Mexico, U.S. Industry's Cries Get Louder" (April 20, 1996).

Counterfeiting of driver's licenses and other documents are crimes and have become serious problems in the United States. More than twenty million motorists hold California driver's licenses, and the California Department of Motor Vehicles fears that at least twenty-five thousand were fraudulently issued by California employees who were fired after bribery was discovered. The bribery started when California began issuing counterfeit-proof driver's licenses. The demand for the new licenses caused a black market, where state employees would sell the new counterfeit-proof driver's license for a bribe of $200 to $1,000. See the *New York Times* article "Bribery Is Cited as California Fights a Rise in Fake Licenses" (August 3, 1997).

It was discovered that the Montana Freemen gave weekly seminars on how to use computers to generate false financial documents such as counterfeit money orders. Until arrests were made, more than 800 people traveled to the Freemen Montana Compound from more than thirty states to learn the forgery techniques. The FBI estimated that the Freemen issued more than $19.5 million in counterfeit money orders and bad checks, which 10 percent of the companies and banks failed to identify as fakes. See the *New York Times* article "Officials Say Montana 'Freemen' Collected $1.8 Million in Scheme" (March 28, 1997).

Trafficking in Stolen Goods

The crimes of trafficking in stolen goods are defined by the statutes of each state and ordinarily include (1) receiving (a single act), (2) concealing and possessing (continuing acts), and, in some states, (3) buying and transferring. In determining the statute of limitations for these offenses, the Supreme Court of Minnesota held in the 1981 case of *State v. Lawrence*:

> The crime commonly known as "receiving stolen property," when used in a short-hand sense, is a misnomer, since it includes a number of different legal concepts in addition to and separate from receiving. The offense includes not only receiving, but concealing; . . . it includes buying; and . . . it also includes possessing and transferring. The issue here is whether any of these terms may be deemed continuing in nature. The two most likely descriptions of defendant's conduct are possession and concealment. Does either, or both, apply? In answering this question we should keep in mind that a crime is not continuing in nature if not clearly so indicated by the legislature. . . .
>
> Both possessing and concealing are distinguishable from receiving in that the latter connotes a single act. Behind possessing and concealing, however, is the notion that property is being kept from someone in violation of a duty to return and this duty to return continues. One of the reasons for including possessing and concealing as crimes is to be able to prosecute even though the time has run out on receiving. Surely this serves the purpose of the statute, which is to deter trafficking in stolen goods.
>
> * * *
>
> We hold, therefore, that either concealing or possessing stolen goods is a continuing offense for the purpose of the statute of limitations. We hold this defendant may not assert the statute of limitations as a bar where he kept the goods he stole in his house and garage, thereby not only possessing the goods but making their discovery more difficult for the owner.

To convict of trafficking in stolen goods, the state is ordinarily required to prove

- that the property involved was stolen property,
- that the defendant received, concealed, possessed, purchased, or transferred the property as forbidden by the statutes of that state,
- that the defendant knew the property was stolen.

"Stolen" means that the property was obtained as a result of a theft, burglary, robbery, or any other form of theft crime, such as shoplifting or obtaining property by deception.

The Fence and Fencing Stolen Property[22]

A *fence* is a person who traffics in stolen property (receiving, concealing, possessing, buying, transferring, and so on). A fence acts as a middleperson and pays the thief for stolen property, which the fence in turn attempts to merchandise at a profit to himself or herself. The compensation paid by the fence to the thief is usually a small fraction of the value of the goods. The report of the President's Commission on Law Enforcement and Administration of Justice makes the following observations regarding fencing in the United States:

Nearly all professional theft is undertaken with the aim of selling the goods thereafter. Although the thief himself may retail his stolen merchandise, he probably will prefer to sell to a fence. He thereby increases his safety by reducing the risk that he will be arrested with the goods in his possession, or that they will be stolen in turn from him. He also avoids the dangers associated with the disposal process itself. In addition, large quantities of goods which may be perishable or otherwise quickly lose their value, or for which there is a specialized demand, will require a division of labor and level of organization beyond the capacity of an individual thief operating as his own retailer. The professional thief thus needs a "middleman" in the same way and for some of the same reasons as the farmer, manufacturer, or other producer.

* * *

Some fences engage in fencing as a supplement to their legitimate businesses, often on a more or less regular basis. The consultants learned of clothing and appliance dealers who regularly serve as outlets for stolen goods. The major outlets for stolen jewels in one of the cities studied were reported to be legitimate jewelry merchants. Other fences deal primarily or wholly in stolen goods, and are therefore professional criminals themselves.

Some narcotics pushers act as fences, taking stolen goods instead of cash for narcotics. While dealing with addicts is generally regarded as more dangerous than dealing with nonaddicts, it is also more profitable. The addict in need of a "fix" does not bargain well.

Little research has been done on fencing, despite its central role in professional crime. More information is needed about the nature of the market for illicit goods and the extent to which demand for various types of goods affects the incidence of theft. More should also be learned about the relationship of legitimate and illegitimate markets. Little is known about the pattern of distribution of stolen goods. When stolen automobiles are excluded, only a very small proportion of the total amount of goods stolen is returned to its owners. The redistribution of goods through theft and resale might constitute a significant subsidy to certain groups in our society; its curtailment might have significant side effects which should be explored. Finally, it would be desirable to have more information about the organization and operation of large-scale fencing operations, to aid in the development of better methods of law enforcement.

When Property Loses Its Character as Stolen Goods

United States v. Monasterski

U.S. Court of Appeals, 6th Circuit (1977) 567 F.2d 677, 22 CrL 2357

Three juveniles were caught attempting to steal tires from a railroad boxcar. The juveniles cooperated with FBI agents and delivered some of the tires to the defendant, whom they identified as their prospective fence. The defendant was convicted of receiving stolen property (the tires). In reversing the defendant's conviction, the Sixth Circuit Court held that once the thieves were caught, the tires lost their character as stolen goods and could no longer support the defendant's conviction. The Court further held:

> In accord with the common law rule, one cannot be convicted of receiving stolen goods when actual physical possession of the stolen goods has been recovered by their owner or his agent before delivery to the intended receiver. We further hold, also in accord with the common law rule, that the term "agent" means any person with a right to possession or control over the goods.

The Alabama Supreme Court followed the common law rule that goods that had never been stolen or goods that had lost their stolen character could not support a conviction of the crime of receiving stolen property. (See *Ex Parte Walls,* 711 So.2d 490, 1997.)

Florida, however, changed the common law and enacted a law taking away this defense from a person charged with the crime of dealing in stolen property. Florida Statute (1995) 812.028(3) permits criminal convictions in Florida for endeavoring to traffic in stolen property without proof by the state of Florida that the property was actually stolen. (See *Capaldo v. State,* 679 So.2d 717 [1996].)

Possession of Criminal or Burglary Tools

All states probably have statutes making the possession of criminal or burglary tools a criminal offense.[23] The usual elements of this crime are as follows:

- The defendant had a device or implement in his or her possession
- Such device or implement was suitable or capable of being used in committing burglary[24]
- The defendant intended to use such device or implement to break into a building, dwelling, or depository with the intent to steal

Like the crime of receiving stolen property, possession of burglarious tools is also difficult to prove. The difficult element to prove in receiving stolen property is knowledge by the defendant that the property was stolen. In possession of burglarious tools, the difficult element is intent by the defendant to use such device or implement to break into a building, dwelling, or depository with the intent to steal. Possession of ordinary work tools will not ordinarily be sufficient to justify a conviction for possession of burglarious tools. There must be additional evidence of intent to use such tools for burglarious purposes.

Cases in which most convictions have been obtained can be divided into the following categories:

- The defendant was apprehended committing or attempting to commit a burglary using the tool or had the tool in his or her actual or constructive possession.

- The defendant was in the possession of a specifically designed or adapted tool under circumstances in which a judge or jury could infer the tool's use for an illegal purpose of entry.

Destroying or Damaging the Property of Another

Vandalism and Graffiti Vandalism

No U.S. city, town, or village escapes the physical and psychological disfigurement caused by vandalism to public and private property. Vandalism is a serious problem in most public transport systems, costing millions of dollars in large cities. Schools are often hit hard, with broken windows, break-ins, broken property, and spray paint used on walls.

Veteran law enforcement officers observe that vandalism (criminal damage to property) occurs in cycles. In the summertime, public parks are hit. Benches are piled up, debris is thrown into lagoons, and beaches are littered. If buildings are left vacant, they sometimes are vandalized to the point where they must be razed. Criminal damage to private property varies considerably and is a constant source of citizen complaint to law enforcement agencies.

Many states and cities have passed laws making parents of minors responsible for damage their child causes. The state of Kansas imposes liability upon the homeowner's insurance company, which gives the owner of damaged property the right to collect damages from the insurance company.[25]

In 1990, one 18-year-old did more than $500,000 damage by graffiti vandalism in Los Angeles. The Los Angeles City Attorney said that it was "the worst case of graffiti vandalism we have seen in Los Angeles . . . or anywhere else in the nation [by a single individual]."

Near Tampa, Florida, three teenagers pulled down more than a dozen traffic stop signs for kicks one night. Other teenagers driving home after bowling were killed when their car drove into an intersection and was hit broadside, killing the occupants. The teenagers who took the stop sign down were convicted of three counts of manslaughter. See the *Milwaukee Journal Sentinel* article "Three Friends Get 15 Years for Fatal Stop-Sign Prank" (June 21, 1997).

Arson

One of the first concerns of a fire investigator is the fire's origin. Fires can be classified by their causes as accidental fires, natural fires (caused without human intervention), arson (fires of incendiary origin), and fires of unknown origin.

Many fires are started accidentally, as when children play with matches or when people are careless with cigarettes, cigars, or pipe ashes. Some fires are of natural origin and occur without human intervention. These fires occur because of spontaneous combustion, defective heating units, faulty electrical appliances or wiring, and the like.

Arson is the deliberate, willful, and malicious burning of a building or personal property by a person. Arson is the easiest of the major crimes to commit, the most difficult to detect, and the hardest to prove in court.

Arson kills an estimated five hundred to one thousand people every year in the United States, in addition to injuring thousands of others. More than a billion dollars in property damages occur every year plus the loss of millions of dollars in jobs and in property taxes to local governments. Arson also causes fire insurance rates to increase significantly, passing the costs of arson on to the general public.

Essential Elements of Arson

All states have enacted statutes that define arson. In general, most statutes require that the state prove the following elements:

- That there was a fire and that some part of the building or personal property was damaged. Some courts require an actual burning of part of the property. In the 1992 case of *State v. Williams*, 600 N.E.2d 962, the Indiana Court of Appeals held that soot and smoke constituted "damage" within the meaning of the Indiana arson statute. Attempted arson or conspiracy to commit arson may also be possible criminal charges.[26]

- That the fire was of incendiary origin and was willfully and intentionally set. This is the required proof of corpus delicti (that a crime was in fact committed). For a fire inspector to testify in court that he or she "suspected" arson or that the fire was of "unknown origin" is insufficient to prove corpus delicti.[27] An expert witness is usually required to testify specifically that arson did occur. The witness must then be able to support his or her statement with specific evidence.

- That the accused committed or was party to the crime of arson charged. Like all other crimes, the evidence required to convict a person of arson is proof beyond a reasonable doubt.

Trespass

In its broad sense, the word *"trespass"* means an unlawful act against a person, property, or right of another. For example, court decisions today continue to speak of the trespassory taking of property, meaning that the property was wrongfully taken. Murder, assault, and battery are trespassory acts because they are wrongful and unlawful acts that violate the rights of other people.

However, in its usual and more common use, trespass refers to a wrongful intrusion on the land or into the premises of another person. All states have statutes that reflect this usual and common concept of the offense, and when newspapers use the word, they are usually using it in this limited sense.

A variety of trespass statutes can be found in criminal codes and municipal ordinances. The trespass to land statutes make the unlawful entry on land (when the land has been posted or the person notified to stay off) a criminal offense if the entry or the remaining on the land is without the consent of the owner or the person in lawful

Arsons Receiving National Attention

Devil's Night in Detroit

On an average day in Detroit, Michigan, sixty fires are reported in the city. An arson spree began in the early 1980s during the Halloween period. The worst year was 1984, when 816 fires were reported during the last three days of October. Public awareness, community programs, action by public officials, and over 33,000 volunteers who patrolled the city streets for three nights cut the number of fires to less than 150 for the three nights. A curfew forbidding anyone under 18 from being outside after dark without a parent or guardian was also ordered.[a]

Burning of black southern churches

During 1995–96, more than seventy fires of suspicious origins burned black churches in the South. Congress enacted a new federal law to combat the burning of black churches, and two men were convicted under this law in 1997 when one of the men admitted to informants that he started the fire as a racial act. The *New York Times* article "New Law on Church Arson Leads to 2 Convictions" (June 5, 1997) states that about the same number of fires also struck white churches in the South during this same period.

The biggest arson investigation

For three days after the first Rodney King verdicts in Los Angeles, arsonists turned the city into a series of fires that caused extensive damages. Federal, state, and city officials launched the biggest arson investigation ever organized. Aided by statements of witnesses, photographs and videos taken, and other evidence, more than sixty-five suspects were charged in 1992.

Nightclub arsons

Arson or accidental fires of nightclubs often result in many deaths and injuries. In 1990, a man deliberately torched the Happy Land nightclub in New York City, which resulted in eighty-seven deaths and many injuries. A petty grievance was the reason given for setting the fire.

Burning out a neighborhood drug house

When neighbors find that a neighborhood house is being used to sell drugs, they sometimes burn the drug house if the problem is not eliminated lawfully. Two men were acquitted by a Detroit jury for burning what they believed to be a drug house. See the *New York Times* article "2 in Detroit Acquitted of Arson in Fires at House Tied to Drug Deals," (October 7, 1988).

[a]Other forms of "wilding" also increase on Halloween night. Some wilding results in property damage. Unfortunately, some result in injury and even death. In New York City, young men in Halloween masks waving knives, bats, lead pipes, and a cleaver attacked groups of homeless people while yelling "Trick or treat." Nine homeless men were beaten and cut, and one was killed. Five young men were arrested and charged in the Halloween rampage against the homeless people.

possession. Trespass to dwelling statutes and ordinances forbid the entry into homes and residences unless it is with the consent of an occupant.

Other trespass statutes and ordinances forbid entry into specific places, such as schools with classes in session, unless the person has legitimate business or is a parent. Trespass statutes generally have a section dealing with entry and also a section pertaining to "failure to depart." (Also see trespass cases and material in Chapter 11.)

The Crime of Defiant Trespass

In the case of *Commonwealth v. Groft,* 623 A.2d 341 (Pa.Super. 1993), the defendant (a 56-year-old man) refused to leave the home of his mother after repeatedly being told to find another place to live. He was convicted of *defiant trespass*, which the court described as follows:

> The crime of defiant trespass occurs when a person remains in a place where he is not privileged to remain after notice of trespass is given. . . . The offense is defined by statute as follows:
>
> (b) Defiant trespasser.—
>   (1) A person commits an offense if, knowing that he is not licensed or privileged to do so, he enters or remains in any place as to which notice against trespass is given by:
>   (i) actual communication to the actor; or
>   (ii) posting in a manner prescribed by law or reasonably likely to come to the attention of intruders; or
>   (iii) fencing or other enclosure manifestly designed to exclude intruders.
>   (2) An offense under this subsection constitutes a misdemeanor of the third degree if the offender defies an order to leave personally communicated to him by the owner of the premises or other authorized person. Otherwise it is a summary offense. 18 Pa.C.S. § 3503(b).

New Jersey has a similar statute. *See State v. Morse,* 647 A.2d 495 (N.J.Super. 1994).

Product Tampering

Since 1982, product tampering has cost the lives of twelve people in the United States. The offense of poisoning over-the-counter drugs and food products was described by a high-ranking federal official as "an insidious and terrible crime. It is a form of terrorism not unlike planting a bomb in some public place to gain media attention, notoriety, or some sick sense of control over human life."

During a one-year period in 1986, the federal Food and Drug Administration (FDA)was involved in nearly seventeen hundred cases of actual tampering or hoaxes. The FBI investigated more than three hundred of these incidents. Although it is rare that a product is actually contaminated or poisoned, crimes related to product tampering include the following:

- *Extortion:* After seven people died in the Chicago area in 1982 from cyanide-laced Extra-Strength Tylenol, James Lewis tried to use the killings in attempting to extort $1 million from the manufacturer of Tylenol. Lewis was convicted in a federal court in 1983.

- *Threats to tamper and/or threats to allege tampering:* Another form of extortion that attempts to obtain money from manufacturers, who incur huge costs and loss of market and sales in tampering cases.

- *Attempts to create the basis of a civil lawsuit:* A person fakes a tampering case to make it appear that a person in a family has been the victim of random tampering.

- *Covering up a murder by attempting to make it appear that the victim was killed by random tampering:* A Seattle woman was convicted in 1988 under the 1984 Federal Consumer Tampering Act. She laced Excedrin capsules with cyanide to kill her husband and collect $176,000 in life insurance. Then she planted other cyanide-laced Excedrin capsules in stores to make it appear that her husband was the victim of a random killer. Unfortunately, an innocent victim also died from the poison. The Seattle woman was convicted of two counts of homicide under the Consumer Tampering Act and three other counts of placing cyanide in three other Excedrin bottles.

Product tampering cases that have received national attention include the following:

- In 1982, cyanide was placed in Extra-Strength Tylenol in Chicago; seven people were killed.

- In 1986, cyanide was placed in Extra-Strength Tylenol in Yonkers; one person was killed.

- In 1986, rat poison was placed in Contac in Orlando or Houston; no deaths resulted.

- In 1986, cyanide was placed in Extra-Strength Excedrin in Washington state; the wife of one of two victims was convicted.

- In 1991, cyanide was placed in Sudafed in Washington state; two people were killed.

- In 1993, in the Pepsi tampering scare, the FDA reported that thirty-nine "storytellers" in twenty states were arrested for lying that a consumer product had been tampered with. The FDA reported that none of the reports of syringes in soft drink cans turned out to be authentic.

- The Federal Consumer Tampering Act, 18 U.S.C.A. Section 1365, also forbids tampering that reduces the efficacy of a drug designed to save a life or alleviate bodily injury, as well as tampering that turns a drug into a poison. In *United States v. Cunningham,* 103 F.3d 553 (7th Cir. 1997), a nurse was convicted of tampering when she used the painkiller Demerol belonging to a hospital allegedly to feed her addiction and substituted a harmless liquid without informing anyone.

The crime of consumer product tampering receives a great deal of attention and concern because all societies are vulnerable to such acts. Millions of dollars have been invested in tamper-proof packaging. Most consumers are well aware of the remote problem that the product they purchase may have been tampered with in a way that could seriously hurt them or someone in their family. It is hoped that product tampering will diminish as a crime, just as aircraft hijacking did in the middle and late 1970s.

Federal statutes and the laws of most (if not all) states also make the following conduct criminal:

- Tampering (altering) or destroying evidence of a crime
- Tampering (altering) a financial document such as a check, or a document such as a will or a mortgage
- Tampering (altering) an odometer of a motor vehicle that is to be sold to another person
- Tampering with a witness or a potential witness by telling the witness what to say or what not to say

SUMMARY

Criminal fraud can take as many forms as criminals have imaginations. These crimes generally involve intentional acts or misrepresentations that trick the victim to part with money, goods, or services. States and the federal government have a variety of criminal statutes available to prosecute fraudulent activity. The federal mail fraud and wire fraud laws provide a way for the federal government to pursue criminals in this area, because many times the criminals use the mails or communication devices over which the federal government exercises control and jurisdiction.

The Internet has proven to be a location where fraudulent activity is made possible. Internet securities fraud has increased substantially in the past few years, and prosecutions under federal securities laws have also increased. In these prosecutions, the prosecution must not only prove that false Internet information caused a victim to lose money, but it must also show that the defendant's actions were intended to cause that loss or his or her own gain.

Receiving stolen property is a crime that includes various acts such as possessing, buying, or selling stolen property. To be convicted of the crime, the person must know the property was stolen. Possession of burglary tools is itself a crime if the person in possession intended to use the tools to break into a building with the intent to steal.

 ## BOOK-SPECIFIC WEB SITE

For chapter-related Web links, quizzing activities, and case and news updates, go to the *Criminal Law,* Eighth Edition, book-specific Web site at **http://info.wadsworth.com/ gardner.**

QUESTIONS AND PROBLEMS

1. A nationally known football player was approached by a man who stated that he was a great fan of the player. The man said that he wanted to show his appreciation, and offered to sell the player an expensive automobile with only a few thousand miles at less than one-fourth the retail price. The player agreed;

the vehicle was delivered; cash was paid for the vehicle. The player was told that he would receive the title to the car in a short time through the mail, but he never received the title. The vehicle was determined to be stolen, and the true owner demanded that the vehicle be returned to him. May the owner recover the vehicle? Has the football player committed a criminal offense? How would this matter be settled?

2. A burglar apprehended in the act with burglarized goods fears a long prison sentence. He agrees to cooperate, and the stolen goods are returned to him. The burglar sells the goods to his regular fence. The fence is arrested and charged with receiving stolen goods. Are the arrest and the charge of receiving stolen property valid? Would it stand up in court? State your reasons.

3. In the state of Washington, defendant Clark was given permission to use Dennis Noll's car to run some errands and return at noon. Instead, he drove the car to Colorado, hundreds of miles away.
   a) If Clark were apprehended days later driving Noll's car, what would Clark likely be charged with in your state?
   b) If Clark abandoned Noll's car in Colorado after his trip, what would he likely be charged with in your state? Explain. *State v. Clark,* 96 Wash.2d 686, 638 P.2d 572 (1982).

INFOTRAC COLLEGE EDITION EXERCISES

1. Go to InfoTrac College Edition and, using the subject search term *Enron Corporation*, find an article discussing the possibility of criminal charges against Enron or its accountant, Arthur Andersen LLP. What new information, if any, makes such prosecutions more or less likely?

2. Go to InfoTrac College Edition and, using the subject search term *insurance fraud, subdivision prevention*, find an article on how states and insurance companies are fighting that fraud. Do you think those efforts will make a dent in the problem?

3. Go to InfoTrac College Edition and, using the subject search term *Internet securities fraud*, find an article discussing a criminal prosecution of a perpetrator of a "pump and dump" or "cyber smear" scheme. The Internet defendants generally contend that the securities laws were not intended to apply to their activities. Are they having any success with those arguments?

NOTES

1. Twenty-five of the one hundred Pentagon contractors have been found guilty of fraud. Boeing, Grumman, and Teledyne made payoffs to obtain confidential Pentagon documents. Contractors who overcharged the government were Rockwell, GTE, General Electric (Matsco Division), and Emerson Electric. Fairchild Industries and Northrop falsified test results or failed to test. Harris Corporation was convicted of contract kickbacks.

The federal False Claims Act was passed during the Civil War to prevent war profiteering by military suppliers. The "whistle-blower" section of the False Claims Act rewards people who report fraud on the federal government with 15 percent of the amount of money recovered. The Internal Revenue Service has a similar reward provision for people who report federal tax fraud.

2. Investigating fraud in Medicaid and Medicare programs is discussed in two *FBI Law Enforcement Bulletins*: "Medicaid Fraud Control" (October 1992) and "Health Care Fraud" (October 1992).

See the *New York Times* editorial "Fraud and Waste in Medicare" (August 1, 1997) and other news articles reporting that federal auditors estimated $23 billion in fraud and mistake loss in Medicare payments in 1996. These losses fell into the following categories: (1) "raw fraud," which for the most part was services not provided; (2) a gray area requiring the exercise of judgment; and (3) the antikickback provision forbidding payment for referrals.

3. See the *New York Times* article "Agents Uncover Rampant Food Stamp Fraud" (September 11, 1994), which estimates that in a $24 billion program, $2 billion is used for fraudulent purposes.

4. See the *New York Times* articles "Living Lavishly, Getting Welfare Checks: (While He Lived in the) Trump Tower" (October 7, 1994) and "Officials Say Woman Used 15 Aliases in Welfare Fraud" (May 20, 1994).

5. *Health Care Fraud,* 38 American Criminal Law Review 913 (2001).

6. *Id.*

7. 42 U.S.C. 1320(a)–7(b).

8. 55 *Medicine and Health,* i. 36, p. 2 (2001). TAP illegally enticed doctors to prescribe its prostate cancer drug over a competitor's drug by selling its drug for one price to the doctor but telling Medicaid and Medicare that the price was higher, permitting the doctors to be reimbursed from the Medicare and Medicaid programs at the higher price.

9. Bait and switch schemes usually consist of an attractive bargain that is offered at an eye-catching low price. The bargain is the "bait" to lure customers into the store. The "switch" to get the customer to buy a higher-priced item is done by knocking the quality of the advertised item or stating that it has been sold out or that it is not available on the premises.

10. Religious and charitable scandals of the 1990s included the following:
- The president of United Way and two employees were convicted of the theft of $1 million from the fund. See the *New York Times* article "United Way's Ex-Chief Indicted in Theft" (September 14, 1994).
- Evangelical television ministers received national attention in a series of scandals. Jim Bakker of the PTL Network was convicted after a six-week trial of defrauding his followers out of $159 million. He offered promises of lifetime vacations that he could not provide and used $3.7 million for his opulent lifestyle, which included a fleet of Rolls Royces and an air-conditioned doghouse.
- Promising to double your money with contributions from anonymous donors, officials from the

Foundation for New Era Philanthropy cheated charitable and nonprofit groups out of at least $115 million. The president of the Philadelphia foundation, John G. Bennett, received a sentence of twelve years in prison for the biggest charity fraud in U.S. history. Victims were major charity organizations, Ivy League universities, museums, and colleges. See the *Milwaukee Journal Sentinel* article, "Founder of Defunct Charity Sentenced to 12 Years in Prison" (September 23, 1997).

11. See the *New York Times* article "Allstate Acts to End Auto Accident Fraud: Company Sues Los Angeles Doctors and Lawyers for $107 Million" (February 22, 1998). Also see the *FBI Law Enforcement Bulletin* article "Automobile Insurance Fraud Pays . . . and Pays Well" (March 1986). The article tells of the largest auto insurance fraud in the history of New York state, which was broken up in the mid-1980s.

12. 165 New Jersey Law J. 1 (2001).

13. 650 A.2d 876 (Pa. Sup. Ct. 1995).

14. The *pyramid scheme,* or the *Ponzi swindle,* has a long history in the United States. Immigrants are particularly vulnerable to the swindle because crooks within their own group gain their confidence and cheat them.

Carlo Ponzi engineered one of the first great frauds in the early 1920s in Boston. Ponzi took advantage of his fellow Italians, including family members and his parish priest. He then reached beyond Italian immigrants to defraud more than twenty thousand people of more than $10 million before his scheme collapsed. Ponzi fled to Brazil, where he died a pauper. See the *New York Times* article "Immigrants Swindle Their Own, Preying on Trust" (August 25, 1992), telling of the problems of modern immigrants who are cheated by people within their groups.

15. See the *New York Times* article "Four at Syracuse Financial Firm Indicted in Pyramid Scheme" (June 27, 1997).

16. See the *New York Times* article "In a Poor Land, a Classic Swindle Leaves Rage and Emptier Pockets" (February 1, 1997).

17. An FBI sting operation in 1996 led to the arrest of forty-six brokers, promoters, and executives in New York City. See the *New York Times* article "46 Charged in Stock Fraud Sting by F.B.I." (October 11, 1996).

Also see the 1981 case of *Carpenter v. United States,* 484 U.S. 19, 108 S.Ct. 316. Mr. Winans was a former reporter for the *Wall Street Journal* and wrote a column on stocks in that paper. Winans and others were convicted of profiting by trading on advance knowledge of stocks that were going to be touted (praised) and stocks to be downgraded in future columns. This enabled the insiders to take advantage of the predictable impact on the prices of these stocks.

18. 38 American Criminal Law Review 405 (2001).

19. *Id.*

20. *Id.*

21. See also the U.S. Supreme Court case of *Schmuck v. United States,* 489 U.S. 705, 109 S.Ct. 1443 (1989).

22. Many states and cities require pawn brokers to register and comply with requirements seeking to limit and prevent pawn brokers from dealing in stolen goods. Following is the Indiana Loan Broker Act. (See 602 N.E.2d at 1066.)

IC 23-2-5-4 (1988) requires that "[a]ny person desiring to engage or continue in business of loan brokering shall apply to the commissioner for registration under this chapter," while IC 23-2-5-16 (1988) provides, "[a] person who knowingly violates this chapter commits a Class D felony." Thus, a violation of the Act consists of "(1) knowingly, (2) engaging or continuing in the business of loan brokering, (3) without having registered with the securities commissioner." *Flinn v. State* (1990), Ind.,

563 N.E.2d 536, 541. Finally, a loan broker is "any person who, in return for any consideration from any person, promises to procure a loan for any person or assists any person in procuring a loan from any third party, or who promises to consider whether or not to make a loan to any person." IC 23-2-5-3(a) (1988).

23. The English refer to this offense as "Going Equipped for Stealing." See J. W. Williams's *Moriarty's Police Law,* 21st ed. (London: Butterworths, 1972).

24. See 33 A.L.R.3d 798 (1970).

25. See *Catholic Diocese of Dodge City v. Farmers Insurance Co.,* 825 P.2d 1144 (Kan.App. 1992), in which the property damage was more than $18,000.

26. If the completed crime of arson cannot be proved beyond a reasonable doubt, the state may then consider charging attempt to commit arson (or in an appropriate situation, conspiracy to commit arson).

27. See *Hughes v. State,* 6 Md.App. 389, 251 A.2d 373 (1969), in which the Court pointed out that mere presence of the accused at the scene of a fire is not proof beyond reasonable doubt that the fire was willfully and maliciously set. In *Hughes v. State,* a fire chief testified that he could not determine the cause of the fire. The Court reversed the defendant's conviction, holding that the evidence was legally insufficient to establish the corpus delicti of the crime of arson.

18

Rape and Related Sex Crimes

CONTENTS

KEY TERMS

rape

sexual assault

corroborative evidence

after-the-date rape

report of rape rule

false reporting

rape shield laws

homosexual rape

statutory rape

incest

sex predator laws

registration laws
for sex offenders

Sexual relations (nonmarital) become a crime in the United States if

- there is a lack of consent,
- they are with a minor incapable of legally consenting,
- they are with a mentally deficient person or an adult incapable of consenting,
- they are performed in public,
- they are performed for profit (prostitution),
- they are between a therapist and a patient and in violation of the laws of that state.

Sex crimes occur often in the United States. The term "sex crime" includes a broad classification of offenses that range from serious offenses to nuisance offenses and private offenses between consenting adults.

The enforcement and definition of the more serious offenses are generally uniform throughout the United States, but the enforcement of lesser offenses varies considerably from state to state and somewhat from community to community within each state. To illustrate the wide range of sexual offenses, the following classifications are used:

1. Sexually motivated crimes in which violence is used or threatened:
   - Murders of lust or sexual perversion
   - Forcible, violent rapes
   - Sadistically motivated offenses, in which sexual excitement is derived from inflicting pain or injury on other people
   - Kidnapping or abduction when violence is threatened or used
   - Forceful and violent sexual attacks on children
   - Pedophilia (committed by mentally ill people who lust for children, are capable of kidnapping them, and, after using them sexually, are capable of killing them)
   - Forcible sodomy or forcible fondling
   - Pyromania (a persistent impulse to set fires, in many cases accompanied by a desire to derive sexual excitement from watching a building burn)

2. Offenses against children and mentally defective or deficient adults, in which violence is not used or threatened:
   - Statutory rape or sexual intercourse with a child
   - Sexual intercourse with a person known to be mentally deficient or defective
   - Abduction or "enticement" when force is not used or threatened
   - Incest in which force or threat of force is not used but the victim is not legally capable of consenting to act
   - Child pornography (exploitation and exhibition of children for financial and sexual purposes)

3. Offenses that violate the right of privacy:
   - Offensive touching of the person of another
   - Window peeping (form of voyeurism)

4. Commercial offenses that are profit oriented:
   - Prostitution (male and female)
   - Pimping and pandering
   - Sexual perversion
   - Sale or possession of child pornography or other obscene material or presentation of obscene acts or films
5. Offenses that are not physically dangerous but are against public policy:
   - Forms of voyeurism
   - Public nudity forbidden by a specific statute or ordinance
   - Sexual acts in public places
   - Public nudity such as:
     - College and fraternal-type "streaking"
     - "Mooning" (displaying the derriere from such places as a moving vehicle)
     - Nonhumorous exposure to women and children ("flashing")
   - Obscenity not done for profit
   - Nuisances and other public indecencies
6. Private offenses between consenting adults (in states that have such statutes):
   - Fornication
   - Seduction
   - Adultery
   - Bigamy
   - Incest (sexual intercourse between people related within the degree in which marriage is prohibited)

Forcible Rape of Women and Girls

Rape is one of the most underreported crimes. The crime is one of degradation as well as violence, and fear of reprisal and embarrassment contributes to the victim's hesitation to report it. Those who do report it must confront the trauma of the encounter with the police, the investigation of the crime, and the ordeal of trial.[1]

Many reasons are given for not reporting rape. If the victim knows her assailant (which is often the case in a nonreported rape), she may not report the crime because of fear of retaliation or because she does not want to get the man in trouble. The *after-the-date rape* victim may have the same feelings. The rape victim who has never seen her assailant before may believe that the police will not be able to solve the crime and therefore conclude that the trouble and embarrassment of reporting the crime would be useless. Other women may either distrust the police or dislike the prospect of having to relate their shocking experiences to male police officers. Many law enforcement agencies now have female officers available for women who find it easier to tell such matters to another woman.

Capacity to Commit Forcible Rape

Vaginal rape is the most common form of rape, with women and girls being the victims not only to rape, but also to **sexual assaults** and batteries. Women of any age or status may be the victims of rape, including prostitutes.[2]

In one-third of all sexual assaults reported to law enforcement agencies, the victim was younger than age 12. Females were more than six times as likely as males to be the victims of reported sexual assaults, including forcible fondling. The U.S. Department of Justice July 2000 report (#182990) states that 54 percent of the victims of forcible sodomy were minor males.

Under the common law, a husband could not rape his wife. A husband could be charged with assault or battery if he used considerable force to compel his wife to have sexual intercourse with him against her will. All states have changed this common law concept, which was called the "common-law marital exemption" to the crime of rape.[3]

Today, a husband can be charged as a party to the crime of rape, either as a principal or as an aider and abettor, if he assisted, hired, encouraged, or procured another man to rape his wife. Although only rarely does one woman rape another woman, a few appellate cases concern a woman who was convicted as a party to the crime of the rape of another woman after it was proven that the woman hired, encouraged, assisted, or procured a man to rape the victim.[4]

In the 1981 case of *State v. Thomas,* the defendant was found guilty of two counts of first-degree criminal sexual conduct when he forced a woman, at gunpoint, to perform fellatio on her husband.[5] The defendant then forced the woman to perform fellatio on himself. The Supreme Court of Tennessee affirmed the two convictions, holding that a "defendant who forces an innocent party to commit armed robbery, burglary, rape, incest, etc. is guilty as the only principal, even though the defendant does not commit the crime with his own hand." (See Chapter 4 on criminal liability.)

The Burden of Proof in a Sexual Assault or Rape Case

In all criminal cases, the state has the burden of proving all essential elements of the crime beyond reasonable doubt. In a sexual assault or rape case, the state must prove beyond reasonable doubt that

- The crime of sexual assault (or rape) did occur (proof of corpus delicti). If both adults consented to a sex act, then the crime of rape did not occur.

- The defendant was the person who committed the crime. When the offender is a stranger, identification often becomes a critical issue because of recall problems, lookalike problems, and the excitement and trauma of the situation.

- The sex act was done "without consent" and "against the will" (as defined by many states) or in states following the wording of Section 213.1 of the Model Penal Code, when "he compels her to submit by force or by threat of imminent death, serious bodily injury, extreme pain or kidnapping."

The Importance of Corroborative Evidence in a Rape Case

A rape conviction could rest solely on the uncorroborated testimony of the victim.[6] However, *corroborative evidence* (evidence affirming and supporting statements of the victim) is very important in most cases.

Statistics show that in as many as 30 percent to 40 percent of the cases that come into the offices of prosecutors in large cities, rape charges are not issued. Lack of corroborating evidence is probably the principal reason. Statements of the complaining witness can be corroborated and affirmed by the following:

- Scratches, bruises, injuries, torn clothing, or blood stains from either the victim or the suspect

- Witnesses who heard screams or the sounds of a struggle, or observed either party before, during, or immediately after the assault

- Color photographs of bruises, black and blue marks, lacerations, cuts, scratches, or other injuries to either party, as these injuries will disappear within a few days through the healing process

- Blood, semen, saliva, or nail scrapings taken from the victim or suspect, as well as pubic and head hair obtained at the scene of the crime and from the bodies of the victim and suspect. Such genetic material could result in a positive DNA identification of the offender.

- Weapons or instruments that may have been used to force the victim to submit to the assault

- Buttons, torn clothing, or other items that the victim or suspect may have lost in the struggle

- Soiled or stained clothing of the suspect and victim that contains blood, seminal stains, or other evidence of the crime

- Fingerprints found at the scene of the sexual assault or elsewhere that can be used to corroborate or to identify the suspect

- Observations by doctors and nurses and samples of fluids from vagina, rectum, or oral cavity showing that forcible intercourse had occurred

- If DNA evidence from blood, semen, saliva, and so forth is available, it could prove the identity of the offender almost conclusively.

Whether the state has a strong or a weak case in going to trial in a rape case depends on the physical evidence available and the ability of the complaining witness to testify. Lack of corrobative physical evidence and/or the inability of the complaining witness to testify effectively could cause the case to be viewed as weak.

Possible Responses to a Threat of Rape

Studies show that most women, especially young women, fear rape more than any other crime. How should a woman respond to an imminent threat of rape?

Should she scream, fight back, and try to escape?

Studies show that women who resist decrease the odds of completed rape by 80 percent. But they increase the likelihood of being physically injured. Experts say that it is better to be raped than to risk being permanently injured or killed.

Should she try to talk the man out of it?	Women have tried many different tactics in trying to avoid rape. They have pretended to be pregnant, or have stated they have a sexually transmitted disease, or have AIDS. They have fainted, cried hysterically, acted insane or vomited, urinated, or acted very ill.
Should she grit her teeth and bear it?	This is an available option that the victim might choose. Or the victim may be able to combine one or both of the above two in an effort to avoid being raped.

An *FBI Law Enforcement Bulletin* article entitled "RAPE: The Dangers of Providing Confrontational Advice" (June 1986) discussed the question of a woman's response to rape and provided the following advice:

> Different motives operate in different offenders and, therefore, what might be successful in dissuading one type of assailant might, in fact, only aggravate the situation with a different type of offender.
>
> Victims must tailor their type of resistance to the environment in which the attack is occurring.
>
> [T]he success of resistance behavior depends largely on the victim's ability to apply it.
>
> We suggest to those who speak publicly on [this] subject to avoid offering single solutions to their audiences.

Different Sexual Assault Statutes Require Different Degrees of Proof

Sexual assault and rape statutes in the fifty different states are worded in many different ways. Prosecutors must be prepared to prove all the essential elements of the crime that they have charged beyond a reasonable doubt.

In both of the following two cases, the victims knew the defendants. The defendants in both cases used little or no force.

Case and State	Facts of the Case	Wording and Requirement of the State Statute
People v. Iniguez, Supreme Court of California, 872 P.2d 1183 (1994)	While the victim was asleep in the defendant's house, he took her clothes off. She testified that she froze when she woke up and "just laid there" and submitted because she feared he would become violent if she did not submit. The conviction was affirmed.	The wording of the state statute that was charged required a showing that the rape was "accomplished against a person's will by means of force, violence, or fear of immediate and unlawful bodily injury." (no requirement of proof of actual resistance by victim).

(continued)

Case and State	Facts of the Case	Wording and Requirement of the State Statute
Commonwealth v. Berkowitz, Supreme Court of Pennsylvania, 641 A.2d 1161 (1994)	Just repeatedly saying "no" was not enough under this statute. In a college dorm room, the defendant closed the door, placed the victim on the bed, and raped her as she repeatedly said "no." No physical or threatening force was used in removing her clothes and raping her. The victim did not testify that she feared violence if she did not submit.	The rape statute required "forcible compulsion" in achieving sexual intercourse rather than terms of nonconsent. Pennsylvania has an indecent assault crime that has no requirement of forcible compulsion and is defined as indecent contact without consent. This should have been the criminal charge for the facts in this case.

Under "threat of force" and "forcible compulsion" statutes, prosecutors must show that the victim's resistance was overcome by the threat of the use of force, causing the victim to submit to the rape. It must be shown that the victim had a genuine and real fear that imminent force would be used.

The California courts have held that "While generally the woman has the power to determine for herself the extent to which she feels she can safely resist, . . . her conduct must always be measured against the degree of force manifested and each case must be resolved on all of the circumstances present."[7]

The Maryland Court of Appeals pointed out that the "vast majority of jurisdictions have required that the victim's fear be reasonably grounded in order to obviate the need for either proof of actual force on the part of the assailant or physical resistance on the part of the victim."[8] Pointing out that the reasonableness of a victim's apprehension or fear was plainly a question of fact for a jury to determine, the Maryland Court of Appeals held:[9]

It was for the jury to observe the witnesses and their demeanor, and to judge their credibility and weigh their testimony. Quite obviously, the jury disbelieved Rusk [defendant] and believed Pat's [victim] testimony.

* * *

Just where persuasion ends and force begins in cases like the present is essentially a factual issue, to be resolved in light of the controlling legal precepts. That threats of force need not be made in any particular manner in order to put a person in fear of bodily harm is well established. . . . Indeed, conduct, rather than words, may convey the threat.

* * *

That a victim did not scream out for help or attempt to escape, while bearing on the question of consent, is unnecessary where she is restrained by fear of violence.

Defenses in Acquaintance Rape or After-the-Date Rape

More than one-half of the forcible rapes that are reported are committed by friends, acquaintances, or relatives. The after-the-date rape (or dates who rape) case can be particularly difficult to prove unless evidence of actual physical violence exists. Because of the friendly and sometimes close relationship that existed between the parties, defendants could use the following arguments in court:

Yes, the parties had sex, but

She consented	and her conduct shows she consented (after all, she invited me up to her apartment, or she came up to my apartment late at night).
I honestly thought she consented	"It is a defense to a charge of forcible rape that the defendant entertained a reasonable and good faith belief that the female person voluntarily consented to engage in sexual intercourse" (California Jury Instruction 10.23).[10]
She never did say "no"	and I thought that because she didn't say "no," she was consenting.
She consented, then changed her mind during the sex	and did not clearly communicate her change of mind.
The manner in which the woman dressed was sexy and provocative and her conduct (such as placing her hand on the defendant's upper thigh)	led the defendant on, and she did not object until things got out of hand (a well-known professional football player was acquitted in a 1987 rape trial using this defense).
She consented, but later developed guilt feelings and regretted what she did	but before and during the sex, she consented. (This defense is sometimes used with the "groupie defense." Athletes and performers charged with rape often use this defense, arguing that the victim pursued and pestered them.)

Convictions for Lesser or Other Offenses in Weak Rape Cases

A rape case can be classified as a "weak" case if there is a lack of corroborating evidence, if the woman is an ineffective witness or becomes so upset that she cannot testify effectively, or if the woman's conduct had been such that it could be interpreted as giving consent to the sex. Other factors that should also be considered are the effectiveness and persuasive abilities of the defense lawyer and the type of witness that the defendant might be.

In anticipating such problems, prosecutors could file a number of charges, including lesser charges to fall back on. Examples of such charges are as follows:

- *Sexual battery or sexual assault.* For example, see the case of *People v. Margiolas*, in which the rape charge was dropped because of lack of evidence of resistance, and the defendant was convicted of a misdemeanor "sexual battery," because he admitted that he forcibly unbuttoned the woman's blouse despite her verbal as well as physical objections.[11]

- *Statutory rape, when the victim is underage.* In the case of *Michael M. v. Superior Court of Sonoma County* (*California*), a forcible rape of a 16½-year-old girl was committed by the defendant, who was then 17½ years old.[12] Because the state was unable to present proof sufficient to obtain a conviction for forcible rape, the defendant was charged with and convicted of statutory rape. The U.S. Supreme Court affirmed the conviction. The California prosecutor stated in his brief that the statutory rape statute "is commonly employed in situations involving force, prostitution, pornography, coercion due to status relationships, and the state's interest in these situations is apparent."

- *Burglary.* As an unlawful entry into a building or dwelling with intent to commit an offense (in some states a felony) or intent to steal, burglary convictions were sustained in the following cases in which the male defendants had no right to enter the premises of the women: *State v. Felt*, 816 P.2d 1213 (Ore.App. 1991), in which a former lover had forced intercourse after a date; *State v. Weber*, 814 S.W.2d 298 (Mo.App. 1991), in which the defendant kicked in the door and entered the victim's home for the purposes of committing rape; and in *Cladd v. State*, 398 So.2d 442 (1981), the Supreme Court of Florida sustained the conviction of burglary when the separated husband broke into the wife's home twice, severely beating the wife on the first break-in.

The Report of Rape Rule and the Effect of Delay in Reporting

After a sexual assault, the victim could be confused and fearful of her assailant. This could result in a delay in reporting the crime. A long delay could raise questions of the credibility of the victim, it could substantially diminish the possibility of obtaining physical evidence of the rape, and it could prevent the person receiving the report of rape from testifying as to the statements and circumstances.

A person to whom a rape victim has excitedly reported a rape can testify as to the statements and circumstances under the "report of rape" or excited utterance exceptions to the hearsay rule.[13] Such testimony is important corroborative evidence in proving a rape charge.

Because a child may delay for some time in reporting a sexual assault, state statutes and court decisions give children more time in reporting sexual assaults. In the 1993 case of *Battle v. United States*, 630 A.2d 211 (D.C.Ct.App. 1993), a 14-year-old girl did not report the sodomy (oral sex) for approximately six weeks. However, the Court allowed the testimony of a police officer and the child's aunt as to the report of rape. In the *Battle* case, the girl was living with her mother and the mother's live-in boyfriend (Battle). The girl testified that Battle threatened her with further violence if she told anyone of the incident.

The Serial Rapist

Every large U.S. city has had the problem of the serial rapist, who rapes over and over, most often using the same modus operandi. Research of the behavior of serial rapists before, during, and following the commission of the crimes show that

- The majority of serial rapes were premeditated.
- The "con" approach was used most often in initiating contact with the victim.
- A threatening presence and verbal threats were used to maintain control over the victim.
- Minimal or no force was used in the majority of instances.
- The victims physically, passively, or verbally resisted the rapists in slightly over 50 percent of the offenses.
- The most common offender reaction to resistance was to verbally threaten the victim.
- Slightly more than one-third of the offenders experienced a sexual dysfunction, and the preferred sexual acts were vaginal rape and forced fellatio.
- Low levels of pleasure were reported by the rapists from the sexual acts.
- The rapists tended not to be concerned with precautionary measures to protect their identities.
- Approximately one-third of the rapists had consumed alcohol prior to the crime, and slightly less reported using some other drug.
- The most common postoffense behaviors reported by the rapists were feelings of remorse and guilt, following the case in the media, and an increase in alcohol and drug consumption.
- Criminal sexual sadists are often serial rapists. Sexual sadism is described as "a persistent pattern of becoming sexually excited in response to another's suffering. . . . [T]o the sexual sadistic offender, it is the suffering of the victim that is sexually arousing." *FBI Law Enforcement Bulletin* (February 1992).
- "While the above characteristics may not apply to every rapist, they can be helpful in learning more about offenders, their behavior, and the heinous crime of rape." *FBI Law Enforcement Bulletin* (February 1990).

False Reporting

The *FBI Uniform Crime Reports* state that "a national average of 15% of all forcible rapes reported to police were determined by our investigations to be unfounded. In other words, the police established that no forcible rape offense or attempt occurred."

Note, however, that sexual assault is not the only offense subject to *false reporting*. About the same percentage of burglaries and auto thefts are also falsely reported primarily for the purpose of obtaining insurance money. Armed robberies of single-employee businesses are sometimes falsely reported to the financial benefit of that employee, and one can only speculate about the number of homes, businesses, and other buildings that are destroyed in "accidental" fires.

Rape Shield Laws

Most states have enacted **rape shield laws** forbidding the use of evidence of a rape victim's past sexual conduct with others and evidence of her reputation. Under the protection of rape shield laws, women appearing as witnesses in a sexual assault case therefore do not have to defend their reputations or past sexual conduct.

Before rape shield laws, a victim's reputation was deemed "fair game" by defense lawyers, and the victim could be forced to defend her entire sexual history. Rape shield laws were enacted to encourage the reporting of sexual assaults and to forbid evidence that would prejudice a jury. Such evidence is also irrelevant to the issue of guilt or innocence before the court.

However, exceptions are made in rape shield laws to allow the introduction of relevant, probative evidence at trial. In the U.S. Supreme Court case of *Olden v. Kentucky*, 488 U.S. 227, 109 S.Ct. 480 (1988), the defendant sought to prove that the victim made up her charge of sexual battery against him in order to protect her relationship with her boyfriend. The U.S. Supreme Court reversed the defendant's conviction, holding that his Sixth Amendment right to conduct reasonable cross-examination had been violated.

In the case of *Miller v. State*, 779 P.2d 87 (1989), the Supreme Court of Nevada pointed out that prior fabrication of an accusation of rape is also relevant evidence.

Homosexual Rape

Males may be raped by forcible anal sodomy and other forms of *homosexual rape*. Such offenses are not as common as rape of women except, as reports indicate, within prisons. The extent of this problem in U.S. prisons is unknown, because the thousands of jails and prisons have more than one million inmates. Victims of such crimes, whether they are male or female, have remedies in both civil and criminal courts.

The 1990 civil lawsuit of *Redman v. County of San Diego*, 896 F.2d 362 (9th Cir. 1990), was filed because Redman was raped in a San Diego jail. Redman was an 18-year-old detainee awaiting trial when he was transferred from a "young and tender" jail cell to a unit with a homosexual, where the rape occurred.

The defendant in the case of *Boone v. United States*[14] testified that he used a razor blade in self-defense because he feared that the complainant was going to forcibly commit anal sodomy on him. Because the trial judge did not believe the defendant and concluded that the issue was weak, he did not give a jury instruction on self-defense. The Court of Appeals reversed, holding that this issue should have gone to the jury. Pointing out that a woman who had alleged such facts after cutting up another person would be entitled to instructions on self-defense, the Court held that the results should be the same "unless we are to make sexist differences."

Statutory Rape

All states have statutes that make sexual intercourse with a female who is not the wife of the perpetrator a criminal offense if the female is under the age stated by the state criminal code. This crime is called **statutory rape.** The origin of current U.S. statutes goes

Old Rape Laws and New Sexual Assault Laws

Under Old Rape Laws And The Common Law

- Only females could be the victims of rape.

- Only a male could directly commit the crime.

- A husband could not rape his wife (under the common law, however, the husband could be charged with assault and battery).

- Rape was defined in one (or at most a few) degree.

- Rape was defined only as the insertion of the penis into a vagina by force and against the will of the female.

- Common law rape did not include the crime of offensive touching (however, this could be charged either as disorderly conduct or assault and sometimes battery).

- "Utmost resistance" and resistance were required under the old common law.

- Rape was classified as a crime against sexual morality.

Statutory Changes Enacted In Most States During The Last Thirty Years

- Any person (male or female) may be a victim.

- Any person (male or female) can directly commit the crime. (See the 1986 case of *State v. Stevens,* 510 A.2d 1070 (Me.), in which the Court held that an adult woman could be charged with having sexual intercourse with a 13-year-old boy.)

- A husband can be charged with the rape of his wife under the law of states that have made this change from the common law.

- A variety of degrees of criminal conduct are defined in more specific language.

- "Sexual intercourse" is broadly defined not only as vaginal intercourse, but also "cunnilingus, fellatio, anal intercourse, or any other intrusion, however slight, of any part of a person's body or of any object into the genital or anal opening of another, but emission of semen is not required." Section 940.225(5)(c) of the Wisconsin Criminal Code

- Many modern sexual assault laws include the offense of offensive touching in that they forbid "sexual contact" (intentional touching of an intimate part of another person's body without consent for sexual gratification).

- "Utmost resistance" is no longer required for the crime of rape. Instead, many states require proof that the sex act was done "without consent" and "against the will" of the victim.

- Sexual assault is more often classified as a crime against a person.

back to the English statute of 1275, when the age of consent was set at 12 years. In 1576, the age was reduced to 10 years. California, for example, enacted its first statute in 1850 making the age 10. In 1913, it was fixed at 18, where it remains.

In 1981, the California statutory rape statute was challenged before the U.S. Supreme Court, when it was alleged that the statute unlawfully discriminates on the basis of gender, because men alone were criminally liable under the statute. The Court upheld the power of the states to enact such statutes in the case of *Michael M. v. Superior Court of Sonoma County,* holding:

We are satisfied not only that the prevention of illegitimate pregnancy is at least one of the "purposes" of the statute, but that the State has a strong interest in preventing

Types of Rapes or Sexual Assaults

Type Of Rape	Characteristics	Most Common Defense Used
Forcible rape by a stranger	It is reported that about half of the reported forcible rapes occurred between strangers.	Victim or other witnesses have identified the wrong man (mistaken identification).
Forcible rape by an acquaintance, friend, or relative	Many of these offenses are not reported to law enforcement agencies. The after-the-date rape is particularly difficult to prosecute unless substantial evidence is available.	Victim consented to the sexual act.
Nonforcible rape in which the victim is under age of consent	All states have laws that protect infants and children from sexual seduction by adults. Such statutory rape or SIWAC (sexual intercourse with a child) laws punish as a major crime such sexual intercourse (or sexual conduct) when committed with a child.	Sex act did not occur, or the defendant made an honest mistake as to the child's age (not permitted as a defense in most states).
Nonforcible rape in which the victim was mentally defective or diseased and incapable of giving consent	This type of criminal statute seeks to protect people who are mentally incompetent and incapable of giving consent to sexual acts. The offense requires that the state show that the defendant knew of the mental incapacity of the victim.	Defendant denies that he knew of the mental incapacity of the victim or that any sex act occurred.
Nonforcible rape in which the victim is unconscious[a]	Such statutes seek to protect people who are unconscious (the defendant is aware of this condition). Some statutes also forbid sexual intercourse with a person known to be in a stupor. Such stupor could be caused by alcohol or drugs.	Defendant asserts that the person was conscious and consented or that no sex act occurred.
Rape by use of a date rape drug	Rohypnol ("Roofies") and GHB are odorless, nearly tasteless, and potentially lethal to a victim. By slipping one into a drink, they are used to drug and sexually assault women.	The woman has no memory of what happened and most often there are no other available witnesses. With no witnesses, it is important to obtain a urine sample immediately to prove the presence of a date rape drug.
Sexual intercourse obtained by threats other than threats of violence, which would be forcible rape	In the few states that have enacted a statute such as this, the threat might be to disclose information that the victim did not want disclosed. Today, job-related sexual harassment is remedied through civil proceedings or in other ways.	No threat was made or implied, or no sexual act occurred.

[a]Some states also have a sexual battery statute creating the crime of sexual battery of a victim physically helpless to resist. Florida makes this conduct a crime in Sec. 794.011(4) of the Florida Criminal Code. Proof of the use of physical force is not required under the Florida statute. Other states can achieve the same results under existing criminal statutes.

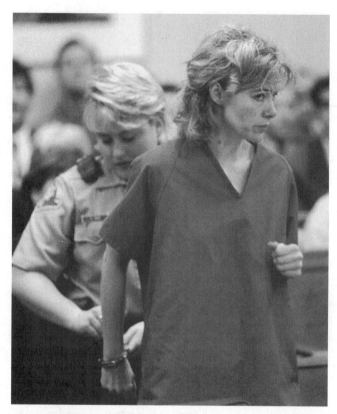

Former grade school teacher Mary Kay LeTourneau has her hand-cuffs removed for a 1998 court hearing in Seattle, Washington. National attention focused on her because as an older woman she took advantage of an underage boy, reversing the usual sex roles. Her affair with the 13-year-old boy resulted in the birth of a baby. She was placed on probation, but she violated the terms of her pro-bation by continuing to meet with the boy. Her probation was then revoked, and she was resentenced to seven and a half years in prison.   AP/Wide World Photos

such pregnancy. At the risk of stating the obvious, teenage pregnancies, which have increased dramatically over the last two decades, have significant social, medical and economic consequences for both the mother and her child, and the State. Of particular concern to the State is that approximately half of all teenage pregnancies end in abortion. And of those children who are born, their illegitimacy makes them likely candidates to become wards of the State.

We need not be medical doctors to discern that young men and young women are not similarly situated with respect to the problems and the risks of sexual inter-course. Only women may become pregnant and they suffer disproportionately the profound physical, emotional, and psychological consequences of sexual activity. The statute at issue here protects women from sexual intercourse at an age when those consequences are particularly severe.[15]

Sexual Misbehavior, or a Felony?

An 18½-year-old high school senior has a 15-year-old girlfriend. They have sex together, with both parties consenting. Is this a case of "kids will be kids," in which both parties are sexually active? Some law enforcement officers, prosecutors, and judges point out that young men have been doing this going back to the horse-and-buggy days. Are they correct? Do such comments condone and approve of such behavior?

If the girl's parents discover what is going on and angrily demand prosecution, should a prosecutor charge the young man with a felony? Or if high school officials come upon the couple during a sex act and demand that an example be set, should the young man (an adult) be charged with the felony of having sex with a minor?

If the girl did not consent to the sex, the case would uniformly be charged as rape (or forcible sexual assault). However, when the parties are both young and both consent, few of the cases are charged criminally.

Should such cases be left to the discretion of parents, law enforcement officers, and prosecutors, as they have been in past years? Or should state legislative bodies provide additional laws governing such situations? An example of such a proposed enactment provides:

Criminal charges cannot be issued if the child consents and the offender is no more than four years older than the victim (for example, a 19-year-old has sexual relations with a 16-year-old).

Honest mistake as to the age of the minor is not permitted as a defense in most states forbidding statutory rape. Nor would consent by the child be a defense. Investigation could even show that the child was a willing participant in the sex acts.

Incest

The crime of *incest* may be committed by adults within a family, but the public concern and prosecution are generally for cases involving children. Like statutory rape, the crime does not require a showing that force was used (or threatened) or that the victim did not consent. Incest was not a crime under common law, nor was it statutorized in England until 1908. Before that time, the offense was dealt with by the English ecclesiastical (religious) courts. Probably all the states have statutes making the offense a crime.

An article entitled "Incest: The Last Taboo" in the *FBI Law Enforcement Bulletin* (January 1984) states:

One thing every State has in common is the prohibition of marriage between parents and children, between siblings, between grandparents and grandchildren, uncles and nieces, and aunts and nephews.

Incest is usually defined as sexual exploitation between persons so closely related that marriage is prohibited by law. While this definition indicates that there is sexual intercourse, it is important to note that not all incestuous relationships involve intercourse. The term "intercourse" refers specifically to sexual activity between two individuals of the opposite sex. Beyond this usual definition are two other types of sexual child molestation that are closely related to incest and share some common features.

The first type, psychological incest, does not require that the individuals be blood relatives. It only requires that the adult assume the role of a parent. This type of incest extends to other nonrelated family members as well, such as step-uncles and aunts and step-siblings. This type of incest often occurs in families that include a step-parent, a foster parent, or a live-in boyfriend of the mother.

The second type of incest involves sexual contact between persons of the same sex, such as father/son, mother/daughter, or siblings of the same sex. Because father/son and mother/daughter incest are basically unstudied areas, very little can be written about their frequency of occurrence, the dynamics of the situation, the traumatic effects, or mode of treatment. It is known that in these types of incest, the parent is usually either a latent or overt homosexual.

The article also points out that an estimated 60,000 to 100,000 female children are sexually abused annually and that 80 percent of sexual abuse is not reported. It is believed that incest affects more than 10 percent of all American families, with at least 5,000 cases of father/daughter incest.

Penalties for incest, the article reports, range from ninety days to life imprisonment. Enforcement, however, is practically impossible unless a member of the family cooperates. Unfortunately, the credibility of the child victim is often attacked and severely questioned.

In 90 percent of cases, the victim is female and the abuse may commence while the child is too young to realize the significance of the problem. When the child becomes knowledgeable about what has happened, or is happening, the child will probably feel guilt, betrayal, confusion, and fright.

The defendant in the case of *Hamilton v. Commonwealth* was convicted of both rape and incest, resulting from a single act of sexual intercourse with his then 10-year-old daughter.[16] The Supreme Court of Kentucky held that the two convictions for the single act violated double jeopardy and vacated the incest conviction. The conviction for rape was affirmed with the life imprisonment sentence.

An unusual case involving a 52-year-old man (father) and his 31-year-old daughter is the 1991 case of *State v. Lubitz,* 472 N.W.2d 131. When the father would not break off the sexual relationship, the daughter complained. After counseling did not work, a prosecutor issued a two-count incest complaint when the father continued the relationship. The Supreme Court of Minnesota affirmed the conviction.

Other Laws That Seek to Achieve Public Safety

In addition to rape shield laws and laws making it easier to prove sexual abuse of children, states have enacted some or all of the following laws that seek to protect children and women from dangerous sexual offenders.

Sex Predator Laws Under Which Sexually Dangerous Persons Could Be Held Indefinitely

Some sex offenders are considered treatable by doctors, but other sex offenders are not treatable. Sex offenders often start with minor offenses such as public exposure and sexual touching. If the offender continues such conduct, the crimes could become more frequent and more violent—such as kidnapping, raping, and killing.

Statutes Seeking to Protect Children

All states forbid adults from having sexual intercourse or sexual contact with a child and make such conduct a crime.[a] Children who have not reached the age of majority are deemed not capable of giving consent to sexual intercourse. The offense of having sexual intercourse with a child is called statutory rape or SIWAC (sexual intercourse with a child).

Law enforcement officers sometimes come upon persons having consensual sexual relations in cars, parks, and other public places. If the parties are both adults, they often are warned and released. However, charges could be brought against them. If one or both of the parties are minors, most law enforcement officers would bring the parties to the police station or sheriff's office, where the parents would be called and asked to come down to the station. After the parents are informed of the facts, the minors are released to the parents, who can then determine what further action will be taken, if any.

In your state: *Statute #*

Sex with a child under age _____ is _____

How would the following be charged in your state?

                                     Statute #

Sexual abuse of a child   _____

Enticing a child for immoral purposes _____

Sexual exploitation of a child   _____

Incest involving a child   _____

Exposing a minor to harmful material _____

Other statutes   _____

Does your state have a "sexually dangerous person" statute (or chapter)?   _____

Does your state have a child abuse reporting statute?   _____

[a]The exception to this is the adult who is legally married to a child because the sexual relations are therefore marital relations.

If the sex offender is treatable, treatment programs should be provided. If the offender cannot be successfully treated, the offender could fall into the category of being mentally ill and dangerous to others. The U.S. Supreme Court held in the 1992 decision of *Foucha v. Louisiana,* 112 S.Ct. 1780, that sex predators or sexually dangerous persons may be constitutionally deprived of liberty indefinitely in civil commitment proceedings.

Such laws are called "sexually dangerous person" or "*sex predator*" or "sex offender" or "psychopathic personality" laws, depending on which state you live in. One of the problems addressed by such laws is the problem of pedophiles who lust after children.

Megan's Law: Registration Laws and Notification Laws for Sex Offenders

Many states have *registration laws for sex offenders* released to live in a community again. For example, California courts held that requiring registration of a defendant convicted of a misdemeanor indecent exposure violation did not violate the offender's constitutional rights. *People v. King,* 1993 WL 196860 (Cal.App. 1993).

Sexual Incidents That Received National Attention

Sexual violence as a weapon and tool of war	It is now recognized that sexual violence has been used for many years as a weapon of terror and a tool of war. Thousands of women were forced into prostitution and sexual enslavement by Japan during World War II, but the crime of sexual slavery was not charged until February 2001, when the Hague War Crimes Court convicted three Bosnian Serbs of rape and sexual enslavement.
Clergypersons, therapists, and doctors	Continue to make the news for sex acts committed while providing pastoral or medical services or counseling. Many states make it a criminal offense for a therapist to have sex with a patient. See 812 P.2d 797 (N.Mex. 1991); 499 N.W.2d 31 (Minn. 1993); 397 S.E.2d 1 (Ga. 1991).
The longest and most expensive criminal trial in U.S. history[a]	The McMartin Preschool case ended in 1990 when a California jury acquitted a 62-year-old woman and her 31-year-old son after six years and costs estimated at $13.5 million. The charges of sodomy, rape, and oral copulation were based on statements of 4- and 5-year-old children.
"No-name" DNA arrest warrants	DNA evidence (genetic fingerprints) is used to convict sex offenders and also to clear and free the innocent. "No-name" arrest warrants are being obtained by prosecutors to stop statutes of limitations from running when DNA evidence is available but the identity of the offender continues to be unknown. The no-name warrants can be held for years until a suspect somewhere in the United States matches up with the genetic code of the guilty person.
Parental liability for sexual assaults by minor child	A Wisconsin civil jury found a 15-year-old boy's conduct was "willful and wanton" in making sexual contact with a 10-year-old girl on twenty occasions. Because Wisconsin limits parental liability to $2,500 per incident, the judgment against the boy's parents was limited to $50,000. *N.E.M. v. Strigel,* 95-0755, Supreme Court of Wisconsin.
College rapes and sexual assaults	In an April 2002 report, the National Institute of Alcohol Abuse and Alcoholism estimated that an average of 192 students every day are raped by their dates or sexually assaulted after drinking. See the *New York Times* article "Study Calculates the Effects of College Drinking in the U.S." (April 10, 2002).

[a] Other day care cases that shocked the United States include the Little Rascals Day Care Center in Edenton, North Carolina, and the Wee Care Day Nursery in Maplewood, New Jersey. See also *State v. Felix,* 849 P.2d 220 (Nev. 1993), and *State v. Michaels,* 625 A. 489 (N.J.Super. 1993). In the *Felix* case, the Supreme Court of Nevada reversed the convictions of two day care workers, holding that "Almost all of the events described . . . were false and incredible. The undisputed medical evidence established that most of the assaults . . . alleged could not have happened." Similarly, sexual abuse charges against Margaret Michaels, a nursery school teacher in New Jersey, were reversed.

In 1998, a Massachusetts judge ruled that children who had appeared as witnesses in a day care sexual abuse case had been so manipulated in interviews with investigators that their testimony was "forever tainted." All criminal charges were dismissed against a 74-year-old woman who had died of cancer while awaiting trial, and a new trial was ordered for the woman's daughter. (See the *New York Times* article "Citing Tainted Testimony, Judge Sets New Abuse Trial," June 13, 1998.)

After listing states enacting such laws, the Arizona Court of Appeals in the case of *State v. McCuin*, 808 P.2d 332 (1991), affirmed the validity of the Arizona statute and held as Illinois did that

> the purpose of the statute is to aid law enforcement in preventing future sex offenses against children. . . . Protection of children from sex offenses is very much part of the State's unquestionable interest in protecting the health, safety and welfare of its citizens. As such, the registration requirement at issue here clearly serves a legitimate governmental purpose.

In addition to registration requirements, many states have included a notification requirement in their law.[17] The statute known as Megan's Law was enacted in New Jersey as a result of 7-year-old Megan Kanka, who was raped and murdered in 1994.

SUMMARY

Rape is a crime of violence. Rape was defined in a June 2001 report issued by the U.S. Department of Justice (NCJ 168633) as "sexual intercourse forced on the victim through physical or psychological coercion. Forced sexual intercourse includes vaginal, anal, or oral penetration by the offender(s), including penetration by a foreign object. Victims can be male or female, and the rape can be heterosexual or homosexual."

The government must prove all the essential elements of the crime that is charged, whether the crime is sexual assault or another felony.

Defendants who use the corpus delicti defense (that no crime was committed) put before the jury (or judge) the question as to whether the woman consented. This defense is used when the parties have known one another or were dating.

In rape by stranger cases, the defense is usually that the government has charged the wrong man and mistaken identity has occurred.

 ## BOOK-SPECIFIC WEB SITE

For chapter-related Web links, quizzing activities, and case and news updates, go to the *Criminal Law*, Eighth Edition, book-specific Web site at **http://info.wadsworth.com/ gardner.**

QUESTIONS AND PROBLEMS

1. In 1993, newspaper stories told of former cult leader David Koresh (Branch Davidian, Waco, Texas) having sex with girls under 15 years of age to whom he was not married. Koresh preached that all women in the cult, in fact all women, belonged to the Lamb (Koresh). If such an incident occurred in your state and evidence was available to prove it in a courtroom, could Koresh be charged and convicted of a

crime? What crime? If it was shown that the girl consented, would this be a total or partial defense?

2. The civilian girlfriend of a U.S. Marine private came onto a military base and partied with enlisted personnel over a three-day weekend. When the private's sergeant found the woman in the barracks room, he threatened that he would accuse the private of violation of barracks regulations unless the girlfriend agreed to have sexual intercourse with the sergeant. Two weeks after having sex with the sergeant, the woman reported him. The sergeant was convicted of rape and extortion and appealed his conviction to the U.S. Supreme Court. Do the circumstances permit inferences that the civilian woman consented to the sex but later changed her mind? Does the two-week delay in reporting the incident support this conclusion? Should testimony of other female witnesses concerning other similar acts of extortion by the sergeant (defendant) be permitted to overcome the two-week delay in reporting? Should the convictions of both rape and extortion stand? *U.S. v. Hicks,*

24 M.J. 3, 41 CrL 4097 (CMA 1987), cert. denied 484 U.S. 827, 108 S.Ct 95 (1987).

3. In the late afternoon, a Milwaukee police officer came upon a young man and woman in a parked car engaged in what the officer concluded to be sexual activity. Because it was a cold day and the woman was partially undressed, the officer did not have the parties get out of the car, which is standard and required procedure of many police departments.

Instead, the officer cautioned both adults and told them to move on. The young man started the car and drove away with the woman. An hour later, the woman walked into a nearby suburban police department and complained that she had been raped. She stated that the driver of the car had a gun pressed against her when the police officer was talking to the couple. She stated that she did not ask for help because of fear for her life. Should the officer be disciplined for not following departmental procedures in this case?

INFOTRAC COLLEGE EDITION EXERCISES

1. Go to InfoTrac College Edition and, using the keyword search term *rape* and subdivision *causes,* find the article containing responses to the review of the book *Why Men Rape* written by Palmer and Thornhill. (You will recall this review was the subject of InfoTrac College Edition Exercise 3 in Chapter 7. Which side of the question do you join?)

2. In the same *rape* search, go to the subdivision *care and treatment* and find the article discussing the care and treatment of rape. What are the physical, psychological, and legal factors to be considered in the treatment of rape?

NOTES

1. The Supreme Court of Oregon in *State v. Bashaw,* 672 P.2d 48 (1983). The Supreme Court of California used the often-used quote of Lord Hale in the case of *People v. Gammage,* 828 P.2d 682 (1992). Lord Hale was the Chief Justice in England from 1671 to 1676 and wrote:

It is true rape is a most detestable crime, and therefore ought severely and impartially to be punished with death; but it must be remembered, that it is an

accusation easily to be made and hard to be proved, and harder to be defended by the party accused, tho never so innocent. 1 Hale, *The History of the Pleas of the Crown* (1st Am. ed. 1847) p. 634.

Because of this type of thinking, courts in the state of California were required until 1975 to give a jury instruction in rape cases that stated in part that "A charge such as that made against the defendant in this case is one that is easily made and, once made, difficult to defend against, even though the person accused is innocent. . . . Therefore, the law requires that you examine the testimony of the female person named in the information with caution."

2. An admitted prostitute may be the victim of a rape. In the case of *People v. Gonzales,* 24 CrL 2194 (N.Y.Crim.Ct. 1978), the defendant did not pay the agreed fee for sexual services but obtained them at the point of a revolver. The highest court in New York affirmed the defendant's conviction for rape.

In the 1993 case of *People v. Powell,* 506 N.W.2d 894, the defendant claimed the woman was a prostitute who accused him of sexual assault after he failed to pay her. The Michigan Court of Appeals held that this was an attempt to place the "questionable" evidence before the jury and would not permit the allegation. The woman was employed as a topless dancer.

3. Lord Hale (an English judge) gave the reason for the "marital exemption" more than two hundred years ago as "the wife hath given up herself in this kind unto her husband, which she cannot retract." See *People v. M.D.,* 1992 WL 147704 (Ill.App. 1992).

The Supreme Court of California observed that the law originally required "utmost resistance" from women in order to prove that the crime of rape had occurred. *People v. Barnes,* 721 P.2d 110 (1986). Not only did the woman have to resist to the "utmost" of her physical capacity, but it also had to be shown that the "resistance must not have ceased throughout the assault." The former rape statute of the state of Wisconsin (former Section 940.01) required "utmost resistance" by a woman until the mid-1970s.

Courts and states have moved away from what the Supreme Court of California has properly called the "primitive rule" of utmost resistance. The modified rule was stated by the Supreme Court of California in the case of *People v. McIlvain,* 130 P.2d 131 (1942), as follows:

A woman who is assaulted need not resist to the point of risking being beaten into insensibility. If she resists to the point where further resistance would be useless or . . . until her resistance is overcome by force or violence, submission thereafter is not consent.

4. See 131 A.L.R. 1322, 84 A.L.R.2d 1017.

5. 619 S.W.2d 513 (Tenn. 1981).

6. See *Gilmore v. State,* 855 P.2d 143 (Okla.Cr. 1993); *Cole v. State,* 818 S.W.2d 573 (Ark. 1991); *Wealot*

v. Armontrout, 740 F.Supp. 1436 (W.D.Mo. 1990); and *Case v. State,* 458 N.E.2d 223 (Ind. 1984).

7. *People v. Hunt,* 72 Cal.App.3d at 194, 139 Cal.Rptr. at 676 (1987).

8. *State v. Rusk,* 289 Md. 230, 424 A.2d 720 (1981).

9. See also *State v. Reinhold,* 123 Ariz. 50, 597 P.2d 532 (1979); *People v. Hunt,* 72 Cal.App.3d 190, 139 Cal.Rptr. 675 (1977); *State v. Dill,* 3 Terry 533, 42 Del. 533, 40 A.2d 443 (1944); *Arnold v. United States,* 358 A.2d 335 (D.C.App. 1976); *Doyle v. State,* 39 Fla. 155, 22 So. 272 (1897); *Curtis v. State,* 236 Ga. 362, 223 S.E.2d 721 (1976); *People v. Murphy,* 124 Ill.App.2d 71, 260 N.E.2d 386 (1970); *Carroll v. State,* 263 Ind. 86, 324 N.E.2d 809 (1975); *Fields v. State,* 293 So.2d 430 (Miss. 1974); *State v. Beck,* 368 S.W.2d 490 (Mo. 1963); *Cascio v. State,* 147 Neb. 1075, 25 N.W.2d 897 (1947); *State v. Burns,* 287 N.C. 102, 214 S.E.2d 56 (1975), cert. denied 423 U.S. 933, 96 S.Ct. 288 (1975); *State v. Verdone,* 114 R.I. 613, 337 A.2d 804 (1975); *Brown v. State,* 576 S.W.2d 820 (Tex.Cr.App. 1978); *Jones v. Commonwealth,* 219 Va. 983, 252 S.E.2d 370 (1979); *State v. Baker,* 30 Wash.2d 601, 192 P.2d 839 (1948); *Brown v. State,* 581 P.2d 189 (Wyo. 1978).

10. However, "if a result of self-induced intoxication, the defendant believed that the female was consenting, that belief would not thereby become either reasonable or in good faith" (California Jury Instruction 4.20).

11. 117 Ill.App.3d 363, 453 N.E.2d 842 (1983). See also *Florida v. Meyers,* 466 U.S. 380, 104 S.Ct. 1852, 35 CrL 4022 (1984), in which the defendant was convicted of sexual battery. The conviction was affirmed by the U.S. Supreme Court.

12. 450 U.S. 464, 101 S.Ct. 1200 (1981).

13. Report of rape could also be made to a medical professional and be admissible under statements for the purposes of medical diagnosis or treatment. Report of rape is also known as the fresh complaint or the outcry rule.

14. 483 A.2d 1135 (D.C.App. 1984).

15. 450 U.S. 464, 101 S.Ct. 1200 (1981). Most states probably make their statutory rape statutes applicable to both females and males. There certainly is a

justifiable need for states to protect children from adults, whether the child is a girl or a boy.

16. 659 S.W.2d 201 (Ky. 1983).

17. To compel registration under Megan's Law and habitual sex offender laws, the crime of failure to register under these laws has been created. The Ohio courts and other courts have held such laws to be constitutional and do not constitute cruel and unusual punishment (see *State v. Douglas,* 586 N.E.2d 1096, 1989). New York's Megan's Law went into effect in 1996 after studies showed that, as a group, convicted sex offenders have a high rate of recidivism. See the *New York Times* article "First Arrests in New York in Offender Notice Law" (July 6, 1996).

19

Prostitution and Related Crimes

CONTENTS

KEY TERMS

prostitution

procuring, promoting,
and pimping

public place

obscenity

pornography

sexual exploitation
of a minor

voyeurism/invasion
of privacy

sexual harassment

telephone harassment

Prostitution

The crime of *prostitution* can be one of at least three nonmarital acts:

1. Engaging in sexual relations with another person for a fee or something of value
2. Offering (or soliciting) to engage in sexual relations with another person for a fee or something of value
3. Requesting (or agreeing) to pay a fee or something of value to another person for sexual services and acts

The *fee* or *something of value* is most often money. Members of either sex may now be convicted of prostitution, as distinguished from the past, when only women could be convicted. Most (if not all) state prostitution statutes forbid prostitution by males selling sexual services to other males. Males who offer to pay a woman to engage in sex acts may also be charged with the crime.

Prostitution is often referred to as the world's oldest profession and is described in history's earliest written records. The Bible, for instance, makes many references to whores and whoremongering. Prostitution is an activity that grows and recedes, depending on the changing mores and morals of a particular civilization. Many believe that, like the poor, it will always be with us.

Throughout the world, efforts have been made to suppress, control, organize, or discourage prostitution, with varying degrees of success. Prostitutes range from the common streetwalker to the privately kept woman or man. In England and France, prostitution is legal, but publicly soliciting customers is against the law. In some countries, particularly in the Orient, government-inspected houses of prostitution are allowed.

Efforts to decriminalize prostitution in the United States have met with little success. Only one state (Nevada) has legalized prostitution. In Nevada, each county has the option as to whether prostitution will be legalized. Fifteen of Nevada's seventeen counties have decided to remove the legal restraints against prostitution.

Procuring, Promoting, and Pimping for the Practice of Prostitution

Many prostitutes operate without pimps or other people procuring or promoting for them. Some prostitutes, however, have pimps, who procure customers and provide protection and bail as needed. In addition to pimps, other people could obtain money by procuring and promoting prostitution.

Procuring, promoting, and pimping for prostitution are forbidden by state criminal codes. Because of financial gains, this group of people has a motive to encourage and coerce young people into prostitution. They increase the volume and extent to which prostitution is practiced and often gain a vicious hold over the prostitutes who work for them. Following are a few of the many pimping, promoting, and procuring prostitution cases that have come before appellate courts:

- The owner of a hotel who rented out rooms knowing that rooms were being used for prostitution could not be convicted of solicitation for this conduct alone. *State v. Alveario*, 381 A.2d 38 (N.J.Super. 1977).

- An adult bookstore that offered live entertainment was shown to be a house of prostitution. A forty-five-count indictment was issued. *State v. Wright,* 561 A.2d 659 (N.J.Super. 1989).

- "Massage parlors" in three Wisconsin counties were charged with prostitution-related offenses for engaging in a continuing criminal enterprise over an eight-year period. *State v. Evers,* 472 N.W.2d 828 (Wis.App. 1991). (For material on the crime of continuing criminal enterprise, see Chapter 21.)

- The defendant was a photographer who arranged to have a 17-year-old girl seduce a pizza deliveryman while he filmed the sex act. The defendant then had sex with the girl. He was convicted of pandering and *sexual exploitation of a minor.* The Iowa Supreme Court would not permit his mistake-of-age defense, and he appealed to the federal courts, where his convictions were affirmed. *Gilmore v. Rogerson,* 117 F.3d 368 (8th Cir. 1997).

- Under the federal Travel Act (Mann Act), prosecutors must show that the escort service violated state law and used interstate facilities for an unlawful activity (prostitution business). *United States v. Jones,* 909 F.2d 533 (D.C.Cir. 1990).

Statutes That Require Proof That the Crime Was Committed in a "Public Place"

Definition of a "Public Place"

Private sex acts between consenting adults are rarely charged as crimes, even if they violate specific sections of criminal codes. Public sex acts, however, are charged as criminal conduct, and the statute often requires proof that the crime was committed in a *public place.* The following cases illustrate:

- The Supreme Court of Arkansas quoted other state courts in defining a public place as a place where the forbidden conduct "could be seen by a number of persons if they were present and happened to look." *State v. Black,* 545 S.W. 2d 617 (1977). If proving that the crime was committed in a "public place" is a problem, there generally are one or more alternative offenses in a state criminal code that do not have the requirement of "public place."[1]

Cases on the issue of what is a public place are as follows:

- The defendant appeared nude in the presence of a female baby-sitter in the bedroom and bathroom of his home. The Georgia Court of Appeals held that the defendant's behavior converted his bedroom and bathroom from a private zone into a "public place" in affirming his conviction under the Georgia public indecency statute. *Greene v. State,* 381 S.E.2d 310 (1989).

- Two men were observed masturbating in the common area of a highway rest room with exposed penises. The Michigan Court of Appeals affirmed their convictions for two counts of gross indecency, holding that the area was a public place. *People v. Lynch,* 445 N.W.2d 803 (1989).

- Defendants were seen having sex in a car parked on a well-lit public street so that the interior was readily visible to passersby. The highest court in New York affirmed the

Old Offenses That Are No Longer Crimes or Are Seldom Charged

Offense	Definition	History
Bigamy (or polygamy)	Marriage to two or more spouses at the same time	Statutorized in 1604 (prior to that time, it was an ecclesiastical crime in England). In recent years, it has been seldom prosecuted in the United States.[a]
Adultery[b]	Voluntary sexual intercourse in which one or both parties are married to another person (parties not married to one another). About half the states continue to make adultery a crime, but these old laws are rarely enforced.	Goes back in history to old Roman law. A Wisconsin woman admitted in a contested divorce hearing in 1990 that she had had an "affair"; she received national attention when she was charged with the two-year felony. Charges were later dropped.
Homosexuality	Sexual relations between persons of the same sex	For many years was a crime in all states. A few states continue to forbid this conduct in their criminal code. While public acts would be a crime, prosecution is rare for private conduct.
Fornication	Voluntary sexual intercourse between two unmarried people	Formerly a crime in all states. Most states have removed this offense from their criminal codes.
Seduction	Enticement by a male of an unmarried woman of prior chaste character to have sexual intercourse	Was a crime in early English law and in many states.
Miscegenation	Intermarriage (and in some states living together) of people of different races (generally white and black)	Was a crime in some of the states. Such statutes were declared unconstitutional by the U.S. Supreme Court. See the case of Loving v. Virginia in Chapter 1.
Buggery (or bestiality)	Any type of sexual intercourse with an animal	A statutory offense in England until 1967.
Abortion	Causing the expulsion of a human fetus prematurely	Previously a crime in all states. States may not now make abortion a crime until the third trimester of pregnancy. Some states no longer have a crime of abortion (see Chapter 12).
Blasphemy, profanity, and indecent language	Cursing or reviling God; unbecoming, not decent, or impious language	Can no longer punish for language violations unless the language falls within one of the crimes listed in Chapter 10.
Crimes against transgenders	The term "transgenders" covers cross-dressers, homosexual drag queens, and persons who believe they are both male and female.	An assortment of criminal laws were used in past years against transgenders (persons who either believed they were born in the wrong body or are intersexed).

[a]Utah banned polygamy as a required precondition to becoming a state in 1890, but over the years the practice of polygamy in Utah has never completely disappeared. See the New York Times article "A House, 10 Wives: Polygamy in Suburbia" (December 11, 1997) and also the Newsweek article "Secrets in the Desert" (August 10, 1998).

[b]Adultery remains a crime in the U.S. armed forces, where dismissal from the service is often the punishment. In 1997, the Air Force prosecuted sixty-seven cases for adultery, including Lt. Kelly Flinn, who was the first woman to pilot a B-52 bomber.

Prostitution

Prostitutes may operate (1) independently, (2) under the control of a pimp, (3) as part of an organized syndicate, or (4) with people other than those already mentioned.

Prostitution fuels the illegal drug business because many prostitutes use their earnings to buy drugs. The *FBI Law Enforcement Bulletin* (August 1988) also points out that the crimes of theft, robbery, and assault and battery are frequent by-products of organized prostitution services.

Type of Operation	*Type of Complaint Received by Law Enforcement Agencies*
Streetwalkers (and prostitutes who operate out of taverns and bars)	■ From business establishments (such as restaurants and hotels) when streetwalkers hurt business by driving customers away ■ From homeowners when streetwalkers are walking in their neighborhood ■ From women who have been mistaken for prostitutes by cruising men ■ From men who have been embarrassed or annoyed by prostitutes ■ From customers complaining of theft, robbery, and so on of their wallets, credit cards, or other personal property This is the form of prostitution most visible to the public. It is also the most dangerous for women because they are exposed to violence and robbery by strangers and to arrest by police.
Call girls	Generally, only customer complaints Unless call girls have developed their own customers, they must rely on others to pander for them. Pimps, bartenders, cab drivers, and others, could be used to refer customers to call girls.
Prostitution via the Internet, pagers, cellular phones, and fronts such as escort services and massage parlors	Used generally in combination with "call girl" services. On-line prostitutes say the Internet is a natural medium for selling sex because it is anonymous and connects with many potential customers.[a]
"Sex-for-drugs" prostitution	Public health officials are very concerned about the spread of disease linked to sex-for-drugs prostitution.
Brothels and houses of prostitution	State laws forbid houses of prostitution. In the case of *State v. Mueller,* 671 P.2d 1351 (1983), one woman was selling sex in her apartment with no street or public solicitation and only consenting adults involved. She argued that she had a right of privacy in her home to do as she wished. The Supreme Court of Hawaii affirmed her conviction, holding she had no right to practice prostitution.
Combining prostitution with con games, robbery, extortion, theft of money, credit cards, and so on	*FBI Law Enforcement Bulletin* article "Knock-Out Dates: Flirting with Danger," (January 1993), tells of women who pick up men in hotels, restaurants, and bars to rob them or steal from them after placing a drug in their drink to incapacitate them. For an example, see the case of *U.S. v. Pasucci,* 943 F.2d 1032 (9th Cir. 1991 where a business man was caught by an extortion ring.

[a]See the *New York Times* article "Prostitutes on Wane in New York Streets But Take to the Internet" (February 22, 1998). The article points out that in a crackdown in 1994, New York police made more than 9,500 prostitution arrests for that year. But for the years of 1996 and 1997, fewer than 2,000 arrests were made for each year. New York police believe prostitutes have "adopted more . . . technological means to stay ahead of the police."

Because Prostitution Fuels the Illegal Trade, Cities Use One or More of the Following to Discourage the Crime

- Increased fines and jail sentences for prostitutes and johns
- Cracking down on male johns to discourage this activity
- Increased use of the "loitering to solicit prostitution" ordinance or statute
- Filing a civil lawsuit against people with five or more prostitution or loitering for prostitution arrests, as was done in San Diego and Milwaukee. The civil court would then declare loitering by such people in certain areas of the city to be a public nuisance and also forbid them from flagging down cars and loitering at bus stops throughout the city. Violations would lead to a civil forfeiture of up to $2,000, or jailing if the forfeiture is not paid. One of the people in Milwaukee had 18 arrests for prostitution and 124 loitering for prostitution arrests. Police in San Diego reported that the lawsuit virtually eliminated street prostitution in specific areas of San Diego.
- Confiscation of the johns' cars under forfeiture statutes
- City placing newspaper ads listing names of prostitutes and johns (a few cities also place pictures of the johns in the ads)
- Compulsory AIDS tests for convicted prostitutes and johns (A California statute mandating the testing of people convicted of prostitution for AIDS was upheld in the 1990 case of *Love v. Superior Court*, 226 Cal.App.3d 736, 276 Cal.Rptr. 660)

convictions for public lewdness, holding that the interior of the car was a public place when casual passersby could see and were likely to see the partial nudity and the sex acts. *People v. McNamara*, 585 N.E.2d 788 (1991).

- A public self-service laundry was held to be a public place when the defendant exposed his penis to a college woman and began to masturbate. *People v. Jones*, 583 N.E.2d 623 (Ill.App. 1991).

Most crimes can be committed in either a public or a private place. Rape, murder, robbery, theft, and so forth can be committed in either a public or a private place. Sexual crimes against children can be committed either in a public or a private place:

- Lewd conduct with a minor. *State v. Peltier*, 803 P.2d 202 (Idaho App. 1990).
- Indecent liberty with a child. *State v. Williams*, 829 P.2d 892 (Kansas 1992).
- Aggravated felonious sexual assault. *State v. Morse*, 607 A.2d 619 (N.H. 1992).
- The crime of official misconduct when a woman teacher of students 10 to 12 years of age showed her students sexually explicit magazines, had them cut pictures out of the magazines, and discussed her sexual proclivities with the students. *State v. Parker*, 592 A.2d 228 (Sup.Ct.N.J. 1991).

Touching or Other Conduct Done to Arouse Sexual Desire

Touching a private part of another person's body could be (1) accidental, (2) consented to by the other person (children are not capable of consenting to sexual touching), or (3) necessary in the care of the person, or for medical reasons. Touching could be in a friendly, joking, or loving manner, or the contact could be to discipline a child (spanking), or in a hostile or angry manner.

Sexual crimes, such as sexual touching, require that the state show the touching was for sexual gratification. Lewd and lascivious conduct or behavior with a child statutes often require that it be shown that the defendant "had the specific intent to arouse or gratify either child's sexual desires or his own." *State v. Rollins,* 581 So.2d 379 (La.App. 1991).

Following are examples of crimes having the requirement of a showing that the conduct was intended to arouse sexual desire:

- The California lewd and lascivious acts with a child statute requires that the touching be done "with the specific intent to arouse, appeal to, or gratify the sexual desire of either party." *People v. Carson,* 890 P.2d 1115 (1995). The California Supreme Court also held that the lewd touching can occur through the victim's clothing and does not require contact with the bare skin or with "private parts" of the defendant or victim. *People v. Martinez,* 1995 WL 641969 (1995).

- Most state statutes include the buttocks as an intimate part of a person's body. To be a sexual battery or disorderly conduct or another sex crime, it must be shown that the touching was intentional, was without consent, and was for purposes of sexual gratification. *State v. Osborne,* 808 P.2d 624 (N.Mex. 1991), and other cases.

- The defendant offered a teenage boy a ride, made sexually suggestive inquiries of the boy, and then pressed his entire hand on the inner thigh of the boy in a manner suggestive of an intimate massage. The Massachusetts Court of Appeals affirmed the conviction of the defendant for indecent assault and battery. *Commonwealth v. Lavigne,* 676 N.E.2d 1170 (1997).

Obscenity

Obscenity, or Hardcore Pornography

As pointed out in Chapter 10, **obscenity** is not protected by the First Amendment. The test used to identify obscenity was established by the U.S. Supreme Court in the 1973 case of *Miller v. California* and includes the following guidelines:

- Whether "the average person applying contemporary community standards" would find that the work, taken as a whole, appeals to the prurient interest (prurient interest would be appealing to the sexual interest, causing a person to become sexually aroused)

- Whether the work or communication depicts or describes, in a patently offensive way, sexual conduct specifically defined by the applicable state law (called the "contemporary community standards" test)

- Whether the work or communication, taken as a whole, lacks serious literary, artistic, political, or scientific value.[2]

Defense lawyers defending a client charged with selling or presenting obscene material will generally request a jury trial and then show the following as evidence in establishing "contemporary community" standards:

- Lists of the sex films a guest could obtain on pay-for-view channels while staying at local hotels and motels

- The erotic films and material that local people were buying from their cable and satellite providers

- The number and locations of video stores selling X-rated and adult films and information on the size of their inventories

- Movie houses that show X-rated or adult films

- X-rated or adult material available on the Internet

- Night clubs or taverns that feature nude or seminude entertainment locally

- Sale of adult and X-rated material in local stores and material in local newspapers (especially free street papers)

Using the above evidence makes it very difficult (if not impossible) to obtain criminal or civil convictions for obscenity violations.

Protecting Children Against Sexual Exploitation

Child Pornography

The U.S. Supreme Court has repeatedly held that states have a compelling interest in "safeguarding the physical and psychological well-being of a minor" and that "the use of children as subjects of pornographic materials is harmful to the physiological, emotional, and mental health of the child." *Osborne v. Ohio,* 110 S.Ct. 1691 (1990).

Because of these reasons, child *pornography* is treated differently from adult pornography. Adult pornography is sold openly in many communities throughout the United States. Child pornography is outlawed by the federal government and most states.

The child pornography laws of the majority of states and the federal government do not require obscenity as an element of the crime.[3] If a child or children are shown engaged in sexually explicit conduct, possession of such material is a crime under the federal pornography law and the laws of most states.

Five categories of conduct and attempted conduct are made crimes under the federal law and the laws of most states. The crime of child pornography broadly includes the following:[4]

- Production of child pornography (for example, filming a child or children engaged in sexually explicit conduct)

- Advertising child pornography

- Possession of material, knowing that it depicts minors in sexually explicit conduct

- Trafficking in child pornography (importation, distribution, sale, loan, gift, exchange, receipt, or transportation of material, knowing that it depicts minors engaged in sexually explicit conduct)

- Procurement of child pornography (buying, selling, or transporting child pornography or inducing, coercing, or kidnapping a minor for the purposes of producing child pornography)

Regulation of Nudity by States or Municipalities

Nudity by itself is not obscene, lewd, or indecent but may be regulated by specific statutes and ordinances as follows:

Place of Nudity	Manner in Which Nudity May Be Regulated
Public nudity (public beach or public place, such as street)	May be forbidden or regulated by a specific statute or ordinance.
Nude entertainment or nudity in a place licensed to serve alcoholic beverages	May be forbidden or regulated under the authority given to states by the Twenty-First Amendment of the U.S. Constitution to regulate the sale and use of alcohol. The U.S. Supreme Court stated that "the broad sweep of the 21st Amendment has been recognized as conferring something more than the normal state authority over public health, welfare, and morals." *California v. LaRue,* 409 U.S. 109, 93 S.Ct. 390 (1972).
Nudity in a private place (a nudist camp, for example), or in a stage play, or in a movie (the musical *Hair,* the play *Oh Calcutta!* and the opera *Salome* have nude performers)	May not be regulated unless the conduct or display is obscene. Nudity, by itself, is not obscene, lewd, or indecent.
Nudity used for sexual gratification	For example, see the case of *People v. Garrison,* 82 Ill.2d 444, 45 Ill.Dec. 132, 412 N.E.2d 483 (1980), in which the defendant stood behind a storm door in his home exposing his penis to a woman standing outside. The Supreme Court of Illinois held that this was not private conduct and that the defendant had no right of privacy. If a jury found that the defendant exposed his body "with intent to arouse or to satisfy (his) sexual desire," the defendant could be found guilty of the Illinois public indecency statute.

Child pornography could be depicted in magazines, books, motion pictures, videos, and by other means. Most state statutes forbid live performances, and some specifically forbid the use of computers. The federal government and some states forbid visual depictions or advertisements of child pornography "by any means including by computers."

Other Laws Protecting Children Against Sexual Exploitation

In addition to criminal laws that seek to protect all persons from sexual violence, the federal government and most states have criminal laws forbidding the following conduct (or attempt to commit):

- Selling or buying babies or children in violation of state law is generally forbidden. Federal statute 18 U.S.C. 2251A forbids the transfer, sale, purchase, or receipt of a child when such transfer is for the production of child pornography.

Fighting the International Child Sex Trade

Representatives of 134 countries met in Yokohama, Japan in December 2001 to fight the fast-growing world sex trade in children. The first international meeting was held in Stockholm in 1996. UNICEF estimates that every year one million youths (girls and boys) are forced into the sex trade.

Most of these children are from poor countries or are poor illegal immigrants living in industrial countries. Using the Internet and cellular telephones, pedophiles can reach the children by playing online. The governments of the 134 countries pledged increased efforts to stamp out the thriving sex trade by tougher laws and by coordinating police efforts against the child sex trade.

- Use of the mail or other means of transportation of child pornography is forbidden by federal statute 18 U.S.C. 2252. Such transfer could be within a state (intrastate) or between states (interstate). The federal law forbids transfer "by any means, including computer." The federal statute also applies to importation by any means from a foreign country.

- Federal statute 18 U.S.C. 2258 forbids the use of minors in a foreign country to produce child pornography for importation into the United States.

- The Mann Act (18 U.S.C. §§ 2422 and 2423) forbids enticing, persuading, or inducing any person (including children) to travel across a state border for prostitution or for any sexual activity for which any person may be charged with a crime.

- Federal statute 18 U.S.C. Section 2423 also forbids a person from traveling in interstate or foreign commerce for the purpose of engaging in sexual activity with a person under 18 years of age. (Twenty-one countries now permit police to arrest for this crime in an effort to stamp out the growing sex trade in children between nations.)

- Federal statute 18 U.S.C. Section 2243 forbids sexual assault of children on federal property or on airlines. Because sexual activity is forbidden with children under 18 years of age, all the above federal criminal laws apply not only to young children but also to teenage girls and boys.

Pedophiles and the Internet

A pedophile is a person (usually a man) who is sexually attracted to children. The pedophile is capable of enticing children, sexually exploiting them, and then, possibly, murdering them.

Before the Internet came along, pedophiles were isolated, lonely, and hunted individuals. Authorities had child pornography pretty much under control.

Pedophiles almost immediately gravitated to the Internet[5] because it offered them anonymity and immediate contact with children. The Internet can store photographs and allow meeting with other pedophiles online so they can share their interest and experiences.

Virtual Child Pornography

In *Ashcroft v. Free Speech Coalition,* 122 S.Ct. 1389 (2002), the U.S. Supreme Court held that the Child Pornography Prevention Act of 1996 (CPPA) was overbroad and unconstitutional. The Court concluded the CPPA did not limit its prohibition to only obscene materials, but included all depictions of sexual conduct between children. It noted that the movie *Traffic,* which won an Academy Award, had depicted sexual conduct of a 16-year-old girl. This established that not all depictions of such sexual conduct constituted obscenity.

The Court also held the CPPA would not be upheld under the logic of *New York v. Ferber,* 458 U.S. 747 (1982). *New York v. Ferber* upheld child pornography laws that were broader than general laws prohibiting obscene materials on the theory child pornography exploited and damaged the children involved in the pornography. Since no real children are involved in "virtual" sexual contact, no children have been exploited.

Today, child pornography from Russia, Indonesia, the United States, and other countries is available on Web sites. The number of Web sites exploded from 403 in the year 2000 to 1,391 in 2001. American federal law enforcement officers made the biggest child pornography bust in U.S. history, arresting more than a hundred customers of a Fort Worth, Texas, company that was operating globally in the child pornography business.

The names of another thirty thousand alleged buyers of child pornography were obtained in the raid on the Texas company. Investigators concentrated on those suspects with prior convictions of molesting children and the suspects who were presently working with children. The names of the thirty thousand alleged buyers were turned over to state and local law enforcement agencies in hopes that pedophiles can again be driven underground.

Movies, Videos, and Photographs

X-Rated Films and Videos

The X-rated video business is a multibillion-dollar business in the United States. European and Asian producers also have large sales throughout the world.

Are producers of X-rated videos and films, who pay adults to perform sexual acts that are filmed for movies and videos, engaged in the business of prostitution? This issue was before the courts in the case of *California v. Freeman,* 109 S.Ct. 854 (1989).

Freeman was convicted of pandering under the California Criminal Code for hiring adults to perform sex acts, which he filmed and sold. The Supreme Court of California reversed the conviction, holding that Freeman's conduct was not prohibited by the California prostitution and pandering laws. The U.S. Supreme Court affirmed the ruling of the California Supreme Court.

Because a new law expanding the California pandering and prostitution statute was not able to work its way through the state legislature, California has become the capital of the United States for X-rated and pornographic films and videos.[6]

Nude Photos of Children Taken by Family Members

Many family photo and video collections have pictures of young nude children. But when children are no longer babies and have begun to develop sexually, are pictures taken by parents and stepparents sexual abuse? This question has been before a number of U.S. courts.

Mr. Oakes took color photos of his physically mature 14-year-old stepdaughter, showing her fully exposed breasts. He was convicted in a jury trial and sentenced to ten years in prison. The Massachusetts Supreme Judicial Court reversed the conviction, holding the statute to be overbroad. The U.S. Supreme Court vacated the Massachusetts Supreme Court ruling and remanded the case for further hearings. *Massachusetts v. Oakes,* 109 S.Ct. 2633 (1989).

However, the convictions of other defendants in similar situations were affirmed. In *Perry v. State,* 568 So.2d 339 (Ala.Cr.App. 1990), the defendant not only photographed his 15-year-old daughter but also her 14-year-old friend. In *Brackins v. State,* 578 A.2d 300 (Md.App. 1990), the conviction for child sexual abuse was affirmed in the semi-nude photographing of a 12-year-old stepdaughter.[7]

In 1997, protesters in twenty-nine states demonstrated in front of Barnes & Noble bookstores, which were selling two books picturing nude children. Most local prosecutors refused to issue criminal charges, and the bookstores refused to discontinue the sale of the books. The age of the photographed children apparently was below the age of puberty. It was reported that a grand jury in San Francisco refused to issue an indictment after reviewing the books. (See the *Milwaukee Journal Sentinel* article "Amid Protest, Sales Boom for Book of Nude Child Photos," September 19, 1997.)

Voyeurism and Other Criminal Invasions of Privacy

Until recent years, Peeping Toms who trespassed or were not in a public place were often charged as a disorderly person (or with disorderly conduct). Many states now have *voyeurism* laws or *invasion of privacy* laws in their criminal codes. An example of such law is Ohio Criminal Code Section 2907.08(A), which reads:

> No person, for the purpose of sexually arousing or gratifying himself or herself, shall commit trespass or otherwise surreptitiously invade the privacy of another, to spy or eavesdrop upon another.

These laws have been toughened in many states by provisions forbidding "video voyeurism" or "video stalking." The terms "upskirting" and "downblousing" describe offenses that are charged under invasion of privacy statutes. Examples of conduct charged under these laws are as follows:

- A California man videotaped three different women at three different times as he had sex with them. The women did not know and did not consent to the filming. Police learned of the tapes when the man showed the videos to friends. He was convicted under California's invasion of privacy law forbidding filming or recording of confidential communications without the consent of participants. *People v. Gibbons*, 263 Cal. Rptr. 905 (1989).

- A Wisconsin man received a year in jail for lying under oath for posting nude pictures of his former girlfriend on the Internet.

- An apartment manager secretly installed a video camera in a shower used by college women living in his building. After several months of filming the women taking showers, the camera was discovered and the man was criminally charged under the Wisconsin Criminal Code.

Harassment as an Offense

Cities and states have enacted offenses entitled "harassment," "mashing," "hassling," and so on, which prohibit such conduct as improper accosting, ogling, insulting, pursuing, following, molesting, and touching a person of the opposite sex. The primary purpose of such statutes and ordinances is to protect women and young people from behavior that can be menacing and threatening. There are different types of harassment.

Sexual Harassment

Sexual harassment can be a criminal or a civil offense. It is defined as unwelcome sexual advances or requests for sexual favors that may be combined with other verbal or physical conduct of a sexual nature. Ordinarily, women and girls are the victims of sexual harassment, but occasional cases concern men who are the victims of unwelcome sexual advances that amount to sexual harassment. Workplace sexual harassment could occur when

- the boss expects submission by an employee to sexual harassment as an explicit or implicit term or condition of employment

- pay raises, promotions, type of work, and so forth are used as a reward for submission to sexual harassment and providing sexual favors

- such conduct interferes with work performance or creates an intimidating, hostile, or offensive working environment

The U.S. Supreme Court held in 1986 that sexual harassment that caused a hostile or abusive work environment, without showing an economic loss, violated Title VII of the Civil Rights Act of 1964 (42 U.S.C. §§ 2000e–2000e-17). In the case of *Meritor Savings Bank v. Mechelle Vinson*, the female bank employee was subjected to public fondling and sexual demands, to which she allegedly submitted out of fear that she would lose her job.[8]

The U.S. Supreme Court ruled in 1993 that harassment need not result in a "tangible injury," but that it had to be more than "merely offensive" conduct or words. Holding that there could not be "a mathematically precise test," the Court held that a "hostile or abusive" environment violates the law. *Harris v. Forklift Systems, Inc.*, 114 S.Ct. 367.[9]

In two 1998 cases, the U.S. Supreme Court held that corporations and other employers are potentially liable for the conduct of supervisors, whether the employer was aware

A community group in Milwaukee used this billboard to discourage prostitution, which was a problem in their neighborhood.   Courtesy of Eileen Gardner

of it or not. The cases held that an employee who refused unwanted sexual advances but suffered no job consequences may still bring a lawsuit. The cases are *Burlington Industries v. Ellerth,* 118 S.Ct. 2257, and *Faragher v. City of Boca Raton,* 118 S.Ct. 2275.

Telephone Harassment

Before 1966, few states had criminal laws dealing with harassing, abusive, or obscene telephone calls. However, because of the increased volume of complaints received during the 1960s, all the states and the federal government have now enacted statutes making such telephone calls criminal offenses.[10]

Harassing, abusive, or obscene phone calls include the deliberate obscene call, threats, the cruel hoax, bomb scares and threat of bombs, and the "silent" call, in which the person answering the telephone hears nothing or hears breathing on the other end of the line. Criminal charges may be issued in all of these cases if it is apparent that the call was deliberate and made with intent to harass, abuse, or threaten another person. However, charges should not be issued if it appears that the person has dialed a wrong number and simply does not explain the error.

The Illinois *telephone harassment* statute, which outlaws "harassment by telephone," was found to be constitutional by the Illinois Supreme Court in the 1979 case of *Parkins v. Illinois.*[11] The appeal to the U.S. Supreme Court was dismissed for want of a substantial federal question.

Criminal Charges Relating to HIV Infections

AIDS, which is caused by HIV infections, became a fast-growing epidemic in the early 1980s. Because there is no cure for AIDS at the present time, there is great public concern of the risk of infection and the risk of death caused by HIV infection.

People who have AIDS and people infected with the HIV virus can spread the deadly disease to others either intentionally or by negligence. The danger of transmitting HIV infection from one person to another has caused some state legislatures to enact new criminal laws. However, most criminal charges are issued using criminal laws that existed prior to the AIDS epidemic.

Examples of criminal charges and convictions of HIV-infected people for conduct that jeopardized the health of others include "knowingly transferring bodily fluid containing HIV virus" (848 P.2d 394, Idaho; 610 N.E.2d 208, Illinois; 802 S.W.2d 28, Texas); "intentionally exposing sexual partners to HIV" (832 P.2d 109, Washington); "reckless conduct by HIV-infected person" (396 S.E. 301, Georgia); "aggravated assault" (1992 WL 59832, Pennsylvania; 30 MJ 53, U.S. Military); "assault with intent to murder" (545 N.E. 2d 834, Indiana); "assault with dangerous weapon" (669 F. Supp. 289 and 48 F.3d 784, federal prisons); "attempted murder" (621 A. 2d 493 New Jersey; 834 S.W. 2d 559, Texas).

SUMMARY

Prostitution fuels the illegal drug trade because many prostitutes use their earnings to buy drugs. Theft, robbery, and assault are reported to be frequent by-products of organized prostitution services.

This chapter presents material on the crimes of prostitution, procuring, promoting, pimping, obscenity, the child sex trade and child pornography, voyeurism, and harassment as a crime and civil offense. The problem of HIV-infected persons who either intentionally, recklessly, or negligently jeopardize others is also discussed.

 ## BOOK-SPECIFIC WEB SITE

For chapter-related Web links, quizzing activities, and case and news updates, go to the *Criminal Law,* Eighth Edition, book-specific Web site at **http://info.wadsworth.com/ gardner.**

QUESTIONS AND PROBLEMS

1. The following problem is taken from the National Institute of Justice publication *Problem-Oriented Policing:* At 1:32 A.M., a man we will call Fred Snyder dials 911 from a downtown corner phone booth. The dispatcher notes his location and calls the nearest patrol unit. Officer Knox arrives 4 minutes later.

Snyder says he was beaten and robbed 20 minutes before but didn't see the robber. Under persistent questioning, Snyder admits he was with a prostitute who he had picked up in a bar. Later, in a hotel room, he discovered the prostitute was actually a man, who then beat Snyder and took his wallet.

Is it likely that most victims in this type of case will cooperate with the police in attempting to apprehend the robber? Could the police, a prosecutor, or a judge effectively force a victim such as Snyder to cooperate? Explain.

2. Mr. Osborne was a friendly man. As he greeted a young house guest of his family, he hugged the minor and grabbed her buttocks. Mr. Osborne was cautioned and warned a number of times because of this conduct with women and girls. When the conduct continued, the matter was referred to the police and a prosecutor. Could he be charged with a crime under the laws of your state? If your answer is yes, state the offense and elements that would have to be proved to obtain a conviction. See *State v. Osborne*, 808 P.2d 624, 49 CrL 1063 (N.M. 1991).

3. During spring break in 1998, a beach club in Panama City Beach, Florida, ran a "Sex on the Beach" contest. Participants in the contest simulated sex acts with winners in the contest, receiving prizes of $500. The winners were determined by the crowd of onlookers.

When local police heard of the contest and viewed a videotape of the event, three women who exposed themselves and went very far in the simulation were arrested. If this occurred in your state, what criminal charges (if any) could be used and who should be charged? See the *Pensacola News Journal* article "'Sex on the Beach' Contest Draws Trouble: City Leaders Worry About Area's Image" (May 2, 1998).

INFOTRAC COLLEGE EDITION EXERCISES

1. Go to InfoTrac College Edition and, using the subject search term *child pornography*, find the article discussing "virtual" child pornography under the Child Pornography Prevention Act of 1996. What are the free speech issues raised by criminal prosecutions under that Act?

2. Go to InfoTrac College Edition and, using the subject search term *obscenity* and the subdivision *laws*, find an article discussing obscenity available on the Internet. What can public libraries do to limit access by children using library computers to Internet sites with so-called adult content? What are the issues here? See *Mainstream Loudoun v. Board of Trustee's of Loudoun County Library*, 24 F.Supp.2d 555 (E.D. Va. 1998). Do you think the *Loudoun* case should be reversed or affirmed on the basis of *U.S. v. Playboy Entertainment Group*, 120 S.Ct. 1878 (2000)?

NOTES

1. In states where public intoxication is a crime or ordinance violation, it must be shown that the person was intoxicated in a public place. The Supreme Court of Iowa pointed out that a "right of public access is the touchstone of the . . . definition of a public place." (476 N.W.2d at 56). The majority of state courts hold that a motor vehicle on a street or highway is a public place for criminal statutes such as public intoxication, soliciting an act of prostitution, and public indecency in which the state must show "public place."

2. 413 U.S. 15, 93 S.Ct. 2607 (1973).

3. In 1977, the U.S. Congress enacted the federal Protection of Children Against Sexual Exploitation Act (18 U.S.C.A. § 2252). The federal child pornography law was upheld as constitutional by the U.S. Supreme Court in the case of U.S. v. X-Citement Video, Inc., 115 S.Ct. 464, and the state of New York child pornography law was upheld in the case of *New York v. Ferber*, 458 U.S. 747, 102 S.Ct. 3348 (1982).

4. This material is adapted from the U.S. Department of Justice publication entitled *Child Sexual Exploitation: Improving Investigations and Protecting Victims* (1995).

5. States and the federal government may forbid and regulate obscenity and child pornography, but "indecent material" is ordinarily different from either obscenity or child pornography.

In 1996, the U.S. Congress enacted the Communications Decency Act, which made it a crime to send or display "indecent material" on the Internet in a way that it was available to minors.

In 1997, the U.S. Supreme Court held that speech on the Internet is entitled to the same high level of First Amendment protection that is given to books and newspapers. The Supreme Court declared the 1996 Communications Decency Act to be unconstitutional in the case of *American Civil Liberties Union v. Reno,* 138 L.Ed.2d 874.

The level of protection given to the Internet is therefore higher than the protection given to radio, television, and cable broadcasts.

6. In the 1990 Arizona case of *State v. Taylor,* 808 P.2d 314, the Arizona courts distinguish between "Prostitution and Theatre." The defendant was convicted of four counts under the Arizona prostitution statute for paid performances in which "sexual contact" occurred. The Arizona case distinguishes this case and statute from the California *Freeman* case.

7. See the *New York Times* article "Family Photos or Pornography? A Father's Bitter Legal Odyssey" (January 30, 1995), which tells of a 45-year-old businessman who was arrested, handcuffed, and taken from his home. The man took 110 photographs of his nude 6-year-old daughter for an art class he was taking. The article tells of similar incidents in Ohio and California.

8. 477 U.S. 57, 106 S.Ct. 2399 (1986).

9. The Paula Jones lawsuit against President William Clinton was settled by an out-of-court payment to Paula Jones. Proceedings in the case had commenced when the U.S. Supreme Court held that the lawsuit for alleged sexual advances against a sitting president of the United States could not be deferred until the president's term of office ended. (See *Clinton v. Jones,* 137 L.Ed.2d 945, 1997.)

10. In addition to statutes forbidding abusive, harassing, or obscene telephone calls, federal statutes also forbid other abusive use of the telephone, such as the Consumer Credit Protection Act (Public Law. 95-109 Stat. 877), which prohibits debt collectors from "placing telephone calls without meaningful disclosure of the caller's identity"; from "engaging any person in telephone conversation repeatedly or continuously with intent, to annoy, abuse, or harass any person at the called number"; and from "us[ing] obscene or profane language or language the natural consequence of which is to abuse the hearer or reader."

11. 77 Ill.2d 253, 396 N.E.2d 22, 27 CrL 4055.

20

Drug Abuse
and Alcohol-Related Crimes

CONTENTS

KEY TERMS

controlled substances

Uniform Controlled
Substances Act

usable amounts

possession with intent
to deliver

drug "rip-off" cases

drug-induced deaths

drug paraphernalia

driving under the
influence

"booze it and lose it" laws

Drug Abuse

The Frightening Drug Problem

The American public is aware of the staggering problem of illegal drugs in the United States. Public opinion polls show that the drug problem is a major concern of Americans. Aspects of the drug problem are presented almost daily in newspapers and on television.

Illegal drugs have shattered many lives, caused suicides and murders, and caused serious health problems in many people. Illegal drugs have disrupted many American communities and also the economies of many poor countries elsewhere in the world.

Drug lords all over the world have become rich and powerful. They build private armies to protect their illegal operations and to become richer and more powerful. In the Caribbean alone, it is estimated that billions of drug dollars are used every year to tempt law enforcement officers and government officials. The Partnership for a Drug-Free America points out that

- Americans spend billions of dollars yearly for the purchase of illegal drugs.[1]
- Many organized criminal groups, gangs, and terrorists depend on drug money.
- Millions of Americans use illegal drugs every year.

Drugs have become readily available to anyone seeking them. Not only are drugs easily available, but better quality drugs are sold illegally at prices lower than ever before. The prices and quality make them available to the poor and the young.

Illegal Drug Users

The war against illegal drugs is being fought on the *supply side* and on the *demand side*. Cocaine, heroin, crack, and marijuana are produced and grown for the most part outside the United States. Great efforts are being made to prevent illegal drugs from entering the United States. However, efforts to win the *supply side* war have been going on since the 1950s with what is estimated as 90 percent of the illegal drugs getting into the United States.

The *demand side* problem is that millions of Americans are willing to pay billions of dollars yearly for illegal drugs. More money is spent annually in the United States on illegal drugs and legal alcohol than is spent for clothing.[2] The United States is the biggest market in the world for illegal drugs and the profits are huge, so criminals will take great risks to bring the illegal drugs into the country. The users of illegal drugs can be classified as follows:

- *The "situational" drug abuser* is a person who will use illegal drugs for a specific or "situational" purpose, such as to accomplish some other objective. A person who is under a great deal of stress or tension might use a drug such as marijuana to relax. A performer or a truck driver might use a stimulant, or an upper, to stay awake.
- *The "party" or the "weekend" user* is a drug abuser who might use drugs for kicks or just for the experience. These users and the "casual user" are great sources of profits for drug pushers.

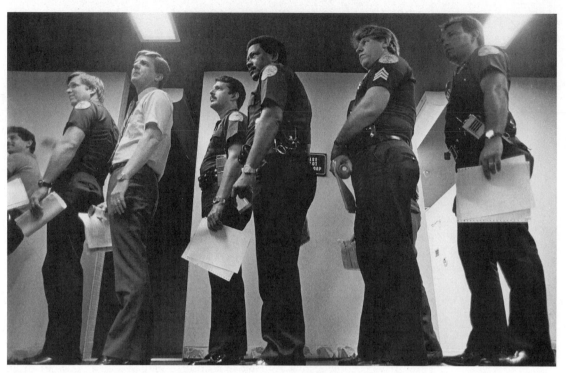

After illegal drug use was disclosed in their departments, officers volunteered to take urine tests to show they were not using drugs. These officers are waiting with their paperwork and sample bottles to take urine tests at police headquarters.   © Bettmann/CORBIS

- *The drug addict* is physically and/or psychologically dependent on drugs. He or she cannot perform daily without drug support. Addicts have a "monkey on their back," which could be very expensive to support. To raise the money for the daily supply of drugs ($50, $100, or even $150 per day), addicts steal, break into cars, commit burglaries, rob, snatch purses, or push drugs. Women or men who trade sex for drugs are the most susceptible to AIDS.

Drug Laws in the United States

If You Drank a Bottle of Coca-Cola in the Year 1905, You Would Probably Not Know That It Contained Cocaine

The first law enacted in the United States was an antiopium-smoking ordinance passed in San Francisco in 1875 because of the opium smoking problem there.[3] This was one of the few restrictions in the United States at that time.

In the 1880s and 1890s, people in the United States could concoct and sell to the American public practically any drug or drug compound they wished. Drugs were available in stores, through mail-order catalogs, or through traveling vendors and peddlers. Little was known at that time about the effect of drugs on human beings. Drug promoters claimed the drugs cured sickness and other human problems.

A German firm, for example, marketed a newly discovered drug in the 1890s as a cough suppressant. The name the firm gave the drug is well known today—heroin.

Heroin did a wonderful job of suppressing coughs, but years passed before people realized the terrible evils and misery of addiction to heroin. Other drugs and compounds that often contained either cocaine or heroin were advertised and promoted as cures for everything from ingrown toenails to cancer. Medications were sold that guaranteed sex rejuvenation, the growing of hair on bald people, the enlargement of women's breasts, a cure for arthritis, and so on.

Cocaine was used in Coca-Cola, a very popular soft drink even in those days. Cocaine was not replaced by the drug caffeine in Coca-Cola until 1906.

With the use of cocaine and heroin in some everyday products, U.S. President William Howard Taft's statement of 1910 that "the misuse of cocaine is undoubtedly an American habit, the most threatening of the drug habits that has ever appeared in this country," is understandable today.

In 1906, the Federal Pure Food and Drug Act was enacted because of the concern over heroin addiction. The FDA requires that a firm or person who wishes to market and sell a drug in the United States must show that

- the drug or medication is not harmful to humans, and

- the drug or medication will do what it is advertised to do.

Another law enacted at the time was the 1915 federal Harrison Narcotics Act.

The Uniform Controlled Substances Act

Today, the federal government and all of the states in the United States have enacted the *Uniform Controlled Substances Act*, which was approved by the National Conference of Commissioners on Uniform State Laws in 1970.[4] The purposes of this Act have been stated as follows:

> This Uniform Act was drafted to achieve uniformity between the laws of the several States and those of the Federal government. It has been designed to complement the new Federal narcotic and dangerous drug legislation and provide an interlocking trellis of Federal and State law to enable government at all levels to control more effectively the drug abuse problem.
> Uniform Controlled Substances Act, 9 U.L.A., Commissioners' Prefatory Note, p. 188 (1979).

In their Uniform Controlled Substances Acts, most states forbid and make it criminal conduct to

- manufacture[5] or deliver a controlled (forbidden) substance,

- possess with intent to manufacture or deliver a *controlled substance*,

- create, deliver, or possess with intent to deliver a counterfeit substance,

- offer or agree to deliver a controlled substance and then deliver or dispense a substance that is not a controlled substance,

- possess a controlled substance,

- knowingly keep or maintain a store, dwelling, building, vehicle, boat, or aircraft, or other place resorted to by persons illegally using controlled substances,

- acquire or obtain possession of a controlled substance by misrepresentation, fraud, forgery, deception, or subterfuge.

The Uniform Controlled Substances Act has five schedules of controlled substances according to their potential for abuse, degree of accepted medical use, and relative physical danger to the abuser. These schedules are summarized by the U.S. Bureau of Justice Statistics *1992 Report on Drugs, Crime and the Justice System*, as follows:

Schedule	Abuse Potential	Examples of Drugs Covered	Some of the Effects	Medical Use
I	Highest	Heroin, LSD, hashish, marijuana, methaqualone, designer drugs	Unpredictable effects, severe psychological or physical dependence, or death	No accepted use; some are legal for limited research use only
II	High	Morphine, PCP, codeine, cocaine, methadone, Demerol, benzedrine, dexedrine	May lead to severe psychological or physical dependence	Accepted use with restrictions
III	Medium	Codeine with aspirin or Tylenol, some amphetamines, anabolic steroids	May lead to moderate or low physical dependence or high psychological dependence	Accepted use
IV	Low	Darvon, Talwin, phenobarbital, Equanil, Miltown, Librium, diazepam	May lead to limited physical or psychological dependence	Accepted use
V	Lowest	Over-the-counter or prescription compounds with codeine, Lomotil, Robitussin A-C	May lead to limited physical or psychological dependence	Accepted use

Types of Possession of Controlled Substances

The most common criminal (or ordinance) illegal drug charge is that of possession of a controlled substance.[6] Possession must be proved in order to sustain the arrest and conviction. Proof of possession may be either of the following:

- *Actual possession* is possession on the person of the defendant, or within an area of his or her immediate control and reach. Actual possession may be within a container (such as a purse, package, or suitcase) that the defendant may be carrying or has within reach. Actual possession may also occur in a vehicle when the controlled substance is under the seat of the person or in the glove compartment of the vehicle owned or driven by the defendant.

- *Constructive possession* of a controlled substance occurs when illegal drugs are in a place immediately accessible to the accused and subject to his or her domination and control. Examples of constructive possession would be drugs found in the trunk of a car the defendant owned or was the driver of, or in a home or business place controlled and dominated by a defendant to such an extent that a strong inference of possession could be drawn by a judge or jury.

(See Chapter 3 for additional material on possession.)

To Convict of Possession of an Illegal Drug, Must the State Present a "Usable Amount" as Evidence?

State courts differ on the question as to whether a "trace" amount of an illegal drug (that is, an amount so small that it is unusable) will sustain a conviction for possession of that drug.

In the case of *People v. Mizell*,[7] the highest court in the state of New York followed the "majority" of the states and held that "any amount of an (illegal drug) is sufficient to sustain a conviction for possession." In the *Mizell* case, cocaine "residue" found on the sides of vials was used to support the criminal charge and conviction for possession. The conviction was affirmed, with the Court holding that the "cocaine residue—though unusable—is nevertheless a controlled substance" under the criminal code of the state of New York.[8]

However, other courts follow the "usable quantity rule" and hold that a blackened residue or a useless trace amount will not sustain a criminal conviction for possession of an illegal drug. Courts holding that a usable quantity of drugs must be presented include California[9] and Florida.[10]

Delivery of Controlled Substances

The acts that are prohibited under the Uniform Controlled Substances Act, as listed in Florida's Criminal Code Section 893.13, are as follows:

> [I]t is unlawful for any person to sell, purchase, manufacture, or deliver, or possess with intent to sell . . . a controlled substance.

Delivery of an illegal drug can be either an actual delivery, or it could be the crime of possession of a controlled substance with intent to deliver (sell or transfer).

In most of the actual delivery cases that come into criminal courts throughout the United States, the government presents evidence showing that the accused sold (delivered) illegal drugs to an undercover law enforcement officer. In other actual delivery cases, the state proves its case by producing a witness to the illegal drug transaction (either the receiver of the drugs or an observer of the delivery). Videotapes or a film of the delivery could also be used as evidence.

The Crime of Possession of a Controlled Substance With Intent to Deliver (Sell or Transfer)

In the typical criminal case of "*possession with intent to deliver* (sell)," the state presents evidence showing that the accused had possession of a large amount of an illegal drug (more than he or she would personally use). A combination of the following evidence is

Possession of a Small Amount of Marijuana

The offense of "possession of a small amount of marijuana" is charged in different ways throughout the United States.

Criminal offense	*Civil offense*	*Legalizing this conduct*
If the person is charged and convicted under a statute and could receive a jail sentence, the conviction is a criminal conviction and the person has been convicted of a crime.	If the only penalty that can be imposed after conviction is a money fine, the conviction is for a civil offense and is similar to a speeding ticket or a parking ticket. Under these circumstances, the offense of possession of a small amount of marijuana has been "decriminalized" as it is no longer charged as a crime.	If neither criminal nor civil punishment is imposed for possession of a small amount of marijuana, the conduct has then been legalized and is no longer a crime or a civil offense. Alaska is reportedly the only state that has legalized possession of a small amount of marijuana by adults. See *Allam v. State,* 830 P.2d 435 (Alaska App. 1992).

State and Federal Clash over the Medical Use of Marijuana

Eight states have passed laws permitting the use of marijuana for medical purposes. But federal drug law has no medical use exception for marijuana and the federal government began major crackdowns in 2001 on the medical use of marijuana in California. This angered many local state officials and caused concern to doctors who could lose their license if they write prescriptions for the use of marijuana.

also generally presented: that the accused also possessed scales and/or small plastic bags with evenly weighed-out illegal drugs, a large amount of money, a pager, or a cellular phone. Evidence that the accused did not have a job but lived very well and drove an expensive car could also be presented.

The evidence presented by the government must be sufficient to justify a conclusion by the fact finder (jury or judge) that the accused possessed the illegal drug with intent to deliver (sell or transfer) to another person. To do this, the U.S. Supreme Court requires that there must be a "rational connection"[11] between the facts presented and the conclusion drawn by the fact finder.

Drug "Rip-Off" Cases

In *State v. Glover,* 594 A.2d 1086 (Me. 1991), the defendant wanted to rip off the buyer and, instead of cocaine, delivered two bags of baking soda at $50 a bag. His conviction for attempted trafficking in cocaine was affirmed. Glover's buyer was an undercover police officer.

Other states, such as Iowa, have statutes that make the delivery or possession of a "simulated controlled substance" a crime. A simulated controlled substance is a substance "represented to be [an illegal drug] . . . and because of its nature, packaging, or appearance would lead a reasonable person to believe it to be a controlled substance." Iowa Statute 204.401(1).

In *State v. Henderson,* 478 N.W.2d 626 (Iowa 1991), the Iowa Supreme Court affirmed the defendant's conviction of possession of a simulated controlled substance.

Criminal Liability for Drug-Induced Deaths

Drug overdose cases occur regularly in every city in the United States as drugs have become purer, cheaper, and easier to obtain. Cocaine is particularly dangerous because it is an unpredictable killer that can cause life-threatening complications that are not related to the dose taken, the length of use, or the manner in which the drug is taken. Swallowing an "eight ball" of cocaine (an eighth of an ounce) can easily cause acute cocaine intoxication and death.[12]

A number of states have enacted laws that make people who illegally manufacture, distribute, or dispense illegal drugs strictly liable for a death that results from the injection, inhalation, or ingestion of such a drug.[13]

Such laws are often called *Len Bias* laws. Len Bias was a basketball star at the University of Maryland when he died as the result of using cocaine. The following case illustrates:

State v. Ervin

Superior Court of New Jersey (1990) 242 N.J.Super. 584, 577 A.2d 1273

Ervin purchased cocaine, which he and his girlfriend shared. She died as the result of using the cocaine. He was not only charged with possession of cocaine but also possession with intent to deliver and causing a drug-induced death, in violation of the New Jersey *Len Bias* law. In sustaining the conviction for the drug-induced death, the Court held:

> The New Jersey Legislature has determined that manufacturing, distributing and dispensing certain illegal drugs, including cocaine which is the substance involved in the present case, are criminal activities which, like the crimes enumerated in the felony murder statute, pose inherent dangers to others including those who use the drugs. Defendant has shown us no basis upon which to conclude that that determination is irrational.
>
> * * *
>
> We hold that the absolute or strict liability feature of N.J.S.A. 2C:35-9, limited as it is to deaths which are the proximate consequences of inherently dangerous illegal activities, does not violate due process of law.

Possession or Sale of Drug Paraphernalia

State criminal codes and the federal government make the possession or sale of *drug paraphernalia* a crime. The Federal Criminal Code defines drug paraphernalia as "any equipment, product or material of any kind which is primarily intended or designed for use" with illegal drugs.[14]

Some products have only one use and that is as drug paraphernalia. For example, "bongs," which are water pipes used for the smoking of marijuana, were called "hardcore paraphernalia by virtue of (their) physical features . . . (because bongs have) no alternative uses."[15]

An example of an item that has more than one use is inositol, an optically inactive alcohol. Inositol is a common cocaine-cutting ingredient. Because inositol has dual purposes, the government has to establish that the inositol was "primarily intended" as drug paraphernalia. *United States v. Mishra,* 979 F.2d 301 (3rd Cir. 1992).

Drug paraphernalia charges and convictions are most often obtained when the item or paraphernalia is seized with drugs such as marijuana, cocaine, and other drugs. In the

This officer is listing items that may or may not violate the drug paraphernalia laws. The federal criminal code defines drug paraphernalia as objects that are "primarily intended or designed for use" with illegal drugs.   © James L. Shaffer

1994 case of *People v. Feld,* 641 N.E.2d 924, an Illinois appellate court held that the state failed to establish that boxes and small wooden pipes were drug paraphernalia. The defendant, a manufacturer, was not apprehended using the boxes and wooden pipes in drug use.

The federal Mail Order Drug Paraphernalia Control Act (21 U.S.C.A. § 857) was upheld in *Posters 'N' Things Ltd. v. United States,* 969 F.2d 652, 51 CrL 1369 (1992), cert. granted 113 S.Ct. 1410 (1993). The defendant in this case sold scales and substances commonly used by cocaine dealers to dilute cocaine. The defendant advertised the products for such use, and purchases were made in such large amounts that it showed that dealers rather than other users were buying the items.

Other Statutes and Laws Used in the War on Drugs

Subject Matter of Law	Problem Addressed by Law
"Drug Kingpin" statutes	The federal government and many states have created a separate crime of being the leader of a narcotics trafficking network. Many criminal codes punish this offense with life imprisonment. New Jersey is one of the states that does and defines "drug kingpin" as follows in New Jersey Statute 2C-35-3:

(*continued*)

Toxic Waste From Illegal Drug Labs

Every year, law enforcement officers seize hundreds of clandestine methamphetamine labs. About twenty percent of the illegal labs are found because of a fire or an explosion at the lab.

Methamphetamine (also known as ice, crank, go, poor man's cocaine, or meth) is a highly addictive central-nervous-system stimulant. Meth is one of the few illegal drugs that people without any chemical expertise can manufacture on their own. In 1998, 1,654 meth labs were seized—most in rural areas of western states.

Of the thirty-two chemicals that can be used to make or "cook" meth, one-third are extremely toxic and also reactive, explosive, flammable, and corrosive. For every pound of meth produced, between five and six pounds of highly toxic waste is generated.

Cleanup is a big mess and is dangerous. Law officers have to take protective measures. As toxic waste is dumped on the land and into streams, sewage systems, lakes, and landfills, hazardous material teams have to be called. Cleanup costs often exceed $100,000. In these cases, criminal charges for violation of environmental laws can be added to the drug charges. (See Chapter 23 on environmental crimes.)

Subject Matter of Law	Problem Addressed by Law
	A person is a leader of a narcotics trafficking network if he conspires with others as an organizer, supervisor, financier or manager, to engage for profit in a scheme or course of conduct to unlawfully manufacture, distribute, dispense, bring into or transport in this State any substance classified in Schedule I or II, or any controlled substance analog thereof
Additional Imprisonment for Using or Carrying a Firearm During and in a Relation to Drug Trafficking crime	The Federal Criminal Code (18 U.S.C.A. § 924(c) and the statutes of most (if not all) states provide for additional punishment for a person using or carrying a firearm during and in relation to a drug trafficking crime.[16]
Nuisance laws and drug house abatement statutes and ordinances	Landlords are often warned that if they allow tenants to sell drugs from the landlord's property, an abatement or nuisance proceeding could be started against the property. Drug houses could also be taken over by a state or local government because of failure to pay taxes, or they could be condemned because of fire or code violations.
Forfeiture of property	Under the Controlled Substance Act and other forfeiture statutes, the following may be seized under

(continued)

Subject Matter of Law	Problem Addressed by Law	(continued)
	court order: (1) instruments of the crime (such as vehicles or watercraft used to commit the crime), (2) profits of the crime (money from drug dealing, stolen goods, and so on), and (3) proceeds of the illegal act (homes, condos, yachts, farms, or other luxury goods purchased from profits of the crime). If the offender did not pay taxes on the profits of drug dealing, the Internal Revenue Service may take action against drug traffickers.	
Use of communications facility to further a drug violation	The use of a communications facility to commit or facilitate a drug violation is a crime itself under federal law if the defendant has a prior conviction for a felony drug violation. (See the 1998 case of *United States v. Mankins,* 1998 WL 65317 [5th Cir. 1998].)	
Possession of wiretapping devices, illegal bugs, and eavesdropping equipment	Title 18, Chapter 119, of the Omnibus Crime and Safe Streets Act makes it illegal to own, manufacture, or sell eavesdropping and wiretapping equipment specifically designed for "the surreptitious interception of wire, oral or electronic communications." Only law enforcement agencies are permitted to buy or use such devices and then only with a court order. Some drug dealers and other criminals illegally possess and use these devices.	
"Schoolyard" or "schoolhouse" laws	In an attempt to keep drugs from schoolyards and neighborhoods, "schoolyard" laws were passed that increase jail time for dealing drugs within one thousand feet of an elementary or secondary school.	
Loss of financial aid and loans for a year for students who are found guilty of simple possession of an illegal drug such as marijuana	Over nine thousand students lost financial aid in the year 2000 under a law enacted by Congress in 1998. Federal college aid can be lost for longer periods for repeat or more serious drug offenses.	

Alcohol-Related Crimes

Alcohol as a Drug

Alcohol is a drug used by an estimated 95 million Americans in some form and in varying amounts. It is a mood-altering drug used by many people as a tranquilizer. It has been observed that if alcohol were discovered today for the first time, the FDA would be obligated by law to forbid its over-the-counter sale without prescription. This statement

"Sniffing," "Bagging," and "Huffing" Inhalants

Inhalants are chemicals that give off fumes or vapors that slow the body's reactions and cloud thinking when breathed in. Many common household products are inhalants

The Partnership for a Drug-Free America estimated in 1998 that

- one out of every five school-age children has tried getting high through the use of an inhalant; and

- one out of every two of these children can name three or more common products that produce a high when inhaled.

Common products available to kids that will produce a high include glue, gasoline, correction fluid, felt-tipped markers, and others. The Partnership for a Drug-Free America estimates that there are more than twelve hundred products available to kids that are capable of producing highs and states that the use of inhalants has become an "epidemic."

Inhalants can be "sniffed" (inhaling the substance into the nose directly from the container), "bagged" (dumping the substance into a bag and inhaling the fumes), or "huffed" (soaking a rag with a mixture, putting the rag to the mouth, and inhaling the fumes).

Inhalants can cause suffocation, a heart attack, or even death. Common symptoms in a child (or an adult) of inhalant use are staggering gait and uncoordinated walk and movement, delirium, slurred speech, chemical odor on breath, body, or clothes, loss of appetite, intoxication, nausea and/or vomiting, belligerence, or impaired hearing.

For further information, call or write the National Clearing House of Alcohol and Drug Addiction.

is made because alcohol is an addictive drug and because it is toxic—it is a poison. But alcohol has, for a long time, been part of our economic, social, and cultural environment. Because of the beverage's long history of social acceptance and our society's economic dependence on it, it continues to be sold openly on the market.

Alcohol's Relation to Crimes and Deaths

British and U.S. studies of accidental deaths in the 1980s and a National Institutes of Health study in 2002 showed that alcohol has a high relationship to deaths caused by drownings, chokings, burns and fires, and falls.[17] A pedestrian who is intoxicated was reported 3.5 times more likely to be killed or injured in a traffic accident.

Alcohol is the most widely abused and misused drug in America and in many other countries of the world. Alcoholism is one of the biggest health problems in the United States, just behind heart disease and cancer. Excessive use of alcohol is also a factor causing heart disease and cancer.

When public drunkenness was prosecuted as a crime throughout the United States, it was always high on the yearly list of crimes.[18] Alcohol continues to be an important factor in many disorderly conduct, battery, assault, rape, child abuse, domestic relations disputes, and criminal damage to property cases occurring in the United States every year. The movement from other drugs to alcohol is sometimes condoned by parents, who in their relief that their children are not involved in the use of other forms of drugs, do not recognize the dangers inherent in the use of alcohol.

The 2002 National Institutes of Health study surveyed drinking among the 8 million college and university students in the United States. The study showed that most students drink moderately or not at all, but 44 percent of students drink in binges.

Alcoholic-related student deaths numbered 1,445 students a year—4 per day. An additional 1,370 students suffered injuries (some very serious) tied to drinking, and an estimated 192 students are raped or sexually assaulted daily after drinking.

1998 Report on Alcohol and Drug Problems of Prison Inmates

The majority of the 1.7 million prisoners in U.S. jails and prisons have substantial alcohol and drug abuse problems. A national study released in 1998 found that illegal drugs and alcohol helped lead to the imprisonment of 80 percent of U.S. prisoners (four out of five of the inmates).[19]

The report released by the National Center on Addiction and Substance Abuse at Columbia University found that 80 percent of the prisoners had been high when they had committed their crimes or had stolen to support their habits or had a history of drug and alcohol abuse that led them to commit crimes.

The study reported that alcohol was the drug most closely associated with the violent crimes of murder, rape, assault, and child and spousal abuse.

Twenty-one percent of state prisoners were convicted of a violent crime while under the influence of alcohol alone. (Three percent were high on crack or powder cocaine, and 1 percent on heroin.)

Drunk Driving: The Criminal Homicide Causing the Most Deaths

Almost fifty people are killed every day in the United States because of *driving under the influence*. In addition, about one million people are injured. The National Highway Traffic Safety Administration estimates the yearly costs of drunk driving to be $45 billion.

Tougher laws and the wide acceptance of the use of designated drivers have helped reduce deaths caused by drunk driving by 29 percent in the ten years ending 1996. The 1997 death of Princess Diana in a high-speed Paris, France, crash received great public attention when the driver of the Mercedes sedan was reported to have a high blood-alcohol level.

The punishment for drunk driving has been increased, and state laws such as forbidding or curbing happy hours by taverns and clubs have been enacted by some states. Victims of drunk driving are reminded that they may commence lawsuits in most states under "dram shop"[20] laws that permit civil lawsuits under some circumstances against bars and individuals furnishing or selling the alcoholic drinks.

Debates have occurred in the legislatures of all states as to what the blood-alcohol limit should be in that state. Organizations such as MADD (Mothers Against Drunk Driving) urge that the limit of 0.10 percent be reduced to 0.08 percent, pointing out that the lower limit is still higher than in most European countries and Japan. Insurance companies and the American Medical Association join MADD in pointing out that alcohol can unravel driving skills subtly and insidiously, long before persons look and act drunk.

Experts now point out that it is the driver with a drinking problem who is the problem. Too many people with severe alcohol and/or drug problems continue to drive while impaired and under the influence. Problem drinkers continue to drink and drive even

Driving and Alcohol

Does your state regulate the following conduct or have the following laws?

Conduct   *Statute*

Driving a vehicle while under the influence   First offense   _____
of alcohol or drug. (Does motor vehicle
include watercraft, aircraft, moped, etc.?)   Second offense   _____

                                                      Third offense   _____

The legal drinking limit is?   _____

Drinking and driving age is?   _____

"Booze it and lose it" statute (administrative license
revocation laws that give police the right to seize licenses
of drivers who fail or refuse sobriety tests)   _____

Punish refusal of driver to take Breathalyzer or other test
when lawfully requested?   _____

Bans open containers of alcohol beverage
in motor vehicles?   _____

While driving under the influence:

- causes property damage?   _____

- causes serious injury to another person?   _____

- causes the death of another person?   _____

Leaving scene of accident (failing to stop and report)

- property damage?   _____

- injury to person?   _____

- fatal accident?   _____

Could law enforcement agencies in your state set up sobriety
checkpoints?   _____

after their licenses have been revoked. They are generally the danger on the highway. One expert commented on the problem drinker, stating that often, "He doesn't give a damn, especially after drinking."

"Booze It and Lose It" Laws

More than thirty states have passed *"booze it and lose it" laws*, which give the police the authority to immediately seize the driver's license of people who fail or refuse sobriety tests. After these new laws became known to the drinking public, a dramatic drop occurred in nighttime fatal crashes. The National Safety Board estimated that if all fifty states adopted such laws, two thousand lives could be saved in the United States each year.

Many states have laws that take away the driver's licenses of motorists under age 21 who drive after drinking even a small amount of alcohol.

When Is a Person Driving, Operating, or "in Physical Control" of a Vehicle?

States forbid operating motor vehicles, watercraft, snowmobiles, and aircraft while under the influence of alcohol or of a controlled substance. In most drunk driving cases, either a police officer or a witness testifies to seeing the defendant drive a vehicle while he or she was intoxicated. But when no witnesses are available to testify as to the driving, courts have ruled as described in the following list in answer to the question of when a person is driving, operating, or "in physical control" of a vehicle. All of the following defendants were under the influence:

- *Defendants who were found asleep behind the wheel of their vehicle:*
  Yes, engine was running. *State v. Dey.* 798 S.W.2d 210 (Mo.App. 1990).
  No, vehicle was in a ditch with engine off. *State v. Block,* 798 S.W.2d 213 (Mo.App. 1990).
  No, key was in the "off" position. *Stevenson v. City of Falls Church,* 416 S.E.2d 435 (Sup.Ct.Vir. 1992).
  No, engine was running but vehicle was "parked." *State v. Mordacq,* 585 N.E.2d 22 (Ind.App. 1992).

- *Defendant turned on the ignition of vehicle:*
  Yes. *State v. Hines,* 478 N.W.2d 888 (Iowa App. 1991).

- *Defendants were sitting behind the wheel of their vehicle; the engine was off, but they were intoxicated:*
  Yes, in the two Minnesota cases of *State v. Starfield,* 481 N.W.2d 834 (1992), and *State v. Nelson,* 483 N.W.2d 739 (1992).

- *California requires "volitional movement of vehicle." Mercer v. Department of Motor Vehicles,* 809 P.2d 414 (Sup.Ct.Calif. 1991).

SUMMARY

All states and the federal government have enacted the Uniform Controlled Substance Act of 1970. Under this law, which is part of the criminal code of your state, the following are crimes:

- Manufacture or delivery of an illegal drug

- Possession with intent to deliver an illegal drug

- Delivery or possession with intent to deliver a counterfeit substance

- Offering or agreeing to deliver an illegal drug and then deliver a substance that is not a controlled substance

- Possession of an illegal drug

- Knowingly allowing a store, dwelling, building, vehicle, boat, aircraft, or other place to be used by persons using illegal drugs

- Obtaining possession of an illegal drug by misrepresentation, fraud, forgery, deception or subterfuge.

BOOK-SPECIFIC WEB SITE

For chapter-related Web links, quizzing activities, and case and news updates, go to the *Criminal Law*, Eighth Edition, book-specific Web site at **http://info.wadsworth.com/ gardner.**

QUESTIONS AND PROBLEMS

1. Is the following conduct made an offense under the laws of your state, county, or city:
   a) Drinking a bottle of beer in a moving motor vehicle?
   b) Drinking an alcoholic beverage from an open container while sitting in a motor vehicle parked in public parking lot?
   c) Public drunkenness?

2. An intoxicated man waved to a police officer as the man urinated on the sidewalk at 4:10 A.M. in front of the main Honolulu Police Department. The man was arrested and convicted of open lewdness. How would this incident probably be handled in your community?

INFOTRAC COLLEGE EDITION EXERCISES

1. Go to InfoTrac College Edition and, using the keyword search term *drunk driving* and the subdivision *laws,* find the article discussing the so-called glove-box defense. Should that defense ever be permitted? Can a state pass a law that convicts anyone sitting behind the wheel of a car who fails the blood-alcohol test, even if they were not operating the car but only drinking in the car?

2. Go to InfoTrac College Edition and, using the keyword search term *drug abuse* and the subdivision *laws,* find the article describing the many ways athletes can use drugs for performance-enhancing reasons.

3. Go to InfoTrac College Edition and, using the keyword search term *drug abuse* and the subdivision *crime*, find the article discussing the results in California under Proposition 36, which requires treatment rather than incarceration in many drug-related crimes. Should other states adopt the California approach?

NOTES

1. In 1998, the National Institute of Drug Abuse estimated that there are four million drug addicts in the United States (two to three million hooked on powder or rock cocaine, eight hundred thousand are heroin addicts, and the remainder are addicted to other drugs).

In addition, millions of people who are not addicted use illegal drugs. The U.S. General Accounting Office (GAO) reports that federal, state, and local governments will spend $3.2 million in 1998 to treat and provide medical care to addicts. The GAO estimates that other costs—drug-related crime, prevention, and lost productivity—will total more than $60 billion a year.

2. A U.N. report in 1997 estimated that the illegal drug trade makes up 8 percent of world trade. This illegal industry is estimated at between $400 billion and

$1 trillion worldwide. It is as large as the worldwide trade in textiles and bigger than the sales of iron or steel. See the *Pensacola New Journal* article "U.N. Report: Social Costs of Drug Abuse About $120 Billion" (November 16, 1997).

3. The Opium War, which Great Britain waged against China from 1839 to 1842, was conducted to force China to permit the importing of opium into China. China had silk and many other goods to sell to the world but would not buy goods from Britain and other nations. As a result, the British ran up a huge trade deficit. To pay off this deficit, the British commenced selling opium to the Chinese and established a British colony at Hong Kong. When the Chinese government tried to stop the sale of opium, the Opium War began.

To supply the opium trade, opium was grown in the British colony of India and shipped to China to be traded for Chinese exports. By 1850, India's largest export was opium, exceeding the export of Indian cotton textiles.

American shippers also brought opium into China to sell in exchange for goods from China. The biggest American trader was Warren Delano (the grandfather of President Franklin Delano Roosevelt). Delano became a very wealthy man in the trade with China. But this trade created thousands of opium addicts and was denounced in churches and in newspapers throughout the United States. After trading in opium was forbidden, illegal shipping and trading in opium continued to supply this deadly drug. See the *New York Times* articles "The Opium War's Secret History" and "Hong Kong's Colonial Ghosts" (June 22, 1997). Also see the book, *Opium: A History* by Martin Booth (St. Martin's Press, 1998).

4. This Act replaced the 1933 Uniform Narcotic Drug Act and the 1966 Model State Drug Abuse Control Act.

5. A designer drug is a drug that is cheaply made from chemicals and is sometimes similar to a commonly known illegal drug. New designer drugs come on the market regularly. To prevent the invention, manufacturing, and distribution of designer drugs before they are permanently scheduled in the Uniform Controlled Substance Act, the U.S. Congress enacted a law permitting the quick and temporary placement of a new designer drug in the federal Controlled Substance Act.

If this law had not been passed, a new designer drug could be sold throughout the United States for up to a year before it was permanently made a part of the Uniform Controlled Substance Act. The U.S. Supreme Court unanimously upheld the quick scheduling of new designer drugs in the 1991 case of *Touby v. U.S.,* 111 S.Ct. 1752.

6. Many courts hold that a person cannot be convicted of possession of a drug solely because the drug is in the person's body. See *State v. Thronsen,* 809 P.2d 941 (Alaska App. 1991), and *State v. Vorm,* 570 N.E.2d 109 (Ind.App. 1991). However, people with an illegal drug in their bodies could be charged with the crime of "being under the influence of a controlled substance." See *Junior v. State,* 807 P.2d 205 (Sup.Ct.Nev. 1991).

7. 532 N.E.2d 1249 (N.Y. 1988). Surprisingly, tests done by the Argonne National Laboratory in 1997 showed that many $1 and $2 bills circulated in Chicago, Miami, and Houston were tainted with microscopic traces of cocaine. The chemists conducting the tests stated that $1 and $2 bills are used to wrap "rocks" (chunks of solid cocaine chipped off a cocaine brick). The rock is then sold. Paper money is used instead of newspaper because the money does not transfer ink to the cocaine as newspaper does. Dollar bills are also rolled into tubes and used to snort cocaine powder.

Defense lawyers have used these findings in cocaine possession cases. The report also states that people who handle cocaine-tainted money do not show traces of cocaine on their person except when money comes into contact with large amounts of cocaine immediately before a person handled it. See the *New York Times* article "Cocaine Turns Up in Many $1 and $2 Bills" (September 23, 1997).

8. The Court of Appeals of South Carolina held that ordinarily a measurable quantity is necessary, but when the cocaine was the "remnant of a larger amount previously possessed in the past," the conviction was affirmed. The cocaine residue was in a crack pipe. *State v. Robinson,* 411 S.E.2d 678 (1991). In *State v. Wood,* 1994 WL 250015 (N.M.App. 1994), the cocaine residue was in syringes (conviction sustained).

9. *People v. Rubacalba,* 1993 WL 428266 (Cal. 1993).

10. *Lord v. State,* 616 So.2d 1065 (Fla. App. 1993).

11. See *County Court of Ulster County v. Allen,* 442 U.S. 140, 99 S.Ct. 2213 (1979).

12. See the *Harvard Medical School Heart Letter* article "Cocaine: An Unpredictable Killer" (April 1992). The article points out that until 1914, cocaine was an ingredient in many cough syrups and home remedy medications sold in the United States. The article also notes that cocaine was used in Coca-Cola until it was replaced by caffeine in 1906. The Harrison Drug Act of 1914 classified cocaine as a narcotic in 1914 and limited its use to prescription medical purposes. The article states that cocaine "then went underground, where it remains (today)."

13. If a person was committing a felony in supplying an illegal drug that directly caused a drug-induced death, a prosecutor could issue a criminal charge of felony murder in addition to other criminal charges if the case met the requirements of the felony murder law of that state. (See Chapter 13 of this text for a discussion of the crime of felony murder.)

14. 21 U.S.C.A. § 863(d).

15. *U.S. v. Dyer,* 750 F.Supp. 1275 (E.D.Va. 1990).

16. In the 1995 case of *Bailey v. U.S.* 116 S.Ct. 501, the U.S. Supreme Court held that to violate § 924(c), the weapon had to be actively deployed and not just left sitting in a closet or nightstand drawer. In the 1997 case of *Muscarello v. U.S.*, 118 S.Ct. 1911, Muscarello was convicted of dealing marijuana. He kept his gun in the locked glove compartment of his pickup truck.

17. *Harvard Medical School Health Letter* (September 1993) citing *British Medical Journal* and *Southern Medical Journal*. The April 2002 report is entitled *A Call to Action: Changing the Culture of Drinking at U.S. Colleges.* The study was done by the National Institute of Alcohol Abuse and Alcoholism, which is a branch of the National Institutes of Health. (See the *New York Times* article "Study Calculates the Effects of College Drinking in U.S.," April 10, 2002.)

18. While many states have decriminalized public drunkenness, other states continue to make public drunkenness a crime. In cities and states in which public drunkenness is not a crime, a person who is intoxicated in a public place is often ignored if not getting into trouble or endangered. If such people are a problem, they could be taken to a detoxification center (if available) or a homeless shelter. Such people could also be arrested for disorderly conduct or another offense.

19. The former head of the White House national drug policy, Gen. Barry R. McCaffrey, stated that the 1998 study was consistent with recent U.S. Justice reports showing that more than 60 percent of adult males arrested in the United States for felonies had tested positive for at least one illegal drug. See the *New York Times* article "Alcohol or Drug Link Found in 80 percent of U.S. Prisoners" (January 9, 1998).

20. Most states have "dram shop" liability laws under which taverns and bars can be liable to innocent victims of alcohol-related accidents and crimes. Social hosts who provide alcohol can also be liable under the laws of some states. Providing alcohol to an under-age intoxicated minor creates the greatest civil liability under dram shop laws.

Authors' note

The 2002 National Institute of Alcohol Abuse and Alcoholism report arrived at the finding that 192 students are sexually abused each day after drinking based upon the following:

The report found that 2% of 400,000 college students stated that they had sex while they were too drunk to give consent. The estimate that 192 students are sexually assaulted daily is arrived at by adding this number and the number of reported student sexual abuses per year.

21

Terrorism

CONTENTS

KEY TERMS

terrorism:
  domestic
  international
  the crime of terrorizing
  bioterrorism
  anthrax as a terrrorist
  weapon

treason

sedition

sabotage

Terrorists are criminals who use force and violence in the pursuit of extreme political goals. They will take innocent lives to make political statements.

Terrorists could be domestic or international. They could be nonstate (acting on their own) or they could be sponsored and act for another nation. They could be protected or sponsored by a nation or a group.

Terrorism can be cheap and relatively easy. Terrorists use surprise and vulnerability to their advantage. A handful of dedicated individuals can cause great harm. Timothy McVeigh and Terry Nichols killed 168 people in seconds by blowing up the Alfred P. Murrah Federal Building in Oklahoma City. Less than a hundred foreign terrorists killed thousands on September 11, 2001.

Terrorism has existed for ages. In the first century, the Zealots used terrorism to fight the Roman occupation of Israel. In the twelfth century, a group of Shiite Muslims called the Assassins used terrorism against Persia. In 1901, an American president, William McKinley, was killed by an American terrorist. Four European heads of state were assassinated by terrorists between the years 1894 and 1900.

Terrorists can be religious or ethnic zealots. They could be persons seeking to avenge a perceived wrong. They could be maniacs who get their kicks out of violence. They could be oppressed people angry or desperate enough to use bombs and guns.

Terrorists differ from other criminals because they commit their crimes to send a political message or to retaliate for a wrong that they believe has occurred. They may seek a change as antiabortionists did who wanted to stop abortions by burning down abortion clinics and shooting abortion doctors.

Terrorism is also a form of warfare that has existed since wars have been waged and conducted. Northern Ireland has witnessed terrorism for more than a half century. To persons who are believers in the cause of the terrorist, the terrorist could be viewed as a hero. To the great majority of the civilized world, terrorists are criminals.

Early Terrorist Acts in the United States

One hundred years ago, anarchists (people who believe organized government is evil) used terrorism to convey their political message. In 1885, after a Chicago anarchist newspaper warned of a bombing, a bomb exploded in Haymarket Square, an open square in Chicago. It killed one policeman and seriously wounded seven other people. Two editors of an anarchist newspaper and two other men were convicted on evidence of their involvement in the bombing and were hanged.

In the years between 1894 and 1900, four European heads of state (the president of France, the prime minister of Spain, the empress of Austria, and the king of Italy) were assassinated by anarchists. President McKinley's assassin, an anarchist, stated before his execution, "I don't believe we should have any rulers. It is right to kill them."[1]

In 1910, the *Los Angeles Times* newspaper building was bombed in a labor dispute. In 1916, one year before the United States entered World War I, an antiwar bombing in San Francisco killed ten bystanders. In a 1920 protest against the stock market and capitalism, a wagon bomb set off on Wall Street killed thirty-three people in New York City.

Domestic Acts of Terrorism in the United States (1985–2000)

Theodore Kaczynski, acting as the "Unabomber," sent sixteen bombs in packages that killed three and injured twenty-eight people in the years from 1978 to 1995. Kaczynski was apprehended after eighteen years of bombing. His bombing was aimed at bringing down the technological system.

During the 1990s, there were bombings, torchings, and shootings at abortion clinics in the United States and Canada by antiabortion extremists. Five people were shot to death; many were injured and one person was killed in the bombings. These violent acts sought to scare and discourage abortion workers and women considering abortions.

Many torchings of buildings and other property damage were done by animal rights extremists who were protesting against rodeos, circuses, zoos, universities, restaurants, and other groups using animals. No deaths occurred, but the disruptions caused the U.S. Congress to create the crime of "animal enterprise terrorism."

A Japanese terrorist cult shocked Japan and the world in 1995 when it released several canisters of a deadly World War II nerve gas, sarin, in a Tokyo subway, killing twelve people and injuring more than five thousand.[2]

As mentioned earlier, less than one month after the Tokyo subway attack, the Alfred P. Murrah Federal Building in Oklahoma City was destroyed by a massive bomb, killing 168 people and wounding more than 500. Three men have been convicted of the bombing and murders of the innocent victims.

Timothy McVeigh[3] received the death penalty, and Terry Nichols was sentenced to life in prison without parole for the bombing of the Oklahoma City building. Although McVeigh and Nichols are reported to have no formal ties to militia or patriot groups, they believed that a "New World Order" was to be imposed by the United Nations, and they expressed hatred for federal law enforcement agencies. While on death row, McVeigh wrote an essay, which was published in a magazine with ties to right-wing militias. McVeigh stated that the Oklahoma City bombing was "morally equivalent" to military actions by the United States against foreign governments.

The October 1987 issue of the *FBI Law Enforcement Bulletin* lists extremist groups operating in the United States in this period. Groups listed by the magazine are as follows:

- *Leftist Groups:* Weather Underground, Black Liberation Army, and Black Panther Party were listed as responsible for twenty-one bombing and sixteen terrorists acts.

- *Antigovernment and white supremist groups:* Committed four bombings, armed robberies, assaults, and one murder.

- *Puerto Rican leftists groups:* Committed seventy terrorists acts of bombings, assassinations, armed robberies, and rocket attacks, most of which were in Puerto Rico.

- *Jewish extremists:* Committed twenty incidents of terrorism, including extortion and threats against persons deemed anti-Semitic or "overtly supportive of Arab efforts . . . not in the interests of Israel." Two members of the Jewish Defense League were arrested in Los Angeles in December 2001 and charged with conspiracy to bomb a Los Angeles mosque and the office of a U.S. Congressional member whose grandfather was Lebanese.[4]

- *Supporters of terrorism in Northern Ireland:* Committed the following crimes in the United States:
  - Illegal purchases and transport of weapons to Northern Ireland
  - Illegal transfers of money to Northern Ireland
  - Assisting in the illegal presence of Irish terrorists in the United States to obtain funds and weapons

If an organization is designated and named as a foreign terrorist organization in the United States by the State Department, it is a crime for Americans to support the group either by money or with other meaningful assistance.

Terrorism by Muslim Extremists Against the United States (1985–2001)

The following terrorists acts were committed by Muslim extremists against the United States from 1985 to 2001:

- Pan Am Air Flight 103 was blown out of the sky over Lockerbie, Scotland, killing all 259 on board the aircraft and 11 people on the ground.
- Seven bombings of U.S. overseas buildings occurred from 1985 to 1998. Over 150 people were killed and over 2,000 injured. Many of the dead and injured were foreign nationals working for the United States. The locations were U.S. Air Force bases in Spain and Germany, a military training center and military barracks in Saudi Arabia, and the U.S. embassies in Kenya, Tanzania, and Peru.
- A truck bomb damaged the New York World Trade Center in 1993, killing six people and injuring more than a thousand. Sheik Omar Rahman and nine other militant Muslims were convicted of this attack and also a conspiracy that, if carried out, would have destroyed the United Nations building and many other New York City landmarks.
- The U.S. naval ship *U.S.S. Cole* was seriously damaged in a suicide bombing in the Middle Eastern country of Yemen, killing seventeen sailors and injuring thirty-nine.
- On September 11, 2001, four U.S. commercial aircraft were hijacked by nineteen terrorists. Two planes loaded with jet fuel were deliberately flown into the 110-story twin towers of the New York World Trade Center, causing the towers to collapse. One aircraft was flown into a section of the Pentagon in Washington, D.C., while passengers in the fourth aircraft fought with the hijackers, causing the plane to crash in Pennsylvania. Total casualties for the day remain unknown but will be in the thousands.

The Use of Anthrax in a Terrorist Attack

Anthrax can be a bioterrorist weapon used by terrorists. It has been known since it was described as the fifth plague of Egypt in 1491 B.C. Anthrax was used in World War I by the Germans. Japan and the United States, along with other major powers, developed anthrax bombs during World War II but did not use them.

The Crime of Terrorizing (Terrorism by Threats)

The *California Street Terrorism Enforcement and Prevention Act* prohibits willful threats to commit a violent crime if the threat "on its face and under the circumstances in which it is made [is] so unequivocal, unconditional, immediate, and specific as to convey . . . a gravity of purpose and an immediate prospect of execution." (See *People v. Dias*, 1997 WL 18994, 1997.)

A *South Dakota jury instruction* on the crime of terrorizing:

A person is guilty of Terrorizing if, with intent to place another human being in fear for his or another's safety, the person: Threatens to commit any crime of violence or act dangerous to human life.

See South Dakota Supreme Court in *State v. Carlson*, 559 N.W. 2d 802 (1997).

The *Working Papers for the Proposed Federal Criminal Code* explaining §§ 1614 and 1616 (menacing in which a defendant uses threats to deliberately put another in fear):

The threat may be a prank, or may be made in anger; while there may be no intent to inflict actual injury, such acts can be intended to cause fear. Such deeds have been traditionally punishable as misdemeanors.

But there can be deeds deliberately designed to instill fear in a large number of people, or to so affect an individual as to disrupt normal life patterns. In short, the proposal conceives of a type of assault, in form of threat, which warrants more than a misdemeanor punishment.

Present Federal law already recognizes that some forms of threat can be quite serious. . . . These laws make no distinction, however, between the relatively harmless expression of anger and a threat more serious in its impact. The proposed statutes would permit differentiation between a serious and a relatively minor threat against an individual.

. . . [I]t is the making of such threats that will be illegal under the proposed statute, regardless of whether the defendant actually plans to carry out the threat.

In October 2001, contaminated letters containing a deadly, potent, pure strain of anthrax began to appear in U.S. mail. The letters containing concentrated anthrax were delivered in Washington, D.C., New York City, Boca Raton, Florida, and Reno, Nevada. Anthrax was being used as a biological terrorist weapon in the United States.

Five persons died from anthrax and others became ill but recovered. The source of the anthrax is believed to be domestic, but as of the date of this writing, the identity of the terrorist remains unknown. A large reward has been offered for information.

Criminal Charges Against Terrorists

After the 1995 terrorist attack that destroyed the Oklahoma City federal building, Congress enacted the Federal Antiterrorism Law, 18 U.S.C.A. Section 1331, which gives the federal government jurisdiction to act against terrorism toward the United States, whether it occurs in the United States or elsewhere in the world.

More than 2,800 persons died on September 11, 2001, when terrorists hijacked two commercial airplanes loaded with passengers and jet fuel and slammed into the twin towers of the World Trade Center in New York City. Another hijacked plane was flown into the Pentagon in Washington, D.C. In the fourth hijacked aircraft, passengers fought with the hijackers, causing the plane to crash in western Pennsylvania.   AP/Wide World Photos

Because the federal government has thousands of crimes in the Federal Criminal Code, terrorists have been and will generally be charged under existing federal or state criminal law. For example, the first person to be criminally charged for the September 11 terrorist attacks is Zacarias Moussaoui, a 33-year-old French citizen of Moroccan descent.

Moussaoui is charged with "conspiracy with Osama bin Laden and Al Qaeda to murder thousands of innocent people in New York, Virginia and Pennsylvania on September 11, 2001." The six counts of conspiracy are conspiracy to commit acts of terrorism, to commit aircraft piracy, to destroy aircrafts, to use airplanes as weapons of mass destruction, to murder government employees, and to destroy property. Four of these six counts carry a maximum sentence of death. (See Chapter 4 for material on the law of conspiracy.)

Other Possible Criminal Charges Against Terrorists

Treason   Treason is the only crime defined in the U.S. Constitution. Article III, Section 3, provides: "Treason against the United States, shall consist only in levying War against them, or in adhering to their Enemies, giving them Aid and Comfort. No Person shall be convicted of Treason unless on the Testimony of two Witnesses to the same overt Act, or on Confession in open Court."

Treason is a difficult crime to prove. In the history of the United States, treason has been charged only some thirty times. Aaron Burr was charged with treason in 1807 and, after a trial, was acquitted on a technicality. After World War II, Tokyo Rose, among others, was convicted of treason and served seven years in prison for urging American military to desert during World War II.

Sedition

All democratic countries have had to pass laws to protect their governments from overthrow by the use of force and violence. The **sedition** law now in effect in the United States is the Smith Act of 1940. It forbids advocating the forceful overthrow of the U.S. government, the distributing with disloyal intent of materials teaching and advising the overthrow of the government by violence, and organizing or helping to organize any group having such purpose.

The U.S. Supreme Court affirmed the conviction of an officer in the American Communist party in the 1951 case of *Dennis v. United States*.[5] At that time, Communist literature distributed in the United States urged the violent overthrow of the U.S. government. Following the conviction of Dennis, the American Communist party stopped urging the violent overthrow of the U.S. government and now advocates change through peaceful and lawful means.

Sabotage

Sabotage is made a crime by 18 U.S.C.A. § 2155. The offense forbids damaging or injuring national defense material or national defense utilities "with intent to injure, interfere with, or obstruct the national defense." In the 1987 case of *United States v. Johnson*, 41 CrL 2205, the defendant was convicted of sabotage when he put a bolt in an airplane's engine intake because he was "angry," "upset," and "thinking about all of my problems." The defendant was an airman with the U.S. Air Force.

Immigration Offenses

Because most of the September 11 terrorists entered the United States through the front door (that is, presenting themselves at a port of entry), immigration procedure and law have become stricter.

Every day, approximately one million people seek entry into the United States. Some try to sneak in, while others present themselves at one of the hundreds of ports of entry on the Mexican or Canadian border or ports on the Atlantic or Pacific Coasts. About three thousand of these people are intercepted every day as suspects in illegal entry or other immigration offenses.

Antiterrorism Laws Enacted by U.S. Congress[a]

Year	Popular Name/Citation	Purpose of law
1903 and 1918	Immigration Act of 1903 and Act of 1918	Permitted exclusion of aliens advocating overthrow of government or affiliating with organizations who did so.
1940	Alien Registration Act and Smith Act of 1940	Requires deportation of aliens violating Act of 1918. Forbids advocating the forceful overthrow of the U.S. government, distributing with disloyal intent materials teaching and advising the overthrow of government by violence, and organizing any group having such purpose.
1950	Internal Security Act of 1950, 50 U.S.C.A. § 402	Further regulated actions of resident aliens.
1976	Foreign Sovereign Immunities Act, 28 U.S.C.A. 1602	Permits civil lawsuits by persons injured by terrorists against nations supporting those terrorists.
1978 and 2000	Foreign Intelligence Surveillance Act of 1978 as amended by the Act of 2000	Gives government broad power to conduct electronic and other surveillance of suspected terrorists.
1984	Hostage Taking, 18 U.S.C.A. § 1203	Makes it a federal crime to take an American citizen hostage anywhere in the world if purpose is to coerce person or government.
1996	Antiterrorism Act of 1996, 18 U.S.C.A. § 2332(d)	Makes it a crime for U.S. citizens to support any group listed as a foreign terrorist organization by either money or with other meaningful assistance. Also makes it a crime to enter into a financial transaction with a nation designed as a supporter of terrorism.
1996	Iran and Libya Sanctions Act of 1996, 50 U.S.C. § 1701	Places sanctions on persons or nations that engage in trade with Iran or Libya.
2001	U.S.A. Patriot Act of 2001, Pub. L., 107-56 Title III	Criminal penalties and forfeiture rules for money laundering by or for terrorist organizations.
	Title IV	New rules for protecting U.S. borders.
	Title V	Removes obstacles to investigating terrorism; pays rewards and uses DNA to identify terrorists.
	Title VI	Payments to victims of terrorism.
	Title VIII	Strengthens criminal laws against terrorism. New crimes governing attacks against mass transportation systems, harboring terrorists, or providing support to terrorists.

[a]Over the years, states have also enacted many antiterrorism laws and other laws protecting the state and the state government.

About half of the illegal immigrants in the United States have entered as visitors. They arrive in the United States as tourists, but they have no intention of returning to their homes. They stay on and melt into U.S. society, hoping that in time they can become legal residents.

They may buy a forged green card to pass as a legal and permanent resident. They may become a legal resident by marriage or work or through the visa lottery. About half of those who overstay their visits become legal residents (246,000), while in a four-year period, about 332,000 of those who overstayed their visits eventually return home.

Every year, more than one million people are detained for illegal entry or other offenses and are returned to their native country. Most of the detained people are not referred for criminal prosecution.

Illegal entry or reentry into the United States accounts for about 46 percent of the suspects investigated. Harboring or bringing in foreign citizens with forged or inadequate documents accounts for about 38 percent of the criminal offenses investigated. Misusing visas or permits accounts for approximately 8 percent of the offenses, and frauds and forgery involving passports and other documents comprise another 8 percent, according to the Immigration and Naturalization Service.

Other seldom used federal offenses that are punished very severely include "the crime of mailing a lethal substance" and "threatening to use a weapon of mass destruction."

SUMMARY

Terrorism is an old crime that has been used for centuries by angry extremists seeking to retaliate and to force a nation to make changes. The motives of terrorists differ from other criminals in that they commit crimes in an angry effort to achieve an extreme political goal.

Because terrorists violate existing federal and state laws, they are ordinarily charged under existing federal and state criminal law. Usually the federal government prosecutes them. However, a state could also bring criminal charges if the criminal laws of that state were violated. Under the dual sovereignty doctrine (see Chapter 9), both a state and the federal government could bring criminal charges if criminal conduct violated the criminal laws of two or more sovereign governments.

 ## BOOK-SPECIFIC WEB SITE

For chapter-related Web links, quizzing activities, and case and news updates, go to the *Criminal Law*, Eighth Edition, book-specific Web site at **http://info.wadsworth.com/ gardner.**

QUESTIONS AND PROBLEMS

1. Some states created the crime of terrorism in their criminal code many years ago. Review the criminal code of your state to determine whether your state has a specific crime of terrorism. What conduct does this law forbid?

2. Does your state criminal code contain the crimes of sedition and/or sabotage? How are these crimes defined?

3. A group of people opposed to the killing of young calves are peacefully demonstrating with signs on the sidewalks in front of a very popular restaurant in your city. The group is peacefully urging people not to use the restaurant because veal dishes are featured on the menu. The owner of the restaurant angrily complains to the police. Have criminal violations occurred? Could this situation escalate into a situation in which arrests would be made?

INFOTRAC COLLEGE EDITION EXERCISES

1. Go to InfoTrac College Edition. As you might expect, the number of articles on terrorism has grown substantially after September 11, 2001. Using *terrorism* as a search term, find articles discussing the following topics:

   a) The prevalence of terrorists in Latin America and the likely effect they will have on the United States

   b) Where are we heading in this "war" on terrorism? What does it hold for the future, in the opinions of futurists, that is, persons who study the political and social environment for purposes of predicting the future?

   c) Why do some of the members of the Muslim religion regard the United States as the enemy of Islam? What are the roots of the Muslim rage, as seen through the eyes of a moderate Muslim? How widely is that rage shared? What should the United States do to counter that rage?

2. Using the same search term, find an article discussing the most recent antiterrorist legislation passed by the U.S. Congress, the U.S.A. Patriot Act of October 2001. What are some of the provisions of the Act that might cause concern for civil libertarians?

NOTES

1. After McKinley's death, President Theodore Roosevelt stated that anarchism was "a crime against the whole human race." The United States passed immigration laws that excluded anarchists from entry into the country.

2. See the *New York Times* article "How Japan Germ Terror Alerted World" (May 26, 1998). The article states that one of the Japanese cultists testified that the cult's plan was to kill millions of people throughout Tokyo and also at nearby American military bases, where thousands of American service people and their family live.

3. McVeigh was found guilty by a jury of all the charges against him, which were the federal crimes of (1) conspiracy to use a weapon of mass destruction, (2) use of a weapon of mass destruction, (3) destruction by an explosive, and (4–11) the eight counts of the murders of the eight federal law enforcement officers killed in the blast. All three men were charged in federal courts for federal crimes.

A third man, Michael J. Fortier, pleaded guilty to four federal charges and was sentenced to twelve years in prison. Because of his cooperation, this sentence was a reduction from the long sentence he would have received. One of the federal criminal charges was the federal criminal charge of "misprision of a felony." Fortier had known of the planned bombing but had not warned anyone. See Chapter 23 on the federal crime of misprision of a felony.

4. *See* the *New York Times* article "Followers of Rabbi Kahane Subjects of Terror Inquiry" (December 16, 2001).

5. 341 U.S. 494, 71 S.Ct. 857 (1951).

22

Organized Crimes and Gangs

CONTENTS

KEY TERMS

organized crime and gangs

crimes of:
  money laundering
  smurfing
  loan-sharking

corruption of public officials

RICO

continuing criminal enterprise

The Dangers of Organized Crime and Gangs

Gang violence and organized crime have been serious problems in American cities for many years. In 1967, the President's Commission on Law Enforcement stated:

> In many ways organized crime is the most sinister form of crime in America. The men who control it have become rich and powerful by encouraging the needy to gamble, by luring the troubled to destroy themselves with drugs, by extorting the profits of honest and hardworking businessmen, by collecting usury from those in financial plight, by maiming or murdering those who oppose them, by bribing those who are sworn to destroy them. Organized crime is not merely a few preying upon a few. In a very real sense it is dedicated to subverting not only American institutions, but the very decency and integrity that are the most cherished attributes of a free society.

Terrorism is a type of organized crime, but it is different in that terrorists commit their crimes for political purposes. Other criminals in organized groups commit their crimes primarily for profit and greed.

Many gangs are organized in ethnic groups (Asian, Hispanic, Russian, Irish, Jewish, and so on). Gangs are also organized according to their primary goals (terrorist, drug gangs, robbery, shoplifting, and so on). Other organized gangs include motorcycle groups such as the Hell's Angels, the Outlaws, the Pagans, and the Bandidos.

The organization known as the Skinheads is reported to have members in thirty countries. Street gangs that have acquired notoriety include the Crips, the Gangster Disciples, the Bloods, and the Folk Gangsters.

The Los Angeles youth gang known as the Bloods has demonstrated that gang members can effectively be recruited in jails throughout the United States. The Bloods (known for their colored bandannas, sophisticated code language, and violence) are reported to have spread from California cities to 123 cities nationwide since their origins in the 1970s.

Jail inmates sometimes join gangs such as the Bloods for protection within the jail. Gang rules such as hand signals, code language, and hierarchy are taught. The name "Bloods" reflects the requirement that blood must be spilled to get into the Bloods gang, and a member's blood will be spilled if he tries to leave. "Blood in, Blood out" describes an initiation rite in which an innocent person's blood is shed in a random attack. This is often accomplished by slashing a pedestrian on a street corner or other public place with a box-cutter knife.

Criminal Profits: Where Do They Go?

The Crime of Money Laundering [1]

Criminals and racketeers do not report to the Internal Revenue Service that they support themselves and their families by committing crimes. They need a source of reportable income for income tax purposes in reporting to federal and state tax departments. The reportable income must be large enough to justify the standard of living of the criminals and their families.

Changing Times and Changing Organized Criminal Groups in the United States

1919–1933	When beer and other alcoholic drinks were made illegal in the United States (Prohibition), the Mafia and other gangs moved in to capitalize on the demand for the prohibited products. After a series of turf and other gang wars, Al Capone emerged as one of the strong leaders. Capone went to a federal prison not for the many murders, robberies, rackets, and other crimes he committed, but instead for federal income tax fraud.
1930s–1980s	With the end of Prohibition in the United States, the Mafia looked for other illegal sources of income. There was a market for illegal gambling, which they moved into. Extortion (blackmail) of businesses that were forced to pay protection money, loan-sharking, skimming, prostitution, and other crimes of opportunity were also committed.
1960–present	With the legalization of many forms of gambling in the United States in the 1980s and 1990s, organized crime lost much of a lucrative market. Those Mafia families that had gone into illegal drugs found tough law enforcement and risks of long jail terms, intense competition from gangs, and a lack of a reliable foreign source of illegal drugs. Mafia families tended to go into corruption of unions and establish monopolies in such businesses as vending machines, and profit from bid rigging, extortion, or control of businesses in construction, waste disposal,[a] and other areas. New ethnic and other gangs took over many forms of racketeering in the United States from the Mafia.
September 11, 2001	Many terrorist acts had been committed prior to September 11, but the events of this date shocked the civilized world and caused over a hundred nations to declare war on the Osama bin Laden terrorist organization and the Talibans who had sheltered Al Qaeda.

[a]The conviction of John Gotti in 1992 and the convictions of sixteen men involved in organized criminal activities in New York City in 1997 hurt Mafia shakedowns in the construction and garbage-hauling businesses, extortions in New York wholesale food and produce markets, the milking of union pension and welfare funds, payoffs for obtaining jobs and contracts in new construction, and control of trucking in the garment district. See the *New York Times* article "Two Convicted as Masterminds of Mob's Hold on Private Garbage Collection" (October 22, 1997).

The *New York Times* article "Officials Say Mob Is Shifting Crimes to New Industries" (February 10, 1997) tells that the Mafia is moving into new frauds in health insurance, prepaid telephone cards, and small Wall Street stock and bond brokerage houses.

Therefore, acquiring a legitimate business is common. Legitimate businesses can be profitable in themselves. "Dirty" money might be held until it can be "laundered" through a legitimate business and returned in a "clean," reportable form to the owner. The owner then reports this amount to federal and state tax departments.

Shipping cash out of the United States is necessary in illegal drug trafficking to pay for further shipments of narcotics from South America and elsewhere in the world. Laundering dirty money can also be done outside the United States. This service, when combined with banking criminal dollars, can be profitable.

Under federal law, financial institutions (such as banks and savings and loans) are required to report currency transactions over $10,000. Currency transaction reports (CTRs) are used by governmental agencies to determine whether tax fraud or criminal activities such as *money laundering,* illegal drug transactions, racketeering, and so on are occurring.

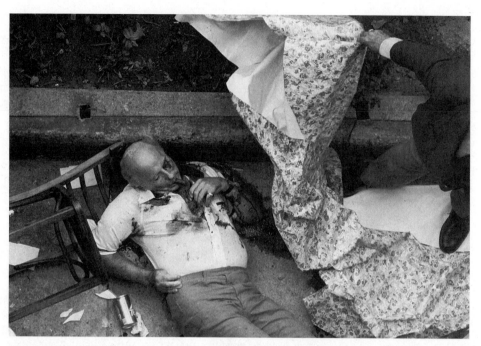

Many of the old Mafia leaders have been killed as Mafia boss Carmine Galente was killed in 1979. Four men surprised Galente as he was having lunch in a New York restaurant and killed him and his companions with shotguns and automatic weapons.   © Bettmann/CORBIS

Money laundering is now called the world's third largest business.[2] A major drug dealer's success is directly linked to his or her ability to move dirty money through the system undetected. The amount of illegal drug money moved within the world's money system is immense. The United Nations estimates that there are more than 21 million people in the world who abuse cocaine and heroin and that 30 million people abuse amphetamine-type stimulants.

In shipping money out of the United States to purchase new drug shipments and to launder money, criminals must find a friendly country and bankers willing to cooperate with criminals. Before the fall of the Noriega government, Panama was the leading banking system for criminals from all parts of the world.[3]

To ship money out of the United States to a tax haven, the criminal violates a number of laws, including a requirement that a declaration be made when more than $5,000 is taken out of the United States. Because illegal drugs are a major source of profits for criminals, law enforcement officers are not only looking for illegal narcotics coming into their country but are also on the alert for large cash shipments going out of the country.

Currency Transaction Reports and "Structured Transactions"

With drug trafficking revenues as high as $300 billion a year, many drug dealers and other criminals reap huge profits. A large amount of such criminal profits is spent purchasing expensive cars, homes, condos, jewelry, furs, clothing, and other luxuries.

Businesses and financial institutions in the United States are required to report cash transactions of $10,000 or more under the Currency Transaction Reporting Act (31 U.S.C.A. § 5311). The CTRs filed by businesses, banks, and other financial institutions are used to determine whether tax fraud or money laundering is occurring. Further investigation could then lead to illegal drug dealings and racketeering.

Unfortunately, businesspeople who want to make profits will sometimes cooperate with drug dealers and other criminals seeking to hide cash transactions. Car dealers, real estate agents, and jewelers can illegally agree to structure a transaction. In a structured transaction, the buyer makes a series of payments in cash or cashier's checks of under $10,000 over a period of weeks. When the sales price is reached, the dealer or real estate agent turns the car or condo over to the buyer. For a $50,000 Mercedes-Benz or Rolls-Royce, six or seven payments under $10,000 would be the structured transaction. This illegal practice is sometimes called *smurfing* and is made a crime by the Federal Money Laundering Control Act of 1986 (31 U.S.C. § 5324).

Another illegal way of avoiding the CTR requirement is to put the title to an expensive car or piece of real estate in the name of a third party. The question is then raised how the third party obtained the $50,000 in cash to purchase a Mercedes-Benz and whether he or she is driving the vehicle or living in the condo.

Loan-Sharking as a Criminal Investment and as a Criminal Banking Venture

Loan-sharking has always been a profitable source of income for organized crime and racketeers. Not only is it a profitable criminal investment, but the loan shark often acts as a banker for criminals.

The loan shark finances criminal ventures such as narcotics purchases. Such loans are made at high rates of interest. Failure to repay a loan could result in brutality or death. Gamblers can borrow money from loan sharks to pay their gambling debts, or they may find if they run up a gambling debt that it has been turned over to a loan shark for collection.[4]

People threatened by a loan shark for collection of a large debt will sometimes become police informants or government witnesses as a way out of their dilemma.

When Legitimate Businesses Are Taken Over by Criminals

When a legitimate business is taken over by criminals, some or all of the purchase money might be from illegal operations. The legitimate business is used only to launder limited dirty money and to provide an image of legality for salaries and income that are reported to state and federal tax departments.

Other legitimate businesses, however, are used for an assortment of other crimes such as fraudulent stock sales, bankruptcy fraud, and arson of business property.

Corruption of Public Officials

In 1967, the President's Commission on Law Enforcement stated:

All available data indicate that organized crime flourishes only where it has corrupted officials. As the scope and variety of organized crime's activities have expanded, its need to involve officials at every level of government has grown. And as government regulation expands into more and more areas of private and business

RICO (Racketeer Influenced and Corrupt Organizations) Act [a]

RICO forbids a person or persons from

- Using income received from a pattern of racketeering activity to acquire an interest in an "enterprise." An enterprise is defined as "any individual, partnership, or corporation, association, or other legal entity, and any union or group of individuals associated in fact although not a legal entity." 18 U.S.C.A. § 1961 (4). The U.S. Supreme Court held that this included both legitimate and illegitimate "associations in fact." *U.S. v. Turkette,* 101 S.Ct. 2524 (1981).

- Acquiring or maintaining an interest in an enterprise through a pattern of racketeering activity.

- Conducting or participating in the affairs of an enterprise through a pattern of racketeering activity.

- Conspiring to commit any of the above offenses.

Criminal penalties

Fines up to $25,000 and/or imprisonment not longer than twenty years for each offense plus forfeiture of interests acquired in violation of RICO.

Civil penalties

"Any person" may commence a private civil action for treble damages and attorney fees when the forbidden conduct causes injury to "business or property."

The statute numbers of the RICO Act in your state are _____

Designated potentially associated statutes

Mail and Wire Fraud Statutes The two elements for these federal crimes are (1) formation of a "scheme or artifice to defraud" and (2) use of the mails or wires to further the fraudulent scheme.

Travel Act Statute This statute forbids travel in interstate commerce or use of any facility in interstate commerce with intent to (1) distribute the proceeds of unlawful activity, (2) commit any violent crime in furtherance of unlawful activity, or (3) manage, promote, or establish any unlawful activity.

Extortion (Hobbs Act, 18 U.S.C.A. § 1951) This defines extortion as "the obtaining of property from another, with his consent, induced by wrongful use of actual or threatened force, violence, or fear, or under color of official right."

Unlawful Labor Payments (violation of the Taft-Hartley Act, 29 U.S.C.A. § 186[a][b]) The making of payments by employers or their representatives to a union official, and the receiving of payment by a union official from employers or their representatives, is forbidden. (Specific intent, such as in bribery, need not be proved, and only general intent is required.)

[a]18 U.S.C.A. §§ 1961–68, first enacted by Congress in 1970.

activity, the power to corrupt likewise affords the corrupter more control over matters affecting the everyday life of each citizen.[5]

In 1983, the Attorney General of the United States, in testifying before the Senate Judiciary Committee, cited instances of huge payments to law enforcement officials to ignore organized criminal activities. He stated, "The dollar amounts are so great that bribery threatens the very foundations of law and law enforcement."

The Crime of Continuing Criminal Enterprise (RICO)

Most organized criminals and gangs are engaged in *continuing criminal enterprises,* which are ongoing criminal businesses. In 1970, the U.S. Congress enacted a criminal statute with such broad provisions that it has been called the "new darling of the prosecutor's

Illegal Gambling in the United States

During Prohibition in the United States (1919–1933), organized crime made huge profits selling illegal beer and alcohol to the many people who wanted to drink.

With the legalization of beer and alcoholic drinks, organized crime turned to other illegal activities. It is widely believed that until the 1970s, illegal gambling was the greatest money-maker for organized crime.

With the legalization of many forms of gambling in the United States and with the effective use of RICO, profits from gambling dropped rapidly, while the risks in illegal gambling went up. Illegal gambling is no longer as attractive to criminals as it previously was. Today, some forms of gambling continue to be illegal.

Distinguishing illegal gambling from friendly gambling   For a game of chance or a lottery to be illegal, it must violate a specific law or ordinance. Illegal gambling is often distinguished from legitimate commercial promotions by the fact that illegal gambling or lotteries have (1) a prize, (2) consideration, and (3) chance elements.

Therefore, a company that wishes to run a promotion can offer a prize if the customer does not have to buy anything or pay anything (no consideration). Or instead of a chance element, there is a skill element (writing an essay, or naming a new product, and so on).[a]

The federal crime of gambling: 18 U.S.C.A. § 1955

(b) As used in this section—
  (1) "illegal gambling business" means a gambling business which—
    (i) is a violation of the law of a State or political subdivision in which it is conducted;
    (ii) involves five or more persons who conduct, finance, manage, supervise, direct, or own all or part of such business; and
    (iii) has been or remains in substantially continuous operation for a period in excess of thirty days or has a gross revenue of $2,000 in any single day.

The Federal Professional and Amateur Sports Protection Act (Public Law 102-559) prohibiting sports gambling   Section 3702 makes it unlawful for states or individuals to sponsor, operate, advertise, promote, or license a lottery, sweepstakes, or betting on one or more competitive games in which amateur or professional athletes participate.

Several exemptions are provided, including betting on parimutual animal racing, or jai alai, and some casino betting.[b]

[a]When is gambling a "social game" between friends, between neighbors, or in an office or factory pool? The Court in the 1991 case of *State v. Hansen,* 816 P.2d 706 (Or.App.), cited Oregon Statute 167.117(4)(c):
'Social game' means:
(a) A game, other than a lottery, between players in a private home where no house player, house bank or house odds exist and there is no house income from the operation of the social game; and
(b) If authorized pursuant to ORS 167.121, a game, other than a lottery, between players in a private business, private club or place of public accommodation where no house player, house bank or house odds exist and there is no house income from *the operation of the social game.*" ORS 167.117(13). [Emphasis added.]

Friendly gambling (office or factory football pool, neighborhood poker game, and so on) can be distinguished from commercial gambling by some or all of the following factors:
- Where the game is played and who the players are
- Size of the pot
- Whether the house takes a percentage of each pot
- Whether the players bet against the house and the house acts as the banker, and whether the house acts as the dealer in such games as blackjack, craps, and so on
- Other factors such as the type of game played

[b]Sports betting is a big business in the United States, with billions of dollars wagered each year. Much of the betting is legal, but some of the betting could be in violation of state and/or federal law, and it also could be in violation of the National Collegiate Athletic Association rules.

Gambling scandals occurred in 1994 at Northwestern University and in 1996 at Boston College, where thirteen football players were suspended.

nursery." The Racketeer Influenced and Corrupt Organizations (**RICO**) Act was enacted as Title IX of the Organized Crime Control Act of 1970.

RICO has proved to be a valuable tool in the fight against organized crime in the United States. Since 1980, senior mob figures from Los Angeles, New Orleans, New York, Cleveland, and Philadelphia have been convicted. The former head of the New York Gambino crime family, John Gotti,[6] was convicted under the RICO statute and received life imprisonment without parole. In 1997, Vincent Gigante, believed to be the head of the New York Genovese family, was also convicted under the RICO law. Among the jury findings that sent Gigante to prison was the finding that Gigante plotted unsuccessfully to murder his rival, John Gotti.[7]

To convict under RICO, it must be proved that the defendant was part of a criminal "enterprise" and that the defendant committed two felonies, such as murder, arson, or extortion, within a ten-year period. Under RICO, prosecutors can tie together evidence of many crimes and, if convicted, the defendant receives a stiff sentence.

Former FBI Director William Webster pointed out that it was not until the early 1980s that law enforcement officers and prosecutors figured out how to use RICO effectively. Many states have enacted similar statutes ("little RICOs") that are part of their state criminal code. With the federal RICO, every criminal transaction involving the use of the mail, telephone, or interstate communication creates the potential for criminal prosecution or a civil lawsuit.

Other Uses of the RICO Racketeering Law

In the 1983 case of *Russello v. United States,* 104 S.Ct. 296, the U.S. Supreme Court acknowledged that the primary purpose of RICO was to strike at the "source of economic power" of organized crime and gangs.

The racketeering law has also been used against other criminal activities, as the law does not limit the use of RICO only to organized crime and gangs. RICO convictions have been affirmed by the U.S. Supreme Court when the racketeering law was used against illegal activities by antiabortion groups, violations by brokers and traders at the Chicago Board of Trade, Taft-Hartley violations, and porn shop violations.

SUMMARY

Organized crime and gangs are very serious problems in the United States and other democratic countries. A survey of over four thousand law enforcement agencies in the United States in 1996 identified over thirty thousand gangs with membership in excess of eight hundred thousand.

Terrorism is a type of organized crime whether the terrorism is domestic or international. The crime of continuing criminal enterprise has been proven to be effective in combating domestic organized crime.

BOOK-SPECIFIC WEB SITE

For chapter-related Web links, quizzing activities, and case and news updates, go to the *Criminal Law,* Eighth Edition, book-specific Web site at **http://info.wadsworth.com/ gardner.**

QUESTIONS AND PROBLEMS

1. An unusual case (also discussed in Chapter 15) came before the U.S. Supreme Court in 1997. Over a period of time, a sheriff and his deputy were requiring bribes from a prisoner for contact visits with the man's wife and sometimes his girlfriend. The officers were paid $6,000 a month and $1,000 per contact visit, which was twice a week.

   Because the prisoner was a federal prisoner housed in a county jail for a federal fee, both the sheriff and his deputy were charged and convicted of federal bribery and also the RICO violation of continuing criminal enterprise. Should the convictions be affirmed? Was this a continuing criminal enterprise? *Salinas v. United States,* 118 S. Ct. 469 (1997).

2. The Republic of the Philippines brought a RICO action against Ferdinand Marcos (the former president of the Philippines) and his wife, Imelda, for systematically stealing, bribing, and looting money and valuables from the Philippine people during the years Marcos was president. Was this a continuing criminal enterprise? *Republic of the Philippines v. Marcos,* 862 F. 2d 1355 (9th Cir., 1988) review denied 109 S.Ct. 1933.

INFOTRAC COLLEGE EDITION EXERCISES

1. Go to InfoTrac College Edition and, using the keyword search term *organized crime* and the subdivision *investigations,* find the article discussing corruption investigations in Youngstown, Ohio. What could happen to the representative to Congress named in that investigation if he is charged and convicted of a crime? Can he keep his seat in Congress?

2. Go to InfoTrac College Edition and, using the search term *organized crime* and the subdivision *laws,* find the article reviewing RICO prosecutions in 1999 or 2000 in the *American Criminal Law Review's Annual Survey of White Collar Crime.* What is the advantage of RICO laws to the prosecution?

NOTES

1. See the *FBI Law Enforcement Bulletin* article "Laundering Drug Money" (April 1990).

2. See the book *The Laundrymen: Inside Money Laundering, The World's Third-Largest Business* by Jeffrey Robinson (New York: Little, Brown, 1996).

3. In what is called the "biggest drug bust in history," the United States invaded the Republic of Panama in 1989 to stop the money laundering and to stop the use of Panama as a transfer point for shipments of illegal drugs from South America to the United States.

General Noriega surrendered to U.S. forces because he feared death from his countrymen. Noriega was convicted of drug charges in the United States and is now in a federal prison (ee Chapter 9).

4. A 1997 study of gambling addiction conducted by the Harvard Medical School and financed by the gambling industry concluded that 1.29 percent of young and old adults in Canada and the United States had compulsive gambling disorders.

However, the percentage of problem gamblers among people with alcohol or drug substance abuse problems or mental disorders was found to be 14.29 percent. Other specialists on gambling believe that up to 5 percent of the general population and as many as 25 percent of substance abusers are compulsive gamblers. See the *New York Times* article "Compulsion to Gamble Seen Growing" (December 7, 1997).

The need for money to gamble could cause compulsive gamblers to steal from employers, family, friends, or others. Compulsive gamblers also borrow money from other people, including loan sharks. The inability to repay gambling loans leads to further difficulty. Children and dependents of compulsive gamblers are often deprived of necessities needed for their well-being and education.

5. President's Commission of Law Enforcement, page 6.

6. Both Gotti and LoCascio were convicted under the RICO Act. Gotti was convicted of five murders, including the killing in 1985 of Paul Castellano, who was Gotti's predecessor as the crime boss of the Gambino family.

Sammy Gravano's book is entitled *Underboss: Sammy the Bull Gravano's Story of Life in the Mafia* (Scranton, PA: HarperCollins, 1996).

7. For years, Vincent Gigante (the "Chin," or the "Robe") presented himself as being mentally ill and not competent to stand trial. His lawyers argued that Gigante had a tested IQ of 70 and was not capable of running a Mafia crime family. Gigante was often seen walking on the streets of New York wearing a bathrobe and mumbling incoherently to himself.

Prosecutors argued that Gigante was a murderous Mafia boss and the head of the powerful Genovese family crime group. A series of mobsters who turned informants testified that Gigante was not a feeble old man but was a top Mafia leader. See the *Milwaukee Journal Sentinel* article "Mafia's 'Odd-father' Gets 12-Year Term in Prison" (December 19, 1997).

23

Contempt, Crimes by Public Officials, and Crimes Against Government

CONTENTS

KEY TERMS

contempt: civil and criminal

perjury

subornation of perjury

tampering with evidence

bribery

espionage

economic espionage

environmental crimes

Contempt

Contempt is the willful disregard of the authority of a court of law or of a legislative body. Acts that delay, impede, or frustrate the functioning or the dignity of a court or legislative body may be held to be in contempt of that body. The deliberate, willful, and contumacious (obstinate) disobedience of a lawful order is a common reason for finding a person in contempt. The U.S. Supreme Court held in the 1975 case of *Maness v. Meyers:*

> We begin with the basic proposition that all orders and judgments of courts must be complied with promptly. If a person to whom a court directs an order believes that order is incorrect the remedy is to appeal, but, absent a stay, he must comply promptly with the order pending appeal. Persons who make private determinations of the law and refuse to obey an order generally risk criminal contempt even if the order is ultimately ruled incorrect.[1]

Contempt and contempt proceedings originated in early England, when English kings gave their judges the power to punish conduct that interfered with the functioning of the courts. Although many American states have statutes defining contempt, the offense of contempt remains today in England as a common law misdemeanor. The following example of contempt received national attention in November 1983.

EXAMPLE: In a hearing before the U.S. Supreme Court, *Hustler* magazine publisher Larry Flynt became angry and shouted obscenities at the nine justices. The hearing concerned a civil libel suit by a vice president of *Penthouse* against *Hustler.* Flynt wanted to argue the case himself, but the Court refused and appointed a lawyer to represent him. Flynt (who was in a wheelchair, paralyzed in a 1978 assassination attempt) was taken to a jail and booked on contempt charges. Flynt apologized later, and the charges were dropped.

Civil Contempt

Contempt is classified as either civil or criminal. *Civil contempt* is used to compel people to do something they are obligated to do. *Criminal contempt* can be used to punish people for what they have done. When Larry Flynt shouted obscenities at the nine justices in the courtroom of the U.S. Supreme Court, he was immediately found in criminal contempt and jailed.

Civil or criminal contempt is sometimes used in divorce cases, child custody cases, and other matters to compel people to comply with court orders. Following are a few of the thousands of contempt cases that occur every year in the United States:

- Refusal to answer questions before a grand jury after being granted immunity could mean jailing for contempt, as in the Susan McDougal case (twenty-one months) and in the case of *Shillitani v. United States,* 86 S. Ct. 1531 (two years).

- Failure to comply with a court order, as in the divorce case of *Morgan v. Foretich,* 564 A.2d 1 (twenty-five months for contempt in hiding a child).

- Newsperson failure to provide information as ordered by court (only a few states have enacted a newsperson privilege law protecting confidential sources of news information).

- Failure to pay court-ordered child support money when the defendant has money to make such payments.

People who are jailed for failing to answer questions or to comply with the order of a court have the key to their own jail cell. If they comply, they can then walk out of the jail.

Criminal Contempt

Criminal contempt is designed to protect the public interest by ensuring the effective functioning of the judicial and legislative systems. In 1968, the U.S. Supreme Court stated in *Bloom v. Illinois* that "criminal contempt is a crime in the ordinary sense; it is a violation of the law, a public wrong which is punishable by fine or imprisonment or both."[2] The Court quoted Justice Oliver Wendell Holmes in stating that "these contempts are infractions of the law, visited with punishment as such. If such acts are not criminal, we are in error as to the most fundamental characteristic of crimes as that word has been understood in English speech." The defendant in the *Bloom* case was sentenced to twenty-four months in prison for submitting a falsely prepared will for probate. His demand for a jury trial was denied. In holding that in serious contempt cases the defendant had a right to a jury, the Court stated:

> Prosecution for contempt plays a significant role in the proper functioning of our judicial system; but despite the important values which the contempt power protects, courts and legislatures have gradually eroded the power of judges to try contempts of their own authority. In modern times, procedures in criminal contempt cases have come to mirror those used in ordinary criminal cases.[3]

Other examples of people who were found in criminal contempt include the defendant who hit his defense lawyer in *United States v. Wright,* 854 F.2d 1263 (11th Cir.), and a defendant who gave the judge the finger in *Mitchell v. State,* 580 A.2d 196, 48 CrL 1082 (Md. 1990).

Direct and Constructive Contempt

Contempt is also classified as either direct or indirect (constructive) contempt. Direct contempt is committed in the immediate presence and view or hearing of the court or legislative body. Acts of violence, insulting or abusive language, or failure to obey a proper order of the court or the legislative body are examples of conduct that have been held to be in direct contempt. Direct contempt may be punished summarily, because the person is present before the court or the legislative body at the time.

Constructive, or indirect, contempt arises from matters not occurring in or near the presence of the court or the legislative body but that nevertheless tend to obstruct or delay the functioning of the court or legislative body. Failure to appear as ordered or as required is an example of conduct that could be found to be in constructive contempt. Constructive contempt may not be punished summarily, because the person is entitled to procedural due process. This entitles the person (1) to an opportunity to show cause, within a stated time, why an order adjudging one in contempt should not be issued (2) to a hearing after receiving notice of its time and place, (3) to a reasonable time for preparation of one's defense, (4) to a statement of facts constituting the contempt charged, and (5) to service on him or her of a copy of any writing or document filed in support of the alleged contempt with such matters set out in an order issued by the court determining to cite the person for contempt.

The Requirement of Intentional Wrongdoing

In the 1976 case of *Commonwealth v. Washington,* the Supreme Court of Pennsylvania quoted other courts, holding:

> There is no contempt unless there is some sort of wrongful intent. *Offutt v. United States,* 98 U.S.App.D.C. 69, 232 F.2d 69, 72 (1956), *cert. den.* 351 U.S. 988, 76 S.Ct. 1049, 100 L.Ed. 1501 (1956). "[A] degree of intentional wrongdoing is an ingredient of the offense of criminal contempt." *In re Brown,* 147 U.S.App.D.C. 156, 454 F.2d 999, 1006 (1971). "Willfulness is, of course, an element of criminal contempt and must be proved beyond a reasonable doubt." *United States v. Greyhound Corporation,* 508 F.2d 529, 531 (7th Cir. 1974).[4]

In the *Washington* case, the defendant overslept and failed to appear in time at his trial. In reversing his contempt conviction, the Pennsylvania Supreme Court held:

> Were we to accept the prosecution's argument, any person, judge, attorney, witness, or party, who comes into the courtroom late can be held guilty of contempt of court, regardless of the reason for the lateness. We cannot accept such a conclusion. Unless the evidence establishes an intentional disobedience or an intentional neglect of the lawful process of the court, no contempt has been proven. Such is the case here.
>   Judgment of sentence reversed.

In the 1976 case of *People v. Harris,* the defendant failed to pay a fine imposed for a prior criminal conviction.[5] Although the defendant showed that he had no money and was unemployed, he was found in contempt for failure to pay the fine. The Illinois Court of Appeals reversed the contempt finding, holding that there was no showing that the defendant willfully placed himself in a position to be unable to pay the fine.

Language by a Witness or Attorney That Would Justify a Contempt Finding

While answering a question on cross-examination, a witness used the expression "chicken shit." As a result, the witness was found to be in direct contempt for the use of this term in a courtroom. The U.S. Supreme Court reversed the defendant's conviction in the case of *Eaton v. City of Tulsa,* holding:

> This single isolated usage of street vernacular, not directed at the judge or any officer of the court, cannot constitutionally support the conviction of criminal contempt. "The vehemence of language used is not alone the measure of the power to punish for contempt. The fires which it kindles must constitute an imminent, not merely a likely, threat to the administration of justice." *Craig v. Harney,* 331 U.S. 367, 376 (1947). In using the expletive in answering the question on cross-examination "it is not charged that [petitioner] here disobeyed any valid court order, talked loudly, acted boisterously, or attempted to prevent the judge or any other officer

Contempt

Classification	Type	Procedure used to punish
Civil contempt is remedial and is used to force people to do what they are lawfully required to do (answer questions, identify themselves, pay support money as ordered by a divorce court, and so on).	*Direct contempt* is committed in the immediate presence and view or hearing of the court or legislative body.	*Summary process* Only direct contempt may be punished summarily. If the court or legislative body does not act at the time the contempt is committed, notice and an opportunity for a hearing must be given to the person.
"*Criminal contempt* is a crime in the ordinary sense; it is a violation of the law, a public wrong which is punishable by fine or imprisonment or both." U.S. Supreme Court in *Bloom v. Illinois*, 391 U.S. 194, 88 S.Ct. 1477 (1968).	*Constructive,* or *indirect, contempt* is committed out of the presence or hearing of the court or legislative body. Although the matter or incident does not occur in or near the presence of a court or legislative body, it must tend to obstruct or delay the functioning of the court or the legislative body.	*Contempt hearings* Notice and an opportunity for a hearing (plus other due process rights) must be given for constructive (indirect contempt) and for direct contempt when the court or legislative body does not act immediately.

of the court from carrying on his court duties." *Holt v. Virginia*, 381 U.S. 131, 136 (1965); see also *In re Little*, 404 U.S. 553 (1972). In the circumstances, the use of the expletive thus cannot be held to "constitute an imminent . . . threat to the administration of justice."[6]

The Power of Legislative Bodies to Punish for Contempt

Constitutions grant legislative bodies the power to legislate. To inform themselves as to what laws and measures should be enacted, legislative bodies must gather necessary information on which to base their decisions. They therefore have the power to hold hearings and make investigations into matters relevant to their jurisdiction to legislate. Neither Congress nor the state legislatures possess the general power to make inquiries into the private affairs of citizens that are not relevant to measures they may be considering. Legislatures possess inherent power to protect their existence and their power to proceed in their legislative functions. The following case came before the U.S. Supreme Court in 1972:

Groppi v. Leslie

Supreme Court of the United States (1972) 404 U.S. 496, 92 S.Ct. 582

A former Catholic priest, Father Groppi, led a group who seized the Wisconsin Assembly chamber and held it for a short time. Father Groppi was arrested and held in jail. Two days after the incident, the Wisconsin Assembly voted to hold Groppi in contempt and gave him six months in jail as punishment. The U.S. Supreme Court unanimously held that the action violated Groppi's due process rights, as he received a jail sentence without any notice of the hearing and there was no opportunity for him to appear and defend himself.

Crimes by Public Officials

If all people were angels and were to live in peace and harmony with one another, then, as James Madison observed in *The Federalist Papers* of the 1780s, there would be no need for governments. But people are not angels, nor are they governed by angels (as Madison also pointed out almost two hundred years ago).

The U.S. Supreme Court observed that "nothing can destroy a government more quickly than its failure to observe its own laws, or worse, its disregard of the charter of its own existence."[7] In 1928, Justice Louis D. Brandeis stated in his dissenting opinion in *Olmstead v. United States:* "Our Government is the potent, the omnipresent teacher. For good or ill, it teaches the whole people by its example. . . . If the Government becomes a lawbreaker, it breeds contempt for law; it invites every man to become a law unto himself; it invites anarchy."[8]

Cicero wrote long ago in *Pro Cluentio 53* that "we are in bondage to the law in order that we may be free." Calvin Coolidge observed, while president of the United States: "Wherever the law goes, there civilization goes and stays. When the law fails, barbarism flourishes. Whoever scorns the law, whoever brings it into disrespect, whoever connives at its evasion, is an enemy of civilization. Change it if you will . . . but observe it always. That is government."

Some of the Crimes Committed by Public Officials and Other People

Some of the many offenses committed by public officials and private individuals are as follows:

- Unauthorized (or excessive) use of force (assault and battery)
- False imprisonment
- Unauthorized wiretapping (federal felony) or bugging (state offense)
- *Perjury*[9] and *subornation of perjury* (the crime of perjury consists of knowingly and materially testifying falsely while under oath; the crime of subornation of perjury is committed when another person is induced or knowingly permitted to testify falsely)
- Official misconduct and misconduct in public office (using the powers of one's office to obtain a dishonest advantage for oneself, or falsifying an entry in a record or report)
- Aiding, assisting, or permitting the escape of a prisoner
- Intimidating witnesses, prisoners, or others
- *Tampering with evidence* or falsifying evidence
- Misprision of a felony. Some states and the federal government have codified this old common law crime. In 1998, Michael Fortier pleaded guilty to misprision of a felony (and other crimes) because he failed to warn officials of the plot to blow up the Alfred P. Murrah Federal Building in Oklahoma City. See the *New York Times* article "Sentencing the Man Who Failed to Warn of a Fatal Conspiracy" (May 13, 1998).

    Federal courts define the crime of misprision of a felon as follows: "[T]o sustain a conviction . . . for misprision of felony it was incumbent upon the government to prove beyond a reasonable doubt (1) that . . . the principal had committed and completed the felony alleged; . . . (2) that the defendant had full knowledge of that fact; (3) that he failed to notify the authorities; and (4) that he took . . . affirmative steps to conceal the crime of the principal."[10]

- *Bribery*. The U.S. Supreme Court held that to violate the federal gratuity statute (18 U.S.C.A. § 201(c)(1)(A), the government must prove a link between the thing of value given to a public official and a specific "official act" for which it was given.[11]

  The federal court in the case of *United States v. Arthur* described the crime of bribery as follows:

  > Not every gift, favor or contribution to a government or political official constitutes bribery. It is universally recognized that bribery occurs only if the gift is coupled with a particular criminal intent. . . . That intent is not supplied merely by the fact that the gift was motivated by some generalized hope or expectation of ultimate benefit on the part of the donor. . . . "Bribery" imports the notion of some more or less specific quid pro quo for which the gift or contribution is offered or accepted.[12]

- Extortion by a public official or employee in violation of the Hobbs Act, 18 U.S.C.A. § 1951. The public official or employee obtains payment because of his or her office and by use of "force, violence or fear." In *United States v. Swift,* the defendant was a city sewer director who received payments from a contractor in return for approval of payments made for work done on sewage pumping stations.[13] Another example of extortion under the Hobbs Act is as follows:

  > A bail bonds agent who was also an alderman in a small town conspired with members of the police department to extort money from travelers passing through town in exchange for dismissal or reduction of drunk driving charges against the travelers. *United States v. Stephens,* 964 F.2d 424 (5th Cir. 1992).

- Fraud and corruption.

Crimes Against Government

Espionage

Spying or being a party to *espionage* is forbidden by all democratic countries. Giving or selling national military or defense secrets to a foreign nation is a serious felony. A shocking number of Americans were charged with or convicted of spying. Most spies today sell secrets for money.

- *Aldrich Ames* was an alcoholic for years, yet he worked for the Central Intelligence Agency and received regular promotions within the organization. On a civil servant's pay, he bought an expensive home in Washington, D.C., for cash, and he drove a Jaguar. To obtain the money to live a luxurious life, Ames delivered vast amounts of highly secret documents and information to the Soviet Union, which paid Ames millions of dollars. Ames betrayed at least a dozen of the United States's best spies working within Russia. All were jailed, and most were executed. Ames and his wife were taken into custody in 1994 after nine years of espionage.

- *Robert P. Hanssen* was convicted in May 2001 of selling highly sensitive national secrets to Russia for fifteen years. Hanssen was a high-ranking FBI counterintelligence agent. It is believed that Hanssen also corroborated information that Aldrich Ames provided to the Russians.

- *John A. Walker Jr.* headed a spy ring of family members and friends. Officials called it the most damaging espionage conspiracy in decades. Walker received life imprisonment and said the Soviet Union paid $1 million for his information on military communication codes.

- *Jonathan Jay Pollard* provided secret information to Israel that was available to him as a U.S. Navy intelligence analyst. He received a long prison sentence. See *United States v. Pollard,* 959 F.2d 1011, review denied U.S. Supreme Court, 52 CrL 3033 (1992).

- The highest ranking military officer to be convicted of spying was German-born *George Trofimoff*, a retired Army Reserve colonel. He was convicted in September 2001 of selling military secrets for more than twenty years to Russia. Ronald A. Pelton was convicted of selling military secrets from the National Security Agency to Russia. A former FBI agent, Richard W. Miller, became involved with a Russian woman and provided national secrets to Russia.[14]

The Economic Espionage Act of 1996[15]

To fill in the gaps in existing federal and state laws,[16] the U.S. Congress enacted the Economic Espionage Act in 1996. The new law creates a federal felony that punishes the theft, misappropriation, wrongful alteration, or delivery of trade secrets.

Trade secrets are essential to maintaining the health and competitiveness of many segments of the U.S. economy. Potential violators of the law could be people seeking to sell or obtain trade secrets for a foreign government, or for a foreign or domestic corporation, or to benefit in another way from the illegal access to valuable information, data, and technology.

Violators who are apprehended could be charged under this law, state laws, patent and copyright protection laws, or computer crime statutes.

In May 2001, the FBI arrested three employees of Lucent Technologies and charged them with conspiracy to commit wire fraud to steal Lucent's highly classified trade secrets and sell them to the Chinese government. Lucent is the largest maker of communication equipment in the United States and was in serious financial trouble in 2001, laying off thousands of its employees.

Obstruction of Justice

The offense of obstruction of justice was a common law misdemeanor that is now part of the criminal code of the federal government and states. The offense seeks to protect the judicial system, both civil and criminal, from intentional acts that would hinder, corrupt, or impede the functioning of the system. Attempting to influence a juror, destruction or suppression of evidence, and seeking to prevent a witness from testifying or attending a trial are some of the acts that have justified charging the offense of obstruction of justice.

In the early days of the law, resisting, hindering, or obstructing a law enforcement officer was a common form of obstruction of justice. Many states, however, have made this offense a separate offense from obstruction of justice.[17] For example, Chapter 843 of the Florida Criminal Code is entitled "Obstructing Justice." Within Florida Chapter 843 are eighteen separate offenses, two of which forbid "resisting an officer." Tampering with evidence (destroying, concealing, or altering) is found in Florida Chapter 918.

A police officer was charged with obstructing justice in 1991 when he pretended to find a bag of cocaine in the vicinity of a person who had just been arrested. An Illinois Court of Appeals held that the officer could be convicted of obstructing justice for attempting to "frame" the arrested person in the case of *People v. Hollingsead,* 210 Ill.App.3d 750, 155 Ill.Dec. 216, 569 N.E.2d 216. The officer's defense was that he was just joking, and then that he was attempting to obtain a confession from the arrested person.

A Philadelphia doctor was convicted in 1997 of obstruction of justice and harboring a fugitive when he voluntarily changed fingerprints and dramatically changed the appearance of a drug lord wanted by federal officials. (See the *New York Times* article "Surgeon Is Convicted of Disguising a Fugitive" (February 28, 1997).

Tax Evasion

To operate and provide services, government needs money. Former U.S. Supreme Court Justice Oliver Wendell Holmes pointed out that taxes are the price we pay for civilization.

Much of the money needed to fund government services and activities is obtained through taxes. Deliberate tax evasion and tax fraud are generally punished as crimes. Tax evasion cases that have received national attention are the following:

- In 1973, the vice president of the United States, Spiro T. Agnew, resigned after pleading no contest to tax evasion charges.

- Socially prominent hotel owner Leona Helmsley was convicted of failure to report and pay taxes on $1.8 million in 1990. She was sentenced to four years in prison and fined $7.1 million.

- In the 1920s, gangster Al Capone and his gang had an extraordinary grip on Chicago. Law enforcement officials were unable to convict Capone of any of the many felonies they believed he had committed, but they were able to convict him of income tax fraud and send him to prison. Capone was one of the first people to be convicted with the use of the "net worth" method (circumstantial evidence). The U.S. Supreme Court affirmed the use of the net worth method in the 1954 case of *Holland v. United States,* 348 U.S. 121, 75 S.Ct. 127.

Drug dealers and other criminals who live lavishly as a result of their criminal activities must show "legitimate" income to support their high lifestyles. To do this, they must launder dirty money and create sources of "legitimate" income. They then pay taxes to state and federal governments on their declared incomes.

In 1985, a prominent Mafia leader was tried. The jury heard a tape recording of the Mafia leader talking to a friend in which the Mafia leader stated, "I surround myself with accountants and lawyers." The Mafia leader had in mind what happened to Al Capone

Crimes Uncovered by the Watergate and Whitewater Investigations

Watergate The burglary that led to a Whitehouse cover-up that led to a presidential resignation.

After the botched break-in of the National Democratic Headquarters at the Watergate apartment building, the White House became involved in a cover-up that then led to

- the resignation of President Richard Nixon,
- eighteen months in prison for former Attorney General John Mitchell for perjury and cover-up conspiracy,
- seven months in prison for Jeb Magruder for perjury and conspiracy to obstruct justice,
- thirty-three months in prison for E. Howard Hunt for burglary, conspiracy, and wire-tapping,
- a prison term for James McCord Jr. for burglary,
- eighteen months in prison for H. R. Haldeman for perjury, conspiracy, and obstruction of justice,
- prison terms also for John Ehrlichman (eighteen months), John Dean (four months), and Chuck Colson (eighteen months).

After Richard Nixon resigned, his successor, President Gerald Ford, pardoned him (see Nixon, R., in keyword index).

Whitewater The six-year investigation of the Arkansas business dealings of President and Mrs. Clinton.

Neither President nor Mrs. Clinton was accused or found guilty of any wrongdoings, but fourteen other people were convicted as wrongdoers:

- Former law partner of Mrs. Clinton, Webster Hubbell, pleaded guilty to felonies of tax evasion, mail fraud, and concealment by scheme.
- Former Arkansas Governor Jim Guy Tucker found guilty by jury of conspiracy and mail fraud. Pleaded guilty to conspiracy to defraud the IRS.
- Whitewater land development partner of the Clintons, Jim McDougal, convicted by jury of eighteen felonies in collapse of his savings and loan, which cost taxpayers $73 million.
- Susan McDougal convicted by jury of four felonies, then served eighteen months for failure to answer grand jury questions as to Whitewater.
- Former judge, David Hale, pleaded guilty to two felonies.
- Little Rock appraiser, Robert Palmer, pleaded guilty to conspiracy.
- Convicted of felonies: William Marks (one) and Christopher Wade (two).
- Convicted of misdemeanors: Stephen Smith (one), Larry Kuca (one), Attorney John Haley (one), Banker Neal Ainley (two), Charles Matthews (two), and Eugene Fitzhugh (one).
- White House adviser Bruce Lindsey was named an unindicted coconspirator in a case that ended in mistrial.

and wanted to avoid being prosecuted in a net worth tax case. He was convicted, however, of other criminal violations.

Environmental Crimes

It is reported that today the United States alone produces approximately 125 billion pounds of hazardous waste annually.[18] If not properly handled and disposed of, this waste can foul air, pollute land, poison water, and seriously affect persons, animals, fish, and agriculture.

Until the 1980s, little was done to regulate disposal of hazardous waste. FBI Director William S. Sessions quoted American conservationist Paul Brooks: "In America today [1970s], you can murder land for private profit. You can leave the corpse for all to see, and nobody calls the cops." Sessions pointed out that unfortunately "this was the case 20 years ago. No one could call the police, because no laws had been broken."[19]

In the 1980s and 1990s, laws were enacted to protect public health and the quality of the environment. The U.S. Congress added criminal sanctions to a host of environmental laws and in 1990 enacted the Clean Air Act Reauthorization. Vigorous enforcement of these laws has been said to be a top priority.

The Environmental Protection Agency (EPA) and the Department of Justice's Environmental Crimes Section are among the federal agencies combating *environmental crimes*. All of the states have enacted laws and authorized agencies within each state to enforce these laws.[20]

Voting Law Violations

The federal government and each state have laws regulating voting. Violations of some of the voting laws have been made a crime. For example, falsely claiming to live in a state or district in order to vote is a voting fraud and a crime. A commissioner from the city of Miami was arrested in 1998 and accused of conspiring to cover up a scheme in which voters falsely claimed to live in his district so they could vote for him. See the *New York Times* article "Miami Official Is Arrested in Election Fraud Inquiry" (May 29, 1998).

There have been many illegal political contributions to both major political parties in the United States. Foreign political campaign contributions are illegal. In January 2001, Indonesian billionaire James Riady paid a record $8.6 million criminal fine, and his California LippoBank pled guilty to eighty-six misdemeanors for political contributions made to the Bill Clinton 1992 presidential campaign.

Other Criminal Violations

It is reported by the President's Commission on Law Enforcement that the federal government alone has more than twenty-eight hundred crimes in the Federal Code. The President's Commission also points out that each state has the same number or more crimes in their state statutes. The following are a very few of the many crimes reported in daily newspapers:

- States often make the failure of an employer to withhold income taxes on employees' wages and salaries a crime. Under California law, employers who fail to withhold can be charged with a felony. (See the *New York Times* article, "California Raids a Business That Refuses to Withhold Taxes," May 3, 2001.)

- State election laws sometimes make it a felony to induce a person to vote if the inducement is worth $1 or more. A New York woman came to Wisconsin and passed out packages of cigarettes to homeless men as an inducement to vote in the presidential election of 2000. She was fined $5,000. (See the *Milwaukee Journal Sentinel* article "$5,000 Settles Election Case," May 4, 2001.)

- It is a federal crime to use marriage as a means of evading the immigration laws of the United States. Twenty persons were indicted on charges that they fraudulently obtained marriage licenses to gain permanent resident status for illegal immigrants in Chicago. (See the *Milwaukee Journal Sentinel* article "20 Accused of Marriage to Gain Residency," November 18, 2000.)

- States often make failure to report for jury duty when summoned a crime. In Wisconsin, the misdemeanor is punished by a $40 fine and ignorance of the law is not a defense. (See the *Milwaukee Journal Sentinel* article "County Prosecuting Jury Service No-Shows," October 31, 2000.)

- Bootlegging whiskey has made millionaires of some families in the Appalachian hills of Virginia and West Virginia. Cigarette smuggling is a problem in the Detroit area. Both crimes cause federal and state government to lose tax revenue. The federal government claimed a loss of $2.9 million in unpaid federal taxes for one moonshiner alone. (See the *New York Times* article "Alleged Bootleggers Face Sobering Case," September 9, 2001, and the *Detroit Free Press* article "Cigarette Smugglers Busted," May 20, 1997.)

- A federal court and jury held that the federal government was not guilty of any wrongdoings in the 1993 deaths of 80 Branch Davidians at the cult's compound in Waco, Texas. Also the federal government settled the final civil lawsuit in regard to the 1992 siege and assault at Ruby Ridge, Idaho. As compensation for the killing of a wife and child, the federal government paid the family $3.1 million.

SUMMARY

With twenty-eight hundred federal crimes and the same number or more in each of the states, there are more crimes than any one person can state they know well. This chapter and other chapters in this text seek to present those crimes generally charged and best known to the legal and law enforcement communities.

This chapter briefly presents both civil and criminal contempt, crimes that define conduct public officials should avoid, and crimes against government.

BOOK-SPECIFIC WEB SITE

For chapter-related Web links, quizzing activities, and case and news updates, go to the *Criminal Law,* Eighth Edition, book-specific Web site at **http://info.wadsworth.com/ gardner.**

QUESTIONS AND PROBLEMS

The following were presented in the May 2000 brief on *Police Integrity* published by the National Institute of Justice. Please answer each scenario indicating whether (1) this is criminal conduct violating your state criminal code or (2) this is not criminal conduct (assume there is no local law enforcement regulation forbidding this conduct).

1. A police officer runs his own private business in which he sells and installs security devices, such as alarms, special locks, and so on. He does this work during his off-duty hours.

2. A police officer routinely accepts free meals, cigarettes, and other items of small value from merchants on his beat. He does not solicit these gifts and is careful not to abuse the generosity of those who give gifts to him.

3. A police officer stops a motorist for speeding. The officer agrees to accept a personal gift of half the amount of the fine in exchange for not issuing a citation.

4. A police officer is widely liked in the community, and on holidays local merchants and restaurant and bar owners show their appreciation for his attention by giving him gifts of food and liquor.

5. A police officer discovers a burglary of a jewelry shop. The display cases are smashed, and it is obvious that many items have been taken. While searching the shop, he takes a watch, worth about two days' pay for that officer. He reports that the watch had been stolen during the burglary.

6. A police officer has a private arrangement with a local auto body shop to refer the owners of cars damaged in accidents to the shop. In exchange for each referral, he receives payment of 5 percent of the repair bill from the shop owner.

7. A police officer, who happens to be a very good auto mechanic, is scheduled to work during upcoming holidays. A supervisor offers to give him these days off if he agrees to tune up the supervisor's personal car. Evaluate the *supervisor's* behavior.

8. At 2:00 A.M., a police officer on duty is driving his patrol car on a deserted road. He sees a vehicle that has been driven off the road and is stuck in a ditch. He approaches the vehicle and observes that the driver is not hurt but is obviously intoxicated. He also finds that the driver is a police officer. Instead of reporting this accident and offense, he transports the driver to his home.

9. A police officer finds a bar on his beat that is still serving drinks half an hour past its legal closing time. Instead of reporting this violation, the police officer agrees to accept a couple of free drinks from the owner.

10. Two police officers on foot patrol surprise a man who is attempting to break into an automobile. The man flees. They chase him for about two blocks before apprehending him by tackling him and wrestling him to the ground. After he is under control, both officers punch him a couple of times in the stomach as punishment for fleeing and resisting.

11. A police officer finds a wallet in a parking lot. It contains an amount of money equivalent to a full day's pay for that officer. He reports the wallet as lost property but keeps the money for himself.

INFOTRAC COLLEGE EDITION EXERCISES

1. Go to InfoTrac College Edition and, using the keyword search term *offenses against the environment*, find the periodical reference to corporate crimes against the environment. To what extent can a corporate officer be charged personally with violation of a criminal law protecting the environment?

2. Using the keyword search term *contempt*, find an article discussing the tension that exists between a court's right to compel testimony and use its contempt power to do so, and the right of a newsperson to keep her "sources" confidential. When, if at all, should a newsperson be allowed to refuse to name her source? What if that source could provide valuable information to an important investigation?

NOTES

1. 419 U.S. 449, 95 S.Ct. 584 (1975). However, in the *Maness* case, the U.S. Supreme Court held that a lawyer is not subject to the penalty of contempt for advising his client, during a civil trial, to refuse to produce material that would incriminate him. The Court held: "The privilege against compelled self-incrimination would be drained of its meaning if counsel, being lawfully present, as here, could be penalized for advising his client in good faith to assert it."

2. 391 U.S. 194, 88 S.Ct. 1477 (1968).

3. New Jersey courts have held that "before a judge makes a contempt determination the accused should be permitted to speak." 357 A.2d at 276 (1976). In the case of *In re Logan Jr.,* 52 N.J. 475, 246 A.2d 441 (1968), the Court held: "The pronouncement of guilt before according that opportunity places the defendant at the disadvantage of trying to persuade a mind apparently already made up, and also puts the judge in the possibly embarrassing position of reversing himself if such persuasion results."

4. 466 Pa. 506, 353 A.2d 806 (1976).

5. 41 Ill.App.3d 690, 354 N.E.2d 648 (1976).

6. 415 U.S. 697, 94 S.Ct. 1228 (1974). In a dissenting opinion, Justice William H. Rehnquist suggests "a flat rule, analogous to the hoary doctrine of the law of torts that every dog is entitled to one bite, to the effect that every witness is entitled to one free contumacious or other impermissible remark."

7. *Mapp v. Ohio,* 367 U.S. 643, 81 S.Ct. 1684 (1961).

8. 277 U.S. 438, 48 S.Ct. 564 (1928).

9. In 1968, the President's Commission on Crime noted that perjury has always been widespread and that there must be more effective deterrents against perjury to ensure the integrity of trials. Another writer commented that few crimes "except fornication are more prevalent or carried off with greater impunity." See "Perjury: The Forgotten Offense" in *The Journal of Criminal Law & Criminology* 65 (1974).

10. Court in *U.S. v. Stuard,* 556 F.2d 1, 22 CrL 2337 (6th Cir. 1977), quoting *Neal v. U.S.,* 102 F.2d 643 (8th Cir. 1939). See also *Pope v. State,* 284 Md. 309, 396 A.2d 1054 (1979).

11. *U.S. v. Sun-Diamond Growers of California,* 119 S. Ct. 1402 (1999). In other criminal cases concerning the biggest sting operation conducted by the FBI, more than sixty lawyers, bailiffs, judges, and other persons in the Chicago court system were indicted for bribery. Operation Greylord was conducted because money was used to buy and fix criminal and civil Chicago court cases. Other criminal charges resulting from Operation Greylord included mail fraud, racketeering, and obstruction of justice.

12. 544 F.2d 730 (4th Cir.). The decision of the Court continues as follows:

This requirement of criminal intent would, of course, be satisfied if the jury were to find a "course of conduct of favors and gifts flowing" to a public official in exchange for a pattern of official actions favorable to the donor even though no particular gift or favor is directly connected to any particular official act. *U.S. v. Baggett* (4th Cir. 1973) 481 F.2d 114, *cert. denied* 414 U.S. 1116 (1973) (Travel Act prosecution involving alleged bribery of Maryland County Commissioner). Moreover, as the Seventh Circuit has held, it is sufficient that the gift is made on the condition "that the offeree act favorably to the offeror when necessary." *U.S. v. Isaacs* (7th Cir. 1974) 493 F.2d 1124, 1145, 15 CrL 2002, *cert. denied* 417 U.S. 976 (1974) (construing Illinois statute in a Travel Act prosecution). It does not follow, however, that the traditional business practice of promoting a favorable business climate by entertaining and doing favors for potential customers becomes bribery merely because the potential customer is the government. Such expenditures, although inspired by the hope of greater government business, are not intended as a quid pro quo for that business: they are in no way conditioned upon the performance of an official act or pattern of acts or upon the recipient's express or implied agreement to act favorably to the donor when necessary.

13. 732 F.2d 878 (11th Cir. 1984). In the 1992 case of *Evans v. U.S.,* 504 U.S. 255, 112 S.Ct. 1881, the U.S. Supreme Court held that a demand or other act of inducement by the public official was not necessary to convict of extortion under the Hobbs Act.

14. In 1997 and 1998, the following people were convicted of spying for money: the highest ranking CIA officer ever convicted, Harold J. Nicholson, sold secrets to Moscow for $300,000; a low-level CIA employee and two civilians were convicted for delivering classified documents to East Germany between 1979 and 1984; and a former FBI supervisor, Earl E. Pitts, was convicted of selling classified information to Russia for $244,000. A dismissed CIA agent, angered by his firing, tried to extort $500,000 from the CIA for his silence. When the CIA would not pay the money, Douglas F. Groat told two foreign nations how the United States spied on them.

15. The law's complete name is the Federal Economic Espionage and Protection of Trade Secrets Law (Public Law 104-294, Stat. 3488, 1996). For a more complete discussion of this law, see the *FBI Law Enforcement Bulletin* article "The Economic Espionage Act of 1996" (July 1997).

16. See the *New York Times* article "F.B.I. Says 3 Stole Secrets From Lucent" (May 4, 2001).

17. An example of "resisting law enforcement" is *Jackson v. State,* 576 N.E.2d 607 (Ind.App. 1991), in which the defendant refused to provide identification under circumstances that obligated him to do so. An example of "interfering with an officer" is *State v. Peruta,* 591 A.2d 140 (Conn.App. 1991), in which a jury found that the defendant, a news cameraman, interfered with law enforcement officers at the scene of a fatal automobile accident.

18. See the *FBI Law Enforcement Bulletin* article "Environmental Crimes Prosecution" (April 1990).

19. See the *FBI Law Enforcement Bulletin* article "Director's Message" (April 1991).

20. Examples of environmental criminal charges include illegal storage and disposal of hazardous waste (New York, 768 F.Supp. 957, 1991), illegal landfill (New York, 751 F.Supp. 368, 1990), illegally discharging pollutants into navigable waters (993 F.2d 395, 1993), causing hazardous waste to be transported to unpermitted facility (980 F.2d 27, 1992), discharge of waste water with excessive pollution levels (755 F.Supp. 771, Ill. 1990), unlawful storage and disposal of hazardous wastes (766 F.Supp. 873, Wash. 1991), violations of the Clean Water Act (784 F.Supp. 6, reversed in part 3 F.3d 643, 2d Cir. 1993, N.Y. 1991), and reckless disposal of hazardous waste (586 N.E.2d 1239, Ill. 1992).

Appendix A

Applicable Sections of the U.S. Constitution (Ratified in 1788)

Preamble

WE THE PEOPLE of the United States, in Order to form a more perfect union, establish Justice, insure domestic Tranquility, provide for the common defense, promote the general Welfare, and secure the Blessings of Liberty to ourselves and our Posterity, do ordain and establish this CONSTITUTION for the United States of America.

Article I

Section 1   All legislative Powers herein granted shall be vested in a Congress of the United States, which shall consist of a Senate and House of Representatives. . . .

Article II

Section 1   The executive Power shall be vested in a President of the United States of America. . . .

Article III

Section 1   The judicial Power of the United States, shall be vested in one supreme Court, and in such inferior Courts as the Congress may from time to time ordain and establish. . . .

Article IV

Section 4   The United States shall guarantee to every State in this Union a Republican Form of Government, and shall protect each of them against Invasion; and on Application of the Legislature, or of the Executive [when the Legislature cannot be convened] against domestic Violence. . . .

Article VI

This constitution, and the Laws of the United States which shall be made in Pursuance thereof; and all Treaties made, or which shall be made, under the Authority of the United States, shall be the supreme Law of the Land; and the Judges in every State shall be bound thereby, any Thing in the Constitution or Laws of any State to the Contrary notwithstanding. . . .

American Bill of Rights (Ratified in 1791)

Amendment 1

Congress shall make no law respecting an establishment of religion, or prohibiting the free exercise thereof; or abridging the freedom of speech, or of the press; or the right of the people peaceably to assemble, and to petition the Government for a redress of grievances.

Amendment II

A well regulated Militia, being necessary to the security of a free State, the right of the people to keep and bear Arms, shall not be infringed.

Amendment III

No Soldier shall, in time of peace be quartered in any house, without the consent of the Owner, nor in time of war, but in a manner to be prescribed by law.

Amendment IV

The right of the people to be secure in their persons, houses, papers, and effects, against unreasonable searches and seizures, shall not be violated, and no Warrants shall issue, but upon probable cause, supported by Oath affirmation, and particularly describing the place to be searched, and the persons or things to be seized.

Amendment V

No person shall be held to answer for a capital, or otherwise infamous crime, unless on a presentment or indictment of a Grand Jury, except in cases arising in the land or naval forces, or in the Militia, when in actual service in time of War or public danger, nor shall any person be subject for the same offence to be twice put in jeopardy of life or limb; nor shall be compelled in any criminal case to be a witness against himself, nor be deprived of life, liberty, or property, without due process of law; nor shall private property be taken for public use, without just compensation.

Amendment VI

In all criminal prosecutions, the accused shall enjoy the right to a speedy and public trial, by an impartial jury of the State and district wherein the crime shall have been committed, which district shall have been previously ascertained by law, and to be informed of the nature and cause of the accusation; to be confronted with the witnesses against him; to have compulsory process for obtaining witnesses in his favor, and to have the Assistance of Counsel for his defence.

Amendment VII

In suits at common law, where the value in controversy shall exceed twenty dollars, the right of trial by jury shall be preserved, and no fact tried by a jury, shall be otherwise reexamined in any Court of the United States, than according to the rules of the common law.

Amendment VIII

Excessive bail shall not be required, nor excessive fines imposed, nor cruel and unusual punishments inflicted.

Amendment IX

The enumeration in the Constitution, of certain rights, shall not be construed to deny or disparage others retained by the people.

Amendment X

The powers not delegated to the United States by the Constitution, nor prohibited by it to the States, are reserved to the States respectively, or to the people. . . .

14th Amendment, Ratified 1868

Amendment XIV

Section 1   All persons born or naturalized in the United States, and subject to the jurisdiction thereof, are citizens of the United States and of the State wherein they reside. No State shall make or enforce any law which shall abridge the privileges or immunities of citizens of the United States; nor shall any State deprive any person of life, liberty, or property, without due process of law; nor deny to any person within its jurisdiction the equal protection of the laws. . . .

Appendix B
Glossary of Legal Terms

accomplice One who aids another in the commission of a crime. An accomplice is generally treated the same as a principal.

actus reus The criminal act.

administrative crimes Crimes created by government administrative agencies under specific authority and guidelines granted to the regulatory or administrative agency by law of that state or the federal government.

affirmative defense A defense to a criminal charge in which the defendant generally admits doing the criminal act but claims an affirmative defense such as duress (he or she was forced) or entrapment (see Chapter 7).

arraignment Formal assertion of criminal charges against a defendant.

assault In many instances, an assault is an attempt to commit a battery, but many states also make other conduct an assault. Could be combined with a charge of battery to constitute the crimes of "assault and battery" (see Chapter 14).

battery A successful assault, in which the victim is actually and intentionally (or knowingly) struck by the defendant.

benefit of clergy A medieval limit on capital punishment. People convicted of a capital crime entitled to claim the benefit of clergy (by the fifteenth century, anyone who could read) could not be executed for their offense. By the end of the eighteenth century, the privilege had been eliminated for most crimes.

bill of attainder Legislative act that inflicts punishment without trial; prohibited by Article I, Sections 9 and 10, of the Constitution.

burglary Unlawful entry into the premises of another with intent to steal or commit a felony. Two hundred years ago in England, an illegal entry into the home of another by force and at night was punishable by death if the entry was done to steal or commit a felony (see Chapter 15).

capital punishment Inflicting deadly injury as punishment for criminal conduct.

certiorari A form of review of lower court decisions by the Supreme Court. Certiorari is discretionary with the Court, and most petitions requesting it are denied. Traditional legal doctrine is that no conclusion can be drawn from a denial of certiorari.

clear and present danger The test used to judge governmental restrictions on speech.

common law The earliest type of law. Common law was created by judges based on custom, usages, and moral concepts of the people. Most law today is statutory law enacted by legislative bodies (see Chapter 2).

common law crimes Crimes created by judges.

condonation Forgiveness of the criminal act by the victim. Normally not a defense to prosecution.

contempt Failure or refusal to obey a court order (civil contempt), or interfering with the functioning of a court or legislative body (criminal contempt). Criminal contempt that occurs in the presence of the court can be punished summarily; other criminal contempts require the normal prosecution procedures.

corporal punishment Inflicting nondeadly physical injury as punishment for criminal conduct.

corpus delicti In all criminal cases, the government must prove that the crime charged was committed (corpus delicti) and that the defendant was party to the crime (committed the crime or was an accomplice). (See Chapters 7, 13, and 18.)

criminology The sociological and psychological study of the causes, development, and control of crime.

double jeopardy A defense, stated in the Fifth Amendment, to prosecution on the grounds that the defendant has been tried before on the same charge, and acquitted.

due process The constitutional guarantee that criminal arrests and trials must meet certain minimum standards of fairness (procedural due process), and that laws not violate constitutional rights (substantive due process).

duress A defense to criminal prosecution on the grounds that the defendant was forced to commit the criminal act.

entrapment The defense that a law enforcement officer used excessive temptation or urging to wrongfully induce the defendants to commit a crime they would not have ordinarily committed.

ex post facto Criminal law made retroactive to punish prior conduct not criminal when done. Prohibited by Article I, Sections 9 and 10, of the Constitution.

extortion Obtaining property by threats of future harm. Differs from robbery in that robbery requires threat of immediate harm.

federalism The principle defining the division of power between the states and the federal government, in which the federal government has only those powers specifically delegated in the Constitution.

felony The most serious grade of crime; usually includes possibility of prison sentence.

felony murder All states and the federal government have felony murder statutes that punish as murder the causing of death of another while the defendant is committing a felony of violence. A felony murder conviction does not require a showing of malice or deliberate intent to kill (see Chapter 13).

fighting words Speech that, because it will likely incite immediate violence, is not protected by the First Amendment.

forensic Pertaining to courts of law.

habeas corpus A writ that compels the authority holding a person in confinement to explain the basis for that confinement. Used frequently as a method for state and federal prisoners to attack the constitutionality of their imprisonment. Both the federal government and states have some form of a habeas corpus law, often called "postconviction relief" laws.

hearsay Secondhand evidence. Hearsay testimony results when one person, the witness, testifies that he or she heard another person, the third person, say something. Such testimony is generally not admissible in trials if it is offered to prove the truth of what the third person said.

immunity An exemption from criminal prosecution, which can be limited to prosecution for a specific crime (transactional immunity) or for any crime related to the testimony or conduct for which immunity is granted (use immunity). Diplomats and legislators also enjoy immunity from prosecution in many circumstances.

inchoate crimes Criminal acts that lead to or are attempts to commit other crimes.

indictment A formal criminal charge brought by a grand jury against a defendant.

injunction A court order prohibiting a person from engaging in defined conduct. A violation of an injunction can be criminal.

interdiction The name given the government's attempts to stop the import of illegal drugs into this country.

justification The general doctrine of nonliability for actions otherwise criminal, based on recognized categories of excuse. Self-defense, necessity, and duress are examples of justification categories.

lesser included offense A criminal offense that is necessarily included in commission of some other offense. The crime of unlawful entry (or breaking and entering) is included in the crime of burglary. Normally, one cannot be convicted of both offenses for the same acts.

M'Naghten Rule The insanity defense rule requiring proof that defendants did not know the scope or character of their actions.

Magna Carta The document signed by King John in 1215 giving certain rights to his nobles. Successive kings affirmed this charter before Parliament.

malum in se Evil or wrong in itself. Murder is wrong with or without a law prohibiting it.

manslaughter Criminal homicides other than murder. Most states provide for two degrees of manslaughter, voluntary and involuntary.

menacing Intentionally placing or attempting to place another in fear of immediate serious physical injury.

mens rea The criminal intent or state of mind.

misdemeanor Offenses that carry punishment of a degree less than felonies. Usually misdemeanor crimes do not involve prison sentences.

misprision of a felony Failing to report or concealing a known criminal.

Model Penal Code Proposed criminal law developed by the American Law Institute, a group of lawyers, judges, and teachers. Many states have modeled their criminal codes on the MPC.

necessity A defense to criminal prosecution on the grounds that the harm to be avoided outweighed the harm caused by the crime committed. Necessity will not justify taking another person's life.

no contest plea A plea to a criminal charge that does not admit guilt, but does not contest the charges filed. In most instances, this plea will be treated as a guilty plea for sentencing and other purposes. (Sometimes called "nolo contendere.")

nuisance speech Speech that, because of its intrusive quality, may be regulated in time and place of its exercise.

nulla poena sine lege The principle of legality; no act should be made criminal or punished without advance warning in the form of legislative act.

obscenity Communication that the average person, using contemporary community standards, would find appeals to the prurient interests or depicts sexual conduct in a patently offensive manner and, taken as a whole, lacks serious artistic, literary, political, or scientific value.

overbreadth The constitutional law doctrine that invalidates laws that regulate conduct so broadly as to interfere with individual freedoms.

police power The inherent power of every state and local government, subject to constitutional limits, to enact criminal laws.

presumption A rule of law that the trier of fact shall assume the existence of a state of facts without evidence being produced. Presumptions are rebuttable or irrebuttable.

privilege A defense to criminal prosecution on the grounds that the person was in good faith discharging some duty of his or her public office when the criminal act occurred.

proximate cause The ordinary and probable cause of a result.

prurient A prurient interest is an excessive, shameful, or morbid interest in sex.

rape shield laws Laws passed by many states to limit the extent to which defense attorneys in a rape case can inquire into the victim's past sexual life.

recidivist One who is a habitual criminal.

regulatory offenses Crimes relating to conduct affecting the health and welfare of the general public in areas in which federal or state governments may lawfully regulate the conduct. Manufacture and sale of drugs and storing and selling food for human consumption are examples of areas in which the government can regulate and thus create regulatory crimes. Many regulatory crimes are "strict liability" and require no guilty intent.

RICO The Racketeer Influenced and Corrupt Organizations Act. Passed by Congress to enable prosecutors to charge all people engaged in unlawful activity who own or invest in an enterprise that affects interstate commerce.

scienter A form of specific intent requiring a showing that the actor knew of the existence of certain facts. For example, one cannot be guilty of possession of stolen property if one does not know property is stolen.

sedition The crime of advocating the forceful overthrow of the established government. In this country, the Smith Act makes such advocacy a crime.

sexual assault The crime in most states that includes the crime of rape, as well as other lesser degrees of assault.

sexual harassment Unwelcome sexual advances, with or without physical contact; in the workplace, creation of a "hostile environment," such as belittling or embarrassing an employee or co-worker who has refused sexual advances, can be sexual harassment.

shoplifting Stealing goods from retail stores by concealment, generally on the person of the defendant. Commission does not require removal of the goods from the store.

solicitation Attempting to get another to commit a crime.

specific intent The intent necessary for one or more elements of an offense. Murder, for example, requires the specific intent that the act be done intentionally or purposely.

status crimes Criminal laws that punish a status, such as drug addiction, with no act requirement.

statutory crimes Crimes enacted by a legislative body and signed into law by the state governor or president of the United States. Statutory crimes make up the vast majority of crimes enforced in the United States today.

statutory rape Sexual intercourse with a minor female under a certain age, usually 18. Consent and, generally, mistake as to age are not defenses to this crime.

tort A noncontractual civil wrong.

transferred intent The doctrine that one who intends to inflict harm on one person but injures another instead is presumed, for purpose of criminal prosecution, to intend the actual result.

uttering Putting into circulation a check known to be worthless.

venue In criminal prosecutions, the proper location for the criminal trial. Venue is usually in the county in which the crime is alleged to have occurred.

vicarious liability Criminal liability of one person, with or without culpability, for the criminal acts of another. Usually imposed when the defendant occupies some relationship to the person committing the crime, such as employer-employee, that charges the defendant with the duty to control the other person.

void for vagueness The constitutional law doctrine that invalidates criminal laws written in such a manner as to make it unreasonably difficult for a defendant to know whether or not conduct is prohibited by the law.

***Wharton* Rule** The requirement that crimes needing more than one person for commission, such as bigamy, require three or more people for a conspiracy conviction.

Table of Cases

Index

Photograph Credits

This page constitutes an extension of the copyright page. We have made every effort to trace the ownership of all copyrighted material and to secure permission from copyright holders. In the event of any question arising as to the use of any material, we will be pleased to make the necessary corrections in future printings. Thanks are due to the following authors, publishers, and agents for permission to use the material indicated.

Chapter   2.   **21:** © Bettmann/CORBIS

Chapter   3.   **88:** AP/Wide World Photos

Chapter   6.   **113:** © Michael Brennan/CORBIS   **119:** AP/Wide World Photos

Chapter   8.   **172:** AP/Wide World Photos

Chapter   9.   **189:** © Bettmann/CORBIS

Chapter 10.   **214:** © Bettmann/CORBIS

Chapter 11.   **238:** AP/Wide World Photos   **244:** AP/Wide World Photos

Chapter 14.   **297:** AP/Wide World Photos   **310:** AP/Wide World Photos

Chapter 15.   **334:** AP/Wide World Photos

Chapter 16.   **363:** AP/Wide World Photos

Chapter 18.   **404:** AP/Wide World Photos

Chapter 19.   **426:** Courtesy of Eileen Gardner

Chapter 20.   **432:** © Bettmann/CORBIS   **438:** © James L. Shaffer

Chapter 21.   **453:** AP/Wide World Photos

Chapter 22.   **462:** © Bettmann/CORBIS